HEALTH, FOOD, AND NUTRITION IN THIRD WORLD DEVELOPMENT

International Development Resource Books
Pradip K. Ghosh, editor

Industrialization and Development: A Third World Perspective
Urban Development in the Third World
Technology Policy and Development: A Third World Perspective
Energy Policy and Third World Development
Population, Environment and Resources,
and Third World Development
Health, Food, and Nutrition in Third World Development
Economic Policy and Planning in Third World Development
Development Policy and Planning: A Third World Perspective
New International Economic Order: A Third World Perspective
Foreign Aid and Third World Development
Multi-national Corporations and Third World Development
Economic Integration and Third World Development
Third World Development: A Basic Needs Approach
Appropriate Technology in Third World Development
Development Co-operation and Third World Development
International Trade and Third World Development
Disarmament and Development: A Global Perspective
Developing South Asia: A Modernization Perspective
Developing Latin America: A Modernization Perspective
Developing Africa: A Modernization Perspective

HEALTH, FOOD, AND NUTRITION IN THIRD WORLD DEVELOPMENT

Pradip K. Ghosh, *Editor*

Foreword by Gamani Corea, Secretary-General of UNCTAD

Prepared under the auspices of the Center for International Development, University of Maryland, College Park, and the World Academy of Development and Cooperation, Washington, D.C.

International Development Resource Books, Number 6

(G/P)

Greenwood Press
Westport, Connecticut • London, England

Library of Congress Cataloging in Publication Data

Main entry under title:

Health, food, and nutrition in Third World development.

(International development resource books, ISSN 0738-1425; no. 6)
Bibliography: p.
Includes index.
1. Public health—Developing countries.   2. Food
supply—Developing countries.   3. Nutrition—Developing
countries.   4. Medical policy—Developing countries.
5. Nutrition policy—Developing countries.   6. Developing
countries—Economic conditions.   I. Ghosh, Pradip K.,
1947-   .   II. Series.
RA441.5.H43   1984   363.8'09172'4   83-26504
ISBN 0-313-24142-2 (lib. bdg.)

Library of Congress Catalog Card Number: 83-26504
ISBN: 0-313-24142-2
ISSN: 0738-1425

First published in 1984

Greenwood Press
A division of Congressional Information Service, Inc.
88 Post Road West, Westport, Connecticut 06881

Printed in the United States of America

10 9 8 7 6 5 4 3 2 1

To
Johan Galtung

"THE ULTIMATE OBJECTIVE OF DEVELOPMENT
MUST BE TO BRING ABOUT A SUSTAINED
IMPROVEMENT IN THE WELL-BEING OF THE
INDIVIDUAL AND BESTOW BENEFITS ON ALL. IF
UNDUE PRIVILEGES, EXTREMES OF WEALTH AND
SOCIAL INJUSTICES PERSIST, THEN DEVELOPMENT
FAILS IN THE ESSENTIAL PURPOSE."

- UNITED NATIONS GENERAL ASSEMBLY
RESOLUTION 2626 (XXV), 24 OCTOBER 1970.

Contents

LIST OF TABLES

PART II

STATISTICAL INFORMATION AND SOURCES

LIST OF FIGURES

HEALTH PROGRAMS AND POPULATION GROWTH

THE PRIORITY OF NUTRITION IN A NATION'S DEVELOPMENT

The Third World

Afghanistan
Republic of Afghanistan
Algeria
Democratic and Popular
Republic of Algeria
Angola
People's Republic of Angola
Argentina
Argentine Republic
Bahamas
Commonwealth of the Bahamas
Bahrain
State of Bahrain
Bangladesh
People's Republic of
Bangladesh
Barbados
People's Republic of
Barbados
Benin
People's Republic of Benin
Bhutan
People's Republic of Bhutan
Bolivia
Republic of Bolivia
Botswana
Republic of Botswana
Brazil
Federative Republic of Brazil
Burma
Socialist Republic of the
Union of Burma
Burundi
Republic of Burundi

Cambodia
Democratic Kampuchea

Cameroon
United Republic of Cameroon
Cape Verde
Republic of Cape Verde
Central African Empire
Chad
Republic of Chad
Chile
Republic of Chile
Colombia
Republic of Colombia
Comoro Islands
Republic of the Comoros
Congo
People's Republic of the
Congo
Costa Rica
Republic of Costa Rica
Cuba
Republic of Cuba
Dominican Republic
Ecuador
Republic of Ecuador
Egypt
Arab Republic of Egypt
El Salvador
Republic of El Salvador
Equatorial Guinea
Republic of Equatorial
Guinea
Ethiopia
Fiji
Dominion of Fiji
Gabon
Gabonese Republic
Gambia
Republic of the Gambia

Ghana
  Republic of Ghana
Grenada
  State of Grenada
Guatemala
  Republic of Guatemala
Guinea
  Republic of Guinea
Guinea-Bissau
  Republic of Guinea-Bissau
Guyana
  Cooperative Republic of
  Guyana
Haiti
  Republic of Haiti
Honduras
  Republic of Honduras
India
  Republic of India
Indonesia
  Republic of Indonesia
Iran
  Imperial Government of Iran
Iraq
  Republic of Iraq
Ivory Coast
  Republic of Ivory Coast
Jamaica
Jordan
  Hashemite Kingdom of Jordan
Kenya
  Republic of Kenya
Kuwait
  State of Kuwait
Laos
  Lao People's
  Democratic Republic
Lebanon
  Republic of Lebanon
Lesotho
  Kingdom of Lesotho
Liberia
  Republic of Liberia
Libya
  People's Socialist
  Libyan Arab Republic

Madagascar
  Democratic Republic
  of Madagascar
Malawi
  Republic of Malawi
Malaysia
Maldives
  Republic of Maldives
Mali
  Republic of Mali
Mauritania
  Islamic Republic
  of Mauritania
Mauritius
Mexico
  United Mexican States
Mongolia
  Mongolian People's Republic
Morocco
  Kingdom of Morocco
Mozambique
  People's Republic
  of Mozambique
Nepal
  Kingdom of Nepal
Nicaragua
  Republic of Nicaragua
Niger
  Republic of Niger
Nigeria
  Federal Republic of Nigeria
Oman
  Sultanate of Oman
Pakistan
  Islamic Republic of Pakistan
Panama
  Republic of Panama
Papua New Guinea
Paraguay
  Republic of Paraguay
Peru
  Republic of Peru
Philippines
  Republic of the Philippines
Qatar
  State of Qatar

Adopted from THE THIRD WORLD: PREMISES OF U.S. POLICY by W. Scott
Thompson, Institute for Contemporary Studies, San Francisco, 1978.

Rhodesia
Ruanda
  Republic of Ruanda
Samoa
Sao Tome and Principe
  Democratic Republic of
  Sao Tome and Principe
Saudi Arabia
  Kingdom of Saudi Arabia
Senegal
  Republic of Senegal
Seychelles
Sierra Leone
  Republic of Sierra Leone
Singapore
  Republic of Singapore
Somalia
  Somali Democratic Republic
Sri Lanka
  Republic of Sri Lanka
Sudan
  Democratic Republic of
  the Sudan
Surinam
Swaziland
  Kingdom of Swaziland
Syria
  Syrian Arab Republic
Tanzania
  United Republic of Tanzania

Thailand
  Kingdom of Thailand
Togo
  Republic of Togo
Trinidad and Tobago
Tunisia
  Republic of Tunisia
Uganda
  Republic of Uganda
United Arab Emirates
Upper Volta
  Republic of Upper Volta
Uruguay
  Oriental Republic of Uruguay
Venezuela
  Republic of Venezuela
Vietnam
  Socialist Republic of Vietnam
Western Sahara
Yemen
  People's Democratic Republic
  of Yemen
Yemen
  Yemen Arab Republic
Zaire
  Republic of Zaire
Zambia
  Republic of Zambia

Countries which have social and economic characteristics in
common with the Third World but, because of political
affiliations or regimes, are not associated with Third
World organizations:

China
  People's Republic of China
Cyprus
  Republic of Cyprus
Israel
  State of Israel
Kazakhstan
Kirghizia
Korea
  Democratic People's Republic
  of Korea
Romania
  Socialist Republic of Romania

South Africa
  Republic of South Africa
South West Africa
  Namibia
Tadzhikistan
Turkmenistan
Uzbekistan
Yugoslavia
  Socialist Federal Republic
  of Yugoslavia

Abbreviations

ADC	Andean Development Corporation
AsDB	Asian Development Bank
ASEAN	Association of South-East Asian Nations
CARIFTA	Caribbean Free Trade Association
DAC	Development Assistance Committee (of OECD)
ECA	Economic Commission for Africa
ECE	Economic Commission for Europe
ECLA	Economic Commission for Latin America
ECOWAS	Economic Commission of West African States
EDF	European Development Fund
EEC	European Economic Community
EFTA	European Free Trade Association
ESCAP	Economic and Social Commission for Asia and the Pacific
FAO	Food and Agriculture Organization of the United Nations
GATT	General Agreement on Tariffs and Trade
GDP	gross domestic product
GNP	gross national product
IBRD	International Bank for Reconstruction and Development (World Bank)
IDA	International Development Association
IDB	Inter-American Development Bank
IFC	International Finance Corporation
IIEP	International Institute for Educational Planning
ILO	International Labour Office
IMF	International Monetary Fund
LAFTA	Latin American Free Trade Association
ODA	official development assistance
OECD	Organisation for Economic Co-operation and Development
OPEC	Organization of Petroleum Exporting Countries
UNDP	United Nations Development Programme
UNEP	United Nations Environment Programme
UNESCO	United Nations Educational, Scientific and Cultural Organization
UNHCR	Office of the United Nations High Commissioner for Refugees
UNITAR	United Nations Institute for Training and Research
UNICEF	United Nations Children's Fund
UNIDO	United Nations Industrial Development Organization
WFP	World Food Programme
WHO	World Health Organization

Foreword

I am pleased to know of the International Development Resources Book project. The 20 resource books which are published under this project, covering the whole spectrum of issues in the fields of development economics and international co-operation for development, and containing not only current reading materials but also up-to-date statistical data and bibliographical notes, will, I am sure, prove to be extremely useful to a wide public.

I would like to commend the author for having undertaken this very ambitious and serious project and, by so doing, rendered a most valuable service. I am confident that it will have a great success.

Gamani Corea

Secretary-General
United Nations Conference on Trade and Development

Preface

Stimulus for the publication of an international resource book series was developed in 1980, while teaching and researching various topics related to third world development. Since that time, I have built up a long list of related resource materials on different subjects, usually considered to be very important for researchers, educators, and public policy decision makers involved with developing country problems. This series of resource books makes an attempt for the first time to give the reader a comprehensive look at the current issues, methods, strategies and policies, statistical information and comprehensive resource bibliographies, and a directory of information sources on the topic.

This topic is very important because within the framework of the current international economic order, developing an effective heatlh, food and nutrition policy is envisaged as a dynamic instrument of growth essential to the rapid economic and social development of the developing countries, in particular of the least developed countries of Asia, Africa and Latin America.

Much of this work was completed during by residency as a visiting scholar in the Center for Advanced Study of International Development at Michigan State University. Suzanne Wilson and Mary Ann Kozak, students at the University, provided assistance with the project. I am thankful to the M.S.U. Sociology department for providing necessary support services and Dr. James T. Sabin, Vice President, editorial of Greenwood Press who encouraged in pursuing the work and finally agreeing to publish in book form.

I would also like to gratefully acknowledge the encouragement given to me by Dr. Denton Morrison to pursue this project and Dr. Mark Van de Vall who has been an inspiration to me since my graduate school days.

Finally, preparation of this book would not have been competed without the contributions from Samuel H. Preston, Keith Abercrombie, Arthur McCormack, D. Gale Johnson, Fred T. Sai, Michael J. Sharpston, Raymond F. Hopkins and Donald J. Puchala, James E. Austin, Norman K. Nicholson, John D. Esseks, Paul Andre

Finot, Hans-Rimbert Hemmer, Frank Schofield, Frederick L. Golloday, Carl E. Taylor, Amor Benyoussef, Jacob Meerman, Susan Hill Cochrane and Nancy Birdsall, and finally many experts of the Organization for Economic Co-operation and Development. I am also gratefully indebted to Journal of Economic Literature, U.N. Documents and World Bank Publications for the much needed annotations, and a very special thanks to Tom and Jackie Minkel for typing assistance.

For additional resource materials on related topics of international development, please consult the following resource books published by the GREENWOOD PRESS (Westport, Connecticut, London, England).

RESOURCE BOOK NO. 1.	INDUSTRIALIZATION AND DEVELOPMENT: A THIRD WORLD PERSPECTIVE
RESOURCE BOOK NO. 2.	URBAN DEVELOPMENT IN THE THIRD WORLD
RESOURCE BOOK NO. 3.	TECHNOLOGY POLICY AND DEVELOPMENT: A THIRD WORLD PERSPECTIVE
RESOURCE BOOK NO. 4.	ENERGY POLICY AND THIRD WORLD DEVELOPMENT
RESOURCE BOOK NO. 5.	POPULATION, ENVIRONMENT AND RESOURCES, AND THIRD WORLD DEVELOPMENT
RESOURCE BOOK NO. 6.	HEALTH, FOOD AND NUTRITION IN THIRD WORLD DEVELOPMENT
RESOURCE BOOK NO. 7.	ECONOMIC POLICY AND PLANNING IN THIRD WORLD DEVELOPMENT
RESOURCE BOOK NO. 8.	DEVELOPMENT POLICY AND PLANNING: A THIRD WORLD PERSPECTIVE
RESOURCE BOOK NO. 9.	NEW INTERNATIONAL ECONOMIC ORDER: A THIRD WORLD PERSPECTIVE
RESOURCE BOOK NO. 10.	FOREIGN AID AND THIRD WORLD DEVELOPMENT
RESOURCE BOOK NO. 11.	MULTI-NATIONAL CORPORATIONS AND THIRD WORLD DEVELOPMENT
RESOURCE BOOK NO. 12.	ECONOMIC INTEGRATION AND THIRD WORLD DEVELOPMENT
RESOURCE BOOK NO. 13.	THIRD WORLD DEVELOPMENT: BASIC NEEDS APPROACH
RESOURCE BOOK NO. 14.	APPROPRIATE TECHNOLOGY IN THIRD WORLD DEVELOPMENT
RESOURCE BOOK NO. 15.	DEVELOPMENT CO-OPERATION AND THIRD WORLD DEVELOPMENT
RESOURCE BOOK NO. 16.	INTERNATIONAL TRADE AND THIRD WORLD DEVELOPMENT
RESOURCE BOOK NO. 17.	DISARMAMENT AND DEVELOPMENT: GLOBAL PERSPECTIVE
RESOURCE BOOK NO. 18.	DEVELOPING LATIN AMERICA: A MODERNIZATION PERSPECTIVE
RESOURCE BOOK NO. 19.	DEVELOPING SOUTH ASIA: A MODERNIZATION PERSPECTIVE
RESOURCE BOOK NO. 20.	DEVELOPING AFRICA: A MODERNIZATION PERSPECTIVE

PART I
CURRENT ISSUES, TRENDS, ANALYTICAL METHODS, STRATEGIES AND POLICIES, COUNTRY STUDIES

Introduction

This resource book has two multifaceted purposes. Firstly, to document and analyze the current trends in the development of an effective policy related to health, food and nutrition of the third world countries--and to evaluate the progress made by them during the past decade in attaining long term objectives of a sustained economic growth and improvement in the quality of living future populations.

We are all very much familiar with the problems of third world countries, usually described by Latin America (excluding Cuba), the whole of Africa, Asia (excluding its socialist countries, Japan and Israel) and Oceania (excluding Australia and New Zealand). They are plagued by poverty, very high rates of population growth, low growth rates of gross domestic product, low rates of industrialization, extremely high dependence on agriculture, high rate of unemployment, and uneven income distribution. Although the expression "third world countries" no longer has a clear meaning, majority of the international development experts would consider the poor developing countries to belong in the third world irrespective of their affiliation as aligned or non-aligned characteristic.[1]

Secondly, major purpose of this volume is to provide the researchers with the much needed knowledge about the different sources of information and available data related to health, food, nutrition in third world development. These policies in the developing countries have raised many complex issues. While these issues are largely dependent on national policies and priorities, their solution is of international concern.

The pace and pattern of policies related to health, food and nutrition have varied widely among the developing countries partly because of differences in the availability of natural, human and capital resources and in factors such as size and location, and partly because of differences in objectives, strategies and policies of those countries. The issues affecting strategies and policies differ considerably at the present time from those that were important a decade ago and policy design is thus now more complex and difficult than before.

The current concern with problems of poverty and income distribution has intensified interest in development. It has also led to heightened interest in problems of malnutrition and poor health as particularly serious manifestations of poverty and to renewed emphasis on the relationships between population growth and poverty. Up to the present this increased concern has been most apparent in official pronouncements, such as the address presented by Robert McNamara at the World Bank's 1973 annual meeting in Nairobi and the resolutions adopted at the World Food Conference in 1974. In fact, relatively little progress has been made toward achieving a consensus with respect to the changes in policies and programs that will be most effective in mounting "the assault on poverty." [2]

The developing countries as a whole have come to hold an increasingly dependent position in the world food system. Exporters have become importers, reliance on food aid or assistance to meet balance of payments deficits has grown for non-OPEC countries, and efforts to expand production in promising areas, such as the Sudan and Brazil, have yet to be realized. This food dependency and vulnerability to scarcity spills over into balance of payment, developmental and political stability concerns. Barring the global catastrophe envisioned by the Club of Rome, poverty will prove a more intractable problem than low productivity in the third world. Much greater attention will have to be paid to the distribution of income, jobs, and foodgrains in the future if increases in production are to actually reduce hunger, improve health and nutrition.

This volume examines the experience of a substantial number of the third world countries in implementing development plans during approximately the first half of the 1970's and draws some general conclusions for policy action during the years ahead.

Attention has been focused on some of the major problems faced by hard core developing countries and policy issues posed by those problems. However, the development needs of hard-core developing countries are very large and call for much greater interest and attention from world community than has been the case so far. A systematic attack on the acute problems of countries facing extreme poverty and underdevelopment should therefore now be at the center of the policies designed to usher in a new international economic order.

It is hoped that this resource book will be of use not only to those directly involved in the formulation and implementation of development policies but also will help to acquaint a wide reading audience with the thrusts planned by developing countries for accelerated progress. In addition, the intercountry comparative analysis may be of use to planners and policy makers in developing countries, especially from the viewpoint of harmonizing national plans in order to strengthen economic co-operation with respect to health, food, nutrition and development among interested countries.

The plan of the reading materials in Part I of this book and the selection of the pieces represents a specific orientation, or bias. They represent current international issues and trends affecting health, food and nutrition in third world development, analytical methods, strategies and policies for selected third world countries.

Part II includes statistical information and a descriptive bibliography of information sources related to health, food and nutrition and development in the third world countries.

Part III is a select bibliography of books, documents and periodical articles published since 1970, relevant to health, food and nutrition in the developing countries. Annotations for the different titles have been compiled from The Journal of Economic Literature, International Social Sciences Index, U.N. Documents Index, World Bank Publications, Finance and Development, Book Publisher's promotion brochures and the IMF-IBRD Joint Library Publications.

Part IV consists of a directory of information sources. This section is in four parts; United Nations Information Sources, listing of bibliographic sources, titles of selected periodicals published around the world and a directory of institutions involved in research, relevant to health, food and nutrition problems in the third world countries.

[1]Rodwin Lloyd, "REGIONAL PLANNING PERSPECTIVE IN THIRD WORLD COUNTRIES," in TRAINING FOR REGIONAL DEVELOPMENT PLANNING: PERSPECTIVES FOR THE THIRD DEVELOPMENT DECADE, ed. by Om Prakash Mathur, UNCRD, 1981.
Thompson, W. Scott, THE THIRD WORLD: PREMISES OF U.S. POLICY, Institute for Contemporary Studies, San Francisco, 1978.

[2]This is the title of a recent World Bank publication containing policy papers on rural development, education, and health; see International Bank for Reconstruction and Development (IBRD), The Assault on Poverty: Problems of Rural Development, Education and Health (Baltimore: Johns Hopkins University Press, 1975).

Health Programs and Population Growth

SAMUEL H. PRESTON

In the best of all possible worlds, the accomplishment of one social objective would facilitate, or at least not inhibit, the attainment of others. In matters of health improvement, salubrious side effects generally prevail--declines in morbidity and mortality not only prolong healthy life but also generally increase labor productivity, increase investment in human capital, and lengthen valued kinship ties. The only serious drawbacks are demographic. Declines in mortality usually increase the proportion of the population that is outside the labor force age range. Far more important, they appear to produce an extended period of accelerated population growth. The likelihood of such a period is powerfully suggested by the demographic history of virtually every country in the world during the last century.

Nations could have averted the accelerated growth, almost universally induced by successful health programs, only by achieving declines in birth rates that were equal in magnitude to the declines in death rates. Demographic theory and casual empiricism suggested that mortality change should in fact call forth some fertility response. Frank Notestein and Kingsley Davis in their development of demographic transition theory argued that norms and practices supportive of high fertility had evolved in order to ensure social survival under conditions of high mortality. By implication, mortality decline should remove the social underpinnings upon which high fertility had rested. More concretely, under a regime of reduced mortality fewer births would be required in order for parents to achieve a certain family size goal that was framed in terms of surviving children.

The late 1960s witnessed a flurry of research that appeared to support these arguments. Computer simulation made the motivational argument more precise and dramatic. Heer and Smith assumed that

Reprinted with permission of the Population Council, from **POPULATION AND DEVELOPMENT REVIEW**, Vol 1, No. 2, Dec. 1975, (189-199).

parents made an accurate assessment of prevailing mortality conditions and that they procreated until they were 95 percent certain of having at least one son alive when the father was aged 65. Under these conditions and assuming perfectly effective contraception, they showed that net reproduction rates would remain roughly constant as mortality declined to a life expectancy of 62 and would fall precipitously thereafter.[1] The decline in the level of fertility required to reach the presumed target would at least compensate and sometimes overcompensate for the decline in mortality in its effect on population growth. Although the assumptions of Heer and Smith were highly restrictive, there was a strong inclination to accept the results as applying to a more general set of circumstances. Some aggregative empirical studies indeed appeared to support the importance of mortality level for fertility determination. Nations or regions with higher levels of mortality were shown to have higher levels of fertility even after statistical controls had been placed on such factors as per capita income, newspaper circulation, and women's labor force participation. It is possible, however, that such results were simply reflecting the reverse influence of fertility on mortality, or that mortality was merely acting as a "proxy" for another, unmeasured variable. Furthermore, at least one study detected no significant cross-sectional effect of mortality on fertility. Most important of all, inspection of trend data revealed fertility in the majority of developing countries to be quite intransigent even in the face of major mortality reductions.[2]

Although their designs were badly flawed or severely restricted their applicability, the studies suggesting the existence of an important positive link between mortality and fertility were greeted with relief and rapid acceptance by the scientific community. They appeared to exonerate health programs from the blame for accelerated population growth, confirming for some that this was in fact the best of all possible worlds. What had been a potential source of embarrassment to those promoting improved standards of health was rapidly turned into a virtue. According to Carl Taylor:

> The third and most important way in which health programs contribute to economic development is by providing the best prospects of solving the population problem. In order to get acceptance of family planning, it is essential that parents have some assurance that children already born will have a reasonable chance of surviving to adulthood.[3]

Similar sentiments have been repeatedly endorsed by the World Health Organization and the United Nations Department of Economic and Social Affairs.[4] In its well-publicized report, Rapid Population Growth, a distinguished committee appointed by the US National Academy of Sciences advocated mortality reduction in order to promote fertility declines in less developed countries (e.g., pp. 87, 95).

By the late 1960s, the problem of rapid population growth had clearly become redefined as a problem of high fertility. Thus measures designed to reduce mortality were advocated, in part, on the grounds that they would also lead to fertility decline, even though there was an imminent danger that they would accelerate population growth. The likelihood of such an effect should have been obvious from the period's unprecedented rate of world population growth. It is one thing to ask whether mortality levels influence fertility, but for most purposes, the more important question is whether the quantitative influence of mortality on fertility is sufficiently large that the growth consequence of mortality change can be safely ignored. New evidence on this question is not reassuring.

I. RECENT EVIDENCE ON MORTALITY/FERTILITY RELATIONS

A much clearer indication of the likely response of fertility to variation in infant and child mortality has become available through research conducted in the last two years. Much of this work was presented and scrutinized at a 1975 Bangkok conference sponsored by the Committee for International Coordination of National Research in Demography (CICRED). Typically, the research examines relations at the level of the reproductive couple, rather than at the aggregate level where interpretation is muddied by the joint operation of many highly correlated factors and by the simultaneous effects of fertility on mortality.

The results of this work can be simply summarized. In most of the score of populations for which data are available, there is some fertility response to an infant or child death in the family, but in none of the populations is the response even half "complete." That is, most families are unable or unmotivated to replace a deceased child with another live birth, additional to those that would be expected in the absence of a child death. The implications of this behavior for population growth are immediate: reductions in child mortality in a population will typically be accompanied by some reduction in fertility because fewer families will need to replace a child that has died; but since most families would not have replaced the child in any event, the fertility reduction will be smaller in magnitude than the mortality reduction, and growth rates will rise. Only through additional mechanisms of an indirect nature could the acceleration in growth be averted.

The extent to which deceased children are "replaced" in the family seems to vary systematically with the level of socioeconomic development. In general, populations at the highest and lowest development levels exhibit the strongest replacement effects. The accompanying figure illustrates the approximate relation between the size of the replacement effect and level of socioeconomic development. It also cites country populations that provide evidence on the strength of these relationships at various socioeconomic levels.

Populations at the lowest level of development appear to display a stronger replacement effect than those at the next higher level. The reason probably has nothing to do with the volitional responses of parents to child loss; parental control over the number of births is seldom exercised in either group. The mechanism is instead a biological one that operates primarily through breastfeeding. Since lactation has a strong tendency to suppress ovulation, the survival of a child in breastfeeding populations tends to delay a subsequent pregnancy. In extreme cases, Senegal and Bangladesh, the average interval to the next birth when the latest child dies in infancy is 12-13 months shorter than when the latest child survives. A similar difference in intervals has been reported for Saint Patrice, a French village, in the seventeenth and eighteenth centuries. On the other hand, Anhausen, a German village, displayed no difference in mean intervals in the nineteenth century; the apparent reason is the absence of breastfeeding, also suggested by other evidence.[5] Differences of 5-11 months are most common where breastfeeding is frequent and prolonged. Average birth intervals in breastfeeding noncontracepting populations are often around 2.5 years, so that the measured replacement effect can be as high as 40 percent, although a level of 25 per cent is more common,. That is, over the course of a woman's reproductive life, 1.0 fewer child deaths would be associated with about .25 fewer births in populations where breastfeeding is prolonged. Since breastfeeding is commonly more extensive in poorer populations, that is where this type of replacement effect tends to be stronger. It may also be the case that the ovulatory-suppressant effect of lactation is stronger in more poorly nourished populations, although this proposition has not been conclusively demonstrated. In some populations, (e.g. India), this essentially involuntary mechanism is often reinforced by conventional differences in residential and sleeping arrangements and frequency of intercourse that depend on the survival or death of an infant.

In the course of social modernization, the average length of breastfeeding generally declines by major amounts and so does the strength of this involuntary mechanism. For example, in Algeria the average length of breastfeeding is 13.4 months but for literate women it is only 7.5 months and in urban areas it is 11.3 months.[6] Indirect evidence on the average length of breastfeeding in rural and semiurban areas of Peru, Colombia, Mexico, and Costa Rica places it in the range of 3-7 months. Research by Rutstein and Medica demonstrates that the replacement effect is very weak in these populations; in Colombia and Mexico, no replacement effect at all is observed.[7] Here the growth-generating effect of mortality change is expected to be maximal, since none of the short-term effects of mortality change at the family level are attenuated by corresponding changes in fertility. If anything, improved health and mortality in such populations may produce higher levels of fertility by reducing sterility, subfecundity, and pregnancy wastage and by extending the average lifetime of a marriage. In Gabon, for example, mortality is quite high even for tropical Africa but fertility is unusually low because approximately a quarter of reproductive age women are sterile, mostly as a result

Figure 1.
Approximate extent to which dead children are replaced in a family

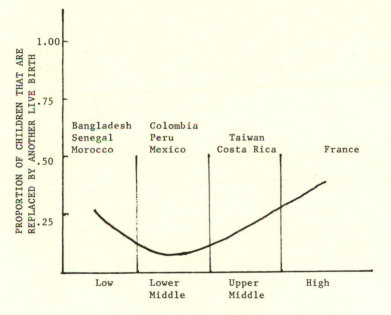

LEVEL OF SOCIO-ECONOMIC DEVELOPMENT

11

of malarial infection.[8] An antimalarial campaign in such a population can be expected to reduce mortality and raise fertility.

There are two plausible explanations for the absence of a volitional replacement mechanism in populations at low levels of development. Either family size goals are not framed in terms of surviving numbers of children, or the goals themselves are so high that childbearing at a near maximum rate would be required to reach them even in the absence of child deaths. In either case, the type of reproductive motivation presumed by Heer and Smith could not be prevalent in these populations. Only when family size goals become sufficiently low that contraception is generally required to avoid overshooting them, can a substantial volitional response be expected. This requirement severely constrains the response of fertility to a change in mortality in the very countries where postulated economic-demographic relations appear to make rapid growth least advantageous.

Taiwan provides the best information on the extent of replacement in a population at intermediate levels of socioeconomic development. One study of 8,178 rural Taiwanese women found that, for women who had produced three births, those who had experience one child death among these first three subsequently bore .29 more children than those who experienced none.[9] Individual-level factors such as income, educational attainment, and birth control knowledge are statistically controlled in this study, so that the possibility of spurious results due to a mutual dependence of mortality and fertility on these characteristics is effectively eliminated. Length of breastfeeding is also controlled, so that the results should not be heavily confounded with this involuntary mechanism. Interestingly, the additional number of births desired was more responsive to variation in child mortality than was actual fertility. The explanation for the discrepancy probably lies in the inability of some women to act upon their desires as a result of subfecundity, loss of a husband, or other intervening reproductive obstacles.

The developed country in which these relations have been most carefully investigated is France. A retrospective survey conducted in conjunction with the 1962 population census interviewed 92,000 women who had completed childbearing and were under age 70. Reconstructed reproductive histories of these women revealed that 61 percent of their births that survived to the time of interview were followed by an additional birth, whereas 74 percent of child deaths were so followed.[10] If we suppose that 39 percent (100 - 61) of women would have stopped childbearing if their latest child had not died, whereas only 26 percent of such women actually did stop, then some 33 percent of those with a deceased child (13/39) actually "replaced" it with a birth that would not have occurred otherwise. This estimate is somewhat crude and varies with the order of birth of the child and with husband's social class. It is nevertheless consistent with the notion that replacement behavior should be strongest in a low fertility-goal setting. Even here it is obvious that replacement is far from complete.

The results thus far have been formulated in terms of the reproductive period of individual women, but the translation into vital rates is direct. Suppose that the responsiveness of fertility to mortality is toward the maximal end of its recorded range,so that women "replace" one-third of their infant deaths. In a country with an initial crude birth rate of 40 per thousand and infant mortality rate of 150 per thousand live births, a major decline in the infant mortality rate to 50 would induce a fertility reduction of $-.10(.33)(.040)$ or $.0013$. The crude birth rate would decline by scarcely more than a point--from 40 to just barely below 39 per thousand--even under such a major mortality change. The effect would be somewhat magnified if mortality also changed for older children and similar replacement behavior were exhibited toward them, but a change of as much as 3 points would be most unlikely. It would take exceedingly careful statistical work to identify accurately a relationship of this magnitude from aggregative cross-sectional or longitudinal data.

II. INDIVIDUAL RESPONSE TO COMMUNITY MORTALITY LEVELS

The evidence cited to this point indicates conclusively that couples are unlikely to respond to variations in the mortality experience of their own children in such a way as to produce completely compensating changes in fertility. If compensation for a change in mortality is to be complete, there must be an additional, "contextual effect": couples must perceive the mortality experience of others or of the community at large and correspondingly adjust their own fertility. Two mechanisms have been suggested whereby such a contextual effect might emerge. They can be labelled "insurance motivation" and "fatalistic resignation." Neither has received an adequate empirical test in any population, so they must be considered conjectural.

The reasoning in support of the insurance motivation link is straightforward. If parents are attempting to secure the survival of a certain number of children to some point past the end of their reproductive period, they must not only react to the mortality experience of their own children but also must anticipate the children's survivorship beyond the point where they could be replaced. Since this anticipation is presumably based on their observation of mortality in other families, an additional mortality-fertility link is created. By itself, this mechanism would at most secure exactly compensating changes in fertility to a change in mortality, assuming that parents accurately assess the death risks of their children. But if the additional assumption is made that parents are more distressed by falling short of their target than by exceeding it, then there is the likelihood that a fertility response will be overcompensatory. In situations of higher mortality there is greater uncertainty about survival, as well as lower average survival.[11] Greater uncertainty gives higher weight to outcomes other than "the" target, and if the child-preference function is skewed toward larger numbers, additional force is added to the higher-fertility impetus.

It was this combination of assumptions--insurance motivation and asymmetric preferences—that produced the striking simulation results of Heer and Smith. Both ingredients are essential to the outcome, which relied additionally on the assumption of perfect contraception.[12] Obviously, it relies as well on the accurate perception by parents of prevailing mortality levels. If these perceptions are formulated with a substantial lag, as is reasonable to expect, then the fertility response will also be lagged. Most importantly, since the survival of offspring in the most hazardous first few years of life need not for the most part be anticipated by parents but rather can be observed and reacted to, the overcompensatory possibility logically applies primarily to mortality among older children whose death rates in most populations are the lowest and show the least interpopulation variability of any age group. Even though a change in the death rates of older children might produce an exaggerated fertility response, the changes themselves tend to be small. For example, as mortality improves from a life expectancy at birth of 50 years (a level now surpassed by less developed countries as a bloc) to one of 65, the probability that a 5-year-old will survive to age 30 typically increases by only 7 percent, from around .88 to around .95. With constant fertility, however, the net reproduction rate would increase by about 23 percent.

The "fatalistic resignation" argument takes the following form. Fatalism—an attitude that events are outside an individual's control—is a significant reason why many individuals fail to exercise control over their fertility. In a less developed country, one of the cheapest and most salient ways in which an individual's life can be altered is probably through health improvements. The demonstration that such changes are within reach may precipitate a psychological change that makes the adoption of contraception (and other innovations) more likely. At the same time, recognition that one's personal future is longer and more predictable can make one more "planful," producing the same effect. Again, this effect probably emerges, if at all, after a substantial lag, since it relies upon individuals' perceptions of and reactions to a mortality change.

A very ambitious attempt to test the importance of community mortality level for fertility has been made in Taiwan. Heer and Wu's study of rural Taiwan was purposely designed to include respondents in villages having substantially differing levels of mortality. Controlling for individual-level characteristics of women in the two villages, including personal experience with child mortality, they find that women in the high-mortality village bear, on average, .35 more children than women in the low-mortality village. However, they are unwilling to attribute this effect to differences in mortality level per se, since the villages differed in most other significant dimensions of modernization as well. A multitude of contextual effects could be represented in their estimate. The importance of other factors is suggested by the fact that perceptions of child survival levels were not significantly associated with desired number of births, which differed by only .06 between women who perceived survival chances to be less than 85 percent and women who perceived them to be greater than 95 percent. Nevertheless, the results are at least consistent with the notion that community mortality level can affect fertility through channels other than the replacement of deceased children within a family.

A good deal of work must be done before the magnitude of contextual effects can be firmly established. Researchers would do well to recognize the many different types of responses available to societies when mortality declines exogenously. Increased production and use of resources, diminished standards of living, and emigration are potential alternatives to fertility reduction, and it is important to study why a particular response or set of responses is forthcoming in a certain setting. Some of the responses need not rely at all upon individual perceptions of mortality change. For example, when population pressure is increased by a mortality decline, a particular inheritance system may result in later marriage and lower fertility without individuals being aware that conditions have changed.

That the sum total of mortality effects typically results in incomplete fertility compensation over periods of at least a half-century is, to repeat, tangibly illustrated by the recent history of world population growth. Birth rates have fallen but not by a magnitude equal to the drop in death rates. Furthermore, most demographers attribute substantial portion of observed declines in fertility to other features of modernization: urbanization, increased literacy, expanded opportunities for women, and so on. Even if the entire decline were ascribed to mortality change, compensation would be incomplete. Most available studies demonstrate that fertility does respond to mortality, and if the "population problem" were defined simply as one of high fertility, mortality reduction policy might provide a promising avenue of attack. But the problem is not fertility but growth, the balance of births and deaths. Current levels of fertility are problematic only in the context of the prevailing imbalance. Continued mortality reduction in less developed countries, no matter how desirable on other grounds, is likely to exacerbate that imbalance.

III. A CONCLUDING NOTE ON HEALTH POLICY

The position that countries or individuals should be "denied" access to all available health resources has been repeatedly labelled as immoral or inhumane. In fact, such denials take place daily around the globe as a result of responsible decisions reached publicly and privately. Individuals don't behave in a way that suggests that their sole concern is prolonging life or improving health, nor do they appear to expect such behavior in their behalf by their governments. No country of the world devotes its entire budget to improving physical health; most goes instead to enriching the years that will be lived in any event. Yet there is no doubt that additional health expenditures could reduce mortality in every country. The point is simply that budgetary decisions necessarily take account of competing desires and even competing moralities.

To assume that they should be based exclusively on one's own conception of what is moral is to deny the legitimacy of those making competing claims. I am not suggesting that the time is ripe for contraction of health programs, only that their levels be set with full appreciation of the positive and negative consequences. The evidence seems clear that the effects of health programs on population growth should rarely count on the positive side.

NOTES

[1]David Heer and Dean O. Smith, "Mortality level, desired family size, and population increase," Demography 5, no. 1 (1968): 104-121. Their unrealistic assumption that contraception was perfectly effective helped to produce a fertility response that was more than compensating. In a low mortality population where fewer births would be required to reach a reproductive target, many more years would have to be spent avoiding an "unwanted" birth. Had they permitted unwanted births in their calculations, the result of mortality decline might well have been an unambiguous acceleration of population growth.

[2]Major examples of aggregative studies that seemed to suggest the existence of a mortality-fertility link are T. Paul Schultz, "An economic model of family planning and fertility," Journal of Political Economy 77, no. 2 (March/April 1969): 153-180; David Heer, "Economic development and fertility," Demography 3, no. 2 (1966): 423-444; and Harald Frederiksen, "Determinants and consequences of mortality and fertility trends," Public Health Reports 81, no. 8 (August 1966): 715-727. On the other hand, Irman Adelman's cross-sectional study turned up no significant link between the two: "An econometric analysis of population growth," American Economic Review 53, no. 3 (June 1963): 314-339. Ansley Coale and Edgar Hoover's classic, Population Growth and Economic Development in Low Income Countries (Princeton, NJ: Princeton University Press, 1958), p. 17, noted the absence of major fertility decline in several developing countries that had experienced a prolonged mortality decline.

[3]"Health and population," Foreign Affairs 43, no. 3 (April 1965): 479. Taylor has been among the most consistent and eloquent advocates of health improvements fo social as well as for humanitarian reasons.

[4]"Evidence accumulates that the reduction of infant mortality may be a prerequisite to the acceptance of family planning. Couples will not wish to prevent pregnancies until they have some assurance that the children they already have will survive" p. 84 of UN Department of Economic and Social Affairs, Measures,

Policies, and Programms affecting Fertility. UN Population Study No. 51. The Director General of the World Health Organization, in an address to the 21st World Health Assembly Organization, stated that, "A minimal level of health seems to be necessary for a family to realize that it can regulate its demographic behavior." International Planned Parenthood Federation, The Relationship between Family Size and Maternal and Child Health. Working Paper no. 5, p.1.

[5] For evidence on differential birth intervals, see papers by Knodel; Chaudhury, Khan, and Chen; and Cantrelle, Ferry, and Mondot in the Proceedings of the CICRED Seminar on Infant Mortality in Relation to Level of Fertility, Bangkok, 6-12 May 1975. To be published by CICRED, Paris, 1975.

[6] Cantrelle, Ferry, and Mondot. A similar urban-rural differential is reported for Senegal.

[7] Shea Rutstein and Vilma Medica, "The effects of infant and child mortality on fertility in Latin America" in Proceedings of the CICRED Seminar. The absence of any replacement effect is surprising since the measured effect also includes the involuntary mechanism. The authors speculate that women experiencing high levels of child mortality may be less fecund than average., thereby masking the involuntary link as well as any volitional response.

[8] Cantrelle, Ferry, and Mondot.

[9] David M. Heer and Hsin-ying Wu. "The separate effects of individual child loss, perception of child survival and community mortality level upon fertility and family planning in rural Taiwan with comparison data from urban Morocco" In Proceedings of the CICRED Seminar. Oddly, child deaths beyond the first evoked a negative replacement effect, such that if two of the three births had died (95 cases), a woman subsequently bore only .13 more children than if none had died (3,001 cases).

[10] The data are presented in Alin Lery and Jacques Vallin. "Attempt to estimate the excess fertility consecutive to the death of a young child" in Proceedings of the CICRED Seminar.

[11] This argument only applies to the point where survival chances of children decline to 5, but mortality in virtually all current populations falls into this range.

[12] See note 1 K. Vencatacharya has done a simulation of Indian conditions, assuming that parents procreate until one son reaches age ten. Asymmetric preferences are still present, but no scope is permitted for insurance motivation. Under these conditions, growth rates rise substantially as mortality declines, contrary to the Heer-Smith results. "Influence of variations in child mortality on fertility: A simulation model study" in Proceedings of the CICRED Seminar.

Population Growth and Food Supplies in Different Time Perspectives

KEITH ABERCROMBIE
ARTHUR MCCORMACK

The World Population Conference held in Bucharest in 1974 placed considerable emphasis on agricultural and rural development as a means of influencing demographic change, and on the urgency of world food problems. There are many references to such matters in the World Population Plan of Action, and they are the subject of no less than five of the conference's 17 substantive resolutions. Furthermore, the conference requested that its discussions be fully reflected at the World Food Conference that was about to take place in Rome. But on the relationship between population and food it was unable to go further than a general statement "recognizing that the solution of the problem of population growth depends largely on a balance between the size of the world's population and the world's production of foodstuffs and volume of available resources."[1]

The World Food Conference, convening in Rome later in 1974, gave little attention to population problems, as was to some extent justified by its preoccupation with the more immediate future up to about 1985. The conference report states:

> Some speakers referred to difficulties caused by the current rapid population growth in the developing countries. . . Although the period of the future on which the World Food Conference was focusing mainly concerned the next 10 years or so, during which time the rate of population growth was virtually predetermined, action should be undertaken now to ensure that population growth was reduced in the more distant future and the size of the task for world food production proportionately reduced. Although it was clear that the food needs entailed by inevitable population growth must

Reprinted with permission of the Population Council, from **POPULATION AND DEVELOPMENT REVIEW**, Vol 2 No. 3 and 6, Sept/Dec. 1976, (479-498).

be met, it was equally clear that population could not indefinitely continue to double every generation, and that at some point the earth's capacity to sustain human life would inevitably be overstretched if present trends continued. Other speakers, however, believed that the role of rapid population growth in causing or exacerbating the world food problem had been exaggerated and could divert attention from the real solution to the problem."[2]

But although the World Food Conference did not spend much time discussing the issue of population and food, it went much further than the World Population Conference. In a most forthright resolution entitled "Achievement of a desirable balance between population and food supply," sponsored by 22 developing countries, the main provisions are as follows:

The World Food Conference

Recognizing that the increasing demand for food is related in particular to the unprecedented population growth, which has doubled the world's population in a single generation,

Realizing that despite improved agricultural technology, an appreciable share of the human race continues to be severely undernourished, and that many millions face actual starvation,

Bearing in mind that land and water resources are limited and further that, due to underdevelopment of such resources in developing countries, it is becoming increasingly difficult to meet the food needs of a rapidly growing world population,

Now calls on all Governments and on people everywhere not only to make every possible effort to grow and equitably distribute sufficient food and income so that all human beings may have an adequate diet...but also to support, for a longer-term solution, rational population policies ensuring to couples the right to determine the number and spacing of births, freely and responsibly in accordance with national needs within the context of an over-all development strategy.[3]

I. DIFFERENT TIME HORIZONS

The World Food Conference was mainly concerned with a time horizon during which the population is largely, though by no means entirely, predetermined. A careful distinction between different time horizons is in fact essential for any meaningful discussion of the relation between population and food supplies.

As regards the population, we must distinguish three groups: first the people who exist already; second, those who, short of catastrophe, will inevitably be added to the population; and, third, those who may or may not be added to the population in the future.

The first group -- the existing population -- already includes very large numbers of malnourished people, who are overwhelmingly to be found among the poorest people in the developing countries. Groups of them regularly become a charge on the conscience of the international community whenever poor harvests threaten them with actual starvation, but their plight even in good years is such that they should be a constant preoccupation.

The second group -- the inevitable increase in the population -- will almost all be in the developing countries. It is estimated, on the basis of the United Nations "medium" population assumption, that 90 percent of the net addition to the world's population between now and the year 2000 will be in these countries.[4] If things continue as they are, very many of them will be added to the number of malnourished people.

It is the third group -- the avoidable population increase -- that was most neglected at the Bucharest and Rome conferences. It is often assumed that nothing can be done that will have a significant influence on the size of the population even as far away as the end of the century. But the United Nations projections indicate that the present world population of 4.0 billion could rise to anywhere between 5.8 and 6.6 billion by the year 2000, depending mainly on the rate at which fertility declines in the developing countries. This potential difference of 800 million people (one-fifth of the present total), almost all of which would be in the developing countries, represents a demand for about 185 million tons of cereals (14 percent of current world production and consumption) even at the present low average level of consumption in these countries. Thus it is not unreasonable to conclude that action taken now to curb population growth could substantially influence the size of the future task for the world's agriculture. And, of course, the farther we look into the future, the greater is this potential difference.

The importance of distinguishing different time horizons applies equally to the possibilities for future food supplies. Most people, unfortunately including many government planners, tend to base their expectations of the future largely on their knowledge of the immediate situation. Since this situation is subject to abrupt changes, mainly as a result of the weather, this has led to swings between optimism and pessimism about future food supplies in relation to population.[5]

These swings have become particularly sharp in recent years, with the greater availability of information and the avid interest of the communications media in predicting the future of mankind. The prevailing opinion of future prospects has switched violently from gloom during the widespread bad harvests of 1965-66 to complacency in the "green revolution" years of 1967-71, and back again to pessimism since the difficulties that began in 1972.

With the better harvests in many developing countries in 1975 and the generally good results in 1976, there are already some signs of a return to complacency about future food supplies. However, it is to be hoped that the attention focused by the World Food Conference on the underlying longer run problems will continue, for some time at least, to convince people that such complacency is as little justified as the extremes of pessimism and optimism.

It should be obvious that the immediate world food situation, which depends so much more on the weather than on the success or failure of man's efforts, must be a very unreliable guide to the future. But there is another school of thought that goes to the other extreme and bases its assessment almost entirely on an estimate of the eventual carrying capacity of the world in terms of food supplies. Where, as in many cases, this estimate is highly optimistic, it provides no guide at all to what will actually happen, and can hardly be used to prove that there is no such thing as a world food problem. This view takes no account of past failures to make full enough use of the undoubtedly great potential, nor of the long and probably difficult segment of the future that has to be got through in order to reach the bright prospect represented by the world's eventual carrying capacity. It is epitomized by the insistence of some delegations at Bucharest that "Mankind's future is infinitely bright"° -- a statement that was modified in the final version of the World Population Plan of Action to "Mankind's future can be made infinitely bright."[6]

What has happened during a fairly long period of the past provides the best guide to what may happen in the future. It must, of course, be combined with a realistic assessment of the changes that appear likely in the past trends, but this should be based on what is feasible in the period under consideration, rather than just long-term potential.

II. PAST TRENDS

Analysis of data on food and population over the past quarter century provides a base from which to look ahead. During the last 25 years or so the average annual rate of increase of world food production has steadily deteriorated. Table 1 indicates that it fell from 3.1 percent in the 1950s to 2.8 percent in the 1960s and 2.2 percent in the first half of the 1970s.

This deterioration partly reflects the fact that it becomes more difficult each year to increase production at the same rate as in the past. Not only does the same percentage increase become larger in absolute terms, but it gets harder and more costly to extend the cultivated area and raise yields.

Some more specific factors in the declining growth rate can also be identified. One is that the high rates of increase achieved in the early 1950s reflected in part postwar recovery, especially in Europe and some of the developing regions. A major factor in North America, from the mid-1950s to the mid-1960s was the accumulation of "surpluses"; this was followed by a brief period of more successful supply management from the late 1960s until the removal of all production controls in the United States in 1973. In some developing countries, the ready availability of food aid may have somewhat dampened incentives to increase domestic production from the mid-1950s to the mid-1960s. Since then (and especially since 1972) virtually all developing countries have aimed to accelerate the expansion of production. During the early years of the "green revolution" (roughly 1967-71) several of them were conspicuously successful. However, in the early 1970s, as in the mid-1960s, many of their efforts to increase production have been vitiated by widespread bad weather, with additional difficulties caused in 1973 and 1974 by the shortage and high price of chemical fertilizers.

Except in the most recent period, when the slowdown has been particularly marked in the developed countries, food production has grown at about the same rate in developed and developing countries. But per capita production has not, because population growth rates in developed and developing countries have diverged dramatically. The long-term averages shown in Table 1 clearly reflect the declining rates of population growth in the developed countries, but they fail to reveal the changes that have occurred in the developing market economies, where population growth has risen from 1.9 percent per annum in 1950 to 2.4 percent in 1975. In actual numbers, the increases are huge: 1.9 percent of the 1950 population of the developing market economies comprised 31 million additional people, and 2.4 percent of their 1975 population 68 million additional people.

In contrast to the continuing large increases in food production per capita in the developed countries, per capita production in the developing countries rose by only 0.6 percent a year in 1961-70 and 0.2 percent in 1971-75. In the developing market economies, in spite of the very good harvests many individual countries enjoyed in 1975, the increase in food production fell behind population growth in 1971-75, with a particularly alarming deterioration in Africa. Even over the longer period, during which food production in the developing countries as a whole has kept slightly ahead of population growth, it has lagged behind in many individual countries. This was the case in 1961-74 in 45 countries, or almost half of the total of 96 developing countries for which the United Nations Food and Agriculture Organization (FAO) publishes data, representing nearly 40 percent of the total population of the developing countries.[7]

Population growth accounts for some 70 percent of the increase in the demand for food in the developing countries and 55 percent in the developed countries. Paradoxically, at the world level the figure is about 80 percent, because the slow population growth in the developed countries is accompanied by a much higher level of per capita demand than the much more rapid growth in the developing countries. The remainder of the increase in food demand comes from higher incomes, but (again somewhat paradoxically) the share of population growth is likely to increase still further in the future, as the income elasticity of demand for food declines with economic development.

In the 86 developing countries for which relevant data are available, the increase in food production in 1961-74 failed to equal the estimated increase in the domestic demand for food, stemming from both population growth and higher incomes, in 58 countries, or about two-thirds of the total. As a result, the food imports of the developing countries have risen very steeply, by 3.3 percent a year in 1961-70 and 7.1 percent a year in 1971-74. Their gross imports of cereals (including rice in milled equivalent) increased from 38 million tons in 1969/70 to 63 million in 1974/75.

The average annual growth of population in the developing countries in 1961-74 ranged all the way from 0.1 percent in Barbados upwards to 3.5 percent in Bangladesh, Colombia, Iraq, Mexico, and Paraguay. It is sometimes argued that rapid population growth is a necessary stimulus for the intensification of production.[8] Although this may be true in a general sense, there is no evidence that the unprecedentedly high rates of population growth in so many of the developing countries today are necessary for the intensification of production or that they lead automatically to it. For example, in the five countries just mentioned, the increase in food production fell behind population growth in three and was ahead of it in two. Taking a larger sample of countries, one of the authors has demonstrated elsewhere that there appears to be no correlation between the rate of population growth and whether the increase in food production has been above or below it.[9] What matters is the response of farmers and governments to the challenge brought by rapid population growth. In some countries they have been notably successful in responding to this challenge, but in others they have not.

III. FOOD SUPPLY AND NUTRITIONAL LEVELS

Unfortunately the challenge does not consist only in feeding the additions to the population. The world has not even been particularly successful in providing nutritionally adequate diets for its existing population. Rapid population growth thus preempts resources that might otherwise be devoted to improving the nutrition of the people who are already here.

Table 2 presents data on food supplies in relation to nutritional requirements in the main regions of the world. The data are in terms of dietary energy supplies, which are now considered the principal nutritional indicator.[10] If dietary energy is adequate, protein is generally adequate too. Conversely, if there is an energy deficit, even where protein supplies are above requirements, part of them will be used to provide energy and thus not be available for their essential protein functions. The data in Table 2 differ from those of per capita food production in Table 1, in that they allow for changes in net trade and stocks and include fish consumption. (Full data are still available only for 1969-71, the last fairly "normal" period before the recent

Table 1
Average Annual Rates of Increase in Food Production,
Population, and Per Capita Food Production,
Developed and Developing Countries 1952–75

Development Status	Food Production[a]			Population			Food Producti[on] per Capita	
	1952 –60	1961 –70	1971 –75	1952 –60	1961 –70	1971 –75	1952 –60	1961 –70
	Percent per year[b]							
Developed Market Economies[c]	2.1	2.5	1.8	1.2	1.1	0.9	0.9	1.4
North America	1.7	2.4	1.9	1.8	1.3	0.9	-0.1	1.1
Western Europe	2.5	2.3	1.9	0.8	0.8	0.6	1.7	1.5
Oceania	2.7	3.4	1.3	2.4	1.9	1.7	0.3	1.5
Eastern Europe and USSR	5.3	3.2	2.1	1.5	1.0	0.9	3.9	2.2
All Developed Countries	3.1	2.7	2.0	1.3	1.1	0.9	1.8	1.6
Developing Market Economies[c]	3.2	2.9	2.5	2.4	2.6	2.6	0.8	0.3 –
Africa	2.4	2.9	0.5	2.4	2.5	2.7	na	0.4 –
Latin America	3.0	3.0	2.7	2.8	2.8	2.7	0.2	0.3 –
Far East	3.3	2.7	2.8	2.2	2.5	2.5	1.1	0.2
Near East	3.7	3.3	3.7	2.6	2.7	2.8	1.1	0.7
Asian Centrally Planned Economies	na	2.8	2.4	na	1.7	1.7	na	1.1
All Developing Countries	na	2.9	2.5	na	2.3	2.3	na	0.6
All Countries	3.1[d]	2.8	2.2	1.9[d]	1.9	1.9*	1.2[d]	0.9

Table 2
Average Dietary Energy Supplies
as a Percentage of Nutritional Requirements,
Developed and Developing Countries, 1961, 1969–71, and 1970–74

Development Status	1961	1969–71	1970–74
Developed Market Economies[a]	115	121	na
North America	118	126	na
Western Europe	118	123	na
Oceania	121	123	na
Eastern Europe and USSR	116	127	na
All Developed Countries	116	123	na
Developing Market Economies[a]	93	97	na
Africa	91	94	90[b]
Latin America	100	106	107
Far East	92	94	93
Near East	89	102	100[c]
Asian Centrally Planned Economies	86	92	na
All Developing Countries	91	95	na
All Countries	100	104	na

NOTE: Based on food available at the retail level after allowing for storage and marketing losses and waste.

na = not available.

[a] Including countries in other regions not specified.

[b] 15 countries only (the corresponding figure for these countries in 1969–71 was 91).

[c] Five countries only (99 in 1969–71).

SOURCE: FAO food balance sheets.

difficulties began in 1972).

In the world as a whole, the supply of dietary energy is more than sufficient to provide nutritionally adequate diets for all of the existing population. If it were distributed strictly in accordance with nutritional requirements, it would feed about 4 percent more people than the present population of 4 billion, or some 160 million more people (about two years of the current population increase). On an even more hypothetical plane, if all of the cereals now fed to livestock were consumed directly by human beings, existing food supplies might be sufficient to provide a largely vegetarian diet for perhaps 1.5 billion more than the present population.[11]

But the available food supplies are very far from being distributed in accordance with nutritional requirements. Their distribution depends partly on ecological factors, but more generally it is influenced by income and purchasing power. Thus, the developed countries consumed more than 20 percent in excess of their dietary energy requirements in 1969-71. These countries, with less than 30 percent of the world's population, consumed almost 40 percent of the total dietary energy supply. In terms of "wheat equivalent" (roughly converting the consumption of livestock products to "original plant calories"), they were responsible for about two-thirds of world food consumption, although it should be noted that even this is only slightly more than their share of production.[12] The developed countries account for only about 13 percent of the world's population growth, but for about 18 percent of the increase in the demand for food. Almost 450 million tons of cereals, or about one-third of world production, are fed to livestock in these countries.

In the developing countries, in contrast, the available supplies of dietary energy were 9 percent below requirements in 1961 and 5 percent below in 1969-71. Supplies in both Latin America and the Near East rose somewhat above requirements in 1969-71, but Africa and the Far East were still more than 5 percent below. Food balance sheet data for more recent years, which are only now becoming available, indicate a slight deterioration in Africa and the Far East in 1970-74, and a slight improvement in Latin America and the Near East. The food production data available for 1975 suggest that there was a substantial recovery in per capita food supplies in the Far East and a further improvement in the Near East, but it is clear that the nutritional situation as continued to worsen seriously in many parts of Africa.

Out of the 96 developing countries for which data are available, only in 39 did dietary energy supplies at the national average level meet nutritional requirements in 1969-71, and only 18 had a safety margin of more than 10 percent to allow for maldistribution within the country. The number of countries with a deficit of dietary energy fell from 74 in 1961 to 57 in 1969-71, but even in the latter period there were still 24 countries (half of them in Africa) where the deficit was more than 10 percent.[13]

National averages provide only a first indication of the food situation. Food is distributed within a country according to income rather than nutritional requirements; and there is even maldistribution within families. Individual requirements also

vary. It is therefore extremely difficult to arrive at an estimate
of the actual number of people even in a single country who do not
receive their nutritional requirements. FAO undertakes the
thankless task of making such estimates at the global level and is
sometimes accused of exaggerating them in order to keep itself in
business. Their most recent estimate is that (excluding China) at
least 460 million people suffered from severe protein-energy malnutrition in 1969-71. Of these, 430 million were in the developing
market economies, where they constituted a quarter of the total
population, and 300 million were in the Far East region, where they
made up 30 percent of the population.[14] These figures are believed
by FAO to be on the low side but, even if they were on the high
side and the true numbers were only half as great, they would still
be appalling.

Moreover the numbers of severely malnourished have increased
considerably since 1969-71, especially in Africa and the Far East.
The limited available data for more recent years indicate drastic
declines in the already very low national average intakes of
dietary energy in a number of countries in at least one year of the
period 1972-74.[15] It is highly probably that worsening
malnutrition has been a main cause of sharply rising death rates in
some countries. In India, for example, the crude death rate rose
from 16.4 per thousand in 1971 to 18.9 in 1972.[16]

IV. LONG-TERM POTENTIAL

The main problems in the short and medium term are caused by the
rate of growth of the population rather than its absolute size,
except of course in those areas, mainly in Asia so far, where the
population density is already uncomfortably high. In the longer
term future the rate of population growth will be reduced (this is
implied even under the United Nations "high" assumption and, as is
indicated below, the reduction appears to have begun already), and
the principal problem will increasingly become the sheer size of
the population.

The farther ahead we look into the future, the easier it is to
be optimistic about food supplies in relation to population. Thus
most of the estimates of the eventual carrying capacity of the
earth in terms of food supplies are highly optimistic. Many of
them, however, are deplorably imprecise in specifying their
assumptions and amount to little more than speculation.

The starting point for such exercises is an assessment of the
potential arable area, and this is usually their most scientific
part. There appears to be little disagreement that the arable area
can be at least doubled. One recent estimate puts the maximum
potential arable land at about 3.2 billion hectares, or a little
more than twice the present level,[17] and another puts it at 3.4
billion.[18]

But in 1965 K. M. Malin blandly told the World Population
Conference in Belgrade that "with new methods and large capital

expenditure" the arable area could be increased more than sixfold, so that, "depending on the intensity of farming," the world could feed from 65 to 130 billion people.[19] Colin Clark, basing himself partly on Malin, estimates that 47 billion could be fed at North American dietary standards, or 157 billion at Japanese standards.[20]

Roger Revelle's much more scientific estimate, prepared for one of the symposia preceding the Bucharest conference, includes a detailed calculation of potential water supply and irrigation. He concludes that, with appropriate technology and sufficient purchased inputs (equivalent to those used in maize production in Iowa), a minimum subsistence diet could be provided for 97 billion people or an adequate diet, including "sufficient high-quality protein," for 50 to 60 billion.[21] Another recent estimate is that, assuming that all growth circumstances that can be influenced by man are optimal, the world is capable of producing 30 times the present amount of food.[22]

Walter Pawley's study of the year 2070[23] has sometimes been misinterpreted as being one of these very optimistic readings of the future. In fact, however, it sets out to demonstrate the highly speculative nature of such exercises by specifying very clearly the kind of assumptions it is necessary to make. His estimate that in 100 years the cultivable area could reach 6 billion hectares, or more than four times the present level, is based on the assumption of two major technological breakthroughs. The first would permit the continuous cultivation of humid tropical soils after the tree cover is removed, and the second would make possible the desalinization of sea water at costs low enough to be economic for irrigation. Then, if three crops a year were grown in the warm zones with perennial irrigation, and if world average yields were five times the present European level, a 50-fold increase in production would be possible. This could feed at North American dietary standards the 36 billion population that would result in 2070 if current trends in population growth continued -- as they obviously will not. If per capita gross domestic product grew at 4 percent a year from now until 2070, effective demand in the developing countries could sustain such dietary levels.

But colossal costs would be involved in such developments. A 70-to 100-fold increase in fertility use would vastly expand the runoff of chemical residues into the lakes and oceans. The potential increases in production would be very unevenly distributed geographically in relation to the population. Above all, there is the problem of timing. When particular technological breakthroughs are made and, even more important, how quickly they can be put into practice, are what matter.

The question of what may actually happen during a given period of time has in fact received more attention in some of the more recent studies. The Hudson Institute envisages a world where in 200 years' time a population of, say, 20 billion (implying considerable reductions in population growth) would both produce and be able to afford an ample diet, but it does admit that during the balance of this century "much suffering and great problems are likely to be witnessed" in "the poorest third of the world."[24] The widely publicized conclusion in the first report to the Club of Rome was that, if current population growth continued and if agricultural yields were doubled, the world would not have enough arable land to feed its population at present dietary levels by some time before the middle of the next century. Even the quadrupling of yields would only put this off until about 100 years from now.[25] Apart from the fact that current population trends obviously will not continue, this model appears to have the eventual breakdown of food supplies built into it, by assuming that the "over-use" of land must lead to erosion. The second report to the Club of Rome does not attempt a world food model, producing instead four very sombre scenarios for south Asia -- to which it provides a fifth, "the only feasible solution," which requires, among other things, "an effective population policy."[26]

All except one of the estimates discussed above are confined to conventional methods of food production. The optimistic view of the Hudson Institute, however, is partly based on the greatly expanded use of novel sources of food supply, such as the conversion of waste products by enzymes and single-cell high-protein organisms, or the highly intensive cultivation of plants in artifical environments.[27] Because such methods largely escape the constraint of available land, they could enormously increase the number of people who could be fed. Unconventional products are also likely to become increasingly important in livestock feeding, making it possible to reduce the rapidly expanding use of cereals for this purpose.

Optimism about the ultimate food production potential of the earth is therefore probably justified. But this is totally irrelevant to the problems involved in increasing production fast enough to keep up with rapid population growth and to provide better diets for the existing population size. There is no guarantee that the world will be any more successful in utilizing its food production potential in the future than it has been in the past. It would be tragic if optimism about the long-term future should lead to complacency and inaction about the more immediate future. Even the more pessimistic estimates carry such danger, for, although they may jolt some people into action, the feeling of hopelessness they induce could also lead to inaction.

V. THE NEXT QUARTER CENTURY

Throughout this article we have stressed the need to distinguish different time perspectives in considering the relation between population and food supplies. It is becoming abundantly clear that the last quarter of this century is likely to be one of the most crucial periods in the history of mankind's efforts to feed a growing population. On the one hand, there is general agreement that, if the right action is taken, population growth can be reduced, the increase in food production accelerated, and the purchasing power of the poorest people raised sufficiently for the virtual elimination of hunger and malnutrition by the end of the century. This could lay the foundations for a widely shared

prosperity in the more distant future. On the other hand, the
alternative is not hard to visualize. If sufficient political will
cannot be found for the massive action that is necessary, there
will not only be widespread starvation but also a gradual drift
downward in the nutritional levels of the poorest people. This too
might lead to eventual prosperity for a stabilized population, but
the reduction in population growth would have resulted from higher
infant mortality rather than deliberate fertility limitation.

FAO's latest projections, revised for the World Food
Conference, extend only to 1985, but they serve to indicate how
quickly the situation might get out of hand.[28] The demand for food
in the developing market economies is projected by FAO to rise by
3.6 percent a year between 1969-71 and 1985. Food production in
these countries, in contrast, increased by only 2.6 percent a year
from 1961 to 1973. If this production trend continues (and it is
noteworthy that the trend in 1971-75, at 2.5 percent a year, was
still below it), these countries would require net imports of 85
million tons of cereals a year (and even more in a bad year) by
1 9 8 5 to meet the effective demand for food. Such import
requirements are much higher than the developing countries' already
very burdensome net cereal imports of 16 million tons in 1969-71
and about 40 million tons in 1975. Although the continuation of
past production trends in the developed countries would generate
exportable supplies far greater than this import requirement, it is
hardly conceivable that imports on such a scale could be financed
either through food aid (for which the World Food Conference's
minimum target was only 10 million tons a year) or on normal
commercial terms.

Hence a substantial acceleration of the increase in food
production in the developing countries themselves is of overriding
importance. FAO estimates presented to the World Food Conference,
based mainly on the detailed country-by-country supply analysis
carried out for the Indicative World Plan,[29] indicate that it
would be feasible to raise the rate of growth of food production in
the developing countries to 3.6 percent a year by 1985, and thus to
meet the increase in the effective demand for food without a
further rise in imports.[30]

The preliminary version of a study under way in the United
States Department of Agriculture (USDA)[31] confirms this broad
picture and takes it further into the future. Under the most
likely of three alternative scenarios for the year 2000, population
growth in the developing countries would average 2.2 percent a
year, and significant progress would occur in institutional
development and in the use of purchased inputs in agriculture, but
foreign and domestic capital would not be sufficient to maximize
production growth. Under these conditions, the cereal import
requirement of the developing countries would rise from 22 million
tons (7 percent of their total supplies) in 1970 to 62 million tons
(8 percent) in the year 2000, and their cereal consumption per
capita would increase from 173 kilograms in 1970 to 221 kilograms
in 2000.

The import demand projected under each of the scenarios falls
well within the feasible capacity of the major exporting countries.
Even the combination of peak levels of domestic consumption and

exports would raise the harvested cereal area in the exporting countries to only 42 percent of their total arable area in the year 2000 in comparison with 33 percent in 1970 and 45 percent in the early 1950s. Yield increases from 1970 to 2000 under the three scenarios range from 25 to 50 percent in most developed countries, and from 50 to 90 percent in the developing countries.

The USDA study assumes that, although energy costs will continue to be high, they will not have much effect on world agriculture up to the year 2000. Neither the FAO projections nor the USDA study, however, consider the possibility of climatic deterioration. Although the evidence is far from conclusive, it would seem prudent to take this contingency into consideration in food and agricultural planning. Apart from increasing the level of stocks required for safety, it would also add considerably to the difficulties of achieving the necessary sustained expansion of production.

Although it is generally agreed that more rapid expansion of food production in developing countries is both essential and feasible, it is becoming increasingly clear that it will take some time before this can actually be achieved. Even with the 4 percent increase in food production in the developing countries in 1975, the rate of increase in the first half of the 1970s was still considerably less than in the 1960s and below the rate of population growth. Several years of such large production increases are needed before real progress can be achieved again. The longer-term deterioration has to be reversed before the necessary acceleration can get under way.

As a result, the developed countries will for some time be called upon to play a much bigger role in the food supplies of the developing countries than was envisaged even as recently as November 1974, when the World Food Conference took place. Their role in food aid, in the rebuilding of stocks, in trade liberalization, and in capital and technical assistance for agricultural development was fully recognized at that time. The World Food Conference also called on these countries to "adopt and to implement agricultural policies which encourage the early expansion of food production while taking into account...world food requirements."[32] It now seems highly desirable that the developed countries carefully plan their food production in the light of world food needs during the next five to ten years. Such planning would be much facilitated by the greater stability that could be provided by an effective and comprehensive international grains arrangement.

One major area of agreement at the World Food Conference was on the need to establish a minimum level of world food security, based on the FAO proposals for an internationally coordinated system of nationally held food stocks. Progress, however, has not been any more successful with respect to this aim that it has on the Conference's other main conclusion that the increases in food production in the developing countries should be accelerated.

It has already been stressed that the immediate situation is not a reliable guide to the future course of food supplies in relation to population, but the main events since 1972 nevertheless serve to demonstrate some of the difficulties that have to be overcome for steadier progress to be resumed. Bad weather was unusually widespread in 1972, and there were simultaneous declines in production in North America, western Europe, eastern Europe and the USSR, the Far East, and China. World food production fell -- not only in relation to population but in absolute terms -- for the first time since World War II. It was possible to meet most of the shortfall, but only at the cost of a large reduction in the cereal stocks that had accumulated, largely fortuitously, in the main exporting countries. Stocks subsequently fell still further, and the first chance to replenish them did not come until 1975, when good harvests occurred in North America and in many developing countries. Although, as in 1972, a large part of the exportable supplies was again imported by the USSR in 1975 (to mitigate the effect of a disastrous domestic cereal harvest on the expansion of livestock production), stocks rose for the first time in three years.

For four years then, in the absence of adequate stocks, cereal supplies depended almost entirely on current harvests. There was starvation in some areas during this period, and it is only by the greatest good fortune that it was not much more widespread. A serious food crisis would still be unavoidable if there were a repetition of the simultaneous crop failures that in several major regions of the world occurred in 1972. At that time there were still reserves of idled land in the United States, as well as large stocks.

For some time, virtually the only remaining food reserve of any size was represented by the cereals that are fed to livestock, mainly in the developed countries. Cereal feeding to livestock was temporarily reduced one-fourth (35 million tons) in the United States in 1974/75 mainly in response to shifts in relative prices, but it remains to be seen whether such reductions could be deliberately achieved to meet the emergency needs of large populations effectively and speedily in the event of widespread shortages.

World cereal stocks (outside China and the USSR, for which there are not data) at the end of the 1975/76 crop season were estimated by FAO to have increased by 10 percent to some 118 million tons. Even with this increase, however, they represent only 13 percent of annual consumption, and remain about 35 to 45 million tons below the 17 to 18 percent of annual consumption that FAO judges a minimum safe level for world food security (a level that of course goes up every year with the growth of population and demand).

The recent difficulties also give special relevance and urgency to the proposal of the Seventh Special Session of the United Nations General Assembly that post-harvest food losses should be reduced by at least half by 1985. This could perhaps increase annual cereal supplies in the developing countries by 15 to 30 million tons, or enough for between 65 and 130 million more people at present consumption levels. It has sometimes been thought in the past that this would be more costly and difficult to achieve than the equivalent increase in production, but the difficulties experienced recently in increasing production sufficiently rapidly alter that picture.

Returning to the longer-term possibilities, the nutritional implications of the projections discussed above are particularly alarming. According to the FAO projections, even if the increase in the effective demand for food in the developing market economies could be met -- by a combination of increases in domestic production, food aid, and commercial imports -- the number of people suffering from severe protein-energy malnutrition would not fall but would in fact rise from 460 million (outside China) in 1969-71 to perhaps 750 million in 1985, almost all of them in the developing market economies.[33] The consequences of not meeting the increase in the effective demand for food would obviously be even more serious.

Further light may be expected to be thrown on this fundamental question by the Model of International Relations in Agriculture (MOIRA). As with the USDA model, only a preview is so far available.[34] The model looks ahead to the year 2010, since, on the basis of a modified version of the United Nations "medium" assumption, the world population is expected to double between 1975 and that year. Its starting point as regards nutrition is that in 1975 about 370 million people received less than their protein requirements. Thus although it uses a different method of measuring the number of malnourished, the model arrives at a figure not far below that of FAO.

The model examines the effects on the number of malnourished people of various combinations of policies. At the worst extreme, the number of malnourished would reach the staggering figure of almost 3 billion (mostly in the densely populated countries of Asia) in 2010. According to the model, the best alternative would appear to be a combination of relatively high income growth outside the agricultural sector, food aid, the stabilization of international food prices at a high level, the redistribution of urban incomes, and the redistribution of incomes in favor of the agricultural sector. But even under these assumptions the number of malnourished would still rise from 370 million in 1975 to 470 million in 2010. The study concludes that "a lowering of hunger will be realized only if income differences within both the urban and the rural populations can be reduced," but the quantification of this in combination with the other policy changes just listed is not included in the summary that is so far available.

The conclusion of the MOIRA model is the same as that of an important study carried out by the International Labour Office (ILO) in preparation for the recent World Employment Conference.[35] This study concludes that the "basic needs" (including nutritional needs) of the poorest 20 percent of the populations of the developing countries can be met by the year 2000 through a combination of rapid economic growth and the redistribution of income. Some of the necessary income redistribution would already be achieved if the major part of the required increase in production were produced by the poorest farmers. But in many developing countries the redistribution of access to productive resources, primarily through agrarian reform, would also be a prerequisite.

The "basic needs" approach to development proposed by the ILO appears to offer the best hope for the elimination of hunger and

malnutrition within an acceptable period. The World Food
Conference resolved "that all Governments should accept the removal
of the scourge of hunger and malnutrition, which at present
afflicts many millions of human beings, as the objective of the
international community as a whole, and should accept the goal that
within a decade no child will go to bed hungry, that no family will
fear for its next day's bread, and that no human being's future and
capacities will be stunted by malnutrition."[36] Regrettably it is
already clear that this ambitious goal cannot be achieved so soon
as 1985, and it is necessary to work out the full implications of
achieving it within a more realistic period, such as the single
generation that now separates us from the end of the century.

Among the implications that have to be studied are the effects
of different rates of population growth on all aspects of the
question. The MOIRA model indicates the expected beneficial
effects of lower population growth on the numbers of malnourished,
but treats population growth as an exogenous variable. The ILO
projections are optimistically based on the United Nations "low"
assumption for population growth.

The elimination of hunger and malnutrition will clearly entail
an even faster growth of food production in the developing
countries than the 3.6 percent a year needed to meet effective
demand without the further growth of imports. The World Food
Conference in fact reaffirmed the target of 4 percent annual
agricultural growth that is a major feature of the International
Development Strategy for the Second United Nations Development
Decade.[37] Although the achievement of such a high rate of
production growth is believed to be feasible, it is likely to be
difficult to sustain for any great length of time. It is therefore
imperative that rates of population growth be slowed down in order
to reduce as soon as possible the size of the task for food
production.

The prospects for a reduction in the rate of population growth
during the next quarter century do in fact now seem somewhat
brighter than before. In the past the United Nations "medium"
projections (which were regarded as the most probable) generally
turned out to be too low when subsequently checked against the
actual growth of population. Recent evidence indicates, however,
that birth rates in developing countries have declined more than
expected, so that the latest "medium" projections may turn out to
be too high.

This appears to be due at least partly to the population
programs carried out in the 1960s and 1970s, and thus the
"developmentalist" theory so prevalent at the Bucharest conference
already seems less plausible than it was thought to be only two
years ago. The idea that a reduction in the rate of population
growth would come automatically and sufficiently rapidly as a
consequence of economic development and social justice had obvious
attractions for those countries at Bucharest that felt they did not
have an acute population problem, as well as for those who feared
that population programs might take precedence over the urgent need
for development.[38] It is now evident, however, that birth rates
have begun to decline in many developing countries without these
preconditions. Worldwide, the birth rate fell from 34 per thousand

in 1965 to 30 in 1974, and the death rate from 15 to 12 per thousand, producing a slight decline in the rate of natural increase from 1.9 percent in 1965 to 1.8 percent in 1974. Although the main influence has been continuing reductions in the already low birth rates of most developed countries, birth rates have also begun to decline in such densely populated developing countries as China, India, Indonesia, the Republic of Korea, Pakistan, the Philippines, and Thailand. They fell particularly sharply in the Caribbean countries, Chile, Costa Rica, Panama, Tunisia and Venezuela, and more slowly in many other developing countries. There was some slowing of the rate of natural increase of population between 1965 and 1974 in Asia and the Caribbean, no change in mainland Latin America and the Near East, and a slight rise in Africa.[39]

It would be difficult to maintain that during the short space of a decade there has been such a change in the economic and social conditions of so large and diverse a group of countries as to fulfill the developmentalist requirements. On the contrary, it would appear that population programs can be successful even if acute poverty is still present, as it will be, in spite of all efforts, in large areas of the world for some time to come.

The increasing numbers of applications to the United Nations Fund for Population Activities for assistance in population programs of all kinds also indicate that the emphasis on developmentalism at Bucharest has not affected the realization of the immediate need for such programs, and that the conference has more probably led to increased concern and action in this regard.

But, in spite of these encouraging signs, it cannot yet be assumed with any confidence that the size of the task for the world's agriculture during the next quarter century will be sufficiently reduced. Population growth will continue to be rapid, even if it is slowing down slightly sooner than was expected. The new encouraging trends may even be temporarily reversed. With commendable caution, therefore, the report from which the above figures on declining fertility are quoted concludes only that they "indicate that the world is at least headed toward, rather than away from, a more slowly increasing population."[40]

Indeed, the immediate effect of improved food supplies and general welfare may often be a temporary increase in the rate of population growth, because of lower death rates, especially among children. But it is only when parents see children surviving who might otherwise have died that they realize that there is no need to give birth to so many children, and that the basis is laid for a long-term decline in population growth rates.

It is thus essential that the influences leading to reduced fertility should be reinforced to the maximum extent possible by suitable population policies, including family planning programs. As was rightly emphasized at Bucharest, such policies and programs have to be conceived as an integral part of economic and social development programs, and not as a substitute for or in isolation from them. They must be seen as a means to arrive at better nutrition and a higher quality of life in general, and not as ends in themselves.

The Malthusian specter is still with us -- perhaps never more

so than in the critical period between now and the end of the
century. However, the specter will not materialize inevitably, as
was believed by its inventor. What happens can be very much
influenced by what is done in such fields as population policy,
agricultural production, and income distribution. If the right
policies are followed, there is some hope that, even with the
greatly enlarged population that must be expected by the year 2000,
at least the worst manifestations of hunger and malnutrition can be
eliminated.

NOTES

[1]United Nations World Population Conference, 1974, "Food
production," Resolution VII, Report of the United Nations World
Population Conference 1974, Bucharest, 19-30 August 1974, E/CONF.
60/19 (New York: United Nations, 1975): 36.

[2]United Nations World Food Conference, 1974, Report of the World
Food Conference, Rome, 5-16 November 1974, E/CONF. 65/20 (New
York: United Nations, 1975): 33.

[3]United Nations World Food Conference, 1974, "Achievement of a
desirable balance between population and food supply,"
Resolution IX, Report of the World Food Conference, cited above,
p. 11.

[4]United Nations, World Population Prospects 1970-2000 as Assessed
in 1973, ESA/P/WP.53 (New York: United Nations, 10 March 1975.)

[5]One of the authors has analyzed these swings in some detail
elsewhere: See K. C. Abercrombie, "Changing views on the man-food
relationship," CERES: FAO Review 4, no. 2 (March-April 1971):
22-26. See also Thomas T. Poleman, "Food and population in
historical perspective," in Thomas T. Poleman and Donald K.
Freebairn, eds., Food, Population and Employment: The Impact of
the Green Revolution (New York: Praeger, 1973), pp. 3018; and D.
Gale Johnson, "Food for the future: A perspective," Population
and Development Review 2, no. 1 (March 1976): 1-5.

[6]United Nations World Population Conference, 1974, Report of the
United Nations World Population Conference, cited in note 1, p.
7.

[7]FAO, The State of Food and Agriculture 1975 (Rome: FAO, 1976):
57. The comparison of the rates of growth of food production and
domestic demand that follows is drawn from the same source.

[8]The main proponents of this argument are Ester Boserup and Colin Clark. See Ester Boserup, The Conditions of Agricultural Growth (London: Aldine, 1965); and Colin Clark, Population Growth and Land Use (London: Macmillan, 1967), pp. 133–138.

[9]K. C. Abercrombie, "Population and food," in Leon Tabah, ed., Population Growth and Economic Development in the Third World (Liege: International Union for the Scientific Study of Population, 1975): Vol. I, 352–354. This chapter discusses in detail (although on the basis of less up-to-date information) many of the subjects that can be only briefly mentioned here. The lack of any significant correlation between the rate of increase of population and food production is confirmed in an unpublished correlation analysis carried out by W. Schulte of FAO.

[10]FAO/WHO, Energy and Protein Requirements: Report of a Joint FAO/WHO ad hoc Expert Committee, Rome, 22 March –2 April 1971, FAO Nutrition Report Series No. 52, WHO Technical Report Series No. 552 (Rome: FAO, 1973). This is the latest in a long series of FAO and WHO expert groups that have assessed nutritional requirements in the light of advancing knowledge. It is the first to consider energy and protein requirements together.

[11]This calculation assumes that all of the cereals fed to livestock are fit for direct human consumption. We know of no estimate of the quantity that is not fit for human consumption, but believe that it would not greatly reduce the overall figure. Part of the cereals that are not fit for human consumption are deliberately made so under "denaturing" regulations.

[12]K. C. Abercrombie, "The international division of labour and of benefits in food and agriculture," Society for International Development, European Regional Conference, 1975, Linz, Austria, 15–17 September 1975, Conf. Doc. No. 21–e (Linz, 1976), p. 13.

[13]United Nations World Food Conference, Assessment of the World Food Situation, Present and Future, E/CONF. 65/3 (Rome: United Nations, 1974): 59–60.

[14]United Nations World Food Conference, Assessment, cited above, pp. 64–67. The most persistent critic of FAO's earlier estimates of the total number of malnourished is Colin Clark. Lord Boyd Orr, FAO's first Director-General, stated in 1950 that "a lifetime of malnutrition and actual hunger is the lot of at least two-thirds of mankind." See John Boyd Orr, "The food problem," Scientific American 183 (1950): 11–15. P.V. Sukhatme has defended this statement as a correct interpretation of the information on nutritional requirements available at the time in "The phenomenon of hunger as FAO sees it," World Justice 5, no. 2 (December 1963): 154–156. Indeed, many of the critics seem to give insufficient weight to the great advances that have been made in nutritional knowledge. Yet, almost a quarter of a century after Boyd Orr's famous statement, Colin Clark was still

accusing him of confusing "two columns in a statistical table."
See Colin Clark, "Population," l'Osservatore Romano, weekly
English edition, 2, no. 302 (10 January 1974): 7. Thomas T.
Poleman, another critic of FAO's earlier estimates, welcomes the
"changes at FAO" implied by the latest estimates, but still
considers them exaggerated. He may, however, wish to reconsider
even this guarded welcome, since the 1,900 kilocalories he
believes is FAO's figure for the average dietary energy needs of
people in south Asia is actually the limit below which they are
considered to be suffering from a severe degree of protein-energy
malnutrition. See Poleman, "World food: A perspective,"
Science 188, 4188 (9 May 1955): 510-518. It should be noted
that the latest FAO estimates have so far been published only in
summary form in the Assessment document for the World Food
Conference. More detailed explanations of the assumptions and
calculations are to be expected in the Fourth World Food Survey,
now in preparation.

[15]FAO, "World food and agricultural situation -- April 1976,"
Monthly Bulletin of Agricultural Econmics and Statistics 25, no.
5 (May 1976): 5-6.

[16]Office of the Registrar-General, Vital Statistics Division,
Sample Registration 7, no. 4 (New Delhi: 1974).

[17]President's Science Advisory Committee, Panel on World Food
Supply, The World Food Problem, Vol. II, Report of the Panel on
World Food Supply (Washington, D.C.: Government Printing Office,
1967): 423.

[18]Pieter Buringh, H. D. J. Van Heemst, and G. J. Staring,
Computation of the Absolute Maximum Food Production of the World
(Wageningen: Centre for Agricultural Publications and
Documentation, 1975).

[19]K. M. Malin, "Food resources of the earth," Proceedings of the
World Population Conference, Belgrade, 30 August-10 September
1965, Vol. 3 (New York: United Nations, 1967): 386-387. In
this field, where speculation and vague assumptions are so rife,
Malin seems to have set an unbeatable record.

[20]Clark, Population Growth and Land Use, cited in note 8, pp. 142-
157. This author takes Malin's calculations seriously. A
penetrating analysis of his own calculations has recently been
made by J. Klatzmann in Nourrir Dix Milliards d'Hommes (Paris:
Presses Universitaires de France, 1975), pp. 205-208.

[21]Roger Revelle, "Will the earth's land and water resources be
sufficient for future populations?" The Population Debate:
Dimensions and Perspectives. Papers of the World Population
Conference, Bucharest, 1974, Vol. 2 (New York: United Nations,
1975): 3-14. This is a great advance on the corresponding study
presented to the previous World Population Conference, and indeed
is one of the most scientific of the available studies. Most of

the assumptions are explicity stated, but some of them seem highly optimistic.

[22]Buringh et al., Computation of the Absolute Maximum Food Production of the World, cited in note 18.

[23]Walter H. Pawley, "In the year 2070," CERES: FAO Review of Development 4, no. 4 (July-August 1971): 22-27. This justly celebrated article is a condensation of a lecture delivered at the Nordic Conference, Stavanger, in 1970. Reference to the text of the lecture, which unfortunately has not been published, is necessary for a full understanding of the author's views.

[24]Herman Kahn and William Brown, "A world turning point -- and a better prospect for the future," Corporate Environment Program, Research Memorandum 13, Hudson Institute, New York, 1975.

[25]Donella H. Meadows, Dennis L. Meadows, Jorgen Randers and William W. Behrens III, The Limits of Growth, a Report for the Club of Rome's Project on the Predicament of Mankind, (London: Earth Island, 1972), pp. 48-52, 141.

[26]Mihajlo Mesarovic and Eduard Pestel, Mankind at the Turning Point, the Second Report to the Club of Rome, (New York: Dutton/Reader's Digest Press, 1974), pp. 115-129.

[27]Kahn and Brown, cited in note 24.

[29]United Nations World Food Conference, Assessment, cited in note 13, pp. 78-107,

[30]United Nations World Food Conference, The World Food Problem: Proposals for National and International Action E/CONF. 65/4 (Rome: United Nations, 1974).

[31]Anthony S. Rojko and Patrick M. O'Brien, "Organizing agriculture in the year 2000," Food Policy 1, no. 3 (May 1976): 203-219. An earlier account of this study was presented at a recent FAO seminar and is summarized in its report. See FAO, Population and Food and Agricultural Development: Report of a Seminar Organized by the International Association of Agricultural Economists in Collaboration with FAO and UNFPA (Rome: Food and Agriculture Organisation, 1976), pp. 32-34.

[32]United Nations World Food Conference, 1974, "Objectives and strategies of food production," Resolution I, Report of the World Food Conference, cited in note 2, p. 5.

[33]United Nations World Food Conference, Assessment, cited in note 13, p. 95.

[34]Jerphaas de Hoogh, M. A. Keyzer, H. Linnemann, and H. D. J. Van Heemst, Food for a Growing World Population: Some of the Main Findings of a Study on the Long-Term Prospects of the World Food

Situation (Amsterdam: Economic and Social Institute, Free University, February 1976).

[35]Tripartite World Conference on Employment, Income Distribution and Social Progress, and the International Division of Labour, Employment, Growth and Basic Needs: A One-World Problem (Geneva: International Labour Office, 1976). Although this report deals fully with the international aspects of meeting basic needs, its main contribution concerns domestic policies. It may be regarded as a first contribution to defining the "new national social order" that is a necessary counterpart of the concept of a New International Economic Order as called for by the United Nations General Assembly.

[36]United Nations World Food Conference, 1974, Resolution I, Report of the World Food Conference, cited in note 2, p. 4. The words quoted echo those of Henry Kissinger in his address to the conference.

[37]United Nations World Food Conference, 1974, Resolution I, Report of the World Food Conference, cited in note 2, p. 4.

[38]One of the authors has elsewhere questioned the correctness of this view and its assumption of a necessary correlation between the success of population programs and general development. See Arthur McCormack, "Population and development at Bucharest and after," International Development Review 17, no. 3 (September 1975): 14-19. Another recent study concludes: "General development ('Take Care of the People and Population Will Take Care of Itself') or specific thresholds such as women's status or popular education or income redistribution are being strongly advanced at present in the post-Bucharest spirit. There can be little doubt that such fundamental social changes would also affect fertlity downward, but they too take time and effort, not to mention (far larger) funds, and they are, after all, the ends for which fertility control is a means, not the other way round. It is precisely the drag that population growth places on such development that is the problem; the question is, can fertility be lowered significantly as a prior aid in the process?" Bernard Berelson and Ronald Freedman "The record of family planning programs," Studies in Family Planning 7, no. 1 (January 1976): 37-38.

[39]Population Reference Bureau, World Population Growth and Response, 1965-1975: A Decade of Global Action (Washington, D.C.: Population Reference Bureau, Inc., 1976), pp. 2-3, 265. The world figures are based on an estimated 1974 birth rate of 27 per thousand in China; if, as some experts believe, a rate as low as 17 is more accurate for China, the world birth rate for 1974 would be reduced to 28 per thousand.

[40]Population Reference Bureau, World Population Growth and Response, cited above, p. 3.

Food for the Future:
A Perspective

D. GALE JOHNSON

The early and middle years of the decade of the 1960s were a period of significant concern about the prospective adequacy of world food supplies. Production shortfalls in grain -- the major source of calories for the world -- occurred in China, the Soviet Union, and South Asia. By 1965 there was serious concern about the possibility of mass starvation in South Asia, and there may have been severe food stringencies, including famine, in China in the early years of the decade. In the United States, the President's Science Advisory Committee undertook a major study and issued a major two-volume report, The World Food Problems, in 1967.[1] Numerous Congressional hearings were held.

By the time The World Food Problems was published, however, the world food situation had eased substantially, grain exports were declining, and world grain stocks were increasing. The rapid spread of the new high-yielding varieties of rice and wheat in South Asia led at least one prominent government official to announce in late 1968 that "the world has recently entered a new agricultural era" attributed to "the sweeping advances in food production in several major developing countries."[2]

The rapid change in the availability of world grain supplies and the sharp increase in grain reserves in the years following 1967 led industrial countries and most developing countries to turn their attention to other and seemingly more pressing problems. As a result, in the period from 1967 through 1972 little was done, at least as a matter of conscious policy, that would contribute to a sustainable increase in per capita food supplies in the developing countries. Will the world's policy makers behave in the same way once the present period of food stringency and relatively high food prices is behind us, as I am confident it will soon be? The answer is likely to be in the affirmative, unless food and population

Reprinted with permission of the Population Council, from
POPULATION AND DEVELOPMENT REVIEW, Vol 2, No. 1, March 1976,
(1-19).

problems are generally accepted as long-run problems requiring continuous attention and effort.

A paragraph from the World Food Conference Assessment of the World Food Situation that emphasizes the world's quixotic attitudes toward food and agriculture merits quotation in full:

> In recent years the prevailing view of the world food situation and prospects has swung from pessimism in 1965-66 to optimism in the "green revolution" years from 1967 to 1970 or so, and subsequently back again to pessimism. It is essential that the widespread concern, which has arisen from the recent events described above, should be directed to the longer-term problems and lack of concern following a few years of good harvests.[3]

What is the nature of the world's food problems? If we accept as the primary objective of food policy the achievement of levels of food consumption that will provide nutritionally adequate diets for a very large percentage of the world's population, it should first be recognized that there is not a single world food problem, but rather a multiplicity of problems. The primary, though not sole, cause of inadequate nutrition is poverty or low income. According to estimates made in the Assessment approximately 25 percent of the population of the developing regions (excluding Asian centrally planned economies) has inadequate intake of energy and protein in contrast to only 3 percent in the developed, or industrial, regions.[4]

Higher-income families in the developing countries generally have adequate caloric intakes, even though the average level of income of the half of the populations with highest incomes is less than a third or half of the US poverty level.[5]

In the recent analyses of prospective per capita food supplies in the years ahead, of which there have been several, the emphasis has been upon increasing the rate of growth of food production as the primary solution to the major world food problems. This emphasis is appropriate if poverty is the primary cause of insufficient food intake.

Poverty occurs or exists for many reasons. In the developing countries one of the main sources of poverty is low productivity in agriculture -- the low output yield per worker and per hectare of cultivated land. Increasing productivity in agriculture and thus increasing the total food supply is one way of increasing real per capita incomes and reducing poverty. A further consideration is that in the developing countries a very large fraction of the total population is directly or indirectly engaged in agricultural production. While the fraction of the population of the developing countries living in rural areas has been decreasing and will continue to decrease, the absolute numbers living in rural areas will probably not decline before the end of this century. Projections of the Food and Agriculture Organization indicate that between 1975 and 1985 the population economically active in agriculture in the developing market economies may increase by 56 million or by more than 12 percent.[6] The projections indicate a reduction in the percentage of the economically active population engaged in agriculture in these countries from 62 percent in 1975 to 54 percent in 1985. At this rate of decline it would be approximately 1990 before half of the economically active population was employed outside agriculture. Thus, growth of real per capita income in the developing countries will be strongly influenced by the growth of real per capita incomes of farm and other rural people for the rest of this century -- and beyond.

I. PROJECTED FOOD SUPPLY AND DEMAND

Within the last two years, four different projections of world food supply and demand for 1985 have been published. Two were undertaken at American universities; one was done for the World Food Conference; and the fourth was by the US Department of Agriculture.[7] While projections can be in error, and often are, the basic similarity of the projection results should not be ignored. The four projections, singly or collectively, do not bear out the prophets of doom, glooms, and mass starvation. However, they all point to an imbalance in the regional distribution of the surpluses and deficits between food supply and demand. While each of the four projections indicates that for the developing countries as a group food production is likely to grow more than population, each also indicates that with a continuation of current policies and past trends food production in the developing countries will fail to keep pace with the growth of demand unless substantially greater investment is made in agriculture in the developing countries than has occurred in the past.

Each of the studies indicates that the developed regions as a group, including the Soviet Union and Eastern Europe, are likely to have a significantly more rapid growth of food production than of food demand. The World Food Conference projections indicate that demand might grow by 1.5 percent annually between 1970 and 1985, while food production, based on past production trends, would increase by 2.8 percent annually.[8] The Iowa State University study projects a potential export availability in 1985 of 180 million metric tons of grain for the developed market economies plus the Soviet Union, assuming medium population growth and historical income growth.[9] The University of California projections indicate a projected export availability of more than 104 million tons of grain in 1985 from North America and Oceania.[10] In 1969-71 the developing countries imported about 24 million tons.

The methodology of the US Department of Agriculture projections did not permit an excess of production over demand for the world for 1985. Thus the export availability projected for the developed countries reflected the import demand of the developing countries. To meet the maximum growth in import demand of the developing countries, as well as an increase in imports by the developed countries from freer trade in agricultural products, would require an annual growth of grain production in the developed countries of 2.8 percent.[11] This is roughly the growth rate of

grain production in the developed countries during the period of
1960-62 to 1969-71.[12] During the latter three years, the three
major exporting countries -- Australia, Canada, and the United
States -- were limiting grain production in an effort to bring
supply into equilibrium with demand at politically acceptable
prices.

In effect, the four projection studies indicate that during
the next decade the food supply-demand situation in the developed
regions will be similar to that of two decades prior to 1972.
Output growth is likely to be greater than demand growth, including
import demand from the developing countries. It is noteworthy
that in the United States during the two decades prior to 1972 the
real price of grain declined.[13]

While the four projections emphasize the substantial increase
in grain imports by the developing countries during 1970-85, the
trends in food consumption in those regions that would emerge if
grain imports per capita remained at approximately the 1969-71
level would be about the same as in the past two decades. In the
World Food Conference projection, food production in the developing
market economy countries grows at approximately the same rate as
population --2.6 and 2.7 respectively.[14] This would imply roughly
constant per capita food consumption during the next 15 years
compared to an increase of about 0.4 percent annually from
1952-72.[15] In the US Department of Agriculture projections, except
the one assuming economic stagnation through the remainder of this
decade, per capita food production in the developing countries was
projected to increase by from 0.1 percent to 1.4 percent
annually.[16] The higher figure assumes a major effort by the
developing countries to expand food production.

I should not leave the impression that there is unanimous
agreement that with reasonable and attainable effort there would be
continued modest improvement in per capita food consumption in the
developing countries during the next decade. Numerous statements
by the officers and staff of the Overseas Development Council give
a much more pessimistic view. Their major publications imply that
the events of the early 1970s portend a substantial worsening of
the world food supply situation, especially as it affects the lower
income populations of the developing countries. Thus, in By Bread
Alone Brown and Eckholm's view seems to be that the world has
entered " . . . a period of more or less chronic scarcity and
higher (food) prices."[17] The cause of this situation is that
" . . . the soaring demand for food, spurred by both continuing
population growth and rising affluence, has begun to outrun the
productive capacity of the world's farmers and fishermen."[18]

As a private group that devotes its energies to the problems
of economic development, with special emphasis upon food and
agriculture, the views of the Overseas Development Council warrant
serious consideration. It should also be noted that the
pessimistic appraisal of the prospects for improving per capita
food consumption in the developing countries through increased
production in those countries has been the view that has received
most attention in the popular or general media. As a result of the
acceptance of this pessimistic view, in many cases attention has
been addressed to -- I might argue diverted to -- measures to

reduce food consumption in high income countries as a means of meeting the food needs of the poor countries.

II. THE FUTURE OF REAL FOOD PRICES

A number of arguments have been advanced in support of the view that food will be more expensive, in real terms, in the future than in the past decade.[19] If real food prices were to increase significantly, it would mean that supply was lagging behind demand. The implications for the world's poorer people would be serious, indeed. It would almost certainly mean that an even larger share of their meager incomes would be required to maintain what is an already nutritionally inadequate diet in far too many instances. I shall now turn to an examination of these arguments.

There are grounds for believing that real grain prices in international markets will be somewhat higher in the future than during the four or five years prior to 1972. The primary reason is that international grain prices were depressed during that period by the overvaluation of the American dollar and, to a lesser extent, the Canadian dollar.[20] For the countries whose currencies are closely related to the dollar, the increased imports of agricultural products by countries whose currencies have appreciated in terms of the dollar will result in high grain prices. To some considerable degree the impact of the overvaluation of the dollar was offset for the American farmer by annual direct payments of US $3 billion to $4 billion from 1968 through 1972.

But this source of increase in the international prices of grain -- perhaps of the order of 10-15 percent in the long run -- is not what the pessimists have had in mind. As I understand their position, it is that the expansion of supply required to keep pace with the growth in demand will result in significantly higher unit costs of production of food products. Such a development is possible, but is it likely? If so, it would represent a reversal of the trend toward <u>lower</u> real prices of grain for the past six decades. In the United States, between 1910-44 and the 1971 crop year, the real farm price of feed grains and hay declined by 40 percent; the real price of food declined by 37 percent.[21] Yet, the declines in real farm prices in the United States, as measured here, have been somewhat less than the declines in real export prices from the major grain exporting areas.[22]

Why is it expected that the real cost of producing grains will increase? The reasons appear to be the following: First, there is relatively little uncultivated land remaining in the world, and, in particular, all of the diverted acreage in the United States, the main food-exporting country, has been returned to production; second, increasing yields will increase costs in part because of diminishing physical returns to fertilizer; and, third, the price of farm inputs -- especially those based on petroleum products -- will be substantially higher in the future than in the past.

The first two reasons for rising real costs of grain can be said to be either incorrect or irrelevant or both. There are substantial possibilities for expanding the cultivated land area in Africa, South America, South East Asia, North America, and Australia.[23] It is true that the potential for expanding cultivated land in parts of Asia is relatively small, but this does not mean that the real costs of producing grains must increase. It is not at all certain that cultivating additional land is generally a significantly lower-cost means of expanding output than increasing yield per acre. Thus, in the United States, the answer for the past several decades appears to be that it has generally been cheaper to expand output through higher yields than by adding new land; some new land has been brought into cultivation, but far more has been retired.[24] Also, it is clearly possible to increase yields in the developing countries. Even though yields have increased in the developing countries in the past three decades, they are still much lower than in the industrial countries.[25]

The second reason for higher cost -- increasing yields will result in higher costs because of diminishing returns to fertilizer -- is not a valid one. While higher yields may require more fertilizer per unit of output, it need not follow that real costs per unit of output will increase due to the higher yields, because fertilizer is only one of many inputs used in grain production. As yields increase per unit of land, the productivity of other inputs increases and thus contributes to lower costs, if the returns to these resources remain constant. In addition, farmers do not continue to operate on a single fertilizer-yield function; rather, the function changes over time. As farmers use fertilizer for longer periods of time, they learn how to use it more effectively through a multitude of adjustments such as better-adapted seed varieties, greater plant density, timing of application, location of fertilizer in the soil, and more effective types of fertilizer.[26]

There is a possibility that the prices of farm inputs having a significant energy component, and, in particular, the price of fertilizer, will be substantially higher in the future than in the past. The Tennessee Valley Authority estimates indicate that a fourfold increase in the price of natural gas -- from US $0.20 per thousand cubic feet to $1.00 per thousand cubic feet -- would increase the plant gate price of a ton of urea by $22.00 or approximately 24 percent.[27] It now appears that a price of $1.80 per thousand cubic feet of natural gas, which is equivalent to oil at $11.75 per barrel, is a more realistic expectation for the next several years. At this price of natural gas, the increase in the gate price of urea would be about $46.00 per ton, or an increase of 50 percent compared to the 800 percent increase in the price of natural gas.

But there are many other factors that affect the price and cost of nitrogen fertilizer. One important factor is technology and size of plant. Thus, for instance, with a natural gas price of $1.80 per thousand cubic feet, the cost of producing nitrogen fertilizer with 1974 technology would be less than the cost with free natural gas and 1960 technology.[28]

Another factor affecting the cost of fertilizers in the developing countries is the low ratio of output to capacity. In such countries most of the nitrogen plants operate at 60-70 percent of capacity.[29] If capacity utilization were increased to the level achieved in the industrial countries of approximately 90 percent, fertilizer costs would decline significantly. Protectionist trade policies practiced by many developing countries, notably vis-a-vis their fertilizer industries, impose unnecessarily high costs on their farmers.

It is a serious error to assume that the three- or fourfold increase in world prices of fertilizer between 1972 and 1974 was primarily due to the increase cost of fuel for the production of nitrogen fertilizer. The Tennessee Valley Authority attributed much of the price increase to the failure to expand fertilizer production capacity during the unprofitable period from about 1968 through 1972. When demand increased in 1973, there was no new capacity to come into production, and the consequence was a rapid increase in fertilizer prices.[30]

The TVA analysis seems to be borne out by recent price developments in the international fertilizer market. By mid-1975 international prices of urea had declined to about $160 per ton compared to prices of over $350 per ton in late 1974 and early 1975.[31]

This is not to suggest that there will be no increase in the real price of fertilizer. Real energy costs are up and are likely to remain significantly above the 1972 level even if nitrogen production is expanded significantly in the Middle East. Further, the future price of fertilizer must be high enough to provide a return on the investments required to expand production. Prior to 1973 the price of nitrogen fertilizer provided a very low return on investment because demand had lagged behind the productive capacity of the industry for several years. TVA estimates indicate that, with a natural gas price of $1.50 per thousand cubic feet, raw material costs account for less than 45 percent of the gate price of urea; return on investment accounts for a major share of the remainder.[32]

I do not believe that a valid case has been made for significant increases in the real costs of producing grains in the years ahead. It has only been asserted. The improvements in methods of production that we have seen over the past four decades can continue into the future -- and will if appropriate efforts are made to discover and implement lower cost approaches to producing grains and other foods. As I will argue below, if the appropriate conditions are established, there are major potentials for relatively low-cost increases in output in the developing countries.

But even if real prices of internationally traded food soon return to the pre-1972 level, this will hardly be sufficient to achieve a significant improvement in the per capita food supplies in the developing countries. Significant improvement in the food situation in the developing countries requires three things: (1) increasing the growth rate of food production in the developing countries compared to the past two decades; (2) achieving a relatively high rate of per capita income growth; and (3) reducing the rate of population growth.

III. INCREASING FOOD PRODUCTION

There are two main alternatives for increasing food supplies in the developing countries -- increased production and increased imports. For most of the developing countries significant further increases of food imports do not represent a viable alternative. The anticipated increase in demand for grains in the developing market countries for 1970 to 1985 is approximately 240 million tons according to the projections made for the World Food Conference.[33] Only a relatively small part of this increased demand is likely to be met by additional imports. While the major grain exporters will probably have the capacity to increase exports to the developing countries, it is most improbable that the developing countries would (or should) choose to use their limited foreign exchange earnings to import large additional quantities of grain, or that the industrial countries would provide the grain as aid.

If as much as one-fifth of the increased demand were met by increased grain imports of 50 million tons annually, the added cost in foreign exchange might be as much as $8 billion. This cost is well beyond reasonable expectations of what could be afforded by the developing countries and what the major industrial countries are likely to provide as aid.

There is a large potential for increasing the growth rate of food production in the developing countries. In some countries there can be substantial increases in the cultivated area; in all countries there can be large increases in yields. The much higher grain yields in the industrial countries than in the developing countries do not appear to be due to more favorable weather or soil. In fact, with the potential for double and triple cropping that exists to a far greater degree in the developing countries than in the temperate zone industrial countries, the potential annual production from a hectare of land is almost certainly greater in the developing than in the industrial countries.

It is instructive to compare the development of yields in the industrial and developing countries over the past four decades. During 1934-38 grain yields per hectare were the same at approximately 1.15 tons. Grain yields were static in the developing countries between 1934-38 and 1952-56, while yields in the industrial countries increased to 1.37 metric tons per hectare. During 1969-70 grain yields averaged 2.14 tons in the industrial countries and 1.41 tons in the developing countries. It is worth noting that grain yields in the developing countries in 1969-70 were slightly higher than in the industrial countries in 1952-56.[34]

The necessary conditions for significant increases in food production in the developing countries are well known. The main conditions are a major expansion of agricultural research in the developing countries; adequate supply of modern inputs required to increase yields; incentives sufficient to encourage farmers to make the required adjustments; and expansion and improvement of transportation, marketing, and processing institutions. In addition, increased investment in human capital and improved communications are desirable not only because of the contributions to increased agricultural output, but also through assisting farm people in the long-run adjustments that they must make to economic growth.[35]

IV. AGRICULTURAL RESEARCH

In 1965 it has been estimated that only 11 percent of the world's publicly supported agricultural research was undertaken in Latin America, Africa, and Asia.[36] Agricultural research has had a major role in the approximate doubling of grain yields in the industrial countries over the past four decades. Obviously many other factors have had a role -- the reduction in fertilizer costs, improved pest and disease controls, and more effective control of weeds. But for all of these changes, the research results can be said to have been a necessary condition. Without hybrid corn, for example, lower-cost fertilizer would have had only a modest impact on yields.

If the industrial nations are sincere about increasing the food supply in the developing countries, they will support a major expansion in agricultural research, both basic and applied, in the developing areas. The expenditures required are not large. It has been estimated that total expenditures on publicly supported agricultural research in 1965 were a little more than one billion dollars for the world; private research relevant to agriculture was almost certainly less than that. What is required is a long-term commitment by the United States and other industrial countries to provide support for agricultural research throughout Africa, Latin America, and Asia.

There are a number of multilateral and bilateral ways that the industrial countries could assist agricultural research. One is through regional centers, and, in fact, it appears that much of the international funding, both private and public, of agricultural research is now going to such centers. While regional centers are important and can make significant contributions, it is necessary that national research capabilities be developed. Such capabilities are required to adapt varieties to local conditions; to continue the fight against the predators of nature -- insects and disease; to provide the capacity for independent discovery; and to create centers for developing the scientists and researchers for the future.

There are substantial risks involved when new grain varieties are introduced into agricultural regions that lack viable agricultural research institutions. Such institutions are also required to adapt varieties to meet local tastes, just as it has been necessary to modify the high-yielding varieties of rice to meet the taste patterns of South Asia. When one grain is the major food, it is important that it be a grain that is liked.   All people, rich and poor, have their likes and dislikes.

There are a number of particular research programs that deserve the highest priority.   Root crops, which serve as the main food for upwards of a tenth of the world's population, have received little emphasis.   A major research effort is required to eliminate the tse-tse fly, which, according to the Preparatory Committee of the World Food Conference, would add "7 million square kilometers to agricultural lands, an area larger than the agricultural area of the United States."[37]

If the industrial nations among them were to commit themselves to provide $1 billion annually for a decade and half that amount for the subsequent decade, great strides could be made to bring the benefits of agricultural research to all the major climatic zones of the developing world.   Additional scientists need to be trained, but the facilities for such training are readily available in the United States and elsewhere.

V.   ADEQUATE SUPPLY OF MODERN INPUTS

Man, land, and seed are not enough to achieve grain yields of 2.5 to 3.0 tons per hectare, which will be necessary in the developing countries by the end of this century.   Plant nutrients adequate for such a yield must be added to the land; plant populations dense enough for high yields require protection from diseases and insects; water supplies, where irrigation is required or desirable, need to be reliable and controllable.

Some of the modern inputs, such as pumps and pipes for irrigation, can be produced economically in the developing countries.   However, developing countries, in their efforts to industrialize, should not make the mistake of maintaining and encouraging farm input industries where the costs are substantially greater than import costs.   High-cost fertilizer or high-cost insecticides only add to the costs of food and inhibit the growth of output.

There are two possible developments, both largely outside the control of the developing countries, that could contribute substantially to the availability of modern farm inputs -- international trade liberalization and peace in the Middle East.   I shall comment briefly about each of them.

VI.   INTERNATIONAL TRADE LIBERALIZATION

It is infrequent when a link is made between the liberalization of international trade and per capita food supplies in the developing countries.   It is unfortunate that there is so little understanding of the role of trade in increasing incomes and food supplies in the developing countries. The industrial countries have been willing to go to a considerable distance in removing barriers to trade in industrial products produced by other industrial countries, but they have been most reluctant to lower the barriers to their imports of agricultural products and labor-intensive manufactures produced from the developing countries. It seems rather odd that it is accepted that there are gains from trade among industrial countries in industrial products, yet little progress has been made in extending the same advantages to the developing countries where their products are competitive with either the industrial or agricultural products of the industrial countries.

The present round of General Agreement on Tariffs and Trade negotiations provides an opportunity for reducing the barriers to trade on labor-intensive industrial products, such as textiles, and on farm products that cannot be competitively produced in temperate zones, such as sugar and numerous fruits and vegetables. The additional foreign exchange earnings made possible by reduced trade barriers would permit the developing countries to obtain modern farm inputs at the lowest possible cost. There would be less need to engage in high-cost production of such inputs if the low-cost products of the developing countries had ready access to international markets.

VII. PEACE IN THE MIDDLE EAST

A stable and durable peace in the Middle East could make a significant contribution to the food supplies of the developing countries. Higher yields will require substantially larger amounts of fertilizer, especially nitrogen. The lowest-cost area in the world for producing nitrogen fertilizer is the Middle East. The Middle East has enormous reserves of natural gas that could serve as the base for a large fraction of the world's output of nitrogen fertilizer. More natural gas is flared (wasted) in the Middle East than is consumed by the entire petrochemical industry in the United States. The transportation costs of the fertilizer to the rest of Asia would be lower than from the other major areas of low-cost production.

There has been a significant increase in nitrogen fertilizer production in the Middle East following the major developments in the technology of production in the mid-1960s. The unstable political situation, however, has seriously inhibited the very large capital investments that are required. If there were a durable peace, there is no reason why such investments would not be made and a very large supply of nitrogen fertilizer be made available. As suggested by the cost calculations outlined above, the nitrogen fertilizer could be produced at relatively low cost even if the price of crude oil were to remain substantially above the 1972 levels. While some of the natural gas supplies of the

Middle East will find their way into European markets, it is likely that the gas will return most to its owners by being transformed into a finished product in the region. The production of nitrogen fertilizer is one of the profitable activities that peace would make possible.

There are those who point out that it would be dangerous to concentrate the production of nitrogen fertilizer in the Middle East. To do so, it is claimed, would only add another economic weapon, in addition to crude oil, that could be used in the future. Perhaps so; no one could say that such would not be the case. But we live in a world in which many risks must be taken. In my opinion, the benefits to the developing world of a substantial increase in the supply of nitrogen at relatively low cost are worth the risk. Increasing grain yields in the developing countries to at least the level of current yields in the industrial countries will require enormous amounts of nitrogen fertilizer. A durable peace in the Middle East is of great importance to the poor people of the world.

VIII. ADEQUATE INCENTIVES

The growth of food production will be disappointing unless farmers are provided with adequate incentives. The ready availability of the products of agricultural research and modern farm inputs is not enough. The utilization of these products must be profitable. These seem like self-evident statements and they are. Yet we still find many governments, especially among the developing countries, that follow short-run and shortsighted policies of holding down the prices of major farm products. India, for example, has generally held the price of rice below world prices. It is not surprising that the new high-yielding varieties of rice have failed to be adopted as rapidly or as extensively as the new wheats, since the price of wheat has been kept much above world prices.

IX. THE SHORT RUN

The measures that can increase the rate of growth of food output in the developing countries admittedly require time. Expanding fertilizer output in the Middle East would require a minimum of three years, while significant results from expanded research activities would almost certainly take much longer. The factors that will affect food supplies in the developing countries for the rest of the decade, except for changes in incentives, are already at play. Whether the developing countries can escape food shortages over the next two or three years will largely depend upon climatic conditions and the capacity of the industrial countries to respond if adversity should strike.

X. INCREASING INCOMES

Those measures that increase the rate of growth of food production
will contribute to an increase in the growth rate of real per
capita incomes. Increased yields, both per worker and per unit of
land, generally lead to increased real incomes. This is not true
for everyone living in rural areas, since the techniques that
result in increased yields may not be applicable in all
agricultural regions. Thus, if increased yields and total output
of the major food crops result in lower prices, those regions not
participating at all or participating only partially in the
increased yields can suffer losses in real incomes.

   This possibility was considered to be a serious potential
adverse consequence of the new high-yielding varieties of rice and
wheat. These were -- and still are -- adapted to irrigated areas
and often only to irrigated areas with above average quality of
water control. It was also feared that the high yields would cause
significant declines in the demand for farm labor, and thus
landless laborers would suffer severe losses of employment. Some
also argued that the higher returns from the high-yielding
varieties would induce landlords to dispossess tenants and operate
their farms with hired labor.

   It is true that the high-yielding varieties, as well as other
approaches to increasing yields, generally result in lower labor
requirements per unit of output. But in most cases, the increase
in output has been greater than the reduction in labor use per unit
of output, and as a consequence the aggregate demand for labor has
increased. This is likely to be a general phenomenon until certain
types of farm machinery are introduced. While the introduction of
tractors and associated machinery can result in reduced labor
demand, other types of machinery, such as mechanical pumps powered
by motors, may still make it possible to increase labor use in an
area due to increased output, more than offsetting the reduced
input per unit of output.[38]

   The lower grain prices that some feared would result from the
high-yielding varieties did not occur to any significant degree, if
at all. During the latter part of the 1960s, when the
high-yielding varieties were being adopted, grain output growth did
not outstrip the growth of demand. What is often ignored in the
uncritical fear of adverse price effects from increased yields is
that demand is also growing in the developing countries, and that
if grain yields increase significantly this will contribute to
faster economic growth and, in turn, an increase in the demand for
grain.[39] Obviously, there is some rate of increase of grain output
in the developing countries that would result in a decline in real
grain prices. But this rate of output growth appears to be
significantly greater than any that has been achieved in the past
two decades.

Further, for at least some years to come, a faster rate of grain output than of grain demand growth could be offset in the developing market economies by reducing imports. Of course, this would force some adjustments on the industrial countries, but real grain prices could be maintained in the developing countries.

Finally, some decline in real grain prices in at least some of the developing countries would have positive benefits and could be consistent with rising real incomes of farmers. A number of the developing countries have used price supports and control of imports to hold wheat prices substantially above world market levels. Where the new high-yielding wheat varieties have been introduced and account for a significant fraction of total wheat output, it would appear reasonable to pass some of the economic benefits along to consumers.

XI. POPULATION GROWTH

While it is quite possible to increase food production at a rate equal to or greater than the rate of population growth, two points merit strong emphasis: first, significant improvements in per capita food supply are likely to be achieved only as birth rates decline and the rate of population growth is reduced in the developing countries; second, while the governments of the densely populated developing countries can look forward with a fairly high probability to a maintenance of existing levels of per capita food production and perhaps to some improvements, for the next two decades, it may become increasingly difficult for food output growth to keep pace with unchanged population growth as we look beyond the present century. This is not to say that food output growth rates of 2.5-3.5 percent cannot be maintained for a long time to come, but it does seem reasonable to become concerned about such high output growth rates as we look further and further into the future.

But I think the first point is perhaps the more important and the more pressing. Assuming that population in the developing countries were to continue growing at 2.5 percent annually for the remained of this century, then an increase in food production of 109 percent (3 percent annually) would increase per capita food consumption by only 13 percent. An increase in food production of 135 percent in the 25-year period would increase per capita production by 27 percent.

However, it will not be an easy task for the developing countries to increase food production even by 3 percent annually. To do so will require substantial investments in irrigation, research, and production facilities for fertilizer and farm equipment, and in transportation and marketing facilities. And what will be achieved? An increase in per capita food production that is so modest that a significant fraction of the poorer people in the developing countries will realize little or no improvement in their diets.

If, however, population growth were to reduced to 2 percent annually for the remainder of this century, a 3 percent growth in food production would result in a 28 percent increase in per capita food production. With that large an increase in per capita food production and the larger increase in per capita incomes that would be associated with a slower population growth, at least during the transition to the slower rate, there could be a significant improvement in the diets of the poorer segments of the population.

XII. FOOD, ECONOMIC GROWTH, AND POPULATION

Even if there were no significant interrelationships between increased per capita growth rates of food production and of income, on the one hand, and population growth rates, on the other hand, it would be, of course, desirable to achieve relatively high growth rates for food and income. However, it seems to me -- a nonspecialist in demography -- that increasing per capita food supplies and per capita incomes would have some effect in reducing population growth. One effect would be through further increasing the percentage of the population living in urban areas in the developing countries. A second effect would be that higher per capita incomes might have a number of direct and indirect effects upon birth rates -- increased levels of schooling that would affect the cost of children, improved access to medical facilities and contraceptive information, opportunities for greater investments in material and financial assets for old age security, and the intangible effects of greater confidence in and hope for a more satisfactory future for the parents and children.

In any case, it seems unlikely that increased per capita food supplies and higher incomes would result in increasing population growth rates in all but the very poorest of the developing countries. For most developing countries, further reductions in death rates will come more slowly than during the past two decades when life expectancy increased from 35 to 40 years in 1950 to 52 years recently.[40] Thus, any reduction in birth rates should fairly soon be followed by reduction in population growth rates.

XIII. THE ROLES OF FOOD AID

I have not mentioned food aid up to this point. This has been deliberate since I do not believe that large-scale and continuous food aid commitments serve any useful purpose in improving food supplies in the developing countries.[41] However, food aid on a modest scale can meet some useful objectives. One may be as part of the support of specific agricultural development projects, such as new land settlement where food supplies may be required during the first season. Another may be the use of food aid to assist in maintaining school attendance by the provisions of meals in schools. A related program for which food aid could be of value would be in providing supplementary foods for certain vulnerable groups, such as pregnant and lactating women and young children.

It may also be desirable for the industrial countries to provide food aid to the developing countries to meet emergency conditions. The major accomplishment of US food aid has been its capacity to meet emergency needs for food cause by such natural disasters as floods, cyclones, and earthquakes. The concept of emergency could be extended to significant departures below trend production caused by adverse weather conditions or other factors that can have a significant effect on a single year's grain production. If developing regions or countries were assured that any shortfall in grain production in excess of some given percentage, such as 6 percent, from trend production would be met by outside sources, a substantial stability of grain consumption could be achieved at modern cost. Such a program would have few disincentive effects with respect to either production of the holding of stocks or reserves in the developing countries.[42]

XIV. CONCLUDING COMMENTS

The foregoing arguments suggest there is cause for cautious optimism that the food supply situation of the developing countries will continue to improve over the coming decades. But if significant improvements in per capita food production and consumption is to be achieved, it will occur only if the governments of the world give serious and continuing attention to the measures required to increase the food production capabilities of the developing countries. It is not at all certain that governments will give sufficient attention to these problems. One has to admit that little has occurred during the past three years, when there has been so much emphasis upon food crises and problems, to give one much hope that once grain prices decline and the food situation continues to ease, governments will act with greater foresight than they did from 1967 through 1972.

NOTES

This article draws to a substantial degree upon the author's monograph, World Food Problems and Prospects (Washington, D.C.: American Enterprise Institute for Public Policy Research, 1975.).

[1] President's Science Advisory Committee, The World Food Problems, 2 vol. (Washington, D.C.: US Government Printing Office, May 1967).

[2] Lester R. Brown, "A new era in world agriculture" (USDA 3773-68), paper presented at the symposium on World Population and Food Supply, Kansas State University, Manhattan, Kansas, December 1968, p.1.

[3] United Nations World Food Conference, Assessment of the World Food Situation: Present and Future, E/Cong. 65/3 (Rome: United Nations, 1974), p. 29.

[4] United Nations, Assessment, p. 66. Thomas T. Poleman has questioned the reliability of the estimate that 25 percent of the population of the developing countries has inadequate supplies of calories and energy. He points out, correctly in my opinion, that the estimate is based upon limited data of questionable reliability. See "World food: A perspective," Science 188, no. 4188 (9 May 1975): 515-516. This issue of Science is a special issue on food and contains many excellent articles.

[5] See United Nations, Assessment, pp. 62-64 for a discussion of the relationship between food, energy, and income in the developing countries.

[6] W. Schulte, L. Naiken, and A. Bruni, "Projections of world agricultural population," Monthly Bulletin of Agricultural Economics and Statistics 21, no. 1 (January 1972): 1-10.

[7] The four studies are: United Nations World Food Conference, Assessment of the World Food Situation: Present and Future, E/Conf. 65/3, 1974; Economic Research Service, US Department of Agriculture, The World Food Situation and Prospects to 1985, For. Agric. Econ. Rpt. no. 98, December, 1974; L.L. Blakeslee, Earl O. Heady and C.F. Framingham, World Food Production, Demand and Trade (Ames: Iowa State University Press, 1973); and University of California Food Task Force, A Hungry World: The Challenge to Agriculture (Berkeley: University of California Division of Agricultural Sciences, July 1974).

[8] United Nations, Assessment, p. 90.

[9] Blakeslee, World Food Production, p. 218. In 1969-71, net grain exports from the developed market economies and the Soviet Union were 34 million tons; in 1974-75 approximately 60 million tons.

See Economic Research Service, US Department of Agriculture, World Agricultural Situation, WAS-7, June 1975, p. 24.

[10]University of California Task Force, A Hungry World, p. 190.

[11]ERS, USDA, The World Food Situation, p. 36.

[12]ERS, World Agricultural Situation WAS-7, p.24.

[13]ERS, USDA, The World Food Situation, p. 28.

[14]United Nations, Assessment, pp. 87 and 90.

[15]United Nations, Assessment, p. 30.

[16]ERS, USDA, The World Food Situation, p. 36.

[17]Lester R. Brown with Erik P. Eckholm, By Bread Alone (New York: Praeger Publishers for Overseas Development Council, 1974) p. 6.

[18]Brown with Eckholm, By Bread Alone, p. 1.

[19]Real food prices reflect changes in nominal or actual prices adjusted for the effects of general price level changes.

[20]G. Edward Schuh, "The exhange rate and US agriculture," American Journal of Agricultural Economics 56, No. 1 (February 1974): 1-13.

[21]In both calculations, prices received have been adjusted for direct government payments as though the total of such payments represented a net addition to prices and incomes, thus moderating the magnitude of the measured decline. I have elsewhere argued that the direct payments did not increase net farm incomes by more thn one-third to one-half of the gross payments received. See D. Gale Johnson, Farm Commodity Programs: An Opportunity for Change (Washington, D.C.: American Enterprise Institute, 1973), p. 48.

[22]Farm prices in the United States in 1971 included farm program payments, and an export subsidy was paid on wheat. No such distortions existed in 1910-14.

[23]"While in some developing countries the practical ceiling on land development may have been reached, in a large part of the developing world there remain land resources which are either unutilized or are utilized in production processes with very low returns. The largest °land-reserves' in the developing countries are in South America, Africa and in parts of Southeast Asia. All of these regions suffer from specific limitations...but modern technology is increasingly able to cope with the problems and one may expect some very major development programmes for cultivated land in these regions." Preparatory Committee of the World Food Conference, Preliminary Assessment of the World Food Situation:

Present and Future, United Nations, E/Conf. 65/PREP/6, April, 1974, p. 65.

[24]Total cropland (excluding cropland used only for pasture) in the United States in 1950 was 409 million acres, in 1969 total cropland was 384 million acres (H. Thomas Frey, _Major Uses of Land in the United States: Summary for 1969,_ ERS, USDA, Agr. Econ. Rpt. No. 247, 1973, p. 4). Cropland harvested declined from 352 million acres in 1949 to 286 million acres in 1969, ibid., p. 9.

[25]Theodore W. Schultz has given strong emphasis to the limited role of land in agricultural production: "...only about one-tenth of the land area of the earth is cropland. If it were still in raw land in its natural states, it would be vastly less productive than it is today (italics in the original). With incentives to improve this land, the capacity of the land would be increased in most parts of the world much more than it has been to date. In this important sense cropland is not the critical limiting factor in expanding food production.
"The original soils of Western Europe, except for the Po Valley and some parts of France, were, in general, very poor in quality. They are now highly productive. The original soils of Finland were less productive than most of the nearby parts of the Soviet Union, yet today the croplands of Finland are far superior. The original croplands of Japan were vastly inferior to those of Northern India. Presently, the difference between them is greatly in favor of Japan. There are estimates that the Gangetic Plains of India could, with appropriate investments, produce enough food for a billion people...
"Harsh, raw land is what farmers since time immemorial have started with; what matter most over time, however, are the investment that are made to enhance the productivity of cropland." The food alternatives before us: An economic perspective," Agricultural Economics, University of Chicago, Paper Nol 74:6, 25 May, 1974.

[26]In a study of adjustments in the use of nitrogen fertilizer in the Corn Belt, Wallace Huffman found that there was a major change in the fertilizer corn yield function between 1959 and 1964. The function became much flatter, and, even through nitrogen use per acre of corn increased 150 percent between 1959 and 1964, the marginal productivity of nitrogen declined very little. See Wallace Huffman, "The contribution of education and extension to differential rates of change," unpublished Ph.D. dissertation, University of Chicago, 1972, pp. 27–34.

[27]Tennessee Valley Authority, "World fertilizer market review and outlook," in US Senate Committee on Agriculture and Forestry, _US and World Fertilizer Outlook,_ 93d Congress, 2d Session, March 21, 1974, p. 106. Natural gas at $0.20/MCF is equivalent to petroleum at $1.54 per barrel; at $1.00/MCF for natural gas the equivalent petroleum price is $6.53 per barrel.

[28]Tennessee Valley Authority, "World fertilizer market." For a 200 ton per day plant using the older technology, the gate pricce of a ton of urea if natural gas were free would be about $164. With natural gas at $1.80/MCF the gate price would be $140 for a plant producing 1000 tons of ammonia per day. Interpolations made by the writer.

[29]Tennessee Valley Authority, p. 80.

[30]Tennessee Valley Authority, p. 68.

[31]ERS, USDA, World Agricultural Situation, WAS-7, June, 1975, p. 19.

[32]Tennessee Valley Authority, p. 102.

[33]United Nations, Assessment, p. 84. The projected increase is from 385.7 million tons in 1970 to 628.5 million tons in 1985.

[34]Grain yields from FAO data.

[35]Space limitations prevent more than noting the importance of the expansion and improvement of marketing, transportation, and processing institutions and increased investment in human capital and improved communications. For the role and importance of investment in human capital, see Theodore W. Schultz, Transforming Traditional Agriculture (New Haven: Yale University Press, 1964), Chap. 12.

[36]Estimates made by Robert Evenson and Yoav Kislev in Agricultural Research and Productivity (New Haven: Yale University Press, 1975), p. 16. Unpublished estimates provided by the authors indicate that in 1970 approximately 15 percent of publicly supported research was in the developing countries. China is not included due to lack of data.

[37]Preliminary Assessment of the World Food Situation: Present and Future, p. 66.

[38]Lester Brown, in arguing for selective mechanization of farms in developing countries, gives the following example: "Traditional methods of irrigation, using human or animal power, often do not supply enought water to meet minimum crop needs...One study of pumping costs in India found that it costs 495 rupees to pump 10 acre-inches of water by hand, assuming a 40-foot lift. With draft animals used to provide the power to operate a Persian wheel, the cost drops to 345 rupees. But the really startling gain is the decline of cost to 60 rupees with the use of a diesel engine. As more water becomes available and production is boosted, more labor is required for land preparation, planting, fertilizing, weeding and harvesting, and threshing." (By Bread Alone, p. 218).

[39]In the ERS-USDA model of rates of growth in production and demand

for grains in the developing market economies, four different
assumptions are made concerning increases in grain production and
the rates of economic growth for 1970-85. The extreme cases
assume annual growth rates of grain production of 2.7 and 4.1
percent. In these two cases the rate of growth of demand was
projected as 3.0 and 3.9 percent. Thus most of the higher rate
of grain output growth was offset by a higher rate of growth of
demand for grain and the real price effects would be minimal
(ERS, USDA, The World Food Situation and Prospects to 1985,
p.36).

[40] Bernard Berelson, "World Population: Status Report 1974,"
Reports on Population/Family Planning, no. 15. (January 1974):
7. In the same publication the following is stated: "Whichever
is the cause and whichever effect -- and the influence appears to
run in both directions -- high birth rates are the companion of
poverty. Countries with the highest birth rates are usually
those with the least productive economies, the lowest
urbanization, the highest illiteracy, the lowest percentage of
children in school, and the lowest availability of medical
personnel" (p. 9).

[41] Space does not permit development of the arguments for the
ineffectiveness of large-scale food aid. I have developed these
arguments in World Agriculture and Disarray (New York: St.
Martin's Press, 1973), pp. 161-180.

[42] For fuller development of this proposal, see Yail Danin, Daniel
Sumner, and D. Gale Johnson, "Determination of optimal grain
carryovers," Office of Agricultural Economics Research,
University of Chicago, Paper no. 73:12.

The Priority of Nutrition in a Nation's Development

FRED T. SAI

All societies have known, for short or long periods, what it means and costs to go hungry. Among the approaches existing to resolve the problem of inadequate nutrition in developing lands is that of convincing the leadership that the situation is real and begs immediate attention. There are different ways to make the established order face reality and then implement a rational programme benefiting all of society, but especially mothers and infants. A coherent scheme is described here.

I. STATEMENT OF THE PROBLEM

Throughout human history and in all societies, the importance of acute hunger to individual and national well-being has been recognized. The lessons of famines resulting from droughts, floods, locusts or wars are too well known. Yet the more subtle forms of 'hunger', such as chronic undernourishment and individual or mixed deficiencies of nutrients, are yet to be considered a serious threat to national development. The reasons for this are many. The science of nutrition is relatively new, even to medicine. Most national development plans are concerned with immediate and pressing economic problems; policy makers like to be identified with programmes which yield visible results in a very short time. The populations and groups most adversely affected by poor nutrition -- especially women and children -- are relatively silent in most countries. And the argument has not been made convincingly enough that good nutrition would make a direct

From **IMPACT OF SCIENCE ON SOCIETY**, Vol XXIV, No. 2, 1974, (131-141), reprinted by permission of the publisher, UNESCO, Paris.

contribution to development, or that poor nutrition would retard progress directly or indirectly by diverting resources from more profitable programmes.

It is necessary, therefore, for nutritionists and health workers to demonstrate convincingly to administrators and policy makers these problems of poor nutrition, that good nutrition deserves a priority rating in national development plans, and that the nutrition component of these plans can be properly executed and their impact evaluated in a reasonable span of time. There are direct and indirect indices for demonstrating the nutritional problems of people, which could be used when making a case for a place to be given to the question of nutrition in national development.

Demographic Considerations

The size of the population, its age and sex distribution and its rate of natural increase are of great importance. In most of Africa, the population is increasing very rapidly (at a rate of about 2.5 per cent per annum). Food production has not been keeping pace consistently with this natural rate of growth, so the gap between the population and its food supply is increasing in some areas. There is a high fertility rate, meaning that a large proportion of the women are either pregnant or nursing at any given time, thus increasing their demand for food. The average women in Africa south of the Sahara has between six and eight completed pregnancies during her fertile life. Twenty per cent of the population are under 5 years of age and up to almost 50 per cent under 15. The young group, with proportionately higher food requirements, are non-contributors to its supply, and the greater their numbers the more the food resources are strained.

There is a very rapid migration of young adults to towns in search of jobs and improved social status. The main urban centres in Africa are growing at rates of between 7 and 12 per cent per annum. Young people are leaving the farms and joining the ranks of the food buyers. Many remain unemployed for prolonged periods and their nutrition, as well as that of their children, suffers. The seriousness of the nutritional problems of such migrant groups has been stressed previously [1]. Their nutritional status and that of their dependants are thus largely related to their earning power, but the negative effect of such heavy emigration from rural agricultural areas on food production has not been stressed enough.

The growth and development of children are good indices of national nutritional status and can be used to demonstrate differences between regions, groups and classes of the same country. It is known that the children of poorly fed mothers are smaller at birth than those of the adequately fed. Low birth weight is associated, in turn, with the inability to thrive and with higher neo-natal mortality. Children are usually breast-fed, and do reasonably well up to 6 months or so. Graphs of growth of

African and European children during the first 6 months show a very satisfactory comparable growth performance. From 6 months onward the African children lag behind and, by the age of 2, there is quite a divergence with the African child showing almost no growth in the second year. It is from the age of about 6 months that supplementary foods should enter the child's diet. For a variety of reasons either no supplements are given or else gruels of maize, sorghum, cassava or yams with their relatively poor protein are served. These foods are adequate in neither quality nor quantity, and the growth rate reflects this.

In developing countries, there are differences between the growth rates of children -- from well off 'elite' families and those from poorer homes -- which can be used to demonstrate the importance of good nutrition. (See Fig. 1.) Regional differences within the same country are also important. Children from the drier sub-Sahara zones are generally thinner for their age and height than those of the coastal zones; the adults are usually tall and thin, and their weight ratio is less satisfactory than that of Africans in the forest and coastal belts. The weight of adults is a fairly sensitive index of current nutritional state. Research work in Africa has demonstrated that adults in the sub-Sahara regions may lose more than 2 kg in weight during the pre-harvest period known as 'the hungry season'.[2] This weight is regained immediately after the harvest. Such fluctuations in weight cannot be good for maximum productivity.

Morbidity and Mortality

Rates of specific illness due to nutritional deficiency and deaths resulting from these would provide the most satisfactory evidence of the scale of the nutrition problems of any country. Unfortunately the figures that are available are not very dependable. some reports hardly mention malnutrition as a cause of death, although our knowledge of the areas would lead one to suspect widespread malnutrition. Apart from being a direct cause of death, malnutrition can act synergistically with infections and other illnesses which are then registered as the basic cause of death. Even some health authorities accept these registered causes of death, and thus fail to demonstrate the critical importance of nutrition.

Protein-calorie malnutrition (PCM) (discussed elsewhere in this issue of Impact) is a very important cause of morbidity and mortality in children from about 6 months to 4 years of age. Overt clinical cases have been estimated at between 2 and 10 per cent for various countries in Africa. Where growth retardation to a severe enough degree has been used as the indicator of PCM, then as many as 40-50 per cent of all African children in the same age group are malnourished at some time or other. When untreated, the death rate from overt PCM alone may be as high as 20-50 per cent depending on the type of malnutrition. A study in Latin America (see Table 1)

Table 1. Nutritional deficiency as an associated cause of death in children under 5 years,[1] in Latin America, 1968–69

Place	Percentage with associated nutritional deficiency in selected causes of death			
	All causes	Diarrhoeal disease	Measles	Respiratory systems
Cities				
Cali, Colombia	39.9	51.3	65.3	39.8
Cartagena, Colombia	43.7	64.0	94.1	36.1
Kingston, Jamaica	31.7	40.6	–[2]	23.8
La Paz, Bolivia	40.7	67.3	50.4	24.6
Medellin, Colombia	50.7	62.0	83.8	29.1
Monterrey, Mexico	49.2	64.6	70.2	21.3
Recife, Brazil	59.8	70.3	74.3	50.9
Resistencia, Argentina	57.0	67.3	66.7	50.0
Ribeirao Preto, Brazil	67.1	75.4	70.8	56.0
San Juan, Argentina	36.9	68.4	–[2]	8.3
San Salvador, El Salvador	42.5	48.3	69.2	28.7
Santiago, Chile	38.8	52.1	–[2]	30.6
San Paulo, Brazil	45.2	62.9	51.9	32.6
Rural or suburban				
Chaco, Argentina[3]	48.1	66.9	53.8	24.5
Franca, Brazil	48.9	68.8	–[2]	45.5
San Juan, Argentina	38.6	61.5	36.4	35.2
San Juan, Argentina[3]	39.2	53.3	35.7	38.9
San Salvador, El Salvador[3]	44.4	54.6	78.4	39.5

1. Neonatal deaths excluded.
2. Percentage not calculated for base less than 10.
3. Rural areas.
Source : Modified by J. D. Wray from Table 25, *Inter-American Investigation of Mortality in Childhood: Provisional Report.* Washington, D.C., Pan-American Health Organization, 1971.

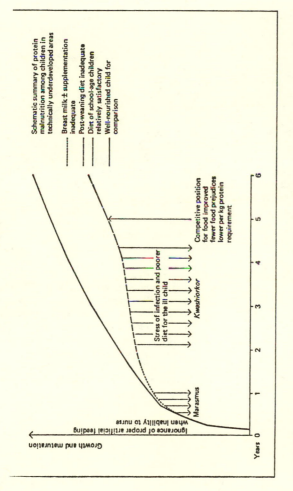
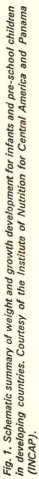

Fig. 1. Schematic summary of weight and growth development for infants and pre-school children in developing countries. Courtesy of the Institute of Nutrition for Central America and Panama (INCAP).

has shown that, in thirteen cities and five rural or suburban areas, malnutrition was an associated cause of death in 30 to more than 60 per cent of all deaths in children under 5 years of age. The general death rates of this age group are therefore an indirect indicator of the importance of nutrition.[3]

It must be remembered that in some countries as many as 50 per cent of all children born alive do not reach the age of 5 years. If malnutrition is such a basic contributor to these deaths, then there is no escaping its importance. From the various rates mentioned, one can easily calculate the national wastage of child life attributable to malnutrition; apart from this, there is the cost to the nation of attempts to treat such an eminently preventable condition.

In most developing countries with poorly developed health services, no more than a small fraction of sick children receive adequate treatment. The costs of treating malnutrition can be calculated thus: in Accra, Ghana, an average of 500 cases of PCM were being treated a year (1970), so at U.S.$240 per case this works out to U.S.$120,000 per annum. If we assumed the rest of the country treats another 500, the total cost of PCM treatment to the public treasury would be U.S.$240,000. Over-stretched funds and hospital beds are thus being 'misused'. The indirect costs to the nation of pregnancies ending in live births, but with no children surviving to age 5, must be truly staggering. Alan Berg has given estimates of what malnutrition costs in The Nutrition Factor: its Role in National Development[4].

Among women, the best indication of poor nutrition is obtained during pregnancy and the lactation period. Most women in Africa do not gain weight commensurate with the needs of pregnancy.. During normal pregnancy a woman should weigh 6-9 kg more at term than before pregnancy. Some actually lose weight during lactation so that these women may, in fact, be milking the flesh off their bodies for their children. The baby in the womb is a parasite and all of its body, including its stores of vitamins and minerals, have to be derived from the mother. If the mother has inadequate supplies, the child hardly gets enough and the mother become depleted. The lack of extra nourishment, therefore, coupled with frequent unplanned pregnancies leads to high maternal morbidity and mortality, or at the very least to premature aging.

A Rise in Calorie Intake

Every country depends on its working groups for its economic progress, so it is almost axiomatic that a hungry nation cannot achieve its full potential. The evidence in Africa to support this statement is not very impressive; more information must be obtained. The productivity of agricultural and other workers in Africa, however, is known to be comparatively low. Although much research is still needed to isolate the role played by other environmental factors, there can be no doubt that chronic undernourishment contributes to this condition.

Theoretically, therefore, it would seem that an increased calorie intake should automatically lead to an increased output; if this does not happen, then restricted output is not attributable solely or mainly to calorie deficiency. But this line of argument ignores the known fact that the productivity of labour is influenced in no small measure by educational and psychological factors which are more deeply ingrained than the simple lack of food, although prolonged undernourishment does sap strength. Merely increasing food for an adult labor group, however, may not increase output. What happens when food intake is further restricted is much more important among adults. Experiments which cut down the food intake of labourers will show reduced productivity, perhaps even immediately.

In Accra and many other parts of Ghana, labourers go to work on an empty stomach and have their breakfast at mid-morning. Their rate and efficiency of work decline appreciably before breakfast. In other countries, it has been noticed that providing breakfast for a work force or schoolchildren makes for better work output and cuts down absenteeism.

All these factors serve to illustrate that the problem of nutrition is a serious one at the national level. But a problem does not earn a priority rating for planners simply because it affects a large number of people by causing disease or sapping strength. The opportunities for solving the problem must be actually or potentially available. To cite an example from medicine in Africa, there is the case of yaws. Yaws was a common disease in Africa, affecting a large number of people, both young and old, and causing much disfigurement. It was not a very rapidly fatal disease; it certainly did not compare with malaria as a cause of morbidity and mortality. As soon as penicillin proved its efficacy against yaws, however, practically all the African nations undertook to fight against the malady. In a few years yaws was almost completely wiped out from many parts of the continent. Yet malaria remains a serious concern.

The problem with nutrition is that it does not lend itself to one-time solutions, and its complexity tends to discourage any efforts at all. Poor nutrition is therefore widespread; it causes much ill health and death, and may be responsible for underproduction.

It must be mentioned that there are certain things in life which are not quantifiable in economic terms. After making valiant efforts to justify by economic arguments that nutrition be given priority, the humanitarian arguments should not be forgotten. What price happiness? How much do smiles and laughter, in a home where children are living happily and growing well, mean to a nation? What is the negative effect of unhappiness, however caused? No one knows, but these things should be considered. In parts of Africa there are long periods of mourning when work ceases. Should a reasonable fraction of these deaths be due directly or indirectly to malnutrition, then preventing their occurrence will not only increase happiness but also raise the output of work.

II. WEAK POINTS IN THE FOOD CHAIN

It would be necessary to analyse in some considerable detail the major causes for the state of affairs described thus far so that remedial action can be specific. In considering the food chain -- production, marketing, preparation and consumption -- various weaknesses immediately become obvious in all developing countries. Let us discuss some of these.

Food Production, Processing and Storage

In many countries food production is very poorly organized. It is in the hands of peasant farmers who have maintained with little change the agricultural practices, including cropping patterns, from one generation to the next. Usually food production is based on the staples, all other food crops being auxiliary. In many parts of Africa, men help to clear the land and to sow. After that it is women's work until the harvest. Elsewhere, women have responsibility for non-staples such as green leafy vegetables, peas, beans and tomatoes. There are areas where the vegetables that are eaten are only those that are gathered.
Whether cultivated as crops or simply gathered, production per acre is relatively low. Everything is at the mercy of nature. When the rains are good and timely, things are usually fine; but any deviation from the normal, such as too much or too little rain, storms at the wrong time, or droughts, would interfere with the crops. The periodic famines of India, Pakistan and Bangladesh caused by floods or droughts and the cyclical famines of the Sahelian region of Africa are catastrophes of major dimensions which affect the rest of the world.
The main staples of rice, wheat, maize and the starchy roots, and fruits such as yams, cassava and plantains, are all prone to various diseases and parasites which man has to keep in check. In addition, the crops themselves may be food for vermin and insects. Proper harvesting, processing and storage are therefore necessary in the warm, humid climates in which man's competitors for food thrive so easily.

Unconsumed Cereals

An estimated 10-30 per cent of all food grain produced in tropical Africa is never consumed by man. There are countries where corn is buried underground for storage purposes, its owners being lucky to retrieve 50 per cent. Even where reasonably constructed traditional barns and silos are used, insects still attack the stored grain. A saving of the grain thus lost may in some cases amount to a 40-50 per cent increase in the food available over the year. In countries with only one harvest season, the lack of processing and good storage accounts for the cyclical undernourishment that is accepted as almost the normal state of things. A typical example is the sodure or 'hungry season' of the Sahelian region in Africa. Practically no effort is made to store green leafy vegetables. Where there is more than one rainy season, this poses no problems; otherwise, there are entire months when none of the major sources of vitamins and minerals are available. Pulses and legumes are very difficult to store, and the amount wasted is even greater than for cereal grains.

Food processing, even elementary treatment with insecticide, is not sufficiently widespread in developing countries. The excessive concern during the last decade with the adaptation of large silos for use in the rural areas of developing countries has looked almost like trying to use a 'jumbo jet' for travel between villages in Africa. The first element in the processing chain, namely individual farmyard protection of grain, is often absent. This (coupled with poor transport facilities) has meant that a farmer may not readily see the crop he has produced translated into cash; thus he has no encouragement for working harder in the future.

Transportation and marketing facilities are other major obstacles in the food chain. Even in countries with good trunk roads, the small 'feeder' lanes so vital for bringing produce from farms may be poorly developed or completely lacking. Thus, when the harvest is good, food may be rotting on farms just a short distance from arterial roads, with consequent high prices in urban areas. The road systems and the economy may be such that food by-passes needy villages and even large conglomerates on its way to major urban centres. In times of plenty, this situation can further reduce the price fetched by foods.

Food Purchasing

In most rural areas only a small proportion of the family diet is acquired by purchase. The staple is almost invariably produced by the family. Such cash as may be obtained from sale of farm produce is used mainly to buy small quantities of fish, meat and oils for sauces and condiments. Note that in agricultural areas, the cash comes from the sale of surplus staple. Thus a poor harvest of the staple crop adversely affects nutrition in a more complex manner. Town dwellers normally have to purchase all their food; the availability of cash is thus the major determinant of adequate nutrition. The more experienced townsmen know their markets well and have more cash and steadier incomes, whereas rural immigrants are often poor earners, dwelling in peri-urban slums and as a group their nutrition is generally bad.

Preparation and Consumption at Home

Poverty and ignorance can combine to make a household select only cheaper foods or those known traditionally as the correct foods. There is little real knowledge of the qualitative aspects of foods, nor of the different requirements of various physiological groups. Many households store food badly. Other than in some very special groups such as are found in China and India, the preparation at home of green vegetables and pulses and beans does not conserve their nutrients or improve their digestibility. There is, indeed, a greater variety of foodstuffs not considered good for children where the justification lies in the mode of preparation or storage.

Among some Latin American populations, for example, milk was not considered good for children. This is understandable if one remembers the consequence of drinking non-pasteurized milk. Peas and beans, if badly prepared or given in too large quantities, cause flatulence and various stomach upsets. The destruction of water-soluble vitamins by some types of African cooking is appalling. Therefore, apart from gross wastage on farms and during transport and marketing, there is also nutrient wastage within the household.

The distribution of food within the home, or the 'pecking-order', is often contrary to true physiological needs. The better protein foods are often high prestige foods and it is the male members of the household who have first choice of all the meals, women and children coming last. When all these factors are taken together, serious nutritional problems are likely to affect some groups.

Family or Household Size in Relation to Nutrition

There are not many good studies on the relation of household size to nutrition. We can say that among communities suffering from marginal nutrition, poorly spaced childbirth depletes the mothers of minerals such as iron and calcium and of vitamins such as folic acid. As already mentioned, absence of weight gain during pregnancy and premature aging nare the price many women pay for having children. The children arrive under weight, and the frequency of PCM is higher among poorly spaced children. In towns, given the same income levels, the larger the peri-urban household in terms of children, the poorer its nutrition.

Infection

The load of infection is heavy on populations in developing countries. Measles, whooping cough, diarrhoeal diseases are all too frequent especially in the weanling. The pneumonia-diarrhoea complex is a syndrome which brings fear to many homes since it is associated with high death rates. During these infections, children lose their appetite, or they may have various foods withdrawn from their diet on the wrong premise that these are bad for children who are ill. All this, together with an excessive drain of nitrogen from the body, makes illnesses frequent precursors and companions of malnutrition, as Table 1 has shown.

III. REMEDIES: PREPARING THE GROUND

There is a need to have acceptance at the highest possible governmental level of the fact that (a) food and nutrition problems are serious enough to warrant their consideration in planning national development and (b) every nation, however inadequate its base of planning, outht to have some kind of national food and nutrition policy. It is not easy to propose one simple method by which any national government can be made aware of this issue. Whatever method appears feasible at any given time should be accepted as the correct one.

Individuals who are respected and have contacts with ministers of state can be made aware first, so that they can convince these officials. Wives and friends of ministers of state may be involved. It is necessary to get only those high officials who have direct responsibility (such as ministers of health or agriculture) since they may not be either powerful or vocal enough in governmental circles. Any strong minister, or even secretary of the ruling political party, may be the right person to convince before the government is ready to listen and take action.

It is necessary to have at the highest possible governmental level some form of machinery to keep nutritional problems under constant review, to suggest solutions and to plan programmes and activities. Owing to the complex nature of nutritional programmes, interministerial nutrition committees or commissions have been tried in many places. Theoretically this is a sound approach but, in practice, they have not worked too well in many African countries. Their unsatisfactory performance may be because of a lack of trained personnel, insufficiency of funds, or inability to identify satisfactory projects which can be seen as politically and economically advantageous. To establish a commission on nutrition when there is no highly trained nutritionist with a functioning research unit available is unlikely to yield satisfactory results.

If there exist such an individual and such a unit, then the specialist should be the secretary of the nutrition commission, and his unit could provide the service secretariat. The commission could consist of the ministers of agriculture, health, education, community or rural development and economic planning. It would be useful to add members from university departments of food science and nutrition or food and nutrition research institutes. Major women's organizations may be represented, as well as individuals known for their standing in the society and interest in the subject. A total membership of about fifteen is usually satisfactory, since the commission will establish standing committees to include persons who are not necessarily members of the commission itself.

Simply obtaining governmental acceptance (and even setting up a good secretariat) is only the first step and will not, of itself, achieve much. There must also be a massive and overt commitment of several important governmental agencies as well as mobilization of all the resources of the people themselves.

IV. GOVERNMENTAL AGENCIES AND THEIR ROLE

Ministry of Agriculture

There is a great need for ministries of agriculture in developing countries to reorient their approaches to peasant food production. Large-scale, heavily capitalized agriculture has only a limited role in food production in many parts of the developing world at the present time. If this is not recognized, not only would agriculture be following the wrong direction in terms of production efficiency but it would also contribute directly to rural unemployment and urban migration — and both of these would aggravate further the problems of food and nutrition. In many parts of the world there are traditional methods of improving the fertility of soil and, with little further scientific input, the yield per farmer per hectare might be considerably improved. Better selection of seeds and the judicious use of fertilizer (even at the peasant level), coupled with properly organized co-operatives for the collection, processing and storage of produce, all these can help to increase the total quantity of food produced and distributed. The disproportionate emphasis on cash crops in many countries must be altered.

Agricultural extension services could be made more food- and nutrition-oriented than they are at present. This might mean the retraining of agricultural extension officers and home economists in agriculture to be a vanguard corps, linking government, farmers and households. Programmes such as the home economists' retraining programmes now under way in Africa, under the auspices of the United Nations Economic Commission for Africa, are likely to be of very great significance in this field.

Health Services

In many countries nutrition has been seen, unfortunately, as a health problem only. Health has a role to play in nutrition, and it is the responsibility of ministries of health to expand their preventive services in such a way as to achieve: (a) the rapid control of infections; this would contribute indirectly to the preservation of nutrients in the body, especially among children; (b) the presence of a cadre of health educators who should be able to assist in the community nutritional education programmes; (c) better training of health staff for activities in nutrition.

Ministries of Education, Social Welfare

Formal education is directly associated with the ability to achieve responsible nutritional status, although to what extent economic factors intervene in the process is not too clear. One thing is certain: in most social services, the more educated seem to fare better than the less educated or the completely illiterate. The school system would appear, therefore, to be a very important area for the inclusion of programmes aimed at better nutrition for the family. In this respect, it is gratifying to know that many countries are examining their programmes of early education to determine to what extent formal training can be altered so as to (a) reduce the number of people who want to flee the land but (b) relate this more closely to agriculture and other more land-based production. These programmes can be successful only if agriculture is made attractive in terms of job content and rewards.

Involvement of the People

There are many community leaders and agencies that can all be used for getting people involved in programmes aimed at the improvement of their own nutrition. Many past programmes have been geared so specifically to nutrition alone as to have very little meaning for what may be the major concerns of the community. Among the rural poor, food and nutrition have to be viewed as only one component of general developmental requirements. Governmental and non-governmental agencies should sit with the people, and plan and work with them. The provision of adequate water, cleansing of the environment, even assistance with better laying out of villages, would create indirectly an atmosphere within which good nutrition intervention programmes could be mounted. The programmes should take into account the social and cultural facts underlying the nutritional problems that have been encountered. They should recognize the total effect, practices, and preferences of the area and establish those which can be harnessed for good.

Since the most vulnerable groups are infants, young children, pregnant and lactating women, it would be best to give them a priority rating in these programmes. For better infant nutrition the first essential is adequate breast-feeding. Programmes ought to encourage prolonged lactation. Regulation of fertility is necessary for maintenance of lactation as well as for better nutrition of the mother; this should be emphasized. Package-deal programmes, including these elements, should be evolved at the community or even homestead level, if they are to succeed.

Priority Programmes

It is impossible in a general paper, unrelated to a particular country or region, to make a list of priorities. The United Nations in resolution A/RES/2848 (XXVI) produced a list of sixteen items (see below) for dealing with the strategy to solve the protein nutrition crises in developing countries. These same features can be made part of any nutrition programmes; the important thing is for each nation to select those issues on which to concentrate.

V. A FINAL WORD

For over a decade now, various international agencies have been grappling with the nutrition problems of the world. Many of the approaches have been overly simple and their aspirations high; it is not surprising to learn that they have been unsuccessful. The complex interrelationships of the food and nutritional problems with other developmental questions have not been fully exploited. Unfortunately, solutions are not easy. There is no doubt that general economic uplift of a people, coupled with responsible education, will make for better nutrition. Improved nutrition of a people, however, can also be a direct input to alter their aspirations so they they may join more fully in the better economic development of their countries and local areas. This circular relationship has to be recognized and accepted in order that nutrition receives its proper place in development programmes.

At the present time the major impact of nutrition problems is on infants and young children, and pregnant and lactating women. The international community is being called upon to assist with the development of intervention programmes which will make for amelioration of these problems among these groups in the shortest possible time. But no international activity can have any hope of success unless the problems are recognized within nations and even among local communities as pressing ones to which there can be solutions -- if people are willing to apply themselves.

Essential elements of a strategy statement
on action to avert
the protein crisis in developing countries

1. Make every effort to increase the production of food crops, particularly through the exploitation of new high-yield varieties, bearing in mind the special need for an expanded production of protein-rich pulses and oilseeds.

2. Encourage accelerated and expanded research designed to improve the nutritive value of cereal proteins through genetic engineering.

3. Encourage accelerated and expanded research designed to develop high-yielding pulses, legumes and oilseed crops.

4. Encourage the increased production of animal proteins, particularly through research on increasing forage yields and production.

5. Make every effort to prevent an unnecessary loss of protein-containing foods in field, storage, transport and home.

6. Encourage increased production from marine and fresh-water fishery resources.

7. Encourage the development, distribution and promotion of formulated protein foods.

8. Facilitate the application of science and technology to the development of new protein sources in order to supplement conventional food resources.

9. Develop and support regional and national centres for research and training in agricultural technology, food science, food technology and nutrition.

10. Conduct informational and educational campaigns related to protein production and consumption.

11. Improve protein utilization through the control and prevention of infectious diseases.

12. Review and improve policies, legislation and regulations regarding all aspects of food and protein production, processing and marketing so as to remove unnecessary obstacles and encourage appropriate activities.

13. Give special attention to the protein needs of vulnerable groups.

14. Initiate intervention programmes aimed at insuring that vulnerable groups will receive the most appropriate type and a sufficient quantity of food by the most effective means.

15. Recognize the important relationships between family size, population growth and the protein problem.

16. Recognize the role of economic development and social modernization in solving the protein problem.

NOTES

[1] SAI, F. The impact of urban life on the diets of rural immigrants and its repercussions on the nutritional status of the community. Ghana Med. J., December 1967.

[2] Ghana national nutrition survey, 1961-67. Accra, Government of Ghana, during the years indicated. (Mimeo. reports)

[3] Inter-American investigation of mortality in childhood (provisional report). Washington, D. C., Pan-American Health Organization, 1971.

[4] BERG, A.; MUSCAT, R., The nutrition factor. Washington, The Brookings Institution, 1973. (This is a broad survey of the role of nutrition and nutritional education in national development.)

Health and the Human Environment

MICHAEL J. SHARPSTON

Health has an obvious and fundamental influence on human welfare; and if the health of the bulk of the population in a developing country can be improved, this could well have a major impact on over-all welfare distribution. This was the basis of the World Bank's Health Sector policy paper released in 1975.

In recent years, two trends have tended to increase the Bank's interest in health in developing countries. First, there has been a growing realization in the development community as a whole that gross national production (GNP) per capita alone is not an adequate measure of development and of its effect on human welfare. The result -- both outside and inside the Bank -- has been increased attention to income distribution and to the social sectors.

The second recent trend has been a growing awareness of the problems of pollution and of the ecological effects of man-made changes in the environment. In 1970 the World Bank Group established the Office of Environmental Affairs "...to review and evaluate every investment project from the standpoint of its potential effects on the environment." Environmental concerns in Bank projects cover a wider field than human health, but health is often a major issue. For example, water resource projects, such as irrigation or hydroelectric schemes, can have an important effect upon the incidence of certain diseases, especially in a previously arid area, where new breeding places for disease-carrying insects can be created. Thus both because of a desire to avoid health problems and because of an active interest in improving welfare, the Bank became increasingly involved in health considerations.

From **FINANCE AND DEVELOPMENT**, Vol 13, No. 1, March 1976, (24-28), reprinted by permission of the publisher.

I. WHAT AFFECTS HEALTH LEVELS?

Before formulating a sensible health policy either for the World Bank or for the developing countries, perhaps the most fundamental question to be answered is: "What really determines the overall health level of a population?" One obvious and possible answer is health services and the number of physicians or hospital beds; yet there is clear evidence that at best this is only a very partial answer. For example, in the "west" -- Northwestern Europe and the United States -- life expectancy at birth rose from about 35-40 years in the eighteenth century, to 50-55 by 1900 (in Sweden it rose from below 35 in 1755-76 to over 55 by the first decade of the 1900s). Yet, very little indeed of this progress can be attributed to medical science. By 1900 major discoveries in medicine and surgery had already been made, but only smallpox vaccination would have been in sufficiently general use to have had a significant effect on mortality in the population as a whole. One must, therefore, look to other factors -- better nutrition, a slow improvement in hygiene habits and (from about 1870) the effects of a series of public health measures.

Similarly, in 1970, a country-wide health survey in Thailand found that, on the average, sickness occurred twice a year per person, but that only 17 per cent of the population utilized public sector health facilities during a year. Private clinics were important in Bangkok, but in the rural areas 61 per cent of the people applied self-treatment, sometimes with the aid of a pharmacy. Yet, despite this low coverage of the population by health services, health in Thailand and many other countries of the developing world has improved very substantially since World War II. Evidence of this is the population "explosion" most of which can be attributed to decreased mortality rather than increased fertility. Average life expectancy at birth in the developing world has increased from about 32 years before World War II, to about 49 years at the end of the 1960s. Though this is still far short of the 70 years or more now typical of a developed country, it represents a very dramatic fall in mortality, over a rather short period. Some of the fall is attributable to major health campaigns (a notable example is malaria) control in the South Asian subcontinent, but a large residual is left, which can only be explained by other factors. However, before one can understand fully how these other factors operate, it is first necessary to examine rather carefully what the real health problems of a typical developing country are and what causes them.

II. THE ECOLOGY OF POVERTY AND DISEASE

Man, the organisms which give him diseases, and the vectors (such as flies) which help transmit disease are all part of an ecological system. It is the interaction of man and his environment which determines the incidence of disease. Curative health care services very rarely affect the incidence of disease, though they may mitigate its effects. Rather, the disease pattern of a society intimately reflects its standard of living, and indeed its whole way of life.

One very important factor affecting the pattern of disease is he high level of fertility -- typical of most developing countries and typical also of the poverty syndrome. This has an obvious effect on the age structure of the population. In any country, it is the old and the very young who are most susceptible to disease. Developing countries have proportionately very few old people, and many young children. As a result, diseases such as cancer and cardiovascular conditions are a far smaller part of the disease pattern than in developed countries. On the other hand, up to a half of all deaths may be those of children under five.

In addition, the high level of fertility common in the developing world, and the short interval between births, also have a direct impact on health, largely because less nutrition and care are available for each successive child. Morbidity (sickness) and mortality in a large family are higher, and later children in the family are at a particular disadvantage. Furthermore, from the third child onward, the risks to the general health of the mother increase. High fertility can cause health problems at a community level as well. Population pressure on the land may lead to overcropping and hence to poor general nutrition. Excessively rapid urbanization and overcrowding create major health risks. Population growth makes it harder to provide safe or sufficient water supply, garbage disposal, and sanitation for the community or other social infrastructure. More generally, population growth may slow the improvement of educational levels and per capita income; and, under a market system, tend to increase the inequality of income distribution. All these factors tend to have a strong detrimental effect on overall health conditions.

III. MALNUTRITION-DISEASE SYNERGISM

One of the most significant effects of the existence of large families living in poverty is malnutrition, which is of considerable importance as a direct cause of death. Still more importantly, nutritional deficiency is frequently an associated cause of death among young children, and is also a major factor in the widespread occurrence of immaturity (low birth weight and other similar characteristics, whatever the length of the pregnancy), often in its turn an associated cause of death in babies. In a major study of Latin America, a comparatively well-fed part of the developing world, "nutritional deficiency" or "immaturity" were the primary causes of death for only 6 per cent of deaths of children under five, but one or the other was an associated cause in 57 per cent of all deaths. Mere exposure to a disease agent need not produce clinical disease and very frequently does not do so. Malnutrition is of such significance essentially because it hampers the body's resistance. Malnutrition acts "synergistically" with disease agents to increase the incidence of clinical disease and aggravate its severity. Equally, disease can bring on malnutrition by increasing food requirements at a time when effective food absorption is often diminished.

IV. DISEASES FROM HUMAN WASTES

The most important single group of diseases in the developing world are those whose transmission cycle depends upon contamination by human wastes of food, drink, water, or soil. For most diseases generally, and for nearly all diseases in this group, man is the reservoir of infection; without contamination of the environment by the wastes of infected human beings, the disease cycles would come to an end. Among the diseases in this group are typhoid, dysentery, cholera, polio, and hepatitis. Diarrheal disease, also in this group, is probably the biggest single cause of death in children under five, and is a major cause of illness among adults. In Latin America, diarrheal disease was responsible for 26 per cent of deaths under five years of age in Sao Paulo, Brazil, and no less than 43 per cent in rural El Salvador.

Many worm diseases also belong to this group, including tapeworms, hookworms, and bilharzia (also called schistosomiasis). These diseases only rarely cause death in adults; rather, they are diseases of life, a continuing burden on the sufferer. Case studies in Bangladesh, Sri Lanka, and Venezuela found infestation rates at age six to be 95 per cent, 95 per cent, and 93 per cent, respectively. A recent World Bank case study of the labor force engaged on civil construction at three sites in West Java, Indonesia, found 85 per cent infested.

Both water supply and sanitation bring about major changes in the man-disease ecological system. Essentially, all the various techniques for sewage disposable, or for the provision of a safe water supply, are intended to break the tight transmission cycle upon which a high prevalence of these diseases depends. With good water supply and sanitation, isolated cases may still arise -- there may even be epidemics, or sporadic outbreaks of a disease problem -- but disease is much less likely to be an endemic phenomenon, a part of the ecological "scenery".

V. AIRBORNE DISEASES

Airborne diseases are the second most important group. They are transmitted by the breathing-in of the disease agent, and include tuberculosis, pneumonia, diptheria, bronchitis, whooping cough, meningitis, influenza, and measles. Crowded, ill-ventilated housing fosters the spread of these diseases, especially if windows are blocked against the cold. One study (Ruth R. Puffer, Carlos V. Serrano, and Ann Dillon, The Inter-American Investigation of Mortality in Childhood (Pan American Health Orgnization/UNICEF, 1971) showed that in rural Viacha, Bolivia, on the high Altiplano, almost two thirds of all death of children under five years were caused by airborne diseases (and in Viacha over one child in ten dies even before the age of one).

Malnutrition, diseases caused by the contamination of the environment by human wastes, and airborne diseases form the core of the disease pattern of the developing world. This disease pattern is intimately related to large families with children born at short birth intervals, inadequate housing, water supply, sanitation, nutrition, and general hygiene. All these factors work together, and reinforce each other to emerge as the basic pattern of poverty and disease.

There are, of course, other important diseases, but they are generally more limited to particular areas or certain ways of life. The mundane diseases of the core disease pattern really take the biggest toll. In a major study of 22 locations in eight Latin American and Caribbean countries, diseases from contamination by human wastes, airborne disease, and nutritional deficiency were responsible in all except two cases (both in Jamaica) for over 70 per cent of the deaths of children under five that were not due to congenital anomalies and birth-related causes.

Africa probably does have particularly difficult problems because its climate makes it ecologically very suitable for certain diseases. Nevertheless, in many ways the disease pattern of much of the present developing world is not so different from that which existed in many of today's developed countries at about the turn of the century. It is, essentially, a disease pattern of poverty; and, in fact, the higher socioeconomic (largely urban) groups in a developing country do have markedly different health problems from the bulk of the population. They have much more housing than the rest of the population and often have smaller families. Their disease pattern will correspond more to that of a developed country than to that of a developing country, with influential members of this group requiring health care for the chronic and degenerative diseases typical of later life. Evidently, the health problems of the higher socioeconomic groups are minor compared to those of the poor, rural, or urban. However, these groups are of considerable significance in determining the effective health priorities of a developing country, both because of their economic power in terms of effective demand, and because of their sociopolitical influence.

VI. PRESENT HEALTH SERVICES

We can now examine the type of health and health-related services available in a developing country. As regards water supply and sanitation, in the poorest developing countries most of the rural population defecate in the fields, and indeed this continues to be the case until people reach quite high income levels. In few developing countries does more than a small portion of the rural population have access to functioning modern water supply systems. In the urban areas, water supply and sanitation services are somewhat better; but usually they are very inadequate, particularly in shanty-town areas, and such sanitary facilities as exist are often not well utilized.

Whereas in the United States expenditures on health services now average well over $400 per capita a year, in many developing countries expenditure is probably less than 1 per cent of this amount. Costs, however, are not nearly so different; a hospital can easily cost $8,000 per hospital bed, and $2,000 a year in recurrent costs (depreciation and interest on capital excluded). A doctor's salary in some parts of Africa may easily be $10,000 a year -- less than in the United States, to be sure, but still about one quarter of U.S. levels, whereas financial resources are only one hundredth. Any rational discussion of health policy must bear such factors in mind. High-level medical manpower is also very scarce in most African countries, although less so in Latin American and Asia. To take an extreme case, in 1970 Upper Volta had little more than one physician per 100,000 persons, as against one per 700-800 persons in the United States. Most developing countries also have much less physical infrastructure for health services than the developed world. For example, Indonesia recently had rather under 2,000 persons per hospital bed, as against about 120 per bed in the United States.

VII. THE ALLOCATION OF RESOURCES

These statistics are traditional measures of health services, and although they do serve to give some idea of the limited availability of resources at a national level, they also show that there is gross distortion in the allocation of these resources. In nearly all developing countries, the bulk of government health expenditure is allocated to curative services. A large part of government funds is spend on hospitals, particularly on in-patient services. Hospitals, in turn, are concentrated in the urban areas, and most of the patients also come from the same urban area; organized referral is usually of insignificant importance. Some rural inhabitants go to an urban center, but even so, most of the medical care serves a few urban people.

Thus, in early 1969, Greater Accra contained about 8 per cent of the total population of Ghana, but over 45 per cent of all doctors in the country. Again, 55 per cent of Ministry of Health doctors worked at the three largest hospitals in the country, and the situation for nurses was similar. By contrast, the Upper Region of Ghana, with a population of nearly 1 million, had seven government doctors and five mission doctors, 2 per cent of all doctors for 10 per cent of the population; furthermore, all were non-Ghanaians, even the Regional Medical Officer. Within regions also, there was a heavy concentration of health services in the regional capitals. Thus, in the populous and prosperous Ashanti Region, 34 out of the 36 Ministry of Health doctors worked at Okomfo Anokye Hospital; one worked in the Regional Office; and only one was stationed outside the regional capital. Even after allowance for patient migration into the city for treatment, there were over six times as many Ministry of Health doctors available to care for the population of the regional capital as there were for the rest of the region.

The reasons why doctors (government of private), congregate in the principal towns and the government doctors stay in the large hospitals are not hard to find. The economic opportunities are in the large towns -- and government doctors often do have private practices, whether or not it is officially permitted. Even if a doctor comes from the rural areas originally (and, in fact, most come from better-off households in the cities), by the time he has completed his training he usually has adopted the outlook of an urban professional man; his friends will live in the cities, and that is where the bright lights are. Furthermore, he is likely to associate high professional status with the sophisticated treatment of "interesting" cases; this will usually only be possible at a few major hospitals. Politically, private sector doctors will usually be able to determine where they practice, and so also will public sector doctors -- doctors are a tight elite, with an arcane expertise that touches the frightening mysteries of life and death; few laymen will tackle them on their own terrain. In any case, the lay elite -- politicians, civil servants, even trade union leaders -- are also nearly all urban, and will want "proper" (that is, Western) level of treatment for themselves and their families.

The result is that in most countries the doctors stay almost exclusively in the main towns, perhaps after a token year or so of exile in the hinterland, soon after becoming qualified. Additional output of doctors by the medical schools only leads to unemployment or underemployment of doctors in the capital cities, probably couples with emigration; this, for example, is the case in the Phillippines. The rural areas remain without doctors. On the other hand, the mere fact that doctors remain unemployed will not necessarily prevent the building of new medical schools; the output of doctors is frequently determined by the political power and social aspirations of middle-class parents.

VIII. HEALTH COVERAGE

This impressive array of factors tends to concentrate the resources of the health services in a few urban areas. Bearing this in mind, we can examine the three main reasons why health coverage in developing countries tends to be low. The first reason is geographical: it is known that the great bulk of patients at a health facility come from the immediate vicinity, say, within five miles. For example a study in India showed that attendance at a dispensary halved for every half mile distance from it. Yet much of the population of most developing countries is dispersed and outside the immediate vicinity of a health facility. The second reason is administrative: it is very difficult to get referral systems to work. The transport from outlying areas to urban hospitals is not available, and few developing countries have an administrative control system strong and ruthless enough to prevent those in the immediate vicinity of a hospital from pre-empting the available beds. The third reason is cultural: particularly in Latin America, a peasant may feel that a doctor looks down on him, and prefer to go to a "curandero" or traditional healer. In Asia, people may have more faith in traditional healers, or go to western doctors only for certain conditions. Thus even in the cities many people do not make use of official health services. An example of the effects of "cultural distance" is Cali, Colombia, where one study found that despite a doctor-to-population ratio of 1 to 910, 17 per cent of children who die are not seen by a physician, and another 19 per cent have no medical attention during the 48 hours preceding death. The combined effect of geographical, administrative, and cultural distance is that for many developing countries the official health services may be a small and rather unimportant part of the total health care picture. Often other factors are of far more significance -- such as self-treatment, use of traditional healers, advice from pharmacists or "injection men," and among better-off groups in the cities, private practice.

The effect that the concentration of official health services in urban hospital facilities has upon the available health statistics is also significant. Even in a developed country, a health service "discovers" the illnesses for which it is looking; in New York City, reported cases of lead poisoning were one in 1950, but 1,925 in 1971, after lead poisoning attracted professional interest. In the same way, because official health services devote most of their resources to large urban hospitals with few pediatric beds, and in particular tend to collect their statistics from such sophisticated facilities, the picture the statistics tend to portray is that the important health problems of the country are the degenerative diseases of the more affluent and elderly city dwellers. There is thus a self-justifying circle; if a developing country adds a large kidney unit to its new teaching hospital, kidney problems will come to figure large in the health statistics -- and in this way the emphasis on sophisticated and expensive kidney treatment facilities will be "justified."

IX. WHY HAS HEALTH IMPROVED?

To some extent, major health campaigns have been a factor in the improvement of health in developing countries since World War II. Official health services for individuals, however, have probably had too low a coverage in many developing countries to have had much impact on overall national health levels. In any case, there is a limit to what conventional health services can achieve in an unchanged physical and social environment. For example, the medical school in Cali, Colombia had a program for hospital care of premature infants, with survival rates comparable to those in North America; but 70 per cent of the infants discharged from the premature nursery were dead within three months.

The existence of some attempt at modern water supply and sanitation in the towns of the developing world could well be one reason why health today in developing countries is better in the towns than in the countryside, whereas in nineteenth century Europe the reverse was the case. However, health in developing countries has also been improving in the rural areas -- as the population explosion shows -- and since water supply and sanitation usually remain very inadequate in such areas, there must be some other factor.

The most likely factors leading to health improvement, then, are a rise in the levels of nutrition and the slow spread of modern ideas of personal hygiene. Across the developing world, per capita incomes are rising, and transport systems are improving; the result is more food, better quality food, fewer localized food shortages, and a more varied diet. In other words, the principal factor behind the improvement in health and hence the population explosion in developing countries is probably not any form of health measure, but economic development itself.

Better health can increase production, increase the benefits of consumption, and improve the efficiency of investment for either purpose. As one example, a fall in morbidity can improve the efficiency of education or work time, and increase the benefit to the individual of his leisure time. A rather different type of possibility is that control of disease problems may open up new fertile land, permit exploitation of mineral resources, or increase trade and tourism. For example, the Panama Canal could only be built after disease problems had been brought under control. Again, in the past few years efforts at malaria control have permitted new settlements on fertile land in Ethiopia, Nepal, and Sri Lanka. Settlement of fertile land is one of the main anticipated benefits of the major project against "river blindness" now getting under way in West Africa.

To take another rather different situation, certain human diseases also affect animals, so that there is scope for programs, which improve human and animal health simultaneously, and facilitate exploitation of animal resources for meat or as stronger draft animals. Equally, provision of a good supply of water in an arid area may benefit livestock development or permit extra crop production, as well as benefiting human health. Or, again, everyone knows it is a waste if rodents eat crops while they are in storage; but it is just as much a waste when ingested food is eaten away by parasites within the body, when fever increases the metabolic demand for calories, or when enteric disease impairs intestinal absorption. Furthermore, if people are ill, there is a good chance that they will spend resources on attempted remedies (effective or not); it is, therefore, quite legitimate to count avoided costs of treatment as a benefit from better health.

Changes in health do, of course, affect population growth, and this must also be considered. In general, better health and nutrition -- whatever their cause -- tend to increase the ability to reproduce healthy babies with a good chance of survival; what one then has to consider is how the will to reproduce is affected.

Historical experience is varied, but on the whole, it seems likely that a decline in the birth rate is significantly related to a fall in the infant mortality rate, but that the birth rate falls less. It should be a deliberate aim of health policy to reinforce the link between a decline in mortality and a decline in family size, by having health workers recommend the benefits of smaller families, for the health benefit to the individual family, as well as on economic grounds.

X. BALANCED DEVELOPMENT

Probably the most appropriate framework in which to analyze health policy is to view better health as part of a balanced socioeconomic development in the human environment. Better health is one aspect of man achieving more positive control of his environment and as such it helps to justify and facilitate planning of his future -- social or economic, public or family affairs. Within this framework there are a large number of linkages. For example, family planning improves nutrition; nutrition improves health; health can improve attitudes to family planning and to development as well as directly increasing production. Emphasis on health is probably not essential for economic development (except for control of specific diseases in certain regions). However, better health in its own right should surely be one of the aims of development; and improving the health of the poorer members of a developing country could be a very important way of increasing their welfare.

Perspectives on the International Relations of Food

RAYMOND F. HOPKINS
DONALD J. PUCHALA

The international system of production, distribution and consumption of food is managed by states, corporations and international organizations. International organizations play minor roles in the food regime, principally as arenas for policy coordination among state bureaucracies and as agents for modest multilateral programs. All of these actors work within the framework of a set of norms, rules and practices that constitutes a global food regime. Currently, the regime is undergoing change. Growing demand for food, tighter connections among markets, and greater reliance on technology have increased the importance of international adjustments. American preponderance in shaping regime features and insuring food security through reserves has declined. The dramatic price rises and rationing of international food supplies that occurred during the "crisis" of 1973-74 exposed serious deficiencies in the existing regime. At least five world food problems -- potential shortages, instability, insecurity, low productivity and malnutrition -- continue as real or potential threats. To solve these problems the norms of the current regime that has existed since World War II are seriously under challenge. Re-evaluation and reform of the major principles characterizing the food regime are needed.

Securing adequate food is one of the oldest problems confronting political institutions. Historically this intimate connection between food and politics has emerged in diverse forms. From the "minimal government" of nomadic herdsmen and hunting-gathering peoples and the complex despotisms found in societies relying on irrigation to the elaborate regulations for food growing and marketing in most contemporary states, procuring of food has been a central factor shaping political patterns and, in most cases, encouraging substantial government intervention[1]. It is small

From **INTERNATIONAL ORGANIZATION**, Vol 32, No. 3, Summer 1978, (581-616), reprinted by permission of the publisher, University of Wisconsin Press, Madison.

wonder then that as food systems have become increasingly global, with national markets linked together and technology diffusing rapidly, demands for solving food problems have shifted to the international arena. Unfortunately, in recent years the contemporary international system has been unable to deal effectively with global food problems.

This essay will discuss some of the most notable of these inadequacies. In addition, we will introduce a set of concepts for describing and explaining what will be termed the international relations of food. Guided by the conceptual framework designed in this chapter, this special issue of International Organization will explore the international relations of food, with particular emphasis upon the capacities of national and international institutions involved in promoting the production, distribution and consumption of basic food stuffs among the earth's peoples.

I. GLOBAL FOOD PROBLEMS

It hardly needs saying that the stimulus to the efforts which produced this volume is the consensus among editors and authors that there are global food problems. Problems, in the sense we use the term, are conditions of production, distribution or consumption that are sufficiently undesirable to at least some actors in the system that they initiate calls for change. It should be noted that there is a lively debate among experts over the dimensions and severity of world food problems. The controversy stems from many sources including differences in analysts' disciplinary training and ideological perspective, as well as from the varying data they call upon, the different forecasting and other methodological techniques they employ, and from crop conditions prevailing at the moment of analysis. In the judgments that follow, our approach has been to consider the literature carefully, to see points of consensus among otherwise contending writers, to evaluate others' conclusions and to frame our own arguments in the light of the best systematic evidence. Our analysis steers a rather unspectacular middle course between the positions of those who unrealistically minimize food problems and those who view them as so severe as to conclude that world-wide starvation will soon be upon us.

We suggest that five important food problems exist. First, we face the threat of chronic food shortages in some regions, most notably in South Asia and Africa, and their attendant economic, political and human consequences. Second, current arrangements lead to undesirable instability in supply bound up with unreasonable fluctuations in prices, unpredictable markets, and undependable trade flows. Third, certain countries encounter the problem of security of food imports, especially where imports represent either important elements in national standards of living, or, more crucially, where they represent hedges against starvation. A fourth problem results from the low productivity of agriculture and related poverty in many less developed countries.

Such conditions represent a barrier to both food production and general economic development as well as a costly waste of human resources. Fifth, there is <u>chronic malnutrition,</u> especially among underprivileged groups and classes in certain countries and regions.

Each of the five problems is significant and hence deserving of extended analysis. For this reason we have asked several of our authors to discuss particular dimensions of the global food problem. Nicholson and Esseks, for example, deal with problems of underproduction and food scarcity in less developed countries. Seevers and Johnson each address the problem of market and price instability. Paarlberg takes up the issue of import security and studies characteristic responses to it. In separate articles, Christensen and Austin analyze problems of rural poverty and malnutrition.

The five global food problems are obviously interrelated. Each is a cause of one or several of the others, and all lead to or follow from fundamental distortions of supply or demand for food. What makes the interrelatedness of global food problems analytically perplexing is that various elements of distributional distortion affect different countries and populations in different ways, sometimes at different times. As a result the universality of the food system tends to be blurred. Several of the essays in this volume are addressed to the interrelatedness of the dimensions of the world food problem. Destler shows how the very multi-dimensionality of world food problems creates a complex and at times contradictory policy process as the United States Government deals with food and agricultural issues. Nau examines how global considerations further complicate food policy making and lead to a multifaceted and multimotivated international diplomacy. Austin explores problems of international institutional proliferation and the consequent problems of coordination that follow as the interrelatedness of food affairs defies attempts to organize internationally.

The truism underlined in this volume is that no single or simple policy, indeed no unilateral one, can solve all of the global problems of food. Nonetheless, as several of the authors individually suggest, and as the anthology as a whole implies, practicable steps toward coordinating national and international action can significantly alleviate the severity of world food problems.

As preview and overview to more detailed analyses in the essays that follow, let us look more closely at each of the problems on the agenda of world food diplomacy.

Food Shortages

Food shortages in recent years were responsible for the dramatic increases in the price of grain and other basic foodstuffs in the early 1970s and for heightened domestic and international

Table 1   Average wheat export prices, 1968–1976[1]

Dollars/bushel (60 lbs.) averaged for grades and varieties

Year	United States	Canada[2]	Australia[3]
1968	1.69	1.96	1.42
1969	1.67	1.89	1.38
1970	1.74	1.71	1.33
1971	1.69	1.70	1.40
1972	1.86	1.89	1.54
1973	3.55	4.37	2.77
1974	5.16	6.22	3.72
1975	4.79	5.52	3.11
1976[4]	3.98	4.34	2.96

1. Source: United Nations, Monthly Bulletin of Statistics, Vol. XXX, No. 12, (December, 1970), p. 165.
2. Canadian dollars.
3. Australian dollars.
4. Figures are for June, 1976.

Table 2   World food reserves, 1961–67 to 1976

Year	Reserve stocks of grain	Grain equivalent of idled US cropland	Total reserves	Reserves as days of annual grain consumption
		(MILLION METRIC TONS)		
1961–67	151	70	220	89
1968	144	61	205	71
1969	159	73	232	85
1970	188	71	259	89
1971	168	41	209	71
1972	130	78	208	69
1973	148	24	172	55
1974	108	0	108	33
1975	111	0	111	35
1976	116	0	116	43
1977	171	0	171	48[2]

Source: Lester Brown, The Politics and Responsibility of the North American Breadbasket, World Watch Paper #2, Worldwatch Institute, October, 1975, p. 8; USDA, Foreign Agricultural Circular (September 19, 1977), p. 2.
1. Based on carry-over stocks of grain at beginning of crop year in individual countries for year shown. Stocks include those held by both exporting and importing countries.
2. Authors' estimate.

political interest in food problems. The shortages that developed between 1972 and 1974 were particularly severe due to the convergence of an extraordinary cluster of causal factors. These factors include unfavorable weather conditions in major grain producing regions, shifts in American and Canadian reserve policies, unprecedented Soviet interventions into grain import markets, high fertilizer prices, the world energy crisis, and a failure in the Peruvian anchovy catch. Analysts tend to refer to the years 1973-1974 as a period of "scarcity crisis" for the global food system, and several of the contributors to this volume use these years as a baseline for their analyses. The term crisis carries emotional loading and using it too frequently tends to destroy its analytical relevance. Therefore, we do not insist that readers accept that the years 1973-1974 were crisis years in world food affairs. It should be understood, however, that they were years of extreme and rapid change in global food supply and price conditions. Furthermore, they were dangerous years because food supplies had dwindled to the point where major famines would have occurred if conditions had deteriorated further. The gravity of the situation as it developed between 1972 and 1975 is captured rather dramatically in two sets of indices -- (1) grain export prices, and (2) reserve stocks of grains. These are reported in Tables 1 and 2.

Note in the tables how prices began their steep rise and total reserves began their deterioration in 1972. Although some American idle land was put into production in 1973 to meet the situation, prices continued to climb and total reserves dwindled. However, the key factor affecting the price at which grains moved internationally in this period is not the total working stocks in the world, but rather the stocks of exporting countries. Many large importing countries maintain working stocks that are practically never available for export and hence not directly a factor in international market prices. Therefore, it is the stocks of the exporting countries that both provide security backup for world food needs and constitute the major variable affecting prices and control over markets.

Comparing Table 3 with Table 1 indicates that the price of wheat mounted in 1973 and 1974 as supplies tightened and, most dramatically, as the stocks of exporters declined.

World prices became most extreme in 1974 (the first half of 1974 to be exact)[2] when they peaked at postwar highs, nearly four times above 1968 levels. Although world reserves fell to a two-decade low -- where the world held only thirty-three days consumption of grain in storage -- actual stock scarcity conditions among exporters became less severe by the end of 1974 and succeeding years. But, as of 1976, world reserves (Table 2) were still critically low. There had been no replacement of importers' reserves and the import-dependent world was still eating largely from month to month. During 1977, with production at or above trend for the second year, surpluses began to build, especially among exporters. But how these will affect the per capita food available globally, currently or in the future, is uncertain.

The years 1972-75, then, are benchmarks in the analysis of global food problems. By hindsight, their greatest significance

Table 3 Wheat in world trade

WHEAT PAST CARRYOVERS (MILLION METRIC TONS)

Year	Exporting countries beginning stock	Working[1] stocks	Total export use	Beginning stock as % of total use
Av. 60/61– 70/71	42.7	10.4	68.3	.64
71/72	44.4	12.6	75.5	.59
72/73	41.4	12.8	88.3	.47
73/74	22.7	15.0	82.3	.28
74/75	19.8	14.0	80.5	.25
75/76	22.3	13.7	87.1	.26

Source: International Food Policy Research Institute, communication with Barbara Huddleston.
1. Stocks committed to specific future uses and hence unavailable for alternative allocations.

Table 4 The changing pattern of world grain trade, 1934–1938 to 1976[1]

Region	1934–38	1948–52	1960	1970	1972–73	1976[2]
			(MILLION METRIC TONS)			
North America	5	23	39	56	89	94
Latin America	9	1	0	4	−3	−3
Western Europe	−24	−22	−25	−30	−18	−17
E. Europe & USSR	5	—	0	0	−26	−27
Africa	1	0	−2	−5	−1	−10
Asia[3]	2	−6	−17	−37	−38	−47
Australia & N.Z.	3	3	6	12	7	8

Note: Positive numbers indicate net exports; negative numbers indicate net imports.
1. Figures derived from Lester Brown, Table 1.2, p. 11, and *Potential Implications of Trends in World Population, Food Production and Climate*, OPR-401, United States Central Intelligence Agency, Washington, August, 1974, p. 15.
2. Preliminary estimates of fiscal year data.
3. Includes Japan and Asian Communist Countries.

lies in the fact that they prompted a long overdue and sober analysis of the global food system. It must be borne in mind, however, that regardless of the apparent uniqueness of contributing factors, shortages in 1973 and 1974 fundamentally reflected the global growth in demand for food stimulated by rapidly expanding population. Scarcities in export-import markets in 1973 and 1974 were extraordinary only as regards their unprecedented severity. Improvements in supply conditions since 1975 by no means suggest that food scarcity is on the way to being overcome, either in world trade or in poor countries.

Tables 4 and 5 depict some longer-run developments in the global food system. They dramatically document growing demands upon the stocks of food exporters as (1) an increasing number of countries have had to turn to imports to feed their populations and (2) the degree of external dependence of importing states has also increased during the last two decades.

The period from roughly 1950 to the present has witnessed a dramatic shift toward world dependency (especially Asian) upon North American grain surpluses, and this, hypothetically speaking, is projected to increase even more dramatically over the next ten to fifteen years.[3]

We say "hypothetically" because projections of North American output suggest that export supplies will not be available to meet import demands to the end of the next decade, except at higher levels of prices (and correspondingly reduced demand), unless the growth of population and income in less developed countries is reduced and rates of growth in food production in these countries are raised dramatically. Even if high prices should push back demand, such a textbook "equilibrium" adjustment would not signal a solution to the problem of food scarcity. Indeed, it would most likely signal mounting hunger among the poorest people in the poorest countries.

In addition to the food import needs of the less developed world, projected to be at least 86.4 million tons in 1990 (Table 5), import demand over the next several years will be increased by the growing needs of customers such as Japan, Western Europe and the Soviet Union, unless these countries manage major strides in the direction of self-sufficiency. By a conservative estimate, needs in these areas will climb from 30-40 million tons in 1972-76 to the neighborhood of 45 million tons of food and feed grains in 1985.[4] It should also be noted that the "Asian" figures in Table 4 probably do not properly anticipate Mainland China's possible emergence as a major food importer. The expansion of China's agricultural production is estimated at between 2 and 2.69 percent per annum. While this rate has remained constant for several years and may be keeping pace with population growth, the instability of weather conditions in China would suggest at least some occasional severe shortages.

As noted, the growth of demand for foodstuffs world wide is largely attributable to rapid population growth, especially in Asia and Africa. But heightened demand is also linked to shifts toward higher protein diets in more affluent countries. In food deficit and poor countries population growth remains rapid, ranging from 2.0 to 3.5 percent last year. By contrast food production in these countries as a group has averaged 2.9 percent per year for the past fifteen years, and declined to 1.7 percent in the early 1970s.[5] For Bangladesh to be self-sufficient by 1990 her food production growth rate would need to rise from 1.5 percent to 4.5 percent for the next twelve years. Even if bumper crops produced in South Asia in 1975 and 1976 were to continue, scarcities in that region would be likely to persist. The dramatic 1975–77 rise in grain production in South Asia put the region back near its longer-run trend of yearly increase. But, even at this level, output in the region remains one to three percent below what is needed for meeting domestic economic demand for food. As expanding population threatens food supplies in poorer countries, consumers in industrialized countries, notably in the United States, Japan and Western Europe and recently in the Soviet Union, are buying more meat, thus inflating global demands for feed grains. As economic development progresses in parts of the Third World there is good reason to believe that further shifts to meat diets will occur, at least among the more privileged classes.

Given projected uncertainties in export supplies over the next decade, estimates of the capacities of deficit countries to increase domestic production become important and revealing. Unfortunately, many of these assessments are rather pessimistic for a variety of reasons. Some analysts, for example, cite the rising ecological problems that will accompany the use of more land for crops, and more intensive use of fertilizers and other agro-chemicals.[6] Others point out that diminishing returns from land-saving technologies are already being encountered, that marginal land brought into production is frequently ruined by erosion or desertification in short order, and that rising relative prices for energy and other basic input resources point to a tightening supply situation (current oversupply notwithstanding). In addition, there has been a marked secular decline in funding of basic agronomic research in the United States and elsewhere, and some experts at least, suggest that this may have ushered in a levelling in the growth of output that is irreversible in the short run.[7] Recent initiatives in funding for agricultural development are encouraging, but their impact will be felt only over the longer run.

Despite the notable pessimism, however, it is fair to say that the preponderance of those who have looked into production problems in agriculture can identify adequate capacity in the years ahead to meet growing demands, including demands based on a desire for better diets. Notably, the capacity in question is the capacity of less developed countries to increase <u>domestic</u> production. But this will only be realized if research and technology gains are acted upon, if requisite investments are made, and if all other varieties of output-enhancing opportunity are grasped. For several less developed countries, including those discussed by Nicholson and Esseks, this means stemming declining rates of growth of domestic food production. For others it means pushing agricultural growth rates toward four or five or six percent per year. Even if such optimistic production potentials were approached, instability and occasional acute shortages are likely as long as sizable, readily distributable reserves do not exist.

Instability

Instability marked by extreme and erratic fluctuations in commodity prices has come to characterize and confuse international agricultural markets in recent years. Price instability tends to skew rewards from market participation toward those participants who can best afford to speculate. Conversely, it imposes penalties from market dependence on those who can least easily and least quickly adjust to fluctuation, namely lower income countries in general and lower income consumers in particular. Beyond adjustment effects, fluctuating world food prices also tend to wreak havoc with public and private economic planning, again, most notably in less developed countries where planners must estimate food costs in their national development plans.

One can look at the global food problem in terms of conditions of increasing scarcity, as we did in the previous section. But, in addition, one can also view the problem in terms of fluctuations or deviations around the basic trend lines. From the latter perspective what we observe is that global supplies of foodstuffs fluctuate markedly and erratically from year to year due mainly to changing weather conditions, variations in farmers' planting strategies, and government-promoted incentives and disincentives. But until very recently, major fluctuations in production have prompted only minor changes in price due to the fact that during the 1950s and 1960s the United States and Canada accumulated large reserves in periods of surplus and were able to release them in periods of shortage, thus buffering price shifts. They acted in a duopolistic manner to manage international grain markets. But large public reserves no longer exist, and North American policies no longer encourage accumulation. Therefore, unless policies and capacities change, we have a situation wherein even mild shifts (less than 2 percent) in world supply can and do bring about abrupt and extreme fluctuations in price. Observe in Figure 1 how outputs of wheat in the major exporting countries have varied in the past two decades (due in large measure to changes in planting related to variations in government support policies). By contrast, note in Figure 2 how prices remained relatively (indeed remarkably) stable through the 1950s and 1960s, despite the varying supply conditions, and then how they moved rapidly upward in the early 1970s. The price rise is accounted for by the elimination of publicly held reserves, aggravated by the onset of worldwide inflation and the tightening of international supplies discussed in the previous section. As already shown in Table 1, prices continued to fluctuate erratically from 1972/73 onward (jumping approximately 300 percent on the average between 1973 and 1974, when world production dropped by roughly 4 percent from trend, and then later dropping by approximately 20 percent between 1975 and 1976, when world production increased by roughly 9 percent.[8] This, of course, is in great contrast to the 1950s and 1960s, in which increases or decreases in production of up to 35 percent resulted in price changes of only two to three percent.

Price instability in international food markets exacerbates

Table 5 Annual grain consumption by main uses, 1970–1990

	ACTUAL CONSUMPTION		PROJECTED DEMAND[1]	
	1970	*1980*	*1985*	*1990*
Developed Countries		(Million Tons)		
Food	160.9	163.1	164.1	164.6
Feed	371.5	467.9	522.7	565.7
Other Uses	84.9	100.6	109.5	116.4
Total	617.3	731.6	796.3	846.7
		(Kilograms)		
Per Capita	576	623	649	663
Developing Market Economies		(Million Tons)		
Food	303.7	409.3	474.5	547.2
Feed	35.6	60.9	78.6	101.9
Other Uses	46.4	64.1	75.4	88.5
Total	385.7	534.3	628.5	737.6
		(Kilograms)		
Per Capita	220	233	240	246
Developing Centrally Planned Economies		(Million Tons)		
Food	164.1	200.5	215.2	225.3
Feed	15.3	38.7	48.7	61.4
Other Uses	24.6	32.6	36.0	39.1
Total	204.0	271.8	299.9	325.8
		(Kilograms)		
Per Capita	257	290	298	304

1. FAO projections based on "trend" GDP growth and U.S. "medium" population projections.
Source: In *Overseas Development Council (1977) The United States and World Development Agenda* (New York: Praeger Publishers), p. 184; adapted by the ODC from: *Food and Agriculture Organization of the US (1975) Population, Food Supply and Agricultural Development* (Rome: FAO), p. 28.

hunger in a number of ways. For one thing instability created by shortages can lead to "windfall" profits for those who control supplies, especially when prices rise far above levels needed to stimulate additional production. In such cases the extraordinary profits constitute largely a tax on consumers by producers. Within some states these excess gains are captured by grain dealers (private or public), credit agencies and other intermediaries rather than by farmers. When supplies are in excess, producers suffer as prices plummet. Marginal producers facing such market forces can be wiped out; supplies, moreover, may drop more than needed to adjust to the market and a new cycle of instability follows.

Second, and equally important, excessive fluctuations in commodity prices undermine planning, both for individual farmers and for import-dependent states. In selecting the most profitable (and efficient) crop or mix of crops a farmer must estimate the prices he is likely to receive. When these fluctuate widely, rational decisions about planting are impossible. Similarly, development planners in most developing countries can see their efforts rendered useless when food prices fluctuate widely, drawing off funds for development to pay for expensive imports or, when their countries are producers, excessively rewarding or punishing their rural sector. Government marketing boards and controls on agricultural prices through tariffs and domestic price supports are common buffers used in Europe and many developing countries to alleviate price instability by insulating producers, consumers or both from market extremities. Seevers, in his essay below, discusses such practices under the rubric "market separation." When such devices work well, they transfer the cost of adjusting to price fluctuations onto national treasuries, directly or ultimately at the expense of public policy goals or taxpayers' pocketbooks. In addition, evidence from less developed countries suggests that market intervention programs are poorly or corruptly managed. As a result, they do not stabilize income, they seldom stabilize prices of agricultural inputs such as fertilizers (which also fluctuate widely and particularly at times of food price fluctuation), they often act as revenue-raising or income subsidizing rather than stabilizing devices, and they tend to keep acting after necessities for intervention have eased. The problematic record of market separation notwithstanding, public authorities can be expected to continue such practices, not only in the expectation that wide and erratic price fluctuations will continue in international food markets, but also because they are intimately linked to domestic politics.[9]

In developed food exporting countries large fluctuations in prices and export demands stimulated political discontent among farmers, as currently in the United States and recurrently in several Common Market countries. On the other hand, in food importing developed countries, fluctuating prices tend to raise fears about availability of supply and to provoke political problems accordingly. Although as Johnson argues below some price instability may be beneficial as it signals changing supply conditions and often prompts market-adjusting behavior, recent price instability seems to have exceeded what might theoretically be beneficial to the matching of international supply and demand.[10]

Security of Food Imports

    Food imports in many poor countries have become a chronically
recurring "crisis." Food is transferred internationally via two
channels: trade and aid. Both of these channels have become less
reliable sources of supply. Price inflation in foodstuffs and
competing demand from industrialized importing countries such as
Japan and the Soviet Union limits LDC access to the international
commercial system. Industrial countries' willingness to extend aid,
which has fluctuated more according to both domestic and
international political expediencies than to needs for food,
similarly constrains LDC access to the international concessional
system. What periodically changes this import problem into an
import crisis is that many of the most populous less developed
countries, notably India and Bangladesh, possess extremely limited
capacities to adjust to internal shortfalls. Periodically,
internal crop failures and the absence of internal reserves leave
imports as the only difference between meager diets and starvation.
If such imports are not obtainable at crucial times, famine or near
famine conditions ensue with their attendant national and
international political disruptions. In Africa, for example,
successful coups in Niger and Ethiopia were directly related to
drought and famine, and the whole Sahelian region suffered turmoil
with international dimensions. Needless to say, even the threat
that imports will not be available when needed breeds tension and
insecurity, as illustrated by the role of food in Japanese-American
diplomacy.
    For reasons already discussed imports of food deficit LDCs.
Clearly, if the supply and demand projections discussed earlier are
at all reliable, it is unlikely that adequate supplies will be
available on future world markets. There simply wiln not be enough
food to meet importers' demand even if exporters increase
production to predicted maximums! Least of all, under these
conditions, will very much food be available on concessional terms.
In addition, it has been argued with some merit that food imports,
and especially those that came gratis or on concessional terms,
have aggravated poorer countries' development problems. They add
to long-term debt, they often encourage the continuation of
policies emphasizing urban industrialization that were responsible
for inadequate food production in the first place, and they tend to
encourage tastes and food consumption preferences that lead to
continuing dependency upon imports. Nevertheless, regardless of
the second best solution that concessional imports represent, some
guarantee of food supplies or food aid will certainly be needed by
deficit states in the foreseeable future.[11] Otherwise supply crises
will recur, and, at the very least, these will cloud and confuse
rational efforts toward internal development.

Low Productivity and Poverty

Low productivity and poverty plague millions of the world's populace engaged in agriculture, a point made both forcefully and compassionately in Cheryl Christensen's contribution to this volume. The rural populations of the less developed countries, constituting 60 to 90 percent of these nations' peoples, account for more than half of the world's population. As a rural labor force they are a key potential resource for greater food production. In addition, of course, these poor people are in most need of more and better food. Their low productivity is at the heart of the supply side of the world food problem.

We cannot explore the problems of rural underdevelopment in any depth; they are beyond the scope of this volume. To say the least, the problems are immense, their manifestations are almost as varied as the peoples and institutions of the Third World, the literature on these problems is voluminous, and prescriptions for their solution are numberless.[12] In the most general way, it could be said that low productivities in peasant agriculture in Asia, Africa and Latin America follow basically from the underemployment of land and labor. Technologies that would heighten the productivities of these factors are often not available. But, more fundamentally what are lacking are educational facilities and sources of credit that would enable farmers to use more productive technologies and markets that would offer inducements to technological innovation.

Still, to look at problems of rural underdevelopment simply in terms of standard economic categories is to treat them superficially. Broader and deeper questions have to do with why backwardness often perpetuates itself when knowledge, and sometimes even capital, are available to overcome it. The search for answers to such questions leads one to explore the social, economic and political factors inside under-producing countries, and the international context within which these factors exist. One needs to ask rather sensitive questions about who benefits from things as they are and who would stand to gain or lose economically, politically or otherwise if agricultural modernization were actually to come about. Although it is dangerous to generalize, politically powerful traditional elements in less developed countries who oppose land reform or other rationalizations of holdings are often major obstacles to rural development. There are other obstacles. For instance, modernizing elite factions usually prefer urban industrialization to investing scarce capital in agriculture; credit institutions (indigenous and international) balk at the high risks and uncertain outcomes in rural sector investments; and private and public agencies in developed countries see their interests challenged by the emergence of food processing industries in LDCs which would help to bring peasant agriculture into the cash economy. One could go on to cite even more unsavory obstacles to rural development such as programmatic racism and ethnic repression. At its crux, the problem is usually political, and the sad commentary is that peasants tend to be politically powerless.

Some forces do push vigorously for rural modernization and increased productivity in LDCs, and on balance the situation is not totally discouraging. The contribution by Nicholson and Esseks below offers a rather positive assessment of some LDC efforts at agricultural modernization. In addition, as Austin and others point out, international institutions such as the World Bank, the Organization of Economic and Community Development and the European Communities (EC) have lately begun encouraging greater attention to agricultural modernization and attempting to gear their aid strategies accordingly. The United States Agency for International Development (USAID) also has been involved in this task for many years with comparatively increased efforts in the 1970s. Still, given the decline in percapita real aid flows over the last decade, progress toward heightened peasant productivity is likely to be slow and halting in years ahead, perhaps too slow and too halting to meet scarcity crises projected for the 1980s. Ironically too, given the meager diets of rural populations in less developed countries, most of these people constitute an enormous latent demand for food. Should they achieve increased productivity, increased demand would accompany it. For this reason, expanding output of such poor farmers is not an important threat to developed country export interests in agriculture.

Malnutrition

Malnutrition is both the most general and the most basic world food problem. By shifting attention from production and aggregate distribution problems to the actual consumption of food, the most intractable elements of world food problems are revealed. These are dramatized by Austin's contribution to this volume. Malnutrition, estimated to afflict between one half and one billion people, is substantially a product of poverty.[13] People generally suffer from protein and/or caloric deficiencies because they or their families cannot afford more or better food. The inequality of income that determines undernourishment is an international problem, as illustrated by low daily calorie intakes in Africa, Asia and Latin America. For instance, the average calorie intake of Brazilians in 1n64-66 was adequate in aggregate statistical terms, but 44 percent of the Brazilian population was probably malnourished.[14] Malnutrition deserves special attention not only because it is so widespread, but because different targets and different institutions are required to solve it than rather simply to raise productivity. Poor farmers and poor urban workers are debilitated by the effects of malnutrition. High underemployment and unemployment in poor countries may reflect the weakened health and low energy levels of undernourished people, and, to close a vicious circle, undernourished people are naturally the products of under- and unemployment. Even with successful steps to increase the aggregate amount of food available in the world and in each food deficit country, chronic malnutrition with its long-run debilitaion of human capacities may continue largely unabated.[15]

Global nutrition problems have been the subject of concrete efforts by national and international groups, including church groups, foundations, development banks, ministries responsible for overseas aid and foreign trade, and US agencies. Political pressure for even greater efforts has been generated by numerous voluntary associations in developed states and by Third-World lobbying for the New International Economic Order, as at the 1977 FAO Conference. But so far, pressure has been diffusely targeted at a problem with no self-evident solution and has had little real impact on actually reducing malnutrition.

II. FOOD SYSTEMS AND FOOD REGIMES

While the nature and severity of world food problems provide the context for the analyses contained in this volume, the focus of our collective effort is upon the international relations of food. There is presently, and has been for some time, an active international diplomacy of food affairs -- communication among governments about food and agricultural issues, proliferating international organizations and bureaucracies concerned with food questions, countless international meetings and conferences, a good deal of official buying and selling, and all manner of bargaining with regard to commodities, money and technology. Paralleling these public activities are broad ranges of private venturings into international food affairs, from marketing to investing, to education and lobbying, to humanitarian projects of impressive scope. But, what exactly has been the impact of all this? Are peoples better fed because of it? Might they be better fed without it? Or, do we have here a case of the proverbial "sound and fury," signifying very little?

Our volume is designed to explore the effects of the contemporary international relations of food upon human welfare, most notably nutritional well-being. We are not agronomists, hydrologists, biologists or other technical specialists in the agricultural sciences, and we therefore do not claim insights or aspire to new knowledge in matters of making things grow better, faster and in greater quantity. Here, we can but acknowledge the findings of colleagues in other disciplines and their implications. As social scientists, we begin from the assumption that food systems are social systems as much as they are biological ones, and food problems are political and institutional as much as they are agricultural. Food production, distribution and consumption are purposeful acts, following implicitly or explicitly from calculated decisions taken within contexts of formal or informal social institutions. Understanding such decisions within such contexts is essential to understanding food systems and their impact upon human welfare. Much of the work contained in the essays to follow was informed, and guided, by these assumptions; much was also based on a common set of analytical concepts which it will be useful to make explicit.

First, throughout the volume the concept "global food system" is rather narrowly defined. It has been necessary to specify carefully this concept because it embodies many of our dependent variables, i.e., the outcomes we are trying to understand. Therefore, regardless of what the term "global food systems" might mean in other contexts, here it refers to three interconnected functions -- production, distribution and consumption -- and to their means of interconnectedness via public and private transactions. By "transactions" we mean bargains or other manners of agreement that initiate flows of commodities, capital, information, technology or personnel. Such flows, of course, link production to distribution to consumption. Structurally, the global food system is composed of centers of production, centers of consumption and channels of distribution (and exchange). Typical centers are countries and regions and, as noted below, channels are commercial and concessional, public and private. It should be understood that most of the transactions that constitute characteristic patterns in the production, distribution and consumption of food at given times are not international transactions (as most food is produced with local inputs and consumed domestically) but some important ones are. These international transactions are of prime analytical interest to the contributors to this volume, both as important characteristics of the global food system and as factors affecting non-international patterns. Food aid, for example, has been frequently cited as an important factor depressing production in recipient countries.[16]

Of central importance to our collective study is the assumption that conditions prevailing in the global food system occur neither haphazardly nor entirely in response to agronomic or economic imperatives. Rather, they occur because people make decisions about production, distribution and consumption that accord with commonly accepted and widely prevailing norms which lend legitimacy to certain practices and declare others illegitimate. Sets of such guiding norms prevailing at given times constitute regimes. We find the concepts "regime" and "global food regime" particularly useful analytically and use them consistently throughout the volume. A regime is a set of rules, norms or institutional expectations that govern a social system. Govern, in the sense we use it, means to control, regulate or otherwise lend order, continuity or predictability. We assume that there is a global food regime that governs the global food system, and we shall attempt to demonstrate in this volume that a specifiable regime has governed international aspects of the food system for some time. Furthermore, we believe that it can be shown that the food regime governs the food system because regime norms influence the transactions which determine the system. That is, the international relations of food affairs are by and large conducted within normative parameters which prescribe certain kinds of transactions and proscribe others. Some norms are formal rules or laws, others exist as informal but institutionalized expectations. Together they influence practices which in turn shape the general behavior of the system as adjustments occur among various parts of the food system to particular actions fostered or tolerated by the regime. Empirically speaking, the existence and nature of the regime is observable in such events as (1) the intensity and directions of flows of food-related transactions among regime participants; (2) the agendas, manifest and latent, of forums where food issues are discussed; (3) the patterns of allocation of public and private resources for solving food problems; (4) the patterns of outcome, recommendation institutionalization and practice reflected in the results of public and private food diplomacy; and (5) the rhetoric, both supportive and critical, of participants.

The usefulness of the "regime' concept is as much in the kinds of questions it raises as in the order it lends to analysis. For example, if indeed there is such a thing as a global food regime which consists of hundreds of specific rules and norms that guide international decisions about food transactions, what in fact are these rules and norms? What are their principal features and what principles seem to underlie them? Furthermore, where, when and how do they originate? How and by whom or what are they maintained or enforced? To what extent are they consistent, coherent and valued (and hence likely to be heavily institutionalized)? When, why and how do they change? Most significant, perhaps, what kind of global food systems do regime norms create? In this last respect it is important to ask and answer questions about the ways in which the global food regime affects participants in the global food system, i.e., those individuals, organizations and populations that either produce, consume and distribute food or directly affect these processes. The regime could affect participants in the system by affecting the values they derive from participation. These might include wealth, power, autonomy, community, nutritional well-being, aesthetic satisfaction in eating and sometimes physical survival. Since any regime conditions the distribution of such values among participants, usually in some skewed fashion, it is important to inquire into the ways that particular regimes condition particular distributions. A good deal of the analysis in this volume pursues such issues.

Readers moving progressively from chapter to chapter will observe the emergence of a comprehensive picture of the global food system. The system appears decentralized into national subsystems where most production, consumption and exchange take place, though still heavily affected by international transactions. In its international aspects the global food system is bifurcated along two dimensions. First, it is clearly divided into surplus and deficit producing countries, that is, exporters and importers, and the dependence of the latter upon the former is apparently increasing (which is not to deny that there are elements of reciprocal dependence in the relationship). Moreover, as Table 6 shows, exporting developed countries are also much heavier grain consumers than are developing country importers, because they consume a large share of grain through feed for animals.

Second, two networks of transactions link producing countries to consuming countries: a commercial network of sellers and buyers and a concessional network of donors and recipients. Commercial channels carry the bulk of food through the food system, as well as the inputs for growing it, and these channels primarily link North America to Europe, Japan, Korea and Taiwan, and recently the USSR and China. Concessional channels run mainly in North-South directions and remain crucial to less developed countries which lack the financial resources to meet all their needs in commercial exchanges. Production, distribution and consumption patterns in the global food system are markedly skewed; the populations in wealthy industrialized countries and the wealthy in some less developed countries are distinctly privileged. The global food system, overall, is inadequate to the needs and aspirations of many of its participants, and these multiple inadequacies, as explained above, are the causes of "world food problems."

Both the nature and the inadequacies of the global food system are influenced but not fully determined by the contemporary global food regime. This regime, as regards the international relations of food, has been American centered and prescribed, and based principally upon national government actions. To some extent it has relied upon multinational enterprises, private interest groups, and formal international organizations to enforce its rules and norms. The regime was fairly stable and institutionalized from the late 1940s until the early 1970s, during which time participants had complementary, congruent, and usually accurate expectations about relationships between their transactions and systemic outcomes.

Norms that guided (and constrained) the international relations of food from the late forties to the early seventies can be grouped into at least eight sets of principles.

1. Respect for the Free Market

Most major participants in the international diplomacy of food between 1948 and 1972 adhered to the belief that a properly functioning free market would be the most efficient allocator of globally traded food commodities and agricultural inputs. They therefore advocated such a market, aspired towards it, at least in rhetoric, and assessed food affairs in terms of free market models. Actual practice deviated rather markedly from free trade ideals.

In fact, cynics might want to suggest that the principle under discussion here could better be labelled, "talk about free trade, but practice mercantilism." Canada and the U.S. have been described as alternate price leaders in a North American duopoly during the 1960s. Yet, whatever the practice, free trade, anti-monopoly ideals remained so strong that deviators were continually compelled to explain and justify their behavior, and such inquiry and defense provided the making for endless debate within international institutions such as the Food and Agriculture Organization (FAO) and the International Wheat Council.[17] Allowing for the impact of the social-political factors that render international market reality different from the ideal of economic theory, a case can be made that food flows through the

international commercial system did in fact reflect norms
maintaining free market aspirations during the postwar era.
Seevers' analysis below fits such an interpretation and advances
the widely held argument that "perfecting" markets would have a
benign impact upon the global food system. Christensen accepts the
realities of "market" norms but criticizes their impact on the food
system.

2. National Absorption of Adjustments Imposed by International
    Markets

     As indicated, relative price stability in international food
markets obtained during much of the postwar era and can be
accounted for in large measure by American (and to a lesser extent
Canadian) willingness to accumulate reserves in times of market
surplus and to release these, commercially and concessionally, in
times of tightness. Such North American behavior made the
international market a much more predictable and acceptable food
allocator than it might otherwise have been, and as a result free
market norms of access and information were fortified. Still, it
must be underlined that it was a rule of the food regime that North
America would adjust domestically in the interest of domestic and
international price stability and stable market shares, and that it
would do this over and over again. Further, both American and
Canadian participants in global food affairs carried out
adjustments that served these de facto norms of market stability
without much dissent from overseas or at home.

3. Qualified Acceptance of Extra-Market Channels of Food
    Distribution

     Food aid on a continuing basis and as an instrument both of
national policy and international program became an accepted part
of the postwar food regime in the years following 1954. Heated
debates took place over the price-cutting and surplus-dumping
practices that followed the adoption of Public Law 480 (later the
Food for Peace Program) in 1954. Eventually, multilateral
concessional food transfers were legitimized by the United Nations
World Food Program in 1962. Bilateral concessional flows were
accepted under terms of the Food Aid Conventions that accompanied
the international wheat agreements of the 1960s. Previously,
acceptance of this practice had been limited to food emergencies
such as those in Europe following both World War I and II.
Otherwise exporters condemned food concessions as dumping and
recipients occasionally sought side-payments for accepting such
food. In a system of free-trade-oriented participants,

acquiescence in extra-market distribution could be obtained only
upon the stipulation that market distribution was to take
precedence over extra-market distribution. More simply, it was
acceptable to American and foreign producer/exporters to give food
away as long as this did not reduce income or distort market
shares. While this qualification implies consistency between the
commercial and concessional norms of the food regime, in practice
there has been a good deal of tension, even within the United
States, and energetic efforts were made to use concessional
transactions to create commercial markets.

4. Avoidance of Starvation

The obligation to prevent starvation as an international norm
was not novel to the postwar period; it derives from more remote
times (although the international community's capacity actually to
muster meaningful relief is recent). There has been and remains a
prevailing consensus that famine situations are extraordinary and
that they should be met by extraordinary means. To fail to do
would be gross immorality according to world-wide standards.
Ironically, the attention to and strength of this norm may be
increasing currently, at the very time that food reserves available
for famine relief remain near their thirty-year low point.

5. Free Flow of Scientific Information

There is some question about the analytical usefulness of
labelling "free information" a norm of the global food regime
because there has been great deviation from it in practice.
Whereas most of the other norms discussed here emerged and
prevailed during the postwar era largely because of American
advocacy and practice, "free information" emerged in spite of
American misgivings. "Freedom of information" about the results of
agricultural research was a principle nurtured by the United
Nations Food and Agricultural Organization and welcomed by those
seeking modern technologies for agricultural development. In these
ways this principle upheld norms for disclosure for the global food
regime. On the other hand, American commercial practice, both
public and private, was to protect certain information for market
advantage. As long as the United States adhered to these practices
the global flow of scientific information about agriculture was
impaired. Many recent developments suggest, however, that American
attitudes and practices with regard to disseminating scientific
information have changed. However, many countries, notably the
Soviet Union, have never accepted the principle of free
information, at least with respect to "timely" (for them strategic)

information.

6. Low Priority for National Food Self-Reliance

Partly because the global food system of the past thirty years was perceived by most participants as one of relative abundance, and partly because of international divisions of labor implicit in free trade philosophies, autarky was not accepted as a norm of the global food regime. Quite the contrary was in fact the case. External sources of supply were accepted as dependable. Markets were accepted as stable. Aid was available both to those who would exchange political allegiance for food, and to those who threatened political deviation if food was withheld. There were, in general, low perceived risks in dependence. Most Communist countries, of course, rejected this principle of "agricultural dependence" in favor of agricultural development and internal adjustments. But the majority of other participants in the global food system acquiesced.

7. Lack of Concern for Chronic Hunger

That international transactions in food should be addressed to alleviating hunger and malnutrition, or that these concerns should take priority over other goals, such as profit maximization, market stability or political gains, were notions somewhat alien to the global food regime of the postwar era. This is not to say that some individuals and organizations were not at work combatting malnutrition. But, in general, it was simply not a rule of international food diplomacy that hunger questions should be given high priority, or even that they should be raised if there were dangers of insulting friendly governments by doing so. As a result, relatively few resources were devoted to alleviating chronic malnutrition globally, and little concerted action was undertaken. Austin argues pointedly below that the result of this has been a continuing deterioration of nutritional conditions among the world's poor in spite of small gains in per capita production.

8. National Sovereignty and the Illegitimacy of External Penetration

It need hardly be pointed out that the global food system of the last thirty years functioned within the confines of the international political system, so that the norms governing the latter necessarily conditioned those of the food regime. Important among these was the general acceptance of the principle of national sovereignty; among the norms this supported was a tendency to define problems as those between states and a consequent proscription against international interference by one state in "domestic" affairs of another. In practice with regard to food this meant that production, distribution and consumption within the confines of national frontiers remained largely beyond the "legitimate" reach of the international community, even under famine conditions, as long as national governments chose to exclude the outside world, as Ethiopia did in 1973.[18] In practice, this meant that many of the poorest and hungriest people of the world could not be reached via the distributive processes of the global food system. The world acquiesced because sovereignty was the norm, and hence the malnourishment of millions was not seen as a collective responsibility in any strong sense.

Some effects of the prevailing food regime upon the global food system during the postwar era are easily discernable. In setting and enforcing regime norms for commercial transactions, the U.S. worked out trading rules through bargaining and formal policy coordination with key importers and other exporters. Communist countries remained peripheral participants with their own rules within Comecon (when the Soviets were exporters), although they occasionally interacted with "western" food traders, playing by the rules when they did. World trade in foodstuffs attained unprecedented absolute levels, and North Americans became grain merchants to the world to unprecedented degrees. Through concessional transactions the major problems of oversupply and instability in the commercial markets were resolved. Surpluses were disposed of in ways that probably enhanced the prospects of subsequent commercial growth for major food suppliers. Especially with respect to grain trading, adherence to regime norms enhanced the wealth and power (i.e., market share and control) of major exporters, most notably farmers and trading firms in the United States. Also enhanced were the nutritional well-being and general standard of living of fairly broad cross-sections of populations within major commercial grain-importing countries. Adhering to regime norms, however, also encouraged interdependencies among exporters and importers which, over time, impeded the international autonomy and flexibility of both.

With regard to concessional food flows regime norms facilitated global humanitarianism and enhanced survival during shortfalls and famines, as in the Indian food shortage of 1965-67. But the norms contribute to huge gaps in living standards between richer countries and poorer ones, they helped to perpetuate large gaps between the rich and poor within countries, and they failed to affect chronic nutritional inadequacies of poor people worldwide. By promoting transfers of certain types of production technology as well as foodstuffs, regime norms also contributed to diffusing more capital intensive farming, specialized rather than self-reliant crop choices, and a sharp rise in productivity (India, for example, doubled her production growth rate after 1950 compared to the

historic trend in the first half of this century). One result has
been cultural; expectations of people everywhere include a growing
demand for "high income' food commodities, as for example wheat and
meat, and a growing reliance upon high technology, high energy
inputs. Over all, the food regime reflected, and probably
reinforced, the global political-economic status quo that prevailed
from the late 1940s to the early 1970s.

Later chapters of this volume suggest that the global food
regime may be changing. For one thing many of the norms seem to be
in question at present, either because they are unacceptable to
increasingly powerful Third-World countries and coalitions, or
because they are no longer acceptable to the United States. Free
trade philosophies, for example, are under assault by exponents of
the New International Economic Order. International market
stability and open market access provided by domestic adjustments
and practices in the United States are no longer guaranteed by the
support of substantial political interests in this country. Other
norms, such as the primacy of market development over economic
assistance goals, are in question because participants widely
recognize that adhering to them would exacerbate the whole range of
world food problems. To take a case in point, almost no one any
longer is discouraging national agricultural developments that
enhance self-reliance in grain crops, and almost no one any longer
is withholding scientific information or technical assistance that
could further such agricultural development. Moreover, capital
intensive technology is out of vogue; labor intensive techniques to
provide rural populations with work are encouraged. To be sure,
elements of carryover and continuity from the postwar regime
persist, and rather intense international debate surrounds the
wisdom of changing norms. Unfortunately, as we write (1978), the
most accurate conclusion concerning the global food regime is a
rather unsatisfactory one. The normative content of the regime is
in flux. Any number of indices suggest that the postwar global
food regime has probably passed into history. Yet its successor
has failed to emerge clearly. The 1970s are unlikely to be years
that produce global consensus on almost anything. For policy
makers these years of regime flux are likely to prove
extraordinarily difficult.

III. PARTICIPANTS: KEY FOOD ACTORS AND INSTITUTIONS

The norms guiding the international relations of food emerge
in the decentralized world polity. They arise from the actions and
interactions of states and other organizations. They are bargained
rules, for the most part, though bargaining capacity tends to be
asymmetric and closely linked to participants' command over the
resources required to make transactions. More simply put, big
buyers and sellers, producers and consumers in commercial networks
and big donors in concessional ones have major (though not
exclusive) influence over food regime norms. At times "global

norms" have entailed little more than universal acceptance of a
major participant's unilateral policies.

The United States and the Global Food Regime

Because of the United States' position as the leading food
exporter, and a huge consumer, especially on a per capita basis,
the decisions of public and private officials in this country have
weighed heavily, often decisively, in setting and enforcing norms
of the global food regime. This is especially true with regard to
the setting of patterns and prices in the international grain
trade, and volumes and direction soft international food aid. In
some instances, the American ability to produce and export huge
yearly surpluses placed this country in the position of supplier of
first, last, and just about only resort for food-deficit
populations overseas. Such quantitative dominance has doubtlessly
amplified American influence over the global food regime. As a US
official responsible for the daily operation of the export
monitoring system, set up in 1974, remarked: "We come very close
to being one market; world grain prices, for instance are set in
Chicago -- it is the Chicago price plus transportation anywhere."
Previously, the US domestic price, less subsidies set by Congress
or the Secretary of Agriculture, largely determined world wheat
prices, and, except for rice where Thailand's influence is
important, North American policies determined the international
prices at which most grains would flow both commercially and
concessionally.
   The preponderance of the United States is declining in some
areas (for instance, US food aid provided 90 percent of the total
in the 1960s but only 60 percent in 1975) and in other areas its
dominance is precarious. The U.S., for example, was the leading
rice exporter nor the decade 1965-1975, while producing less than
two percent of the world's rice. But this position is regularly
challenged by Thailand. More recently, Brazil has been challenging
the US in the soybean market; likewise, competition in beef is
stiffening. Meanwhile, Western European agricultural scientists
have been working with strains and breeds to lower the EC's
dependence on imported North American feedgrains. Agricultural
trade as a proportion of world trade is also declining, from 33
percent in 1950-1955 to 17 percent in 1971-1975. Still, the US
share of world agricultural trade has remained stable, averaging 12
to 15 percent in the period 1950-1977, though rising to 16 percent
during the "crisis" period of 1973-1974.
   American preponderance in the global food system, and US
influence over the food regime, are less challengeable in other
respects. The United States Department of Agriculture (USDA) has
a central role in the global intelligence network which informs
production, consumption and trade worldwide. USDA monitoring and
research activities with regard to world crops (plus complementary
work by the Central Intelligence Agency with special attention to

the Soviet and Chinese situations) are looked upon as highly authoritative. Published intelligence from US sources is used by many other governments, as well as by farmers and multinational agribusiness firms. The contribution of these data-gathering and processing activities to the functioning of the global food system should not be underestimated. Nor should we underestimate the global systemic impacts of American public and private agronomic research, which remains the most extensive in the world. Greater openness and attention to more diverse problems in recent years has heightened further the global impacts of American agricultural research. All of this suggests that American behavior in international food affairs, and above all American public policy decisions with regard to agriculture, have a great deal to do with the functioning of the global food system and the setting and enforcement of the norms that govern it. Understanding the principles and forces that shape US agricultural policy therefore is crucial to understanding the global system. Extended discussion of American policy and policy making is beyond the scope of this essay, but these issues are analyzed in detail by I. M. Destler in this volume.

In general, agricultural policy in this country, both in its domestic and foreign aspects, emerges from public policy processes characteristic of American government generally. Pressures from farm organizations, the agribusiness community, consumers' associations, church and international relief agencies and a great many other factions play a part. Members of Congress, their constituents, committees, debates and election campaigns are important. Various inter- and intradepartmental interests within the administration intervene, including Agriculture, Treasury, State Department and the Office of Management and Budget. Foreign delegations and governments also attempt to influence the domestic political process. Because of the way the process works, United States agricultural policy predominantly serves domestic interests. Yet these interests are often in conflict; this frequently undermines the consistency of policy, even with respect to national goals. Destler discusses these policy issues at length below.

The Role Of International Organizations

National policy decisions (or non-decisions) reverberate through a network of international organizations with food-related missions. Eighty-nine such international intergovernmental bodies were recently listed in a report on American participation in world food politics prepared by the United States Senate.[19] If one were to go on to also count private associations, organizations involved in global food affairs would number in the thousands. It would require research and analysis well beyond the scope of this volume even to begin to map the full structure of the international organizational arena for food. Nonetheless, some mapping is required to help sort out the maze of acronyms and relatively

obscure formal organizations that exist. Figure 3 provides such an
overview map.

What in the diagram is called the "United Nations Food
Network" is a set of functionally interrelated institutions,
individually and collectively mandated to respond to problems in
the global food system as defined by their member-governments and
international staffs. The Food and Agriculture Organization (FAO)
is a specialized agency of the United Nations operating under a
1945 agreement between the FAO Conference and the General Assembly.
It is an autonomous association, responsible only to its members
(currently 136 national governments) and financed by them for its
"regular" budget which largely pays for staff operations. The
charter mandate of the FAO calls on it (1) to collect, analyze and
disseminate information relating to food and agriculture, (2) to
provide an international forum for the consideration of food
problems, and (3) to provide technical assistance to member
countries.[20]

Most closely bound to the FAO (or vice versa) within the UN
network is the United Nations Development Program (UNDP). The main
source of technical assistance in the UN, UNDP was founded in 1966
through a merging of the Expanded Program of Technical Assistance
and the United Nations Special Fund. FAO currently serves as the
executing agency for most projects in food and agricultural
development financed by UNDP, and UNDP reimbursements yearly
constitute the single largest category of the FAO's total
receipts -- about double that of the regular budget of 106 million
(for 1978).

Less intimately associated with FAO, but still importantly
linked, are the World Bank Group, the three regional development
banks, the World Food Program and other "cooperative" programs.
Through an IBRD/FAO Cooperative Program, FAO assists the Bank in
identifying and evaluating projects for possible funding, and it
aids prospective loan recipients in preparing applications. Less
directly, linkages also exist between FAO's Industry Cooperative
Program, its Investment Center and the Bank's International Finance
Corporation, where liaison and exchanged information guide
private-sector investments in food processing and agricultural
development. By way of their capital-raising activities, and via
intraprofessional communication, the World Bank Group is connected
to the Inter-American Development Bank (IDP), the Asian Development
Bank (ADB) and the African Development Bank (AFDB), all of which
finance agricultural development.

The World Food Program (WFP), created in 1966, is essentially
an international food-for-work operation that finances development
projects with payment in kind pledged by members. WFP also
intermittently functions as a disaster and famine relief agency.
Organizationally, it is linked to FAO via appointments to its
governing body, and via joint field operations. Cooperative
programs also link FAO to various other parts of the UN system;
these include a program with the World Health Organization (WHO) on
food standards -- the Codex Alimentarius Commission -- a program
with the United Nations Children's Fund (UNICEF) directed toward
improving nutrition among children, and a program in education
about global hunger and food needs, the Freedom From Hunger

Figure 1. Wheat area and production in the United States, Canada, Australia, and Argentinia

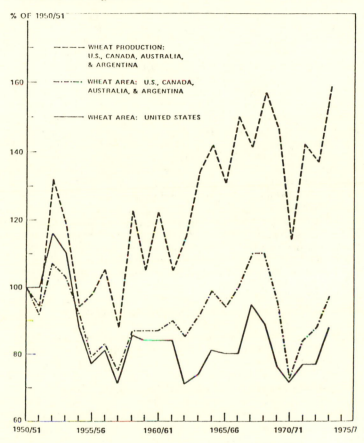

Figure 2. World Export Unit Values for Wheat, 1948–1976

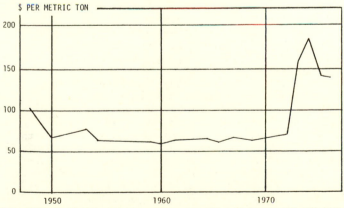

Source: USDA, *The World Food Situation and Prospects to 1985*, p. 25, for years 1948–1972; FAO, *FAO Commodity Review and Outlook, 1975–76.* Figure 1. p. 10. for years 1973–1976, estimated yearly average U.S. No. 2, for years 1973–1975, projected yearly average for 1976.

Campaign (FFHC).

Several new organs were created by the World Food Conference in November, 1974, and these are now operating in the UN food network.[21] Resolutions approved first by the Conference and later by the UN General Assembly established a World Food Council (WFC) as the "highest" institution on world food problems in the UN system. Meeting at the ministerial level, the WFC is composed of 36 countries, nominated by the Economic and Social Council (ECOSOC) and responsible to it. Its composition represents a world fragmented into an industrialized North, an underdeveloped South, a capitalist West and a socialist East. For broad policy issues, the WFC was intended to be the hub of the UN Food Network. Whether it will achieve this status remains to be seen. Until its third annual meeting in Manila, in June 1977, disagreements over its authority and staffing blocked significant action. At Manila, a number of resolutions were passed on food aid, reserves, and policy coordination under multinational aegis. These were supported by the Soviet Union as well as Western and Third World governments. However, these resolutions were essentially hortatory, a point the Soviet government made in explaining its support.

Also authorized at Rome in November, 1974, were the International Fund for Agricultural Development (IFAD) and the Consultative Group on Food Production and Investment (CGFPI). The former, after an initial capitalization of just over $1 billion for agricultural development was raised, began operations in 1977 with the special aim of helping the poorest of the less developed countries. It reports to but is not under the authority of the Secretary General of the UN, and its operations are overseen by a governing board composed of representatives of three categories of countries -- developed-donor, developing-donor (e.g., OPEC) and developing-recipient. The CGFPI, which began operations in 1975, was called into being to encourage larger flows of resources into food production in less developed countries and to coordinate the activities of various international donors. Patterned after the Consultative Group on International Agricultural Research (CGIAR), the group on production and investment is sponsored by the World Bank, the FAO and the UNDP and hosts meetings of representatives of UN donor agencies, the development banks, foundations, donor governments, and recipient countries. As its name implies, it is a consultative organ responsible for collating information and recommending ways to increase, expedite and rationalize aid for agriculture worldwide.

In addition to organs already described, there are several UN bodies which regularly consider food questions as aspects of their broader programs. Significant among these is the United Nations Conference on Trade and Development (UN-CTAD), where intense debate on North-South trade issues, many having to do with the terms of trade for agricultural commodities, has occurred over the years.[22] In many ways, UNCTAD has become as salient a forum for North-South agricultural issues as has the General Agreement on Tariffs and Trade (GATT) for developed western states bargaining on agricultural issues (although there has been little "success" within GATT in lowering trade barriers in the agricultural area!).

Some words of caution are in order before we move from mapping

Figure 3. The United Nations food network

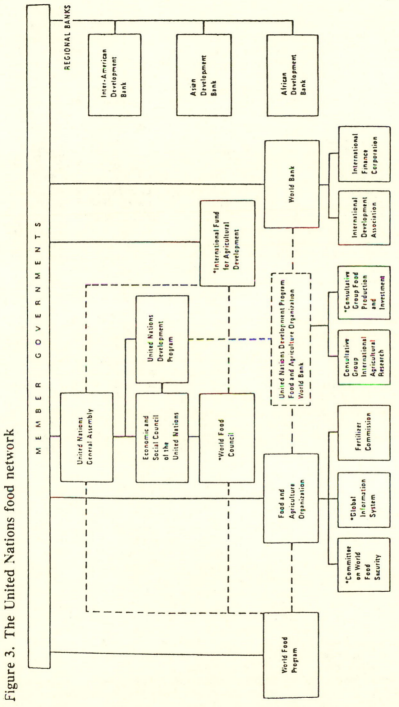

Source: Based upon Figure 3 in Martin Kriesberg. *International Organizations and Agricultural Development.* Economic Research Service. Foreign Agricultural Economic Report No. 131 (Washington: USDA, May, 1977), p. 19.

115

into analysis and evaluation. First, organizations depicted in Figure 3 and briefly highlighted here are by no means the only international food bodies, not even as regards the UN network. For one thing, there are various coordinating committees and ad hoc food groups interlaced among the major institutions such as the Committee on Surplus Disposal of the FAO which monitors concessional sales for possible violations of anti-dumping norms. For another, many of the major organizations noted, the FAO in particular, contain any number of quasi-autonomous, differentially responsible organs within them. Second, the operational world of the groups and associations of the UN network is nowhere nearly as orderly, well-organized or separate as Figure 3 indicates or as the discussion suggests. In reality, redundancy (for good or ill) is rampant, complementarity is often unrecognized or at least unexploited, responsibility and accountability are poorly defined, coordination is difficult, and political bureaucratic competition further complicates the network. Third, let us caution readers against mistaking activity for impact or accomplishment. There is a good deal of activity surrounding the international organization of food affairs, but budgets are modest, authority limited, support from member-states is uncertain at best, and, for myriad political and bureaucratic reasons, organizations tend to be restrained from accomplishing their mandated tasks.[23]

Yet international institutions should not be evaluated in terms of unrealistic criteria. Many global food problems could be more effectively addressed if international organizations were more authoritative, more efficient and more able to command resources in pursuit of global objectives. Contributing authors make this clear in their discussions, and we return to elaborate this point in our concluding chapter. Rather than dwell upon functions international organizations do not (and perhaps cannot) perform given the environment in which they operate, we should note the functions they can and do perform in relation to the global food regime. International organizations in the food area affect, modify and occasionally enforce regime norms in at least four ways: (1) by prodding governments through public and private channels, such as speeches, reports and multilateral conferences, to confront issues that national bureaucrats might otherwise choose to ignore, (2) by collecting information, fostering inter-elite communication and sponsoring research that governments by themselves might take little interest in, (3) by providing international services that governments could not perform for political reasons, and (4) by legitimating unilateral policies or bilateral deals by lending them multilateral imprimatur.

With regard to our point about prodding or stimulating governments, the continuing debate concerning international grain reserves is particularly illustrative. The latest impetus for the idea of a global reserve came from a 1973 proposal by former FAO Secretary-General Boerma. The scheme contradicted American (and Canadian) policies at the time it was articulated, but it did receive collateral support from the number of independent studies by business and academic organizations in the United States and elsewhere. In this way Boerma's initiative became an issue in US policy making and, as Destler shows, it was hotly debated in

Washington during preparations for the World Food Conference of 1974. Ultimately, the State Department's positive position toward grain reserves carried the debate and Secretary Kissinger was authorized to announce US acceptance of the reserve principle and to pledge cooperation towards it realization. He did this at the Rome Conference.

At this point the national debate about principle became an international debate about practice. The United States initially offered a plan for a reserve program of 60 million tons -- considerably larger than that suggested by Boerma. Washington then retreated from this position and fell back upon a scheme for a more limited reserve, nationally held and coordinated. But this by no means settled the question. Eighteen months after the initial pledge at Rome the reserve discussion was centered at the International Wheat Council (IWC) in London, where debate among potential participants in the reserve turned on questions about the total size of stocks, the size of each country's contribution, the method of holding the reserves, the distribution of costs, the conditions for accumulating and releasing stocks, the relation between food reserves and food aid, and the role of international organizations in the reserve undertaking.

By the autumn of 1976 the "food reserve" question was re-injected into American domestic politics as a campaign issue, as candidate Carter became an advocate of international stocks. Shortly after the installation of the Carter administration, Agriculture Secretary Bergland publicly proposed to build a modest US reserve of about 8 million tons,[24] and renewed efforts at the IWC to attain international support and cost sharing for a broader reserve undertaking. The issue may be decided by mid-1978, when the current International Wheat Agreement expires, either with a successful incorporation of new multilateral rules for managing international reserves or with failure and a return to relatively uncoordinated national measures. In the latter case, the United States will return (though less dependably) to its de facto role of principal reserve holder for the world.

While the food reserve story is not yet concluded, our point is made. International organization prompting injected a significant issue into national policymaking that many officials within relevant national governments would have preferred to avoid. When the issue was projected back into the international arena it took the form of a proposal for global collective action, which, if ultimately accepted, could become a new norm of the global food regime.

In areas of information, research and communication, the FAO is both central and significant. As the principal intergovernmental organization for food affairs, FAO participates in or reviews nearly all intergovernmental and transnational activities in the field. FAO's budgets for research and publication are small compared to amounts spent by governments for nationally focused research programs. Yet, the organization's output is substantial: its periodicals, yearbooks and country analyses are frequently cited, and its projections frequently guide national planning and policy making.[25] Its studies in agricultural adjustment have aimed to lower barriers to trade. Its research on

fisheries helped to establish fishing area councils in which
countries could address mutual problems; and through "indicative
planning" reports it reviews the investments and activities of
countries and MNCs on a global scale with the purpose of mobilizing
resources of individual states to address foreseeable problems.

The network of institutions involved in international
agricultural research is centered in the FAO, but it extends beyond
to include national research and development agencies such as the
United States Agency for International Development and Canada's
International Development Agency. It also includes a number of
quasi-public bodies such as the Consultative Group on Food
Production and Investment noted earlier, and the ten international
research centers coordinated by the Consultative Group on
International Agricultural Research. Widespread international
communication about agricultural research is newer still. While a
full assessment of the institutions in this area is premature, it
is fair to credit cooperative international research ventures
during the 1960s with producing the "miracle seeds" for high
yielding dwarf varieties of wheat and rice that led to what some
proclaimed as a "Green Revolution" in food production.

In addition to disseminating information and coordinating the
creation of new knowledge, international organizations have become
increasingly involved in field operations in rural modernization
and agricultural development. Most of these efforts, naturally,
are targeted toward Third-World countries. Some of the development
services of the multilateral agencies are discussed by Austin,
while Nicholson and Esseks cover the problems that poor countries
face. Though still modest, the budget allocations for such
interventionist field programs have expanded rapidly since the
early 1960s, and it has sometimes been the case that multilateral
undertakings have reached countries and peoples denied bilateral
assistance for political reasons.

Fourth, international organizations have influenced the global
food regime, by legitimating practices and patterns of behavior,
thereby turning them into norms. It is not surprising that most
practices legitimated by international organizations are often
simply multilateralized versions of the policies and preferences of
powerful member-states. Yet, there is still something to be said
for member-states' seeking international endorsement, especially if
it creates a barrier to actions that would be detrimental to other
states. Furthermore, multilateral debate, such as at the IWC or
the Rome World Food Conference, has provided reconsiderations and
modifications in national policies that multilateral acceptance
often requires. Contributors to this volume report on a number of
efforts of multilateral legitimation of norms including those for
maintaining a concessional system of food distribution, those
shaping "development" as an international responsibility to be
fostered by the UN and FAO, those maintained by GATT for
strengthening the free trade principles of the commercial system,
and those that foster and direct the international research
network, including the principle of free flows of information.

Despite (or possibly because of) their impact, support for
international food organizations, most notably the FAO, has
declined among industrialized states in recent years. This has

coincided with the increased activity of the poorest states in the United Nations, where the various agencies charged with international welfare tasks have become primary arenas of debate between advocates of a New International Economic Order and their critics. As the global food regime of the postwar era has become subject to increasing challenge, stress and deviation, political leaders in the United States and other industrialized countries have sought to protect their states' very large stakes in the traditional status quo. Part of their strategy has been to deflate universal multilateral bodies, and hence to dampen "populist" pressures by circumventing forums controlled by Third World majorities. Alternatively, these countries' spokespersons have sought to create new specialized institutions with built-in veto opportunities, weighted voting, limited membership or limited authority, and to propose bilateral alternatives to multilateral programs where one-on-one rather than one-against-many bargaining conditions would prevail.

Agribusiness And The Global Food Regime

Multinational agribusiness corporations, the largest and most numerous of which are American, must be included in any discussion of the global food system and regime. As managers of global food transfers, promotors of large-scale production and facilitators of technological diffusion, the MNCs are often links between governments' intended policies and their actual accomplishments. This is especially the case with United States foreign agricultural policy, since the realization of official intentions in trade, aid, and development investment has depended consistently upon the compliance and cooperation of the agribusinesses which actually handle the flows of foodstuffs, capital and technology. The major grain companies, Cargil and Continental, for example, are the effective managers of international sales of wheat, corn, rye and other grains to Europe, Japan, the Soviet Union and other major customers. Similarly, US concessional sales, although approved officially, are actually negotiated between private companies and recipient countries.

Multinational firms also affect global food production and agricultural productivity through their investment decisions. Producer firms such as Esmark, Dole, Kraftco and Nestle affect poorer countries by promoting technological diffusion, altering patterns of land use and impacting upon local patterns of income distribution. Cultural diffusion, also promoted by MNCs, has led to the introduction of western food marketing techniques, from supermarkets to McDonald's "golden arches" throughout the world, and such activities, for better or worse, have also promoted changes in dietary and nutritional habits in many countries.

More analysis and appraisal of the effects of large corporations is included in chapters by Seevers and Christensen. Let it suffice to say here that while intergovernmental

organizations operating in the food area can be criticized for
their limited impact on the global food system, the contrary is
probably true with regard to the MNCs. The large firms have been
both aggressive and effective, but their largely profit-motivated
activities have had mixed effects. Their contributions in
disseminating technology have been impressive. But a goodly
proportion of their investments in the Third World have been in
cash crops which actually compete with food crops, and in food
crops that are exported to richer countries rather than eaten in
poorer ones.[26] Similarly, their marketing activities, their
occasional oligopolistic influence over prices and the secrecy of
their transactions have had unsettling effects upon the food
system. These were clearly in evidence in the case of the Soviet
grain purchases of 1972, where market management by the large
firms, and the secrecy that cloaked it, hindered timely adjustment
to the magnitude of the Russian intervention. Both Paarlberg and
Destler analyze aspects of this Soviet grain deal in their
respective chapters below.

As regards the relationship between the MNCs and the global
food regime, our judgment is that the large firms had little to do
with the setting of the norms that have prevailed in the postwar
era (except perhaps via their influence over US policies).[27] On
the other hand, the regime as a whole has been benign by and large
toward the interests of the big producers and traders.[28] The
companies have profited in the environment that the regime created.
The regime's emphasis upon commercial dealings, its ethos of more
trade and freer trade, its direction of concessional flows through
private transactional networks, its encouragement of research in
more productive technologies (notably a boon to fertilizer
producers), and its relative underemphasis (until the 1970s) on
small farmers in poor countries, who are of little use to MNCs one
way or the other, all created an environment which, in no small
measure helped produce multinational agribusinesses and sustain
their growth.

IV. FOOD SYSTEM AND REGIME IN PERSPECTIVE

For all its complexity of structure and functioning, the
global food system, especially since 1972, has not been functioning
very satisfactorily if we impose standards such as the stemming of
scarcity, provision of security or the maintenance of price
stability. Nor, for that matter has it worked very well to
overcome low productivities in farming in less developed countries
or to improve the basic nutrition of the world's poor.

At the heart of the system's incapacity to respond adequately
and equitably to world hunger is the basic principle that underlies
the norm-setting process of the regime.

The rules of the regime originate as <u>national policies which
are internationally bargained and coordinated,</u> by purpose or
default, by multilateral agreement or unilateral dictate. This

would be satisfactory if national policies (or at least the
policies of those national actors that most influence the regime)
gave high priority to meeting global needs. In fact, as suggested,
the case is exactly the opposite: national foreign policies in
agriculture, because of the political imperatives behind them, have
tended to serve domestic ends ahead of international ones. This
last point, incidentally, tends to be as true for less developed
countries as it is for the industrialized states. The outcome of
this "nationally decided, internationally coordinated" principle
has been a continuing pattern of food flows conditioned primarily
by market forces (from those who can sell, to those who can buy)
unbuffered in recent years by reserves, and by and large
undersupplied in aid. It might be argued that such a system is
about the most that we can expect in a world of separate, sovereign
and unequally endowed states. A number of authors contributing to
this volume, however, are unwilling to accept this.

The political forces shaping norms of the food regime are
largely divorced from the majority of people most severely affected
by problems in the global food system. These are the rural poor of
the Third World. Food trade and aid, investment and information do
not affect these people significantly since they are simply not
part of the modern interdependent world. The poorest peasant of
Asia, Africa and Latin America participate little if at all in cash
economies and hence are neither stimulated nor distracted by price
changes or other supply and demand fluctuations, international,
national or otherwise. They are often unreached, even by their own
governments' policies. Certain theorists, of course, argue rather
persuasively that such isolation in poverty for the peasantry
reflects not their isolation from the world system but their
centrality in it. They are its victims, and their continued
victimization is crucial to its national and international
functioning. Only a revolutionary overturning, it is argued, can
break them out of their poverty. Only one of the authors below,
Christensen, makes the case for revolution. Whether at the center
or the periphery of effects from the international food system,
such peasants, once involved in the causal links of the system, are
both the most vulnerable and least potent group affected, at least
compared to the minor extent of their involvement. Hence sober
eflection upon the norms of the global food regime, as we perceive
them, does drive one to the conclusion that the rules of the system
have focused neither sufficient transactions nor attention upon the
plight of the world's rural poor. By legitimizing ongoing
concessional dealings, the regime might be said to point in this
direction, but the residual role these have played as ways to
"dump" have lessened their effectiveness. Further, intentions over
who should benefit from foreign donations have tended to shift
markedly at the national borders of recipient countries, and the
norm of sovereignty has muzzled international concerns with
internal affairs, often to the detriment of poor people in the
countryside.

Finally, in addition to the broad and endemic inadequacies of
the current food system, which will be difficult to rectify, other
more specific shortcomings can be singled out that are perhaps
easier to deal with. For example, there is currently a lack of

productive resources and relevant technology available to countries
needing to expand their food supply. Furthermore, in many poor
countries public policies actually inject net disincentives to
expanded food production.[29] Added to this are inadequacies in
financial and administrative infrastructure which further hamper
food production. Globally, there is no real control over grain
production, no systematic stockpiling and no controls over trade
and price. National policies in nearly every country, developed
and underdeveloped alike, are still deficient with respect to
nutrition and health. Population policies are rare and largely
ineffectual. While many of these problems could be alleviated by
changes within countries, in many cases the success of what is done
will depend partly upon what is done in other countries, and
partly, too, upon international norms. Global food interdependence
requires collaborative policy efforts to establish rules for a new
global food regime. Without such new norms, and appropriately
compliant behavior, it is likely that the expansion of food
production will occur haphazardly, and too slowly, with little
attention to chronic hunger, little heed of environmental side
effects, and little concern for distributive justice.

NOTES

[1]Lucy Mair, Primitive Government (Baltimore: Penguin, 1962); Karl
A. Wittfogel, Oriental Despotism (New Haven: Yale University
Press, 1957).

[2]FAO,FAO Commodity Review and Outlook 1975-76 (FAO: Rome, 1976),
pp. 8-9.

[3]See USDA, The World Food Situation and Prospects to 1985
(Washington: United States Department of Agriculture, 1974), and
Lester Brown, "The World Food Prospect," Science (Dec. 12, 1975):
1053-59.

[4]International Food Policy Research Institute, Meeting Food Needs
in the Developing World. Research Report #1 (Washington: IFPRI,
February 1976).

[5]Ibid., p. 13.

[6]Eric Eckholm Losing Ground: Environmental Stress and World Food
Prospects (New York: Norton, 1976).

[7]James G. Horsfall and Charles R. Frink, "Perspective on
Agriculture's Future: Rising Costs -- Rising Doubts"
(unpublished paper presented at Symposium on Limits to Growth,
University of Connecticut, October 21, 1975).

[8]FAO, p. 23 for production figures for 1973-74 and estimates for 1975-76.

[9]Peter Katzenstein, "International Interdependence: Some Long-Term Trends and Recent Changes," International Organization, Vol. 29, No. 4 (Autumn 1975): 1021-34.

[10]Odin Knudsen and Andrew Parnes, Trade Instability and Economic Development: An Emprical Study (Lexington Mass.: Lexington Books, 1975). These authors point out that export instability, on balance, encourages economic development and that some degree of instability is probably desirable.

[11]All USDA and FAO projections tend to agree on this point.

[12]Bruce F. Johnston and Peter Kilby, Agriculture and Structural Transformation (New York: Oxford University Press, 1975); Guy Hunter, Modernizing Peasant Societies (New York and London: Oxford University Press, 1969); Yujiro Hayami and Vernon Ruttan, Agricultural Development: An International Perspective (Baltimore: Johns Hopkins Press, 1971); Herman Southworth and Bruce Johnston, eds., Agricultural Development and Economic Growth (Ithaca: Cornell University Press, 1967); Keith Griffin, Underdevelopment in Spanish America (Cambridge: M.I.T. Press, 1969); Keith Griffin, The Political Economy of Agrarian Change (Cambridge: Harvard University Press, 1974).

[13]Overconsumption is also a form of malnutrition. It is not, however, a concern of this volume.

[14]See FAO, Assessment of The World Food Situation, (Rome: FAO, 1974), pp. 49-50, and Shlomo Reutlinger and Marcelo Selowsky, Undernourishment and Poverty, International Bank for Reconstruction and Development, Bank Staff Working Paper no. 202 (Washington: IBRD, April, 1975).

[15]For a general review of malnutrition, see, James Austin, "Attacking the Malnutrition Problem" (unpublished paper presented at the Conference of the Institute for the Study of Human Development, Madrid, Spain, September, 1975). See also Austin's contribution to this volume.

[16]Theodore W. Schultz, "Value of U.S. Farm Surpluses to Underdeveloped Countries," Journal of Farm Economics, Vol. 42 (December 1960): 1028-9, and Clifford R. Kern, "Looking a Gift Horse in the Mouth: The Economics of Food Aid Programs," Political Science Quarterly, Vol. 8 (March 1968): 59-75.

[17]Johnathan Barker, "Peasants Under Capitalism" (unpublished paper given at the International Studies Association Meetings, March 15, 1977).

[18]Jack Shepherd, The Politics of Starvation (New York: The Carnegie Endowment for International Peace, 1975).

[19]U.S. Congress, Senate, Select Committee on Nutrition and Human Needs, The United States, FAO and World Food Politics: U.S. Relations With An International Food Organization, Staff Report 94th Congress, 2nd Session, (Washington: U.S. Government Printing Office, June, 1976), pp. 11-13.

[20]United States Government, FAO Interagency Staff Committee, "United States Objectives in FAO," (Washington, May, 1976).

[21]Thomas G. Weiss and Robert S. Jordan, The World Food Conference and Global Problem Solving (New York: Praeger, 1976), pp. 155-166.

[22]B. Gosovic, UNCTAD, Conflict and Compromise: The Third World's Quest for an Equitable World Order Through the United Nations (Leiden: Sijthoff, 1975), pp. 93-114 and passim.: J.C. Nagle, Agricultural Trade Policies (Lexington, Mass.: D.C. Heath, 1976), pp. 70-97.

[23]For a discussion of budgetary resources, see, United States Department of Agriculture, Economic Research Service, "Multilateral Assistance for Agricultural Development" (Washington: USDA, 1977). For commentaries on national support and political and bureaucratic problems, see, United States Senate, Select Committee on Nutrition and Human Needs, pp. 25-68.

[24]Under current legislation (1977), a U.S. domestic reserve of 35 million tons of grain may be accumulated and held.

[25]Joseph M. Jones, The United Nations at Work: Developing Land, Forests, Oceans and People (Oxford, England: Pergamon Press, 1965), p. 118.

[26]See Michael Lofchie, "Political and Economic Origins of African Hunger," Journal of Modern African Studies (December 1975): 551-567, and Susan George, How the Other Half Dies (London: Penguin, 1976).

[27]Similarly, most poor countries have had little influence on the regime, except as their needs became so apparent as to be impossible to ignore.

[28]It might also be considered to have been largely benign toward the interests of poor countries, though not necessarily poor people in these countries, except where these interests conflicted with those of the major participants in the commercial system.

[29]Abdullah A. Saleh, "Disincentives to Agricultural Production in Developing Countries: A Policy Survey," Foreign Agricultural Supplement (Washington: GAO, March, 1975), p. 1.

Institutional Dimensions of the Malnutrition Problem

JAMES E. AUSTIN

The roots of malnutrition are found in economics, education, agriculture, and health. This multiple etiology requires that approaches to the problem engage many different institutions. These organizations can be viewed as constituting an International Nutrition Institutional Network. The functions of this system are collection and dissemination of information, provision of goods and services, financing, and coordination. Significant problems, however, have been identified in the performance of these functions. These are organizational: poor coordination, vague responsibility delineation, inadequate evaluation, people limitations, and international-national relationships. They are also political: policy vacuum, knowledge gaps, and priority conflicts. Unless these are rectified, the Network's effectiveness will remain severely limited.

As the introductory essay of this volume indicates, widespread, though regionally- and class-concentrated malnutrition is a prime aspect of the world food problem. It is the qualitative dimension, and perhaps the most defiant one since it is not to be overcome by simply raising food production. If malnutrition is to be analyzed as a distortion of the global food system, it is fundamentally a distortion of the distributive function of that system. Many consumers in many places and strata continually receive too few nutrients to sustain energy, health, and sometimes life.

The distributive distortion of the global system that produces malnutrition reflects in part the playing out of some of the norms of the global food regime. It has been the implicit norm that matters of nutrition are not to be treated as very important questions in food diplomacy, especially when raising them would

From **INTERNATIONAL ORGANIZATION**, Vol 32, No. 3, Summer 1978, (811-836), reprinted by permission of the publisher, University of Wisconsin Press.

Table 1 Population with calorie intake below requirements (1975)

Region	Millions of people	% of Total population
Asia and Far East	924	82
Africa	243	77
Near East	112	51
Latin America	94	36
	1,373	71

Source: Shlomo Reutlinger, Marcelo Selowsky, I.B.R.D., Working Paper No. 202, December 1975.

Table 2 Population with daily deficits in excess of 250 calories

Region	Millions of people	% of Total population
Asia and Far East	707	63
Africa	93	61
Near East	61	33
Latin America	71	23
	932	48

Source: Shlomo Reutlinger, Marcelo Selowsky, I.B.R.D., Working Paper No. 202, December 1975.

Table 3 Global income and population distribution—1973

Per capita GNP income grouping	Average GNP per capita	Number of countries	POPULATION		TOTAL GNP	
			Millions	%	Billions	%
Below $200	$ 120	43	1,151	30.1	$ 136	2.9
$200–$ 499	280	52	1,184	30.9	332	7.0
$500–$1,999	1,000	53	531	13.8	530	11.0
$2,000–$4,999	2,800	28	654	17.0	1,871	39.3
Over $5,000	2,970	12	316	8.2	1,896	39.7

Source: *World Bank Atlas*, World Bank 1975.

tend to generate further questions about domestic distributions of food. Low priorities accorded nutrition in food diplomacy led to low funding for programs of international research and intervention, low capacity in international institutions assigned nutritional roles, and consequently low performance from these institutions.

There is currently some evidence that international indifference to malnutrition and its causes is changing, as for example in the United Nations Economic and Social Council's (ECOSOC) designation, "Organizational Arrangements for Nutrition," as a major agenda item of its summer 1977 meeting and The World Food Council's (WFC) decision to include nutrition planning and interventions as the major items for its June 1978 annual meeting. But even if there is new interest, new action will probably require institutional overhaul. After taking stock of the magnitude of global malnutrition, this essay critically examines the structure and capacity of existing international nutrition institutions. Concluding comments focus on prospects for improved institutional efforts.

I. GLOBAL MALNUTRITION

The Magnitude of Global Malnutrition

More than 1.3 billion people, over two-thirds of the developing nations' population, are suffering from some degree of caloric undernutrition. As can be seen from Table 1, the problem is most acute in Asia, the Far East, and Africa. The global daily shortage of calories of the undernourished population is 444 billion calories, which is equivalent to 127,000 metric tons of grain. This means that on an annual basis there is a global calories shortfall equivalent to 46 million metric tons of grains, which is about one-third of all grain traded internationally.[1]

Even if one takes a narrower view of the problem and only focuses on those with daily caloric deficits greater than 250 calories (10 percent), the numbers are, unfortunately, still very large. As Table 2 reveals, the total number of people suffering from these more severe caloric deficits amounts to over 900 million or almost 50 percent of the developing countries' population.

Calorie energy deficiencies are pervasive and primary and almost always signify accompanying protein shortages which reduce the body's growth capacity and disease resistance. The protein deficits are particularly devastating for young children, as the high infant mortality rates in developing countries reveal. Beyond calories and proteins, mineral and vitamin deficiencies affect even larger numbers.

The magnitude of these deficits and the human suffering they inflict clearly make global malnutrition one of the most pressing social problems confronting the world today. It will also be extremely costly to alleviate. The costs of meeting the calorie deficits cited above are estimated at $19 billion.[2] The size of the problem means that large resources must be mobilized and that will require significant assistance from international development agencies if the immediacy of the problem is to be addressed. It will also require sizable allocations from the developing countries' scarce internal resources, creating pressures among the various national agencies and development programs which compete for their pieces of the governments' modest budgets.

Nature of the Malnutrition Problem

    Scarcity of resources is but a reflection of the fundamental causes of malnutrition: poverty, poor nations, and poor people. National incomes are low and what little there is is maldistributed. Table 3 reveals that on a world basis two billion people in 95 countries exist on an average per capita national income of less than $0.60 per day; 60 percent of the population controls only 10 percent of the world's GNP while almost 80 percent of the global GNP is in the hands of only 25 percent of the population.
    Specific country data reveal further the poverty-malnutrition link and also illustrate the particularly precarious nutritional state of the urban poor in most developing countries. Brazil has a national per capita average calorie intake above the recommended daily adult allowance of 2500 calories, but when one disaggregates this average by income strate the adverse nutritional reality of the poor emerges. Calorie intakes of the poorest 20 percent of the households in the Northeast, East, and South are about 40 percent less than those of the highest 20 percent. In all instances the caloric intake of the poorest urban households was less than that of their rural counterparts. Nutritional data for Rio de Janeiro show that this inverse income deficiency correlation tends to hold for other nutrients as well as calories. In India, as well, the urban poor are in the worst nutritional situation. Anthropometric and biochemical indicators also show this urban-rural nutrition pattern. The urban and malnourished are fewer in numbers but appear to experience more severe deficiencies.
    These income and nutritional intake figures raise the basic issue of equitable income distribution. Malnutrition now results not so much from absolute total food shortages as from the uneven distribution of food supplies. China and Cuba had 1974 per capita annual income levels ($300 and $490, respectively) much below Brazil ($900), but the income redistribution in those two poorer countries reportedly has dramatically reduced malnutrition there while it prevails in the richer country. The problem is one of inequity, not just poverty. Malnutrition mirrors income maldistribution. Consequently, effective nutrition intervention programs require resource transfers which begin to shift the

distribution pattern.

Income redistribution is a politically sensitive issue in most nations, and, therefore, nutrition programs run the risk of jangling the nerves of politically significant power blocs. For example, increased taxes on industrialists to pay for government nutrition programs in Colombia and Costa Rica met (but overcame) considerable resistance; similarly, fortification programs of salt in Nicaragua and sugar in Guatemala encountered opposition from processors. Nutrition intervention is almost inevitably political intervention, which practically ensures institutional resistance on one front or another. Nevertheless, in some countries, e.g., India and Chile, nutrition has been used as part of redistribution-oriented political campaigns. Feeding is highly visible and therefore can be a political asset; its basic humanitarian nature may in fact make it a more politically palatable way to effect redistribution than, say, land reform. Thus, nutrition programs find themselves in the ironic position of being blocked by redistribution opponents or being supported by them as a palliation to obviate more fundamental structural changes.

The fact that malnutrition is enmeshed in the poverty web means that it is both a contributor to and consequence of the multiple strands that stifle development. To understand fully the malnutrition problem one should also identify the noneconomic strands and how they are entwined. Malnutrition stems from insufficient food intake in quantitative and qualitative terms, and many factors can lead to inadequate intake other than just low incomes. Four such factors are:

(1) Food beliefs, e.g., certain protein foods are not to be eaten during pregnancy;
(2) health concepts, e.g., food is withheld from sick children;
(3) cooking practices, e.g., nutrient leaching due to excess boiling of rice and discarding of the water; and
(4) intrafamilial food distribution patterns, e.g., the male head of household receives priority in family food allocation, often to the detriment of the small children who are more nutritionally vulnerable.

In addition to the sociological factors, deficiencies in the food production and delivery system itself can constrain intake. Several countries (e.g., Sahelian Africa) simply may not have the natural resources to produce adequate supplies of food imports which often must be limited to less than the needed amounts due to foreign exchange scarcity. Even where the natural agronomic resources do exist, their exploitation is often hampered by lack of the necessary physical infrastructure or institutional mechanisms to realize the food production potential. These inadequacies mean that either output remains low or sizable food losses occur during the seed-to-consumer flow. The net results is the same: lower supplies, higher prices, reduced intake, nutritional deficits.

Malnutrition impinges adversely on overall health status, particularly of young children, through its interaction with

Table 4   International nutrition system: institutional roles

Institutions	Collection & dissemination of information	Provision of goods & services	Financing	Coordination
Primary Nutrition Institutions:				
INCAP	x			
CFNI	x			
ININ	x			
PAG	x	x		
Food for Peace Program		x		
WFP		x		
Voluntary Agencies		x		
CWFS				x
IFS		x		
CFAPP	x			x
WFC		x		x
Secondary Nutrition Institutions:				
Universities and Research Institutes, etc.	x			
WHO	x	x	x	x
UNICEF	x	x	x	x
FAO	x	x	x	x
Ag Research Centers	x			
CGIAR	x			
USDA	x			
IFPRI	x			
UNDRO		x		
Red Cross		x		
IFDC	x	x		
IWC	x			x
National Development Agencies (A.I.D., SIDA, etc.)		x	x	
CGFPI				x
UNDP		x		
World Bank	x		x	
IDB			x	
ADB			x	
IADF			x	

Table 5   Food and nutrition planning in developing countries[a]

Planning/policy status	Number of countries
1. Extensive nutrition interventions but not on a coordinated intersectoral basis.	36
2. Steps being taken toward intersectoral food and nutrition plan/policy.	41
3. Intersectoral food and nutrition plan/policy adopted.	6

[a]Where UNICEF has projects.
Source: UNICEF, "General Progress Report of the Executive Director," p. 55, E/ICEF/642, 1976.

infection. Simplistically stated, undernourishment reduces the body's resistance to disease such that an infection, like measles, which would be relatively harmless to a healthy child, can be fatal to a malnourished child. Or, conversely, a healthy child can be pushed into a malnourished state by reduced nutrient intake or retention due to the advent of sickness. Consequently, improved sanitation and water supply along with other health care measures are important in alleviating disease and malnutrition incidence.

From the foregoing, the multiple etiology of malnutrition is evident. Its roots are found in economics, education, agriculture, and health. This multiple causality indicates the need for a multi-sectoral approach to the problem of combating malnutrition. Such an approach carries very significant institutional ramifications: it requires that multiple institution -- i.e., national and international, public and private, formal and informal groups, programs and organizations -- and professionals from different disciplines and sectors with different resources and inputs all direct their energies toward the common problem. For most existing institutions actively working against world hunger, nutrition has been a largely neglected focal point, usually an orphan to simpler and more obvious concerns about state to state movements of quantities of food. Nutrition interventions can take many different forms: supplementary feeding programs, food fortification, nutrition education, formulated, nutrient-dense foods, agricultural technology, ration shops. Such programs address specific nutritional deficiencies and particular nutritionally vulnerable groups. They go beyond simple food production. With nutrition now beginning to appear on organizational agendas, the newness and unfamiliarity with the problem area is creating both trepidation and institutional resistance. Complicating the situation even further is the requirement for multi-institutional interaction for effective programming. Always difficult in any event, problems of organizational coordination and integration can attain paralyzing proportions at the international level.

II. THE INTERNATIONAL NUTRITION INSTITUTIONAL NETWORK

In one way the "international nutrition institutional network" is coextensive with the UN Food Network." The cluster of public international institutions generally mandated to deal with global food problems is also assigned the general task of enhancing nutrition. Technically, participants in the nutrition network are really a subcluster of groups, programs, committees, and the like -- organizations within organizations -- specifically charged with nutrition-enhancing assignments. Typical international nutrition groups would include the FAO/WHO Protein-Calorie Advisory Group, UNICEF's Child Feeding Program, FAO's Nutrition Division, teams at the regional research centers at work on enriching the protein content of maize, potatoes, etc. In its most extensive definition, the nutrition institutional network interlinks not only personnel associated with public international organizations but also counterparts within national governments and private organizations. To gain proper perspective, the reader should note that this global network of nutrition institutions is extensive, but it is not large in terms of either the number of professionals it includes (hardly more than a few thousand global) or in terms of the resources it commands and dispenses (a small fraction of resources allocated to food aid). In addition, there is some danger that the term "network" may be a bit overworked here; to lend the impression of tightly linked set of institutions bound by a common purpose would be misleading. Actually, the institutional links are often tenuous, and the orientations are diverse. Nonetheless, the organizations are all in the nutrition business in some form. All are directing their efforts toward the alleviation of malnutrition, and all interact with one another.

Beyond the nutrition-targeted institutions are organizations and programs whose activities carry nutritional implications even though their main focus is broader than just nutrition, e.g., agricultural or rural development. These are secondary rather than primary institutions in the nutrition network, but they still must be considered in an overall examination.

The purpose of this section is neither to present an exhaustive institutional shopping list, nor to detail the work of specific nutrition groups. Analysis here is rather directed toward identifying the principal functions that organizations performs in the international nutrition field and illustrating these with brief descriptions of the activities of some of the major actors in the network.

Collection and Dissemination of Information

A fundamental ingredient of most institutional systems is an information flow. For nutrition such an information function encompasses basic and applied research as well as the generation of more operational data such as nutrient supply and nutritional status statistics.

On the research side there exist several institutes which are viewed as international nutrition information centers. Among these are the Institute of Nutrition for Central American and Panama (INCAP), the Caribbean Food and Nutrition Institute (CFNI), the Indian National Institute of Nutrition (ININ) and various universities and research institutes within the United States and other developed nations, including the newly launched United Nations University which has hunger as one of its main research areas. At the World Food Conference, Resolution V gave the World Health Organization, (WHO), United Nations Children's Fund (UNICEF), and the Food and Agriculture Organization (FAO) the responsibility for arranging an internationally coordinated program in applied nutrition research. This effort is designed to increase and improve these and other institutions' ongoing research. At an October 1975 interagency meeting in Rome, it was proposed that the Protein-Calorie Advisory Group (PAG) should initiate coordination of applied nutrition research. Subsequently, the Administrative Committee on Coordination (ACC), the UN system's highest coordinating body, under pressure from the line agencies, reversed the Rome decision and stated that no interagency consultative machinery should be established to coordinate nutrition research as a whole. Additionally, there are several international agricultural research centers (CIMMYT, IRRI, CIAT) carrying out research on basic grain production, with modest emphasis on nutritional aspects. Despite these ongoing efforts, significant nutrition knowledge gaps exist concerning the nature of malnutrition and the means to alleviate it most effectively. Continual probing is needed to provide a sturdier base for directing international efforts.

On the operating data side the FAO and the USDA have traditionally been the major assemblers and disseminators of food production and trade data. Recently the International Food Policy Research Institute (IFPRI) was formed with support from several sources, including the Rockefeller and Ford Foundations, the World Bank, and the Canadian International Development Agency. IFPRI seeks to carry out policy-oriented research that leads to improved food intake by developing country populations; it has a mandate from its Board to give explicit attention to nutrition policy and programs. The World Bank and bilateral agencies play significant roles in shaping and disseminating the research results funded under their auspices or carried out by their own staffs. The World Food Conference also recommended that WHO, FAO, and UNICEF establish a global nutrition surveillance system to monitor the food and nutrition conditions of the disadvantaged groups. WHO is the leader organization, working with the UN agencies as well as other international institutions. This system presumably will be related to the Global Information and Early Warning System established in 1974 under the aegis of the FAO (unfortunately without the participation of the USSR of China). Without reasonably accurate and timely information on food availability and nutritional status, program planning will take place in a vacuum or be based on shaky data foundations. In either case, the effectiveness of international efforts will be diluted.

Provision of Goods and Services

Information provides the basis for action and international nutrition action takes the form of supplying food, supplies, or technical assistance. International food aid flows through bilateral and multilateral arrangements. Of the former, the largest currently and historically has been the US P.L. 480 Food for Peace Program, which sold on concessional terms or donated over $1 billion worth of food in 1976. This food is shipped by the international grain companies, with voluntary agencies such as CARE, Catholic Relief Services, and the Church World Services frequently administering the in-country donated food feeding programs. The major multilateral food aid efforts is the World Food Program (WFP) which is operated under the joint auspices of FAO and ECOSOC. As noted in the previous chapter, the WFP budget for the 1976-77 biennium is $750 million, of which the US has pledged $188 million with the balance coming from other developed nation donors and the oil-rich developing nations.

During emergency famine or disaster situations other organizations are involved in the food relief operations, for example, the United Nations Disaster Relief Office (UNDRO), the League of Red Cross Societies, OXFAM, and other voluntary agencies. Emerging from the World Food Conference was a Committee on World Food Security (CWFS) which was given responsibility for developing an international grain reserve system to handle food emergencies as well as designing other measures to insure greater food security to developing nations. While progress in this direction has been minimal, as Destler explains, the emergence of an international reserve system would be a major step toward reducing the world's nutritional vulnerability.

The fertilizer problem has begun to be addressed institutionally. In 1974 the FAO established the International Fertilizer Supply Scheme (IFS), through which 73,000 tons of fertilizer had been placed as of June 1975 in 30 of the most seriously affected importing nations. This amount is still far less than that financed through bilateral aid. Also, the International Fertilizer Development (IFDC) has been established to carry out research and provide advice. This latter entity perhaps will enable a smoothing out of the traditionally marked peaks and troughs in fertilizer prices and investments, which are due in part to the technology which leads to lumpy investments, and in part to inadequate effective demand data.

The development institutions provide considerable amounts of technical assistance in various areas. One area that has received particular attention has been national food and nutrition planning, which entails assessing nutritional status and designing viable, multi-sector nutrition programs to improve nutritional well-being. A.I.D.'s Office of Nutrition has centered much of its technical assistance activities in this area, accompanied by several other countries' development agencies -- particularly those in Canada, Sweden, the UK, Germany, Norway, and the Netherlands. Also, the FAO was designated after the World Food Conference as the lead agency in promoting the strengthening of national nutrition planning capacities.[3]

The Consultative Group on Food Production and Investment (CGFPI), established in 1975 by the World Bank, the FAO, and the UN Development Programme (UNDP), also stress to governments the importance of planning. Its technical assistance role, however, is somewhat different. The CGFPI Chairman, Ambassador Edwin Martin, described it as follows: "Unlike the World Bank, we have no money to give or lend; we make no decisions like FAO. All we can do is encourage people and organizations to do the right thing by offering what we think is sound advice. In this sense then, our role is one of catalyst or facilitator."[4] The CGPI assembles donor countries, developing nations, and public and private agricultural investors and attempts to stimulate investments which would increase food supplies to the most nutritionally disadvantaged. In effect, the CGPI is an institutional matchmaker using technical advice and institutional prestige as the uniting mechanisms.

Financing

The tab for the research, information dissemination, planning, food donations, agricultural production, and technical assistance activities of the international institutions is picked up by several organizations. The funds for nutrition research come from foundations, national and international development agencies, and the United Nations. It is estimated that world expenditures on nutrition research related to developing country malnutrition, excluding funds for agricultural research, are $20 to $40 million per year. The expenditures for food aid amounted to approximately $2 billion in 1976.

The bulk of international financing goes to food production efforts rather than specific nutrition projects. The 1975 AID appropriation for food and nutrition was $300 million.[5] UNICEF's child nutrition expenditures in 1975 were $15.1 million.[6] The World Bank, Inter-American Development Bank (IDB), and the Asian Development Bank (ADB), destined, in 1976, $2.5 billion for agricultural production. The FAO and UNDP accounted for another $300 million. The newly established International Agricultural Development Fund (IADF) is expected to have a capitalization of about $900 million. The IADF was one of the most financially significant institutional development emerging from the World Food Conference but its thrust is toward food production rather than nutrition per se. Although food aid and nutrition expenditures are sizable, they are small compared to the previously cited $19-billion short-run expenditures that would be needed to remove the current nutritional deficits. Resources are scarce and therefore a premium exists on their efficient use.

Coordination

A prerequisite to efficient and effective use of allocated resources is the coordination of international efforts. When world attention was drawn to the global food crisis by the dramatic crop shortfalls of the early seventies, considerable international institutional activity was generated which gave rise to a host of new coordinating bodies and activities. The World Food Conference, for example, created several institutional coordinating vehicles,

primary among these the World Food Council. As the highest
political body of the UN system dealing exclusively with food, the
council set forth the following as its main functions: "(a) to
monitor the world food situation in all its aspects, including
what international organizations and governments are doing to
develop short-term and long-term solutions to food problems; (b) to
look at the total food picture and determine in its coordinating
role whether the world food strategy as a whole made sense; (c) to
identify malfunctions, gaps, and problem areas; and (d) to exert
its influence, through moral persuasion, to get any necessary
improvements made."[7] Given these functions, the World Food
Council, in one sense, could be viewed as the general manager of
the UN food network performing the overall coordinating role of
interlinking the various food and nutrition institutions. In fact,
in the Council's June 1977 meeting, nutrition planning and programs
were designated as priority items for Council study in preparation
for the 1978 meeting.

Other UN entities are serving as the subcoordinators in
different areas, for example, WHO for global nutritional status
surveillance and FAO for applied nutrition research and nutrition
planning. The old Intergovernmental Committee of the World Food
Program was reconstituted as a 30-member Committee on Food Aid
Policies and Programs (CFAPP) to serve as a forum for consultations
and coordination on food aid policies and operations. An
International Group for Agricultural Development in Latin America
(ICAD/LA) is being organized by the Inter-American Development Bank
to coordinate efforts in removing agricultural production
constraints and in reducing malnutrition in the hemisphere.

Other coordinating bodies that existed prior to the World Food
Conference have expanded their activities. The Consultative Group
on International Agricultural Research (CGIAR), which has been
coordinating the activities of the international agricultural
research centers since 1971, almost doubled its budget from $34
million to $64 million between 1974 and 1976. The International
Wheat Council (IWC), as Destler reports in his essay, has been the
forum for international grain reserve discussions.

Coordination is essential and clearly there is considerable
movement in this direction. Its effectiveness, however, is not so
clear and will be discussed in a moment. As a means of recapping
this section, Table 4 presents a summary profile of the
institutional roles of the various main food and nutrition groups
discussed thus far.

A final addition to this inventory: the most important
institution in the nutrition system is the malnourished family. If
the entire hierarchy of nutrition institutions and the focus on
macro policies and programs fail to understand and meet the needs
of the target families, then even the neatest, most logical,
well-coordinated network is meaningless. Thus one should remember
the critical importance of designing structures and procedures to
overcome barriers to implementation that keep nutrition delivery
systems from reaching needy groups. Christensen argues in her
essay that such barriers are numerous and formidable, especially at
the national level.

III. INSTITUTIONAL PROBLEMS AND PROSPECTS

Despite this multitude of international institutions involved in nutrition, the progress made toward alleviating malnutrition has been far from dramatic. In fact, the numbers of malnourished have increased; we have not even been able to keep up with the geometry of population demography and the erosion of global impoverishment. Although the task is large and the resources scarce, few leaders in the international nutrition community are satisfied with performance to date. The spectre of even worse malnutrition looms ominously on the horizon; thus it is critical that the international nutrition community examine why its performance has not been more effective and try to delineate ways to strengthen its future efforts.

From an examination of published documents and discussions with functionaries from many of the international nutrition organizations, several institutional problems emerge as major areas of concern for the international nutrition system. These concerns fall into two broad categories: organizational and political.

Organizational Concerns

Good intentions and financial resources can be readily squandered by organizational deficiencies. The international nutrition community cannot afford the luxury of ineffectual organization. There appear to be five areas of organizational concern: poor coordination, vague responsibility delineation, inadequate review and evaluation, people limitations, and international-national relationships.

Poor Coordination

A major organizational problem is with inter-institutional coordination. A recent study of the World Food Conference and the UN's role concluded that °Even with the myriad of specialized agencies and bodies of the UN there is as yet no capacity to anticipate and plan responses to new global exigencies or ones that overlap the mandates of several organizations."[8] Furthermore, the authors raise the "central and long-standing question as to whether ECOSOC can achieve a central coordinating role in human welfare within the system of international organizations."[9] Other outside observers have come to similar conclusions: "We are seriously concerned that the UN system....has no effective mechanism for coordinating and managing the tremendous resources made available to it for carrying out economic and social activities in the world community."[10] The problem is also recognized by the UN officials themselves who have to deal with it directly. One put it this way: "I am myself very much concerned with the present situation of interagency coordination which, to say the least, is in my opinion very unsatisfactory, and the programmed and the countries we are trying to serve are the ones who suffer."[11] Exacerbating this problem further is a reported lack of communication among institutions it is rather difficult to coordinate if one does not even know what there is to coordinate.

Coordination problems are certainly not unique to the UN system. Bilateral development agencies have only recently begun to communicate about their respective nutrition activities and have not yet begun significantly to coordinate their substantive field activities. Even less progress has been made on the interface between bilateral and multilateral institutions.

These interinstitutional problems appear to be generic to food- and nutrition-related institutions at the national level and across political systems. The author sat in the office of the Director of Nutrition of a social East African nation and listened to the same lament about the difficulty of attaining coordination among ministries of agriculture, education, health, and finances that he had heard a week earlier in the office of the US Senate Select Committee on Nutrition and Human Needs. In one Latin American nation the inability of the Planning Ministry to achieve adequate coordination with and among the various implementing ministries led a major multilateral development organization to refuse to finance a national nutrition program.

The coordination problem is not just inter-institutional but also within organizations. Most development institutions involved in nutrition also are concerned about other development areas, too. Those activities, e.g., health, water systems, industrialization, do not have nutrition as their central focus, but do have nutritional implications. People carrying out these operations frequently lack the appreciation for, or knowledge of, nutrition to coordinate effectively their efforts with the institutions' nutrition programs. Significant nutrition awareness and know-how has not yet permeated the ranks of loan officers, project managers, and country analysts that constitute the bulk of the professional staffs of the national and international development agencies. Even within institutions specializing in nutrition, particularly universities and research organizations, professionals become prisoners of their particular disciplines and fail to interact with their in-house colleagues from other departments.

Poor coordination is an easy target for organizational critics. Such criticism is frequently responded to by institutional shuffling in the form of new committees and more meetings. As one UN Director put it: "For institutional reasons coordination already receives and undue amount of discussion in UN circles."[12] Too often coordination can simply become a guise for inaction, a meaningless part of the bureaucratic ritual. Coordination requires time and resources; clear benefits must be forthcoming to justify the investment. It is not sufficient simply to point out coordination problems; more often than not they are simply symptoms of other underlying organizational problems.

Vague Delineation of Responsibility

Some point to inadequate leadership as the source of the coordination problem:

--The one major resolution of the World Food Conference on which no institutional follow-up arrangements have been put in place is that on nutrition. The UN family still has divided responsibility with no single dynamic source of leadership for all of us.[13]

--The running battle going on between UN agencies about who has jurisdiction and who should be doing what and who should be in charge of whom is a good example of the leadership vacuum at the international level.[14]

--My personal experience with each of these agencies suggests that a considerable amount of time is spent in conflict with each other.[15]

The failure to delineate institutional responsibilities foster agency rivalries that have been extremely counterproductive. The experience of the evolving role of the Protein-Calorie Advisory Group is illustrative. During the 1960s, the PAG basically concerned itself with providing technical guidelines by drawing on experts from the international scientific nutrition community. By the 1970s many countries had developed their own technical capacity and the era of viewing nutrition as a "technology problem" was passing. As nutrition became more of a development issue other disciplines became involved and the PAG Board was reconstituted to reflect this change. The new function of the PAG was then to advise the heads of the UN agencies on where emphasis should be placed in their nutrition activities. This role encountered resistance from other UN entities, particularly the FAO. The PAG's new role was viewed as an encroachment on the sphere of influence of others. When an institution's boundaries have been trespassed, a not unusual bureaucratic reaction is to counterattack. The UN's Administrative Committee on Coordination (ACC) proposed a Nutrition Subcommittee at the Secretariat level as the new focal point for UN agencies and bilateral agencies and non-governmental organizations. As an adjunct to the Subcommittee, the ACC also proposed a Nutrition Advisory Panel to replace the PAG, with the new group having a broader scope. This proposal, in turn, met vigorous opposition and action was deferred by ECOSOC until its 1977 Summer meeting.

Another example occurred with the World Food Conference follow-up activities in the area of food and nutrition planning. FAO was the designated lead agency in this area and initially proceeded in isolation, presenting its plan to the other UN and bilateral agencies as a fait accompli. FAO's self-image of being the expert in this aspect conflicted with the perception of the other institutions which also felt capable of contributing significantly to this field. Considerable resentment was generated by the perceived imposition of a plan and the presumption of institutional dominance in the planning area. The plan was rejected, to be replaced by a document incorporating all the institutions' viewpoints.

This vagueness in the delineation of responsibility, with the resultant inter-institutional conflicts, is probably due both to the complex nature of the problems being addressed and the institutions' historical emergence as somewhat ad hoc responses to particular problems or pressures. In this regard McKitterick observed that, "These branches of the United Nations have constituted since their inception a kind of world community, attacking its social and economic problems across a broad front and in a largely uncoordinated way."[16] Malnutrition, as one of several socioeconomic problems, is especially complex and multifaceted. Consequently, the problem of where to draw institutional dividing lines is particularly difficult. WHO was given the mandate in health and FAO in food, but nutrition is both a health and food problem. Consequently, both have claim to the nutrition turf. Whereas WHO and FAO were organized with a sector orientation, UNICEF was formed with a target group focus. Given that children are an especially nutritionally at-risk group, UNICEF stakes an additional claim to the nutrition ground. The sectoral vs. the target group focus creates an organizational inconsistency which will inevitably lead to overlap. Additionally, the traditional sectoral definitions simply are inconsistent with the multi-sectoral nature of the malnutrition problem. These UN inter-institutional problems mirror similar rivalries at the country level between ministries of agriculture, health, and welfare. Institutional friction and poor coordination will inevitably continue unless responsibilities and authority are more clearly delineated, operating activities integrated, and a superior arbitrator mechanism created to reconcile turf disputes. Such delineation, integration, and arbitration is not readily forthcoming under the current UN setup and similar organizational voids exist within individual countries. A further reflection of, and in part a contribution to, this vacuum are deficiencies in the review and evaluation processes.

Inadequate Review and Evaluation

Resistance to evaluation is commonplace among institutions: they are threatening, particularly when they come from outside entities. In international agencies in-house reviews often are exercises carried out more to generate the information needed to produce an annual report than to provide a critical assessment of activities. Among the UN nutrition institutions, UNICEF has on several occasions used outside organizations to review both the managerial and strategic aspects of its operations. Perhaps its target group orientation forces it to take a more eclectic and open view. In any case, such frank introspection has been more the exception than the rule in the UN.

Because of the vagueness of nutrition programming responsibilities and because these are often secondary activities for many of the implementing organizations, nutrition operations are particularly at risk of becoming nobody's responsibility. Consequently, nutrition is especially in need of an effectively functioning review and evaluation system. Such review procedures should cut across implementing organizations rather than be just within each entity. Furthermore, they should be conducted by a group which does not have a vested interest in the individual organization and can, therefore, take an objective view. With this approach, program reviews can serve as an oversight net and as an inter-institutional coordinating mechanism.

People Limitations

A fourth organizational concern is one of personnel. A problem common to both international and national nutrition efforts is the staff perspective and limited understanding of nutrition. For example, Dr. Doris Calloway, Professor of Nutrition at the University of California, Berkeley, and FAO consultant, has criticized the FAO for the absence of sufficient qualified nutrition staff and for viewing malnutrition as largely a "food-supply gap" to be remedied by greater output and higher incomes coming from rising GNPs.[17] The international agricultural research centers have been similarly criticized for being fixated on a "grow more" philosophy neglecting the economic, sociological, and distributional aspects of malnutrition. Expanding the professional staffs' nutrition vision and knowledge is a basic task facing the whole gamut of international nutrition institutions from the FAO to the World Bank to Harvard University to the National Ministry of Planning. Nutrition education begins at home.

The other people limitation concerns a bureaucratic affliction reportedly acutely present within the UN system. The highly politicized nature of the institution results in personnel selection too often based on political rather than technical criteria. The net effect is professional mediocrity which is a disservice to the member nations. After a recent six-month sabbatical at FAO, Professor Vincent H. Malstrom commented on the work environment: "There were many evidences that FAO was grossly overstaffed. With no clocks to punch, no real boss to crack the whip, and no fear of being fired, most employees of FAO had found themselves an apparently °ideal' situation -- a well-paid job with little or no work."[18] Viewing the UN as a patronage basket only serves to discourage the many competent professionals in the organization and results in poor service to its constituency. The depoliticalization of personnel selection is a prerequisite to

International-National Relationships

   Another organizational dimension can create serious barriers
to effective action, namely, the unwritten rules of conduct that
govern relations between international institutions and the
countries with which they deal. The tragedy of the Ethiopian
drought as documented by Jack Shepherd illustrates the extreme
case. Between April and November of 1973 more than 100,000
Ethiopians starved to death. The need for good aid was known by the
international agencies but they did not act. "Their
reason -- their only excuse -- was diplomatic tradition and
practice. For in the international community, no aid is given or
even offered, regardless of consequences, without the specific
request and cooperation of the recipient country....Behind the
protective curtain of respect for local sovereignty the second
coverup went along with the Imperial Ethiopian Government's own
coverup and involved every major international relief agency, most
donor nations, and many African leaders. All kept quiet as the
Selassie government requested. One authoritative voice might have
saved thousands; their silence condemned tens of thousands."[19]
   It can be contended that to speak out would be interfering in
the internal affairs of a country. The international community
does have a standard of conduct other than the diplomatic code and
that is the Declaration of Human Rights. It speaks out against the
torture of political prisoners; starvation is simply a different
form of the same. At an operational level, however, one can
contend that an international organization can only operate if it
has the trust of the host country. To receive confidential
information from the government and then use it against them would
destroy the working relationships. Trust and confidentiality are
important elements to preserving a relationship, but there are
times when the cost of maintaining a relationship clearly exceeds
the benefits.
   In normal situations, however, the task is more one of
fostering a meaningful relationship rather than terminating one.
In nutrition, as in some other development areas, three aspects of
the interface between the international organizations and the
country governments are of concern. First, international
organizations have frequently tended to "sell" certain types of
nutrition intervention programs (e.g., high protein foods) that
their research of judgements lead them to consider optimal. This
frequently results in lender or donor needs (rather than country
needs) dictating nutrition strategy. The financial and information
leverage of these international agencies puts the recipient
countries in a dependent position with no outside institutional
vehicle to which they can turn to verify the desirability of the
proposed course of action. The second problem arises because the
various lender, donor, or technical assistance agencies frequently
give conflicting advice or espouse very different approaches. Such
fragmentation only confuses the development process, erodes the
credibility of the international institutions, and strains
institutional relations. The poor coordination among bilateral and

multilateral agencies carries a very real cost in decreased effectiveness at the country level.

Action Options

There are two basic reorganization options: change institutional process or change institutional structure. It was precisely these alternatives that the World Food Conference Resolution XXII focused on when it requested ECOSOC to urgently consider "whether or not rearrangements in the United Nations' system of new institutional bodies may be justified in order to ensure effective follow-up on Conference Resolution V on nutrition."

The Administrative Committee on Coordination opted for the process alternative. After studying the situation it concluded that "The existing arrangements for ensuring appropriate planning, implementation and assessment of nutrition-related activities were not adequate...the system required an action-orientation based on common policies and approaches to nutrition improvement...the rearrangements required were more in the nature of new mechanisms for cooperation and common action than new institutions or bodies."[20]

Given the nature of the organizational concerns identified above, it is far from clear whether this prescription is appropriate. It may be that a bandaid is proposed where surgery is in order. Keeping the old institutions and adjusting their roles is not an easy task. The old roles emerged in a different food and nutrition environment and are often inconsistent with the new needs which are more action oriented. One is confronted with a situation of new roles being imposed on old institutional structures -- square pegs and round holes. This role-structure incongruity requires resolution. The new Director General of the FAO found that 80 percent of FAO's regular budget was "destined to pay for a gigantic centralized bureaucracy in Rome, 11 percent to put out publications that no one reads and the remaining 9 percent to holding meetings and for travel expenses that are largely unnecessary."[21] He has apparently decided to attack the problem through structural and process change via a vigorous decentralization program. This is desirable and is consistent with a more action-oriented country level assistance role for the FAO, but it will undoubtedly generate great internal turmoil and backlash from the affected bureaucrats. It is not clear, however, how nutrition activities will be affected of affect this reorganization. Changing long-standing institutional structures is a tough business. Nonetheless, merely fine tuning existing international nutrition institutions may not suffice to clear away the static or lack of coordination.

Institutional structure has also begun to change through the recent proliferation of food and nutrition institutions. The emergence of new entities from the World Food Conference probably indicates a belief on the part of the developing nations that the existing institutions were not adequate for their needs. However, as Asher argued some time ago, proliferation most likely reflects a tactical maneuver designed to achieve greater political control than was possible through the traditional institutions.[22] Still, not all of the new institutions were prompted by urging from the developing countries. The CGFPI was a US initiative and the IFAD was an OPEC-sponsored scheme. The new organizations may be very useful if they permit the international community to escape the clutches of those bureaucracies still clinging to an unproductive status quo. The concomitant risk, however, is that this multiplication of bureaucracies will only add to the already cumbersome burden of institutional coordination without making any net positive contribution against malnutrition.

The potentially most significant addition to the structure of the international nutrition network is the World Food Council. The WFC provides the system with an institutional focal point that had previously been missing. It provides the logical pivot around which structural changes can be carried out. However, the track record of the WFC has been less than satisfactory. The WFC has encountered active resistance from the other UN agencies which feel their jurisdictional power threatened by the Council; the lines of responsibility and authority remain cloudy and confusing. Furthermore, the participation of non-UN entities remains restricted. Consequently, without basic organizational changes the World Food Council's full potential may well remain unrealized. Under such a reorganization two operating committees could (and should) be established: the Technical Coordinating Committee (TCC) and the Overview Committee (OC).

The TCC would be divided into two subcommittees. One would be concerned with food and nutrition research activities and the other with operational programs. The subcommittees would be chaired by the professional staff of the WFC, supported by a group of outside expert TCC-affiliated consultants, and constituted by the member UN food and nutrition agencies (FAO, WHO, UNICEF, WEP, etc.), bilateral agencies (USAID, SIDA, etc.), and nongovernmental entities (IFPRI, CARE, etc.). The UN system must open up because most of the money and action in food and nutrition are really outside the system. Co-opting and broadly representing the whole international nutrition network within the UN framework is therefore critical to framing UN strategies and executing global-level undertakings. Concurrent with, and perhaps stemming from, this broadened participation must be a concerted effort to depoliticize the operations of the WFC. A high level of professionalism is a prerequisite to credibility and support from the broader nutrition community. If this is garnered, then the WFC could draw on and help channel more efficiently and effectively the significant technical, human, and financial resources existing in the previously described international nutrition network.

The functions of the TCC would be as follows:

(1) To provide a common forum to reach a consensus on problem diagnosis and desired action areas both in research and operations;

(2) Formulate a multi-institutional assistance strategy, including action priorities, for approval by the full Council;

(3) Pinpoint institutional gaps, delineate areas of implementation responsibility and clarify institutional roles;

(4) Integrate the programmatic endeavors of multiple institutions via the formation of multi-institutional task forces aimed at specific food and nutrition problems (e.g., vitamin A deficiencies, food reserves, infection-nutrition interaction, etc.);

(5) Serve as a central nutrition information collection and dissemination vehicle for the international institutions and for individual countries.

The OC, which would consist of a multidisciplinary professional staff, would perform the needed review and evaluation function that was identified earlier as a problem area. The Committee would review the activities of the member institutions of the TCC subcommittee to see if proposed actions were implemented and with what effects. The results would serve as constructive feedback to the TCC and its members for strategy reformulation. Each UN agency would be requested to submit to the OC a nutritional impact statement designating the expected effects of each project they sponsor. The purpose of this would be to heighten nutritional awareness among personnel and to operationalize nutritional accountability.

This reorganization option (see Figure 1) implies more than minor structural and process changes. It would vest considerable power in the WFC in terms of advising, planning, coordinating, arbitrating, communicating, and reviewing. The PAG's functions would largely be absorbed and expanded through the TCC and the OC. The other UN agencies' nutrition activities would come under the TCC auspices. The WFC would be the ultimate nutrition authority within the UN system and nominally within the entire international nutrition system. This implies cutting across multiple institutions in a difficult-to-manage matrix organization. But you have to step over bureaucratic lines if you want to get over bureaucratic barriers. However, for the WFC to carry out this expanded role successfully and for the reorganized international nutrition system to make an increased impact will require the resolution of several political concerns.

Political Concerns

Oiling the organizational machinery is not enough. More development resources are needed as well as a higher priority for nutrition in the allocation of existing development resources. Changing allocations and priorities require political action both internationally and domestically. There appear to be three barriers to more effective political action: policy vacuum, knowledge gaps, and priority conflicts.

Policy Vacuum

Political action requires the delineation of an overall strategy including the specification of priorities. Such systematic planning has generally been absent at both the international and national level. The United States is in the particularly ironic and inexcusable position of aggressively pushing for formal food and nutrition planning in developing nations while being unable to do the same itself. This internal policy vacuum leads to inadequacies in policies vis-a-vis the other international organizations and encourages similar vagueness in their policies. For example, the Senate study of US-FAO relationships concluded that "A coherent, rational and explicit policy consisting of goals, objectives, and priorities for FAO and for the United States as a member of FAO does not exist. What does exist are fragments of policies...US policy tends to be °situation-or-issue-specific.' These policies tends to be negative and reactive rather than positive and creative."[23]

As can be seen from Table 5 only a handful of developing nations have actually adopted an integrated national food and nutrition policy. For most countries nutrition programs have been launched on a rather ad hoc basis rather than being an integral part of an overall development program. Unless nutrition programming becomes systematized it will likely not receive significant attention in the national planning process and will not get a meaningful piece of the national budget. The organizational problems indicated in the previous section hamper this planning process but inadequate knowledge about the problem and the options also hamper action.

Knowledge Gaps

Nutrition is a relatively young science and nutrition interventions a relatively recent addition to the development program portfolio. Consequently, several key questions remain unanswered on both the biological research and field application sides.

For example, it is not clear how critical it is in terms of physical and mental functional performance whether 60 percent, 70 percent, 80 percent, or 90 percent of recommended allowances of various nutrients are consumed and when, and for how long. Such a lack of understanding of the functional significance of nutritional status clearly hampers decisions on the quantity, timing, and direction of nutrition resource allocation. There is also a gap in understanding the relative effectiveness and true costs of alternative interventions, e.g., nutrition education vs. feeding programs vs. price subsidies vs. fortification vs. agricultural production vs. health care. The recent launching of major national food and nutrition programs by a South American country was delayed considerably by the lack of hard data on which nutrition programs would make best use of its scarce resources. Even as finally formulated the effect is still almost "flying blind." This increases the risk of failures and exposes the program to attacks from its abundant critics who are lurking in the wings waiting to pounce. Furthermore, little systematic research has been done on the nutritional impact of government policies dealing with the production, processing, and distribution of food.

These questions have remained unanswered either because of the technical difficulty of the research of the failure to allocate sufficient research funds. A higher priority for research must accompany organizational changes in the international nutrition system if programmatic action is to accelerate. Policy makers need a clearer picture of their options and the expected costs and benefits. This will also require a more systematic collection and dissemination of research results and field experience in a form usable to country planners. Today much of the existing knowledge is not readily accessible to decision makers on an international basis. The WFC could serve an important function here.

Priority Conflicts

Removing the nutrition knowledge gaps will enhance policy formation but policies remain hollow unless they are given a high political priority. Nutrition has not traditionally ranked high on the priority agenda. Within the UN system it has, until recently, received relatively modest resource allocations[24] and has been terribly underrepresented in terms of staff.[25] Nutrition has fared no better in other multilateral institutions; the World Bank has spoken often of the need to confront the malnutrition problem, but to date the level of the Bank's nutrition lending as a percent of its total portfolio verges on tokenism.[26] In developing countries nutrition projects more often than not have consisted of small efforts hidden away in the Health Ministry or feeding programs supported by international food donations and run by international voluntary agencies.

IV. CONCLUSION

Political inaction in nutrition has been due to the knowledge and policy vacuums as well as organizational weaknesses. It should also be recognized that malnutrition is rooted in poverty and the economic roots of poverty are embedded in politics, as Christensen makes amply clear. Alleviating malnutrition will require increased and reoriented resource mobilization and this takes political commitment. Attaining and maintaining sufficiently high priority among policy makers for food and nutrition problems is a major political concern facing the international nutrition system.

The World Food Conference generally receives high marks from the nutrition community[27] for effectively drawing political attention to the world food problem:

> "...It was as good a step forward as was possible at that time. I think the main benefit was a focusing of attention on the problem. Until that time there were many groups in many places talking but no central focus. I think the World Food Conference centralized discussion and attention and in that sense I would rate it a success."
> "...The World Food Conference was good as far as it went. Of course one's expectations have to be tempered by realities of world organizations but I still believe the Conference was important in that it called attention to the size and kind of problem we are facing."
> "...The major contribution of the Conference was that it identified the idea that coordination and cooperation are imperative if we are ever going to have any kind of world food security program."

The Rome Conference did reach reasonable consensus which is more than the earlier Bucharest World Population Conference achieved.[28]

The marks are not so high, however, for the Post-Conference results, but to expect instant breakthroughs is politically naive. Nonetheless, there is considerable concern[29] about the apparent loss of political momentum in this post-Conference period:

> "...If you try to evaluate the Conference in terms of commitments, I cannot be so positive."
> "...The Conference generated more bureaucracy, and I have seen little evidence of any real gains made by the new organizations that were created."
> "...It is too early to evaluate the success or failure of the Conference, but I am concerned with the lack of follow-up with respect to some of the organizations that were set up."
> "...We are going through a kind of no-growth period in hunger problems. They heyday of loose money for food programs is over -- we are in a period of consolidation and tend to look at projects in a much more reserved light. Unfortunate as it may seem, human well-being by itself is not sufficient to justify a commitment of development funds."

"...We are losing momentum in facing the problem. The worst thing that could happen to any kind of world food movement is two good crop years. Attention would shift to other matters and we should have lost the force generated by the Conference. The sense of urgency has diminished which is most unfortunate."

The international nutrition community finds itself in the ironic position of viewing more food as undesirable from a political perspective.[30] The global political system may be in the lamentable situation that more crisis and starvation are the prerequisites to developing the necessary political will to deal with hunger.

This reactive posture perhaps can be averted if the current leadership vacuum is filled. The World Food Council is a significant institutional step toward removing that vacuum. To be effective, however, the WfC's leadership role must be further legitimized and strengthened. A basic impediment to the WFC's aggressive leadership role in the international nutrition network is the tenuous nature of its authority. It is in the difficult position of being a manager with great responsibility but without commensurate authority. Within the UN system the proposed reorganization, especially if accompanied with concomitant budgetary allocations, would create needed authority. In effect, a new leadership strategy requires a new organizational structure. Organizational change becomes a prerequisite to legitimizing the new role of the WFC. An international body cannot readily prevail against the sovereign will of the countries it serves. Thus externally, the WFC's legitimacy comes from the countries' perception of its utility. This perceived utility will be stronger to the extent that countries share Kurt Waldheim's perception that "Our global interdependence as people, and the constantly growing interrelationship between political, economic, social, ecological, and population factors, will make it increasingly difficult for any of us to discuss major world issues except as against the background of commonly agreed goals established by the world community working in concert."[31]

The ultimate viability of the WFC will depend on support from the major international political forces. More specifically, it is the US and the USSR, because of their dominant roles in the world food system and international politics, who could make the WFC and global food system management a reality. The support of the Group of 77 is already present. It is the American and Russian political and economic commitment to the WFC that is needed. This implies the need for a clear delineation of their own national food and nutrition objectives and policies and a further extension of their existing joint efforts in the food area. Political rhetoric must be translated into institutional capacity. This will entail a delegation of food authority and responsibility to a multilateral entity. The need for this joint leadership effort appears clear, the political costs relatively low, and the international benefits large. History, however, makes one somewhat pessimistic about its realization.

Leadership is needed not only on the macro level but also within nutrition institutions throughout the network. Such leadership implies political involvement because food is politics. Jelliffe put it this way: "One of the biggest blocks to implementation is the lack of appreciation by the research workers that -- without becoming politicians -- they have to develop some homespun wisdom as advocates and presenters of their results. The idea that communication by means of a research report is sufficient to get something done is wrong. Advocacy is needed as well."[32]

The leadership and advocacy needs boil down ultimately to individuals. To be an effective nutrition leader and advocate, one's fundamental responsibility must be seen as being to the people, not to institutions or to governments. In one sense the acceptance of that perspective by decision makers throughout the nutrition system is the most basic political challenge. It is also the most difficult to achieve.

In 1963 President Kennedy told the First World Food Conference:

> We have the means, we have the capacity, to eliminate hunger from the face of the earth in our lifetimes. We need only the will.

In 1974, Secretary of State Kissinger told the World Food Conference:

> All governments should accept the removal of the scourge of hunger and malnutrition . . . as the objective of the international community as a whole, and accept the goal that within a decade no child will go to bed hungry, that no family will fear for its next day's bread, and that no human being's future and capacities will be stunted by malnutrition.

In 1985 will someone again have to step forward and urge the world to feed its hungry?

NOTES

[1]The International Food Policy Research Institute estimated that 1974-75 cereal shortfall at 45 million tons, rising to 98-105 million tons in 1985; Meeting Food Needs in the Developing World: The Location and Magnitude of the Task in the Next Decade, Research Report No. 1, February 1976, p. 2. This is not to suggest, however, that the best way to meet nutritional needs is necessarily through grain trade or international food donations.

[2]J. E. Austin et al., Urban Malnutrition: Problem Assessment and Intervention Guidelines. Harvard University, Report Submitted to International Bank for Reconstruction and Development, September 1976. The calculation assumes a cost of $263 per ton including

delivery system costs and the needs to distribute 72 million tons to meet the calorie deficit, including 30 million tons which get drained off through leakages such as storage, consumption by nontarget group individuals, etc.

[3]For further discussion see "The United States, FAO and World Food Politics: US Relations with an International Food Organization," Staff Report of the Senate Select Committee on Nutrition and Human Needs, June 1976, Washington, D.C.

[4]Interview, August 1976.

[5]The authorization was $500 million but was reduced by the Appropriations Committee.

[6]"General Progress Report of the Executive Director," UNICEF, E/ICEF/6422, 1976, p. 16; an additional $43.7 million was spent on child health (Medical care, water supply and family planning).

[7]"Report of the World Food Council," United Nations General Assembly, Thirtieth Session, New York.

[8]Thomas G. Weiss and Robert S. Jordan, The World Food Conference and Global Problem Solving. (New York: Praeger, 1976), p. 143.

[9]Ibid.

[10]Senate Select Committee Staff Report, p. 11.

[11]Personal communication, August 1976.

[12]Personal correspondence, October 1976.

[13]Edwin M. Martin, "Nutrition Problems of the World," The Johns Hopkins University Centennial Symposium on Nutrition and Public Health, November 11, 1976.

[14]Interview, July 1976.

[15]Personal correspondence, November 1976.

[16]Nathaniel M. McKitterick, "US Diplomacy in the Development Agencies of the United Nations," planning pamphlet No. 122, National Planning Association, Washington, D.C., July 1965 p. 13.

[17]Senate Select Committee Staff Report, p. 26.

[18]Vincent H. Malstrom, "Roman Holiday: An Inside Look at the UN Food and Agriculture Organization," Middlebury College Newsletter (Spring 1975), p. 31.

[19]Jack Shepherd, The Politics of Starvation (Carnegie Endowment for International Peace, New York, 1975), p. x.

[20] UNICEF, p. 9.

[21] The New York Times, April 25, 1976, sec. 1, p. 7; note that the FAO budget also supports the country and regional field offices.

[22] See Robert E. Asher, "International Agencies and Economic Development," International Organization, Vol. 22, No. 1 (Winter 1968).

[23] Senate Select Committee Staff Report, p. 2.

[24] For example, UNICEF spent $5.9 million on child nutrition in 1971 and $15.1 million in 1975.

[25] For example, the Nutrition Unit at WHO Headquarters consists of only about five professionals.

[26] In 1976, nutrition loans or nutrition components of other loans were less than 4 percent of total annual agriculture and rural development lending.

[27] Interviews, July and August 1976.

[28] This is not to suggest that consensus is to be equated with success: the disagreements at Bucharest probably provided the dissonance to force a needed rethinking of approaches to the population issue. Nonetheless, post-Conference follow-up was complicated by the lack of consensus.

[29] Interviews, July and August 1976.

[30] There are likely few in the nutrition community who would opt for the food shortfall, but the realities of the political process do create a discouraging dilemma.

[31] Kurt Waldheim, "Keynote Address," The World Food and Energy Crisis: The Role of International Organizations, Richard N. Gardner, ed. (Rensselaerville, New York: Institute on Science and Man, 1974), p. 4.

[32] D. Jelliffe, "Comments on Bottlenecks in Implementation: Some Aspects of the Scandinavian Experience," W. Eide, M. Jul and O. Mellander, Human Rights in Health (Ciba Foundation Symposium Amsterdam, N. Y.) 1974, p. 269.

The Politics of Food Scarcities
in Developing Countries

NORMAN K. NICHOLSON
JOHN D. ESSEKS

Barring the global catastrophe envisioned by the Club of Rome, poverty will prove a more intractable problem than low productivity in the Third World. Much greater attention will have to be paid to the distribution of income, jobs, and foodgrains in the future if increases in production are to actually reduce hunger. The failure of many countries to manage their food supplies adequately and to provide basic food security to their populations is explained both by an urban bias in planning and by the sheer administrative complications and costs of stabilizing the foodgrains markets. For many countries dependency was politically easier. Major efforts to increase basic food production are essential in most developing countries, but the political adjustments associated with that decision may be difficult. The institutional patterns required to induce an agricultural revolution will challenge existing patterns of power and social stratification.

The food problem in many Third World states is basically that they have become or will shortly become incapable of meeting rising domestic demand from population growth and higher personal incomes through increased production or commercial imports. As Hopkins and Puchala discuss, by the mid-1980s the aggregate foodgrain import needs of LDCs and other deficit countries (e.g., Western and Eastern Europe) are expected to exceed the production capacities of exporting states. In the resulting high-priced commercial markets, the poor in many LDCs will be outbid by rich importing countries. Moreover, food aid from developed OECD countries, especially the major grain exporters, is both limited and undependable. In the tight supply year 1973, US aid, which makes up well over half of all food aid, dropped in volume by about 40 percent from the 1972 level; and in 1974 shipments declined by a further 50 percent.[1]

With domestic production decreasing or stagnant relative to

From **INTERNATIONAL ORGANIZATION**, Vol 32, No. 3. Summer 1978, (679-719), reprinted by permission of the publisher, University of Wisconsin Press.

population, commercial imports too expensive, and food aid scarce,
many LDCs are likely to see nutritional levels deteriorate, perhaps
to the point of widespread starvation if the world scarcities of
1973-1975 recur. In the process, there are likely to be attendant
political ills: Mass-scale unrest from soaring domestic food
prices, insatiable demands from public-sector employees for
compensating wage hikes, and increased corruption as governments
distribute relief and ration food.

The developing countries as a whole have come to hold an
increasingly dependent position in the world food system.
Exporters have become importers, reliance on food aid or assistance
to meet balance of payments deficits has grown for non-OPEC
countries,[2] and efforts to expand production in promising areas,
such as the Sudan and Brazil, have yet to be realized. This food
dependency and vulnerability to scarcity spills over into balance
of payment, developmental and political stability concerns. The
riots which occurred because of a rise in food prices in Cairo in
spring 1977 illustrate this point well; the rise (later rescinded)
was brought on by pressure from foreign lending agencies, and by
planners trying to improve production incentives for Egypt's
farmers.

The LDCs do not play a role in creating regime norms, except
through their dependency. Rather they are the target of the
concessional trading system, of funds to foster development, and
requests to undertake "reforms" -- regime practices often
inconsistent with each other and with the domestic policy
preferences of less developed states, as we shall see in detail
later.

I. THE PROBLEM CASES

Not all LDCs face this destiny; only the most vulnerable.
Developing countries can be classified into four groups.[3] The
first group comprises traditional food surplus states, e.g.,
Thailand, Burma, Nepal, Kenya. With reasonably high further
investments and good management in the food-farming sector, these
nations should be able to continue to feed themselves, at least in
basic foodstuffs. The second group consists of financially
self-sufficient states, e.g., Algeria, Indonesia, Iran,
Morocco, Nigeria. Though not self-reliant in food, they have high
foreign exchange earning ability from oil, phosphates, or other raw
materials. A third group of states is more vulnerable. They
cannot afford the import consequences of stagnant food production,
but either have already "made definite progress with the Green
Revolution," e.g., Pakistan, the Philippines, Turkey, or, as in
parts of Latin America, they have unexploited potential in good
climates and underutilized land. The fourth group consists of
severely disadvantaged countries. They face limited
foreign-exchange earning capacities, population pressures (India,
Bangladesh, Sri Lanka), and/or unfavorable climates (the

Table 1 Indices of per capita food production:
1961-74 USDA and FAO estimates

1961-65 AVERAGE = 100

		1961-65 Average	1966	1968	1970	1972	1974	1971-74 Average
A. Stagnant or Declining Output (Africa)								
Benin	USDA	100	92	94	93	91	99	94
	FAO	100	102	104	108	96	106	102
Ethiopia	USDA	100	100	103	100	91	87	91
	FAO	100	101	101	103	99	90	96
Ghana	USDA	100	99	91	88	83	87	87
	FAO	100	93	91	101	104	101	104
Guinea	USDA	100	93	108	106	107	104	107
	FAO	100	97	105	102	94	92	94
Kenya	USDA	100	99	100	95	97	95	94
	FAO	100	109	107	107	102	96	99
Liberia	USDA	100	97	83	83	85	94	89
	FAO	100	98	92	93	95	102	96
Madagascar	USDA	100	105	108	107	107	103	104
	FAO	100	102	102	98	90	93	92
Mali	USDA	100	92	82	87	66	67	68
	FAO	100	98	91	90	74	72	75
Niger	USDA	100	100	98	96	73	71	71
	FAO	100	110	103	96	81	70	73
Nigeria	USDA	100	94	83	96	96	92	93
	FAO	100	88	88	91	85	79	82
Senegal	USDA	100	89	82	66	63	91	82
	FAO	100	91	87	69	59	75	75
Sierra Leone	USDA	100	95	97	94	97	95	97
	FAO	100	111	107	107	109	107	107
Togo	USDA	100	112	115	105	98	93	96
	FAO	100	115	119	114	84	87	89
Uganda	USDA	100	107	109	105	97	85	93
	FAO	100	99	101	108	101	94	98
Upper Volta	USDA	100	91	86	79	68	78	70
	FAO	100	106	106	102	86	60	78
B. Increased Outputs (Africa)								
Ivory Coast	USDA	100	107	107	112	115	128	120
	FAO	100	93	105	111	116	121	119
Malawi	USDA	100	127	106	109	129	123	123
	FAO	100	121	112	109	126	122	122
Rwanda	USDA	100	101	116	121	112	99	111
	FAO	100	106	107	119	112	96	110
Zaire	USDA	100	109	114	122	108	115	111
	FAO	100	107	121	118	115	127	118

155

Table 1   (continued)

C. Widely Divergent Indices

Burundi	USDA	100	107	105	110	107	82	101
	FAO	100	105	105	129	171	181	165
Cameroon	USDA	100	102	105	95	94	95	95
	FAO	100	105	121	122	124	121	122
Tanzania	USDA	100	111	100	102	103	86	97
	FAO	100	110	107	124	114	109	113
Zambia	USDA	100	122	81	92	157	135	129
	FAO	100	113	102	99	99	103	100

D. South Asian Countries

Bangladesh	USDA	100	91	101	95	80	85	85
	FAO	100	91	100	92	78	80	82
Burma	USDA	100	85	92	92	83	88	88
	FAO	100	86	94	94	84	90	90
India	USDA	100	89	100	109	98	95	101
	FAO	100	91	99	105	97	96	100
Pakistan	USDA	100	101	119	132	118	121	120
	FAO	100	99	116	120	114	113	114
Sri Lanka	USDA	100	89	110	120	100	108	102
	FAO	100	96	101	98	93	97	94

Sources: U.S. Department of Agriculture, *Indices of Agricultural Production in Africa and the Near East, 1956-75* (Washington, D.C., 1976, Statistical Bulletin No. 556); USDA, *Indices of Agricultural Production for the Far East and Oceania, Average 1961-65 and Annual 1966-75* (Washington D.C., 1976, Statistical Bulletin No. 555); and Food and Agriculture Organization, *Production Yearbook, 1974* (Rome, 1975), Vol. 1, pp. 29-30.

Table 2   Indices of food imports, 1962-73, based on current market values

1962-65 AVERAGE = 100

	1962-65 Average	1967	1969	1971	1973	1971-73 Average
African Countries:						
Cameroon	100	123	134	190	247	210
Ethiopia	100	159	110	174	152	144
Ghana	100	90	85	87	126	93
Ivory Coast	100	n/a	260	308	412	367
Kenya	100	67	165	224	247	235
Liberia	100	119	95	146	206	168
Madagascar	100	82	120	157	205	168
Malawi[a]	100	84	92	149	205	179
Mali	100	108	184	247	563	364
Nigeria	100	93	147	245	359	292
Senegal	100	106	136	131	237	170
Sierra Leone	100	130	118	151	246	181
Tanzania	100	135	222	268	411	383
Togo	100	138	114	129	255	190
Uganda	100	170	517	561	551	543
Zaire	100	107	97	96	173	131
Zambia[a]	100	n/a	172	297	153	222
South Asian Countries:						
Burma	100	n/a	288	430	236	290
India	100	158	103	67	118	76
Pakistan	100	131	60	67	136	90
Sri Lanka	100	103	90	93	125	102

1971-73 AVERAGE, ALL COUNTRIES = 219

Note: [a]1964-65 average.
Source: Food and Agriculture Organization, *Trade Yearbook, 1968 and 1974* (Rome, 1969 and 1975).

156

drought-prone African states neighboring the Sahara) which threaten periodic or near-chronic food scarcities. In these states (basically in South Asia and sub-Saharan Africa), high population density relative to food-producing resources keeps them close to or below the margin of minimum nutrition (see Austin). They find it difficult to arrange for foreign exchange to cover both currently needed food imports and Green Revolution inputs (fertilizers, irrigation equipment) which might eventually reduce import dependence. Our paper concentrates on these two problem areas.

II. THE SHAPE OF THE PROBLEM

The best assessments of the progress in reducing food insecurity, or lack of it, is the trend in countries' ability to increase per capita food production and to reduce dependence on food imports. Unfortunately, both food output and population estimates for LDCs are often of questionable reliability. We try to illustrate this by producing, in Table 1, two separate time series of per capita food production for each of the 28 countries surveyed -- estimates offered by the Food and Agricultural Organization (FAO) and the US Department of Agriculture (USDA).[4] For 15 of the 23 African states surveyed, the two series agree that food production either failed to keep pace with population (e.g., Ethiopia, Liberia, Nigeria) or improved only a few percentage points from the 1961-65 base (Benin, Guinea, and Madagascar), as the 1971-74 averages in group A of Table 1 show. Staying close to the base index tended not to be much of an achievement, since African states were then and are now among the world's most nutritionally poor countries. According to FAO estimates for the early 1960s, the average daily supply of calories per person in Africa was below the level required for good health and about two-thirds the level prevailing in the developed world.[5] In nine of the above 15 problem countries, the loss of stagnation in food outputs per capita can be attributed in varying degrees to short-term climatic factors, namely the multi-year Sahelian drought of the early 1970s.[6] However, in five of those nine cases, downward or stagnating trends began before the drought.[7] Significantly upward trends -- with per capita food outputs increasing by more than 10 percent -- are displayed by only four of the sub-Saharan African countries surveyed: the Ivory Coast, Malawi, Rwanda, and Zaire (group B in Table 1). For another four states (group C), the FAO and USDA estimates diverge too greatly, underlining the problem of reliable data, and prohibiting sensible conclusions. The FAO, for instance, estimates that in 1974 Burundi had increased its per capita production 81 percent over the 1961-65 base, while the USDA thought it had fallen 18 percent.

Among South Asian states (group D) FAO and USDA estimates indicate that Bangladesh and Burma failed to expand food production as rapidly as population growth and India was stagnant: its 1971-74 average was virtually unchanged from that of 1961-65. The indices for Sri Lanka are too divergent for conclusions. Only Pakistan appears to have achieved significant progress, with the FAO and USDA estimates showing 14 to 20 percent increases in food outputs per person.

A survey of food imports from 1962 to 1973 is presented in Table 2.[8] In 21 sub-Saharan and South Asian countries (i.e., those for which data were available) there was a general, substantial rise in the money value of food imports. If we compare averages for 1971-73 with the 1962-65 bases, we find a mean increase of 119 percent. Some twelve of the twenty countries (see group B, Table 3) could "afford' their increased food bills. The ratios of their food imports to export revenues were no higher in 1971-73 than in 1961-65; export earning rose enough to offset the higher food bill. However, for the other countries (see group A), the reverse was true; food imports became more expensive, relatively as well as absolutely. Relative increase or not, many countries in both groups continued to have high foreign food bills. India's food imports in 1971-73 averaged 16 percent of its total export earnings; Pakistan, 18 percent; Zaire, 20 percent; Sierra Leone, 21 percent; Sri Lanka, 48 percent; and Senegal, 51 percent.

An alternative to focusing on monetary indicators of food import dependence is to look at physical or volume dependence. The "problem" countries identified in Table 3, i.e., those which had relatively higher food import bills (group A), tend also to be those which in 1971-73 were more dependent than in 1961-65 on imported grain relative to total domestic consumption. Such concurrence increases the threat to consumption levels. The increased cost of food imports makes them a conspicuous target for cutbacks by government action. But any cutback will obviously affect consumption most where it depends upon imports (see Table 4).

This likelihood was realized for at least seven African countries where production lagged behind population growth and imports failed to fill the gap. In these states, averages for per capita consumption of cereals, 1973-75, were below 1961-65 baselines (see Table 5). Available data on the seven indicate both lower or stagnant output relative to population and import volumes which did not compensate for this.[9] Consumption by the poorest in these countries, of course, dropped.

In addition to an imbalance between supply and need for food, inequitable distribution of income is also a problem. Malenbaum proposes that in many Third World countries one-third or less of the population consumes more than half of the available food.[10] Even in a country such as India, which has barely managed to match food production to growing population, there are large regional variations in consumption. Differences among classes are even more striking. With continuing population growth projected for the long term, the magnitude of the world population threatens to exceed its capacity to produce food. In the short term, that is in the next decade or two, the inability to provide jobs and income to increasing numbers of the poor, rather than the physical lack of food, is the problem. There are economic and social barriers to meeting the needs of all humans for food. It is a crisis of planning and implementation when production grows but not

Table 3   Food imports as percentage of total export earnings 1962–73

	1962–65 Average	1967	1969	1971	1973	1971–73 Average
A. More Costly Dependence						
Senegal	43.6	41.0	58.5	55.0	64.5	51.3
Sri Lanka	40.5	46.5	44.0	45.0	54.0	48.0
Sierra Leone	18.0	30.1	16.5	22.1	23.5	21.3
Zaire	18.2	17.3	17.0	18.5	21.6	20.3
Pakistan	31.3	31.0	13.2	13.5	24.0	18.0
Ivory Coast	11.0	n/a	15.4	18.2	13.0	16.6
India	32.0	51.0	29.0	16.0	21.0	16.0
Togo	19.0	19.1	11.5	11.4	18.2	15.3
B. Less Costly Dependence						
Madagascar	14.3	10.2	14.0	14.0	13.1	13.0
Ghana	19.3	19.3	16.0	15.5	12.4	12.5
Kenya	14.0	8.0	11.6	14.0	10.0	12.1
Malawi[a]	14.0	8.0	9.1	11.0	11.0	11.1
Tanzania	5.2	5.5	8.0	9.0	10.1	11.0
Cameroon	9.4	11.0	7.0	10.4	8.0	9.4
Liberia	14.0	11.0	6.0	8.4	9.1	8.5
Nigeria	11.1	9.0	10.5	9.0	7.0	8.0
Uganda	2.3	3.4	8.5	8.0	6.5	7.3
Burma	10.0	n/a	5.6	8.6	5.5	6.2
Zambia	4.2	n/a	4.0	9.1	2.8	6.0
Ethiopia	6.0	9.1	5.3	8.0	3.6	5.2

Note: [a] 1964–65 average.
Source: Same as for Table 2.

Table 4   Cereals imports[a] as percentage of total cereals consumption (by volume) 1961–73

IN PERCENTAGES

	1961–65 Average	1967	1969	1971	1973	1971–73 Average
A. Increased Import Dependence						
Ethiopia	.3	.7	.9	1.3	2.7	1.5
Ivory Coast	24.0	20.2	31.5	28.2	29.5	31.3
Liberia[b]	26.2	36.2	36.3	30.0	17.7	26.5
Madagascar	3.8	2.0	3.8	6.0	17.7	13.3
Nigeria	2.4	3.6	4.8	8.3	8.7	7.7
Senegal	76.7	68.3	67.8	79.1	90.0	86.1
Sierra Leone[c]	11.1	15.8	13.0	21.0	18.6	18.7
Tanzania	6.3	4.3	7.6	8.3	16.5	11.6
Upper Volta	1.8	4.4	4.0	7.0	10.5	8.4
Zaire	36.2	31.2	24.9	32.9	38.4	36.4
Zambia[d]	4.7	4.6	11.6	7.7	10.1	9.3
B. Decreased Dependence						
Ghana	25.3	19.0	23.9	21.6	25.7	22.3
Guinea	18.1	18.7	16.4	17.8	13.2	15.7
India	8.3	11.0	4.5	2.3	4.5	2.8
Kenya	5.8	.2	1.1	7.2	3.4	4.2
Pakistan	19.3	26.4	9.9	10.8	9.7	11.3
Sri Lanka	54.6	52.7	48.3	48.2	52.1	49.7

Notes: [a] Wheat, coarse grains, and rice unless otherwise indicated. [b] Rice only. [c] Wheat and rice. [d] Wheat and coarse grains.
Sources: U.S. Department of Agriculture, *Foreign Agriculture Circular: Reference Tables on Wheat, Corn, and Total Coarse Grains Supply-Distribution for Individual Countries* (Washington, D.C. 1976); and ibid., *Reference Tables on Rice Supply-Distribution for Individual Countries* (Washington, D.C., 1976).

consumption. Poverty is as much a part of the world food crisis as food shortages.

The problem of income distribution is one which cannot easily be handled within the context of food policy in isolation from other aspects of national development strategies and international patterns of resource flows. It may be possible, as in the case of Sri Lanka, to heavily subsidize food distribution, to use "food for work" projects to provide subsistence to unemployed workers, or to target relief supplies directly to the destitute where they are geographically concentrated (e.g., the Bengali refugees in Indian camps in 1971), but these distributional solutions are inherently limited in their impact and are difficult to sustain. Thus, although we shall concentrate on the distributional politics and problems of food policy in this paper, we must indicate at the outset that neither concessional supplies of food from the United States nor higher agricultural productivity in the agricultural sector in the Third World will in and of themselves eliminate the hunger problem. Only where these food policies are integrated with programs to redistribute productive assets more equitably and with investment patterns which emphasize maximum employment generation can we expect a substantial reduction in real, as opposed to statistical world hunger.

In summary, we see in the two regions of South Asia and sub-Saharan Africa many countries whose production, import, and/or consumption records are not encouraging. From the early 1960s to the mid-1970s, their per capita food outputs declined or were stagnant; they remained significantly dependent on costly food imports or food aid; and/or their actual consumption levels (at least for cereals) declined. Some countries were "problems" in all three respects, e.g., Ethiopia, Senegal, and Sierra Leone.

By drawing on experiences of these areas, we can anticipate the kinds of policy adjustments and related policy outcomes in LDCs generally as they cope with high production targets, chronic, widespread malnutrition, and threat of mass famine. The discussion that follows is based largely on the experiences of India and selected African countries and is divided into two sections: problems and related policies concerned with distribution and policy problems for food production.

The Politics Of Distribution

The international movement of concessional grain supplies into Third World countries may have one of three possible distributional goals. First, the aid may be intended merely to relieve the intense shortfalls of supplies associated with natural disaster and crop failure -- as famine relief. These programs typically do not make class distinctions among recipients and generally make very limited contributions to the economic rehabilitation of the poor. Second, the food aid may be designed to provide long-term supplements to the income of specific target groups in the form of

Table 5　Indices of per capita consumption of cereals[a] 1961–75

	1961–65 Average	1967	1969	1971	1973	1975	1973–75 Average
A. Lower Consumption							
Ethiopia	100	105	112	107	78	95	85
Kenya	100	91	86	69	88	82	83
Liberia[b]	100	81	80	79	77	76	76
Nigeria	100	78	93	71	69	79	75
Senegal	100	113	105	124	107	86	95
Sierra Leone[c]	100	95	90	117	94	98	99
Upper Volta	100	88	75	79	67	69	68
B. Higher Consumption							
Ghana	100	118	110	121	150	127	137
Guinea	100	128	115	114	106	101	104
India	100	100	105	103	107	105	104
Ivory Coast	100	121	139	141	121	122	119
Madagascar	100	112	103	106	108	118	115
Pakistan	100	107	123	111	117	114	115
Sri Lanka	100	104	110	115	108	102	108
Tanzania	100	87	86	105	126	131	122
Zambia[d]	100	146	154	135	116	123	121
Zaire	100	95	120	133	150	163	157

Notes: [a]Wheat, coarse grains, and rice, unless otherwise indicated. [b]Rice only. [c]Wheat and rice. [d]Wheat and coarse grains.

Table 6 Percentage of government expenditures allocated to agriculture[a]

	1963	1964	1965	1966	1967	1968	1969	1970	1971	1972	1973	Average for all years
Kenya	n.a.	17.9[b]	18.1[b]	14.3[b]	12.4[b]	12.5[b]	12.8[b]	11.0	9.0	10.0	12.1	13.0
Malawi	n.a.	8.8	n.a.	10.4	n.a.	12.5	n.a.	n.a.	11.9	15.4	15.4	12.4
Tanzania	13.6[b]	11.8[b]	8.6[b]	8.3	n.a.	n.a.	n.a.	10.2	11.3	9.5	9.9	10.4
Uganda	n.a.	8.1[b]	6.7[b]	8.5[b]	8.0[b]	8.2	6.6	9.5	8.7	n.a.	n.a.	9.1
Ivory Coast	n.a.	n.a.	n.a.	n.a.	n.a.	n.a.	n.a.	8.8[c]	6.3	6.8	8.7[c]	7.6
Ghana	6.4	5.4	8.8	7.5	7.4	6.5	5.3	5.1	4.9	5.6	6.5	6.3
Rwanda	n.a.	n.a.	n.a.	4.6	5.9	5.1	4.9	5.1	4.6	n.a.	n.a.	5.0
Ethiopia	n.a.	n.a.	3.0	2.7	2.8	4.2	n.a.	3.6	5.0	8.7[c]	8.7[c]	4.8
Sierra Leone	n.a.	n.a.	n.a.	n.a.	n.a.	3.6[b]	3.1[b]	4.8[b]	4.9[c]	3.5[b]	7.8[b]	4.6
Liberia	n.a.	n.a.	n.a.	n.a.	n.a.	1.8	1.8	1.5	2.7	3.8	3.8	2.6

Note: [a] Actual recurrent and capital expenditures, unless otherwise indicated. [b] Fiscal year. [c] Estimated.

Sources: Kenya: Irving Kaplan, et al., *Area Handbook for Kenya* (Washington, D.C., 1967); Kenya, *Economic Survey, 1970* (Nairobi, 1970); United Nation *Survey of Economic Conditions in Africa, 1973* (New York, 1974). Malawi: Harold D. Nelson, et al., *Area Handbook for Malawi* (Washington, D.C., 1975 *Survey of Economic Conditions in Africa, 1973*. Tanzania: Allison B. Herrick et al., *Area Handbook for Tanzania* (Washington, D.C., 1968); *Survey of Econom Conditions in Africa, 1973*. Uganda: Uganda, *Statistical Abstract* [5], 1967 (Entebbe, 1967); 1970 (Entebbe, 1970); and 1971 (Entebbe, 1971); Allison B. Herric et al., *Area Handbook of Uganda* (Washington, D.C., 1969).

subsidized food supplies, "food for work" programs, or highly specialized nutritional programs. These programs often have a very limited clientele and seldom have any immediate impact on the structure of poverty in Third World countries. They are essentially remedial in character rather than developmental. Third, foodgrains programs are designed to stabilize prices and counter inflationary trends associated with the development process in many countries. In the long term, this use of foodgrains probably has the greatest impact on the structure of poverty through the contribution it makes to speeding investment. On the other hand, such a food program has little direct effect immediately on the poor and may well serve to depress agricultural prices and reduce production incentives in agriculture in the recipient country. The two effects are, of course, related. It is difficult to improve the lot of the poor if agriculture is depressed and most of the poor are found in the rural areas. The politics of food distribution will differ greatly depending on the type of distributional strategy intended by the international donor and the recipient government. (It should not be assumed that these two are necessarily congruent).

For twenty years (1954-75) surplus grain stocks moving through the concessional system of the global regime provided (friendly) developing nations with an inexpensive and politically attractive solution to their food problems.[11] In terms of famine policy these stocks supplied the essential "insurance" against erratic weather. But that is not the only function concessional sales and gifts performed. In India, for instance, they were used, somewhat ineffectively, as an anti-inflation device to compensate for extensive deficit financing. It is also clear that, given the apparent stagnation in Indian agriculture and the difficulty of persuading subsistence farmers to part with their produce on the market, American grain was used by Indian planners to avoid the necessity of what they perceived to be fruitless investment in the agricultural sector.

As the amount of food moving in concessional systems decreased relatively and absolutely after 1972, countercyclical policies, once accomplished solely through import policy, must now be controlled by regulation of national foodgrains supplies and markets. This involves the control of price levels, whether for famine, welfare, or anti-inflation reasons. Restriction on the physical movement of grains are likely to be necessary, at least where areas of high demand and high income compete for stocks with areas of high need and low income. Stocks will also have to be maintained as reserve for famine and, once established, the system may prove useful for "buffer stock operations" to even out price fluctuations. Finally, given the collapse of income earning capacity in certain regions due to weather or within certain classes due to the structure of the economy, it may be advisable to target supplies specifically to the "vulnerable population." Each of these functions will require the development of new institutional capacity by the government. The total cost of this operation is likely to be high, and a number of difficult decisions must be made regarding the allocation of costs and benefits of the system.

III. THE INDIAN CASE

In India the distinction between short, intense periods of deprivation (famine) and the growing incidence of continuing destitution is fairly clear. While famines have been largely alleviated, chronic hunger remains a difficult problem. India's institutional development for dealing with the facts of hunger goes back more than two decades and provides many lessons. Moreover, the Indian case is particularly important as it illustrates how even minor shortfalls in production can escalate to major political consequences in the absence of effective management.

As a first step it is important to recognize the magnitude of the task at hand. In 1973, Ali Khusro estimated that India required, at minimum, a buffer stock of about five million tons a year to provide adequate security.[12] Taking into account procurement costs, handling, storage costs, and storage construction, the total cost for each million tons was calculated to be about $119.6 million in non-recurring costs.[13] In fact, a stock of eight or nine million tons has proven barely adequate to cover the deficits of the seventies. The operative costs of the public-sector Food Corporation of India, which handles these stocks, has proven higher than expected.[14] A careful analysis of the costs of the Corporation indicated that for each quintal of grain, purchased at Rs. 80, the necessary mark-up for the Corporation was Rs. 25, or 31 percent (one rupee = $0.13). Furthermore, the longer a stock was held in reserve the larger that figure would be. On a stock of 8.9 million tons handled in 1972-73, losses in storage and handling alone were estimated at a value of $28.0 million. In addition, rising foreign and domestic prices have forced the government of India to subsidize the operation in the amount of $196.3 million in the same year. In comparison, the entire proposed central government expenditure on agriculture for 1971-73 was $584.2 million. This enormous expenditure and a staff of 38,000 at the central level alone (in many cases actual procurement and distribution of grain is handled by state level officials) is the price of a national system of food crisis management.

India's present massive system of foodgrains management evolved slowly after the inflationary effects of the second five-year plan (1956-57 to 1961-62) led to a public outcry against rising prices. At that time, the state's role consisted of little more than allocating imported stocks and making the arrangements for their dispatch to the larger cities. Stocks were not maintained against emergencies, no buffer stock operations were attempted to stabilize prices, and there was no serious attempt to use food stocks as a planning device for economic planning.[15] There were certain left-wing politicians and Planning Commission economists who called for greater control over both imported and domestic stocks, but the flood of American grain during the late 1950s relieved the pressure and delayed full institutional development for nearly ten years. It was only in 1964 that the government of India accepted a proposal for the establishment of a central foodgrains trading organization (Food Corporation of India), and not until 1968 that the organization became fully operative with complete control over interstate movement of foodgrains and sole responsibility for management of imported stocks.

The Food Corporation was but one part of a package of institutional innovations and policy departures undertaken in the period 1960-65. The poor accomplishments of "community" oriented development programs in the fifties and the growing fear of the economic and political consequences of rising prices persuaded the government to adopt a new strategy aimed mostly at the individual commercial farmer. In this context the Corporation was expected to accomplish its ends through market operations and, if need be, to support farm prices in order to provide incentives. From a long-term perspective it was the surpluses of the good years and not the shortfalls of the bad years that were the problem -- for the commercial farmer.[16] The latter problem could continue to be managed through imports.

In 1965, there was already a huge, but chaotic, public operation on foodgrains, characterized by a complex set of arrangements between New Delhi and the respective state governments. Most deficit states were badly in debt in their foodgrains operations, it was impossible to keep track of stocks, and such internal procurement of grain as did take place was entirely at the whim of respective state governments. Many in Delhi, therefore, perceived that the establishment of an autonomous, compact, and professional state trading organization would improve the situation. With its own capital, its own procurement organization, and its own interstate distribution system, the Corporation could reduce costs and confusion. So long as most stocks were in fact imported, this was not a difficult decision to implement.[17]

However, the food crisis of 1967 eliminated any semblance of autonomy for the Corporation. Prices, distribution arrangements, and interstate allocations became matters of intense political concern subject to day-to-day control by the Ministry of Food. Finally, the crisis ended any hope that the Corporation might actually establish itself as an independent force in the markets of the surplus states. As in the past, state governments became reluctant to permit external control of their food stocks and preferred to operate as the "agents" of the Corporation, maintaining their physical control over procurement.

Moreover, many national-level politicians and administrators were not eager to bear the responsibility of controls. As market prices are disrupted, the functions they perform must be absorbed by administrative agencies. These price functions include: adjustment of supply and demand, income distribution, resource allocation, and capital formation.[18] The regulation of the supply of food to one region or section of the population will affect supplies available to other regions and sections. This almost inevitably leads to demand for the extension of government protection to a larger and larger portion of the population. Most importantly, as Myron Weiner argues in Politics of Scarcity, once a government enters into controls, like it or not, it does become responsible for vagaries of weather and market.[19] The administrative and financial cost of the operation aside, the political cost of failure to meet these responsibilities, once accepted, are enormous. Driven to avoid such failure, governments will be tempted to expand their control over the nation's food supplies, both at the production and distribution end of the chain. This, in turn, disrupts existing distribution of functions between public and private sectors, threatens existing distributions of political and administrative authority, and adds massively to the bureaucratic weight of government on the citizenry. The sources of political crisis are far broader than the cries of the hungry.

The moment once accepts the inevitability of securing a substantial portion of its emergency reserves domestically, the problem of price levels presents itself. Those affected by hunger have little income earning capacity and cannot pay market prices for food. A subsidy is the obvious answer. But the cost of a subsidy is not to be measured only in budget terms. On the contrary, Morris Morris argues, the real cost is the missed opportunity for alternative investment.[20] Given the difficulty of raising taxes in Third World countries, the transfer payments which relief expenditure represents are not usually transfers from the rich to the poor but from the poor to the poor. Every rupee of relief could have been used toward productive investment elsewhere.

The alternative strategy is to restrict the price the government must pay for the grain in the first place. One method is a statutory levy on all farmers. This has the advantage of increasing the "market surplus" because it operates even on subsistence farmers. Few state governments were willing to accept the administrative cost of such a measure, however, and no one has forgotten the Congress Party defeats in the 1952 elections in areas where this method was employed.[21] If the government decides to buy in the market, however, the presence of such large "commercial" purchases will tend to force prices up, to the advantage of the better capitalized farmer who can wait to take advantage of the unusually high prices which prevail after the government has drained the market.[22]

For the government of India the Green Revolution has largely resolved this problem. The new hybrid wheats have had a dramatic impact on the northern wheat regions of India, especially in Punjab and Haryana. In an area of high productivity and commercial farming, the procurement task is greatly reduced. The government of India prohibits export of grain from the region, thus limiting demand; the state marketing federations then enter the markets as the monopoly wholesale agents of the government. In 1972, India procured 7.7 million tons of foodgrains internally. Of that total roughly 5 million tons were procured in Punjab and Haryana.[23]

This arrangement is not simply fortuitous, however. The surplus exists because of previous investment in the region which has encouraged commercial agriculture and because of research investments that produced the new technology.[24] Furthermore, it is sustained politically because the state government, in effect, supports harvest prices with its procurement operations and prevents the normal seasonal decline.[25] The stocks thus procured by the state government then become resources in political bargaining with the national leadership. In short, India's food system reflects a continual balance of political administrative, and economic costs in selecting a strategy for securing adequate stocks.

In summary, India now has the capacity to secure and store large reserve stocks, it has the capacity to manage a national foodgrains budget and interstate allocation system (averaging 7.4 million tons between 1969-72), and above all is committed to this as a continuing public function. The cost is high and the system is not free from many difficult problems, but it represents a substantial increase in the institutional capacity of the government. The test of the system in the Bangladesh war proved its utility. Ten million refugees were fed with grain stocks approaching nine million tons with an efficiency that probably few developed nations could guarantee.[26]

IV. THE AFRICAN CASE

No tropical African government has a capability comparable to India. Where they exist, state food marketing agencies appear to lack the purchasing networks, pricing policies, and other means with which to secure large quantities of foodstuffs relative to consumption needs.[27] For example, Kenya's Maize and Produce Marketing Board was charged by statute to ensure adequate supplies of maize through stocking in good years, selling from reserves in lean years, and arranging for imports to cover domestic deficits. However, according to Leys, in both the 1965 and 1970-71 droughts the Board proved unequal to these responsibilities, being unable either to stock sufficiently before the droughts or to prevent illegal exports and a flourishing internal black market during the scarcities.[28]

Kenya has been unusual in tropical Africa for its large grain storage capacity -- with its maize-stocking facilities equal to about a half year's demand.[29] In the other drought-prone states of the region, storage capacity has been very low relative to total consumption needs. Mali as of 1974 could store about 34,500 metric tons or roughly 4 percent of the expected consumption of the staples sorghum and millet for the 1974-75 crop year.[30] Chad's storage capacity in the same year was estimated at only 11,000 metric tons.[31]

The first and last steps in a food distribution system are the same -- identifying the needy. The first step is to identify correctly the start of a crisis and to set in motion the public response mechanisms. The last step in the chain of events is to assure that the food reaches the needy and that the crisis does not destroy their earning capacity. This last point is often omitted in discussions of famine. If the diversion of funds is not to continue ad infinitum, it is essential that those affected by crop failure not be forced to sell their land, tools, or animals. Once this happens the region may take years to recover. The argument is

essentially the same if the target group is not one hit by famine
but one which has been historically destitute. The only way out of
continued dependence on government is to increase their earning
capacity.

Both the identification and management of crises depend to a
large extent on the degree to which governments have already
invested in development in the affected regions. Without
communication facilities and officials penetrating into every
village, hunger may well become widespread before anyone knows
about it. This was the case in Bengal in 1943, where over a
million starved, and in the Sahel and Ethiopia in 1973, where
deaths in both areas may have numbered in the tens of thousands
before their governments became aware of the mass scale of
suffering.

One of the first clear indications of a drought crisis
received by Ethiopia's central government was the appearance on the
outskirts of the capital city itself of about 1,500 destitute
peasants.[32] They had left their farms about 200 miles to the north
in quest of food. Similarly, Sahelian governments began to suspect
a crisis when nomads, with their livestock lost, were reported
flocking to administrative centers to obtain food and water.[33] In
other words, the central governments began to appreciate the
situation only after crops and animals had been destroyed and food
reserved from previous years had been totally consumed. There was
apparently little effective anticipation of the crisis, such as
readying relief stocks so that livestock could have been saved and
farmers permitted to remain in their villages. This lack of
official anticipation seems condemnable since rains had been poor
in the immediately preceding two or more years. The 1972 rainy
season should have been watched with care.

The capacity to monitor, however, was limited by physical and
political obstacles to communication between countryside and
capital. Shepherd reports that in 1973 eight out of ten Ethiopians
"lived a full's day walk from any road."[34] Their needs were
represented to the center, if at all, through a feudal-type system
of governance. In the Sahel the 1970-73 drought tended to be most
severe in northern areas, closer to the desert, where
communications were poor, but also where the inhabitants were
mostly nomads who by tradition avoided contact with government. In
addition, the Sahel's governments, like most of Africa, accorded a
low priority to agriculture in their spending programs (see Table
6) and, hence, had few cadres in food-producing areas who could
develop informed reports on the drought's impact on production.

Yet another factor in the Sahel was the absence of recent-
memory precedent of drought with sufficiently high political costs
to make governments wary. Among such costs (which developed during
1973) were thousands of refugees crowding in and around cities and
towns, severe losses of export revenues (because of reduced
harvests of cash crops and livestock), and numerous starvation
deaths blamed on the incumbent elites by their political rivals.
The last major drought in the Sahel occurred in 1912-14.[35] In
effect there was no "Bengal famine" (India, 1943) to sensitize
central governments to the imperative of preparing for another
mass-impact drought. Adequate preparations would have been costly.

These costs include the development of data-gathering capacities sufficient to assess the food crop and livestock losses, the amounts of food reserves not yet consumed, and the deficits needed to be covered by imports. In the absence of these and other assessments, external relief sources could not determine how much help was needed. For example, on April 18, 1973, the French Foreign Ministry estimated that the drought-afflicted Sahelian states would require 530,000 tons of emergency food before the end of the crop year. The FAO thought otherwise, announcing on April 20th that the need would be 713,000 tons.[36]

Whatever the correct level, relief arrived too late in 1973 to prevent tens of thousands from dying.[37] It arrived late largely because the process of persuading donors to make commitments and to start shipping began too late. And the tragic delay in this process was due mostly to the Sahelian government's own failure to appreciate the seriousness of the drought. It did not declare a "state of emergency" and make urgent appeals for external aid until March 1973, about four to five months after it should have been clear that the 1972 harvests were extraordinarily poor and the pasture cover woefully inadequate.[38] A similarly tragic time gap occurred in Ethiopia: severe crop failures occurred in the fall of 1972 but no request by the Haile Selassie government for foreign relief assistance was made until April 1973.[39]

India's government, having experienced recurring crop failures and knowing their potentially high human and political costs, has invested in elaborate administrative mechanisms to alert it to famine threats and then to implement distributive programs. However, even when adequate staff is in place, the task of spotting the crisis is far from easy. As Morris indicates, distress signals are often difficult to read.[40] High prices may signal growing demand as much as food shortfalls. Migration may be merely the movement of surplus labor to jobs in other areas. Liquidation of assets (cattle, gold, stocks of produce) may be, in effect, a private insurance system at work. If officials are too callous, they flirt with death. If they are too generous, scarce resources and food stocks are depleted unnecessarily or prematurely, development plans are disrupted, and peasants may even be encouraged to take unnecessary risks at public expense, e.g., planting highly valuable but vulnerable crops.

Food administrators in India have concluded over the years that the task of identifying the needy in individual terms is almost impossible. And given the fact that it is also impossible to control the general price level, they seek an intermediate solution -- fair price shops in selected areas. The fair price shop is an outlet for government food stocks at controlled prices (stocks being either imported or domestically procured). This technique targets specific regions of high demand and attempts to supply those regions with a basic minimum ration at controlled prices. This does not, of course, provide jobs for the jobless or prevent the rich from bidding up the prices on the "free" market. Organized workers are easy to target with such a system because they can be identified at their work place. But the bulk of the population must be supplied in its neighborhood, irrespective of income. The number of fair price shops in India at the end of 1972 was 165,000. Although government officials admit they have no clear information on urban-rural distribution patterns or allocation of stocks among cities of different size,[41] they assume that the rural areas can feed themselves and, leaving aside periods of intense famine, have centered public distribution in the cities. It would also appear that the small and medium sized towns tend to be neglected. It is a widespread, though unproven, assumption that the effect of the system is to offset the effect of inflation on the big city work force and not to provide protection for the poor. We shall return to this point, but the system would appear to trade the Punjab farmer a stable price in return for a stable price to the urban worker, neglecting the rural poor and small towns. Overall, the system has little effect on the effective price structure (the one facing most people) and does little to help the destitute.[42] Thus, its determinants must be viewed as almost entirely political. This compromise between the larger wheat farmers, who market most of the grain, and the urban workers/middle class has one efficacious result -- it provides stocks which can be distributed in case of famine. The system has offered no real solution, however, to the problems of the chronically poor.

In the Sahel and Ethiopia during 1972-74, governments were both late in identifying the crisis and in distributing relief supplies. They had no "system" -- even one favoring the better off workers and farmers -- which could be activated once the famine threat was identified. With very few "up-country" food reserves, they had to rely mostly on supplies shipped from abroad and on transportation means which were unsuitable for carrying large quantities of basic foodstuffs inland from ports. Severe bottlenecks developed at ports, along typically single-track railroads leading from ports, and at bridgeless rivers and other natural obstacles. Food spoiled. Other relief supplies were diverted to commercial markets for the profit of local officials.[43]

By late 1974, the high political stakes of mismanaging famine relief became clear. Three civilian governments of drought-stricken countries fell to military coups: those of Upper Volta (in February 1974), Niger (April), and Ethiopia (September). Urban workers protested soaring food prices, student groups blamed government for the suffering of drought victims, and rumours circulated that officials were profiting from sale of relief supplies.[44] Such signs of popular disaffection encouraged the military in their ambitions and gave them grievances with which to justify their takeovers before national and foreign audiences.

The Politics of Production

Besides developing the institutional capability to distribute large quantities of relief supplies with reasonable efficiency and equity, vulnerable LDCs should also follow India's example in trying to increase domestic food production.

In sub-Saharan Africa food farming has tended to be a

seriously neglected sector. The region's governments have spent
relatively little on agriculture (even though from 60 to over 90
percent of their people obtain their livelihoods from that sector).
Among the 10 African countries surveyed, the highest average
allocation was only 13 percent, found in Kenya, the most
industrialized of the states. The lowest was 2.6 percent in
Liberia, and the median 7.6 percent. (See Table 6.) In
comparison, the state government of Punjab (India) devoted 11
percent to agriculture in 1974-75, without taking into account
federal government expenditure in the state.[45] African
governments' relative neglect of agriculture has meant little
research on food crops, weakly staffed extension services for food
farming, and inadequate investments in farm-to-market
transportation so that many areas of potentially significant
surpluses are cut off from town consumers and, hence, have no
incentive to produce in surplus of family and local needs.[46]

What will induce less developed states to invest more heavily
in food farming, as the Indian governments have begun to do? Among
the persuasive local factors may be the 1973-75 famine experiences,
the increasing foreign exchange drain from food imports, and
soaring domestic food prices. Between 1970 and 1974, food prices
rose by a reported total of 74 percent in Tanzania, 85 percent in
Ghana, 102 percent in Zaire, and 145 percent in Uganada.[47] To
these factors might be added external forces in the international
food system, including global regime norms. (See the essays by
Seevers and Christensen.)

V. THE INDIAN CASE

In the early sixties India embarked on what was a remarkable
rural development strategy for an underdeveloped nation. Faced
with rampant inflation and rapidly increasing demand for food,
which threatened to disrupt the entire planning exercise, India
opted for a "quick fix." On the advice of the Ford Foundation, the
government of India decided to concentrate its investment in the
most favored rural areas in order to maximize the marketed
surplus.[48] Technical assistance, credit, roads, electricity, and
irrigation development were poured into districts (particularly in
Punjab and Haryana) with good water supplies and soil fertility,
among other advantages. When the new plant varieties appeared,
this same investment, particularly credit and irrigation, proved
crucial to its adoption by farmers.

In the mid-sixties important new varieties of hybrid wheat and
rice were developed. The attraction of these new hybrid seeds was
the ability to produce a dwarf plant which was very responsive to
high applications of fertilizer. Traditional varieties of grains
typically converted the nutrients provided by heavy fertilizer
applications into the overall growth of the plant rather than into
the growth of the grain. Not uncommonly, the resulting increased
growth of the traditional varieties caused the stalks to break,

lodging the grain on the ground and resulting in heavy crop losses. In these circumstances, the biological capacity for intensifying grain production simply did not exist; and a technological barrier existed to increased food production. The new hybrids, being genetically dwarf, absorbed increased nutrients in the grain, thus removing the constraint and permitting efficacious use of heavy dosages of fertilizer.

The new varieties were "revolutionary" in two senses. Of course, the genetic breakthrough was a discovery of major importance. In terms of most farming techniques, however, the new varieties' requirements were not dramatically different from traditional varieties; only the results were. It was certainly not uncommon to double or treble yields by shifting from the old to the new varieties. This dramatic increase in farm yields and, therefore, in farm income was what made the new varieties truly "revolutionary." Several consequences followed from this production breakthrough. First, a "revolution" occurred in thinking about the problem of agriculture. Farmers who were presumed to be hopelessly backward and conservative by urban-dwelling government planners suddenly switched to these highly profitable seeds, which demonstrated the potential dynamism of peasants when offered a workable technology. This in turn provided an opportunity for new investment in the rural sector to provide public support for the "revolution." Second, the new seeds worked effectively only when combined with plenty of fertilizer and plenty of water. In consequence, the capital outlay of farmers (for wells) and the production expenditures (for seed and fertilizer) increased rapidly and with them risk. This in turn put pressure on governments to assist the revolution through the provision of credit, stabilization of market prices, and investment in rural infrastructure. Third, the new varieties proved very prone to disease, compared with traditional varieties, and the rice, in particular, was very sensitive to variations in climate and growing conditions. This, in turn, necessitated a heavy public investment in agricultural research (and extension) to protect the "revolution" from genetic failures. Even at the time, some were cautious about the potential of this revolution. The success of the technology depended on large fertilizer imports. Many developing nations lacked governmental systems capable of maintaining the administrative and research support to sustain the highly vulnerable technology. Nevertheless, most observers assumed that the world's food problems had been solved. Today we are less optimistic.

In India, the application of Green Revolutionary technology to favored rural areas proved to be an unqualified success. However, it has meant that eight districts with 0.31 percent of India's cultivated area used 11.4 percent of the nation's fertilizer.[49] Extensive and effective use of fertilizer is the key to increasing rural incomes in the Third World.

It was generally recognized that this strategy was one beset with enormous risk because prospects for the future lay in a restricted geographical region and two crops.[50] Many argued that smaller investment spread over wider areas would produce greater aggregate yield responses. These arguments did not prevail, largely because of the uncertainty of farmers' responses in the more backward areas. In many ways the gamble paid off; Punjab and Haryana can now provide 65 percent of India's buffer stock. Although this has eased some of the government's problems, it has increased others. Nothing was done to reduce inter-regional income disparity; in fact the disparity grew. Nor was anything done to reduce the probability of crop disasters in less favored regions. Indian politics has been strongly affected by these choices.

Such a strategy, in retrospect, made sense only if the United States would insure the gamble with its own stocks. No society on the edge of subsistence would ever have taken such a gamble. In the past, farmers and governments alike have preferred to reduce the risks of famine rather than increase the returns of good years. Farmers plan their crop strategies for the worst years. Such a strategy is not applicable today because it is no longer accepted that the agricultural sector is stagnant, and there is an inclination to seek solutions in growth rather than in distributional arrangements. Nevertheless, a policy in which one section of the population secures all the gains of the Green Revolution and another section absorbs all the risks of the global food crises will not prove viable. Nor do enormous transfers of food from the rich to the vulnerable make sense. Rather, a strategy which attempts to increase and protect the productive capacity of each region and population group would appear to be the only viable one for a nation at the margin. It is not enough that governments give more attention to agriculture; they must be concerned with the pattern of that investment.

Greater investment in agriculture is hardly a difficult principle to sell if a nation is close enough to the margin of survival. Unfortunately, the distribution of the costs of such investment still remains to be decided. In most countries of the Third World, and especially in India, agricultural taxes are very low and very regressive. Yet rural incomes have been rising and at least some have derived enormous benefits from public investment. Faced with rising prices and high income taxes, urban interests are likely to take a critical view of rural public investment, focusing on the need first to correct these inequities.[51]

In India the emergence of the commercial farmer, encouraged by the policies of the sixties, has coincided with precipitous increase in government demands in the form of taxes, fees, price controls, etc.[52] This has led to the development, in the early seventies, of the embryos of farm lobbies in several states.[53] Such farm interests were strikingly absent in the decision-making processes of the sixties. It is not that caste and language have disappeared as rural issues. Rather, these appeals are no longer sufficient to win support without sensitivity to the interests and demands of the commercial farming population. In various areas, these farm interests receive further strength from local government systems, cooperatives, and even the new agricultural universities.

Large landed interests had always been a political force in the sub-continent, but post-independence land reforms virtually eliminated this landlord class as a political force in many areas of India. Democratic elections then brought the middle farmers into increasing political prominence: first in the state legislatures, then in the state executives, and finally, by the late sixties, in New Delhi. While never very effective at the national level, the "farm bloc" formed one of the components of resistence to the "leftist" policies of Indira Gandhi in the early seventies. Farm power in the states proved a far more effective buffer to those policies, as programs of further land reform, rural tax reform, and small farmer development were ground to a halt. It was evident that the progressive farm community felt that these new impositions were threats to their newly acquired prosperity and opportunities for social mobility. In Punjab, farm organizations attempted, unsuccessfully, to disrupt government procurement operations. In Gujerat, farm disaffection contributed to the embarrassing defeat of the Congress Party in the 1975 elections -- just before the declaration of emergency. In most states the major institutions serving the rural sector -- land development banks, marketing federations, primary credit cooperatives -- have all come to be controlled by the farming castes and represent an important base for rural political organization. The organized farmer is now a force to be reckoned with in India. This "organization" is not as yet as formalized and national in scope as, let us say, the American Farm Bureau Federation. Nevertheless, a revolution has occurred in that at least some sections of India's farm community can and do now demand changes in policy and improvements in public services to serve their interests.

VI. THE CASE FOR AGRICULTURAL DEVELOPMENT IN LDC'S

It might be expected that the food crisis of 1973-74 would encourage rural investment and perhaps in turn shatter the old alliance of urban and rural elites in many LDCs. The latter would be expected because a heavily regulated urban sector would not accept a virtually unregulated rural sector once economic growth spreads to the farms. In the rhetoric leading up to the Indian political crisis of 1975, for instance, it was evident that the "capitalist" farmer had replaced the "feudal" landlord as the target of the urban left.

Similar shifts in political symbols denote realignments following a change in the rural sector. In Kenya, when African "big farmers" replaced Europeans after the country's independence in 1963, criticism by urban socialists arose. As Table 6 indicated, Kenya's government has ranked among the highest in Africa in terms of the spending priority accorded to agriculture. However, the flow of services (extension, production, and land-purchase credit) tended to favor large-scale farmers.[54] As of 1966 there were reportedly about 750 farms, averaging 800 acres, owned by African civil servants, politicians, and others.[55] While much of the favored position of larger farms relative to government services may have been due to political connections, another factor was those farms' superior capacity to utilize credit and other inputs. A study in Kenya's Nyeri District found a correlation between farmer's progressiveness on this dimension and their receipt of government services.[56] Moreover, whatever greater rural inequality and critical rhetoric government policies did promote seems to have had only minor political impact thus far. Bienen notes that Kenya's former opposition party made little headway with this issue.[57] One reason appears to be that many large holdings are in fact owned jointly by groups of persons. Another is that owners tended to settle numerous relatives on their land.[58] Finally, pressure from landless peasants could be met through opening new opportunities (at least for the first decade of independence) by settling them on formerly foreign-owned farms.

No response by the Third World nations which ignores questions of equity will be meaningful, however, for it is the destitute who represent the reality of the world food crisis. Dandekar and Rath presented the dilemma clearly.[59] In 1960-61, they report, 40 percent of India's rural population and 50 percent of its urban population lived below a consumption level of one half a rupee a day. In the eight-year period (1960-61 to 1967-68) they examined, the net national product more than doubled. Yet consumer expenditure increased by only 4.8 percent. Were this to continue, they argue, "The gulf between the rich and the poor will widen intolerably and inevitably undermine the democratic foundations of the economy." This aspect of the global food crisis will test the will and ingenuity of planners, administrators and above all, of politicians. They must be able to design a development plan that will direct a greater proportion of the growth in national income to the poor and a choice of technology that will provide them with productive employment. John Lewis has called for a "relevant radicalism," radical in its departure from existing trickle-down growth strategies.[60] Too few planners have taken the advice.[61]

However, a development model is emerging among economists of how to handle the inequality concerns. It takes the form of increasing agricultural productivity sparked by public investment in technology and overhead. The consequent increase in farm income stimulates demand which is then met by expanding small-scale consumer goods industries in smaller towns, close to their market. This in turn, it is hoped, will absorb the excess labor supply -- productively. Rising income will hopefully slow population growth and also increase effective (market) demand for foodgrains. These in turn must be supplied by an increasingly productive domestic agriculture. There are variations on this theme but the basic outline is recognizable.[62] The recent history of punjab fits the new development model. Double cropping has increased demand for labor, thus expanding employment opportunities in the small towns.

In many areas, however, the model faces serious institutional obstacles. Where "feudal" landlords are still the rule, land reform and other redistributive measures may be needed. Most of the existing rural institutions may have to be reformed or bypassed because they have been largely captured by local elites who are not inclined to use them to foster greater production.

The widespread weakness of local participatory institutions requires some explanation. The situation is by no means a total disaster. In the Indian state of Gujerat, for example, cotton marketing cooperatives in Punjab appear to have been viable and also to have made credit available even to small farmers if they were able to grow the new high-yielding dwarf varieties. Nevertheless, it is true that rural institutions, even in the Indian sub-continent, have been a disappointment.

There are essentially three explanations for the political weakness of the countryside. First, in areas where the new technology is unsuited, agriculture is still stagnant. There has not been enough economic pressure to divert local institutions away from their traditional preoccupation with distributing patronage to undertaking effective developmental roles. Second, in areas with highly unequal land holding sizes, politics is dominated by patron-client relations. The small farmer is dependent on the larger farmer and cannot bring effective pressure to bear for more widespread dispersion of needed inputs such as credit and water and fertilizer. The benefits, if any, tend to be highly concentrated among the few politically powerful "bosses." Third, even in technically dynamic areas with fairly equitable land holding patterns, the local institutions can be rendered ineffective if poorly designed. This was certainly the case with local governments in both India and Pakistan, where indirect elections favored elite control in local bodies and confusion and overloading of functions inhibited accountability. The combined effect of these technological, social, and institutional problems has tended to hamstring even progressive national government efforts in the past.

Finally, state administrators are often as reluctant to accept innovations as rural elites. This need not be because they are somehow part of the "establishment" but because new departures threaten established bureaucratic power structures. Certainly, the Ford Foundation encountered this kind of resistance in trying to implement a program that would have directly benefited rural elites.[63] This suggests that national governments may have to risk classic "redistributive" radicalism in certain regions if the way is to be opened for new investment and new technology. This being the case, class issues are likely to dominate the politics at the margin. A way out of this conflict and the worst effect of food crises can be found with a combination of political skill and an adequate development model, but success is far from guaranteed. Let us look at three sets of basic decisions which must be made and the factors which inhibit adequate responses.

(1) The greatest problem of a food crisis is that it tends to encourage a concentration on the short-term responses to the detriment of long-term structural changes. This is especially true where the crisis is viewed as a temporary aberration. A recognition of the permanence of the food crisis and the corollary need for major structural changes is a first requisite of adjustment to the crisis. It is probably true that nothing short of pressure from urban consumers will produce the incentives for policy changes. On the other hand, extractive politics to benefit the urban populace may well substitute for investment and rural structural change if the urban elites are too powerful.[64] Conversely, if rural elites prevail, solutions will be sought in higher agricultural prices, mechanization, and expanding farm size. These changes will increase the marketed surplus, increase farm

incomes, but cause hardship for a growing portion of the rural community. Neither of these solutions resembles the labor-intensive consumer goods strategy outlined in the new model. The problem is that in most developing countries it is difficult to imagine the appearance of a coalition of political forces that might produce such policy.

A labor-intensive strategy of development encouragement requires several policy innovations. First, it requires the existence of the small farm, which tends to be more productive per acre than the large farm and also uses labor more intensively. Mere food shortage is not likely to persuade a government to risk a radical land reform by direct redistribution, however, in light of the present economic and political power of landed interests in most LDCs. This means that the single structural change which could absorb the most rural labor is usually precluded. There are undoubtedly alternative ways of influencing farm size, for example, tax and inheritance policy. However, lack of administrative capacity to administer them and lack of any clear theory on how to go about reform tend to eliminate this option even if the political will exists. The other major source of employment opportunities appears to be small consumer goods industries. This solution is inhibited by a lack of appropriate technology, ideological mistrust of "capitalist solutions" in some countries, urban elites' preoccupation with imported luxury goods, and the lack of a dynamic rural sector to provide a market for these goods. In addition to these problems, the small manufacturers' sector faces strong if not overwhelming competition when seeking government assistance -- from heavy industry (supported by international investment), primary commodities development (sustaining food and luxury goods investment), and the growing vested interests of a farmer-dominated cooperative sector. Clearly, there are many more effective claims on public resources than the needs of small industry and market towns. Only public works, supported by landed interests and contractors, is available as a politically popular labor-absorbing program.

The entire farm community will be able to resist urban exploitation on the one hand and increasing concentrations of rural economic power on the other (both inimical to long-term solutions), only if reasonably broad-based rural political participation is encouraged. This may be accomplished by substantial decentralization to local governments, a mass-based party structure, or through lobby activities by broad-based farm organizations.[65] One way or another, however, it must be done. Unfortunately, such structures are often a threat to national or regional leaders, local elites, and to bureaucratic power -- a formidable list of adversaries. In India, the power of the local government (panchayats) and the autonomy of the cooperatives which peaked in the mid-1960s has been steadily eroded in most states. In 1974, for example, in Gujerat state in India, no elected governments at any level continued to function. All governmental functions were being performed by administrators. In the same year in Punjab state, both the Apex Cooperative Bank and the Apex Cooperative Marketing Society had delayed over two years in electing their governing boards due to a combination of fiscal and

political difficulties. Pakistan is still without functioning
rural local governments although the Bhutto regime had been
considering the matter for four years. Yet broad-based rural
political participation appears to be essential to a proper balance
of rural development policies and socially optimal results.

However necessary for effective development over the long run,
such participation may appear in the short term to be politically
too risky. Tanzania, with its program for socialist rural
development ujamaa, is a good example of this paradox. Tanzanian
rhetoric calls for broad popular involvement in government.[66] A
1972 reform significantly increased the powers of local government
at the expense of central ministries. However, one field study
suggests that the farmers themselves have had very little influence
on policy choices.[67] Another source concurs: "(T)he practical
effect of the decentralization policies pursued since 1967 has been
to concentrate decision-making power in the hands of
administrators, technicians, and political commissioners at
Regional and District levels."[68] The problem may derive from the
radical nature of the ruling party's rural development strategy,
the opposition it has encountered, and the government's
unwillingness to give its many farmer opponents formal means to
influence policy. The strategy has been to communalize
agriculture, and it has been strongly opposed by commercial farmers
who feel threatened with loss of income and by poorer peasants who
object to being resettled into new communal villages.[69] As long as
much of the clientele is hostile to its policy purposes, Tanzania's
government, and others like it, may pursue transformationist
strategies only be repressing grassroots participation. The
hostility need not be long-lasting, however, particularly if after
trial and error the strategy proves economically successful.[70]

The other factor which appears to be essential to
restructuring the rural sector is public investment in agricultural
research. It is widely recognized now that a steady program of
agricultural technology is essential to rural modernization and to
reducing production costs while increasing yields.[71] For many
small nations the cost of building educational institutions and
research centers will be high, and there may be advantages to
internationalization. But one way or another relevant research must
be encouraged. Politically, this is probably easier than
institutional reform as much of this effort is within the control
of the national elites. One can be reasonably optimistic about the
future in this area, provided research priorities relate to small
rather than large capital intensive farming.

(2) The second set of strategic decisions for developing
nations as they consider restructuring the rural sector to handle
the emerging food crisis is in defining the proper relationship
between the public and private sector. This involves decisions
about the control of land, the manufacture and distribution of
inputs, and the control of the grain trade. A related set of
decisions concern the development of regulatory policies -- crops,
prices, input packaging, and marketing. The former set of
decisions, regarding nationalization, are typically made on
ideological grounds and not on the basis of any particular theory
of rural development. The latter decisions, regarding regulatory

activity, are usually dictated by the extent to which policy is dominated by governmental purposes. In neither case does the preference, convenience, or efficiency of the farm community appear to be the primary consideration in the decision.

In Indian Punjab, for example, a "crop loan system" specifies the "package" of inputs to be used on a particular crop. Both the loan and the inputs are supplied through the state cooperative system.[72] Yet analysis of the production functions of farmers can find no appreciable difference in the efficiency with which fertilizer is used among farmers relying on the co-ops and those relying on the private sector. Some studies, in fact, suggest that those following the official advice operate less efficiently.[73] In Pakistan Punjab, farmers preferred the larger and more expensive diesel pumps for their tubewells in the mid-sixties, because government regulation of electricity made the more efficient electric pumps too difficult to install.[74] For years in India, until 1965, in fact, foodgrains procurement prices were set without the slightest attempt to calculate the actual cost of production.[75] Extension services more often act as the conduits of official policy than as service agents for the farmer; this has been true in India, Pakistan, Tanzania, and many other LDCs. In spite of these examples, decisions to increase public input or control have not been either entirely pointless or detrimental to farm interests. It simply should be noted that farm preferences typically took a back seat to government needs in these programs.

The basic problem here is twofold. First, policy makers have often failed to treat the farmer seriously as a rational, profit-oriented producer for whom considerations of efficiency are of some significance. This is reflected in the lack of concern for adequate profit incentives. When a government must control and regulate, it usually has been bureaucratic convenience and efficiency which dictated the choice of institutional arrangements and the form of the regulations, not the farmer's. Finally, when restrictions are imposed, too little attention has been paid to finding a mode of enforcement which might contribute mutually to the interests of both government and farmer. There are examples of useful arrangements, but they are all too rare. Punjab's MARKFED (state cooperative marketing federation) exchanges support for harvest season prices for an effective governmental monopoly of wholesale marketing. The Gujerat government trades strict crop and movement controls over the cotton crop for equally strict publicly regulated quality control which improves farm prices.[76]

Far more common are the institutional failures. To assure maximum production rather than maximum profits, extension services have frequently been used to encourage farmers to employ more chemical fertilizer than the farmers found profitable. There are even reports of extension officers being ordered to require farmers to take complex fertilizers they neither wanted nor needed in order to remove stocks that had been over-produced by the factories. This type of unprofessional advice to the farmer clearly weakens the effectiveness of the extension service. Cooperative societies have often been treated as administrative agencies of the government. They are asked to procure foodgrains for government stocks at very low profit margins. They are employed to enforce

the use of certain technology packages favored by the government.
In fact, governments often have preferred heavily bureaucratized
systems of market management rather than reliance on simple market
regulating mechanisms because direct physical control over the crop
was more amenable to traditional bureaucratic procedures than free
market manipulations. The inability of developing nations to
implement policies in the rural areas and the high administrative
costs which are frequently incurred are all too often due to a
failure to reconcile the valid interests of the farmer with the
public interests of the government in new and more efficient and
reciprocal institutional arrangements.

Finally, politicians desiring control and administrators
desiring effective "integration" of policy are far too likely to
encourage the concentration of governmental power in the rural
areas. It is only slowly that India has learned the cost of this
policy.[77] Slowly, however, it has become evident that services
must be institutionally differentiated if specific rural groups are
to be targeted. In addition, it has become evident that
differentiation of functions and multiple channels of access to key
inputs and services may reduce access costs to the farmer and
provide greater flexibility to him in adjusting his combination of
inputs.[78] For example, given the additional administrative and
political complications of using cooperative credit, it may not be
attractive to all farmers. On the other hand, the existence of
extensive cooperative credit undoubtedly has its impact on the
private moneylenders' rates of interest, level of services, etc.
Farmers can be expected to take advantage of the indirect effect of
programs in decisions about borrowing as well.

As poor countries have been and are compelled by food
shortages to take agriculture more seriously, they are forced (many
for the first time) to think much more seriously about the impact
of their administrative procedures, institutional patterns, and
regulatory policies on the rural sector. Most lack information,
experience, and training in evaluating these impacts and taking the
appropriate adjustment effects. Hence, program "errors," even if
high, should not be an excuse for no effort at all.

(3) International relations constitute the third set of
decisions. External relations will continue to play a vital role
in the strategies employed by the Third World nations in their
attempts to handle the food crisis. Small nations and those
vulnerable to recurrent drought will remain dependent on
international reserve stocks. The major grain exporting nations
can help to provide the security which will enable these states to
risk the radical departures in policy and the high investment rates
that will be needed to transform their agricultural sectors.
Imported chemical fertilizer will also continue to be a vital
component of any development strategies. Fortunately, it now
appears that the fertilizer shortages of the 1973-75 period have
been rectified and new production capacity will ensure ample
supplies at least for the next decade.[79] Nevertheless, fertilizer
imports will continue to absorb vital foreign exchange, even if new
production reduces the need for costly food imports.

The continuation of a food import strategy in the face of
rising international grain prices is, of course, a very restricted

solution, generally available only to countries with a strong and reliable export capacity. Furthermore, whether the grain is supplied on commercial terms or as relief supplies under bilateral or international agreements, grave political risks are involved in such dependence. Pakistan and India both felt the pressure from the United States when aid was manipulated to bring a stop to the 1965 war. With the United States supplying most of its fertilizer, Pakistan must be well aware of the intimate connection between the success of its agricultural programs and American views on its nuclear program. The use of food as a diplomatic bargaining tool by the US or other major suppliers may seem ineffective when applied to the Soviet Union; but in the Third World, food dependence can make countries very vulnerable. This last statement should be treated with caution, however. We have stressed throughout that food strategies are the result of a complex set of demands and that there are alternatives available to developing nations. The costs of dependence are not necessarily determining -- they must be weighed against alternatives. Similarly, in encouraging or discouraging import dependence, donors such as the United States should keep in mind their complex goals as well. When used carefully and targeted accurately, food imports can still be used to encourage job creation and to control inflation in the Third World.[80]

Developed states can do much to encourage greater production in the Third World; a most important contribution would be the use of the vast technical capacity of the US to help solve the complex remaining technological problems of tropical agriculture.[81] We should recognize, however, that successful agricultural development will alter diets in the direction of more nourishing but less efficient uses of grain, such as meat, processed foods and milk.[82] The effect of this on poor people who cannot afford these foods may be deleterious, as Christensen argues in this volume. This suggests that poverty and inequality will continue to be at the forefront of international politics in the Third World for some time, regardless of any likely level of "success" in rural development.

Domestic Political Constraints and International Dependency

We can now summarize briefly some of the domestic political factors which inhibit or influence solutions to the food crises in various Third World countries and the potential or real role of international forces upon them. Like any other set of policies, those aimed at coping with food problems involve gains for some and losses for others. In consequence, existing political cleavages will often be increased and new ones may appear. Characteristically, seven forms of political problems appear to surround food issues as increasing population puts pressure on existing supplies and poverty exacerbates hunger in LDCs.

First, and perhaps most severe in the initial stages, are

interregional conflicts within LDCs. Except in small countries food crises are seldom uniformly distributed geographically. Typically, rural growth increases intra-country differences.[83] Planned investment tends to take place in those areas which promise the most return. Typically the problems of the better endowed regions present problems that are both technically and administratively easier to resolve by hard-pressed governments. In consequence, both efficiency and the national interest seem to conspire to increase inequality. There is certainly some evidence of this in India where the Ford Foundation encouraged intensive investment in the best areas for a "quick fix" for the food shortage.

Where geographical cleavages also correspond with ethnic and cultural differences, the redistribution of the gains of growth is even more difficult. The Sahel offers a good example where governmental neglect was largely responsible for the severity of the food crisis there. The ethnic divisions between pastoralists and the farming-town populations on which the region's governments were based contributed to the inadequacy of governmental responses. Even otherwise effective development programs, as in India, have shut ethnic minorities out of the benefits. In India, as elsewhere, minority tribal groups have not fared well at the hands of the dominant group(s).

Nor are different regions likely to have equal access to decision makers. India provides a good example. In Punjab, which is the heartland of the Green Revolution, the success of a farmer depends on his tubewell, a necessity that can easily be secured locally through influence with the local credit cooperative. Electricity, to run the pump, can be assured politically by Punjab's contribution to the central foodgrains pool. In Gujerat state, in contrast, there is little ground water; and it would require a Planning Commission level decision to construct a new dam to provide the needed water. With cotton as the major crop in the region and cotton exports failing, Gujerat has far less influence in New Delhi. Not surprisingly a dam has not been built.

Investments based on the comparative advantage or superior resource base of a given region, therefore, are reasonable policy decisions where ethnic homogeneity or a responsive political structure can provide alternatives or transfer payments to the marginal areas. Where such political mechanisms fail, however, growing tension, conflict, and even separatism may result. In this situation, the current attention of the international aid agencies to the poor developing world may be more important in the political economy of the world than realized. By providing additional resources, new technologies, and foreign pressure, foreign aid can assist the needed transfer payments within LDCs.

The second issue involves the character of rural politics. In most Third World countries rural politics has become the politics of faction and patronage since independence. Rural politics depends, then, on the distribution of favors to clients. Political struggles are for a piece of a very small pie and short of the negative power of rural elites to prevent reform, rural influence is frequently dissipated in factional struggles.[84] This may provide the explanation of why nations with such a large rural population can spend so little on the development of that sector. Coalitions of rural factions may break down as poverty increases and we may well see the emergence of class politics in the villages. For the present, however, the inability of the farmers, save in the most progressive areas, to articulate their economic interest against rural elites and the urban sector is a fact of life in most Third World nations.

The prevalance of factionalism combined with patronage politics is an understandable solution to the political problems of a rapidly changing rural environment. Within the village traditional loyalties are typically shattered by externally induced stresses and strains. As the scale of political organization and the degree of political participation both increase, some basis must be found for alliances among disparate groups with little experience of working in common. The result is loose alliances among diverse segments which trade their support for direct and immediate favors. We have, in effect, a barter political economy. This system is highly efficient in its use of scarce political resources. Divided as it is into factional segments, there is often no majority coalition or stable opposition, merely a dominant faction facing a fragmented opposition. Only those in the dominant faction need to be "paid off" and there is little need to provide "class benefits" or public goods to a farm constituency -- only favors to supporters. Such a system works quite well, even with a bare minimum of divisible patronage, as exemplified by Kenyan politics. It is difficult for such a system to have any progressive impact on public policy. It develops no real pressure for structural change, no real support for the concentration of resources and large-scale, long-term investment. Local elites, well off and benefiting from control of the patronage, have little incentive to challenge the system. They leave policy to the urban elites. Both increasing poverty and rural progress, however, threaten this political order. No matter in which direction many developing nations move, major adjustments in rural politics are in the offing.

The emergence of class conflict is a third component of the emerging poverty of the Third World. In the past, rural social units -- villages, tribes, and estates -- stood against the hostile outside world. Throughout the Third World a growing market orientation combined with increasing population pressure have destroyed that solidarity. One need not assume that that traditional solidarity was necessarily benign, but it was real. In areas experiencing growth, however, customary ties collapse; and rural tension is common. For the first time in many countries, therefore, opportunities have appeared for political leaders to win support from the rural poor who can no longer be controlled by their patrons.[85]

A growing class consciousness among the farm population will, of course, have a mixed effect. On the one hand, it may encourage governments to pay increasing attention to the agricultural sector, which in the long run is probably beneficial. On the other hand, the growing threat of a restive rural poor does not generally incline landowners toward "socially progressive" policies. Curiously enough, redistributive solutions to rising rural poverty make the most sense in those countries which face the least serious resource constraints. In areas such as India and Bangladesh there are undoubtedly areas which might benefit from land redistribution, for example, but in areas like Punjab one could not redistribute further without endangering production. In the final analysis there is simply not enough land to go around. In this context, to paraphrase John Lewis, a good deal of Indian radicalism is irrelevant. In many areas of Latin America and Africa with a dual economy of distinct peasant and modern sectors, however, major redistributive solutions are plausible. In such areas a strong leftist party with a base in the rural poor might be efficacious in forcing incremental reforms. Thus, the growing class conflict in rural areas will undoubtedly mean increased political participation but its significance will depend on the overall resource situation and how that participation is structured. Thus, strong local governments will encourage agriculture but strengthen land-owners against the agricultural laborers. Migration will relieve pressure for land reform but the associated urbanization will increase pressure for lower food prices and greater government control over markets. Unduly rapid commercialization of agriculture without a strong demand for labor and without the political capacity for transfer payments probably encourages extremist movements. Thus, the "new development model" can trigger instability if rural job creation is not achieved.

The fourth element of the merging political crisis is the role of technology. In the early part of this century in India, manufactured consumer goods destroyed a whole class of village artisans.[86] Today in some areas resumption of cultivation and mechanization may be destroying a class of tenant farmers. Pakistan is a good example,[87] as is Ethiopia. Cohen observed in Ethiopia that a rural development program targeted at small farmers had the unintended consequence of dispossessing many of them. Through a demonstration effect, large landowners outside the project area adopted the improved seeds and use of fertilizers which proved successful in the project. And finding that those inputs made mechanization financially feasible and that with machinery they could dispense with tenant farmers, owners drove "thousands of tenants" off the land.[88] The tenants who remained found their rent rising and sale prices of land climbing out of reach, despite their own higher incomes from Green Revolution inputs. Another unfortunate side effect may be dramatically increasing numbers of very small farms, as an expanding population, a land constraint, and a more productive technology combine to constrict the assets available to the poorest.[89] No one would argue that technology "caused " these problems. Rather, there is now good evidence that technological innovation tends to economize on scarce factors in the production process. Sometimes this is labor, as in the United States, or land, as in Japan. Further, these are not simply economic changes, but, as Polanyi argues, these technical changes almost always help to speed up changes in social relationships with associated changes in power relationships.[90]

The Green Revolution technology has been accused of producing potentially dangerous social side effects in the most affected areas. This argument contends that, due to the intensification of production, landlords have been encouraged to resume cultivation of their own land and eject their previous tenants. Furthermore, it is argued, this terminates any social obligations the rural rich may have had to care for the rural poor by turning "tenants" into "wage laborers." The result, it was predicted in the late sixties, would be rapidly growing immiserization and rural insecurity. Events have raised some question about this prediction and necessitated some reservations. First, there appear to be no particular economies of scale in the new technology. Whether, in fact, operational holdings expand in size, increasing the number and vulnerability of those without land or even tenant's rights depends on a number of factors. Among them are the initial degree of inequality of holding sizes, extent of supporting services to small operators available from the government, the availability of a stable water supply, and the flexibility of existing tenancy arrangements. Second, in most areas the new technology has been labor-deepening and has forced up agricultural wages. Whether this is an advantage to the poor or not depends on other factors. A tradition of payment of wages in kind rather than cash will permit workers to share in the increased productivity and rising prices. If off-farm employment is available, workers may in fact combine the high peak season's wages which the new prosperity permits farmers to pay with additional earnings in the slack season. Rising prosperity in the farm sector may in fact encourage the development of localized business investment that will provide those jobs. Ultimately, the logic of the argument was based on the increasing gap between the landowners and the rest of the rural population, a gap widened by the increased productivity of land. One's reaction to this argument depends on how one evaluates the political impact of the increasing gap compared with the significance of a rapidly growing real income. The Green Revolution has undoubtedly raised tension and conflict. But the experience of ten years suggests that, within these specific regions, progress has been sufficient to contain them.

Intra-governmental and inter-governmental problems constitute the fifth aspect of political change. The growing economic integration of the agricultural sector into the national economy has a profound influence on government administration. Technical bureaucracies expand and create tension with old guard law-and-order ministries and traditional generalist civil servants.[91] The scale of social organization adjusts to broadened interdependence of rural communities. Local leaders often become irrelevant to the needs of villagers unless they respond by evolving a new brokerage role that dramatically alters authority relationships in rural areas.[92] New levels of government and administration emerge to correspond to the changing scale and functions of government. This tends, in turn, to exacerbate problems of center-periphery conflict. These questions may be so serious as to virtually stalemate rural institutional development, as they have done in Pakistan recently.[93]

It could be argued, in fact, that the success of the rural transformation, and hence the response to the crisis of food scarcity, depends on the transformation of rural governance structures. Efficient allocation of public goods such as roads,

irrigation and educational facilities, etc., can in most cases only
be made by effective localized authorities. Certainly their
effective maintenance depends upon such decentralization. Of
course centralized control is necessary for sector-wide policies
such as pricing, import-export decisions and credit. Effective
mobilization of the collective self-help capacities of the rural
population, however, demands considerable initiative in devising
and encouraging new economic structures such as water users'
associations and cooperative societies. In short, collective
decision-making capacities need to be expanded at the local level.
For administrators and nationalist leaders who may view power as a
zero-sum game, these are particularly difficult decisions.
Furthermore, the discretionary power invested in these institutions
at the local level is not provided without some risk of wastage,
corruption, and misallocation. A local base for opposition
activity may also be created inadvertently. Drawing the lines of
authority is not easy and new institutions have frequently failed
because it was inadequately done, but the organization of public
authority at the local level is a major variable in the development
process.

The sixth political dimension of the food crisis involves
international dependency. Few Third World nations have the
political capacity or resources to transform the rural sector
without assistance. Yet as the Russian-American conflict spreads
now to Africa and Latin America, as well as Asia, the costs of
dependence become clearer. We have seen the frustration of the
Third World leaders in the Cocayoc Declaration and in other
international gatherings.[94] In the past, aid brought time and
provided external resources for elites. But as the crisis deepens,
time runs out and poverty grows faster than external assistance in
all but a few politically favored states. It seems unlikely that
dependence will be an alternative to domestic reform for many
nations much longer. More important, however, is the fact that
unless the nation in question has the technical, administrative,
and political strength and skill to manage the relationship,
dependence may well distort policy and institutional development as
severely as colonialism did.

Seventh, and finally, "ideological" questions must play an
important role in the emerging solution to each nation's part of
the global food crisis. Insofar as "ideology" implies a model of
the future (in this sense we could use Mannheim's "utopia")[95] and a
broad strategy for the role of government in bringing that future
into existence, one should perhaps encourage it. Many nations,
including those of the West, have been content to minimize the
government's responsibility, dealing with problems in ad hoc
fashion and letting solutions emerge from "market" adjustments.
This would seem unwise if the future global food system will face
shortages anything near as serious as the "doom-sayers" suggest.

The key development problem identified by the Club of Rome, in
political terms, is the inabilty of the future to place demands on
the present.[96] All decision makers discount heavily distant events
in time. The result is that we are often caught by surprise.
Another key problem is that identified by Garnett Hardin as the
"commons" problem.[97] Expendable resources, or those which may be

overtaxed, are poorly managed if responsibility and benefits are separated. From overfishing of the sea to grain shortages flowing from unregulated markets, this classic problem of political economy is becoming more frequent at the international level. An ideology which supports practical management and philosophical wisdom has never been more needed in directing the power of government, certainly those in developing states.

All these political problems are not the direct result of low productivity among the rural populace, or of food shortages, such as occurred in 1973-74. However, increasingly the determinant of economic growth and eventual political order in many developing states appears to rest on how agricultural development is managed. Given the significant vulnerability and hence dependency of many LDCs within the current world food system (especially those in South Asia and Africa), the norms of the global food regime regarding the terms on which concessional food aid and agricultural assistance will be provided become important in determining which pattern emerges in individual countries. In short the countries with the least control over the regime are also the ones most affected -- politically and economically -- by how the system works.

NOTES

[1]These rough percentages are derived from data on food aid shipments of two major kinds: those under Title I of Public Law 480, which provides for sales on concessional terms (20 to 40 years for repayment, low interest rates) and those under Title II of the act, which provides for grants. The data for Title I shipments were given for calendar years as follows: 1972, about 6 million metric tons; 1973, 3 million; and 1974, 1.2 million. Title II figures were given for fiscal years as follows: 1972, 2.5 million metric tons; 1973, 2.1 million; and 1974, 1.4 million. Sources: United States Congress, 1973 Annual Report on Public Law 480 (House Document No. 83-362, Washington D.C., 1973), pp. 8, 50; and "The Annual Report on Activities Carried Out Under Public Law 480, 83rd Congress, as Amended, During the Period January 1 through December 31, 1974" (preliminary draft, Agency for International Development, 1975), pp. 1, 95.

[2]See USDA Economic Research Service, "World Economic Conditions in Relation to Agricultural Trade," WEC 12 (Washington D.C., August 1977), p. 7.

[3]US Department of Agriculture, Economic Research Service, The World Food Situation and Prospects to 1985 (Washington, D.C., 1974), pp. 81-83.

[4]The 28 countries in question were ones for which both FAO and USDA per capita food production estimates were available. See Table 1 for specific bibliographic references.

[5]Cited by Donald Heisel, "Food and Population in Africa," Current History, June 1975): 261.

[6]Ethiopia, Ghana, Guinea, Kenya, Mali, Niger, Nigeria, Senegal, and Upper Volta. Agency for International Development, Special Report to the Congress on the Drought Situation in Sub-Saharan Africa (Washington, D.C., 1975), pp. 17-44.

[7]Ethiopia, Ghana, Mali, Nigeria, and Senegal. See the sources listed in Table 1.

[8]Data on the money value of food imports were available also for 1974. However, world market prices for grain were unusually high that year, as well as in 1973. Including both 1973 and 1974 figures would tend to distort excessively the comparisons in Tables 2 and 3 (that is, the averages for the early 1970s versus the 1962-65 bases). Therefore, we chose to omit the 1974 data.

[9]See the entries for those seven countries in the following sources: US Department of Agricultural Service, Foreign Agriculture Circular: Reference Tables on Wheat, Corn, and Total Coarse Grains Supply-Distribution for Individual Countries (Washington, D.C., 1976) and Foreign Agriculture Circular: Reference Tables on Rice Supply-Distribution for Individual Countries (Washington, D.C., 1976).

[10]Wilfred Malenbaum, "Scarcity: Prerequisite to Abundance," Annals of the American Academy of Political Science, no. 420 (July 1975): 76.

[11]During the decade of the sixties imports of grain averaged 7.7 percent of India's domestic production, for example. More to the point these imports represented 20.4 percent of the marketed supply of grain. See V. S. Vyas and S. C. Bandyopadhyay, "National Food Policy in the Framework of a National food Budget," Economic and Political Weekly, "Review of Agriculture" (March 1975): A2-A13.

[12]Indian Foodgrain Marketing (New Delhi: Institute of Economic Growth, 1973) pp. 18-26. Refer also to John Moore, et. al. Indian Foodgrain Marketing (New Delhi: Institute of Economic Growth, 1973).

[13]The data following on operating costs come from Report of the Committee on Cost of Handling of Foodgrains by Food Corporation of India (New Delhi: Government of India, 1974), pp. 23, 40-41.

[14]These dollar figures were converted from rupees at the official exchange rate then prevailing, one rupee = $0.13.

[15]N. K. Nicholson, "The Politics of Food Policy in India," Pacific Affairs, Vol. 41, no. 1 (Spring 1968):   34-9.

[16]The basic document in this change was the Ford Foundation report, India's Food Crisis & Steps to Meet It (New Delhi, Ministry of Food and Agriculture and Ministry of Community Development and Cooperation, 1959).   Regarding price policy two subsequent reports indicate clearly the direction of thinking, in the Government of India: Agricultural Price Policy in India (New Delhi: Directorate of Economics and Statistics, Ministry of Food and Agriculture, 1966), and Report of the Foodgrains Policy Committee (New Delhi: Department of Food, 1966).   In agricultural policy the innovations are presented in Modernizing Indian Agriculture (New Delhi: Ministry of Food, Agriculture, Community Development, and Cooperation, 1969).   Also see N. K. Nicholson, "Rural Development Policy in India: Elite Differentiation and the Decision Making Process" (DeKalb: Center for Governmental Studies, Northern Illinois University, 1974); D. Brown, Agricultural Development in India's Districts (Cambridge: Harvard University Press, 1971).

[17]This interpretation was derived from extensive interviews by Nicholson in India in 1974 with officers and politicians involved in making the decision or in the early implementation of the decision.

[18]John Mellor, "The Functions of Agricultural Prices in Economic Development," in Comparative Experience of Agricultural Development in Developing Countries of Asia and the South-East since World War II (Bombay: Indian Society of Agricultural Economics, 1971), pp. 122-40.

[19]M. Weiner, The Politics of Scarcity (Chicago: University of Chicago Press, 1962), Chapter 9.

[20]Morris D. Morris, "What is a Famine," Economic and Political Weekly (November 2, 1974), 885; "Needed: A New Famine Policy," ibid., (February 1975); 283. See also N. S. Jodha, "Famine and Famine Policies: Some Empirical Evidence," ibid., (October 11, 1975); 1609.

[21]For a discussion of the politics of decontrol, see Norman K. Nicholson, "Politics and Food Policy in India," thesis presented to the Graduate School, Cornell University, for the Degree of Doctor of Philosophy, June 1966, Chapter 2.

[22]This possibility was demonstrated in the report by the Directorate of Economics and Statistics, Ministry of Food and Agriculture, Report on Market Arrivals of Foodgrains -- 1958859 Season (New Delhi: 1959). The question of the effect of this control system on incentives has frequently been raised in public debate and in academic circles. Several answers are possible. First, the disincentive effect will depend on the extent to which

higher prices would, in fact, be reflected in higher investments by the farmer. It could reasonably be argued that, in the absence of new technology, extensive farm investment was not to be expected. Second, controlled prices may be offset, from the perspective of the farmer, by higher average prices if the government does actually support the price at harvest and in bumper years. Third, some disincentive may be justified by the responsibility of the government to prevent starvation if this is what the grain is actually used for and there appears no other way to do the job.

[23]Statistics on foodgrains production, procurement, pricing, and distribution can be found in Food Statistics, published annually by the Directorate of Economics and Statistics, Ministry of Agriculture, New Delhi.

[24]See N. Krishnaji, "Inter-regional Disparaties in Per Capita Production and Productivity of Foodgrains," Economic and Political Weekly (Special Number, August 1975): 1377. See also John Mellor, The New Economics of Growth (Ithaca: Cornell University Press, 1976). Chapter 3; S. S. John & M. S. Mudahar, "The Dynamics of Institutional Change and Rural Development in Punjab, India" (Ithaca: Rural Development Committee, Center for International Studies, 1974).

[25]N. Krishnaji, "Wheat Price Movement," Economic and Political Weekly (June 1973): A-42.

[26]A review of the relief problems can be found in the following documents: Relief Problems in East Pakistan and India (in two parts), United States Senate, Committee on the Judiciary, Subcommittee to investigate problems connected with refugees and escapees (Washington: June 28, 1971, and October 4, 1971); Senator Edward Kennedy, Crisis in South Asia, United States Senate, Committee on the Judiciary, Subcommittee to investigate problems connected with refugees and escapees (Washington: November 1, 1971).

[27]See the discussions of state agencies in Kenya and Sierra Leone in William O. Jones, Marketing Staple Food Crops in Tropical Africa (Ithaca, New York: Cornell University Press, 1972), Chapters 7, 8.

[28]Colin Leys, Underdevelopment in Kenya (London: Heinemann, 1975), pp. 106-7.

[29]Ibid., p. 108.

[30]See War on Hunger (A Report from the Agency for International Development), vol. 8 (August 1974): 27; and Food and Agriculture Organization, "Mission Multi-Donateurs Dans la Zone Zahelienne: Republique du Niger" (Rome: 1974): 2.

[31]Agency for International Development (US), "Development

Assistance Program: FY 1975, Section Three: Chad, Cameroon, Central African Republic, and Gabon" (Washington: 1975), pp. 1-19.

[32]Jack Shepherd, The Politics of Starvation (New York: Carnegie Endowment for International Peace, 1975), p. 1.

[33]Victor D. DuBois, "The Drought in West Africa: Part I," American University Field Staff Reports: West African Series, vol. 15 (no. 1, 1974): 3.

[34]The Politics of Starvation, p. 4.

[35]Derek Winstanley, "Climatic Changes and the Future of the Sahel," in The Politics of Natural Disaster: The Case of the Sahel Drought, edited by Michael H. Glantz (New York: Praeger Publishers, 1976), p. 198. See also p. 164 of the same volume.

[36]"The Drought in West Africa: Part II" (no. 2, 1974): 6.

[37]A field survey by the US Public Health Service estimated for Mauritania, Mali, Niger and Senegal that "the maximum number of deaths due to famine this year (1973) is calculated at 101,000." Public Health Service, "Nutritional Surveillance in West Africa" (July-August 1973), reprinted in Disaster in the Desert, by Hal Sheets and Roger Morris (New York: The Carnegie Endowment for International Peace, 1974), pp. 131-36. Shepherd reports, "In Ethiopia alone, at least 100,000 people starved to death in 1973 alone . . ." The Politics of Starvation, p. xiii.

[38]"The Drought in Africa: Part II," pp. 2-4.

[39]The Politics of Starvation, p. 17.

[40]"Needed: A New Famine Policy," P. 283.

[41]Report of the Study Team on Fair Price Shops (New Delhi: Ministry of Food and Agriculture, Community Development, and Cooperation, 1966), especially p. 57.

[42]The effect of the distribution on prices in Punjab appears to be one of stimulating prices. See N. Krishnaji, "Wheat Price Movements," Economic and Political Weekly, Review of Agriculture, (June 1973): A-42. On the whole, over the past two decades the index of food prices has risen faster than the wholesale price index and terms of trade have favored the farmer. See, V. S. Vyas & S. C. Bandyopadhyay, "National Food Policy in the Framework of a National Food Budget," Economic and Political Weekly, Review of Agriculture (March 1975): A-2. In fact, the distribution system appears to stimulate demand and as price is determined by demand more than supply -- due to the fact that aggregate production is unresponsive to prices -- the system may actually encourage price increases. See S. K. Chakrabarti, "Relative Prices of Cereals: 1952-70," Economic and Political Weekly, Review of Agriculture (June 1975): A-42; National

Council of Applied Economic Research, Structure and Behavior of Prices of Foodgrains (New Delhi: NCAER, 1969), Chapter 7; R. Tamarajakshi, "Inter-Sectoral Terms of Trade and Marketed Surplus of Agricultural Produce 1951-2 to 1965-6," in Comparative Experience of Agricultural Development in Developing Countries (Bombay: Indian Society of Agricultural Economics, 1972): 141. On the issue of the destitute, see V. M. Dandekar & N. Rath, "Poverty in India," Economic and Political Weekly (January 2, 1971): 25, (January 9, 1971): 106.

[43]John D. Esseks, "The Food Outlook for the Sahel: Regaining Self-Sufficiency or Continuing Dependence on International Aid?" Africa Today, vol. 22 (April-June 1975): 46-7; and The Politics of Starvation, pp. 60-64.

[44]Jean Copans, ed., Secheresses et Famines du Sahel (Paris: Francois Maspero, 1975), pp. 133, 137-38, 140-42; Victor DuBois, "The Drought in Niger, Part II: The Overthrow of President Hamani Diori," American Universities Field Staff Reports: West African Series, vol. 15 (no. 5, 1974): 6-7; and The Politics of Starvation, pp. 49-50.

[45]Punjab Budget at a Glance: 1974-75 (Chandigarsh: Government of Punjab, 1974).

[46]See Uma Lele, The Design of Rural Development (Baltimore: The Johns Hopkins University Press, 1975), Chapters 3, 4, 6.

[47]International Labour Organization, Bulletin of Labour Statistics, 2nd Quarter, 1976, Table 9.

[48]See N. K. Nicholson, Rural Development Policy in India (Dekalb: Center for Governmental Studies, Northern Illinois University, 1974).

[49]See Gunvant Desai, Growth of Fertilizer Use in Districts of India (Ahmedabad: Indian Institute of Management, Center for Management in Agriculture, 1973) Chapter 2. See also Gunvant Desai et. al., Dynamics of Growth in Fertilizer Use at Micro Level (Ahmedabad: Center for Management in Agriculture, Indian Institute of Management, 1973); Brian Lockwood et. al., The High Yielding Varieties Program in India, Part I (New Delhi: Programme Evaluation Organization, Planning Commission, 1971); National Council of Applied Economic Research, Fertilizer Use on Selected Crops in India (New Delhi: 1974).

[50]Even at the time, according to the recollections of those involved in the decision, this was widely viewed as a considerable risk. In fact, most of the field trials of the new seeds were not encouraging and the best economic opinion was against building up a dependence on imported fertilizers.

[51]See Report of the Committee on Taxation of Agricultural Wealth and Income (New Delhi: Ministry of Finance 1972); E. T. Mathew,

Agricultural Taxation and Economic Development in India (New Delhi: Asia, 1968); A. C. Angrish, Direct Taxation of Agriculture in India (Bombay: Somarija, 1972); V. P. Gandhi, Tax Burden on Indian Agriculture (Cambridge: Harvard Law School, 1966); S. L. Shetty, "An Inter-Sectoral Analysis of Taxable Capacity and Tax Burden," Indian Journal of Agricultural Economics, vol. 26 (July-September 1971).

[52] In 1974, for example, attempts were made by the Finance Ministry to pressue the state governments into adopting agricultural income taxes. In addition, although the central government may not constitutionally tax rural income, the income tax laws were amended to take rural income into account in calculating the rate of income tax. Electricity rates were revised upwards by many states during the year and the price of fertilizer was doubled.

[53] The two most obvious were the Kheti Bari Union in Punjab and the Kehdut Samaj in Gujerat. But interviews with Congress party MPs in New Delhi indicated that by 1974 rural MPs from the Northwest were becoming increasingly aware of their common economic interests and some identified the "farm lobby" in the Congress as one of the major components of the attempt to oust Indira Ghandi in 1975 (June).

[54] The Design of Rural Development, pp. 75, 81; and Underdevelopment in Kenya. pp. 101.

[55] Henry Bienen, Kenya: The Politics of Participation and Control (Princeton, New Jersey: Princeton University Press, 1974), pp. 169-70.

[56] Cited by Charles Elliott, Patterns of Poverty in the Third World (New York: Praeger Publishers, 1975), p. 27.

[57] Kenya: Politics of Participation, pp. 181-82.

[58] Underdevelopment in Kenya, pp. 90-91.

[59] V. M. Dandekar & N. Rath, "Poverty in India," Economic and Political Weekly (January 2, 1971); 25; (January 9, 1971); 106. See also P. K. Bardhank, "On the Incidence of Poverty in Rural India of the Sixties."

[60] John Lewis, "Wanted in India: A Relevant Radicalism," Economic and Political Weekly (Special Number, July 1970): 1211.

[61] In 1974, these issues led to the resignation of B. S. Minhas, at that time the leading economist on the Indian Planning Commission. This signaled the impending economic collapse which led to the declaration of emergency in June 1975. His book, Planning and the Poor (New Delhi: S. Chand, 1974) takes on particular significance in the light of subsequent events.

[62] The clearest recent presentation of this model can be found in,

John Mellor, The New Economics of Growth (Ithaca: Cornell University Press, 1976). A two volume work by Sudhir Sen, Reaping the Green Revolution (New Delhi: Tata-McGraw Hill, 1975), A Richer Harvest (New Delhi: Tata-McGraw Hill, 1974), is a comprehensive statement of the problems and solutions. An excellent statistical statement on the Indian case can be found in, "A Report to the Nation on the Downtrodden," Monthly Commentary on Indian Economic Conditions, Indian Institute of Public Opinion, Annual Number, vol. 5, no. 5, (1973).

[63]See N. K. Nicholson, "Rural Development Policy in India: Elite Differentiation and the Decision-Making Process," (Dekalb: Center for Governmental Studies, Northern Illinois University, 1974) pp. 39-43).

[64]A good discussion of the "urban" focus of early agricultural planning in India can be found in C. H. Hanumantha Rao, "Agricultural Policy Under Three Plans," in N. Srinirasan, ed., Agricultural Administration in India (New Delhi: Indian Institute of Public Administration, 1969), pp. 116-19. See also M. Lipton, "India's Agricultural Performance: Achievements, Distortions, and Ideologies," in Agricultural Development in Developing Countries -- Comparative Experience (Bombay: Indian Society of Agricultural Economics, 1972), Chapter 4.

[65]See N. Luyks, "Rural Governing Institutions," in M. Blase, ed., Institutions in Agricultural Development (Ames: Iowa State University, 1971), Chapter 10; N. T. Uphoff & M. J. Esman, Local Organization for Rural Development: Analysis of Asian Experience (Ithaca: Rural Development Committee, Center for International Studies, 1974); D. E. Ashford, National Development and Local Reform (Princeton: Princeton University Press, 1967).

[66]See, for example, statements by Julius Nyerere, President of Tanzania, reprinted in Freedom and Socialism: A Selection from Writings and Speeches 1965-67 (London: Oxford University Press, 1968), pp. 324-25, 353-55.

[67]"As the review of ujamaa carried out under ARDS [African Rural Development Study] noted, "there are only limited formal procedures for local people to influence TANU [Tanganyikan African National Union, the ruling party] officials, leaving little more than good will to assure these officials will, in fact, protect peasant interests." Design of Rural Development, p. 153.

[68]Paul Collins, "Decentralization & Local Administration for Development in Tanzania," Africa Today, vol. 21 (Summer 1974): 25. In the same article Collins suggests that an exception to the concentration trend may be the interaction between local farmers and regional officials by means of Ujamaa Planning Teams which take officials to villages to assist in drawing up feasible and realistic development plans for the villages. Ibid., pp. 23, 25.

[69]See the discussion of farmer opposition to Tanzania's communalization of farming in Design of Rural Development, pp. 155-57.

[70]Chinese experience in this regard is instructive. See B. Stavis, "People's Communes and Rural Development in China" (Ithaca: Rural Development Committee, Center for International Studies, Cornell University, 1974); J. D. Pelzel, "The Economic Management of a Production Brigade in Post-Leap China," in W. E. Willmott, ed., Economic Organization in Chinese Society (Stanford: Stanford University Press, 1972), pp. 387-416.

[71]See R. E. Evanson & Y. Kislev, Agricultural Research and Productivity (New Haven: Yale University Press, 1975); Y. Hayami & V. W. Ruttan, Agricultural Development: An International Perspective (Baltimore: Johns Hopkins, 1971).

[72]Report of the Fertilizer Credit Committee of the Fertilizer Association of India (New Delhi: Fertilizer Association of India, 1968) pp. 92-96.

[73]P. L. Sankhayan, D. S. Sidhu, and P. S. Rangi, "Efficiency and Impact of Various Fertilizer Supply Systems on Production in Punjab," Indian Journal of Agricultural Economics 28 (October/December 1972): 77-84; R. I. Singh, Ram Kumar, & Sri Ram, "Impact of Input Supply Systems on Crop Production in District Moradabad," ibid., pp. 130-36; J. G. Ryan & K. B. Subramanyam, "Package of Practices Approach in Adaptation of HYV," Economic and Political Weekly. Review of Agriculture, (December 1975): pp. A 101-10.

[74]L. Nulty, The Green Revolution in West Pakistan (New York: Praeger, 1972).

[75]This neglect was corrected in the mid-sixties with the establishment of the Agricultural Prices Commission in the Ministry of Agriculture, which prepares cost of production and price recommendations seasonally for the Ministry. The Commission's cost of production calculations are generally disputed by farm organizations which feel they are too low. The Commission also appears to be of the opinion that within broad ranges, prices do not influence the allocation of acreage, input use, etc. For discussions of various aspects of this problem, see Raj Krishna, "Agricultural Price Policy and Economic Development," in H. M. Southworth & B. J. Johnston, Agricultural Development and Economic Growth (Ithaca: Cornell University Press, 1970), Chapter 13. Uma Lele is highly critical of government pricing policies in Foodgrain Marketing in India (Ithaca: Cornell University Press, 1971), pp. 220-23. That this is a widespread problem is argued by T. W. Schultz in "US Malinvestiments in Food for the World," reprinted in Agricultural Development in Developing Countries (Bombay: Indian Society of Agricultural Economics, 1972), Chapter 21.

[76]See N. K. Nicholson, "Local Institutions and Fertilizer Policy: The Lessons from India's Punjab and Gujerat States" (Paper presented to East-West Center Food Institute Conference, INPUTS June 7-17, 1976, Honolulu, Hawaii). Also, "Differential Responses to Technical Change in Gujerat and Punjab: An Analysis of Economic Political Differentiation in India" (Paper presented to American Political Science Association, Annual Convention, San Francisco, September 16, 1975).

[77]A good example is the Small Farmer Program, evolved in the late sixties. It was designed to direct federal resources into programs to help the smaller farmer. Discussions of the problems and programs can be found in V. R. Gaikwad, Small Farmers: State Policy and Program Implementation (Hyderabad: National Institute of Community Development, 1971); Rural Development for Weaker Sections, Report of a Seminar Sponsored by the Indian Society of Agricultural Economics and the Indian Institute of Management (Bombay: I.S.A.E., 1974).

[78]N. T. Uphoff & M. J. Esman, Local Organization for Rural Development: Analysis of Asian Experience (Ithaca: Rural Development Committee, Center for International Studies, Cornell University, 1974), pp. 63-75.

[79]P. J. Strangel & J. H. Allgood, "World Fertilizer Situation 1976-80" (Paper presented to Food Institute Conference, East-West Center, Honolulu, Hawaii, June 7-17, 1976).

[80]See U. K. Srivastava et al., Food Aid and International Economic Growth (Ames: Iowa State University, 1975).

[81]See, for example, W. D. Hopper, "The Development of Agriculture in Developing Countries," Scientific American, no. 235 (September 1976): 196-205.

[82]See J. Janick, C. H. Noller, & C. L. Rhykerd, "The Cycles of Plant and Animal Nutrition," Scientific American, no. 235 (September 1976): 74-87; Roger Revelle, "Food and Population," Scientific American, no. 231 (September 1974): 160-170.

[83]See N. Krishnaji, "Inter-Regional Disparities in Per Capita Production and Productivity of Foodgrains," Economic and Political Weekly (Special Number, August 1975): 1377; P. K. Bardhan, "On the Incidence of Poverty in Rural India of the Sixties," Economic and Political Weekly (Annual Number,

[84]There have been only a few attempts to relate the character of local politics to policy, and they are as yet somewhat primitive. See S. Hadden, Decentralization and Rural Electrification in Rajasthan, India (Ithaca: Rural Development Committee, Center for International Studies, Cornell University, 1974); R. N. Blue & Y. Junghare, "Political and Social Factors Associated with the Public Allocation of Agricultural Inputs in a Green Revolution

Area" (Minneapolis: University of Minnesota, Department of Political Science, 1973, mimeo); B. W. Coyer, "The Distribution of Rural Public Policy Goods in Rajasthan"

[85]Francine Frankel, "The Politics of the Green Revolution: Shifting Patterns of Peasant Participation in India and Pakistan," in T. J. Poleman & D. K. Freebain, eds., Food, Population and Employment (Ithaca: Cornell University Program on Science, Technology, and Society, Praeger Publishers, 1973), pp. 120-51; Jan Breman, Patronage and Exploitation (Berkeley: University of California Press, 1974).

[86]M. L. Dantwala, Poverty in India Then and Now 1870-1970 (Delhi: MacMillan, 1973).

[87]For India, see W. Ladejinsky, A Study on Tenurial Conditions in Package Districts (New Delhi: Planning Commission, 1965); Francine Frankel, "The Politics of the Green Revolution . . ."; Edgar Owens and Shaw, Development Reconsidered, pp. 86-91; W. Ladejinsky, "Agarian Reform in Asia: The Green Revolution and its Reform effects," in R. T. Shand, Ed., Technical Change in Asian Agriculture (Canberra: Australian National University, 1973) Chapter 12; John Mellor, The New Economics of Growth, Chapter 4; L. Nulty, The Green Revolution in Pakistan, pp. 25-40; Hiromitsu Kanepa, "Mechanization, Industrialization and Technological Change in Rural Pakistan," in R. T. Shand, Technical Change in Asian Agriculture, Chapter 9.

[88]John M. Cohen, "Effects of Green Revolution Strategies on Tenants and Small-Scale Landowners in the Chilalo Region of Ethiopia," Journal of Developing Areas, vol. 9 (April 1975); 340-41, 350-51.

[89]In Punjab, for example, farms of under two hectares constituted 17 percent of all holdings. In 1971, they increased in number until they constituted 57 percent of all holdings. N. K. Nicholson, "Local Institution and Fertilizer Policy . . .," p. 23.

[90]Hayami and Ruttan, Chapter 3. See also K. Polanyi, The Great Transformation (Boston: Beacon Press, 1960).

[91]A severe criticism of the recent role of government administration can be found in M. L. Dantwala, "From Stagnation to Growth: Relative Roles of Technology, Economic Policy and Agrarian Institutions," in R. T. Shand, ed., Chapter 13. See also N. K. Nicholson and Silawar Ali Shan, Basic Democracies and Rural Development in Pakistan (Ithaca: Rural Development Committee, Center for International Studies, Cornell University, 1974).

[92]Good discussions of the emergence of brokerage politics can be found in Richard Sisson, The Congress Party in Rajasthan (Berkeley: University of California Press, 1972); and S. Javed Burki, Agricultural Growth and Local Government in Punjab,

Pakistan (Ithaca: Rural Development Committee, Center for International Studies, Cornell University, 1974).

[93]See Integrated Rural Development Programme (Islamabad: Ministry of Food, Agriculture and Rural Development, Government of Pakistan, 1973).

[94]Cocayoc Declaration," Ceres (November-December 1974).

[95]K. Mannheim, Ideology and Utopia (New York: Harcourt, Brace & Co., 1936, Harvest Books ed.), p. 55; Clifford Geertz, "Ideology as a Cultural System," in David Apter, ed., Ideology and Discontent (Glencoe: Free Press, 1964), Chapter 1.

[96]See D. H. Meadows and D. L. Meadows, The Limits to Growth (New York: New American Library, 1972); H. S. D. Cole et al., Models of Doom (New York: Universe Books, 1973); M. Mesarovic and E. Peskel, Mankind at the Turning Point (New York: E. P. Dutton, 1974); E. F. Schumacher, Small is Beautiful (New York: Harper & Row, 1973).

[97]Garnett Hardin, "Living on a Lifeboat," Bioscience (October 1974): 561-68; "Tragedy of the Commons," Science (December 13, 1968): 1243-48; W. M. Murdoch and A. Oaten, "Population and Food: Metaphors and the Reality," Bioscience (September 1975): 561-67.

Some Methods to Improve Nutrition in the Developing Countries

PAUL-ANDRE FINOT

Some of the causes of malnutrition are man-inspired, whether because of cultural or social inclinations or out of ignorance. This often results in food adequate in quantity but not in quality. Other reasons are economic (one-third of the planet's population consumes 70 per cent of its animal proteins), ecological (droughts, floods), demographic, or concern public health. Some solutions proposed here include intelligent use of the scientific processes underlying the production of natural foodstuffs, better education and technology with the aid of international bodies, and self-help at the community level.

It was after the Second World War that an awareness of the problem of malnutrition in the world and of the slow rate of economic development in a large number of countries began to dawn. Aid to the Third World from rich countries, international organizations and private bodies (charitable institutions, scientific organizations and industry) has not reduced the gap which then existed between the highly industrialized countries, which are now living in the throw-away society, and the developing countries whose inhabitants (two-thirds of mankind) do not have enough to eat. Should we think of this as a failure or as a state of affairs which was to be expected in view of the magnitude of the task and the difficulties which it involves? There have of course been many successes at local level (introduction of new crops or of new food products), but these cover only a limited range of the needs which must be met or the reforms which must be carried out if the operation as a whole is to be successful. The primary condition for such success is the integration of measures to improve nutrition into a broader policy of economic, social and cultural development in the countries concerned, which could be given effective help by international as well as private bodies.

From **IMPACT OF SCIENCE ON SOCIETY**, Vol XXIV, No. 2, 1974, (124-132), reprinted by permission of the publisher, UNESCO, Paris.

Human beings must look to nature to supply their vital needs. Failure to supply these needs in full leads to two main forms of malnutrition, one connected with the quantity of food and the other with its quality .[1] When the problem is simply shortage of food, when the amount of food is insufficient to meet the requirements of the organism, the result is undernourishment. This is basically a calorie deficiency: the organism burns up its own tissues in order to compensate for the lack of calories in its food. This type of deficiency, known as protein-calorie malnutrition is characterized by the clinical symptoms of wasting disease (arrested growth, muscular atrophy and loss of weight, sometimes leading to death). It is to be seen in its most chronic form among the very poorest sections of the population, or, sporadically in time of actual famine, in the aftermath of wars or natural disasters, or in exceptionally unfavourable climatic conditions.

The other form of deficiency is of a qualitative nature: the diet is sufficiently rich in calories but does not contain adequate quantities of other essential nutrients such as proteins, essential fatty acids, vitamins, mineral salts and trace elements. The most common type is protein malnutrition which leads to kwashiorkor, the clinical symptoms of which are apathy, diarrhoea, the formation of cedemata, discolouration of the hair, de-pigmentation of the skin and mental retardation, sometimes irreversible. Acute kwashiorkor leads rapidly to death.

I. THE IMPORTANCE OF PROTEINS

The function of proteins in the diet is, on the one hand, to compensate for the wastage of proteins in the organism and, on the other hand, to build up new tissue in the organism in certain physiological conditions (growth, gestation, lactation, disease).[2] The proteins must be supplied in sufficient quantities but they must also meet certain requirements regarding their composition in amino acids. The need for essential amino acids, that is to say those which the organism cannot synthesize for itself (leucine, isoleucine, lysine, methionine, phenylalanine, threonine, tryptophane and valine) varies considerably, depending on the physiological condition of the organism. For example, a growing organism needs proteins with a higher content of essential amino acids than the adult organism does. Lysine in particular is essential for growth and must be present in large quantities in the food of babies and children, whereas relatively small quantities are required by an adult.

A well balanced food protein which contains all the essential amino acids in proportions which correspond to needs will be fully assimilated by the organism and will have maximum biological value. If one of the essential amino acids is not present in sufficient quantity to meet the organism's needs to the full, it becomes a 'limiting' amino acid: the biological value of the protein, which will now only be partly assimilated, will be reduced in consequence. Food of animal origin has been found to be richer in proteins than food of vegetable origin (meat, 49 per cent; powdered milk, 26 per cent, egg, 47 per cent; fish, 75 per cent; soya, 40 per cent; wheat, 12 per cent; maize, 10 per cent; rice, 8 per cent; manioc, 2 per cent). Moreover, animal proteins are better balanced than vegetable proteins, which are deficient in one or more essential amino acids -- methionine in soya and in all legumes, lysine in wheat, lysine and threonine in rice and tryptophane in maize -- which reduce their biological value. Groups whose diet is made up of products of animal origin therefore find it easier to meet their protein requirements than groups whose diet is basically vegetarian.

It is possible, however, to raise the biological value of vegetable proteins to the level of that of animal proteins either (a) by the artificial addition of the limiting amino acid (for example adding lysine to wheat) or (b) by a judicious combination of two vegetable products such that the deficiency of essential amino acids in the one is made good by the high content of the same amino acids in the other. For instance, the value of cereals which are deficient in lysine and rich in methionine will be greatly enhanced by the addition of legumes which have a high content of lysine and a low content of methionine. This is now a well-known nutritional principle which is applied wherever possible to improve the quality of vegetable proteins.[3,4]

II. CAUSES AND VICTIMS OF MALNUTRITION

Measures taken to prevent malnutrition in developing countries aim to ensure that the population receives an adequate supply of food but also to eradicate the various factors which are indirect causes of, or which encourage, malnutrition. These factors must be identified before effective methods of combating them can be chosen.

Geographical factors have a direct influence on food resources. The fertility of the soil, the nature of the terrain, latitude, altitude and the alternation of dry and rainy seasons are determining factors for crop and animal husbandry and necessarily impose restrictions on agricultural resources. The dire effects of malnutrition are, in fact, felt mainly in the most geographically disadvantaged regions in the tropical and subtropical zones which encircle our globe. These geographical factors cannot be changed except by improving the fertility of the soil and by irrigation.

Dietary customs which have taken root over the centuries in different countries are naturally conditioned by the potential resources of local agriculture and are therefore partly linked with geographical factors. They are also influenced by religious factors which make some foods taboo, by sociological factors and by a certain ignorance of the principles of nutrition. Thus in certain areas of the world, priority has been given to the cultivation of certain crops to the exclusion of others, the aim being quantity rather than quality or diversity: in Asia, for example, cereals at present supply 70-80 per cent of food requirements, while in Africa the cultivation of manioc, yams and taro, which have a high carbohydrate content and hardly any protein content, is increasing at the expense of vegetables which have a higher protein content but do not give such a high yield.

In the same way, it is customary in many regions to wean children with food based solely on cereals, which are deficient in the lysine that is essential for growth, to the exclusion of all other vegetable products. This is the reason for the majority of cases of malnutrition. It need hardly be recalled that a large part of India is vegetarian for religious reasons, a fact which also prevents Moslems from eating pork. Similarly, eggs are taboo in certain parts of Africa, as are flatfish and crustaceans in other parts of the world. Thus valuable and sometimes very important sources of protein-rich food are neglected.

These dietary customs must be treated with consideration as they are an integral part of the culture and civilization concerned. The less developed the cuisine the more important these customs are. Any attempt to modify them challenges a set of established values with social, cultural or religious significance. In eating, man seeks a certain psychological satisfaction, a feeling of security and well-being which he experiences when eating traditional food with which he has always been familiar, rather than a biological value corresponding to his physiological needs. Success in introducing new means of nourishment will depend to a large extent on the changing of such customs, and priority should clearly be given to methods which call for as little change in them as possible.

Socio-economic factors are among the most obvious. The problem of malnutrition is not, in fact, a problem of the lack of food or protein but rather a problem of distribution, which is carried out on the basis of economic criteria. Statistically, the world production of protein averages 70 grammes per person per day (including 20 grammes of animal protein); but distribution is such that developed countries consume much more then economically developing countries and this is particularly true of animal protein. One-third of the world's population eats 70 per cent of its animal protein. This imbalance in distribution among the different countries is repeated within each country, as the poorest sections of the population do not have the resources necessary to obtain foodstuffs, and within an even smaller unit, the family itself, where the adult generally serves himself first.

Paradoxically, certain countries export part of their production of animal protein which could be used on the spot if the standard of living were higher or if there were an adequate market or distribution system. In Brazil and in certain African countries meat is exported from areas where the population is suffering from malnutrition because it is too expensive. Egypt, India and Pakistan have developed thriving industries to export deep-frozen shrimps as there is neither a demand nor a market for these commodities in these countries themselves. Peru, which has no network for distributing fresh fish in the interior, is the world's largest exporter of fish meal.

If the standard of living were raised, distribution networks extended and an increasing proportion of the population integrated to the economic market, more people would have access to the 'nobler' foodstuffs.

Demographic factors: a characteristic feature of developing countries is the rapid rise in population. Hygiene and medical care (particularly vaccination) have greatly reduced infant mortality without, however, affecting the birth rate, which is always very high in poor countries. This population explosion leads to increased demand for food in countries where resources are more often than not limited, a phenomenon which tends to reduce still further the amount of food available per inhabitant. The arrival of a new child in a family raises the family's food consumption only very slightly and this naturally affects the other children, who in general eat only what the adults leave them.

Malnutrition is most likely to be prevalent in areas with a high population density, such as Asia, where the land is given over to high-yielding crops leaving little room for the cultivation of vegetables or raising of livestock which would balance the protein intake. A further factor to be mentioned is the drift of rural populations to the towns, swelling the numbers of unemployed and unfortunates who live in shanty towns. Any measure to reduce the birth rate and maintain the rural population would considerably reduce the percentage of undernourished.

III. REMEDIES FOR MALNUTRITION

It is often assumed when talking about malnutrition in the Third World that it could easily be eliminated by distributing the surplus foodstuffs of richer countries, generously offered by charitable bodies or sold at reduced prices by certain governments for political ends. Such measures can only be a temporary expedient. In the long term, the problem of malnutrition must be solved by the countries themselves and must be the task of the governments responsible. They can be assisted in this task by richer countries or the Specialized Agencies of the United Nations, such assistance taking the form not of charity but of a lasting contribution in the field of science, technology and education. General measures in the field of public health and education and more specific measures to improve the traditional diet or to introduce new foods are required if the situation is to be remedied.

Rehabilitation Centres

     One method of combating malnutrition is to set up nutritional
rehabilitation centres whose objectives are twofold. These are (a)
to treat children suffering from malnutrition by supplying them
with their required daily ration of food and (b) to teach mothers
to give their children and the whole of their family the balanced
diet which they need. These centres could be organized to deal
with children suffering from simple cases of malnutrition as
outpatients and to provide a longer period of attention for those
requiring sustained clinical treatment. The establishment of such
centres involves considerable expense, as large amounts of
equipment and teams of specialists are required; part of the labour
is very often supplied by the mothers themselves, who help with
routine chores and looking after the patients while at the same
time receiving training in hygiene and dietetics. Such centres
already exist in many countries, including Colombia, Haiti,
Guatemala and Uganda, and have an important educational role to
play.

Measures To Improve Public Health

     In most regions where malnutrition affects large communities,
it is often accompanied by and sometimes due to endemic disease,
unhygienic living conditions and inattention to personal hygiene.
Such conditions are mainly to be found in rural areas, far from the
towns, where there are few qualified medical staff, and in shanty
towns. In addition to measures to improve nutrition, these
communities require programmes of health education and preventive
measures against such diseases as smallpox, diptheria, measles and
tuberculosis. This is one of the tasks which the World Health
Organization has set itself, and it is working in cooperation with
other international agencies -- the Food and Agriculture
Organization (FAO) and the United Nations Children's Fund
(Unicef) -- to give governments technical assistance in preparing
education programmes, food policies and vaccination campaigns.

Breast Feeding

     In developing countries, kwashiorkor is in most cases a
disease which affects children between 1 and 3 years old who are
being weaned, and the earlier weaning takes place the sooner it
strikes. Mother's milk supplies a considerable amount of essential
nutrients which are not provided by traditional weaning foods. It

now appears that breast-feeding is gradually being abandoned for reasons connected with the changing status of women, their emancipation and their sharing of the role of breadwinner, which means that they are not always able to breast-feed their babies. The abandonment of breast-feeding, which is quite acceptable in industrialized countries where baby foods have so many advantages and are so easy to use, is now beginning to occur in developing countries where the attitude of women in industrialized nations is being copied with a time lag of several years.

The introduction of artificial feeding in certain countries has so many disadvantages, both economic (high price of milk), hygienic (bacteriological contamination of meals) and educational (difficulty in making mothers understand the instructions) that it seems much more sensible to reinstate and return to the natural process of breast-feeding. In this way the child receives the most suitable food, absolute sterility is ensured and an irreplaceable emotional bond is established between mother and child.

The Improvement Of Agriculture

The battle to eliminate malnutrition can be won only if agricultural resources are improved, first, to make good the present shortage of balanced foods and secondly to meet the ever-increasing demand for food resulting from the population explosion. Efforts should be concentrated on two aspects: (a) increased production of traditional foodstuffs and (b) increased production of new strains of cereals (wheat, rice and maize) which have a higher protein content, give a higher yield and are more resistant to disease and difficult climatic conditions. Unfortunately this increase is most necessary in countries where the soil is least fertile and agricultural techniques most primitive.

It can only be achieved through political measures (agrarian reform) and the application of techniques (such as melioration, the use of fertilizers, irrigation and mechanization) which require the assistance of engineers, agronomists and nutrition experts. The 'green revolution' resulting from such measures has enabled several countries to increase their food-producing potential considerably (Pakistan and India), sometimes enabling them to supply all their own needs (Philippines) and sometimes to produce enough to export part of their production (Iran). But these results cannot be achieved without changing the agricultural habits and practices of the rural population and this means that a considerable effort must be put into training.

IV. TECHNOLOGY ASSOCIATED WITH NEW PROTEIN-RICH FOODSTUFFS

The manufacture of protein-rich products and the development of new foods for human consumption call for the application of a very wide range of technologies, first to produce the protein and, second, to manufacture a food on the basis of this protein. The technological processes used for the extraction and purification of proteins include the following:

Extraction with solvents (removal of lipids from meal produced from oilseed plants and fish meal; removal of gossypol, a toxic polyphenol, from cotton meal).

Heat treatments (cooking, sterilization, destruction of trypsine inhibitors in legumes).

Extraction in aqueous medium of variable acidity (elimination of soluble substances such as the flatulent sugars in soya, separation of proteins at their points of electrical neutrality, making the protein soluble).

Hydrolytic treatment with acids, bases or even enzymes (extraction of the nucleic acids from single-cell proteins, improvement of protein solubility); drying processes.

All these different processes are used to prepare products with a varying content of protein and varying functional properties which may make them more or less attractive to potential users.

There exists in addition a whole range of chemical and microbiological methods which make it possible to manufacture amino acids, particularly those which are most often limiting and which, if added to the diet, will balance the protein intake. These protein-rich products can be used in various ways and can be incorporated in different types of foods whose success will depend on their acceptability to the general public and the ease with which they can be used.

In order to reduce the cost price, the food may simply be a dry mixture of various ingredients which the consumer must cook himself. Any given product will naturally be more acceptable if it has been precooked, particularly in the case of children's foods. Cereal products will most often be roller-dried but production in powder form is preferable for milk substitutes, as this increases their solubility.

Where adults are concerned, the texture of food is extremely important and the process of heat extrusion can be considered a turning point in the improvement of foods based on protein enriched cereals. Finally, we might mention a much more sophisticated process, the spinning of protein concentrates, using a technique long known to the textile industry which makes it possible to obtain products with the texture of meat. The choice of the protein substance to be used will depend on its organoleptic properties and also on its functional properties (solubility, capacity to absorb moisture and emulsifying and beating properties, and faculty to combine with cereal products) -- all of which should be gone into thoroughly.

V. POLICY OF ACTION

Efforts to eliminate malnutrition can be successful only if they are accompanied by economic, political and educational measures at government level;

To impose, at national level, programmes to fortify the traditional diet, and to assume responsibiity for a large part of the resulting costs.

To increase production of protein-rich food crops (agrarian reform, green revolution) and foods of animal origin (meat, milk, fish) by subsidizing the means of production (tractors, seed fisheries) and transport and storage facilities.

To encourage production, at national level, of new and cheap, protein-rich foods by making special arrangements with food industries, which will contribute their technical know-how and commercial efficiency.

To promote the new foods among all sections of the population, particularly the poorest sections, using methods of distribution and subsidies which vary according to the degree of poverty and needs (children, pregnant women or nursing mothers).

To train specialists in food science (agronomy, nutrition, food technology).

To increase the purchasing power of the poorest sections of the population in order to integrate them as quickly as possible into the economic market.

When new products are introduced or food habits changed, particular attention must be paid to the problems of marketing. In order to have the best chances of success a new product must have an advantage over the others, either as regards its price or one of its properties (quality, ease of use, taste, functional properties), of which the consumer must be made specially aware. It must also be efficiently presented, distributed and promoted. Its chances of success will depend as much on its suitability to the needs, desires and habits of the public as on methods of promotion (packaging, press and radio advertising, sales demonstration, etc.), distribution and sale.

It should give the consumer the same feeling of satisfaction, well being and security as his traditional food, and at the same

time the certain knowledge that it satisfies his physiological
needs.

VI. FIRST STEPS TOWARDS SUCCESS

In spite of the hard work and enthusiasm of devoted and
resourceful staff, there have been many setbacks in the struggle
against malnutrition in various parts of the world, but there have
also been many successes in countries where the governments, with
the help of international or private agencies, have taken the job
seriously and have made it a national responsibility.

Let us take a few examples. In Asia, the green revolution,
involving the introduction of new varieties of cereals, has created
a valuable source of proteins. In Latin America a protein-rich
product composed of cereals and oil-seed meal and balanced by the
addition of free amino acids has been introduced. Soybean milk,
containing 2.5 per cent of proteins, has been very readily accepted
by the population of Hong Kong, where soya is a traditional food,
and is competing on the market with the most popular soft drinks.
In India modern bread enriched with vitamins, mineral salts and
lysine, has been produced by State bakeries for some time. In
Algeria, a baby food has been successfully introduced on the market
thanks to effective co-operation between the State, international
agencies (FAO and Unicef) and a private firm, while in Mexico
private enterprise encouraged by the government, has, by improving
stockraising methods and introducing a new breed of cattle,
succeeded in creating a dairy industry in a very disadvantaged
area.

There are many examples of local successes, but they usually
solve only one aspect of the problem of malnutrition. In this
field, every avenue must be explored and past failures as well as
successes can be of help in solving, in its various local
manifestations, this worldwide problem.

The Victims Of Malnutrition

Malnutrition, resulting from the factors described in the
article, could affect most countries but it is prevalent in the
countries of Latin America, Africa and South-East Asia, where the
traditional carbohydrate-based diet (maize, manioc, rice) is
lacking in proteins. Certain groups of the population, the
'vulnerable' ones, however, are more affected than others. These
are infants at weaning, the poor, the sick, pregnant women and
nursing mothers.

Unless the family is well-off and can obtain milk for it the
weanling is the easiest prey to kwashiorkor. As it grows, the
child's needs increase but the supply of mother's milk diminishes.
This is more often than not replaced by foods which have a high

starch content (cereals or manioc) but too few proteins, mineral salts and vitamins to meet its needs. The earlier weaning takes place the more serious the effects of this deficiency.

A distinction must be drawn within the impoverished sectors of the population between rural population groups living in particularly disadvantaged areas with limited agricultural resources and urban groups living in shanty towns where unemployment and poverty are rife; the latter do not even have a patch of ground which will supply their minimum requirements. Among such groups, which in normal circumstances have just enough to survive, disease (measles in particular among children), an addition to the family or the need to breast-feed a new-born baby, which all call for a higher food intake, accentuating even further the effects of malnutrition. It is mainly for the sake of these vulnerable groups that effective measures must be taken as soon as possible.

Additives In Traditional Foodstuffs

One very attractive idea is to improve the nutritional value of the traditional basically vegetarian diet of people suffering from malnutrition, first, by adding protein to foodstuffs in which they are almost totally lacking (manioc, yams, taro) or which have a low protein content (cereals) and, second, by adding the necessary amino acids to unbalanced protein foodstuffs (cereals, legumes).

The methods used to introduce these additives differ according to circumstances and possibilities. It is easy enough to add lysine to flour intended for making bread. Rice presents a more difficult problem since a considerable portion of the additive may be lost in the water in which it is boiled; special techniques have had to be developed to overcome this difficulty, but specialized plant is therefore required, which means that the peasant consuming his own produce cannot benefit from such an installation. In the latter case, or where this kind of plant is not available, 'vehicles' such as seasoning or beverages such as tea may be used to balance the diet by providing the necessary vitamins, mineral salts or amino acids.

It is often preferable to enrich the traditional diet with products which are rich in proteins. This necessitates the manufacture of such edibles, and whether or not they are actually used will depend on their functional and organoleptic (sense-provoking) qualities and on the extent to which they are accepted by the population. It therefore follows that new protein-rich foodstuffs should be sought which have organoleptic and biological properties which meet human requirements. Using as a basis the detailed criteria recommended by an FAO committee of experts, a number of sources of protein have been developed or are being developed with a view to improving the food supply; these may be of vegetable, animal or micro-organic origin.

Leguminous and oilseed plants are the plants richest in protein. Leguminous plants yield seeds which contain either starch (peas, beans) or fats (soya)[5] or simply leaves (lucerne)[6] from which proteins can be extracted. Oilseed plants (soya, groundnuts, sesame, cotton, sunflower), once their oil has been extracted, yield a cheap by-product which is rich in protein. This can be used for human consumption as long as the method of extraction used conforms to the requisite hygiene and safety standards and the protein is of good biological value. Industrial techniques make it possible to obtain crude fractions (de-fatted and concentrated meal and isolates) which are rich in protein and therefore very easy to use.

A Good Source Of Protein

Certain products of animal origin which are not at present used as much as they might be could provide a useful source of good protein. In countries with a surplus of fish which is not distributed inland owing to difficulties of conservation or the lack of a distribution network, or where the fish caught is of little market value, the manufacture of fish meal can make a most valuable supplementary contribution to the national diet. Dried skim milk, a by-product of butter manufacture in countries which produce large quantities of milk, is often used as animal feed. It is the cheapest source of animal protein and, because of its high biological value, is used in the preparation of many new protein-rich foods.

Similarly, the use of whey, a by-product of cheese-making which is a contributory factor in the pollution of water in the vicinity of cheese factories, could in the future provide a substantial amount of proteins of very high biological value. Unfortunately these dairy by-products are not available in the countries which need them most and must therefore be imported.

Finally, a source of proteins on which many hopes for the future nourishment of mankind are pinned is that provided by micro-organisms[7]: yeasts, bacteria, mycelium and algae, more commonly referred to as single-cell proteins. Cultures of yeasts, bacteria and mycelium require the use of ferments in which the micro-organisms develop on the basis of various substrates (hydrocarbons, alcohol, methane) providing carbon, and ammonia, providing nitrogent. The great advantage of this method is the speed at which these organisms grow and the small area needed for the cultures, the output per unit of surface area being extremely high. The cost price of protein manufactured by these methods will depend partly on the cost of the substrate used and partly on the degree of purity of the protein extracted.

Algae And Sunlight

Proteins from this unconventional source are at present being used, with a relatively high level of impurities, as animal feedstuffs. If they are to be used for human consumption, these will have to be (a) much researched by biologists to prove that they are entirely harmless and (b) much researched by technologists to reduce the cost price and there will have to be a fundamental psychological change since at present there is a certain wariness about this type of food.

The production of algae, which use sunlight and carbon dioxide, requires quite a large cultivable surface in order to obtain as much sunlight as possible and is only feasible in countries with much sunshine. But one point in the favour of algae is the fact that they have been used for a very long time by the people living around Lake Chad who gather the blue algae (spirulina maxima) which grow there, and by the Aztecs who also used the algae which grew in the lakes of Central America; recently a processing plant for the extraction of these algae was opened on Lake Texcoco in Mexico. In this case, of course, there are practically no psychological barriers to the use of these algae -- quite the contrary in fact, as the Mexicans regard it as a link with the past, a legacy of the civilization of their ancestors.

NOTES

[1]McCANCE, R.; WIDDOWSON, E. (eds.) Calorie deficiencies and protein deficiencies. London, J. & A. Churchill, 1968.

[2]LAWRIE, R. (ed.) Protein as human food. Westport, Conn., Avi Publishing, 1970.

[3]BRESSANI, R.; ELIAS, L.; GOMEZ-BRENES, R. Improvement of protein quality by amino-acid and protein supplementation. In: B. J. Bigwood (ed.), Protein and amino-acid functions, vol. 11. London, Pergamon Press, 1972: Oxford, pergamon Press, 1972.

[4]SCRIMSHAW, N.; ALTSCHUL, A. (ed.) Amino-acid fortification of protein foods. Cambridge, Mass., MIT Press, 1971.

[5]WOLF, W.; COWAN, J. (ed.) Soy beans as a food source. London, Butterworth, 1971.

[6]PIRIE, N. (ed.) Leaf proteins, Oxford, Blackwell Scientific, 1971; Edinburgh, Blackwell Scientific, 1971. _____. Strategies to close the protein gap. New scientist, vol. 59, no. 857, 2 August 1973.

[7]MAURON, J. Technology of protein synthesis and protein-rich foods, Nutr. Diet., no. 18, 1973, p. 24-44.

To Delve More Deeply

ABBOTT, J. The efficient use of world protein supplies. In: J. Porter and B. Rolls (eds), Protein in Human nutrition. London, Academic Press, 1973.

JALIL, M.; TAHIR, W. World supplies of plant proteins. In: Porter and Rolls (eds.), op. cit.

MANOCHA. S. Malnutrition and retarded human development. Springfield, Ill., Charles C. Thomas, 1972.

MILNER, M. (ed.) Protein-enriched cereal foods for world needs. St. Paul, Minn., American Association of Cereal Chemists, 1969.

STILLINGS, B. World supplies of animal protein. In: Porter and Rolls (eds.), op. cit.

TREMOLIERES, J. Nutrition and underdevelopment. In: S. Margen (ed.), Progress in human nutrition. Vol. 1. Westport, Conn., Avi Publishing, 1971.

WORGAN, J. World supplies of proteins from unconventional sources. In: Porter and Rolls, op. cit.

Possible Consequences of Nutritional Improvements for the Economic Development

HANS-RIMBERT HEMMER

The disastrous drought that afflicted the Sahel zone in the early seventies and caused an acute food shortage in this region brought home the unsatisfactory state of nutrition in many developing countries to the politicians who are concerned with development problems. The state of nutrition in a country is essentially identical with the food consumption of the population in that country. Its scale is normally quantified by measurement of the calories and nutrients (such as protein, vitamins and minerals) contained in the consumed food.

A juxtaposition of the information on the nutritional situation gleaned by such quantification with corresponding data on nutritional needs provides evidence of the extent of malnutrition in the developing countries. There can be quantitative as well as qualitative malnutrition. Quantitative malnutrition is a state in which the available food does not meet the indispensable energy requirements. Qualitative malnutrition is a situation in which the amount of food measures up to the indispensable energy requirements but does not correspond in composition, and especially in its content of protein, vitamins and minerals, to the physiological needs.

It was indicated by estimates in the early sixties already that about 20% of the population in the developing countries was suffering from quantitative malnutrition, 33% went short of protein and 50% showed general signs of nutritional deficiencies. At the present time it is thought that the food supply of 1-1.5 billion people is inadequate; over 82% of the undernourished population lives in Asia or Africa. Among children malnutrition is so common that, according to World Health Organization (WHO) estimates, it affects every other child under five years of age in the developing countries.[1]

From **INTERECONOMICS**, July/August 1979, (185-189), reprinted by permission of the publisher.

I. CONCEPT OF ECONOMIC DEVELOPMENT

A definition of the concept of economic development is offered here first to facilitate the examination of the effects of nutritional improvements on economic development.[2] Cardinal to the concept of economic development is the ability of individual members of the community to dispose of goods and services which have an influence on the standard of living which in turn depends upon the extent to which certain needs can be satisfied. Relevant needs are in the view of the UN: Health, food and nutrition, instruction and education, employment and working conditions, housing conditions, social security, clothing, recreation and entertainment, and human liberties. Within these categories of needs a special priority is given to health, food and nutrition, housing conditions and clothing; they are considered "basic needs".[3]

The accessibility of goods and services to the population at large is usually measured by the per-capita income while the distribution of this per-capita income among the individual members of the community is expressed in terms of the Gini coefficient. The concept of economic development is thus capable of precise definition as a time sequence in which the per-capita income of a country rises while the interpersonal income distribution does not "worsen". In view of the very marked inequality of the income distribution in almost all developing countries it may be furthermore assumed that a "worsening" of the income distribution involves an intensification of the income concentration (that means: a higher Gini coefficient). It follows therefrom that the concept of economic development involves a process in which the rise of the per-capita income is attended by at least a constant but as far as possible a decreasing Gini coefficient.

The relative income concentration as reflected by the Gini coefficient has to be taken into account for a consideration of the distribution aspect but does not cover it adequately by itself, for the comprehensive analyses of interpersonal income distribution carried out since the beginning of the seventies have revealed absolute poverty in many developing countries of a sometimes horrifying extent. This absolute poverty is marked by the existence of degrading living conditions including disease; illiteracy, demoralization and also malnutrition; often the victims of this poverty are not even able to satisfy their basic needs.

Seeing that the problem of absolute poverty cannot be gauged adequately by means of the Gini coefficient, the demand for the elimination of absolute poverty must be included in the list of development policy objectives, at least as a complement to the demand for more even interpersonal income distribution. The concept of economic development may thus be defined as follows:

Economic development is a process in which the rise of the per-capita income is attended by an attenuation of absolute poverty; the relative income concentration must not become more acute at the same time. The rise of the per-capita income is to be defined in this context as the growth objective and the attenuation of absolute poverty and the "improvement" of the interpersonal income distribution as the distribution objective. The growth and distribution objectives together present the economic development objective.[4]

II. PRIMARY VERSUS SECONDARY EFFECTS OF IMPROVED NUTRITION

When analyzing the relationship between nutrition and economic development, economists have mostly focused on the question how the state of nutrition has changed in consequence of economic development: Nutrition was taken to be the dependent, economic development the independent variable. Outlays on nutritional improvements were according to this concept a reaction to the economic development process and not designed to speed up the development. The economic analysis thus concentrated on the "passive role of nutrition"; little thought was given to the question of the "active role of nutrition", i.e., to possibilities of influencing the development process by measures of nutrition policy.[5]

The available results of empirical inquiries reveal however a large measure of malnutrition in the countries of the Third World, and as adequate nutrition merits a very high priority among the basic needs, the state authorities are faced with the task of taking measures for an improvement of the state of nutrition so as to raise the standard of living of the inadequately fed populations directly. This objective of nutrition policy is according to Mellor from an ethical-humanitarian point of view of such relevance that all other considerations must be subordinated to it.[6]

This line of argument however ignores the fact that nutrition is one basic human need but not the only one. The situation in regard to the other basic needs -- health, housing conditions and clothing -- deserves equal consideration. Measures to improve nutrition may possibly have negative effects on the satisfaction of other basic needs, with the result that a conflict situation may arise between individual basic needs.

There is also the possibility of an improvement of the state of nutrition in the initial period being detrimental to an improvement in later periods. Measures for an improvement of the food situation are definitely consumption-promoting measures. If the financing of such measures handicaps investive measures which would raise the standard of living in subsequent periods, such an intertemporal conflict of objectives may well arise.

The potential conflicts between these objectives cannot be indicated and possibly eliminated, by reference only to the primary effects of improved nutrition. The secondary effects of such measures on the economic development which may contribute indirectly to changes involving standards must also be explored.

For the comprehension of these secondary effects it should be pointed out once more that the availability of goods and services is cardinal to the concept of economic development. These goods and services are the result of productive activities[7]: Productively applicable resources are brought together in production processes taking place in the country concerned, and the goods and services becoming available are the result of these production processes.

Labour, natural resources and capital are regarded as the major groups of production factors. The stocks of natural resources being essentially constant, any changes in factor stocks of relevance to development are normally limited to the labour and capital factors. Economic development thus presupposes an increase in the availability of productively deployable labour and capital. The term capital stands in this context for that portion of the production of previous periods which contributes to the attainment of production in the period under review. It consists of real capital (such as buildings, mechanical equipment, infrastructure) as well as of human capital, in which term are subsumed all the human capabilities generated in the course of production --the "produced capabilities" which include in particular the education and training acquired by the workforce and the level of technical knowledge prevailing in a country.

To determine the influence of nutrition on economic development the question has to be asked what effect an improved state of nutrition has on the availability and input of the three factor complexes which have been distinguished here -- labour, human capital and real capital. The answer to this question will show which secondary growth and distribution effects arise as a result of measures of nutrition policy.

III. EFFECTS ON THE MANPOWER POTENTIAL

To begin with, the effects of an improved state of nutrition on the quantitative aspects of the workforce, i.e., the manpower potential, will be analyzed.[8] If the available manpower potential is measured in workhours, a change of the available labour can take the form of a change in the number of persons able to work or of their average productive capabilities per hour.

To go by the hitherto available empirical inquiries it may be assumed that an improvement of the state of nutrition tends to lower the birth rate but the average life span may be expected to increase because the improved nutrition leads to a substantial decline especially of infant mortality; this second effect is definitely more potent than the first one so that despite falling birth rates more children will live to working age. The average working life is lengthened at the same time. The numbers of those fit for work will therefore rise persistently owing to nutritional factors.

An improvement of the state of nutrition will furthermore have the effect of increasing the average capacity of the population of working age to perform productive work -- measured in working hours per person -- for the physical capacity for work and the working morale depend in great measure upon the state of nutrition; a certain minimum calorie intake is indispensable for 100% efficiency, and if this requirement is not met, the worker is incapable of persistent activity -- there will be major interruptions. It follows that a larger calorie intake reduces the number of required breaks and thereby increases the number of potential working hours.

Not only the amount of available calories but the qualitative composition of the food intake, especially the supply of protein, vitamins and minerals, is of considerable importance for physical fitness: A deficiency of these nutrients often leads to illness which sometimes results in considerable loss of working time which can be curtailed by minimization of the qualitative malnutrition. A consistent nutrition policy has indeed often resulted in more persistent improvements of the state of health than have traditional measures of health policy (such as provision of more physicians or hospitals) as improved nutrition is a protection against many diseases or speeds recuperation. In either case is the potential labour supply increased.

The development effects of this nutrition-related increase of the potential labour supply to the economy depend essentially on the possibilities for its productive deployment. In the case of a production function with limited substitutional factors, which corresponds largely to the production-technical reality in the developing countries, such productive labour deployment depends upon adequate availability of the required complementary factors -- human capital, real capital and natural resources.

The unemployment prevailing in many countries suggests that this factor conjuncture obtains only very rarely. It is easily forgotten however that unemployment in one sector may coincide with an at least temporary scarcity of labour in another sector (e.g. in agriculture during harvest time); in such a situation the partial labour market imbalances cannot cancel out because of the dualistic structure of the countries concerned and in particular because of intersectoral immobilities. It has also to be borne in mind that a large part of the overt unemployment in developing countries concerns school-leavers who have certain ideas about their careers which cannot (yet) be realized in these countries and refuse to enter supposedly inferior occupations.[9] Unemployed of this type do not normally compete with the labour of the groups affected by undernourishment and malnutrition: The so far available results of empirical inquiries seem to prove on the contrary that the employment problem in the developing countries, like the problem of absolute poverty, is by and large a rural problem. The covert unemployed in the rural areas in particular are likely to benefit from measures of nutrition policy. Nutritional improvements may be counted upon to have positive effects on employment because the thesis relating to the (in most developing countries dominant) covert unemployment calls for qualification under the described aspects of quantitative and qualitative malnutrition: The physical condition of the workers is often such that they cannot work effectively for more than a relatively short time each day; a greater working effort is made impossible by their inadequate nutritional state. Such people have often full-time jobs but do in fact little work.[10] An improvement of the nutritional situation may have an impact not only on the potential labour supply but on the human and real capital resources of the country concerned. The repercussions of nutritional improvements on the capital resources must therefore be considered before definitive statements can be made concerning the employment prospects for the additional labour becoming available due to nutritional factors.

IV. CONSEQUENCES FOR HUMAN CAPITAL RESOURCES

Inadequate equipment with human capital is regarded by several authors as the crucial reason for the underdevelopment of the developing countries. Human capital is in the main created in two ways -- by educational and training measures and by the assimilation of experience in the course of productive activities ("learning by doing"). An improved nutritional situation can have positive effects on both these forms of human capital generation and thus help to overcome a cardinal bottleneck in the development process.

Improved nutrition is known to increase the capacity for mental work markedly.[11] The efficiency of investments in education and training can be enhanced by it: The impairment of the intelligence, receptivity and application of individuals as a result of malnutrition and the effects of illness-induced absenteeism lead to suboptimal use of the capital which has been invested in the education sector because the training results attainable under such conditions compare unfavourably with those which could be obtained under better nutritional conditions. Malnutrition is also partly responsible for the sometimes extremely high failure rates; courses have to be taken a second time and other applicants have to be disappointed. Illness and infant mortality due to malnutrition are also reflected by a high non-completion rate, and even if the stage of education is successfully completed, it may have been in vain because of high mortality rates; as far as the economy is concerned, the investment may have to be written off as a "preproduction loss". This is why in many developing countries investments in education do not become fully effective until adequate nutritional conditions have been created. Measures to improve the state of nutrition may thus have a positive effect on the accumulation of human capital in the countries concerned by inducing productivity gains in the sphere of education and training.

They may also be expected to speed the accumulation of human capital through their effect on the ability to learn. The greater average life expectancy has the result of longer average stays in the production process while temporary working-time losses due to illness are reduced. The workers thus acquire more experience and more human capital is accumulated than would be the case were the state of nutrition not improved. Moreover, the nutrition-related increase of mental capabilities may be expected to lead to improved learning processes, with additional gains of human capital.

V. ACCUMULATION OF REAL CAPITAL

In conclusion the effects on the formation of real capital will be discussed. As pointed out, an improved state of nutrition results in increased productivity of health service investments and of educational and training investments. If the expenditure in these areas is maintained, the effects on the potential labour supply and the accumulation of human capital will be as described. It is however possible that the increased productivity in the health and education/training areas will lead to the diversion to other sectors of part of the resources previously devoted to them. Insofar as this acts as a brake on the increase of the potential labour supply and human capital it will now be possible to step up the formation of real capital. Whether and to what extent an improved state of nutrition will have positive effects on the formation of real capital depends on the attitude of the institutions concerned with development policy. Whether they react to nutrition-related productivity gains in the health, education and training areas by factor diversion can only be established by examination of concrete cases.

To sum up: Economic development can be influenced by nutritional improvements in many ways. These effects on development relate both to growth and to income distribution. Both can be improved by nutritional improvements. The first effect is a higher quantity and quality of available production factors. If this larger or better factor supply is used productively, it will result in production increases leading to faster economic growth. Distributional improvements will occur at the same time because improvements of the state of nutrition will be felt primarily by the population groups at the lower end of the income scale which are in many cases still in a state of absolute poverty. Improvements in income distribution may also occur if the nutrition-related increase of the potential labour supply results in a higher level of actual employment as work is the only possible source of income available to the bulk of the population in developing countries.

Ideal would be a factor conjuncture in which the effects of nutritional improvements on the human and real capital create those job opportunities which are needed to provide employment for the nutrition-induced increase of the labour supply. A kind of "Say's law of nutrition-related increase in employment" would apply to such a situation. But even if this full compensation is not obtained, and improvement of the state of nutrition still meets by virtue of its positive effects on growth and distribution the criteria which have to be satisfied to qualify a measure as "promoting development".

In the face of these development-promoting results one must not overlook however the social costs involved in nutritional improvements. These costs arise because an improved state of nutrition can normally be attained only through reallocation of the available production factors. The production of other goods and services will decline in this case. It is this decline of production which, measured at economic scarcity prices for the goods and services concerned, constitutes the social cost of the nutritional improvements.

Whether the improvement of the state of nutrition on balance accelerates the economic growth and/or improves the income distribution can in the final analysis only be indicated by a comparison of these costs with the social benefits as described in this article. Empirical inquiries[12] warrant however the conjecture that the internal rate of return of many items of expenditure undertaken in order to improve the nutritional situation is, at least in countries with significant malnutrition, certainly not lower than the rates of return which calculations show to prevail for investments for instance in the education sector. Spending on food -- though traditionally treated as consumption -- can therefore be in some measure more productive from a national economic point of view than a large variety of investment outlays.

NOTES

[1] Cf. H.-R. Hemmer, Der Einfluß der Ernahrung . . ., ibid.

[2] On the following cf. H.-R. Hemmer, Wirtschaftsprobleme der Entwicklungslander. Eine Einfuhrung (Economic problems of the developing countries. An introduction). Munich 1978, Chapter A.

[3] Various authors still include education/instruction and employment in the basic human needs. Cf., e. g., D. Schwefel, Grundbedurfnisse und Entwicklungspolitik (Basic needs and development policy), Baden-Baden 1978.

[4] Cf. H.-R. Hemmer, Zur Problematik der gesamtwirtschaftlichen Zielfunktion in Entwicklungslandern (On the problems of the general economic objective function in developing countries), 2nd edition, Saarbrucken 1978.

[5] Cf. K.-H. Lemnitzer, Ernahrungssituation und wirtschaftliche Entwicklung (State of nutrition and economic development), Saarbrucken 1977, p. 14ff.

[6] Cf. J.W. Mellor, Nutrition and Economic Growth, in: A. Berg, N.S. Scrimshaw, D.L. Call (eds.), Nutrition, National Development, and Planning, Cambridge (Mass.) and London 1973, p. 70.

[7]Cf. H.-R. Hemmer, Wirtschaftsprobleme der Entwicklungslander
. . ., ibid., p. 112ff.

[8]This aspect has been discussed extensively in the literature. Cf.
The comprehensive survey in K.-H. Lemnitzer, Ernahrungssituation
und wirtschaftliche Entwicklung, ibid., p. 169ff., and A. Berg,
The Nutrition Factor, Washington 1973, p. 9ff.

[9]R.A. Berry for instance estimates the proportion of such
unemployed in the statistically recorded overt unemployment in
Colombia at 50-60%. Cf. R.A. Berry, Open Unemployment as a
Social Problem in Urban Colombia: Myth and Reality, in:
Economic Development and Cultural Change, Vol. 23 (1974/75).

[10]"To call them underemployed does not seem pertinent"-T.W.
Schultz, Investment in Human Capital, in: American Economic
Review, Vol. 51 (1960), p. 5.

[11]Cf. P. Belli, The Economic Implications of Malnutrition: The
Dismal Science Revisited, in: Economic Development and Cultural
Change, Vol. 20 (1971/72); M. Selowsky, L. Taylor, The Economics
of Malnourished Children: An Example of Disinvestment in Human
Capital, in: Economic Development and Cultural Change, Vol. 22
(1973/74).

[12]Cf., e.g. H. Correa, G. Cummings, Contribution of Nutrition to
Economic Growth, in: American Journal of Clinical Nutrition,
Vol. 23 (1970); H. Correa, Sources of Economic Growth in Latin
American, in: Southern Economic Journal, Vol. 37 (1970/71).

Health Planning in Developing Countries

FRANK SCHOFIELD

Health planning is a management tool with which the politicians and civil servants who administer health services can be helped to obtain and organize resources for the purposes they consider as having highest priority. Health plans are most likely to be successfully implemented when these purposes are made explicit. The political, economic, social and institutional purposes which underlie decisions made in the health sector are as important as those affecting health. Health planning has particular advantages for developing countries, but there are special problems for these countries, too, in the formulation and implementation of their health plans.

Health planning is intended primarily to further the improvement of public health. The planners' task is to allocate efficiently whatever resources can be used for that purpose. In this paper I shall discuss principles in health planning and problems in their practical application, rather than details of planning procedures. The term 'health planning' is used here with a restricted reference, mainly to national, regional or provincial planning.

By first looking at health planning on a small scale we can discern the general outlines of the process. Consider someone with a health problem, some symptoms for which he needs a cure (his objective). He plans the best use he knows of his money, his time and the health services (his available resources) to achieve this. In this planning process his decisions are taken in the context of certain procedures and criteria, such as local customs or rules, his and other people's past experiences, and his own assessment of the nature and progress of his symptoms.

The health worker who is consulted (a medical practitioner, for example) first of all takes a medical history to obtain the

From **IMPACT OF SCIENCE ON SOCIETY**, Vol XXIV, No. 2, 1974, reprinted by permission of the publisher, UNESCO, Paris.

information bearing on the problem, and then plans the management of the treatment (the health programme) to achieve the patient's objective. The doctor's planning is guided only in part, however, by the patient's criteria. The doctor is in command of additional precepts, technical procedures and criteria for making decisions which have been acquired during his professional training and his previous work with similar health problems. Throughout the course of the treatment, therefore, the physician assesses the progress of both their efforts to attain their joint objective -- partly by using the patient's subjective assessments and partly his own technical standards of evaluation.

This example also illustrates the basic theory of health planning for communities and nations. Problems concerning the public's health, or problems in other sectors of national life which are related to health, should be defined and accorded an agreed priority by representatives of the public working jointly with managers and technical experts in the health services. Wherever possible, measurable objectives should be set for reducing significantly each health problem within a specified period of time. Public and technical resources are then identified and allocated to health programmes which are designed as efficiently as possible to achieve the agreed objectives. Within each health programme an information system is set up, which allows the planners and managers to evaluate progress during implementation and thus to keep the programme on course.

Planning, when analysed, nis found to consist of a series of acts of making decisions; and decisions involve making choices. Choices are made of: (a) health problems; (b) the priorities they are to be given; and (c) quantitative or other clear objectives for reducing each problem over chosen periods of time. Then choices are made of the most apparently feasible technical, social and administrative activities which are to be combined to make up a health programme to reach the objectives selected. (At this stage, occasional opportunities may arise for originality in the design of these combinations and the possibilities of effective action outside the health sector must not be overlooked.)

Each of the decisions is taken after reference to criteria. In the planning process these criteria should be made explicit and their comparative influence on each decision should be indicated. The criteria used are determined by the system of values of most importance to the decision-makers. Some of them may be expressed directly in terms of public health (such as death rates or disease rates) but, as will be discussed later, social, economic, political and institutional norms and reasoning are inevitably invoked in large-scale health planning. A very readable paper by Professor Morris Schaefer is listed at the end of this article for those who wish to study further the process of decision-making in health planning.

It is evident that planning is inseparable, in principle, from the process of management. The national health plan document is prepared periodically, at a suitable time to fit into the national planning cycle when there is one; but planning is a continuous function of management, and it is needed at all levels of health work. So many variables -- biological, social and political -- affect a community's health and the functioning of health services that formal revision of health programmes, and sometimes even of the priority problems and the objectives, should be a regular procedure each year and on occasion even more frequently.

I. WHAT, INDEED, IS HEALTH PLANNING?

In the present state of the art we should not claim too much for large-scale health planning. There have been no controlled studies -- they would be very difficult to organize -- which show experimentally that national planning of health services improves the health of the general public more than is being achieved by the traditional, empirical, short-term, ad hoc planning for local communities which is still the only form of health planning undertaken in some countries. Certainly the health effects of most large-scale health planning can only have been marginal up to the present. When health statistics are compared between countries at similar stages of socio-economic development, no important differences appear that could be correlated with the presence of absence of national health planning. It is quite obvious that there are much closer correlations between national health status and general socio-economic factors than between health status and the forms and processes by which the health services are planned and administered.

Here it is probably wise to remind readers what health planning is, and what it is not. It is not solely the budgeting of resources, although there are many so-called health plans which do just that. A document that merely specifies how many hospital beds, health centres, doctors, nurses, how much expenditure on drugs and equipment will be provided in future years is not a real health plan at all. For this should be much more than an account of resources that will be made available. The plan should indicate the purposes for which they are being provided, why those purposes were chosen, how their achievement is to be measured, and how the specified resources will be organized to achieve those purposes. It should describe how feasible this achievement is likely to be and the anticipated constraints to be overcome, what special development efforts will be needed to overcome those constraints, and the form and sources of support those special efforts will need.

Intersectoral Considerations

So far, we have assumed that the objective of health services (and therefore of the health planning process) is to improve

people's health. But this is idealistic; in practice a wider view
is needed. Health services have costs, and if these are provided
other benefits must be forgone. Therefore the social and economic
costs and benefits of attaining specified national health
objectives should be compared with those to be expected if the same
resources were to be used for other desired purposes.

This must bring non-medical planners, economists and, of
course, politicians into the health planning process. These
authorities have a wider range of values, and thus of objectives,
than the saving of life and the prevention of illness and
disability. For instance, the economic returns from investment of
money and manpower and the political advantages for themselves,
their regime and their party will be among the criteria they use to
judge the comparative worth of health compared to non-health
programmes. The existence of national or regional health planning
procedures makes it easier, furthermore, for politicians and
non-medical administrators to introduce such criteria into the
lower level decision-making mechanisms within the health sector
itself, that is, into the management of the health services.
Proportionately the opportunity for vested interests within the
health services to influence health policies and practice for their
own benefit is weakened by the institution of formal health
planning procedures.

As an example of the 'health services' obligations to other
sectors let us take the case of an economically important special
group of the population, such as the workers in major agricultural,
industrial or extractive projects. Investment in such groups could
be of great importance to the future development of the country.
Here an economist is justified in asking for a disproportionate
expenditure on these workers' health and social satisfaction,
because the ultimate benefit-to-cost ratio for the nation as a
whole will be high. Conversely, politically clamorous groups such
as those living in the cities, or the population of a minister's
own constituency, may also for 'policy' reasons receive from a
health plan more than their fair share of health services compared
to the deprived silent majority living in the rural areas. The
latter type of decision can be made even more easily when there are
no formal health planning procedures. Health planning, at any
rate, should bring the reasons behind such decisions into the open.
If it fails to do so the plan will produce dissatisfaction and may
not be implemented. This is a common cause, in fact, of health
plans' failures: the ultimate decision-makers on health policies
either have not been adequately consulted and so do not support the
plan, or else they use the plan to camouflage their real purposes
behind a screen of apparently unexceptional health goals.

These extra-sectoral types of decision-making criteria should
never be ignored, although they complicate the choice of health
problems, objectives, and the choices to be made among the
alternative programmes which the health planning team will present
to the decision-makers. (Usually these key people are themselves
not members of the team.)

Additional parameters become needed now -- not only the
improving vital statistics, incidence or prevalence rates of
disease, case fatality rates, disability rates, cost-effectiveness,

and so on, which the health administrator desires. The economist will feel happy about his chosen health programmes only when their effects can be translated into his economic terms. Similarly the politician will feel frustrated and be non-co-operative in the phase of implementation unless the increased social satisfaction resulting from his favourite health programmes can be expressed, in some way, overtly in the political forum. Planners still have great difficulty in providing useful indices by which to measure the very important non-health effects of reaching or failing to reach what can be called health-related objectives.

Consensus And Rationalization

The better the planning the more explicitly should be stated the differing, and sometimes conflicting, value systems and criteria for decision-making. When these differences and potential conflicts are fully exposed they are finally resolved in either of two ways. The way chosen as appropriate will depend largely upon the cultural milieu in the country where the health plan is being decided. In many cultures the civilized method is to reach a consensus, an agreement among the planners after discreet consultations with the decision-makers on the 'best' system of values and combinations of criteria for that particular choice. Each step leading to this agreement involves a covert system of psychological bargaining among the parties concerned. In other cultures the final decision-maker is supposed to behave in a more heroic fashion, stick his neck out a certain distance, and say 'Thank you all for your work, your advice and the alternatives you have offered for my decision. I acknowledge that the buck stops here. We are going to choose alternative B, and these are the reasons it has been chosen . . .'
The trouble is that we have almost no knowledge of the psychological processes involved in these two stereotypes of decision-making behaviour, of either the implicit rationalizations involved in consensus-reaching or the publicly performed rationalizations of the western-type executive chief. Planners assume that such processes differ from, and are more 'rational' -- meaning more likely to lead to socially beneficial results -- than the 'intuitive', 'arbitrary', 'non-explicit' mental processes that take place in the absence of formalized planning procedures.
So far, however, we have no evidence to support these assumptions. In other fields of intellectual endeavour, such as the arts or natural sciences, consensus by committee would be thought to be counter-productive. Nor, in these domains, are the most creative decisions likely to be reached by leaders who have to justify them publicly in terms of the values that happen currently to be the most fashionable.
At the present stage of development of health planning it

would be manifestly pretentious to call it a science. Many of the hypotheses upon which its procedures are predictated remain unformulated, and none have been put to the test of experimental verification. There is no justification, either, for calling the process an art. It is merely a political and administrative tool, available to decision-makers responsible for health services who genuinely want to be presented with thought-out, feasible alternative options on health goals and on the methods by which resources can best be used to reach them. In contrast, for the decision-maker who has already decided these choices for himself, formal health planning procedures would be an irrelevance. His need would be for managers who could work out training programmes and budgets so that the resources will flow along the channels for which he has a preference.

II. BENEFITS EXPECTED FROM HEALTH PLANNING

In the developing countries the resources for health purposes are scarce, so scarce that they should be allocated strictly to needs and activities which have the highest social and medical priority. The justification for health planning is that it attempts to identify unequivocally these priorities, then to distribute the available trained manpower and money to relevant, well-designed programmes which will meet them. The practical criteria for evaluating a health plan's success are therefore quite clear: at the end of the specified planning period the identified priority needs should have been met to a significant degree -- if possible to such a degree that they have now been replaced by a new set of priorities.

Health planning also has subsidiary advantages which are particularly relevant to developing countries. By describing with clarity the major health activities needed in a country, it indicates the locally relevant service tasks and thus delineates educational objectives for the training of health workers of all categories. A strong and lingering tendency still exists to base medical and nursing teaching curricula on those of the previous colonial mentors, but effective health planning is an important step in improving on the past. Standards should be upheld but the content, attitudes and motivation of students can be switched more easily towards the health problems of their own communities once these have been exactly described and the most feasible practical techniques for dealing with them have been decided.

Another substantial advantage of an explicit national health plan, provided it has been worked out after proper consultations with the most interested parties, is that it will tend to reduce the misunderstandings and diversions of resources away from priority objectives which are caused by sectional interests within the health services. Responsible representatives of professional groups such as the doctors, nurses, sanitarians, technicians and service staff, should be consulted during the planning of the services which they will have to implement. If this has been done well, their enlightened co-operation becomes more readily available to the politicians and administrators who have assumed responsibility for regulating their employment and managing their work.

A health plan which sets measurable health objectives and identifies intermediate steps on the way to achieving them is a strong tool for the managers at all levels within the health services. Measured improvements in the health of the people provide reinforcement of motivation for everyone concerned, health workers and the public. Measured lack of improvement becomes the occasion for an analysis of the reasons, and leads to renewed efforts to overcome the constraints responsible for the disappointing results. This type of feedback is particularly valuable to public health workers, technicians and administrative staff who cannot obtain the same personal contacts and appreciation for work well done which clinicians, nurses and teachers receive from their patients and students.

III. SOUND PLANS ATTRACT NEEDED RESOURCES

A good, well-written health plan can also be one means of attracting resources to the health sector, either from within the country of from outside agencies. Support is easier to obtain for programmes specifically designed to reach socially desirable objectives than for a series of weakly formulated traditional health activities with vague, non-quantifiable goals.

There is a danger, however, that a health plan or part of it might be produced primarily with the intention of attracting these extra resources, and yet fail to make this motivation explicit. This is bad planning, and it prostitutes a health service's function. A health service is intended to improve health, and in doing so to serve other social goals also. Resources attracted and used explicitly for these purposes are justifiably obtained and expended, but not when the cart is put before the horse or the plans confused with the ends. To avoid this confusion, a good health plan will indicate alternatives based upon different resource projections: °We can reach objective X with our current level of expenditure of resources, x. And if we got y resources extra, then we would be able to attain incremental or supplementary objectives X + Y'.

Composition of the Planning Team

The importance of the economist's point of view being represented among those of the health planners has been stressed. If possible this member of the team should represent the national planning commission (if there is one) or the ministry of finance. The viewpoint of the political directorate is even more important. This could be obtained in a steering committee to which the chairman and secretary of the health planning team periodically report progress during the formulation of the plan. Alternatively the chairman must be chosen because he has the confidence of, and free personal access to, the political decision-makers for health programmes. His task then is to ensure at each major step in the planning process -- i.e. for the statements of priority problems, the setting of objectives, and the allocation of available resources to health programmes -- that the technical aspects of decisions made by the planners are understood and agreed in principle by the politicians. Conversely, he ensures also that major political determinants of health decisions are not overlooked in the planners' deliberations or in the document which lays out the plan.

The health personnel on the planning team should, if possible, be generalists and administrators rather than specialists. They should not have anything to gain or lose from the decisions to be made on the allocation of resources. An epidemiologist and statistician are needed to gather and interpret the data from which the information bearing on health problems, on the health services, and on existing operational constraints can be extracted when needed. Clinical specialists and the directors of ongoing public health programmes will need to be consulted for advice and guidance in their technical fields of competence and, as already indicated, so will representatives of the different groups of health workers (or their trade union, if this exists). But the direct representation on the planning team of overt vested interests from within the health services should be avoided if possible.

It has been stressed that the health planning process should make explicit the special viewpoints of economists, politicians and the different types of health worker. But how are the most important points of view, those of the users of the various health services, the tax or health insurance payers and the general public, to be adequately represented?

Official Decisions, Unofficial Influence

The immediate answer to this question is: by the political decision-makers. In theory and sometimes in practice this answer may be adequate. The felt needs of the populations in various parts of a country, however, are not always amenable to political expression. In addition there may be local cultural, economic or social factors which are of great importance in the aetiology of some diseases or in determining the ways in which people use the health services. The health significance of such behavioural patterns may not be evident to the politicians, even those from the same parts of the country. For these reasons, the co-opting of a

national behavioural scientist into the health planning team can be
very beneficial. Sociologists, psychologists or experienced
high-level educators would seem best suited for this function.
Those chosen should not have any other obvious special interest to
advance and they should be encouraged to contact similar colleagues
for information on the beliefs, attitudes and practices relevant to
health of the different cultural or ethnic groups making up the
national population.

For a health plan to be accepted and thereafter implemented,
the decision-makers need first to be identified and then involved
in some way in the major decision-making steps. The real
decision-makers are not necessarily all in officially designated
executive posts in the politico-administrative hierarchy.
Unofficial yea- and nay-sayers may have much more power than
official ones. Particularly when power is concentrated in the
hands of a small elite the advisory role of (for instance) a
leader's personal physician or medically educated old school friend
may far outweigh that of the minister of health or the director of
the government's medical services.

Successful health planning is essentially a political process,
particularly in developing countries. Health scientists,
economists or system analysts from outside the country or from
within the national administration may be of technical assistance
if their services are desired, but the ultimate responsibility for
choosing general health objectives and policies must be placed
squarely upon and accepted by those who have the powers of approval
and implementation. Otherwise, the health planning team will find
it has been wasting its time.

Common misuse of the health planning tool occurs when the
primary motive is to produce a document which can be used as part
of some kind of manifesto. The real, practical feasibility of this
°shadow' plan is of secondary importance, so long as it looks
feasible enough to arouse political enthusiasm. In these cases the
executive managers of the health services will be found not to have
been involved, because the document by itself will serve the
planners' political purposes. Neither the planners nor the
managers need or expect this type of plan to be implemented.

IV. OTHER CONSIDERATIONS IN DEVELOPING COUNTRIES

The benefit-to-cost ratios of simple techniques in preventive
medicine and environmental sanitation are not understood by many
politicians in developing countries, and the advantages these
measures can bring are not appreciated by the people. The
traditional beliefs and attitudes about the causes, and therefore
the prevention, of diseases may continue to differ widely from
those which are held by the planners of the health services.
Therefore very effective programmes such as routine childhood
immunization, chlorinated water supplies, health education to
improve dangerous weaning customs or habits of excretion, may be

thought irrelevant by the public. In most cultures, however, the trend is to accept scientific curative medicine empirically, because its benefits are patent and can be confirmed by personal experience.

When the health demands of the public can be expressed, they may be strident: they are usually overwhelmingly for curative services, whereas the most urgent health needs, from the health manager's and economist's points of view, are for preventive and promotive health programmes.

The public's demands are interpreted in light of the rationalities of politicians, building contractors and other commercial interests, and those of clinical specialists and hospital workers generally. So, while great numbers of the population in rural areas continue to die of inexpensively preventible diseases, one capital city after another is being provided with new prestigious hospitals which in some cases absorb a third to one-half of recurrent health budgets (though producing minimal effects on the people's health).

Formalized health planning -- by providing better information to the decision-makers -- might alter these priorities in some instances. But by taking some of the power to influence health policy decisions out of the hands of public health experts and placing it in those of people more responsive to public demands, formal planning also produces the distinct possibility that these demands could push, even more than at present, the priority national health needs out of sight, and thus reduce still further the present small share of the resources available for prevention.

The ultimate remedy for these short-sighted policies is to be found in another sector, education. In the present circumstances of the developing world, the effects of education are much more beneficial to public health than the effects of the same amount of resources spent on the highly expensive, therapeutic technologies of °up-to-date' hospitals.

Another important problem in practice is how to get new health programmes started and implemented once the health plan is approved. Experienced health-care managers are still scarce in developing countries. Therefore consideration of any programme's feasibility should include the identification by name of its managers and, where appropriate, of the training and experience they will need to do the job. If that is done in the preliminary planning stage, there is usually time for them to get the required training and experience while the other developmental efforts necessary to launch the programme are being undertaken. The potential technical and managerial assistance of international and bilateral health agencies is best utilized in these early developmental stages, but a goal of the planners of any major health programme must be to achieve national self-reliance for that programme once it has been safely launched and set upon its intended course.

V. SOLVING OLD PROBLEMS BRINGS NEW PROBLEMS

Finally, health planners and their decision-makers need a realistic understanding of their ultimate objectives. Public health in developing countries has recently been improving rapidly. This is partly because of broad socio-economic changes, partly through increased control in the physical and social environments, and partly through expansion of health services and improvements in medical science. Improvements lead always to new problems, however, and these are likely to be found more difficult to deal with than the old ones. Professor Jean Hamburger has thoughtfully pointed to some of the problems that are in store (in our journal, World Health).

Millions of people whose counterparts in previous centuries died young are now going to reach old age; but eventually, however good the medical services, all will fall sick of diseases we will not know how to prevent or cure -- yet upon which health services in developed countries are already spending many man-hours and much money to treat pallatively. The public's needs and demands for preventive services and for therapeutic, social and psychological support during illness will alter, but not diminish. As old requirements are satisfied, new ones inevitably will appear.

The biological pressures on human longevity and expanding numbers cannot be fended off indefinitely. The goals of health services and of their planners are therefore no illimitable. Nor are they sufficient in themselves. People everywhere will come to expect better opportunities to enhance the values they can obtain from long and healthy lives.

TO DELVE MORE DEEPLY

HAMBURGER, J. Physicians, biologists and the future of man. World Health, September 1974.

MANGAD, M.; HANNA, W. Jr. Information processing 74; technological and scientific applications in the social sciences and the humanities. Amsterdam, North Holland, 1974. The social and political issues of health care are emphasized.

McEWAN, J. Notions of morality in medical organization and practice. Science, medicine and man, vol. 1, no. 2, 1973.

SCHAEFER, M. Evaluation/decision making in health planning and administration. Chapel Hill, University of North Carolina School of Public Health, 1973. (HADM monograph series, no. 3.)

Search, vol. 6, no. 10, October 1974. Entire issue is devoted to
  health systems, including articles on technology, society and
  medicine; technology, costs and policy-making; advances in health
  care; and technological advances.

Assumptions Implicit in Health Planning

Social planners assume that good planning at high levels in
administrative structures will facilitate the multiple processes of
planning-as-management which go on continuously at the lower
levels. In the health field there is good circumstantial evidence
that, under certain conditions, this is sometimes true.

   Smallpox is a disease which now is close to disappearing from
the world. This would not have occurred as soon as it has without
'macro-planning' on the largest scale -- a world-wide,
internationally agreed health plan to eradicate the disease.
Similarly, at the level of individual nations, the once widespread
tropical disease called yaws has (for practical purposes)
disappeared during the last twenty years from many of the countries
where it used to be endemic. This would not have occurred but for
national health plans which produced programmes for the
methodical, mass administration of preventive and curative doses of
penicillin to predetermined population groups according to
predetermined time-tables.

   These are two successful examples, but there are many failures
which could also be cited. Experience suggests that the optimal
conditions for the successful implementation of large-scale health
programmes are the following:

1. The medical or other technical knowledge and the methods for
    dealing with the health problem already exist and have been
    demonstrated to be effective in conditions similar to those
    being considered in the plan.

2. The objectives are simple, discrete and easily measurable.

3. The political will to achieve the objectives is strong.

4. The effect of an efficient application of the technology is
    permanent, so that the health programme can be limited in time
    and thus in expenditure of resources.

5. The necessary resources are already available or can be
    mobilized rapidly to support the programme.

Those are the circumstances in which the value of health planning is most likely to be evident and incontrovertible. In developing countries, conditions 1 and 2 above are to be found much more commonly than in developed countries. There are many communicable diseases, and also forms of malnutrition, which are now being effectively prevented in the more developed countries but which still cause severe damage to the health, social cohesion and economic welfare of the people in the developing world.

Condition 3 varies from country to country and from one health problem to another. On balance, because public demand for preventive medicine is weak, and, because the economic benefits of health measures have not been clearly demonstrated to the decision-makers in comparison with their costs, the political will to improve their people's health is not strong among the governments of developing countries. Condition 4 unfortunately is not often found, but a number of such opportunities currently exist in the poorer countries while in the developed world they occur more rarely and usually as a result of new scientific discoveries.

The final condition listed above is the one which gives an advantage to the countries with more trained manpower and money. It is paucity of these resources which reinforces the political pessimism about health which has already been noted. The importance of these constraints can be overemphasized, however, in developing countries. Frequently the greatest hindrances to the implementation of successful health programmes appear to be weak motivation, inertia in management and problems in planning such as those delineated in the accompanying text.

How One Nation Views Health Planning as a Social Function[1]

Solution option	Some basic assumptions of solution related to consumers/organizations
More representation of consumers and community organizations in national and provincial health policy-making.	Consumer input is likely to change balance of national, provincial and local health financing priorities. Consumers are interested and qualified to make policies. The political decision process and professional groups of organized medicine will tolerate consumer inputs.
Delegation of authority to local levels to set local planning priorities, with commensurate accountability.	Provincial governments will facilitate consumer inputs. Mechanisms can be found for involving consumers in the planning process. Consumers are interested in local planning and evaluation issues, and qualified to contribute inputs at different levels of the planning process.

Creation of more provincial health services to facilitate the setting up of innovative organizations to deliver higher quality, less costly, more appropriate more accessible consumer-oriented health services (such as community health centers prepaid group practices, health maintenance organizations, hospital mergers, shared hospital services).

Consumer can affect innovation and change in health care.
Consumer wants changes in the delivery of health care.
New innovative health services will be better than what we now have.

More extensive preventive health services, including health education to: (a) arrest the prevalance of health problems arising from home, work and road accidents, diet and exercise and environmental health hazards; (b) change the consumer overdependence on active hospital beds; (c) help the consumer organize his community to ensure that health and welfare needs are met.

Health education programmes can attack many of the factors that cause health problems in man.
Consumer behavior can be modified by different types of health education programmes.
Consumers and communities can be organized into effective action groups to change the relative priorities given to curative (bed) care and preventive care.
Other preventive health programmes can positively affect the health of populations and individuals.

Selective experimentation with: (a) alternative methods of hospital admission and discharge; (b) evaluation of treatment methods, length of stay, and cost of care provided; (c) methods of reducing the cost of hospital care through treatment in less costly but equally effective facilities or

Incentives, both monetary and psychological, can be found to encourage experimentation without penalty to the innovative organization.
Consumers will accept experimental health care systems and not pre-judge 'gimmickry' or accept fads uncritically.
Consumers can be involved in the design and evaluation of experimental health care services, including their comparison with traditional health services.

through better home
care.

Selective experimentation with alternative methods of financing national health services and different methods of paying the doctor.	We do not yet know enough about the diverse ways in which the financing and payment system affect the use of health services. Experimentation is politically feasible within the existing health system. Experimentation will produce policies that are significantly different from what we now have.
Selective experimentation with alternative types of health manpower and with different delegations of task from doctors to para-medical staff, in different types of health teams, and under different renumeration and career structures.	Consumers will accept other health professionals in the treatment process. Other types of health teams will facilitate more effective care at non-exorbitant costs. Doctors will accept other health professionals and the delegation of tasks in a team approach.
Selective experimentation with cost-reducing medical and managerial technologies to improve resource use in patient care (including computers in medical record keeping, patient history-taking, and drug monitoring systems).	The use of such technologies will be accepted by both providers and consumers. Accountability and evaluation of health care can be improved by changes in the way in which data are collected and stored in patient care.

'Selling' a Good Health Plan to Officialdom

What benefits can the minister of health for a developing country expect from a carefully worked out, feasible health plan? The main advantage is political; a good plan will strengthen his ministry's value to the political leadership of the nation. To do this the plan needs to indicate unambiguously the policies which it is supporting, to identify all those who will benefit directly from its implementation, and to describe the social, political and economic advantages to the holders of power of carrying out this plan rather than another -- or rather than continuing without any formal plan at all. To succeed politically, the plan demonstrably should be able to attract support more powerful than the opposition it will encounter among the interests and groups it disappoints.

Institutional benefits to the ministry are obtained by stating clear, measurable objectives and laying down feasible programmes and time-tables. Then the employees can see where they fit in, and what their work is meant to achieve. Here, too, the momentum of the health workers who are satisfied by the plan needs to be sufficient to overcome the hindrances to implementation which will be produced by the unsatisfied. By making the objectives and working methods explicit the administrators can strengthen social compliance within their organization, although thereby they risk to some extent discouraging individual creativity and local initiatives.

The benefits to public health of good planning are difficult to separate from those of good management and from the effects of skilled, conscientious, and socially responsible applications of technology by well-trained health workers. Nevertheless decision-makers at political levels may justifiably take some of the credit, and thus obtain some psychological rewards from measurably reducing ill-health and meeting the related needs of their fellow countrymen and women.

Community Health Care in Developing Countries

FREDRICK L. GOLLADAY

Few developing countries have formulated health policies based upon detailed assessments of the socioeconomic costs and benefits of different approaches to health care. As a result, expenditures for health care in many cases are not as effective as they could be. This realization has produced renewed emphasis on the need to evaluate health care policies and programs in the developing world in order to make them more appropriate to the prevailing needs and resources. Studies, conducted by the countries themselves and agencies such as the World Health Organization (WHO) and the World Bank, have concluded that health care systems need to be expanded and improved at the community level in order to reach the great majority of people who presently do not have access to adequate health care.

Although countries differ in their level of development and in the magnitude of their investment in health, health care systems in many developing countries share certain major characteristics:

--Government expenditures on health in low-income countries are very low.

--The overwhelming majority of people, especially the poorest, cannot easily reach a modern health care facility.

--Most spending is for curative medicine, high-cost hospitals, and highly trained medical personnel.

--Existing program of health care are frequently inefficient in their use of financial and human resources.

Government expenditures on health in low-income countries seldom exceed 2 per cent of gross national product (GNP). Almost half of the 86 developing countries for which data are available spend less than $2 per capita a year on health care; 22 countries spend less than $1 per capita. By comparison, in 1976 the average per capita government expenditures for health were $550 in Sweden

From **FINANCE AND DEVELOPMENT**, Sept. 1980, (35-39), reprinted by permission of the publisher.

TABLE 1. Health expenditure as percentage of gross domestic product[1]

Developing countries (1970)				Developed countries (1973–75)		
	Government	Private			Government	Private
Ghana	1.1	2.9		Australia	5.0	1.5
Honduras	1.9	3.2		Belgium	4.2	0.8
India	0.4	2.1		Canada	5.1	1.7
Pakistan	0.9	1.5		Netherlands	5.1	2.2
Philippines	0.4	1.5		Sweden	6.7	0.6
Sri Lanka	1.8	1.2		United Kingdom	4.6	0.6
Sudan	2.2	1.5		United States	2.4	3.9

Source: Richards, P. J., *Some Distributional Issues in Planning for Basic Needs Health Care; A World Employment Research Working Paper*, Provisional Draft, Income Distribution and Employment Programme, International Labour Office, Geneva, June 1979, p. 3.
[1] These figures must be taken as approximate, since major items may be missing from the public and private side. Comprehensive and accurate data are rarely available; there are often numerous, disparate, and not easily quantifiable sources of finance for health care services within a country. Sources may include the central government, state and local governments, insurance plans, private households, voluntary organizations, employers, lotteries, etc.

239

and $171 in Japan. There is an emphasis in developing countries on high-cost, individual, curative medicine--for example, the operation of expensive, well-equipped hospitals staffed by highly trained medical personnel--and these facilities are concentrated in urban centers. In Ghana, for example, 62 per cent of physicians in 1969 resided in urban areas, where 15 per cent of the population lived. The limited data available suggest that private expenditures for health in developing countries are often considerably greater than the amount spent by governments. In fact, the ratio of private expenditure on health to government expenditure is generally far larger than that in the developed countries (see the table). However, much of the private expenditure is for the services of traditional healers and for drugs of controversial value.

The health problems of developing countries are typically those associated with poverty. However, they are generally more severe than those in industrialized countries and often occur in the form of multiple diseases because the tropical environment encourages the growth of disease-carrying insects and the transmission of disease among the population. In addition, the inadequate housing, clothing, and public hygiene add to the problems of health maintenance. Undernutrition frequently makes people more susceptible to disease and lessens their chance of recovery.

I. INADEQUATE COVERAGE

An estimated 70 per cent of people living in developing countries do not have easy access to a modern health care facility for a number of reasons. Lack of roads and public transportation prevent vast numbers of rural patients from obtaining health care. Pregnant women and small children--those whose needs are greatest--typically find travel especially difficult. An Indian study showed that the proportion of the community attending a dispensary was found to decrease by 50 per cent for each additional half mile between the community and the facility. (H. Frederiksen, Maintenance of Malaria Eradication, World Health Organization, Geneva, February 1964). Research in Africa has concluded that utilization there declines by half for each two additional miles of travel. Where health services are available, supplies of drugs, pesticides, and other essential materials are often unreliable. The resulting interruptions in the services frustrate patients and discourage them from relying on local health facilities. In many cases, the services provided are not adequate. Charges for services or drugs are often not affordable, and people in the subsistence sector frequently do not have the cash to pay for them. Even where care is consistently available, costs of transportation to a health facility and the loss of income frequently exceed the economic resources of many of the poorest people.

Providing health services nationwide will not be easy for any government. Even the most developed countries find that assuring ready access to care is typically too costly and difficult. Developing countries have an acute need for low-cost, self-sustaining, and effective health care systems that can be established and operated within scattered communities.

II. THE STATE OF HEALTH

The urgent need for better health care is quite obvious from a review of the state of the health of the developing world.

About 16 million children under five years of age died in 1979 in developing countries. Five million of these deaths could have been prevented by immunization against the six most common diseases of childhood--measles, polio, tetanus, diphtheria, whooping cough, and typhoid. Nearly 6 million children--all under the age of one year--died as a consequence of the mother's undernutrition during pregnancy. In addition, those who reach adulthood in the poorest countries sacrifice up to a third of their potential working lives by succumbing to fatal diseases.

Much greater human and economic costs are imposed by nonfatal illnesses. Reports are very sketchy, but, even so, the numbers are staggering. At least 5 million children are blinded or permanently crippled in the developing world each year--most of them as a result of polio, a disease for which safe, effective vaccines are available. The WHO estimates that 2-3 million children are severely retarded each year by readily preventable diseases.

The tragedy of disease in developing countries is that many of the most serious health problems are either preventable or curable by simple, inexpensive, and safe methods. For example, a recent World Bank study of health conditions in Mali, West Africa, found that 90 per cent of infant deaths resulted from faulty care of pregnant women and unsanitary delivery practices. Similarly, infant "weanling diarrhea" is a major killer of children in most of the world, yet its prevention or cure is inexpensive and simple. The problem can be avoided by good hygiene and adequate nutrition. Alternatively, body fluids lost because of diarrhea can be restored cheaply at home by administering a solution of boiled water, salt, and sugar by mouth. However, in much of the developing world, ample supplies of safe water and adequate facilities for the sanitary disposal of human wastes are not yet available. Where clean water and sanitation are provided, poor hygienic practices often negate any potential reduction of diarrheal disease.

III. COMMUNITY HEALTH SERVICES

Since on the whole it is the poor and neglected, living mainly

CHART 1
Organization of a community based health system serving about 1 million people

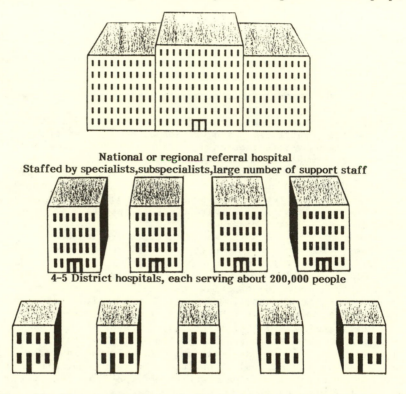

National or regional referral hospital
Staffed by specialists,subspecialists,large number of support staff

4-5 District hospitals, each serving about 200,000 people

20-25 rural health centers or urban polyclinics serving about 40,0000-50,000 people

300 local health posts, each serving about 2,000 to 5,000 people

Source: World Bank Health Sector Policy Paper, World Bank, 1980

in the rural areas in the developing world, who lack essential health care and an understanding of the importance of nutrition and hygienic practices, the problem becomes one of how to serve them best. Many countries are responding by establishing community-level health care facilities that make use of community health workers rather than doctors. But the practical difficulties of too few and too hastily trained health workers, of limited transport, and of inadequate and erratic supplies are compounded in most countries by widespread reluctance to rely upon community health workers. These problems do not mean that the approach itself is incorrect, but rather suggest that in most countries sustained efforts to adapt and strengthen it are required. A large number of developing countries are now implementing a second generation of community health programs that incorporate the lessons of experience from the first.

In order to bring health care closer to people who have been underserved in the past, a three-tiered pyramidal approach to the provision of health services is being used (see Chart 1). The first level is the community health center, the second is the rural or urban polyclinic, and the third is the referral hospital (often at a district level). Community health facilities are being constructed all over the world. These facilities are usually described as health posts, dispensaries, mini-posts, or community health centers. They are typically staffed by locally recruited persons who have been given six months to two years of training. The buildings are typically of local design and materials and are very modestly equipped. These facilities are intended to extend the coverage of the health care system rather than to supplant it. They rely upon existing polyclinics, district hospitals, and health centers for logistical support, supervision, and, in many instances, training. They seek to provide two thirds or more of health care, including supervision of pregnancy, midwifery, care of newborn children, immunization, treatment of endemic diseases (such as malaria), and emergency care for injuries. Tasks requiring complex equipment, such as laboratory diagnosis and surgery, are conducted at higher levels after referral of patients by community health workers. Health and hygiene education are also major responsibilities of community health workers.

Nearly a decade of experience with low-cost health care--in countries as diverse as Botswana, Brazil, the People's Republic of China, India, Iran, Jamaica, and Sudan--is now available. This experience shows that the achievements at recently constructed local health facilities have often been disappointing. One problem has been matching the supply of their services with demand for them. Particularly in Southeast Asia, rural health centers and community health posts are virtually unused--bypassed by patients who prefer to attend larger, more sophisticated facilities. In other areas of the world--most notably sub-Saharan Africa--large numbers of people use community health facilities but receive only minimal attention from staff. In East Africa, many village health workers see up to 90 persons an hour.

Efforts to provide accessible low-cost care have also been frustrated by lack of supplies and personnel. Drugs, dressings, and other materials are often exhausted a few days after receipt.

This is sometimes due to poor planning; however, more often the quantities ordered are adequate for several months, but run out because of improper use--patients may hoard drugs at home or medical officials may overprescribe, for example. Such activities waste funds and may even injure, rather than promote, health. In addition, the sale of drugs on the black market is a common problem. Because dispensers, nurses, medical assistants, and even physicians are ill paid, they may supplement their government salaries by illegal sales of drugs.

A number of countries-especially the smaller, poorer countries--confront severe problems in financing salaries and purchasing drugs. Health budgets are too small, and workers most distant from the capital are the least likely to be paid. Because pharmaceuticals often must be purchased from abroad, foreign exchange constraints are also serious. One Saharan country has been forced to turn to increasingly expensive suppliers as its credit rating with pharmaceutical manufacturers has declined.

The performance of community health workers, too, has often not been as effective as expected. The need for health care in some countries has put so much pressure on health workers that they are almost prohibitied from providing careful diagnosis and precise treatment. Many health workers prescribe three or more drugs to patients when in doubt about the cause of illness, hoping to cover the most common ailments. This practice not only wastes the drugs and supplies but also promotes resistance of disease organisms to drugs such as penicillin, which are widely available at low prices. The type of training given to these health workers also causes problems in many countries. Patients expect health workers to render instantaneous diagnosis, and they distrust the systematic approach of Western health care. Rural health workers are sometimes influenced by community leaders and traditional healers to abandon the practices they have been taught. Since these workers are typically young and of modest social status, they are often unable to resist such social pressures.

Yet another reason community health workers are not as effective as they should be is that they are not trained in the diagnosis and treatment of locally important diseases. This undermines a community's confidence as well as the workers' own confidence in their professional ability. In-service and continuing education, and referral of difficult problems to more sophisticated facilities can minimize this problem. New methods for training health workers are being devised to improve their competence (see Chart 2).

IV. IMPROVEMENTS

Experience from these early efforts in community-level health care provides a basis for improving the second generation of programs now being initiated. Many of the improvements center on the relationship between the health worker and the community he

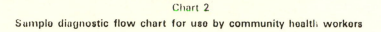

Chart 2

Sample diagnostic flow chart for use by community health workers

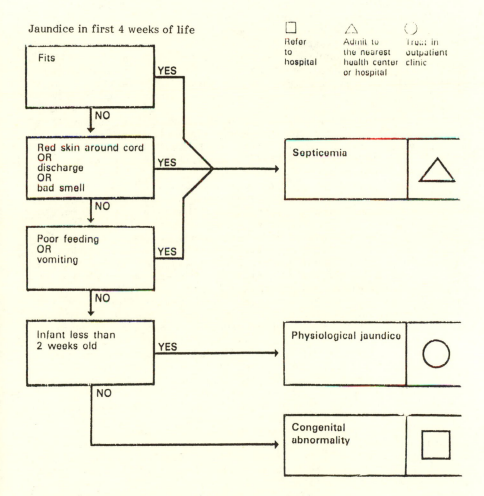

Source: World Health Organization (1978). Flow charts developed by Dr. B. Essex.

serves. If the health worker is to gain the respect essential for him to be effective, he must be given sufficient training, equipment, and supplies so that he is not forced to refer more than a minimum number of patients to higher levels. Very high referral rates undermine the community's confidence in the health worker and also increase the probability of patients' bypassing him. For the same reason, the health worker should be mature enough to enjoy the respect of the community. Early programs exaggerated the importance of formal education for health workers; it is now clear that it is more important for them to have had children themselves and personal experiences with the health crises experienced by the people they will be treating.

Other improvements to existing rural health systems concern supervision. It has been found that, if at least part of the health worker's salary is paid by the government, the operation is more susceptible to discipline than it would otherwise be, since a government salary increases the possibility of sanctions from health officials. Only a very few countries (including the People's Republic of China) have succeeded in making the community responsible for the salary of the health worker without sacrificing efficiency. Moreover, relying solely on local finance tends to favor high-income communities.

Frequent supervision of the community health worker is essential--both to provide in-service training and to ensure that performance meets minimal standards. The insolated, modestly trained health worker is rarely confident of his or her skills and often confronts problems for which he was not trained. Each health worker should be visited regularly by staff from neighboring dispensaries, health centers, and hospitals, as well as from the office of the regional medical officer. Written reports should be used sparingly, but the information that is collected should be promptly analyzed and followed up. Supervision should provide numerous contacts with supervisors to compensate for the inevitable breakdowns in transport, to ensure that a broad range of issues (from clinical care to drug management) is considered, and to reduce the crisis character of visits from the outside. Establishing standards for the use of drugs and supplies and then carefully monitoring the demands of individual health workers are necessary to avoid misuse and/or misappropriation of drugs.

Further, health workers must be made accountable to the community, especially through recognized organizations, such as the local council or village development committee. The community can monitor such aspects of performance as the hours of service, the use of drugs and materials, and the care provided. But how far the health worker should be made formally accountable to the local authorities has to depend on the local situation. In some cases, supervision can be successfully exercised by the community. In others, program directors argue that complaints are resolved most rapidly and effectively if health authorities at a higher level deal with them.

V. PRIORITIES

Building effective systems of low-cost health care will require sustained efforts, continuous modification of approaches, and experimentation. However, the gains in human welfare are potentially dramatic, and the financial costs are relatively modest. The overwhelming importance of good health to individual well-being and to economic performance implies that governments should assign high priority to improving services that contribute to the control of disease.

A simple infrastructure for local health services employing community health workers is important. This primary health care approach would not only extend the effective coverage of basic health care but would also afford a mechanism for surveillance of disease, health education, promotion of family planning, monitoring of sanitation, and targeting of disease control programs. The acceptance of community health workers hinges on their ability to meet a substantial part of the needs of the community. Thus, they must be integrated into a system of supervision, logistical support, and referral. These parallel, supportive programs must be introduced concurrently with the program of community health care.

But community health services should only be part of a wider system. Perhaps the most basic step for most countries is to strengthen programs to control endemic, vector-borne parasitic diseases--especially malaria, sleeping sickness, and schistosomiasis (bilharzia). These programs can be made efficient and be effectively operated without significant changes in the habits and practices of the people who benefit. The basis for such disease-control programs already exists in most of the affected countries.

A second priority is to expand the coverage of childhood immunization programs. These activities require very little effort on the part of those who benefit and generally may be organized without an extensive local infrastructure. Sierra Leone, for example, does this well by employing teams of recruiters, who enlist the assistance of local leaders in gathering together, immediately before the vaccinators arrive in a village, all persons who should be immunized.

Improvements in nutrition, hygiene, and sanitation are also necessary in order to reach the full health potential of most communities. Major investments in these areas will generally be required to improve the quality of services significantly. Moreover, the benefits of greater availability of nutritious foods and safe water will be realized only with marked improvements in the practices of individuals and households. In view of the large investments necessary to improve services, it seems preferable to coordinate these outlays with the expansion of effective primary health care.

RELATED READINGS

World Bank, <u>Health Sector Policy Paper</u>, 2nd edition (Washington, World Bank, 1980)

World Health Organization, <u>The Primary Health Worker</u> (Geneva, World Health Organization, 1980)

Nutrition and Population in Health Planning

CARL E. TAYLOR

The central theme of this paper is that nutrition should be integrated with both health and family planning. To improve program effectiveness, there is increasing need to combine services for nutrition, health, and family planning.

For background, some developments that have occurred in recent years in health planning will be examined. Then a discussion of the evidence for integration will be presented, followed by a final section that reports briefly on three case studies of nutritional planning.

I. PRESENT TRENDS IN HEALTH AND NUTRITION PLANNING

Concern for human nutrition falls between the technical competence of agriculture and health. It has become evident, however, that socioeconomic development and community development require a special focus on nutrition as a neglected area.

Among agricultural experts a common attitude is that all that is needed is to provide food for everyone and nutrition problems will disappear. This all-too-common notion is negated by the general prevalence of malnutrition in food surplus areas. Providing food is only part of the answer. An important challenge is to learn to cope with economic constraints limiting the equitable distribution of food. By providing knowledge of locally available foods which are cheap and nutritious, people can be helped to solve their own nutritional problems.

From **FOOD RESEARCH INSTITUTE STUDIES**, Vol XVI, No. 2, 1977, (77-90), reprinted by permission of the publisher, Stanford University, Food Research Institute.

On the other hand, the inordinately great prevalence of malnutrition has been systematically ignored in the health sector as well. Most nutritional research has been devoted to sophisticated laboratory biochemistry. There has been minimal nutritional epidemiological research and even less on nutrition services and their impact. Little is known about what happens as a result of multimillion dollar expenditures on feeding programs.

The reason for this shared ignorance is that research workers have not bothered to learn what happens to people as a result of what they eat or do not eat. Much energy and expense is devoted to producing and disposing of food for the poor. The reasons for doing so, however, are often not actually to meet nutritional need. For instance, the impact of feeding programs in the United States has received little study because a primary motivation for them has been to maintain economic benefits for American farmers. This means of disposing of food surpluses has been used with only an occasional reference to the rationalization that it was also a good way to redistribute resources.

National Systems of Health Planning

The development of health planning in less developed countries in the past two decades has been notable (19). Whereas planning used to be characteristic only of centralized socialist countries, it has now gained general respectability. The greatest impetus for this emphasis on planning has been the international donor agencies' requirement of systematic planning as a prerequisite for loans and grants in the hope that this will increase accountability. Presumably, where resources are small, planning will help to focus them on high priority problems.

Many less developed countries have established planning units in the health ministry, but only a few function effectively. They tend to have the anatomy of the planning process without the physiology.

If nutritional planning is to be improved, more attention must be paid to how national policies are made and to how the political will to eliminate malnutrition can be generated. Intangibles that affect how decisions are made in varied cultural settings and the mobilization of political and administrative commitment are at present little understood. It will also be necessary to learn how to insure implementation once policies and programs are enumerated. To many elaborate planning exercises end up in multiple volumes which are never implemented or implemented poorly. There is a particular need for developing management methods appropriate to local cultures and administrative patterns. But the best that can be done at this stage is to carry out further case studies designed to yield better understanding of the key factors influencing the political process and the design and implementation of health programs.

When planning first became a serious official activity, widely varying patterns and approaches were developed depending mainly on the political orientation of the country. Around the world, a fascinating convergence now seems to be occurring with a progressive moving together of methods of planning as countries learn from each other's experience. Perhaps the biggest change in health and nutrition planning has been the increasing emphasis on planning from below.

Planning From Below

Planning from below is the term that has been applied both to decentralized decision making within broad directions set by a central planning agency and to programs that call for close involvement of local people both in formulation and implementation. The rationale for adopting it is mostly negative and grows out of awareness of the deficiencies of centralized planning (6). Many local projects have demonstrated that decentralized planning increases local involvement in implementation but it is not clear how these lessons can be best applied to general health services. Planning from below will never have the symmetry and conceptual integrity of a centrally generated plan. Inconsistencies and gaps will have to be accommodated. In setting priorities, professionally determined need will be subordinated to public demand. Allocation of resources will tend to be politicized. Complicated efforts have been required to get consumer representation in United States regional and local health planning agencies, but consumer representatives have learned quickly and eventually have tended to identify with the health services. The process of getting local involvement has been even slower to evolve in less developed countries. Outstanding success in involving the community has been achieved in China, but powerful central control through the Party is also strong. The writings of Freire (7), Goulet (9, 10), and Illich (12) provide challenges for future experimentation.

The question remains, how can political will be generated in mass programs to stimulate peripheral involvement and keep it channeled? It is necessary to learn how to balance responsibilities between central and decentralized parts of the system. Central planners should be responsible for defining broad goals and policies, making major allocations, and setting up data collection and quality control. Within those broad goals, local planners should have considerable freedom to set their own priorities, reflecting a community's own perception of needs, and to work out processes of implementation. Implementation should be a local responsibility, with central planners involved mainly in setting standards and targets. Evaluation can be shared, with local units evaluating concurrently for administrative control of services. Central planners also should make periodic overall evaluations to see if goals have been met and whether objectives should be changed.

The next challenge is to involve communities in their own health care. This is a major new thrust in the World Health Organization and other international agencies. Particularly in rural health services, the experience of the last 20 years has completely changed the old stereotypes away from hospital speciality care.

Growing political commitment is emerging in some countries for comprehensive care based on decentralized health centers and the use of auxiliaries for primary care. Village studies in several countries have shown that a wide gap remains between the health center and the home. Typically, health coverage reaches only 10 to 15 percent of rural populations. This has led to new efforts to identify and strengthen community capabilities to meet their own health needs. In many of the more efficient health projects there has been a tendency to co-opt village volunteers, thus weakening their capacity to carry out their original role of assisting families to solve their own problems without increasing family dependency. New patterns of work need to be developed which are designed to make better use of both organized services and village volunteers, each reinforcing the other.

Nutrition in Health Sector Planning

In the United States, nutrition has been a recognized, but minor, component of health services for many years. The problem has been that activities have become sterotypical and repetitive with little attention to evaluation. As is true of most health indicators, in the United States nutritional status has steadily improved, and the health sector has taken credit for the improvement on the assumption that whatever it was doing was obviously right. Major activities such as feeding programs and nutrition education have been blessed by being little evaluated. Only recently has it become clear that most of the improvement was due to broad socioeconomic development and that specific measures often were irrelevant. In affluent societies people tended to meet their own needs. Now there is growing concern about the poor food habits of many Americans and the relationship to diseases of affluence.

In developing countries much less has been done to promote better nutrition. Programs patterned after those of affluent countries have not worked. Maternal and child health clinics have channeled large amounts of food to vulnerable groups but malnutrition persists. School-feeding programs seem to have been more effective in altering income distribution than in changing nutrition status. Furthermore, it is usually the preschool children who are most seriously at risk, and the children from poor families where malnutrition is more prevalent are not reached by school-feeding programs. Nutrition education may have had some favorable impact, but it has been more than negated by commercial advertising of inappropriate food and of formulas that discourage breast-feeding.

Especially where general socioeconomic development has been slow, present approaches have been unsuccessful (4). Specific program areas that must be taken into account in any program design and that need research attention are examined briefly in the following paragraphs.

Interactions with Infections

Since Scrimshaw, Gordon, and I published the review (22, pp. 367-403) and WHO monograph (23) that defined these interactions, additional research has confirmed their importance. Nutritional effects on host resistance, primarily through cellular immunity, have begun to be defined. Mechanisms by which infections increase metabolic demand have become somewhat more clear, and there is increased awareness of the adverse effects on food intake resulting from loss of appetite and withholding of food during periods of infection. However, there is need for further research on specific relationships such as that between malabsorption and intestinal infections.

Cultural and Biological Correlates of Lactation

The more that is learned about lactation, the more important it is recognized to be. Infant nutrition in poor countries depends so much on lactation that other measures are appropriately called supplemental. From a simple economic viewpoint, breast milk is one of the greatest food resources available to human beings. Because of the significant effect of lactational amenorrhea on fertility, breast-feeding also plays an important role in maintaining child spacing and should be closely related to family planning.

Food Preparation

The preparation of weaning foods needs more study. In poor families the problems of preparing separate foods for young children are great. Gathering fuel and water and cooking take a large part of a woman's day. When a child is given adult foods it often cannot cope with them because they contain too few nutrients for their volume or because they are difficult to digest. The low caloric density of weaning diets appears to be responsible for considerable malnutrition among infants and small children even within families where the total food supplement is adequate (8, pp. 471-78).

Food Combinations

Poverty is only one reason for the poor combinations of food consumed. Most areas grow green leafy plants that would meet many nutrient requirements, notably for minerals and vitamins. Research is needed on easily available items that can be introduced into nutritious combinations with traditional cereals. Rather than trying to make cereals behave like legumes, it would be better to do research on getting maximum production of calories, for example, through tubers, and then to add the other nutrients through available combinations of food.

Relationship between Dietary Levels and Health

Standards of nutritional intake have become suspect. This is especially true because most standards were developed in tests on healthy young men in affluent countries. Is bigger really better in human growth? Countries with chronic food deficiencies might be better off with children who grow up small and lean. But this may seem to be discriminatory, and too little is known about the effect of nutritional level on function.

Cultural Constraints in Food and Nutrition

Nutrition education that ignores local nutritional belief and introduces simplistic solutions from other situations has produced some of the worst examples of developmental colonialism. Very few programs have accommodated local concepts of "hot and cold foods," even though in most countries these beliefs really determine what people eat and when. Common cultural practices such as abstaining from food during infections require anthropological investigation. Many of the most important cultural values are related to food and yet they are treated casually as being mere superstitions.

Measurement Problems

Advancement in understanding requires better measurement methods. My inclination is to urge the use of direct measurements of nutritional status rather than to continue the past emphasis on attempts to measure food supply and demand balances. Increasingly, simple techniques are being developed which measure changes in adults and children in relation to their nutritional environment. Some examples are worth mentioning:

1. Mortality of children of ages 1-3 or 1-5 is probably the most sensitive index of nutritional improvement.

2. Reduced infant mortality follows reduction of mortality of preschool children and may be easier to record because many data systems incorporate this information. Sample surveys can give some information where vital statistics are poor.

3. Weight for age both in cross-sectional surveys and longitudinal growth charts provide some of the most convincing data on child nutrition. Growth charts can also be used as a powerful program and educational tool (14, 17).

4. Arm circumference measures are crude but may help in sorting out the most poorly nourished children (13).

5. Eye changes with vitamin A deficiency are identifiable on survey and in some areas are of primary importance.

6. Simple laboratory tests for anemia and other specific deficiencies are already available and becoming more so.

II. INTEGRATED SERVICES FOR HEALTH. FAMILY PLANNING, AND NUTRITION

Most analyses of the world food and nutrition situation present a gloomy perspective on the interaction between nutrition and population. They correctly stress the negative impact of population growth on world food balances and on achieving the economic and social objectives of development. It is imperative that birthrate reduction follow mortality decline as closely as possible. Well-nourished mothers seem better able to bear children. Since one effect of better nutrition is to increase population growth by reducing mortality, it seems reasonable that nutrition workers should see to it that family planning accompanies effective nutritional programs. A natural mechanism which helps to reestablish the balance between mortality and fertility is that greater child survival increases child spacing because it reduces the frequence with which birth intervals are shortened after a child's death when the biological constraint of lactation is removed. Although breast-feeding is important because lactational amenorrhea helps to maintain birth spacing, there is now evidence which suggests that its contraceptive effect is considerably less pronounced when mothers and children are well nourished.

There are other positive interactions through which better nutrition seems to contribute to reducing fertility. Potentially fruitful topics for further study of the motivational and behavioral factors that influence family-planning practice are emerging from recent studies of programs integrating health, family-planning, and nutrition services which are summarized below.

Unfortunately, a polarization has emerged between those who favor integration of family planning with health services and those opposed (18, pp. 189-99; 27, 97-100). The issue has become symbolic of a major policy issue with millions of dollars of international and national funds for family planning and health care riding on decisions which are being made currently. Some extreme positions have been taken. On the one hand there has been a pervasive but generally unspoken feeling that if health and nutrition activities lower death rates and exacerbate the population problem, then international assistance programs should not support expenditures on health and nutrition. There has also been a tendency for people in health programs to try to obtain some of the family-planning money which has been available in recent years. Such attempts were most common when personnel and facilities for laboriously developed but scantily funded maternal and child health services were co-opted by large family planning programs.

The arguments against integration are usually couched in terms of the urgency of the population problem, the relative ineffectiveness and low status of health services in many developing countries, and the need to bring the birthrate down faster than the death rate where overpopulation is already evident.

The potential advantages of an integrated approach to nutrition, health, and family planning seem much more compelling. To design an organizational structure and procedures for implementing integrated programs is admittedly a difficult undertaking, but five cogent reasons support the argument for administratively integrating this combination of activities.

Aggressive family-planning programs have created resentment and cultural backlash which in its most extreme form results in suspicions of genocidal intent. This is most evident in black Africa, but resentment of compulsory or quasi-compulsory sterilization was a major factor in the recent national elections in India. Where such a backlash occurs, support for family-planning programs is weak and they often fail to have a significant impact on birthrates.

Efficiencies can be achieved by combining personal services which require continuing contacts in the home and clinic. Multipurpose community health workers can readily cover an aggregate of tasks -- nutrition and health education, environmental sanitation, and family planning -- without duplicating key supporting costs such as training, travel time, and facilities which would be required for unipurpose workers. It also should be noted that where health services are inefficient, separate family planning services tend to be inefficient also.

An integrated program is likely to have greater acceptance because village people tend to link family planning with a whole complex of activities associated with mother and child that seem naturally associated. The motivational argument for integration of services capitalizes on improved communication at the interface between the service system and the home and community. By using the rapport created by health care activities which are constantly in demand, ambivalence toward reducing family size can be overcome and acceptance of family planning enhanced. This is especially true among the demographically important younger couples who are just starting to have children.

Finally, there is the proposition that reducing infant mortality rates can contribute to a greater decline in fertility. This proposition, however, has been the subject of a good deal of controversy and needs to be considered in some detail.

Considerable attention has been given to the issue of whether a linkage between falling death rates and falling birthrates through direct and indirect effects of increased child survival can be scientifically demonstrated. In the discussion of the pros and cons of integration, uncertainty about the child survival hypothesis has emerged. At first, it was accepted as common sense, but it has recently been strongly challenged and has become moot.

The Child-Survival Hypothesis

According to the child-survival hypothesis, experience with or fear of child mortality will tend to cause parents to have additional children either to replace those who have been lost or as insurance against expected loss. At a recent conference of the Committee for International Coordination of National Research in Demography (CICRED) in Bangkok, demographers and family-planning experts reviewed much available data and concluded that there was essentially no evidence to support the hypothesis (5). They showed that much of the shortening of birth intervals following child loss which had previously been cited as evidence for the hypothesis could be more reasonably explained by the cessation of the antifecundity effects of lactational amenorrhea. It was argued at the CICRED conference that only if fear of childrens' deaths caused parents to overcompensate by replacement plus insurance births could health expenditures be justified on the grounds that they prevented more births than deaths. The main conclusion of the CICRED conference was that money invested in health care would produce net population growth. As is often true, scientists have taken great delight in debunking what had seemed to be a common sense idea. Nevertheless, the child-survival hypothesis can be redefined so as to continue to provide an important link between child mortality and the birthrate.

As part of the original statement of the theory of the

demographic transition, it had been postulated that a decline in birthrate would almost automatically follow a decline in death rate. Many have become dissatisfied with such a simplistic and mechanistic interpretation of the child-survival hypothesis. My colleagues, Jeanne Newmand and Narindar Kelly, and I have attempted a redefinition of the hypothesis in terms of the following:

1. It is not true that a fall in death rates is a necessary condition for a fall in birthrates. In a few places in Europe birthrates fell before there was significant decline in death rates.

2. It is naive to think that the decision of parents to replace child loss on a one-to-one basis is simply an automatic reflex. The fact is, of course, that motivation for family planning is complex and no one variable can be expected to override other determinants of desired family size. Every partial influence must be examined. This is especially true because of the inexorable demand for improved child care.

3. The practical impact of the child-survival hypothesis is not uniform over time but seems to depend on the developmental level of the country. The insurance effect appears to be greatest when death rates are beginning to fall and birthrates are still high -- precisely the situation in which population growth is most rapid. The replacement effect seems to become evident after general practice of family-planning and lowered family size norms have already placed considerable constraints on fertility.

4. Demographers have tended to classify child-survival effects with the "volitional" as distinct from "natural" causes of family limitation. The volitional causes have been defined to relate to conscious family-planning decisions. Evidence from our studies in the Punjab suggests the need for a third classification of "subconscious expectations" which would also include many of the underlying beliefs that control behavior but that people do not tend to talk about in response to questionnaire surveys (20). This category would also include the motivational influences related to the economic value of children.

5. Of the most practical importance is the probability that child survival effects may be manipulable in contrast to many of the other demographic variables that have been studied. Retrospective data give little indication of the full potential of the interactions. But a direct effort to raise awareness of child survival from subconscious to conscious and personal decision-making levels may be feasible in integrated programs. This opens up the possibility of identifying and systematically using family-planning "entry points" as part of routine maternal and child health services provided by auxiliaries. These are points in the normal care routines where family-planning discussions can be introduced readily and records are designed to show whether appropriate issues were discussed. Although it is frequently alleged that health services are too expensive for

low-income countries, several studies have shown that under village conditions auxiliary-based integrated services for family planning, nutritional surveillance, education, and targeted supplementation, and for simple health care can be provided for less than $2 per capita per year (20).

Evidence supporting this redefinition, with its important implications for integrated programs, has been mobilized from many sources. Time series data show a clear association between the declines in national birthrates and in national death rates. There is also a correlation between the rate of decline in infant mortality and the time that elapses between the onset of a decline in fertility. This time lag has averaged about 11 years in the period since World War II.

Since association does not necessarily imply causation, more weight should be given to nine in-depth studies of relationships between infant mortality and fertility with particular attention to the sequential family-building process in six geocultural areas. Similar data from four other studies associated with action programs were also analyzed. Both types of studies showed that the following wide variety of indicators of higher fertility were associated with a variety of measures of experience or fear of child loss (28, pp. 263-78). The fertility variables were birth intervals, number of births, ideal number of children, parity progression ratios, expected total births, approval of contraception, timing of contraception, and effectiveness of methods of contraception used; the mortality variables were number of child deaths, fear of child loss, loss of child born preceding the measured interval between births, community levels of child loss, perception of child survival, and approval of insurance births. The various data sets included controls for parity, sex, lactation, surviving sons, maternal age, and births in previous year, and many different approaches to statistical analysis were used. Because of the new evidence on the importance of lactation, it seems worth noting that this has its main influence on birth intervals and not on all the fertility variables studied.

There were, however, four studies by Adlakha (1), Alam (3), Heer and Wu (11), and Rutstein (21) which separated the motivational effect from the lactational effect of greater child survival on fertility variables. They demonstrated that subsequent to a child death there was a shortening of the second birth interval after an intervening child had survived, and also that when nonlactating women were separated out they too had a reduced birth interval as compared with controls.

Even more significant in program terms are findings that relate child survival to the use of family planning. Studies of the relationship between child mortality and family planning show that when couples lost a child they were less favorably inclined toward contraception, practiced contraception less often, and delayed first use after birth in comparison with couples who had not lost a child. Perception of increased child survival was associated with greater use of the more effective methods of contraception (26).

From the program point of view the practical challenge is to determine how these motivational variables can be enhanced in mass programs. The spontaneous relationships that have been measured in retrospective surveys indicate only partially what might be achieved through deliberate use of child-survival motivations in integrated programs. If the motivational mechanism is subconscious then direct efforts to make parents aware that their children are surviving and healthy can be used as a family-planning entry point in child care.

Some ten years ago the Rural Health Research Center in India set up long-term prospective research in the Punjab at Narangwal primarily to test the child-survival hypothesis (20). Various groups of villages received different combinations of maternal and child care of family planning provided by auxiliaries in a research design intended to measure differential impact. Conclusive evidence on fertility changes in these groups of villages was not obtained because political pressures created premature termination of the project. Family-planning practice and fertility decline more than doubled in the service villages as compared with controls. In all study groups, however, family-planning practice was still increasing when the study ended. We did not have the five years of observation that we had projected would be necessary to get a plateauing of the curves showing the ultimate impact of each combination of health and family-planning services. Nevertheless, the study did indicate changes in motivational patterns. In the group of villages in which real integration of services was achieved in comparison to four other groups of villages the following differences in attitude were noted: awareness that there were more children surviving than 30 yeas ago increased sharply while in other villages it went down, probably because the health education was stressing hazards to child health. These differences were especially great in low caste groups. Similarly, half of the women from the group of villages with integration said that the greater child survival would influence favorably their decision about how many children they would have as compared with only one-third in other villages. Furthermore, of all women who said that fewer children are dying now than 30 years ago, more than half said this influenced their decisions about how many children to have, while less than one-fifth of those who thought more die said that this influenced their decisions.

Replacement and insurance desires should not be expected to override all other considerations as a motivational force. There is probably a spectrum of responses ranging from lower parity children who are lost even though wanted and are therefore replaced, on to children at higher parities whose births go beyond family expectations so that there presumably would be no tendency to replace further losses. These family level relationships operate within broader community norms and expectations. Where eight to nine children are born and only three to four survive, as in many African villages, insurance and replacement desires may add three or more births. Where an average of four children are born and three survive, the potential replacement desire would undoubtedly be considerably less than one. As child mortality declines, the subconscious expectation of death would also normally decline but only after a lag period. The important issue is where on this spectrum does practical decision making lead to the practice of family planning. An important program component may simply be the education of parents who must understand that survival has improved and that it is no longer necessary to have insurance births. When expectations of survival are high, then replacement desires may become more explicit.

The indirect attitudinal effects of improved health on family decisions may be more potent than the direct effects (15, 24, 25). Expectations of child survival seem to be part of a general subconscious orientation toward the future which also influences attitudes toward development planning and hard work. Field studies to quantify these effects for populations at different levels of mortality and fertility, and in different geocultural regions, could make significant contributions to our understanding of the rationale for integrating health, nutrition, and family-planning services.

III. CASE STUDIES OF THE NUTRITIONAL IMPACT OF FIELD PROGRAMS

The lack of success in implementing most mass nutrition programs requires reevaluation of basic approaches. In recent years I have been involved in two field studies of nutrition and have evaluated a third. These case studies illustrated the need for adjusting planning to the specific local ecology and for knowing how local causal variables act at various levels of development. They also demonstrate that nutrition interventions can produce major change in some situations, but cannot easily do so in others.

Reduction in mortality was achieved at Narangwal in the Indian Punjab with intensive, home-based comprehensive child care by auxiliaries (20). Child mortality from ages one to three was reduced by 40 percent and infant mortality by about a third by a program combining infection control and focused nutritional supplementation based on close surveillance of all children. In controlled trials where groups of villages received different interventions, infection control was more effective for children under two years of age than was nutrition alone. Nutrition alone and infection control had equal impact for children from two to three years old, but significant prevalence of malnutrition continued even after maximum program impact. Longitudinal studies showed that when the amount of grade 2 and 3 malnutrition had been reduced by about half the improvement stopped. A hard core group, mostly girls, continued to have recurrent marasmus in spite of intensive efforts by family health workers because the high parity mothers did not have time to provide adequate care. It was evident that family planning was needed if community malnutrition levels were to be reduced further. Significant improvements in health and nutrition could not have been achieved by increasing food production.

The lessons of Narangwal were applied in a much less intensive form in a Bangladesh intervention program in Companiganj Thana, an

administrative unit in Noakhali District, which is described
elsewhere in this issue (see also 16). The Companiganj Project
confirmed the observations from Matlab Thana that infant and child
mortality falls after the rice harvest and then rises before the
next harvest. Clearly here is one situation where just supplying
food makes a difference. Percentages of children with third degree
malnutrition also fluctuated between a preharvest level of 22
percent and a postharvest level of 14 percent. Conditions were
especially bad during the famine in 1975. A health care program
which includes subsidized sale of a cereal-pulse mix that is
prepared in local mills has led to some improvement in nutrition,
but the family-planning program takes much of the time of the
project workers.

In Cornwall County, Jamaica, effective nutrition care was
provided by community health aides who were rural nomen trained in
short courses and assigned to visit regularly a group of homes in
rural neighborhoods -- supervised by medical students doing a
field rotation (2, pp. 1166-69). Improvements in mortality and
nutritional status seemed related most to the weighing of children
every month by community health aides. This identified for mothers
the fact that a child who was not gaining weight was a sick child.
As Jamaican mothers are very capable and food is available, they
were able to correct the problem once it had been recognized.

These three case studies obviously represent a spectrum in the
range of activities that need integration. In Bandladesh infant
mortality ranges from 150 to 200 per 1,000 live births or more
during famines. The obvious need is to provide food to target
groups in association with family planning to try to change both
fertility and mortality. In the food surplus Punjab where infant
mortality ranged around 100 per 1,000, a more comprehensive care
program of nutrition and infection control provided an opportunity
to show what could be done through total integration of services.
In Jamaica, with infant mortality below 40, the primary need seemed
to be simple surveillance to identify lack of weight gain.

IV. PROGRAM DEVELOPMENT

Programs which provide comprehensive coverage for rural
populations must depend on auxiliaries. The Narangwal program
employed auxiliary nurse-midwives who had high school education
plus two years of nursing training. They learned the Narangwal
routines in six weeks. The average cost for the comprehensive care
was less than $2 per capita per year.[1]

At Companiganj there was no trained pool of personnel to draw
on and village women were recruited and trained for six weeks. The
range of responsibilities was reduced in comparison with the
Narangwal pattern. About half of the village workers are
illiterate but to date they are doing as well as the literate
women. The costs here are about $1 per capita per year.

A major question is how much can be done to get villagers to assume responsibility for their own health and nutritional care. A first step should be that people gather the data needed to make their own community diagnosis. Then, village people can be trained for the following kinds of tasks: weighing children, providing nutrition education, giving out information and supplies for family planning, and simple health care. This approach offers hope of meeting the challenge of working at the interface between health services and communities to strengthen the capacity of the people to solve their own health problems. The key to effective implementation is supportive supervision that is primarily educational.

V. CONCLUSION

The integrated approach to providing health, family planning, and nutrition should fit in with broad-based intersectoral development. It has particular appeal because it is made up of a package of flexibly adjustable components which include specific measures that people already want. It promises efficiency in the use of limited resources. It provides coverage for complete populations with considerable potential for getting services to the rural poor. By improving the health and survival of parents and their children there is hope that the attitudes toward planning and working for the future can be changed. Another important consideration is that an integrated program resolves many of the ethical dilemmas associated with programs focused on single activities, especially family planning. Finally, the integrated approach provides an opportunity for meaningful interactions to improve mutually beneficial relationships between service personnel and communities.

NOTES

[1] The cost is based on detailed functional analysis studies which included careful work sampling. We were able to record time allocation in minutes per week and detailed cost data. Detailed household socioeconomic data also were gathered over the four years of the study.

CITATIONS

1. Arjun Adlakha, "A Study of Infant Mortality in Turkey,"
Ph.D. dissertation, University of Michigan, Ann Arbor, 1970.

2. Michael H. Alderman, Barry Levy, James Husted, and Ryan
Searle, "A Young Child Nutrition Programme in Rural Jamaica,"
Lancet, May 1973.

3. Igbal Alam, "The Relationship of Infant-Child Mortality
to Fertiity in Cebu, Philippines," Ph.D. dissertation, The Johns
Hopkins University, Baltimore, 1973.

4. Alan Berg, The Nutrition Factor, The Brookings
Institution, Washington, D.C., 1973.

5. Committee for International Coordination of National
Research in Demography, Seminar on Infant Mortality in Relation to
the Level of Fertility, Bangkok (Thailand), 6-12 May 1975, Paris,
1975.

6. V. Djukanovic and E. P. Mach, Alternative Approaches to
Meeting Basic Health Needs in Developing Countries, a Joint
UNICEF/WHO Study, World Health Organization, Geneva, 1975.

7. Paul Freire, "Cultural Action for Freedom," Harvard
Educational Review and Center for the Study of Development and
Change, Monograph No. I, Cambridge, 1970.

8. Stanley N. Gershoff, "Science: Neglected Ingredient in
Nutrition Policy," Journal of the American Dietetic Association,
May 1977.

9. Denis Goulet, The Cruel Choice: A New Concept in the
Theory of Development, Atheneum Publishers, New York, 1973.

10. _____, The Uncertain Promise: Value Conflicts
in Technology Transfer, IDOC/North America, New York, 1977.

11. David M. Heer and Hsin-ying Wu, "The Effect of Infant and
Child Mortality and Preference for Sons Upon Fertiity and Family
Planning Behavior and Attitudes in Taiwan," in J. Kantner, editor,
Population and Social Change in South East Asia, Lexington Books,
Lexington, Massachusetts, 1975.

12. Ivan Illich, Medical Nemesis: The Expropriation of
Health, Pantheon Books/Random House, New York, 1976.

13. Derrick Jelliffe, The Assessment of the Nutritional
Status of the Community, World Health Organization Monograph No.
53, Geneva, 1966.

14. Maurice King, Medical Care in Developing Countries, Oxford University Press, Nairobi, Kenya, 1966.

15. Wilfred Malenbaum, "Health and Economic Expansion in Poor Lands," International Journal of Health Services, 3, 2, 1973.

16. Colin McCord, "The Companiganj Rural Health Project: A Joint Venture Between Government and Voluntary Agencies," Contact 34, Christian Medical Commission, World Council of Churches, Geneva, August 1976.

17. David Morley, Paediatric Priorities in the Developing World, Butterworth and Company, London, 1973.

18. Samuel H. Preston, "Health Programs and Population Growth," Population and Development Review, I, December 1975.

19. Wiliam A. Reinke, editor, Health Planning: Qualitative Aspects of Quantitative Techniques, Department of International Health, Johns Hopkins School of Hygiene and Public Health, Baltimore, 1975.

20. Rural Health Research Center (India), The Narangwal Population Study: Integrated Health and Family Planning Services, Rural Health Research Center, Narangwal, Punjab and Department of International Health, School of Hygiene and Public Health, Johns Hopkins University, Baltimore, 1975.

21. Shea Rutstein, "The Influence of Child Mortality on Fertiilty in Taiwan: A Study Based on Sample Surveys Conducted in 1967 and 1969," Ph.D. dissertation, University of Michigan, Ann Arbor, 1971.

22. Nevin Scrimshaw, John Gordon, and Carl Taylor, "The Interactions of Nutrition and Infection," American Journal of Medical Science, 237, March 1959.

23. _____, The Interactions of Nutrition and Infection, World Health Organization Monograph No. 57, Geneva, 1968.

24. Carl Taylor, "Health and Population," Foreign Affairs, 43, 3, 1965.

25. Carl Taylor and Francoise-Maries Hall, "Health, Population and Economic Development," Science, August 11, 1967.

26. Carl Taylor and Harbans Takulia, Integration of Health and Family Planning in Village Sub-Centres: Report on the Fifth Narangwal Conference, November 1970, Rural Health Research Center, Narangwal, Punjab, 1970.

27. Carl Taylor, Jeanne Newman, and Narindar Kelly, "Interactions Between Health and Population," Studies in Family

266   Carl E. Taylor

Planning, 7, April 1976.

    28. _____, "The Child Survival Hypothesis,"
Population Studies, 30, July 1976.

Monitoring and Servicing National Health

AMOR BENYOUSSEF

I. INTRODUCTION

The purpose of this article is to review recent work dealing
generally with methodological and technical issues in health and
development. It also presents examples of the use of the social
sciences, including health demography and economics, and their
application to the question of health services delivery. It
finally analyses some countries' experiences in Africa, Asia and
Latin America in dealing with the delivery of health services to
the underserved rural and nomadic populations. In this connection
the author's views are offered on the methodology and findings of
some WHO country-assisted programmes in the area of health services
delivery.

The overwhelming magnitude of unmet health needs in many
countries throughout the developing world underlines the evidence
of inability of 'scientific medicine', as it is now known, to meet
the needs of non-industrial underprivileged populations. In fact,
this should not be directly related to the failure of scientific
medicine as such, but to the adopting of health-care delivery
systems unable to meet the needs and possibilities of
non-industrial populations. 'These failures, combined with the
apparent success of a completely different approach to health care
currently witnessed in some isolated regions of the world, has led
to the concept of health care community-based or 'primary' health
care.

Health care is one of the most important of all human
endeavours to improve the quality of life and yet a large
proportion of the world's population has no access to health care

From **INTERNATIONAL SOCIAL SCIENCE JOURNAL**, Vol 29, 1977, (397-418),
reprinted by permission of the publisher.

at all, and for many of the rest the care they receive does not alleviate their problems.[1] The spectacular advances of medical science have not touched the majority of the people in the world. The majority of the developing world's population still suffer and die from the same diseases which afflicted their forefathers. There is a rising clamour to provide medical care to all the people in a country and simultaneously a growing awareness that the biomedical sciences by themselves cannot solve the problem of how best to deliver the scarce health care resources to large numbers of people.

Other methodologies for analysing and managing complex social systems are essential if we are to make even a beginning in providing medical care to all the population. Stallones[2] expressed this opinion when he wrote that:

> medical care has little, if any, effect on the health of a community [because] from a community health viewpoint medical care always comes too late. The major benefits that have accrued to us in the past hundred years have resulted from the operation of non-specific influences not under our [i.e. medical profession] direction while scientific advances have been based very solidly on Aristotelian logic and reductionist philosophy. Our obsession with reductionism has led us to ignore the very real values of a systems-oriented approach. Three notions--that an effect has a complex web of antecedents; that a cause produces an intricate ramification of effects; and that modification of one element of a system may be transmitted into distant responses--open the door to a genuinely ecologically oriented approach to the prevention disease.

It is impossible to plan for health care without considering the circular causation at work between the health field and the whole social environment. Myrdal[3] cautions against oversimplifying our understanding of health by isolating it from other socio-economic, institutional and policy factors of the development process.

However, it has long been held true that medical care cannot be considered merely in terms of costs incurred and material benefits accrued, but also must be justified on the basis of relief of pain and suffering. As Candau[4] points out:

> It is amazing to see how great a part of their resources poor people are willing to use, and do in fact use, in order to alleviate the suffering caused by ill health, though of course their sacrifices may be ineffective.

In order to relate these viewpoints an intersectoral modelling of health and the socio-economic environment in developing countries has been developed which attempts to relate environmental factors to fertility and mortality rates and which simultaneously investigates the maximum feasible expansion of health services. At a macro-level this effort relates the health sector to other sectors relevant to socio-economic factors and their interactions and stimulates the dynamic behaviour of the overall system; at a micro-level it examines the expansion of health services.[5]

II. POPULATION COVERAGE AND USE OF HEALTH SERVICES

General Framework

We know, of course, that providing health services is much more problematic in developing than in developed countries. Resources are in short supply. Ratios of the numbers of doctors, nurses and other professionals to the population may be of the order of 10 to 100 times smaller than those pertaining in the more affluent societies. The availability of hospitals and of modern medical technology is perhaps even less equitably distributed among the nations of the world. Even within developed countries, moreover, the distribution of medical care facilities is highly skewed. However, the tendency for both technological and manpower resources to mainly concentrate themselves in urban centres, and particularly in the primate cities of the developing countries, is even more pronounced. The result is that while in the urban areas of many developing countries substantial facilities may exist, rural areas may frequently have almost a complete dearth of manpower, facilities and modern technological resources for medical care.

Moreover, facilities are frequently inadequately staffed, maintained and supplied. It is not uncommon, especially at the periphery, to find hospitals or dispensaries without even minimally adequate supplies or standing idle because there is no one to offer care. Problems of organization and administration combine with difficulties in transportation to aggravate this situation of acute scarcity.

At the same time, among the rural populations which constitute the majority of the peoples of most developing countries, modern medicine is usually seen as no more than an ambiguous good. The theories and practices of Western medicine often clash violently with the accepted maxims and values of traditional society. Frequently, both the canons of folk practice and the existence of native practitioners seem to satisfy most of the medical needs of most of the people most of the time. When modern Western medicine, whether under governmental or private sponsorship, comes to the hinterland of developing countries it usually comes both as a strange and perhaps fearful innovation and as a competitor of established ways of obtaining help for the sick.

On the other hand, the need for medical care is very high among the populations of developing countries, characterized as they are by high degrees of poverty, unchecked exposure to communicable diseases, and low life expectancy. These needs are particularly great among infants and young children, but it is probably fair to say that the level of need of populations in the typical developing countries is substantially greater than for those of the more affluent societies where medical services are more available.

We may summarize the foregoing considerations by making three generalizations which, broadly speaking, apply in most developing countries of the world:

Even within developed countries, the distribution of medical care facilities is highly skewed. However, in the developing countries, the tendency for both technological and manpower resources to concentrate in urban centres, and particularly in the primate cities, is even more pronounced.

Facilities which do exist are frequently inadequately staffed, maintained and supplied. It is not uncommon, especially at the periphery, to find hospitals or dispensaries without even minimal supplies or standing idle because there is no staff to offer care.

Problems of organization and administration combine with transportation difficulties and further aggravate the situation.

These generalizations seem not to hold when 'Western medicine' is understood, accepted and the need for it felt by the people concerned.

There are two types of explanations regarding utilization of health services in developing countries. They concern respectively (a) health facilities; and (b) population characteristics. Health services utilization rates depend upon a complex set of factors relating to the interaction between individuals who perceive a need for service and the specific practitioners or facilities which are available to them.

Health Facilities

It is generally assumed that the greater the expertise and sophistication, the more effective the results of modern medical care. This is still highly controversial but has led, especially in developed countries, to an increasing tendency towards specialization on the part of physicians and other health workers and towards concentration of services in hospitals and other complex facilities where multiple and complex technologies are available for the treatment of the ill. In developed countries, there is evidence that the utilizing public is increasingly taking advantage of the more sophisticated facilities both in terms of the focus of care which they select and of the type of practitioner which they visit.

Population Characteristics

   As the population becomes knowledgeable about different levels of sophistication of medical services, it is reasonable to make two hypotheses about the utilization of services in the various types of medical facilities: (a) populations will tend differentially to choose the facility providing the most sophisticated of services; and (b) the productivity rate (i.e. the number of cases seen per professional worker, or other similar measure), will be greater in facilities possessing a large range of services and technical sophistication than in those providing fewer services. Some medical-care planners, believing that these hypotheses will be borne out by the evidence, have argued that the whole notion of providing unsophisticated 'minimal' service centres to remote rural populations needs to be reconsidered.
   Demographic and social factors which differentially affect the coverage and utilization of health services in developed countries probably operate in developing regions but often with increased force. Studies on utilization of health services in the developed countries have repeatedly suggested that the rates of utilization vary. according to such parameters as socio-economic status, education, urban/rural differences and according to a number of culturally determined attitudes. So-called 'predisposing' or 'enabling' factors have been clarified and defined for the first time in a recent international study on health care.[6]
   It has been known for many years that socio-economic status is associated with differences in the degree of utilization of physicians and other health services in industrialized countries. The different utilization rates reflect both the economic barriers to service and the differential demands among population subgroups for such services. Poverty appears to inhibit the use of health services in at least one way. These effects are likely to be more marked in developing than in developed countries because of the greater relative differences in affluence and because of the scarcity of health resources.
   Health care is a commodity: when health insurance is unavailable, economic, social, cultural and logistic barriers are obviously of tremendous importance. In developing countries, the reality of the economic barriers associated with poverty are greatly magnified, and even minimal charges may make the use of health care prohibitive for poor families. In many developing countries medical services are offered free by the government, but for the very poor, the problem of obtaining medical care may often conflict with the need to work in order to support a family. Besides, the distance the rural poor would have to travel constitutes a constraining factor. On balance, economic barriers as such are probably less of a hindrance to obtaining medical care in developing countries than they have historically been in 'free enterprise' countries.
   Plato's observation that there are two kinds of medicine, one for the rich and one for the poor, is true for most of the world. Where medicine is controlled by the mechanisms of the market, these

differences are reflected in a differential quality of the care available. Where economic barriers are removed through charity or the provision of public medical care, the wealthy often feel, correctly or not, that they can purchase better care and associated amenities through private medical practice. Public or charity clinics often have social characteristics which deter many of the poor from making full use of their facilities. The bureaucracy, impersonality, unpleasant facilities and long waiting time which often characterize hospital outpatient departments are also deterrents to use of medical care. When ethnic and other cultural differences are involved, the social distance between providers of care and recipients is sometimes so marked that medical encounters become aversive to those in need. It is generally believed that demographic, economic, social, cultural and logistical barriers also operate with a high degree of force upon the populations of developing countries. In many, mere distance is a major predictor of who will use health services. Physicians and other health workers in developing countries usually represent the advantaged, if not the elite, classes of society; by virtue of their education and training they may find it difficult to communicate with uneducated groups.

Attitudinal factors seem to also play a major role. Among the psychological manifestations of poverty are a number of attitudes which inhibit the utilization of medical care, including a lack of sophistication and understanding about need for care and a similar lack of appreciation of modern medicine. Above all, the poor, no strangers to problems of all sorts, may come to have a higher threshold for the vicissitudes of health; apathy comes to be a presiding symptom of poverty. The greater the degree of poverty the more pronounced are its psychological concomitants.

Finally, urban/rural status and 'modernizing' characteristics constitute still another set of factors. In developed countries, use of medical services tends to be higher for urban residents than for those in rural areas. Apparently, the demand for medical care in relation to need among rural dwellers is often lower than it is among urban people.[7] This may reflect the results of poverty (so often a rural phenomenon), educational differences, or differential perceptions of the adequacy of available medical care facilities. In developed countries differences between rural and urban areas have become less marked over the last fifty years. In most developing countries, however, these differences are still pronounced.

The Tunisia Study--Methodology and Findings

A review of the present state of knowledge of the factors involved in the utilization of health services shows that few studies are concerned with developing countries and rural areas of developed countries; that there is little multidisciplinary research; and, above all, that few studies are action-oriented.

This complex question, which is a cause of concern for the health authorities and a subject of controversy among research workers, needs to be clarified. In the study of the interaction of health services and their users a multi-disciplinary approach permits the identification of medical, demographic, ecological and socio-economic determinants as well as organization and management factors. Analysis of the adequacy of health services requires statistical analysis of both supply and demand in terms of cost and consumer satisfaction. This is an essential element in the planning, management and evaluation of health services.

The Tunisian study,[8] carried out with WHO assistance between 1969 and 1972, emphasized that both the factors having to do with the distribution and type of facilities in various regions of developing countries and the demographic and socio-economic factors characterizing their populations interact to determine actual levels of utilization of health services. The investigators worked out a technically simple and reasonably inexpensive methodology. This requires population sample surveys, the investigation of health services, and methods of analysis aimed at developing statistical indices. These methods were applied in a study carried out in the Governorate of Nabeul, Tunisia, by the Tunisian Ministry of Public Health and WHO. In each of seven zones (three urban and four rural) a sample of the population was selected for study on the basis of a household survey and analysis of medical records.

The household survey was used to ascertain which factors in a given population discriminate high and low levels of utilization. In all, 678 (446 urban and 232 rural) households, comprising 3,808 individuals, were interviewed. The estimated utilization rates, based on five years' use of the health services by persons whose medical records could be retrieved (38.5 per cent of the total sample), differed appreciably between the urban (88.5 per cent) and rural (46.2 per cent) zones, although the numbers of visits per illness were practically identical. The estimated utilization rates for the entire study population were appreciably lower (49.7 per cent and 19.8 per cent). An analysis of the eighty-six diagnoses found revealed that 30 per cent of the medical and social workload of the health services studied fell into four categories: acute bronchitis (10.6 per cent in urban zones and 13.9 per cent in rural zones); influenza (5.9 per cent and 3.4 per cent respectively); diarrhoea (7.7 per cent and 9.5 per cent); and vaccinations or inoculations (7 per cent and 3.2 per cent). Three categories accounted for almost half of the conditions treated by the health services: diseases of the respiratory system, major gastro-intestinal disorders, and skin diseases. There was little difference in the diagnostic pattern between urban and rural zones.

The questionnaire used in the survey covered demographic and socio-economic patterns of respondents, their perception of the need for care and advice, their experience of the health services (including their attitudes towards them and their staff), and self treatment and recourse to traditional medicine. Users were initially grouped into four categories in order to identify the relation between the extent to which they used the services and their attitudes and socio-economic characteristics. For the analysis, only two categories were taken into consideration:

households making extensive use of the services--i.e. those 90 per cent or more of whose members had a medical record--and those less than 50 per cent of whose members had such a record. The difference between urban and rural users was striking, as is shown in Table 1.

Statistical analysis revealed that those who made extensive use of the health services were generally more literate than those who did not, and that socio-cultural and economic differences existed between the two categories. In the urban and rural households studies, frequent users of the services were in general better acquainted with the means of preventing communicable diseases. On the other hand, respondents who lived in rural zones--particularly those who rarely made use of the services--complained that relations between physicians and patients and the care and medico-social advice provided were inadequate.

The study suggests that the utilization of health services may be regarded as an indicator of modernization and, hence, that improvement in health may depend not only on the impact of the health services but also on the process of change in society. This is an important issue for almost 80 per cent of the world's population and shows that the future development of health and education must be linked with overall development, of which community primary health care would form an integral part. This would entail adapting health and other aspects of development--such as education, agriculture, environmental health and transport--to the needs of the population.

To the extent that the population studied in Tunisia is representative of developing countries, the survey supported these conclusions. It demonstrated that: (a) utilization of health services is low in comparison to that which has been observed in more developed countries; ambulatory health services are used most often for treatment of the common communicable diseases, and 85 per cent of all patients are seen only once per episode of illness; (b) although some health services were available and accessible freely to all the population studied it was estimated that only 50.5 per cent utilize them in a given year; (c) utilization rates are strikingly higher among urban than rural residents; (d) respondents from high-user households were especially likely to have the following characteristics: urban residents who were literate had cultural traits such as reading newspapers, speaking French, watching television and participating in social and economic meeting. They tended also less often to admit being influenced by traditional medical practices, believed in the capabilities of modern medicine to prevent as well as treat illness, and were satisfied with the health services.

III. HEALTH, MIGRATION AND URBANIZATION

For many years it has been noted that urban life is associated with an increased risk of disease. Greenwood,[9] writing in the

1920s, attributed some of this increased risk to crowding, and consequent increased transmission of infectious diseases; both epidemiological and experimental[10] studies provided strong support for this hypothesis. More recently[11] it has been noted that many chronic, non-infectious diseases occur more frequently among urban residents. This difference cannot be as easily explained, and several theories have been put forward as to why urban life poses a hazard to health. They generally fall into two categories: (a) that increased risk of disease is attributable to environmental contaminants found in urban areas and (b) that persons migrating from rural to urban areas are exposed to deleterious social stress. The latter hypothesis has served to make a useful distinction between the health of urban dwellers generally and that of persons who have migrated to the city.

Large-scale migration to cities is occurring throughout the world, particularly in the developing countries. In order to clarify the health consequences of such migration, the World Health Organization has promoted several pilot studies.[12]

There are several ways whereby urban life could have deleterious health effects:

Environmental contaminants existing within a city may cause new diseases or aggravate existing conditions. The urban migrant finds himself exposed to such potential health hazards as air and water pollution, heavy traffic, and occupational hazards that he has not experienced in the rural area. According to this hypothesis, one would expect to find an increase in specific diseases associated with certain environmental contaminants. Also, within the urban area there might be observed a gradient of disease, depending on the concentration of the contaminants. This approach also implies that the migrant's health would be no worse than that of the other urban dwellers. There is evidence that severe and unusual environmental hazards may produce acute increases in mortality for many causes, for instance the 1966 Eastern Seaboard air pollution experience[13] and certain conditions such as chronic bronchitis have been related to air pollution in several countries. The fact, however, that almost every cause of mortality and morbidity is increased in many urban areas argues against the specific impact of environmental contaminants. Finally, there is evidence that disease rates are higher in farm-born persons who have migrated to cities, than amongst the urban-born.[14]

That crowding and more numerous social contacts may afford greater opportunities for the transmission of infectious diseases has recently been critically analysed by Cassel,[15] who has pointed out that the relationship between crowding and health is far more complex than originally envisaged. If crowding simply resulted in increased transmission of infectious diseases, then the urban dweller should have higher rates of these diseases only, particularly those that are airborne. But, as already noted, the rates for almost every disease are higher among urban dwellers. This theory is also difficult to evaluate because crowding is associated with other health hazards such as poor nutritional level and unavailability of adequate medical care. Finally, little is known about detailed social networks of persons who migrate to cities. It is conceivable that some migrants experience fewer social contacts after adopting urban life.

Adequate health care in a rapidly expanding urban area is certainly a major problem for the urban communities of the developing countries. Yet, in these same countries rural health services are even less developed, and it is more typical for a migrant to go from a rural area where there is virtually no medical care available, to an urban area where there is some, however inadequate. Furthermore, migrants may be different from the general population with respect to disease levels. It is well known that cities attract sick persons because of their medical care facilities. Stallones[16] has pointed out that within the United States there is a positive correlation between the physician-population ratio and mortality from coronary heart disease. There is no evidence, however, that most migrants go to cities because of an illness. This effect could operate in a more subtle way if the migrant differed from the non-migrant by having higher levels of genetic or acquired risk factors. It would be very important, therefore, to study the health status of migrants before they even decide to migrate. Such a study, now being conducted in the Tokelau Islands, may indicate whether this is an important factor.

Finally, the notion that has gained considerable support in recent years is that social change somehow imparts a risk to disease. Syme has written extensively about the relationship between coronary-heart disease and mobility.[17] The mobility may be generational--men living in adult circumstances which are quite different from those in which they were reared; persons who have changed jobs frequently seem to have higher disease rates; as do those who change their residence often; and those who do not move themselves, but whose world moves about them. Increased risk of coronary heart disease has been attributed, as Syme has put it, to moving from a world where the rules of the game are clear and known to one where different and unknown rules apply. Henry and Cassel[18] have reviewed a considerable body of experimental animal investigations that tend to support the idea of patho-physiological mechanisms responsible for this increase of disease, which remain to be elucidated, although there is some evidence that complex hormonal changes are involved.

Such ideas about social stress have generated interest in how the migrant adapts to urban life and whether those who adapt easily and quickly experience fewer health problems than those who adapt poorly. What can help a migrant to cope? It is intuitively appealing that social support such as having family or friends already in the urban area or the availability of community agencies may ease the migrant's adaptation. Some support for this hypothesis comes from a recent study at the University of North Carolina, where it was found that pregnant women who experienced a life crisis had far fewer complications of delivery if they possessed psycho-social assets.[19]

There are a number of methodological problems that must be solved in studying the health effects of urban migration. A somewhat ideal study might measure relevant health and social factors in a cohort of rural people before they have decided to migrate, remeasure these factors after the decision to migrate has been taken but before migration actually takes place, and then continue to remeasure these factors at intervals after arrival in the urban area. Repeat examinations would have to be done on different samples of the cohort since the examinations themselves might influence adaptation and such a study would be very long-term. It is unlikely that a large-scale study of this type would be feasible. A compromise used on a number of occasions has been to compare rural to urban residents. A refinement of this approach is to compare rural people to similar people who have migrated to the city, and a further refinement would be to try to measure adaptation to urban life and relate this measure to the health of urban residents. Both these latter approaches were attempted in a study in Senegal.

The Senegal Study: Methodology and Findings

The Senegal Collaborative Study[20] was carried out from 1970 to 1973 by WHO, the University of Dakar, and the Office de la Recherche Scientifique et Technique Outre-Mer, Dakar-Centre, with the technical assistance of the Ministry of Public Health and Social Affairs and other ministries of Senegal. Its object was to assess the effects of urban migration on the health of a sample of Serer migrants from the rural district of Niakhar, some 100 kilometres from Dakar, who were resident in the city at the time of the study. The urban sample was compared to a sample of the rural population of Niakhar from the triple viewpoint of socio-demographic situation, physical and mental health, and housing and the immediate environment. The analysis of findings from the urban sample included the identification of some of the factors associated with adaptation to urban life.

In the non-medical parts of the study,[21] the demographic, economic and socio-cultural aspects of urban migration were investigated. The distribution by age group, sex and marital status showed that the urban migrant population tends to be younger than the rural population and that it includes twice as many single females. Traditional religious practices remained important in the rural area but decreased in significance in Dakar among the urban migrants; this may reflect the greater influence of Islam among the urban population. As might be expected, the educational level, as measured by school attendance and number of years spent in school, was much higher among urban than among rural dwellers; it was also markedly higher among adult males than females. Comparisons of socio-economic conditions between the rural and urban samples showed differences in diet, food, consumption, clothing, and housing that reflect a change in attitudes and behaviour as a consequence of acculturation and urbanization. Finally, the way in which rural and urban dwellers perceived and dealt with health problems did not differ greatly. However, while males migrating to the city continued to trust both folk and modern therapy, females in Dakar tended to believe more in modern medicine.

Three areas of medical concern were studied in particular:[22] precursors of coronary heart disease (CHD), anaemia, and infectious diseases. Little difference was observed between rural and urban populations for most of the precursors of CHD measured, except that the urban samples had higher levels of cholesterol and the males smoked more cigarettes. Anaemia was more common in the rural area in both sexes. Among infectious diseases, malaria, intestinal parasites, and tuberculosis were more prevalent in the rural samples. Schistosomiasis was quite common in both the urban and rural samples. Mental health was assessed through a questionnaire covering various psychiatric conditions of a mild, moderate or severe nature and by subsequent evaluation procedures. In general, the frequency of these conditions was similar in the urban and rural populations, though psycho-physiological reactions and brain syndromes were more common among the urban sample, whereas depression and fatigue were more common among rural people. There was no difference in the rate of anxiety between the two groups. It also appears that there may be certain groups, such as young single women, who have difficulty in adapting to urban life and may be at a high risk for certain diseases. If a subsequent study should bear this out, such groups might well benefit from special social services.

IV. PRIMARY HEALTH CARE

In a recent publication[23] of the World Health Organization it was suggested that primary health care could be called 'Health by the People', which can be both a philosophical and a practical idea. Philosophically one can believe that community organizations, using their powers of self-determination, should be the starting point of health care services. Practically, since there is seldom enough money in most developing countries to consider any other course of action, community organization must be the starting point.

Primary health care is an approach shaped around the population it serves. It uses methods and techniques that are appropriate, inexpensive and acceptable to the community. In so far as possible, the manpower, materials and funds for the project are generated from within the community itself. The major efforts of primary health care are undertaken at the most peripheral community level practicable. However, it should at the same time be an integral part of the regional or national health system and should be fully integrated into the national health system. The WHO publication lists five functions for community organizations: setting priorities, organizing community action for problems which cannot be resolved by individuals (for example, water supply and basic sanitation), legitimizing the primary health care worker, financially assisting the services, and linking health activities to wider community goals.

The community can set health priorities, by using the fourfold criteria of community concern for the problem, its seriousness, its point prevalence and its susceptibility to management.[24] Once the priorities are determined, appropriate action can be taken, requiring primary health care workers who can be selected, trained, financed and inspired by the community. The concept of the primary health care worker is, by now, well known. This worker is neither a doctor, a nurse, a sanitary engineer, nor a nutritionist but, to an extent, performs at a local level some of the duties of each of these roles.[25] The fact that he is a trusted and accepted member of the community is often as important as his training.

It has been found[26] that in time the primary health care worker, along with the community organization, comes to recognize the binding relationship between specific local health problems and, to an extent, the wider regional socio-economic situation in general. Urban malnutrition, for example, can be seen to be closely connected with food production in the rural areas of the country which, in turn, may be linked to the political situation as in China or the United Republic of Tanzania. It should be noted that primary health care and the primary health care worker depend on the use of feasible modern scientific knowledge and health technology, as well as on accepted and effective traditional healing practices and linkage with other tiers of the health advice system, from which the primary health care worker should have adequate supervision, referral services for his patients and training facilities.

A review article[27] dealing with the literature of primary health care deplores that most material lacks documentation and often extols one form of primary health care at the expense of another. The review concludes that the literature can be divided into three groups: conceptual and methodological, evaluative and descriptive.

The conceptual articles are primarily technical, often theoretical works which may never be transformed into working systems. The evaluative literature describes the frustrations of attempting to perform statistical analyses on non-quantifiable data. Descriptive papers may be distorted by the political viewpoint of the author. In general, one could say that most inquiries into primary health care are still in the developmental stage. However, this need not be disquieting, since primary health care is a service to the people, attempting to meet their needs, which properly bears little relation to cold, impassionate, impersonal 'science'.

One recent publication[28] devises a framework for categorizing methods of measuring the various aspects of the quality of health care. This approach could perhaps be useful in making decisions regarding where and how to expand services.

The great bulk of literature on primary health care falls into the third or empirical descriptive category. In the following section we shall adopt this approach to present a selection of currently existing primary health care activities, chosen to represent a broad range of types and a variety of ecological, socio-economic and political settings.

Before doing so, however, it is worth noting that in a recent publication[29] the World Bank Group discusses primary health care in relation to rural economic development. Independently and at a technical level, this reaches nearly the same conclusions as the WHO/Unicef group concerning the need for primary health care and the importance of linking it to the other aspects of rural development.[30]

One of the findings is that the health conditions of the poor everywhere are basically similar. Their core disease pattern consists of the faecally-related and air-borne diseases and malnutrition. Together these account for the majority of deaths among the poorest people in developing countries. The study notes that there is a marked association between the per capita income in a developing country and its health status and that one way to raise the general level of health in a region is simply to raise its standard of living. This relationship between per capita income and health can be seen in comparing certain African countries, which have the lowest per capita incomes and report the lowest levels of health, to certain Latin American countries, which are among the wealthiest of the developing nations, and have health conditions approaching those of the developed world. It is concluded that:[31]

> public health expenditures to improve the quality of life of the poor can be justified on moral and economic grounds, although the complex and dynamic interaction of demographic, social and cultural forces affected by the health workers make it difficult to say, on economic grounds, how large such expenditures should be.

Some Illustrative Country Experiences

China: A Persuasive Health Approach

In China, the entire population has been fundamentally oriented towards disease prevention and primary health care through the guiding inspiration of the top political leadership, particularly the late Chairman Mao Tse-tung.[32] In the early 1950s and 1960s, mass health and sanitation campaigns were organized to secure the personal involvement and commitment of each individual as a patriotic duty to the country and to himself. Mass education drives instructed people to build sanitation facilities and keep their neighbourhoods clean. Everyone was encouraged to practise preventive health care, to 'fight against his own disease' as an enemy to be conquered, and to help his neighbours.

In 1965, Chairman Mao issued the 'June 26 Directive' which put the spotlight on the health needs of China's large rural population and on the inability of the existing health services to provide for them. This led to the so-called 'barefoot doctors', locally recruited rural youths who receive three months of formal training in the use of both traditional Chinese and Western medicine, followed by supervised on-the-job training. The 'barefoot doctors' serve in the rural communes as regular agricultural workers, and provide health care on a part-time basis to the production teams (the smallest subdivision of a commune into which all of rural China is divided) each of which numbers from 100 to 200 people. Each commune supervises between ten and thirty production brigade health stations covering 500 to 3,000 people. The care provided by the 'barefoot doctors' includes treatment of minor illnesses, prevention and health education in both health stations and in the fields; in addition they supervise volunteer health aids who deal with sanitation problems.

There are now over a million 'barefoot doctors' in China, not counting the analogous worker doctors in the factories and the Red Medical Workers active in every city lane. One of the most important tasks of China's health workers is the reduction of the birth rate, which has been quite successful due to constant vigilance, person-to-person contact and educational activities.

Because primary health care is part of the national health system which is administered in decentralized fashion at the community level, health facilities are locally planned and financed and the benefits differ somewhat in the urban and the rural settings. Urban factories maintain health and welfare funds to which are allocated respectively 10 per cent and 2-3 per cent of total salaries; these percentages are said to be 'mandated by the State' and are not considered as tax deductions from wages. Workers' health treatment expenses are free, as they are charged against the fund, whereas neighbourhood lane clinics meet their expenses by charging a fee to patients, except in those clinics where a 'co-operative medical system' has been introduced and patients pay only an annual premium.

In rural China, some 70 per cent out of the production brigades now have a co-operative medical care system, where each member who desires coverage contributes a fixed annual amount which is supplemented by contributions from the production brigade and, in some cases, from the production team welfare funds. There are considerable variations, so that while under some arrangements all the needed services are thus covered, in others a small additional visit fee is charged.

For most visits to the doctor in China, including visits to the 'barefoot doctor', the patient must pay at least a small 'registration fee'.

Primary health care appears to be an essential echelon integrated into the highly structured Chinese national health system. As such, it is an important element in the system's stated priority to provide accessible health care to all, particularly to those who had no access to it in the past.

Perhaps the most remarkable feature of the primary health care programme in China is the extent of its coverage. With its linkage to the mass health popularization campaigns in their emphasis on the strengthening of health care in rural areas, where 85 per cent of China's population live, its pervasive roots anchored in the population of closely knit neighbourhood, team and local residents' health stations, the Chinese PHC programme appears to have developed a comprehensive network for professional, supervised and responsible health care at the grass roots, on the way to achieving practical full health care coverage for China's large population.

United Republic of Tanzania: Population Relocation Helps Simplify Medical Care

Primary health care in the United Republic of Tanzania is being promoted in the framework of the government's commitment to improving basic health services in the rural areas as an integral part of the country's overall socio-economic development.[33]

A major obstacle to the development of this large country has been the widely dispersed situation of its population. Recently, an original attempt was made to solve this problem by grouping the population into larger, economically viable communities called Ujamaa villages, consisting of 100 to 500 families working together collectively. This strategy has greatly facilitated the provision of essential amenities such as wholesome water and basic health services, as well as raising farm productivity; these villages also serve as bases for mass health and sanitation campaigns and help make easier the treatment of communicable diseases and the health education of the population.

Nation-wide emphasis is placed on self-reliance and disease prevention. There is strong community participation in planning and villagers' involvement is encouraged in the construction of their own health facilities, such as health posts, of which there is one in each village. They choose and support their own medical helpers, who staff the health posts and provide treatment for minor ailments. Other primary health care facilities include rural dispensaries (one for 600 to 8,000 inhabitants) which provide higher-level diagnosis and treatment as well as maternal and child health services and mobile health teams which provide health care in areas where institutional coverage is very thin.

Since this young programme started (1972/73), it has already achieved primary health care coverage of over 3 million people by health posts in some 5,500 Ujamaa villages, and about 13 million people are served by 1,555 dispensaries, backed up by 69 health centers and 128 hospitals; it is vigorously progressing towards fuller and more comprehensive coverage. The Tanzanian primary health care programme has met with considerable success and, due to its heavy emphasis on minimization of cost and its relatively modest resource requirements, its approach offers great replicability, particularly for certain neighbouring African countries which have been co-operating in various aspects of health services.

Venezuela: A Pyramid of Simplified Health Care

Primary health care in Venezuela is identified with the 'simplified medicine' scheme adopted in 1962 by the Ministry of Health, as an organized and homogeneous effort to provide basic health care to the country's dispersed rural population.[34] The programme grew out of the pressing and hitherto unmet need for health care by people living in scattered, remote areas and for whom, due to the shortage of trained health staff and other facilities, there was no hope of obtaining professional medical attention. The scheme represents a simple, practical approach to the provision of at least some rudiments of health care and attention to the rural population.

Primary health care in the 'simplified medicine' scheme is essentially preventive and curative and is based in a network of village dispensaries or rural health posts, each one staffed by one auxiliary health worker specially trained for the job. They are the 'front line' integral part of the developing National Health Service which is itself anchored on the centrally administered regional network of the 'Co-operative Health Service', extant in thirteen out of the twenty-three political units of the country and comprising three other higher levels, considered as a necessary supporting structure for the community based front line. These include: the medicatora or rural health post staffed with a doctor and a few auxiliaries and providing medical care to semi-rural and intermediate populations and support for the peripheral level, including sick beds in areas of reasonably high population; the health centre, which is the focal point of the health district (of which there are eighty-five throughout the country) offering regular hospital facilities and professional staff for basic medical services; and a fourth level, represented by the State and/or regional services providing specialized hospital facilities (mental, tuberculosis, etc.).

The health auxiliary is the essential primary health care worker in Venezuela. He or she staffs the rural dispensary, serving from 500 to several thousand people, and must be on call at all times for emergencies, in addition to the regular eight-hour work day. To be selected for training a candidate must be aged 18-40, a permanent resident in the locality of action, be acceptable to the local leaders, and have had six years of primary schooling. Training lasts four months and is geared to a detailed manual of instruction, complemented by a period of in-service training with the nurse-supervisor. Emphasis is placed on the 'human' approach, confidentiality of patient treatment and on the observance of the limits of the auxiliary's competence by referring complex cases to higher levels of service. The training period is sanctioned by a formal certificate to the effect that the auxiliary can perform his functions only in a rural dispensary under the regulations of the health service. In the auxiliary's duties, maternal and child health has priority. This calls for regular follow-up of pregnant women, encouragement of institutional deliveries, supervision in the hygienic and prophylactic procedures of local midwives and collaboration with them for home visits in cases of home deliveries. Another major function of the auxiliary is carrying out curative treatment of illness cases he is able to identify. Health education is given to waiting patients, through home visits, special mothers' classes, children's clubs and community meetings. Other functions include registration of vital events (unofficial) and vigilance concerning certain communicable diseases.

Auxiliaries have been increasingly playing roles of promoters of the general well-being of communities, spurring on community developmental activities such as home and agricultural improvement and some have become the real leaders in the community. At the end of 1973, 792 health auxiliaries had been trained and the PHC network numbered 315 dispensaries and 496 medicaturas, covering an estimated population of 280,000 (out of a rural total of 2.3 million). The programme is government-financed but communities are encouraged to participate in the maintenance and running costs of the dispensaries and contribute in kind for their construction and equipment.

The 'simplified medicine' scheme has the merit of making operational a comprehensive alternative to the previous situation of a chaotic plethora of unrelated and gap-ridden health care schemes. Although its progress has been slowed down by administrative and staffing problems, it has managed to extend health care coverage to many previously neglected areas and has been well received and utilized.

Cuba: A Political Approach to Health Problems

At present Cuba has a health service system available to nearly all of its population, with a referral system ensuring that each patient receives the appropriate level of care. This has not always been the situation. Before 1959, a considerable part of the rural population had no access to any form of health services. The change has come about because of the political revolution in 1959, after which time health care was considered an excellent political investment. Health services are free and run by the State on the principle that the health of the population is a government responsibility, that health services should be available to the total population and the community should actively participate in health work.

Numerous auxiliary personnel were trained and, in 1961, the decision was made to require six months' service in rural areas by all new medical graduates. Measures were taken to achieve complete geographical and population coverage in the whole country. The curative doctor of former times has been replaced by a corps of workers with a comprehensive view of medicine--preventative, environmental, rehabilitative and curative. Perhaps even more decisive for health has been the food distributed to the population. Impressive results have been seen in some areas. For example, mortality from diarrhoeal diseases dropped from 68 deaths per 100,000 population in 1962 to approximately 15 per 100,000 population in 1972. Other health indices have also improved, but not so dramatically. The infant mortality rate was 33 in 1958 and 27 in 1973, and the crude death rate has dropped from 6.5 to 5.8 in the same period.

Niger: Voluntary Workers Help Keep Health Expenses Low

The Republic of Niger has been relying on voluntary workers to cover the elementary health needs of populations living in remote areas. In 1963, the first village health workers were trained to give basic treatment, develop hygiene and improve basic nutrition in their villages. By 1970, various pilot projects were integrated, training was gradually extended and organized so that by 1974 Niger had 780 village health workers and 467 village midwives. At the same time, rural dispensaries were upgraded to rural health centres where regional health action plans could be devised, the midwives and village workers trained and continuing education carried on. Cost is kept to a minimum since the village health workers are volunteers and are not paid. The only expenses are for the training and refresher courses, the medical supplies and the petrol used in transporting the worker and the supplies.

In 1970 a pilot project was initiated in the Department of Marodi where the major diseases were infectious or parasitic and infant malnutrition was widespread. Village pharmacies were opened and village health workers and birth attendants trained. Once a month the village pharmacy is supervised by a nurse from the nearest health establishment who checks the general state of cleanliness of the village, replenishes the supply of free drugs and checks on any incompetence or unwillingness shown by the village health workers. The improvement in health care at the village level is such that it is rare for a village to refuse to develop its own set of village health workers.

Sudan: A Multi-disciplinary Approach to Primary Health Care

In 1975 an in-depth study was made on health programming following which the Sudan, with the assistance of WHO, prepared a 'National Health Programme'.[35] Two related long-term plans also prepared with the assistance of WHO deal specifically with the problem of primary health care in the Southern Region and the four other regions of the country, particularly in the least favoured provinces of the east and west in which the population is mainly rural and nomadic.[36]

These studies evaluate methods and procedures used in the

Sudan for the national programming and formulation of the primary health care programme. Within this framework health programming and health programme formulation depend upon the global decision-making process based on technical, demographic, cultural, socio-economic, financial and political/administrative considerations. In practice programme formulation activities took into consideration broader indicators which inspired the Sudan studies with a truly intersectoral approach.

This approach was designed within the overall framework of socio-economic development, using the following steps: definition of objectives, preparation of strategies, analysis of constraints inherent in these strategies, development of health programmes out of these strategies, estimates of cost in terms of development (capital) and recurrent expenditures, establishment of timetables for pre-implementation and implementation phases.

This methodology included also the development of criteria and setting of objectives for the primary health care programme as a whole, defining strategies for rural and nomadic populations, analysis of constraints and fixing timetables, and finally making programme cost estimates on an annual basis.

The Sudanese experience illustrates how pertinent and important factors other than purely medical can be, especially in terms of strategies for coverage of rural and nomadic populations. These strategies will rely heavily on the participation of the population within the overall framework of community development schemes.

V. CONCLUSION

During the past decade various individual groups and some governments and international organizations have approached the massive problems of poverty, sickness, disease and death, via the route of primary health care. In some cases, existing services were extended from urban centres out to the villages, in others series of interconnected political, economic and social measures, were introduced, while others still started with basic improvements at the village level. The methods used were not the same, yet in each instance a degree of success can be reported. By the use of simple, basic health techniques and the provision of food, education and assistance in financing, the health of many communities has dramatically improved.[37] None of these contrasting approaches include enough data to make it possible to say that any one method is quicker, cheaper or more effective than another one. All are, to some extent, successes when viewed from within (i.e. by their own subjective criteria) yet not all appear viable, or even beneficial, in the long-term. Nevertheless, it is encouraging to note that the possibility for change does exist and that there is no single method that is universally applicable.

There are several questions that can legitimately be asked concerning primary health care.

Is it true that primary health care is the best approach in developing countries? It is at least one approach and action is generally preferable to inaction. If the choice is between offering primary health care or no health care at all, then the answer is obvious.

Is primary health care merely another passing fad in medical care, or is it the wave of the future? In certain countries (China, Venezuela and the United Republic of Tanzania for example), primary health care is so well entrenched that it is hard to think of it as a transitory phenomenon. In other countries the reverse may be true.

Should one be optimistic about the results of primary health care? Achievements in basic health are usually determined by the dedication of the planners and implementation of the health schemes. In some cases the results have been highly rewarding, in others disappointing. Projects that were realistically conceived, well planned and highly motivated, usually succeeded. Others, lacking these basic ingredients, often failed.

What are the areas of primary health care that need further attention? Co-ordination of local, regional and national health efforts needs to be refined and improved; training courses for the primary health care worker must be maintained and brought into focus; coverage should be continuously extended until all segments of the population have access to health care services.[38]

What lessons can be learned from national primary health care experiences? Primary health care is not an easily obtainable goal. It requires years of trial, error and sometimes even failure, to attain a workable and manageable system. It is necessary to persevere through seemingly insurmountable obstacles if the goal is to be reached. Patience and endurance, more than energy and daring, may be the human qualities needed to instigate and bring to fruition a primary health care system in developing countries.

The experience in Africa, Latin America and Asia over the past ten years points to the need for a multidisciplinary approach where health priorities are understood within the general framework of rural development. Such an approach permits epidemiologists and administrators as well as socio-economic planners, social scientists and statisticians to contribute to a better understanding of complex socio-medical priority problems. This understanding must be the basis for health policy-making within the overall development process.

Over the past twenty years, the African, Latin American and Asian experience in this field points to the need for a close time of situational analysis and action. This essentially implies an emphasis on modifiable factors in research and development, together with an effort to minimize financial and human costs compatible with the scarcity of resources and management constraints.[39]

NOTES

[1] J. Bryant, Health and the Developing World, Ithaca, N.Y., Cornell University Press, 1969.

[2] R. A. Stallones, 'Environment, Ecology and Epidemiology', WHO Chronicle, Vol. 26, 1972, p. 294-8.

[3] G. Myrdal, Asian Drama: An Inquiry into the Poverty of Nations, New York, Pantheon, 1968.

[4] M. G. Candau, 'WHO and Socio-Economic Development', WHO Chronicle, Vol. 25, 1971, p. 441-4.

[5] B. Christian, D. Ray, A. Benyoussef and T. Tanahashi, 'Health and Socio-Economic Development: An Intersectoral Problem', Social Science and Medicine (in press).

[6] Health Care: An International Study, Oxford University Press, 1975.

[7] R. Grass, 'Primary Health Care: A Review of the Literature Through 1972', Medical Care, Vol. XII, No. 8, August 1974, p. 638-47.

[8] A. Benyoussef and A. F. Wessen, 'Utilization of Health Services—Tunisia', Social Science and Medicine, Vol. 8, 1974, p. 287-304; A. Benyoussef, A. F. Wessen, T. Phan Tan and H. Souissi, 'Services de Sante: Couverture, Facteurs et Indices d'Utilisation', Bulletin de l'Organisation Mondiale de la Sante, Vol. 51, 1974, p. 111-32.

[9] M. Greenwood, Epidemics and Crowd Diseases, New York, Macmillan, 1935.

[10] L. T. Webster, 'Experimental Epidemiology', Medicine, Vol. 25, p. 77, 1946.

[11] N. A. Scotch, 'Socio-cultural Factors in the Epidemiology of Zulu Hypertension', Am. J. Publ. Hlth., Vol. 53, 1963, p. 1905; S. L. Syme, M.M. Hymen and P. E. Enterline, 'Some Social and Cultural Factors Associated with the Occurrence of Coronary Heart Disease', J. Chron. Dis., Vol. 17, 1964, p. 277; J. Cassel, 'Health Consequences of Population Density and Crowding', Population Growth, Consequences and Policy Implications, chapter XII, Baltimore, Md., John Hopkins University Press, 1971.

[12] A. Benyoussef, 'L'Etude de la Sante des Migrants en Ville', Proc. Colloques internationaux du CNRS, la Croissance urbaine en Afrique Noire et a Madagascar, Bordeaux, Oct. 1970, p. 93-110, Paris, Editions du Centre national de la Recherche scientifique (CNRS), 1972.

[13] M. Glasser, L. Greenburg and F. Field, 'Mortality and Morbidity during a Period of High Levels of Air Pollution', Archs Environ. Health, Vol. 15, 1967, p. 684.

[14]Syme, Hymen and Enterline, op. cit,; W. Haenzel, D. B. Loveland and M. G. Sirken, 'Lung Cancer Mortality as Related to Residence and Smoking Histories', J. Nat. Cancer Inst., Vol. 28, 1962, p. 947.

[15]op. cit.

[16]R. A. Stallones, 'Environment, Ecology and Epidemiology', WHO Chronicle, Vol. 26, 1972, p. 294.

[17]Syme, Hymen and Enterline, op. cit.; S. L. Syme, N. O. Borhani and R. W. Buechley, 'Cultural Mobility and Coronary Heart Disease in an Urban Area', Am. J. Epidem., Vol. 82, 1965, p. 334.

[18]J. P. Henry and J. C. Cassel, 'Psychosocial Factors in Essential Hypertension: Recent Epidemiological and Animal Experimental Evidence', Am. J. Epidem., Vol. 90, 1969, p. 171.

[19]K. B. Nuckolls, J. Cassel and B.H. Kaplan, 'Psychosocial Assets, Life Crisis and the Prognosis of Pregnancy', Am. J. Epidem., Vol. 95, 1972, p. 431.

[20]A. Benyoussef et al., 'Health Effects of Rural/Urban Migration in Developing Countries--Senegal', Social Science and Medicine, Vol. 8, 1974, p. 243-54; A. Benyoussef et al., 'Sante, Migration et Urbanisation : Une Etude Collaborative au Senegal', Bulletin de l'Organisation Mondiale de la Sante, Vol. 49, 1973, p. 517-37.

[21]ibid.

[22]ibid.

[23]K. Newell (ed.), Health by the People, World Health Organization, Geneva, 1975.

[24]Barbara S. Hulka and John C. Cassel, 'The AAFP-UNC Study of the Organization, Utilization and Assessment of Primary Health Care', American Journal of Public Health, Vol. 85, June 1973, p. 494-501.

[25]Thomas W. Bice, Kerr L. White, 'Factors Related to the Use of Health Services: An International Comparative Study', Medical Care, Vol. VII, No. 2, March/April 1969, p. 124-33.

[26]Kerr L. White, 'Primary Medical Care for Families--Organization and Evaluation', The New England Journal of Medicine, Vol. 277, No. 16, October 1967, p. 852-74.

[27]J. Broyelle, L. Brams, F. Fagnani and L. Tabah, 'Recherches sur les Besoins de Sante d'une Population', Bulletin de l'INSERM T., Vol. 24, 1969, p. 613.

[28]K. Smith, 'Health Priorities in Poorer Countries', Social Science and Medicine, Vol. 9, 1975, p. 121-3.

290   Amor Benyoussef

[29] World Bank Group, The Assault on World Poverty, Problems of Rural Development, Education and Health, Baltimore, Johns Hopkins University Press, 1975.

[30] V. Djukanovic and E. P. Mach, Alternative Approaches to Meeting Basic Health Needs in Developing Countries: A Joint UNICEF/WHO Study, Geneva, World Health Organization, 1975.

[31] World Bank Group, op. cit.

[32] Jerome S. Beloff and M. Korper, 'The Health Team Model and Medical Care Utilization', Journal of the American Medical Association, Vol. 219, No. 3, 1972; WHO Chronicle, Vol. 29, May 1975.

[33] ibid.

[34] ibid.

[35] Sudan, Democratic Republic of, National Health Programme 1977/78-1983/84, Khartoum, 1975.

[36] Sudan, Democratic Republic of, Primary Health Care Programme, Southern Region, 1977/78-1983/84, Juba, 1976; Sudan, Democratic Republic of, Primary Health Care Programme, Eastern, Northern, Central and Western Regions, 1977/78-1983/84, Khartoum, 1976.

[37] Newell (ed.), op. cit.; Djukanovic and Mach, op. cit.

[38] F. Schofield, 'Health Planning in Developing Countries', Impact of Science on Society, Vol. XXV, No. 3, 1975; A. A. Idriss, P. Lolik, R. A. Khan and A. Benyoussef, 'Sudan: National Health Programme and Primary Health Care, 1977/78-1983/84', Bulletin, World Health Organization, Vol. 53, No. 4, 1976, p. 461-71 (see also by same authors 'The Primary Health Care Programme in Sudan', World Health Organization Chronicle, Vol. 30, 1976, p. 370-4).

[39] ibid.

Food Crisis in the Developing Countries and Aid Policy

ORGANIZATION FOR ECONOMIC COOPERATION AND DEVELOPMENT

I. INTRODUCTION

Nowhere is the division of the world into rich and poor countries so marked as in the food sector. In the developed countries, the scourge of hunger has practically disappeared, except for a few areas, and the population as a whole consumes more food than it needs to keep alive. In the developing countries, on the other hand, under-feeding (general calorie deficiency) or malnutrition (unbalanced diet, especially as regards protein), or a combination of the two, affect broad strata of the population.

In certain countries or regions, the food situation is so precarious that any occurrence which reduced food production or imports is liable to bring millions of people to the brink of famine. The years 1972, 1973 and early 1974 abounded in such occurrences: natural disasters such as the drought in the Sahel area, bad harvests, the energy crisis, shortage of fertilizers, rise in the price of staple foods, etc., all combined to create a highly dangerous situation. The experts feared that, once again, the developing countries were heading towards famine. Are these fears justified? And if so, what can the donor countries and agencies do to avert the impending crisis, and to create greater security of world food supplies?

This chapter is divided into three parts:

--an assessment of the food situation in the developing countries and an outline of the probable short-term trends.

--a brief recapitulation of the main proposals submitted to the World Food Conference in November 1974, for ensuring, in the longer run, a minimum level of security in world food supplies.

From **DEVELOPMENT CO-OPERATION**, 1974, (61-84), reprinted by permission of the publisher, Organization for Economic Co-operation and Development, Paris.

—a survey of the role of assistance in expanding food production in the developing countries, especially in four key sectors: food crops, livestock farming, fishing and storage.

II. FOOD SITUATION IN THE DEVELOPING COUNTRIES AND PROBABLE TRENDS

a) Food shortage and nutritional deficiencies

The scale of food shortage and nutritional deficiencies in the developing countries is not easy to determine. It is, however, universally recognised that there is a minimum requirement, "a nutritional poverty line", as Indian economies call it, below which serious under-nourishment occurs. This "poverty line" appears to be difficult to estimate and experts are still far from reaching agreement on this subject. The FAO experts have fixed the minimum requirement for all developing countries at an average of about 2,284 calories per head per day, although these food needs are not uniform, and vary, as Table 1 shows, from region to region according to stature, climate and activity. Estimates of minimum protein needs also vary considerably and are still a subject of discussion. However, one point seems to be clear[1]: protein needs depend directly on the extent to which calorie needs are covered, hence priority should be given to the latter.

Practically nowhere in the developing countries are the minimum calorie requirements satisfied, the deficiency being greatest in Asia, the Far East and Africa. It was calculated that in 1970, about 400 million people, comprising 220 million in the Far East, 68 million in Africa, 37 million in Latin America and 34 million in the Near East, had an inadequate energy protein intake.[2] These figures were compiled for average years, leaving such disasters as drought or war out of account. It is, moreover, the case that the above statistics conceal wide disparities between countries and between ethnic groups, income levels, age classes and sexes. The countries showing the greatest deficiencies are as follows: in Asia, the Indian sub-continent and the highly populated areas of the Indo-Chinese peninsula; in Latin America, the countries bordering the Andes and the Caribbean area; and in Africa, the countries South of the Sahara, especially in the Sahel area.

The food situation also varies according to the level of economic development, and still more, in any given country, as between the rich and poor classes. In Brazil, for example, it has been calculated[3] that families with an income of less than 500 cruzeiros per year (about 60 per cent of the population) consume under 2,250 calories per head per day, whereas families with incomes of over 1,200 cruzeiros per year enjoy a standard of food consumption comparable to that found in the wealthiest industrial countries (over 3,500 calories per head per day). The same

TABLE 1. ESTIMATES OF AVERAGE PER CAPUT FOOD SUPPLY BY REGION IN 1970

Regions	Calories (per head per day)			Protein (g. per head per day)
	Minimum requirements	Intake	per cent of requirements satisfied	Intake
Developed countries................	—	3,150	123	94
Developing countries...............	2,284	2,210	97	56
of which:				
Africa.........................	2,335	2,160	93	56
Latin America...................	2,383	2,530	105	65
Near East	2,456	2,500	102	69
Asia and Far East...............	2,223	2,080	94	51

Source: FAO, *Agricultural Commodity Projections,* 1970-1980 (Table 3), Rome 1971, and *Assessment of the World Food Situation, Present and Future,* World Food Conference.

TABLE 2. WORLD POPULATION AND CEREAL PRODUCTION
(Annual average 1970-72)

	Population		Cereal production		
	million	% of total	million tons	% of total	tons *per capita*
World	3,665	100	1,268	100	0.35
Developing countries ..	1,761	48	374	30	0.21
Developed countries[1] ..	728	20	434	34	0.60
Centrally planned countries	1,175	32	460	36	0.39

Sources: FAO, Production Yearbook 1972: World Bank Atlas 1973.

1. Greece, Spain, Yugoslavia, Israel and South Africa are included in this category to achieve consistency in the construction of, this table.

TABLE 3. TREND OF FOOD PRODUCTION PER HEAD 1969-1973
(Index: average 1961-1965 = 100)

	1969	1970	1971	1972	1973
Developing countries ..	102	103	102	99	100
Latin America	102	103	100	99	100
Far East	102	104	102	96	101
Near East........	104	103	102	107	98
Africa	102	102	102	100	95

Source: Assessment of the World Food Situation, Present and Future, *op. cit.*

conclusion can be drawn from studies carried out in Colombia, Peru, Madagascar and India, to mention only a few.[4]

Income levels also determine the composition of the diet. In poor countries and classes, cereals and starchy foods provide the main source of calories, whereas in wealthy countries and classes there is much greater variety. Cereals cover two-thirds of the calorie intake in Far Eastern countries, and more than half in North and West African countries, hence their great importance as food for the developing countries. Wheat consumption varies according to the region: it is very low in West Africa, but high in North Africa and the Near East. Rice provides nearly half the calorie requirement in the Far East and India. Starch foods predominate in the food intake of the West African countries.

Lastly, diet depends not only on climate, type of soil and level of income, but also on socio-cultural customs. In the developing countries, women and children are generally less well-nourished than men. This situation is particularly unfortunate when it is remembered that undernourishment causes irreparable damage to the physical and mental health of the individual in the first few years of his life, and one has also to remember that three-fifths of the population in developing countries are under 15 years old. It has been estimated that in these countries about 200 million children under the age of five suffer from nutritional deficiencies of various kinds and for various reasons.

b) Chief causes of the precarious food situation

The precarious food situation is a typical feature of under-development and is associated with a number of factors: poverty, unsatisfactory sanitary conditions, absence of dietetic knowledge, and socio-cultural customs detrimental to the food intake of certain groups. The main cause is a rate of growth of food production which cannot keep up with the pace of demographic growth, combined with a lack of foreign exchange to meet the growing cost of food imports. Moreover, in 1972 and 1974, several factors arose at an international level to make matters even worse.

i) Inadequate volume of agricultural production

The inadequate volume of food production in the developing countries is one key factor. The gravity of the situation can be summed up in two figures: the developing countries produce only 30 per cent of the food consumed in the world as a whole, whereas they contain nearly 50 per cent of the world's population. Admittedly, these statistics do not tell the whole story, as a

TABLE   4.   RATE OF GROWTH OF FOOD PRODUCTION
(Percentage annual increase)

	1952-62			1962-72		
	Popul- ation	Prod- uction	Production per head	Popul- ation	Prod- uction	Production per head
Developed countries	1.2	2.5	1.3	1.0	2.4	1.4
Developing countries	2.4	3.1	0.7	2.5	2.7	0.2

Source and coverage: Ibid. See footnote 1 to table IV.2.

TABLE   5.   THE CHANGING PATTERN OF WORLD GRAIN TRADE
(+) = net exports: (—) = net imports

Million metric tons.

Regions	1934-38 annual average	1948-52 annual average	1960	1966	1972-3 Prelim.	1973-4 Prelim.	1974-5 Prelim.
Latin America	+ 9'	+ 1	0	+ 5	— 4	(+ 2)	(+ 7)
Africa	+ 1	0	— 2	— 7	— 5	(— 8)	(— 6)
Asia (incl. Japan and China)	+ 2	— 6	—17	—34	—35	(—37)	(—41)
North America	+ 5	+23	+39	+59	+84	+90	+65
Western Europe	—24	—22	—25	—27	—21	—21	—13
USSR and Eastern Europe	+ 5	—	0	— 4	—27	— 9	— 6
Australia and New Zealand	+ 3	+ 3	+ 6	+ 8	+ 9	+ 8	+12

Source: Up to 1972-73, figures derived from Lester R. Brown, " The next crisis? Food ", *Foreign Policy*, Winter 1973-1974; and for 1973-74 and 1974-75, figures calculated on the basis of information supplied by the United States Department of Agriculture.

TABLE   6.   IMPORTS AND EXPORTS OF CEREALS BY DEVELOPING
COUNTRIES IN 1972

Million metric tons.

Regions	Imports	Exports	Balance
Developing countries............................	36	14	—22
of which:			
Africa	5	1	— 4
Latin America	10	7	— 3
Near East	5	1	— 4
Far East	15	5	—10

Source: FAO, *Trade Yearbook*, 1972.

substantial proportion of food production is drawn from subsistence farming, and is not recorded in the statistics, but they give some idea of the problem.

While still very inadequate, food production in the developing countries has advanced at a rate of 2.7 per cent per year during the last 10 years--a higher rate than that recorded in the developed countries over the same period: 2.4 per cent. However, these production gains were almost entirely absorbed by demographic growth: 2.5 per cent per year during the same period, so that food production per head improved very little, and was, in fact, lower in 1972 than it had been throughout the period 1960-1965.

Furthermore, the rate of increase of food production has tended to fall off in the last few years. This trend is especially alarming if one considers that demand is steadily increasing, given the improvement of economic conditions for some strata of the population in a number of less-developed countries. The data collected on the rate of growth of food production for the periods 1952-62 and 1962-72 is shown in Table 4.

These general figures for developing countries naturally conceal wide disparities according to the country, year and crop concerned. A recent report by the FAO[5] indicates that food production has risen less fast than population in 24 countries,[6] including nine African countries and nine Latin American countries, and less fast than demand in 39 countries, including India and Pakistan, which represent two-thirds of the total population. On the other hand, in 30 countries the increase in food production seems to have equalled or exceeded the growth in domestic demand.

In addition, the results have varied widely according to the year concerned. The poor crops in 1965 and 1966, especially in India, were succeeded by four years of good crops from 1967 to 1970, followed by two more lean years in 1971 and 1972. The good crop years coincided with the development of high yield varieties, especially of wheat and rice in Latin America and Asia. Very considerable progress was achieved in such countries as India and Pakistan, which even approached the point of self-sufficiency for a time. Several observers believed in that period that this Green Revolution would radically change the outlook for agriculture in the developing countries, but progress fell off in the early seventies.

The reasons for the insufficient growth of food production in the developing countries are many and complicated, arising out of both cyclical and structural factors.

Bad weather conditions have obviously played a decisive part in the famines of India and, more recently, in the Sahel area. War and internal strife prevented the development of agricultural production, particularly in Bangladesh in 1971 and 1972. These external events have exacerbated more deep-seated structural and institutional weaknesses.

A rise in production implies in some cases an increase in the cultivated area (which would be possible nearly everywhere except in South-East Asia) and in other cases an improvement in yields and/or crop intensity. The latter would involve the development of new, stronger varieties, better adapted to climatic conditions, increases in the use of fertilisers and pesticides,the development of training, credit and marketing facilities, and the extension of irrigation networks (the lack of irrigation being one of the chief bottlenecks hindering the spread of high-yield varieties of rice in Southern Asia). Now, in these respects, nearly everything remains to be done. Credit facilities have grown considerably, but mainly for the benefit of the big landowners, while the small farmers have only exceptionally been able to profit by them. Advisory services too often lack material resources, personnel, and appropriate extension methods and programmes. It has proved very difficult to integrate smallholders in the marketing system and secure remunerative prices for their produce. All these elements have too often been developed independently of each other, instead of forming parts of one whole. Lastly, the inadequate level of official investment in the agricultural sector, the fixing of prices at a level detrimental to the farmer, and the absence of effective land reform measures, have in different degrees checked the development of agricultural production.

ii) Growing burden of food for the developing countries

    Many developing countries which were net grain exporters before the war have gradually become net importers over the last 20 years, whereas the United States and Canada have emerged as the main grain export centres controlling "a larger share of the world's exportable supplies of grain than the Middle East does of oil", in the words of Lester R. Brown[7] (see Table 5).
    Consequently, developing countries have increasingly become dependent upon developed countries for their cereal imports. The main deficit area has been Asia. Gross cereal imports by developing countries rose from 12 million tons between 1949 and 1951 to 34 million tons between 1966 and 1968 and to 36 million tons in 1972 (see Table 6).
    According to World Bank calculations,[8] these imports might reach 43 and 52 million tons in 1974 and 1975 respectively.[9] Cereal imports alone cost about $3 billion per year from 1970 to 1972, and total imports of foodstuffs over $9 billion. To form some idea of the burden presented by these food imports on the developing countries' balance of payments, suffice it to say that during the period 1970-1972, they amounted to an average of 14 per cent per year of their total imports. The percentage was still higher for such countries as Sri Lanka, Egypt, Ivory Coast, Mali, Vietnam (Rep. of) and Senegal, where it exceeded 20 per cent. Furthermore, gross cereal imports (together with food aid), represented in 1972 about 10 per cent of the developing countries' total cereal availabilities, and 14 per cent in such regions as Latin America and Africa. However, in the 1960's and even in the beginning of the 1970's, the burden of payments was mitigated by the availability of food aid which represented up to 45 per cent of total cereal imports during peak periods and an average of about 30 per cent during the 1970-72 period. This share dropped abruptly in

TABLE 7. TREND OF PRODUCTION OF WHEAT AND RICE
FROM 1961-1965 TO 1973

Million tons.

	1961-65 (average)	1965-70 (average)	1970-71	1971-72	1972-73	1973-74 (Prov.)
Wheat						
World	254	315	318	354	346	321
Developing countries	49	58	65	(70)	(78)	(71)
Rice (milled)						
World	253	285	307	309	293	321
Developing countries	141	159	175	174	165	183
Far East	125	140	154	153	143	162

TABLE 8. TREND OF WHEAT AND FLOUR STOCKS 1960-61, 1974-75
(Stocks at the opening of the respective crop season)

Million metric tons.

Years	Argentina	Australia	Canada	EEC	USA	Total
1960-61	1.2	1.7	16.3	5.4	35.7	60.3
1965-66	3.6	0.7	14.0	5.6	22.3	46.2
1970-71	0.8	7.2	27.5	4.1	24.1	63.7
1971-72	0.7	3.5	20.0	4.6	19.9	48.7
1972-73	0.5	1.4	16.0	6.1	23.5	47.5
1973-74	0.5	0.3	10.0	4.9	11.6	27.3
1974-75 (forecast)	0.1	0.5	9.2	6.0	4.6	20.4

Source: FAO, Intergovernmental Group on Grains, September 1973, and April 1974.

TABLE 9. RECENT TREND OF EXPORT PRICES
OF THE MAIN FOODSTUFFS (1971 - JUNE 1974)

$ per ton.

Commodity	1971	1972	1973	Jan. 1974	March 1974	August 1974
Wheat (U.S. No. 2)	62	70	139	214	191	170
Rice (Thailand)	129	151	368	538	603	520
Maize (Yellow No. 2)	58	56	98	122	126	115
Soya	126	140	290	261	265	236

1973, given the sudden reduction of volume of food aid.

iii) Food crisis in 1972, 1973 and 1974

During the 1960's, and up to 1972, the slight gains in production per capita achieved by the developing countries were accompanied by a considerable increase in food production in the industrial countries. The output of wheat rose at a fast rate, the output of rice less rapidly (see Table 7). Three-quarters of the output of wheat, and nearly half the output of rice, came from OECD countries and centrally planned economies. This situation had released surpluses and led to the setting up of large cereal stocks which, in turn, generated some price stability. From 1960 to July 1972, the wheat price varied very little,[10] and the rice price rather more.[11] This situation of abundant supplies and price stability played a regulating function on the world market, and food transactions took place in the best possible conditions. After 1972, however, several events occurred which upset this equilibrium.

iv) Drop in world food production, disappearance of surpluses and erosion of stocks

For the first time since the Second World War, world wheat production declined in 1972, mainly because of the poor crops in the Soviet Union. This setback coincided with bad harvests of rice and coarse grains in other parts of the world.

The drought caused ravages, not only in the Sahel area properly so-called, but in other parts of West Africa (Cameroon, North Nigeria), East Africa (Ethiopia), Central Africa (especially Chad), and South Africa (Botswana). In Asia, following the failure of the monsoon in 1970 and 1971, floods devastated some regions of Bangladesh, India and especially Pakistan, and did considerable damage to the rice crops.

The world grain market had to cope with higher demand, especially from the Soviet Union, which purchased 28 million tons of wheat in 1973—more than any other country in the course of history; by comparison, India imported only 10 million tons to remedy the shortage in 1965-1966. Massive purchases were also made by China and several European countries. As a result of this strong demand, stocks dropped sharply in the course of 1973.

At the beginning of 1974, the OECD countries' wheat reserves stood at about 21 million tons, barely enough to cover three weeks' world consumption (see Table 8). Stocks of rice and coarse grains also declined substantially.[12]

v) Rise in prices of the chief cereals, and impact on imports of foodstuffs by developing countries

As demand rose faster than supply, prices shot up. Between July 1972 and January 1974, wheat, rice and soya prices trebled, while maize and sorghum prices doubled.

These price rises entailed a considerable increase in the developing countries' expenditure on grain imports which was further augmented by the fact that, far from diminishing in volume because of the higher prices, their grain imports rose by 20 per cent from 1972 to 1973; the increase from 1973 to 1974 will probably be higher still (see section (IV) above). On the basis of these forecasts the World Bank estimated the <u>additional</u> cost of grain imports, by comparison with the average for 1972 for all developing countries, at $5.2 billion in 1973 and $8.4 billion in 1974 (Table 10). These figures are probably too high, as the 1974 reference prices used in calculating them were the opening prices for the year;[13] given the drop in prices since the month of March, this now seems to be an over-pessimistic assumption. However, the forecasts give some idea of the scale of the expenditure which has to be borne, especially by such counties as Bangladesh, Indian, Egypt and Korea (Rep. of). Furthermore, for some small countries like Senegal, the additional expenditure incurred will represent something between one-quarter and one-third of their total average annual imports from 1970 to 1972.

vi) Shortage of fertilizers

Coinciding with this rise in the price of basic foodstuffs, the price of fertilizers, which has tended to fall from 1967 to 1971, rose sharply from 1972 onwards, especially from 1973. The price of urea (nitrogenous fertilizer) increased from $46 to $225 and that of TSP (phosphate fertilizer) from $43 to $150 per ton, between 1971 and 1974. This abrupt rise was mainly due to the general increase in demand, the inadequate growth of supply, the repercussions of the energy crisis on the production of nitrogenous fertilizers and lastly, the rise in the cost of maritime transport.

Such a situation was bound to have disastrous consequences, both for the developing countries' balance of payments (already hard hit by the rise in commodity prices) and for fertilizer consumption in those countries. It so happens that fertilizers are essential for the high-yield varieties on which any hope of a rapid expansion of food production depends.

Fertilizer consumption has increased rapidly in the developing countries over the last few years. It amounted to close on 10 million tons in 1972 (of which 60 per cent was nitrogenous fertilizer, 27 per cent was phosphate fertilizer, and the remainder potash fertilizer). A little over half of total consumption was

TABLE 10. ESTIMATED ADDITIONAL COST OF GRAIN IMPORTS
FOR SOME DEVELOPING COUNTRIES IN 1973 AND 1974
(BY COMPARISON 'WITH THE AVERAGE 1970-1972)

Country	1973			1974		
	Cost in $ million	% of total imports in 1970-72	% of GNP 1971	Cost in $ million	% of total imports in 1970-72	% of GNP 1971
Total developing countries...	+ 5,176	8	—	+ 8,376	13	—
Bangladesh	+ 337	—	7	+ 413	—	8
Sri Lanka	+ 85	21	7	+ 111	27	9
India	+ 255	11	0	+ 667	28	1
Pakistan..................	+ 105	13	1	+ 303	36	4
Egypt	+ 369	44	5	+ 603	73	8
Philippines	+ 84	7	1	+ 167	13	2
Senegal	+ 79	32	8	+ 70	28	7
Korea (Rep. of)...........	+ 430	19	5	+ 564	25	6
Brazil	+ 221	6	1	+ 125	3	0
Mexico...................	+ 179	7	1	+ 283	11	1
Chile	+ 142	15	2	+ 323	33	4

Source: World Bank and OECD Secretariat.

TABLE 11. PRODUCTION, CONSUMPTION, IMPORTS AND EXPORTS
OF FERTILIZERS IN THE DEVELOPING COUNTRIES IN 1972

Thousand tons.

Developing Regions	Nitrogenous fertilizers		Phosphate fertilizers		Potash fertilizers	
	Cons.	Imp.	Cons.	Prod.	Cons.	Prod.
Africa	368	275	284	426	162	274
Latin America.	1,486	906	1,043	479	698	24
Near East.....	887	600	373	231	25	—
Far East......	2,978	1,082	986	511	588	—
Others	6	6	1	—	—	—
Total	5,725	2,870	2,686	1,647	1,474	298

Source: Foreign Agriculture, January 28th, 1974.

TABLE 12. IMPORTS OF MANUFACTURED FERTILIZERS BY DEVELOPING COUNTRIES, 1971-1974

Type of fertilizer	1971		1972 estimates		1973 estimates		1974	
	m. tons	$ m.	m. tons	$ m.	m. tons	$ m.	m. tons	$ m.
Nitrogenous	2.3	311	2.5	341	2.6	462	2.0	900
Phosphate	1.0	126	1.2	183	1.4	275	1.1	380
Potash	1.3	96	1.5	101	1.8	138	1.8	170
Total	4.6	533	5.2	625	5.8	875	4.9	1,450

Source: IMF. Imports of fertilizers by developing countries, April 1974.

TABLE 13. FAO PROJECTIONS OF LDC FOOD DEMAND AND SUPPLY GROWTH (ANNUAL RATES) TO 1985, ASSUMING " MEDIUM " POPULATION AND " TREND " GDP GROWTH RATES

% per annum.

	Population	GDP	Food demand	Food supply
Developing countries	2.7	6.3	3.6	2.6
of which Africa	2.9	5.9	3.8	2.5
Latin America	2.8	6.1	3.6	2.9
Near East	2.9	9.3	4.0	3.1
Far East	2.6	5.2	3.4	2.4
Developed countries	0.9	4.5	1.5	2.4

Source: " Assessment of the World Food Situation, Present and Future ", op cit.

covered by domestic production in the developing countries, including the oil-producing countries, while a little under half was covered by imports (see Table 11).

Imports thus play a vital part in the developing countries' fertilizer supplies. With the rise in prices, the cost involved may have grown by $200 million between 1972 and 1973, and by $575 million between 1973 and 1974 (see Table 12). The biggest increases were faced by India, Turkey, Vietnam and Thailand.

The developing countries may have serious difficulties in obtaining supplies of fertilizer on the world market during 1974. Several exporting countries, notably the United States, Japan, the Netherlands and Germany, have either been obliged to slow down nitrogenous fertilizer production because of raw material shortages or have been unable to step up their output sufficiently to cope with the steady rise in domestic and external demand. As a result, certain developing countries found it impossible to import the quantities of fertilizers which they desired at the beginning of 1974. According to the very piecemeal information available, the shortfall in 1973-74 seems to have been 20 per cent for Pakistan, 30 per cent for India and 30 per cent for Bangladesh.[14]

c) Probable Trends in the Food Situation

The statistical data now available only enable us to assess the food situation in 1973 and to begin to measure its consequences. Any attempt at projection into the future must be approached with the greatest caution.

For the shorter term, the drop in grain production which occurred in 1972, mainly in the USSR, did not recur in 1973. In that year, world crops of grain, i.e. wheat, rice and coarse grains, were excellent both in the developed and in the developing regions. On the basis of FAO indices, the world's food production in 1973 was estimated to have increased by four per cent in volume and by two per cent per capita. At least two thirds of the world increase was due to the record crop in the USSR: 110 million tons compared with 86 million in 1972. Developing countries also had good harvests in 1973 although results varied according to the region. There was a distinct recovery in the crop situation in Asia and Latin America, but a worsening in Africa and the Near East. Algeria, Ethiopia, Morocco and Zambia experienced a serious setback in their production for the second year running. For all developing countries combined, the wheat crop was ten per cent lower than in 1972, but on the other hand, the rice crop was excellent and certain countries, e.g. Bangladesh, India, and Thailand, achieved substantial gains.

With regard to the 1974 harvest, early optimism concerning the United States wheat crop has since faded, because of recent drought in the American wheat belt. Since the United States provides about half of the wheat entering world trade, the United States harvest is of paramount importance. Previous forecasts that the current

United States crop may exceed last year's 47 million ton harvest by
22 per cent have been progressively reduced to only 7.5 per cent,
on the basis of conditions prevailing in August 1974. Nor are
prospects encouraging for the USSR and Canada: the USSR harvest is
likely to be much lower than in 1973 and the Canadian wheat harvest
has been reduced because of summer rains.

It is therefore doubtful whether stocks will be reconstituted
at a level commensurate with world food security: in July 1974,
wheat stocks were at their lowest level for 20 years. As for food
aid, expectations of a possible increase in United States aid now
appear less realistic. In addition, supplies of cereal entering
the international market might also be sharply reduced.

Preliminary estimates of 1974-75 world grain trade indicate
that total wheat and coarse grain exports are expected to decrease
from 146 million tons in 1973-74 to 124 million tons in 1974-75.
The main reduction will be in United States exports which are
expected to drop from 75 million tons in 1973-74 to 50 million in
1974-75. This will only partially be compensated by small
increases from other exporting countries such as Australia and
Argentina. Developing countries may accordingly find difficulty in
purchasing required cereal imports on the world market. Much will
depend on the scale of purchases by the USSR and China. Present
forecasts indicate that USSR wheat imports might be lower in
1974-75 than in 1973-74, but that Chinese imports will remain at a
high level and possibly even be increased over the level of
previous years.

Having reached record levels in February/March 1974, grain
prices dropped between March and June but rose again thereafter.
For example, the wheat price (f.o.b. Gulf), which exceeded $200 per
ton in January 1974, declined to $140 in early June but increased
to $170 in August. The price of rice remained high, mainly because
of the very restricted markets. It is still too early to decide
whether the present trend will continue, but there seems every
likelihood that prices will remain much higher than in the past
even if they settle at a level somewhat below the record prices of
the early months of 1974.

As to the longer term, the FAO has recently projected the
world growth of food demand and of supply up to 1985. Its
projections for developed countries suggest that food supply will
increase at a rate of 2.4 per cent while demand will only grow at a
rate of 1.5 per cent leaving a surplus for trade or concessional
sales (see Table 13). In developing countries, on the other
hand, FAO projections indicate that the demand for foodstuffs will
probably rise by 3.6 per cent per year (2.7 per cent to cover the
population increase, and 0.9 per cent due to higher demand per
head). However, prospects for food supply in developing countries
are expected to fall far short of this target: a rate of growth of
2.6 per cent only is expected. The failure of supply growth to
match demand growth will be smallest in Latin America and largest
in Africa. In order to fill the gap, cereals will have to be
imported from abroad. According to FAO projections, the cereals
deficit for cereal importing developing countries could amount to
about 85 million tons per year by 1985. In the case of a year of
bad harvests or natural disasters, the cereal requirements could

rise to some 100 million tons or even more.

The longer-term trend of production in the developing countries will depend on a host of factors, but it seems certain that if supplies of fertilizers are cut down, the prospects of improved yields will diminish accordingly. Yet all forecasts for 1974 bank on a cut in fertilizer imports by the developing countries, especially nitrogenous fertilizers. Preliminary prospects[15] for 1980-81 point to an expected world deficit of about seven million tons in nitrogen supply. However, the situation may be retrieved, once the production capacity now being installed comes into operation. China, which takes about 50 per cent of Japan's exports, may become self-sufficient within a fairly short time, thus releasing part of Japan's fertilizer exports for the countries of South-East Asia.[16] Special measures have already been taken by some OECD countries to allot priority to exports to the developing countries and these measures could be expanded. Finally, if the drop in fertilizer imports does materialise, it might ultimately be counterbalanced by an increase in the production capacity of fertilizer plants in the developing countries, which at present operate, in general, at about 60 per cent of capacity. The Tennessee Valley Authority experts estimates that, if these plants operated at only 80 per cent of capacity, the developing countries could become self-sufficient in nitrogenous fertilizers, and perhaps have a small surplus left over for export.[17] However, the reasons for this low capacity utilisation seem to be so deepseated that substantial improvement cannot be expected in the very short term. There are also moves to set up new plants in developing countries, especially the oil-exporting countries, but their effects will not be felt straight away.

Whatever the trend of the world food situation in 1974 and 1975, the 1972-73 crisis may at least have succeeded in drawing the attention of governments and aid agencies to the necessity of taking more effective measures to cope with the food problem which continues to dog the developing countries.

III. HOW CAN A MINIMUM LEVEL OF WORLD FOOD SERVICES BE OBTAINED?

The crisis of 1972-73 brought out the necessity, for all countries, of having a sufficient margin of security to make good the inadequacies of agricultural production, to deal rapidly with emergencies and to eliminate excessive price fluctuations. The search for ways and means of ensuring a minimum of world food security has been going on for some years. Several solutions are now under study: a) development of national storage policies: b) formulation of a minimum world food security plan (under FAO auspices); c) definition of an international policy for the adjustment of agricultural production.

a) Development of National Storage Policies in the Developing
Countries

A great many developing countries, which are importers of
foodstuffs have no storage policy, whereas others, conscious of
their vulnerability to bad harvests, maintain national reserve
stocks of food (especially in East Africa, Central America
and certain parts of East Asia). It was, indeed, thanks to the
existing food stocks that India, for example, was able to make good
the grain shortages resulting from the poor crops in 1972-73,
without unduly increasing her imports. It would therefore be
desireable, in future, for a growing number of developing countries
to adopt a storage policy and to build up reserve stocks. Some
countries have, in fact, announced their intention of taking such
measures.
However, the building up of national stocks in the developing
countries raises certain problems. In the first place, these
stocks represent, as it were, a frozen asset, and as such should be
kept to a minimum, especially in the poorest countries; but how is
the minimum level to be determined? In addition, the maintenance
and management of these stocks represent a heavy burden for certain
countries' budgets. How can that burden be lightened? Active
steps should therefore be taken to work out appropriate storage
methods and techniques, especially for the hot, wet countries where
it is difficult to keep foodstuffs. Lastly, it should be possible
to mobilise these stocks rapidly, and despatch them promptly to the
distressed areas. Such mobility implies the development of
infrastructure. In all these fields, the donor countries and
agencies could provide assistance.
FAO estimates show that funds of the order of $200 to $300
million (excluding purchase of grains) would be required for a
five-year action in order to create adequate storage facilities and
technical services in 48 developing countries which either have a
storage policy or expressed interest in adopting one. If external
sources were to fund for instance 75 per cent of the programme's
total cost, about $150 to 225 million would be required from donors
in the form of financial or technical assistance. Additional aid
would be needed to fund the initial food stocks.

b) Minimum World Food Security Plan

With the aim of protecting humanity from the uncertainties
affecting agricultural production, the Director of FAO proposed, at
the November 1973 Conference, to draw up a minimum world food
security plan. A draft International Undertaking concerning
general objectives and guidelines for this Plan was endorsed by the
FAO Council in July 1974 and was presented for approval to the
World Food Conference in November 1974. Thereafter practical

measures will have to be worked out concerning its implementation. The purpose of this Undertaking is to ask all countries, developed or developing, to build up minimum security stocks. Stocks would be built up in the rich countries, taking into account not only domestic demand and normal trade requirements, but also the developing countries' needs, especially in the matter of food aid. The developing countries, for their part, would have to build up their own reserves. Very flexible co-ordination of the various policies would be arranged through regular exchanges of information on the level of the stocks, the present and anticipated size of crops, and the available grain supplies, import requirements and food aid requirements.

This Plan seems fairly modest in its aim, as it merely attempts to institute some co-ordination. Yet its exact definition and implementation come up against difficulties which may well delay its application. In particular, at what level do stocks represent a minimum of world food security? What role should be allotted to each country in the constitution of stocks? Will the USSR agree to fall in with the Plan, as the FAO Member countries wish? Moreover, the market situation is such that it is hard to reconstitute large stocks at present. Lastly, the cost and management of stocks sets certain problems, particularly for the developing countries, as mentioned above.

With regard to the fundamental question of the quantity which constitutes a minimum security level, it has been agreed that its determination would be left to each country's own decision. However, an ad hoc FAO working party would examine the techniques for assessing the desirable minimum size of national stocks along with some other practical problems. The FAO Secretariat has recently estimated that total carryover stocks corresponding to 17-18 per cent of world consumption of cereals might be judged a minimum "safe" level for world food security. (This would compare with a carryover of 25 per cent in 1970 when there were surpluses and of 11-12 per cent in 1974 in a period of shortage). Therefore at the 1974 level of consumption, this "safe" carryover would amount to some 230 million tons for the entire world and to 150 million tons excluding China and the USSR.

Notwithstanding the difficulties which would have to be overcome in implementing this Plan, prospects more limited in scope have already been put forward with a view to building up contingency stocks only. A proposal for the creation of a small International Food Reserve for Emergencies which would enable the World Food Programme to increase substantially its relief operations will be put forward at the World Food Conference. The planned level of this Reserve would be of the order of 500,000 tons of cereals plus small quantities of other foodstuffs essential for relief operations. A part of this Reserve would be prelocated in strategic places. The rest would be on call when required. Criteria for cost-sharing would need to be formulated so that all interested governments could take part. It would also be necessary to define criteria for application and guidelines for management. Provision for the regular replenishment would also be included.

c) International Agricultural Adjustment Policy

With a view to tackling the basic problem of food shortage in the developing countries, mainly resulting from unbalanced agricultural production and trade in the world as a whole, the FAO has for some time been working on the formulation of an "International Agricultural Adjustment Policy". This is a far more ambitious project than all those referred to so far, its object being no less than the development and harmonisation of national agricultural and trade policies in the interests of the international community as a whole. In the context of this strategy, a series of measures would need to be taken at national, international and intergovernmental level, to ensure a massive increase in agricultural production in the developing countries and its stable, co-ordinated growth, and to stimulate the trade in agricultural commodities from those same countries. Various measures have been proposed: directives for the development of agricultural production, massive aid to agriculture, adoption of trade liberalisation measures in the developed countries, extension of the generalised system of preferences to cover agricultural products, conclusion of price stabilisation agreements for certain basic foodstuffs, etc. Consultation machinery should be set up to speed up the achievement of these objectives.
These are, very broadly stated, the chief proposals under study at present, on which the donor countries and agencies will be asked to state their position in the course of the coming months.

IV. DEVELOPMENT ASSISTANCE FOR FOOD PRODUCTION IN THE DEVELOPING COUNTRIES

Any abatement of the food shortage in the developing countries will mainly depend on the progress accomplished by them in agricultural production, particularly in three basic sectors: food crops, animal husbandry and fishing. At the same time, large quantities of foodstuffs could be salvaged to feed the population if appropriate measures were taken to improve storage facilities, destroy vermin and parasites and avoid wastage.
Most of the donor countries and agencies recognise the necessity of giving priority to the development of agricultural production in the developing countries, and of stepping up their assistance in this sector to remedy the shortage of food. In the past, a large proportion of traditional donors' assistance to the agricultural sector was geared to the development of tropical crops for export (in particular tea, cocoa, coffee, oil-seeds, etc.) and only occasionally to food crops for the benefit of the local population. In the last few years, however, this trend has been to some extent reversed, and direct aid in the food sector is making headway. Furthermore, it should not be forgotten that aid to the

export sector can bring considerable side benefits to the food crop sector and in some cases appears to be the best means of stimulating the rural sector as a whole.

It is impossible from the available statistical data, to distinguish between aid given to the food and non-food sector. Calculations on the volume of agricultural assistance for 1972 indicate that at least $500 million--representing about 7 per cent of net official bilateral development assistance--were committed for direct or indirect development of agricultural production.[18] Estimates for 1973 point to a figure somewhat higher: about $800 million, of which $600 million was in the form of capital projects and technical assistance and a further $200 million in fertilizers. This amount represents about 8 per cent of bilateral ODA and 12 to 15 per cent of what was reported as capital project assistance. These amounts are, indeed, large figures, but small by comparison with the needs, and ways and means of increasing agricultural assistance should be actively sought.

Moreover, if assistance is to make any effective contribution to the development of food production, it should not be restricted to isolated projects which are likely to pay off quickly, but should provide the basis for real rural development. Nearly all donor countries and agencies accept the arguments for increasing food production under integrated development projects which may embrace such diverse sectors as infrastructure, education, public health, credit and marketing, etc. However, the introduction of such improvements has not got far beyond the experimental stage. As examples, a project for the development of rice-growing launched by the EEC in the Segou area of Mali allots great importance to educational activities (such as a functional literacy campaign for 20,000 country people, the construction of five community development centres, enlargement of a training centre for rice growers); an Indo-Norwegian project for the development of fishing in Kerala concentrated on the improvement of sanitary conditions and the institution of a more efficient marketing network, in conjunction with the building of a fishing fleet, the establishment of fish processing plants, and the installation of refrigerating capacity.

The horizontal integration of sectors should, moreover, be accompanied by some integration of the means of action: supply of capital equipment and inputs, development of research and technical assistance, food aid, etc.

Donor countries and agencies should try to step up yields through the transfer of modern means of production and the initiation of pilot projects and demonstration farms. In addition to projects which artificially create optimum growth conditions, i.e. starting with the rural environment as it now is. Integrated rural development projects involving many small holders rather than a few well-to-do farmers, where the aim is to reduce production costs using simple methods that can be widely adopted, would make an effective contribution to the development of food production.

Having defined the perspective which donor countries and agencies should adopt in addressing themselves to the development of the food sector in the developing countries, we shall briefly consider their achievements and problems in the four key sectors mentioned above: development of food crops, livestock farming, fishing and storage facilities. Some general comments will be added on assistance policies for research and training. For example, a number of "mass operations" have taken place in Africa (e.g. in Mali, Senegal, Dahomey) with the help of France.

a) Development of Food Crops

The flow of aid has done much to expand wheat and rice-growing in the developing countries especially through the cultivation and propagation of high yield varieties, and the supply of seed, fertilizers, insecticides and other pesticides. On the other hand, it has done little for coarse grains (maize, sorghum, millet), starch roots (potatoes, cassava), or pulses (chick-peas, broad beans), although these products often represent the basic staple foods in developing countries. However, several countries and agencies are becoming aware of this deficiency and taking steps to remedy it.

Past experience shows that the use of modern inputs (seed, fertilizers, pesticides, etc.) pays off quickly, as the tropical climate enables several crops of the high-yield varieties to be grown per year, and the farmer's response to the new possibilities in a developing country seems to be just as positive as that of his counterpart in the developed countries. However, such modern inputs can only produce the expected results if a number of conditions are fulfilled: (1) development of irrigation or appropriate moisture conservation procedures, as high-yield seeds need a minimum supply of water; (2) supply of seed and fertilizer in good time and in sufficient quantity, which implies the existence of suitable storage, transport, distribution, credit and marketing facilities; (3) acquisition of the necessary know-how for the use of such sophisticated means of production, hence the importance of advisory and technical assistance services; (4) adaptation of new seeds to the type of soil and the vagaries of the climate, hence the need to develop applied research; (5) if necessary, prices for both inputs and crops to allow the farmer to cover his costs and make a profit. Some thought will also have to be given to creating markets for the sale of the produce.

Having regard to the many conditions to be fulfilled, the integrated development projects referred to above seem to provide the best framework for the provision of inputs. France and the United Kingdom provide small quantities of inputs, especially in the framework of integrated projects where these inputs represent only one element in the overall aid package. The United States has provided a large proportion of its assistance in the form of means of production supplied under integrated agricultural sector loans. However, the bulk of US assistance in this sector has been given in the form of commodity loans. Shipments under commodity loans totalled $737 million from 1965 to 1972, but the annual amount of loans of this type has greatly diminished since 1968, especially

since the virtual suspension of US food aid to India, one of the
chief recipients up to 1972.   Large quantities of inputs have also
been provided by Canada and Japan in the form of commodity loans.
Norway, a minor donor, but a large-scale exporter of fertilizers,
has granted part of its assistance to the agricultural sector in
the form of fertilizer grants.

i) Fertilizers

      Assistance has come in two main forms: finance for the import
of fertilizers and loans for the increase of fertilizer production
capacity.   Fertilizer plants have been built, for example, in
India, Korea (Rep. of), Indonesia and Brazil with AID loans
totalling $150 million (1965-71) and in Taiwan and Morocco with
Export-Import Bank credits in 1972.   Loans for the building of
fertilizer plants were also provided by Japan and Germany.   India
has also benefited from Italian export credits and United Kingdom
grants for the construction of various complexes.   India's
fertilizer production capacity has been largely built up with
Western assistance. It is no accident that high-yield varieties
have spread rapidly in this region.
      The   recent difficulties experienced by the developing
countries in procuring fertilizers, and the effects of reduction of
shipments on the spread of high-yield varieties, induced FAO and
some donor countries to take special measures to resolve the
problems.   An ad hoc Group on fertilizers was set up by FAO to
review the fertilizer situation periodically, and to investigate
the short-and medium-term market trends. This Group now comprises
40 governments and several international agencies, e.g. UNCTAD, the
World Bank Group and UNIDO.   In addition, a special FAO Fertilizer
Programme administered by the FIAC (Fertilizer Industry Advisory
Committee), was launched to supervise the distribution of
fertilizers to farmers and ensure their more effective use through
the widespread provision of technical assistance. The idea of
setting up an International Fertilizer Fund has been proposed on
several occasions, and recently by the Delegates for Sri Lanka and
New Zealand at the first session of the FAO ad hoc Group on
Fertilizer.   Such a Fund could help to finance fertilizer imports
by the countries hardest-hit by recent oil and commodity price
developments. The Indian Minister of Agriculture further suggested
the establishment of buffer stocks, especially of nitrogenous
fertilizers, perhaps financed by the World Bank and administered by
FAO.   Recently an International Fertilizer Supply Scheme was
adopted by the Council of FAO in July and is to be presented to the
World Food Conference.   It provides a framework for concerted
action by governments, governmental and non-governmental
organisations and industry to increase the supply of fertilizers to
developing countries. This scheme comprises, among other things,
the establishment of a fertilizer pool and the setting-up of an
information system. However, present proposals   need further

elaboration before being adopted by the international community. Lastly, technical assistance ought to be supplied to develop the production capacity of fertilizer plants in developing countries where such plants operate at an average of only half their total capacity. The United States has already offered assistance in this respect but so far only a limited number of developing countries have requested such aid.

ii) Seeds

The provision of high-yield seeds also raises some difficult problems. At the moment a large proportion of seeds are supplied by a few donor countries, mostly under project assistance. They are also supplied by international research institutes which helped to evolve high-yield varieties (such as the International Centre for the Improvement of Maize and Wheat in Mexico and the International Rice Research Institute in the Philippines). It should be possible to grow crops for seed-production in the developing countries themselves. Here, much remains to be done. Various initiatives have already been undertaken in Africa by research institutes of several donor countries, for example IRAT (Institut de recherches agronomiques et tropicales et de cultures vivrieres—Institute of Agricultural, Tropical and Food Crop Research—in France). Some projects have already been launched with foreign assistance both at national level (e.g., the Uganda Seed Multiplication Scheme financed with the United Kingdom assistance) and at regional level. As examples of the latter, a West African Rice Development Association (WARDA) was set up recently to provide germinating material and to test the new varieties in different areas; in the Middle East, under the Arid Lands Agricultural Development Programme (ALAD), seed is carefully selected to start nursery seed plots, and young researchers are trained to follow the progress of each crop from sowing to harvest; they subsequently take home the seeds which they think most suitable for cultivation in their own country. Research is also conducted on the evolution of stronger varieties, better suited to the climate concerned and generally required less water and fertilizer.

These initiatives, which were originally confined to cereals such as rice, have increasingly been directed towards coarse grains (maize, barley, millet, sorghum) and to starchy roots and pulses. It should not be forgotten that a marked improvement in food availabilities in some developing areas, especially in Africa, can only be achieved by increased production of these crops. A fresh impetus has been given to their development by international research institutes set up specially for this purpose, such as the International Institute for Tropical Agriculture (in Nigeria), the International Centre for Tropical Agriculture (in Colombia), the International Potato Centre (in Peru) and the International Crops Research Institute for the Semi-Arid Tropics (in India) which is mainly responsible for a world research programme on sorghum-growing. The International Development Research Centre in Canada is also concentrating research on sorghum, millet, cassava, chickpeas and broad beans, to list only a few, and is undertaking development projects for growing these various crops. A large proportion of the projects initiated by these institutes involves the training of young technicians who come from university research institutes, or from agricultural extension services in developing countries. An International Board for Plant Genetic Resources, with headquarters in FAO, was created in 1974 to help in the creation of a network of plant gene collections in order to conserve characteristics which would be of value in breeding plants with higher yields, better food values and greater resistance to pests and diseases.

iii) Pest Control

Much remains to be done in the matter of controlling crop pests. To understand fully the scourge represented by an invasion of locusts, it should be remembered that a swarm can destroy up to 80,000 tons of plants in a single day—enough to feed half a million human beings for one year. Such rough calculations show how greatly food supplies could be increased if effective measures were taken to minimise the locust threat. A number of research institutions are already tackling these problems. For example, in the United Kingdom the Centre for Overseas Pest Research has set up four units specialising in the control of the principal types of pest among which: the Anti-Locust Research Centre, the Termite Research Unit and the Tropical Pesticides Research Unit. In France, various institutes, concentrating on tropical research and grouped under GERDAT, pursue similar lines of research. Other countries also possess research units working on these problems. Assistance is granted to help spread the use of products developed by the donor countries; it also supports the direct promotion of small local research centres in developing countries which are in close touch with the problems involved.

iv) Agricultural Equipment

Simple, well-adapted equipment needs to be evolved for use on a number of crops; several research institutes are currently looking into the possibilities: for example, a Research and Experimental Centre on Tropical Agricultural Machinery (CEEMAT) has been established in France. In the United Kingdom, the National Institute of Agricultural Engineering specialises in the conception and design of elementary agricultural machinery. The University of

Wageningen in the Netherlands, in collaboration with FAO, is conducting research activities on the adaptation of agricultural tools to make them suitable for high-grade varieties of rice in India, Senegal and Nigeria. Japan contributes to the financing of agricultural technology and mechanisation centres (in particular in Malaysia and in Bangladesh). There are strong arguments, however, for improving existing types of equipment for different soils and climates; certainly the problem of training users would be simplified.

b) Development of Livestock Farming

The livestock farming sector is already receiving substantial assistance from some donor countries (especially Australia, Switzerland, Denmark and Japan), and some international agencies (especially the World Bank and IDB). This sector should, in future, be given greater emphasis, especially bearing in mind that: (i) there is a considerable shortage of animal protein throughout the developing countries, while meat and dairy products could provide the local populations with the protein sources they lack: (ii) the effective demand for meat is expected to rise by 4.5 per cent per year in the eighties, which should enable livestock farmers to draw additional income by supplying local and export markets; (iii) milk and meat production in developing countries should make it possible to cut down imports and release foreign exchange for the purchase of capital equipment; (iv) the development of livestock farming can be coupled with the utilisation of land otherwise unsuitable for farming, and assist rotation; (v) lastly, extensive livestock farming would be a source of natural fertilizers (dung, liquid manure) which are often more effective than manufactured fertilizers.

During the 1960's, assistance to livestock farmers was mainly extended for the development of flocks of sheep and herds of cattle in temperate or semi-temperate regions, with the object of providing meat for export (hence the vast scale of livestock farming projects in Latin America). For some years past, however, a growing number of assistance projects in tropical and semi-tropical regions have been concerned not only with cattle and sheep farming, but also with pig and poultry farming. Recent projects have been increasingly intended for developing small farms and for meeting local demand. A new impetus should be given to this type of project and at the same time, a better balance should be achieved between the growth of livestock herds and the growth of pasture. For instance, in the Sahel area the size of herds should have been limited, at least temporarily.

Assistance projects for livestock farming have been oriented in three main directions: (i) improvement of livestock farming conditions; (ii) control of animal diseases and development of veterinary services; (iii) selection of new breeds. Furthermore, the development of livestock farming has often proceeded in conjunction with the development of food crops and fruit and vegetable production under integrated projects (for example, the Danish Government's Agricultural and Livestock Project at Mysore in India).

i) Improvement of Livestock Farming Conditions

This type of assistance may cover extremely varied activities: improvement of livestock farming methods and structures; development of training facilities; research on animal feeding; installation of slaughter houses and cold stores. These various alternatives can be illustrated by some examples. In 1971 the EEC, whose activities in the livestock farming sector are still limited, launched a study on livestock farming structures in Africa, and ways and means of modernising them. To follow up this study, some pilot projects were launched in South-East Mauritania on the protection of livestock, the development of advisory services and new farming methods, and the improvement of water wells. The World Bank introduced a project for grouping nomads in co-operatives and livestock farming companies. Some "state ranches" have been established in Africa.

Technical assistance is allotted great importance in most livestock farming projects. This makes it possible to improve livestock farming methods, which have often remained archaic, and to develop the appropriate advisory services. As an example, a Dairy Training Centre was set up in Uganda in 1968 for all English-speaking African countries, with the help of Denmark. Several projects are concerned with the development of milk production (in particular Danish projects in Iran, Thailand and Zambia, and a project for the modernisation of the dairy industry in Peru, implemented with United Kingdom assistance). Research is now in progress on the improvement of animal feeding and fodder supplies. It has been pointed out that pasture is possibly the most over- and under-exploited resource in the developing countries, and that is is essential to achieve a better balance. In addition, an increasing quantity of nutritious feeds should be produced at lower cost. A project launched by the International Centre of Tropical Agriculture in Colombia aims to improve pig feeding by using cassava. Lastly, meat processing can be improved by establishing up-to-date slaughter houses, cold stores and packing plants. As an example, Denmark granted in 1973 financial and technical assistance to the State of Mysore in India both to set up slaughterhouses and to establish the first training centre for slaughterhouse personnel in the region. An international livestock centre for Africa, with headquarters in Ethiopia, was recently established to help improve livestock production systems.

ii) Control of Animal Diseases and Development of Veterinary Services

Several research institutes receive assistance for investigating the techniques of animal disease control in the developing countries. Examples are the Centre for Overseas Pest Research and the Centre for Tropical Veterinary Medicine in the United Kingdom, and the French Institute of Animal Husbandry and Tropical Veterinary Medicine, which have been conducting research for many years on animal diseases in tropical regions, and training personnel specialising in tropical veterinary medicine. More recently, the International Laboratory for Research on Animal Diseases has been set up in Kenya to deal with these problems.

Large scale drives for the eradication of such diseases as rinderpest, neck threadworm (river blindness) and the tsetse fly in Africa, have been launched by WHO with the help of donor countries and agencies. The latter have also helped to develop veterinary services and centres of veterinary medicine in the developing countries. For example, a veterinary project was carried out in Ethiopia with United Kingdom assistance. Under this project, a team of British veterinarians is co-operating with the Ethiopian veterinary services. Apart from general investigations into animal diseases in Ethiopia, they are starting to control rinderpest, to vaccinate livestock and to train local veterinarians.

iii) Breeding

Various projects have been introduced for improving stock, either through artificial insemination (for example, a Belgian project in Tunisia and a Danish project in Botswana), or by crossing local livestock with selected breeds from donor countries (for example: crossing Indian with Danish stock). The latter practice has on occasion ended in failure with hybrids unable to withstand tropical conditions. Research is in progress in various institutes on breeding problems (in particular in the Bognor Animal Husbandry Research Institute in India, which receives assistance from Australia).

c) Development of Fishing

Fishing could constitute a very promising sector for development assistance, insofar as it is a rich source of protein like the livestock sector. It is, indeed, regretable that people living on the shores of seas, lakes or rivers abounding with fish, should not draw greater benefit from these sources in their diet. Yet fish consumption is very low in the developing countries as a whole (an average of less than 5 kg. per head per year in such countries as Brazil, Mexico, Kenya and India).

Very few projects have as yet been introduced for the expansion of fishing in the developing countries. Only a few donor countries (in particular Norway, Canada and Japan) have devoted substantial sums to this purpose, most of the others attaching minor importance to this sector.

Estimates made under the Indicative World Programme[19] put the annual world production potential of main water species (fish, crustacea and molluscs) at about 118 million tonnes, only half of which was utilised in 1970. However, wide disparities exist as between areas and species. Some species are close to extinction, and call for protection; others, on the contrary are plentiful. A map showing the possibilities by area would be extremely useful. Protection of fish species should be ensured by international agreements; but such agreements are extremely difficult to conclude, as fishing is subject to national jurisdiction, and fishing rights are often the subject of litigation.

Several donor countries (e.g., Norway, Canada and the United Kingdom) have recently helped to finance studies on the prospects of developing fishing, especially along the coast of India, in Lake Rudolf in Kenya, and off the coast of Trinidad and Tobago. A feasibility study was undertaken, with Canadian assistance, to study the possibilities of undertaking an integrated development project for the Niger, Chad and Cameroon fisheries.

Several donor countries are also considering the development of forward and backward production linkages such as the modernisation of fishing equipment. For example, Canada has provided assistance for the motorisation of fishing vessels in Senegal; and in 1971, the EEC launched a project for the development of fishing in the Central Delta of the Niger. This project involves the despatch of teams to advise and train fishermen, the installation of marketing centres, and the implementation of a technical research programme. Technical assistance plays an important role in training advisory and research staff. Several Research Institutes have been set up and developed with foreign assistance, in particular the National Inland Fisheries Institute in Thailand, and the National Institute of Navigation and Fisheries in El Salvador (with Canadian help), the Training Centre for Fishing in Sri Lanka (with Japanese help) and the Institute of Marine Biology (with Danish help). The donor countries provide equipment or advisory personnel, or both, as the case may be.

d) Development of Storage Facilities and Pest Control

It has been calculated that, if the losses due to the lack and defectiveness of storage facilities could be eliminated, it would be possible to feed over 10 per cent of the world population with the grain thus saved. This shows the importance that assistance agencies should allot to storage problems. Storage losses stem from various sources: mildew arising from insufficient drying before silage; inadequate protection against bad weather; pests multiplying without the check of natural enemies, etc. Research is being carried out in a number of national and international institutes to determine the most effective way of combating each kind of pest (selective chemical poisons, irradiation, etc.), and of limiting the damage done by excessive mildew. In the United Kingdom, for example, a special centre (Tropical Stored Products Centre) was set up for this purpose, attached to the Tropical Products Institute.

At the international level, an Assistance Group on Storage in Africa (GASGA) was recently set up with the assistance of France, the United Kingdom, the Canadian Research Centre for International Development, and the International Institute for Tropical Agriculture (IITA) in Nigeria. This group is studying, more specifically, present handling and storage systems for cereals in several English and French-speaking African countries. It also proposes to launch research and training programmes with a view to reducing losses.

Apart from research activities, assistance funds have furthered the growth of storage facilities in the developing countries. As an example, the CIDA (Canadian International Development Agency) has contributed to the construction of twelve silos in Algeria. This project, at a total cost of $40 million, is the biggest of its type to be financed by a donor country. Smaller projects have been undertaken, especially by Canada in Senegal and Tanzania and by Sweden in India, Bangladesh and Tanzania. These are only a few examples but they show the directions in which assistance could usefully be extended.

e) Main Trends in Research and Training Activities

The above statement of the position shows the importance attached by donor countries and agencies to research, with a view to increasing food production in the developing countries. With their help, ten international research institutes already mentioned in this chapter, specialising in the growing of certain crops or in the problems of cultivation in certain climatic regions, have been set up, most of them recently in developing countries. These institutes are concentrating on the chief bottlenecks and are stimulating research in the fields concerned, training research workers, evolving new means and methods of production, and testing the results on a large scale in one or more areas. The Institutes receive support from the Consultative Group on International Agricultural Research, which was established in 1971, under the co-sponsorship of the World Bank, FAO and the UNDP, to consider the financial and technical requirements for international agricultural

research and   to organize the necessary financial support.   The
Consultative Group now has 29 members, including, in addition to
the co-sponsors, governments, regional financial institutions and
foundations.   A small Technical Advisory Committee recommends
programmes for acceptance and financing by the Group. Grants by
the members of the Group amounted to $33 million in 1974. This
concentration of effort on well-defined subjects is a rather unique
phenomenon in the history of development aid and represents an
interesting attempt to make a "breakthrough" in a vital sector.
This method might well be extended to other subject areas (such as
population problems).

The donor countries and agencies have also done their best to
bring the activities of their own research institutes more into
line with the requirements of the developing countries in the food
sector. New centres (e.g. the International Development Research
Centre in Canada   or special   units in already established
institutes) are focussing on the study of these problems. However,
too large a proportion of the research work performed in the
developed countries is concerned with cash crops for export rather
than with food for domestic consumption.

Assistance has also done much to promote research in the
developing countries themselves.   Many regional or national
institutes have been established in specialised fields (live-stock
farming, fishing etc.). Much remains to be done, however, not only
for the establishment of new institutes or the development of
existing ones, but also for the promotion of more applied research
work, especially on a project basis. It is also important to link
the findings of research institutes and experimental laboratories
more closely with users' problems.   The improvement of
communication between researchers and users, scientists and
farmers, represents one key problem which will have to be solved if
food production as a whole is to be stepped up.

By comparison with the drive for innovation undertaken at the
research level, assistance in the matter of training in food
production techniques has remained traditional and limited. It is,
of course, extremely difficult to decide what proportion of
technical assistance is to be allotted to the food sector alone
under technical assistance to agriculture, [20] but that proportion
appears to be considerable. Account must be taken, in addition, of
certain training activities in the spheres of health, education,
transport, etc., under integrated projects.

Assistance from donor countries and agencies has certainly
made a substantial contribution to the training of specialists
(particularly in food crop management and live-stock farming), the
development of extension services and agricultural colleges, the
introduction of new extension techniques for "dynamising" the rural
sector (e.g., methods of "animation rurale" initiated by
IRAM--Institut de Recherche et d'Application des Methodes de
Developpement, France), and lastly, the provision of experts to
advise and train the people of the country in the framework of
development projects. An immense task still lies ahead, however,
It is, for instance, important to co-ordinate more systematically
the supply of agricultural inputs with technical assistance, to
generalise methods of "animation rurale", to develop experimental

research stations on the spot and to set up middle or lower level training centres. Assistance should be increased to projects or institutions, such as a training centre in Nepal which teach the average farmer how to improve his yield, without necessarily using modern means of production, simply by improving his methods of cultivation and by setting up new activities such as poultry, farming, horticulture and sheep farming, that are likely to enable him to augment his income and increase his food resources.

NOTES

[1]See also on this subject the study by Mrs. J. M. Mondot-Bernard "Attempted Analysis of the Food Situation in Africa", OECD Development Centre, 1974.

[2]Assessment of the World Food Situation, Present and Future, World Food Conference, 1974.

[3]Development Centre, <u>Employment Series</u> No 1, Table IV-8, Paris, 1971.

[4]Development Centre, <u>Employment Series</u> No 1, Table IV-8, Paris, 1971.

[5]Preliminary Assessment of the World Food Situation, Present and Future, op. cit.

[6]Comprising 9 African countries (Algeria, Zaire, Tunisia, Mauritius, Uganda, Chad, Kenya, Nigeria, Dahomey): nine Latin American countries (including Chile, Uruguay, Paraguay, and several Caribbean countries); two Far Eastern countries (Philippines and Indonesia); and four Near Eastern countries (including Iraq and Jordan).

[7]Lester R. Brown: "The Next Crisis? Food", <u>Foreign Policy</u>, Winter 1973-74.

[8]World Bank-Additional External Capital Requirements of Developing Countries, March 1974.

[9]Recent FAO estimates indicate an even higher figure: 60 million tons in 1973-74.

		1960	1965	1972
[10]Wheat (per bushel)	$	1.7	1.6	1.8
[11]Rice (100 lbs.)	$	6.6	7.2	9.4

[12]Closing stocks in the main exporting countries (million metric tons):

Coarse grains	1971–72	1972–73	1973–74
(Argentina, Australia, Canada, United States	56	40	32
Rice			
(Japan, Pakistan, Thailand, United States)	8	5	3

[13]Price in dollars per metric ton: Wheat = 240; Rice = 350; Coarse grains = 150.

[14]International Chamber of Commerce, Note on Fertilizers, 19th April, 1974.

[15]See FAO background paper for the review of the Fertiliser Market situation.

[16]According to the 1973 record, the relevant percentages are: 58 per cent in volume and 50 per cent in value.

[17]Estimated world fertilizer production capacity as related to future demand, Tennessee Valley Authority, August 1973, p. 9.

[18]This figure includes grants, loans and technical assistance for the following activities: crop and livestock development, production requisites, land and water development, land settlement and rural development, agricultural extension, research and education, agricultural credit and co-operatives, agricultural planning, administration and statistics, processing and storage, forestry and fisheries.

[19]Assessment of the World Food Situation, Present and Future, op. cit.

[20]In 1972, the agricultural sector was allotted 17 per cent of the total number of volunteers, 24 per cent of the advisers, 21 per cent of the operational personnel and 8–10 per cent of students and trainees.

Aid for the Health Sector

ORGANIZATION FOR ECONOMIC COOPERATION AND DEVELOPMENT

I. INTRODUCTION

Health is such an obvious element of a basic needs approach that it is easy to underestimate its significance in the total pattern of development. It is a "basic human need" but it is also: a) a crucial element in improving productivity; b) the best general measure of improvement in the living standards of the mass of the population--an increase in income per head can be concentrated on a minority, but a significant decrease in infant mortality cannot be achieved by a further decrease in the infant mortality of the elite; c) an indirect measure of improvements in a number of sectors (education, infrastructure, nutrition) which are essential contributors to improvements in health status; and d) in the opinion of many experts, the main hope for reducing the rate of population growth, because increased survival rates mean that parents can achieve family wishes or society requirements with a smaller number of births.

The present situation is one of conflicting tendencies. Life expectancy in developing countries has improved sharply since the Second World War, but is still low compared with developed countries. Some illnesses have been largely eliminated from some regions (malaria) or worldwide (smallpox), but others, especially those associated with malnutrition, are still killing millions of children every month.

It is nevertheless possible to be optimistic, for a number of reasons which will be discussed in more detail in this chapter. First, the technical basis for major health improvements exists--the methods of eliminating the main common diseases in

From **DEVELOPMENT CO-OPERATION**, 1977, (103-115), reprinted by permission of the publisher, Organization for Economic Co-operation and Development, Paris.

developing countries are now thoroughly understood. Second, the essential importance of improving health standards is increasingly accepted in the international community--largely thanks to the unremitting efforts of the World Health Organisation. Third, there is an increasing openness to innovation so that the approach to developing countries' problems can be freed from what have often been traditional developed-country systems and structures.

Each of these three reasons for optimism was clearly brought out in the discussions which took place in November 1976 at a meeting of experts on aid for health in the poorer countries, organised jointly by the Development Assistance Committee and the OECD Development Centre, with participation by experts from developing, as well as developed, countries, multilateral agencies and non-governmental organisations. Health was chosen for a major meeting not only because of its intrinsic importance and because it is the basic needs sector, after agriculture, in which the largest number of DAC Members are active, but also because it was thought--correctly, as it turned out--that it could provide an illustration of problems affecting a number of other basic needs sectors. This chapter is largely based on the conclusions and recommendations of the experts' meeting.

II. THE HEALTH SITUATION IN DEVELOPING COUNTRIES

Table 1 summarizes, on the basis of the two most widely-available indicators of health standards, the progress made in the past fifteen years in the various groups of countries and, above all, shows the gap which still separates the developing from the developed countries. The difference is particularly striking for the infant mortality rate, which, in the countries with less than $520 per head, covering over 70 per cent of the population of non-oil developing countries, is over six times the figure for developed countries.

Figures of this kind, however, necessarily give a false impression, by suggesting that the difference between the health situations in developed and developing countries is a matter of degree. In fact, the nature of the health problem in developing countries is so different from that of developed countries as to have a major effect on the whole of the daily lives of the persons concerned. As one writer[1] has put it:

"It is difficult for those living in temperate climates with good standards of public health and medical care to realise the impact of disease on rural communities in the tropics. For example, if you happen to be born and grow up in rural Africa you are liable to harbour four or more different disease-producing organisms simultaneously. And yet as a parent, you must be fit enough to work or your family will starve. In your village every child at times suffers the paroxysms of malaria fever and you and your wife will mourn the death of one or two children from this disease. The snails in the village pond carry schistosomiasis and you do not consider it unusual when your children pass blood in their urine.

You take for granted the disfigured faces and fingerless hands of the beggars in the village street suffering from leprosy. If you live near a river where blackflies breed, one in ten of your friends and neighbours will be blind in the prime of life. You know that waves of killing diseases such as measles and meningitis and perhaps sleeping sickness are liable to strike your village. But, lacking effective remedies, you tend to philosophise in the face of sickness. You make an effort to walk the ten miles to the nearest dispensary when you or your child is ill, but there may be no remedies, and it may be too late . . .".

This quotation draws attention particularly to the health problems caused by the continued prevalence of certain tropical diseases. In fact, several hundred million people in the Third World are affected by these debilitating disease, most of them chronic, sometimes leading to early death. Three of them, malaria, schistosomiasis (bilharzia) and filariasis (parasitic worm diseases) are massive in their impact, affecting hundreds of millions of people; others, such as trypanosomiasis (sleeping sickness), onchocerciasis (river blindness) and leprosy are less important but still affect the lives of many tens of millions.

To some extent, therefore, the health problems of developing countries are specific to their particular geographic situation. But of far greater importance is the set of problems related to the condition of undevelopment itself: essentially, insufficient or specifically deficient food intake, lack of sanitary infrastructure, poor hygiene and ignorance. Many of these problems and their consequences for health are indeed similar to those which prevailed in North America and Western Europe a century ago. While some of them are a direct cause of disease--for example, malnutrition by leading to debilitation and specific deficiency diseases--their main effect is to provide the conditions in which not only do the tropical diseases flourish but also many diseases regarded as uncommon or trivial in developed countries become mass killers.

The third factor which it is important to mention in describing the health situation in developing countries is their population structure. Compared with the developed countries, developing countries have particularly high proportions of their populations: a) under 5 years of age and b) living in rural areas. Numerous studies have shown that rural populations and the very young suffer more from health problems than other parts of the population.

This concentration of health problems on the very young means that a startling proportion of all the deaths each year in the world are accounted for by small children in developing countries. J. H. de Haas estimated in 1967 that the figure was as high as 30 million, out of 60 million deaths world-wide in all age groups.

Studies by the Pan American Health Organisation for Argentina, Bolivia and El Salvador showed mortality rates in children under 5 years to be almost twice as high in rural as in urban areas.

Similar conclusions emerge from studies in other regions.

The high incidence of disease among the very young has especially important implications for one of the other major problems facing developing countries, namely their extremely rapid population growth. Paradoxically, there is evidence that the high levels of infant and child mortality in developing countries may be a factor tending to increase rather than decrease the rate of population growth. The reason for this is that economic pressures and in some cases social customs require that a certain number of children, especially boys, pass the age of puberty in each family. If infant and child mortality rates are high, parents are likely to bring a large number of children into the world as insurance against "wastage". Although the motivations for fertility, conscious and unconscious, still remain largely unexplored, experience has shown that where infant mortality rates have declined sharply a decline in the birth rate has followed. Better health--of infants and children and their mothers--leading to a reduction in the high rates of morbidity and mortality that are characteristic of the poorer sections of the population in most developing countries is thus one basic condition for an eventual slowing down of population growth. Developing countries are slowly coming to recognise this and to change the emphasis of their population programmes from the earlier, strictly medical, family planning approach to a broader concern with "family welfare".

III. THE UNDERLYING DETERMINANTS OF HEALTH STATUS

The previous section has drawn attention to some of the main causal factors contributing to the poor health situation in developing countries, in particular their relationship to poverty and under-development. It would be quite wrong however to draw the conclusion that these health problems can be solved only when incomes reach a much higher level than at present--still less the conclusion that an increase in incomes will automatically lead to their solution. There are encouraging examples of countries which have achieved major improvements in health status in spite of relatively low income, as well as others of countries with relatively high average incomes but with continuing appalling health standards among the rural poor. Recent analysis has shown that much can be done through improvement, sometimes at very little net cost, in the following areas:

    a) food;
    b) clean drinking water and safe disposal of excreta;
    c) education.

a) Food and nutrition

Protein-caloric malnutrition is the world's dominant health problem. Some 500-600 million people in the developing countries (about two-thirds of them in South Asia) are estimated to be undernourished--that is, they do not eat enough food to meet their minimum daily requirements of calories. Protein deficiencies may affect as many as 800 million people. Because of their higher energy requirements, the groups most at risk are small children and pregnant and lactating women. The most extensive and reliable investigation of childhood mortality in the developing world, conducted by the Pan American Health Organisation (PAHO) in Latin America in 1973 revealed that nutritional deficiencies and infant immaturity at birth (itself often due to poor nutrition of the mothers) were the primary cause of 6 per cent, and associated with 57 per cent, of all deaths. Under-nutrition thus probably contributes to more than half the deaths of children under five in Latin America. A comparable calculation in South Asia or Central Africa would probably yield an even higher figure.

The effects of malnutrition are of three main kinds:

a) physical or mental debilitation. The importance of adequate caloric nutrition to meet the requirements of hard physical activity is evident for countries where most work is still carried out by hand labour. More recently, there has been evidence that mental capabilities can also be affected by inadequate protein levels in early years of life.

b) specific deficiency diseases. These include: anaemia (the most widespread, affecting 5 to 15 per cent of adult men throughout the world, and much higher percentages of women and children in developing countries); kwashiorkor (protein deficiency) and marasmus (energy and protein deficiency), estimated to affect 10 to 20 million young children; and rickets;

c) lowered resistance to infections, including particularly diarrhoea (responsible for the largest number of infant deaths) and pneumonia (itself often the result of measles).

The effects of malnutrition are dramatic and the solution apparently simple: more and better food supplies. In fact this is a good example of the major difficulty in dealing with health problems: first, it involves what is conventionally (and above all, administratively) regarded as a distinct sector; second, it is at least as much a question of improved distribution of available supplies as one of increased availability. The problems of increasing food supplies and improving their distribution have been discussed in earlier reports and need no elaboration here. What is important is that this is not merely a question of the number of men, women and children who lie down hungry at night but one affecting their ability to survive.

b) Clean drinking water and safe disposal of excreta

The pathogen agents for many of the tropical diseases, as well as for diarrhoea, dysentery, typhoid and cholera, are transmitted by human faeces, through inadequate hygiene or contaminated water. The transmission of these diseases is interrupted or substantially reduced when drinking water is not contaminated, there is enough of it for washing purposes, and disposal of human excreta is safe. In addition, many infections of the intestinal tract and skin can be significantly reduced by improvements in domestic and personal hygiene, based upon increased availability of water. These water-washed diseases depend on the quantity rather than the quality of water.

The need for improvement of water supplies, especially in rural areas, has frequently been described in terms of the time and labour spent by women and children in carrying water from distant wells and streams. While this aspect is important, it is probably secondary to the health improvements which might follow from better distribution.

c) Education

Both the areas discussed above, nutrition and water supplies, are also indirect illustrations of the importance of education. The availability of adequate food and water is a necessary but insufficient condition for improvement in the health situation. For such improvement to take place, it is necessary that the people concerned be aware of the way to use the new supplies to the best effect. For example, it makes little sense to develop supplies of high-protein foods if, through lack of instruction, traditional feeding methods, especially after weaning, continue to be based on low-protein "fillers". The need for education on health precautions is not a problem only for developing countries (as is shown by the need for special campaigns in developed countries about the dangers of cigarette smoking) but the implications of a lack of health education are necessarily less apparent in countries where the task of ensuring hygienic conditions is largely borne outside the family--for example by the public water authorities or the food processing industry. The problem is more difficult in developing countries, because the natural vehicle for hygiene instruction, i.e the normal education system, does not cover the whole population and, in particular, discriminates against the women who should be the main targets of hygiene instruction. It is perhaps significant that the countries with health standards higher than those generally associated with their income group also have relatively high educational standards.

Furthermore, while the three areas listed above can be considered the most important, they are not the only elements of a policy to improve the health situation. Essential health care has been defined by Dr. Mahler, Director-General of WHO as including, in addition: the protection of houses against insects and rodents; the care of mothers before, during and after childbirth; family planning; infant and early childhood care; immunisation against the major infectious diseases; prevention and control of

TABLE 1. MAJOR HEALTH INDICATORS, BY GROUPS OF COUNTRIES

	Life expectancy at birth (years)			Infant mortality rate (per 1,000)		
	1960	1970	Most recent estimate	1960	1970	Most recent estimate
Non-oil-exporting developing countries:						
Lower-income (\$265/head or less in 1975)	38.6	43.1	43.4	118.7	106.4	95.7
Middle-income (\$266-\$520)	43.2	48.8	51.0	109.0	110.2	97.6
Upper middle-income (\$521-\$1,075)..	52.3	58.2	60.3	68.7	66.4	52.2
Higher-income (over \$1,075)	68.2	67.5	68.4	70.1	47.8	34.0
Oil-exporting developing countries	38.3	44.6	47.4	136.7	101.4	58.8
Developed countries	69.5	71.4	72.4	28.8	17.0	15.0

Source: World Bank.

TABLE 2. BILATERAL ODA COMMITMENTS FROM INDIVIDUAL DAC MEMBERS: HEALTH AND WATER AND SEWAGE, 1974 AND 1975

\$ million.

	Health A		Water supply and sewage B		Total A + B	
	1974	1975	1974	1975	1974	1975
Australia	9.84	20.57	1.35	3.93	11.19	24.50
Austria	0.09	0.96	—	0.01	0.09	0.97
Belgium	(20.20)	(27.00)	—	0.63	(20.20)	(27.63)
Canada	8.12	11.50	46.27	65.15	54.39	76.65
Denmark	2.72	5.33	4.98	—	7.70	5.33
Finland	0.82	2.00	—	—	0.82	2.00
France[a]	147.99	(205.10)	4.66	—	152.65	(205.10)
Germany	31.00	29.80	41.40	43.50	73.30	73.30
Italy		2.00				2.00
Japan	6.00	9.65	0.79	—	6.79	9.65
Netherlands	18.29	25.60	6.70	14.80	24.99	40.40
New Zealand	4.73	1.85	—	—	4.73	1.85
Norway	12.46	21.92	5.43	0.21	17.89	22.13
Sweden	28.30	(34.74)	46.20	22.36	74.50	(57.10)
Switzerland	0.80	0.06	—	5.10	0.80	5.16
United Kingdom	10.71	7.60[b]	8.50	12.95	19.21	20.55
United States	181.00	(179.40)	19.80	56.40	200.80	(235.80)
Total DAC	483.87	585.08	186.08	225.04	670.05	810.12
EEC	21.92	9.20	11.97	18.89	33.80	28.09

a. Includes French Departments (\$86.3 million in 1974).
b. Capital assistance only. Identified health expenditures, including technical assistance, in fiscal year 1974/75 have been reported by the United Kingdom as \$13.3 million.

locally endemic diseases; elementary curative care of all age groups for disease and injury; and unsophisticated health propaganda aimed at promoting increased interest in health care, knowledge of whom to approach in order to benefit from it, and active involvement in the progressive improvement of this care.

One important conclusion of recent studies, which was particularly stressed at the Experts' Meeting, is that a major improvement of health standards can be achieved only by an improvement in a number of directions. While progress in any one of them is likely to be beneficial to a certain extent, its potential will be largely wasted unless there is progress in others.

IV. THE ROLE OF IMPROVED HEALTH SERVICES

It may seem strange that so little mention has been made so far of health services in a chapter on health problems, but this is because their role in improving the situation in developing countries is not greater than those of the other factors mentioned above and because health services of the kind familiar in developed countries are not the best model for the developing countries' situation.

Nevertheless, the extension of health services is clearly a priority in any programme to improve health standards. The size of the challenge is measured by the fact that it is an accepted estimate that some 80 per cent of the population of developing countries have no access to these services at present and that public sector expenditures on health are in many of the poorer countries no more than $2 per head per year, as compared with a range of $141 to $350 per head per year in the OECD countries in 1974. The problems are aggravated by the dispersion of over 70 per cent of the population of developing countries in small rural communities, and the severely limited resources in the form of qualified personnel.

A rural health centre in Africa can be built for the cost of four beds in a teaching hospital, and can provide most of the health care requirements for roughly 20,000 people. In a country such as Zambia, 250 health centers, enough for the whole population, could have been built at the cost of the teaching hospital in the capital. Similar considerations apply to the alternative use of funds for training. Health centres, in contrast to hospitals, can be operated by a variety of men and women with middle-level skills, who, with appropriate training and support, are quite capable of providing the various elements of essential health care.

Perhaps the most important fact to note, with respect to the argument on "quality" versus "quantity" which is often raised (and where "quality" refers to hospital treatment and care by fully qualified medical doctors), is that there is actually no such choice for the majority of potential patients in the low-income countries.

The greatest potential for health improvement in Third World countries lies with their people, in the communities where they live, by widening the base of the health services pyramid. It is in these same communities that water supplies and sanitation should be improved and their improvement maintained, and that the standards of nutrition should be raised. The optimal use of services is when even at the lowest echelon they act themselves as a referral network, supporting and integrating local initiative. To take an example: the target in Tanzania, where public sector expenditures on health are about $3 per head per year, is to have, at the lowest echelon in the system, one dispensary for every 6,500 people by 1980. The effectiveness of services is multiplied when the communities organise themselves at village level for as many of the tasks of health improvement and life improvement as they can carry out.

A number of projects in various developing countries provide convincing evidence of the achievement of local community organisation[2]. An important feature of these projects is that health is but one aspect of economic and social improvement activities. The term "primary health care", often used as synonymous with essential health care or basic health services, also designates these community-based approaches.

a) Training

Training has been defined by WHO as the greatest challenge for the new approach to health, involving the training of large numbers of para-medical personnel. The rationale for staffing basic health services with para-medical personnel does not lie only in the high costs of medical education (for example, in Tanzania it costs $40,000 to train a medical doctor, less than $2,500 to train a medical assistant). It lies also in the recognition of the banality of diagnosis and treatment for most of the major health problems, for example for such common causes of infant and child mortality as dehydration from diarrhoea. This finding, together with the recognition of the value of early, simple and adequate treatment in the communities themselves, has important implications for training policies. Experience in a number of countries is confirming the potential for training people with much less than a full university education.

At the same time, serious questions have been raised about the appropriateness of training doctors from developing countries to the point where their qualifications are equivalent to those in the industrialised countries, resulting in the best-known form of "brain-drain"[3]. Medical doctors tend to congregate in urban areas (50 per cent of the graduates of the medical school in Nairobi, for example, practise in the capital). Very few medical schools have introduced a session of training in the rural areas for their students. It is clear, however, that medical schools have important roles to play, both in medical research and in producing physicians who can (and who wish to) function as managers, teachers, and supervisors in the health system and staff referral hospitals.

Training of intermediate-level health personnel is far from new. For example, the Ecole Africaine de Medecine in Senegal produced more than 800 medecins africains between 1918 and 1951. They had followed four years of training in simple obstetrical and surgical procedures, preventive medicine, public health and sanitation. Most of them devoted their lives to work in the rural areas. Similar systems were adopted in Fiji, Madagascar, Nigeria and Zanzibar. The functions and levels of intermediate health manpower ("medical auxiliaries") depend on the system adopted by the country concerned. The major question is how to relate training to the major health problems of the country and to the level of general education prevailing in the country. An important consideration is that, in most cases, health workers will have to substitute for the doctor, whether they treat a patient or decide that he should be referred higher up They therefore require technical support for training in diagnostic work.

One innovatory approach is being experimented in Tanzania, under which most basic diagnoses are carried out by staff who undergo a three-year training programme and whose workload is of 150 to 200 patients every morning. To increase the accuracy, repeatability and rapidity of diagnosis, a set of charts has been designed and field-tested by one of WHO's collaborating centres on educational technology in the United Kingdom. These flowcharts, covering 150 of the most common health problems in the country, are one of the factors of success in the performance of basic health services in Tanzania today. In the vast majority of cases, it is claimed, correct diagnosis can be effected by trained medical auxiliaries in less than three minutes. The tool is now being tested for adaptation to the different diseases of three other countries which are introducing health care systems.

The village health worker is at the borderline between health services and community socio-economic development. The variety of experience already acquired in a number of projects suggests that it would be vain to look for a single model. Experts agree that there may be various models within a single country. They also believe that the greatest potential for health improvement might lie with community organisation and community development, but the integration between health services and community development is so far mainly uncharted territory. In this connection, much has been done over the past twenty years for training traditional birth attendants and equipping them with simple tools in a number of developing countries. Trained and, for the most part, untrained traditional midwives, paid in cash or kind by mothers, attend perhaps some 80 per cent of deliveries in the Third World. None of the poorest countries, however, can afford an army of village health workers on the public pay-roll. Most village health helpers, where they exist, are paid for either by customers on a fee-basis, or by the local community, or in some cases not at all.

In some countries this work at community level is performed by

people (usually women) who do not exercise other health
responsibilities. In others, the preference is for multi-purpose
health workers (at varying levels of professional skill). The
multi-purpose worker can, in fact, be seen as the embodiment, in
its simplest form, of the "integrated approach" to health and
family planning that is increasingly commending itself to the
developing countries and to the donor community.

b) Research

For improved planning of health services to meet basic health
needs, one area where much work remains to be done is operational
and applied research in support of the health services themselves.
Training and performance can be improved through the development of
suitable tools to be used (and preferably produced) in the
developing countries. In some instances, the design of simple
tools for mass use and use in village situations may require
applied research from people and institutions in the most advanced
countries. This was the case, for example, for two inventions
which helped reduce time and overcome transportation constraints in
the successful world-wide campaign for the eradication of smallpox:
the bifurcated needle and the use of dried vaccine. The
preparation of salts for oral rehydration of children in such a
form that they can be produced cheaply, prepared and used by anyone
including the mothers, and distributed through existing networks,
is another example of needed appropriate technology. A recent WHO
programme aims at solving more of these problems. The initial
focus is on tools for the immunisation programme, village
obstetrics, oral rehydration and techniques of screening of
nutritional deficiencies.

c) Planning

Above all, given the formidable constraint of resources, the
attainment of the objective of essential health care for all within
a reasonable time horizon requires new and different approaches in
the planning and organisation of health services, as well as a full
appreciation of the linkages with education, sanitation etc. Yet,
as Dr. John Bryant noted in his book on <u>Health and the Developing
World</u>[4], the health sector usually functions in a
profession-oriented, not a system-oriented way. In a Health
Ministry, each department or division has its own area of coverage,
such as hospitals or tuberculosis, and each may function
autonomously. The overall programme of an agency organised in this
way is only the sum of the activities of its departments and not
the result of specific institutional plans to meet specified goals.

The approach which is being sought is in fact a new way of thinking: explicitly describing goals, designing programmes to meet them, studying those programmes in terms of cost and effect with a constant willingness to seek alternative approaches, and continually evaluating the effectiveness of individual programmes and of the whole system, in other words, thinking of health as a system that can be controlled and about which decisions can be made.

This approach is reflected in the recent development of "Country Health Programming" by the WHO, often with the support of know-how from bilateral aid agencies (experience in health planning is rare), for example in Burma, Nepal, Sudan and Thailand, and in the use of systems analysis in the programming of mother and child care in Algeria. Important features of the process are: that the analysis, with full attention to the analysis of constraints, is done by groups of nationals, rather than by small numbers of (foreign) specialists; that it involves representatives of other relevant sectors, and of political, consumers' and other associations, in addition to those of the health sector; and that in several countries it has led to the setting up of planning and evaluation units on a permanent basis. For external donors also, as had already been the case with Tanzania, a goal-oriented national plan provides a more coherent framework for co-operation and co-ordination and a more effective use of inputs.

V. THE ROLE OF DEVELOPMENT CO-OPERATION

The earlier sections of this chapter have attempted to show the importance of the health problem in developing countries, but at the same time the need for approaches which are quite different from conventional health policies in developed countries. This explains why the health sector, with the exception of agriculture, is the one in which the largest number of external donors participate, and yet is probably the sector in which present methods are being most called into question.

a) The Present Contribution

It is estimated that the total volume of official (DAC bilateral and multilateral) commitments for the health sector (including population programmes, water supply and sanitation) in 1975 was of the order of $1.5 billion[5]. (In addition, perhaps more than in most other fields, expenditures by non-profit agencies, especially church-related ones, are particularly substantial). Of this total, bilateral commitments from DAC countries were about $810 million[6] and multilateral commitments about $670 million.

Population programmes accounted for about $200 million and water supplies and sanitation for about $580 million, leaving $700 million in the form of commitments to the health sector defined more narrowly.

Detailed figures for the breakdown among particular forms of the $450 million bilateral expenditure in the health sector proper are unreliable, but it is certain that the more important of these are: hospitals and clinics (including health centres and dispensaries); control of communicable diseases; health manpower development; and mother and child care.

The volume of multilateral commitments in 1975 is estimated to have been as follows (in million U.S. dollars):

	Health, including population	Water supplies and sewerage	Total
WHO	..	..	150
UNICEF	50	--	50
IBRD/IDA	108	160	268
IDB	40	70	110
Asian Development Bank . .	--	65	65
African Development Bank .	--	23	23
Total	(328)	(339)	668

b) The Evolution of Donor Policies

Until about 1970, health aid had concentrated on the establishment and development of facilities at what is now described as the top of the health pyramid: hospitals, most of them in cities, and medical education facilities. A number of donors also supplied substantial numbers of qualified personnel to staff these facilities. More recently, there has been a shift in emphasis, but as yet this has been of differing extent as between individual donors. Some, including Canada, the Scandinavian countries and the Netherlands, now concentrate mainly on rural health centres and hospitals, dispensaries and training centres for rural health personnel. The bulk of United States' health aid (excluding population) is for the development of "low-cost health delivery systems", malaria control and nutrition. While almost all programmes now include some primary health care component, this is limited for some donors by their policy of response to recipient country request, many of which still tend to be for traditional, hospital-centred forms of aid.

c) Reappraisal of the Role of External Aid

Nevertheless, there is general recognition of the need to reconsider the aims and methods of aid in the health sector. This gave particular importance to the conclusions of the November 1976 experts' meeting on aid for health in the poorer countries, in which a remarkably broad consensus was reached among experts from developed and developing countries, multilateral agencies and voluntary organisation.

In particular, there was wide agreement on the following:

a) the improvement of health status requires the meeting of basic human needs in terms of food intake, safe water and adequate sanitation, as malnourishment and contaminated water underlie much of the chronic morbidity, short life expectation and high infant and child mortality in the poorer countries;

b) health care should be extended to the whole population (health services are currently estimated to cover some 15 to 25 per cent of Third World populations). Manpower and financial constraints in the poorer countries make it impossible to expand coverage by extending medical care of a classical or Western-model type. The training and employment costs of a single medical doctor correspond to those of several para-medical health workers. Also, the prevention and treatment of a vast majority of illnesses do not require the skills of a medical doctor;

c) over the last two decades, health policies of the developing countries and external assistance have heavily favoured the development of the top layer of the health services "pyramid": medical faculties and hospitals, mainly in capital cities and other towns. Hospitals now represent an in-built distortion in the allocation of national and aid resources between the needs of the mass of the population and those of a small minority;

d) the most urgent task now and for the decades to come is to favour the development of systems serving the basic health needs of the mass of the population (e.g. immunisation, mother and child care, diagnosis and treatment of the most common diseases, health education, nutrition, sanitation, vector control). Some of these areas are not traditionally part of the tasks of health services, nor do they or their prerequisites normally lie within the sphere of competence of ministries of health. In extended systems, hospitals represent a referral facility for illnesses which cannot be diagnosed and treated at the local level, and medical doctors, a scarce qualified manpower resource, have a role also in the supervision and refresher training of other health workers. Medical education and professional careers at present do not prepare them for this role;

e) because the major health problems of the developing
    countries are closely related to poverty and to the
    environment, health improvement in the poorer populations
    cannot be achieved independently from some measure of
    socio-economic development, nor without the participation
    of the people;

f) the implications of these concepts for positive action
    in health and development policies, and for aid, require a
    major change in perception at decision-making levels,
    going well above and well beyond those in charge of the
    health services themselves. In this context, the
    integration of health aspects in the "basic needs"
    strategy being developed by the ILO and in preparations
    for the Third UN Development Decade Strategy, is of
    particular importance.

The discussion of the role to be recommended for foreign aid
took as its starting point a number of agreed considerations:

a) each developing country will elaborate its own solution
    to its own health problems;

b) aid will be most effective where the recipient country has
    the requisite national policies and a firm commitment to
    primary health care, but aid can sometimes help in the
    establishment of such policies;

c) mass-based or "low-cost" health systems do not necessarily
    mean that total costs (or aid requirements) will change,
    but the nature of expenditure will be different;

d) there should be more collaboration and mutual information
    at four broad levels;
    --among developing countries with similar problems;
    --between developing-country governments and institutions
    and developed-country institutions;
    --among donor countries;
    --at the level of consultation between international
    organisations and bilateral donors, when international
    strategies are reviewed and new areas are formulated, so
    that health aspects are included in the new strategies.

The meeting acknowledged the leadership role of the World
Health Organisation in setting priorities for action at the
international level and in assisting developing countries in
raising the level of health conditions of their populations.

A number of the recommendations addressed to donor agencies
were general in character. These included:

a) that aid agencies explicitly take health factors into
    account in the programming of aid of all types, and that
    health be recognised by aid agencies as a factor which
    affects, and is affected by, all other development
    activities;

b) that donors attach particular interest to the programmes
    of countries which have as a priority the improvement of

the health status of the mass of the population;
c) that aid agencies be prepared to provide in a flexible manner aid in the forms and for the purposes required to promote and support health services and activities which aim at the improvement of the health status of the mass of the population;
d) that aid agencies must recognise the importance of including health components in projects in sectors other than health (e.g. agricultural development, water supply and sanitation, etc.) and of screening development projects to assure that health implications are recognised at the earliest stage of project proposals, with special attention to health hazards in water-related projects (dams, irrigation, etc.).

It was felt that the areas and purposes of particular potential for aid donors are:

a) support for basic health services and primary health care, where the largest aid requirement is for training of para-medical personnel (health workers) and related development-oriented research;
b) assisting developing countries in the planning, analysis and evaluation of measures to affect health, including measures in the fields of health services, environment, population, education, agriculture and nutrition, etc.;
c) current expenditures including for such items as drugs, vaccines, simple diagnostic instruments and other supplies;
d) capital aid and technical co-operation to help provide the infrastructure, equipment and know-how needed in terms of dispensaries, training centres, accommodation for health workers in rural areas, etc., increased national planning, research and evaluation capacity, and national and regional capacity for producing, storing and distributing basic drugs, vaccines, and other items needed for basic health care and health improvement;
e) support for the activities of non-governmental organisations where they can carry out effective programmes;
f) support for communication and education in health and nutrition both through formal education and informal methods;
g) nutritional improvement, through support for planning, more attention to the nutritional implications of agricultural and food aid projects;
h) research, especially operational and applied research to elaborate innovative approaches to the delivery of health services.

It has already been mentioned that population programmes are regarded by many DAC Members as an important part of their aid in the health sector. On this subject, the conclusion of the experts' meeting was as follows:

"Health and fertility are inter-related: as infant
and child mortality rates decrease, parents may wish
to have fewer children: fertility often affects
maternal and child health. Most DAC Members favour the
integration of family planning services within health
care services; some are also conducting pilot projects
for the distribution of means of birth control made
available to communities independently of the provision
of other health measures. Family planning should be
provided on a strictly voluntary basis, in agreement
with the principles of the Bucharest Conference
stressing that people so wishing should have access to
information and means of family planning."

VI. CONCLUSION

Progress in improving the health situation in developing
countries will not easily be achieved, but much can be done, even
with existing knowledge and with no great increase in the financial
resources spent in the sector. The main requirement is that health
should be treated by both donors and recipients as a problem to be
tackled by action in a number of different sectors, recognising
that the beneficial effects of improved health will also be felt
throughout the whole economy and society.

NOTES

[1] Dr. David Rose, of WHO, quoted in Tropical Diseases, WHO, Geneva, 1976.

[2] Some of these examples, notably in Guatemala, Indonesia, Niger
and Yugoslavia, are described in Health by the People, WHO,
Geneva, 1976.

[3] Some countries, for example, Tanzania and Thailand, now require a
minimum number of years of government service from newly
graduated physicians to reduce or delay outflow.

[4] Cornell University Press, Ithaca and London, 1969.

[5] This excludes official aid from such sources as the
centrally-planned-economies and OPEC countries, and other
countries. China in particular is known to supply a considerable
number of health teams, especially in Africa. OPEC countries

occasionally finance the construction of hospitals mainly in Arab countries and are assisting the Sudan in implementing its primary health care plan.   Israel maintains   health aid projects with special attention to ophthalmology.

[6]For a breakdown by donor country, see Table VI-2.

Population Growth and Food Supply in Sub-Saharan Africa

JACOB MEERMAN
SUSAN HILL COCHRANE

The view persists that sub-Saharan African is underpopulated; that its economic growth will be accelerated if its population increases. This view is based on two arguments. First, that modernization (read: industrialization) is facilitated by large numbers of people because they make possible greater specialization and the application of productive modern techniques. Yet three quarters of the countries in the region have populations of less than ten million people. The second argument is that population density is low relative to arable land, which would be more productive if there were more people to work it.

Neither argument is really persuasive. Large numbers do not automatically lead to rapid economic development--the slow growth in India and Bangladesh testifies to this. The key element for economic growth is production stimulated by the effective demand of large markets. For small countries, these have to be export markets. But rising populations in sub-Saharan Africa have led primarily to economic growth based largely upon traditional village agriculture, and this has not increased per capita output. Population growth of this genre could actually reduce total cash income per head because of diminishing returns as more labor is applied to a less productive agriculture. And rising populations in Africa have also made more difficult the training of enough skilled people, on which countries such as Korea and Taiwan based their rapid growth in production (and exports).

It is true that the density of population in the region is very low--on average less than one fifth of that in Asia. But in Asia, more modern technology and better natural conditions--irrigation and double cropping--permit families to cultivate small plots very intensively. In Africa many times more land per capita is needed for survival. Against this measure, much of the region is already crowded: unless new technologies and practices evolve, agricultural output can no longer increase in proportion to additional agricultural labor.

This article presents an opposite argument: sub-Saharan Africa--given its present institutions and endowments of capital

From **FINANCE AND DEVELOPMENT**, Sept. 1982, (12-17), reprinted by permission of the publisher.

Table 1. Comparative yields of basic food crops, 1969–71 and 1977–79

	Sub-Saharan Africa[1]		Developing countries[2]		World	
	1969–71	1977–79	1969–71	1977–79	1969–71	1977–79
Millet						
Yield per hectare[3]	98	94	109	108	110	113
Comparative yield per hectare[4]	104	100	102	101	110	113
Sorghum						
Yield per hectare[3]	92	93	115	151	121	145
Comparative yield per hectare[4]	99	100	105	138	157	188
Maize						
Yield per hectare[3]	114	109	115	126	120	144
Comparative yield per hectare[4]	104	100	141	155	262	316
Rice						
Yield per hectare[3]	108	114	113	129	115	129
Comparative yield per hectare[4]	95	100	130	148	164	184
Roots and tubers						
Yields per hectare[3]	117	117	129	129	110	110
Comparative yield per hectare[4]	100	100	129	129	157	157

Source: World Bank, *Accelerated Development in Sub-Saharan Africa*, 1981, p. 169.
[1] Includes Angola, Benin, Botswana, Burundi, Cameroon, Cape Verde, Central African Republic, Chad, Comoros, Congo, Djibouti, Equatorial Guinea, Ethiopia, Gabon, The Gambia, Ghana, Guinea, Guinea-Bissau, Ivory Coast, Kenya, Lesotho, Liberia, Madagascar, Malawi, Mali, Mauritania, Mauritius, Mozambique, Niger, Nigeria, Rwanda, São Tomé and Principe, Senegal, Seychelles, Sierra Leone, Somalia, Sudan, Swaziland, Tanzania, Togo, Uganda, Upper Volta, Zaire, Zambia, and Zimbabwe.
[2] Includes sub-Saharan Africa.
[3] 1961–63 = 100.
[4] Sub-Saharan Africa in 1977–79 = 100.

341

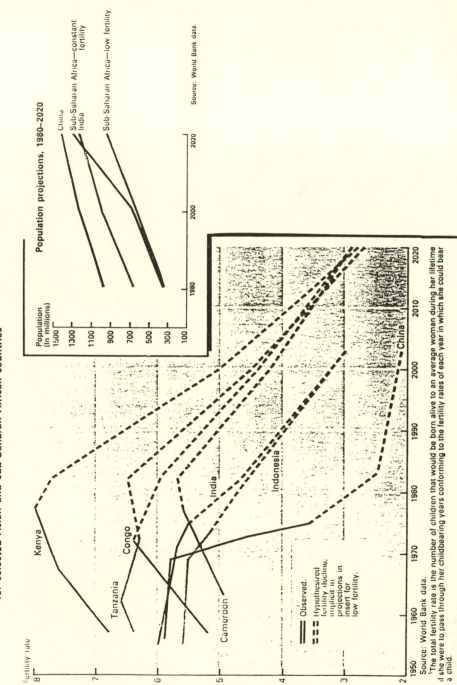

FIGURE 1. Current fertility rates (observed and hypothesized) for selected Asian and sub-Saharan African countries[1]

Population projections, 1980–2020

Source: World Bank data.

Source: World Bank data.

[1]The total fertility rate is the number of children that would be born alive to an average woman during her lifetime if she were to pass through her childbearing years conforming to the fertility rates of each year in which she could bear a child.

342

and technology--is already dangerously close to overpopulation. The rapid growth in numbers projected for the next decades will greatly increase human misery and depress rather than promote economic development. Specifically, rapid population growth will have disastrous effects on the region's ability to increase exports and provide people with food. There must be a search for new ways in which these effects could be mitigated.

I. POPULATION TRENDS

In many developing countries, fertility rates are falling; in some countries, notably China, Colombia, and Indonesia, dramatically. In sub-Saharan, Africa fertility either continues to be very high or is increasing, in part due to some decline in traditional practices that reduce fertility, such as prolonged breast-feeding or sexual abstinence. This situation and the expectation of declining mortality, due to better health care, imply that African population growth, which is already the most rapid in the world, may increase further. Population in sub-Saharan Africa is now about half that of India and a third of China (see chart). If fertility does not decline, in 33 years population will probably exceed that of India and be nearly equal to that of China. If fertility remains constant, in 40 years Kenya's population will increase five times, to 81 million; Nigeria's will increase four-fold, to 341 million. Even under the more optimistic assumption of declining fertility implicit in the second projection in the chart, African population will probably still be three quarters that of India by 2020.

There are two main reasons why reduced fertility in the next few decades is unlikely in sub-Saharan Africa as a whole. First, Africa has low literacy (particularly among girls), high infant and child mortality, and low urbanization. These suggest that existing fertility rates will persist well into the next century. But even if there is an improvement in the factors affecting fertility, these rates may still not decline. Many countries of the Middle East and Latin America have rates of urbanization, income, adult literacy, and child mortality which most African countries will not attain for many decades, yet their fertility levels persist at very high rates. This suggests that the projection for Africa based on constant fertility is more likely than that based on decreasing fertility. Second, average African fertility rates may even increase for the next 20 years or so. (This has already happened in three of the four African countries for which we have adequate statistics--see the chart.) The reason for this is that Africa, perhaps more than any other large region of the world, has had fecundity reduced in the past by poor health. Assuming incomes rise and better diets are possible in future, then health will improve, and both fecundity and fertility may rise.

Implicit in both constant and low projections is the assumption that African life expectancy at birth will increase

FIGURE 2.

The demographic transition

The demographic transition involves several steps. Initially life expectancy is increased as deaths from infectious diseases are brought down. This results in a continual drop in death rates over many decades. This effect has run its course in the industrial nations whose death rate has been about ten per thousand for many decades. Initially as death rates fall, birth rates—and fertility—continue very high. A population explosion is a consequence, since population growth is determined almost exclusively by birth rate minus death rate. Low-income Africa is at this stage. As modernization proceeds, birth rates decrease because couples reduce their fertility. Population growth diminishes. In many industrial countries the birth rate is now very close to the death rate and their populations soon may become stationary.

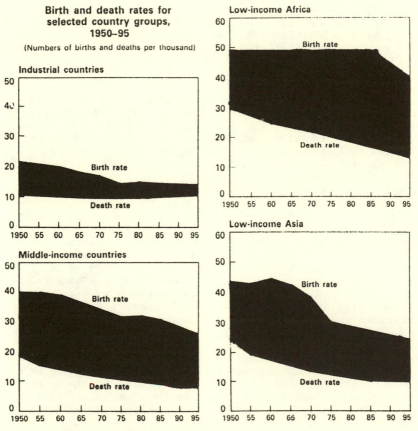

Birth and death rates for selected country groups, 1950–95

(Numbers of births and deaths per thousand)

Industrial countries

Middle-income countries

Low-income Africa

Low-income Asia

Source: World Bank, *World Development Report 1981*.

344

substantially from the current 47 years, which is 10 years below the average for all low-income countries. Nevertheless, at the beginning of the twenty-first century, two thirds of sub-Saharan Africans would still have life expectancies below those of the average middle-income country in 1979. If mortality can be reduced more rapidly--and a successful effort is conceivable throughout the region--population growth would be even more rapid than that now forecast under the constant fertility projection.

II. FOOD SUPPLY

What are the implications of continuing and rapid population growth for African food supply? The region's cereal production is largely restricted to four grains--millet, sorghum, maize, and rice; but the volume of grain production is less, by weight, than 60 percent of the production of roots and tubers. There are two main differences between the output of these crops in sub-Saharan Africa and the rest of the world. First, yields per hectare are lower in Africa than elsewhere. Second, whereas yields elsewhere have increased in the last decade, in Africa they have generally been decreasing or largely constant (see the table).

In the 1960s, agricultural production in the region increased largely in tandem with population; both grew at about 2.3 per cent annually. In the 1970s, however, agricultural output actually decreased some 1.3 per cent a year, while population increased about 2.7 per cent a year. Food imports increased so rapidly that, by 1979, they absorbed more than 14 per cent of the foreign exchange generated by merchandise exports. Imported food grains (including food aid) represented 14 per cent of estimated grain production between 1977 and 1979. Since the urban population absorbed about 20 per cent of total production, and since most of the grain imported was consumed in the cities, it follows that food for African cities has been in large part imported. This growth of food imports is not a consequence of a more efficient division of labor or of an increasing specialization in export crops. The growth in output of all important African agricultural exports except tea has been negligible or negative since 1969-71.

Some of sub-Saharan Africa's poor export performance is explained by Nigeria. With one third of the region's population, it was once the region's largest exporter of agricultural commodities. But since 1960, output in Nigerian agriculture has been decreasing. Today more than 90 per cent of Nigeria's exports are petroleum. This has offset the rapid growth of agricultural exports--more than 6 per cent annually over 1969-79--in countries such as the Ivory Coast and Malawi. But even excluding Nigeria, the region's agricultural growth rate in the last decade has been substantially less than that of population.

Projections of the Food and Agriculture Organization (FAO) suggest that unless there is a very substantial increase in agricultural yields in Africa, the ratio of food produced to food consumed will decline from 86 per cent in 1975 to 70 per cent in 1990 and to 61 per cent in the year 2000. This assumes population growth according to the United Nation's medium-growth projections, which are slightly below the constant fertility projections of the chart. Consequently, food imports, both commercial and food aid, will substantially increase as this century comes to an end. There will also be increased malnutrition among those groups who are, poor and whose food supply is already very uncertain: in much of the Sahel; among landless laborers and the smaller farmers in densely populated rural areas; and among the urban poor in the poorer countries.

III. CAUSES OF LOW PRODUCTIVITY

This performance--falling yields on the farms, decreasing exports, and production falling behind population growth--has several causes. Some of these are of the nature of force majeure; in many countries disruptive civil strife has been associated with reduced output. But a second cause lies in diminishing returns. Africa's traditional agriculture consists of shifting cultivation, long fallow periods, and very limited use of manure, agricultural support services, and supplies. Land has, until recently, been the abundant factor of production. Cultivable land, however, is becoming increasingly scarce. More marginal land has been brought under cultivation, either in zones of lower or uncertain rainfall or on slopes, and this has led to soil erosion and degradation.

Today, population pressure has brought diminishing returns to traditional agriculture in much of the Sahel and the savanna (Niger, Mauritania, the Mossi Plateau of Upper Volta, Senegal's northern groundnut basin, and northern Nigeria), in parts of East Africa (Burundi, Kenya, and Rwanda), Southern Africa (Lesotho, Swaziland, and Zimbabwe), and parts of the West African forest belt (southeastern Nigeria, northern Benin, the western highlands of Cameroon, and the Central African Republic near Bangassou). In these, and other areas, the long fallow period has been shortened, undermining the regenerative power of soils. Consequently, less nutritious crops, which can be grown on very impoverished soils, are more widely cultivated. In the last two decades, production of "inferior" staples such as roots and tubers has increased as rapidly as that of the preferred grains. Fuelwood has become harder to find while overgrazing and disputes between cultivators and pastoral people are more frequent. Moreover, population growth has undoubtedly affected exports, as potential exports such as groundnuts and palm oil are consumed to a larger degree at home. The African share in marketing of groundnut oil, palm oil, and palm kernel oil has dropped precipitously since 1960.

There is also the absence of the Green Revolution--the use of new high-yielding seeds and new technologies in agriculture that has led to dramatic increases in yields in most other parts of the world. This new knowledge--at least for food grains--is largely inapplicable in sub-Saharan Africa: high-yielding rice varieties from Asia are rarely productive in Africa because of plant diseases. And with the exception of the eastern highlands of Kenya, the diffusion of hybrid maize is limited because existing high yielding varieties are not suited to the ecology--the amount and variance in rainfall, sunlight, and transpiration--of most areas in Africa where maize is grown. Moreover, high-yielding technical packages--which combine seeds, fertilizers, and changes in modes of cultivation--have not been developed for African food grains such as sorghum and millet. Other factors also serve to retard introduction of technical improvements, such as poor roads and marketing networks. Information services--radio, extension networks, written materials--are also very underdeveloped.

In addition to these long-term constraints on agriculture, pricing policy has frequently depressed production. The taxes on exports and other cash crops--including the depressing effects of surpluses collected by marketing boards and of overvalued exchange rates--frequently exceed by more than half the value of the crop at the farm gate (that is, the export price less the costs of getting the crop from the farm to on board the ship). Governments have also subsidized the urban population's consumption of imported food grains, such as rice, wheat, and maize, by commandeering large quantities at low prices and in effect driving down the price and restricting the market for local foodstuffs. Frequently, some of the taxes on cash crops have been used for such subsidies. Even without financial subsidies on consumer prices, the widespread import of grains is usually duty-free and often at a very favorable exchange rate; so the consumer gets them at a bargain price. The effect is low prices for agricultural products, which may penalize local production and retard investment and innovation. Farmers with low incomes simply cannot pay for the inputs which most innovations require for their adoption. In general, therefore, some of Africa's agricultural stagnation is caused by government price, fiscal, and trade practices.

The widespread flight from rural areas to the cities--to usually dismal prospects for the unlettered majority--is in part explained by the very low returns to work in peasant agriculture, be these the results of population pressure per se or government policies. The flight is reinforced by the very low prestige of agricultural work. The educated are the first to leave. This rural "brain drain" further contributes to agricultural stagnation, which is exacerbated by extremely low investments in capital formation in African village agriculture.

IV. INCREASING THE FOOD SUPPLY

An entirely different and far more productive agriculture might evolve, if African governments were to fundamentally change their vision. Existing production technology could permit

substantial increases in the yields of many crops if some basic
changes were made in the policies affecting agriculture. One way of
achieving such change would be to make farming profitable.

In the World Bank's experience, agricultural projects in
Africa usually achieve or exceed their production goals when
producer prices are favorable. If prices are very unfavorable,
most of them fail. It is obvious that farmers will substitute a
more profitable individual crop for a less profitable one. But
there is also strong evidence that producers will gradually
change long-run patterns of farming to make the most of
opportunities for applying innovations and new technology in
response to improved general terms of trade for agriculture.

But widespread basic changes are often extremely difficult to
achieve. In many countries interest groups are both dependent on
and a cause of very low returns to agriculture. For example,
eliminating overvalued exchange rates and the mismatch between the
structure of cereal demand (rice and wheat) and the structure of
domestic supply (tubers, maize, and rough grains) is politically
very hazardous because those most injured by such changes are
predominantly the urban constituents from whom governments draw
their basic support. Yet, if the very pessimistic import
projections and tumbling ratio of domestic food production to
imported food are to be avoided, the urban taste for imported wheat
and rice--which now account for about 80 per cent of net commercial
imports of cereals--will need to be curtailed in favor of the
indigenous and far more cheaply produced maize, millet, and
sorghum.

Marketing arrangements will also need to be radically
improved. Typically the government-owned marketing networks have
proven quite costly, when not simply defective, in moving produce
from and inputs to farmers. A greater role for non-government
agents is the solution. Government attempts to control both
producer and retail food prices will also have to be forgone.
These controls and the de jure monopoly on trade that most
governments have granted to the trading parastatals have resulted
in parallel private markets all over the continent. But the
potential that these institutions have for serving the public and
reducing the burden on government through investment in transport
and storage and a systematic approach to developing an adequate and
low-cost supply network is much reduced because of uncertainties
associated with the ambiguous position of private trade and
traders.

Complementing this new approach to price policies and
marketing should be a far greater emphasis on techniques to promote
African's transition out of traditional, low-yielding, shifting
farming systems. This implies more emphasis on agricultural
research, to arrest the deterioration in the production of high
quality seeds; on the operation of irrigation facilities; and on
research to stemplant diseases. In addition, ideas on how best to
modify traditional land tenure arrangements, so that farmers have
an incentive to improve the quality of their soil, are needed to
facilitate the introduction of innovations. The diffusion of small
tools, such as donkey carts and hand sprayers, and productive
inputs, such as pesticides and insecticides, must be

encouraged. Here marketing can play an important role in introducing such new techniques. Highways also need to be repaired and extended. Finally, new basic research to develop higher-yielding food grains and techniques for maintaining soil fertility without fallow periods requires far more attention.

Success here could bring rapid growth in agriculture, which would also bring very rapid growth in effective demand by farmers for the output of other sectors in the economy. That would stimulate development in general.

Development of agriculture will also mean increasing production for export. In some countries strong emphasis on export crops may be desirable. In many countries, hitherto, such emphasis has also been associated with increased production of food crops because the marketing arrangements, infrastructure, and other investments that promoted export production also supported expanded food production. This outcome is not a necessary one, however, particularly if good land is in short supply. In some cases development of agriculture may be most effective through increasing production primarily for export and using some of the proceeds to import food produced more cheaply elsewhere.

V. FAMILY PLANNING

The effect of population growth in diminishing returns to agriculture also lends urgency to the need for family planning. The question facing policymakers in sub-Saharan Africa is not whether or not population will grow--it will grow rapidly--but when growth rates will slow. Experience in Asia and Latin America shows that both development and family planning programs can reduce fertility. China and Indonesia are examples of fertility declines far more rapid than those predicted on the basis of literacy, mortality, and income. In these countries governments have accelerated the demographic transition to lower population growth rates by many means, including increasing access to modern contraceptives, mass education campaigns, and, in China, raising the marriage age.

In 1975, only 8 African countries had even weak family planning programs; they were rarely subsidized by their governments. Today 22 of the 37 African countries for which data are available support family planning. Nevertheless, there is little sense of urgency to the programs; nor have techniques or approaches been worked out that would be most suited to African circumstances. Emphasis on child-spacing as a way to increase the chances of a child's survival is a basic and nearly universal ethic in African villages. It has always been accomplished through prolonged breast-feeding and sexual abstinence. Today, however, there is some use of contraceptives to ensure the required spacing. Thus the traditional ethic provides a rationale for incorporating family planning within maternal and child health programs.

In general, population policy in Africa badly needs

strengthening. This could be done in many ways. Family-planning advice could be recognized as the right of every couple, and providing such advice to all who desire it could be a pronounced basic goal of every government. Governments can encourage widespread family-planning services and supplies, including the availability of cheap or even free contraceptives. Family-planning components can be built into national health care systems to ensure that improved child survival and fertility regulation can be better synchronized. But without increased female education and reduced infant and child mortality, the impact of spacing alone on fertility will be limited. Thus both development and family planning have a role in reducing fertility rates.

VI. A WIDER PROBLEM

In a sense most of the villages of tropical Africa have been suffering from overpopulation for many decades: notwithstanding abundant but not very productive land, in much of the region most villages barely produce enough to feed themselves. Droughts that cause food shortages and even famine are common occurrences. Diet is frequently very poor in general, and in particular during the weeks before the new harvest, and infant and toddler mortality is higher than anywhere else. Poor diet is one reason why dysentery and measles regularly kill malnourished African children.

Population growth in the next decade can only make this situation worse. But the implications for education--an area in which African governments have achieved impressive results and which affects all these sectors--are also serious. To maintain primary school enrollment at the current rate of 65 per cent (which still means an increasing number of unschooled every year) will require increased government expenditures for primary education at about 3.5 per cent a year. To achieve universal primary education by the year 2000 would require expansion at over 6 per cent annually, far beyond the region's capacity. Urbanization will also be a very serious problem. In 35 major capitals, population growth now averages about 9 per cent annually, a rate at which cities double in size every nine years. There are now 28 African cities with populations over half a million. Just 20 years ago there were but three. The urban population will quadruple again in the next quarter century. The majority in these cities will continue to live in slums, usually an entire family (or more) per room, with high rates of disease, little access to public services--good water, sanitation, and medical care--and extremely long journeys to and from work.

Improvement in two areas--breaking the chain of population growth and stagnating agriculture--would help reduce human misery in sub-Saharan Africa. The desired changes can become reality if enough resources, primarily African but also from outside the region, are brought to bear; and if African governments incorporate the needed policies into their political systems.

RELATED READING

Food and Agriculture Organization, <u>Agriculture Toward 2000</u> (Food and Agriculture Orfganization,Rome, 1979).

Timothy King and others, <u>Population Policies and Economic Development</u> (World Bank, Washington, DC, 1974).

U.S. Department of Agriculture, <u>Food Problems and Prospects in Sub-Saharan Africa, The Decade of the 1980's</u>, Foreign Agricultural Report No. 166 (August 1981).

World Bank, <u>Accelerated Development in Sub-Saharan Africa: An Agenda for Action</u> (World Bank, Washington, DC, 1981).

Health Planning and
Population in Africa

NANCY BIRDSALL

Despite common interests, health planners and population
planners have apparently different objectives: respectively to
improve health and reduce mortality, and to reduce rapid rates of
population growth, the objectives appear contradictory. The
seeming contradiction has been heightened by demographic evidence
that post-war rapid population growth in developing countries was
largely the result of public health measures which suddenly lowered
mortality rates.

Population and health planners have agreed on family planning
as a common program where their objectives converge, since family
planning both reduces births and improves the mother's already-born
children's health. However, one school of thought in the
population field maintains that the solution to the population
problem lies not soley in family planning, where the health and
welfare of the family are the motivating force, but in measures
"beyond family planning," where concern with economic development
and societal welfare are paramount. The beyond-family-planning
school maintains that individuals want more children than the
larger society can afford, that family planning permits the
planning of families which are too large. They assert that, in
addition to family planning, changes are required in tax structure,
housing policy, and female employment strategies if childbearing is
to be discouraged (Davis, 1967; Berelson, 1969).

The premise of this essay is that, despite the apparent
contradiction, those in the population field should give priority
to improving health standards and reducing mortality in Africa.

In Africa, cultural, social, and political constraints
militate against a strong public commitment to population
limitation. Studies of the public's attitude toward family size
(Knowledge, Attitude, and Practice of Family Planning, commonly

From **AFRICAN STUDIES REVIEW**, Vol XIX, No. 2, Sept, 1976, (19-33),
reprinted by permission of the publisher.

called KAP studies) have repeatedly demonstrated that African parents do not have more children than they want (Caldwell, 1968 and 1974).[1] In fact, recent evidence suggests the possibility that some African parents have fewer children than they desire, because of subfecundity caused by nutritional and general health problems (McCabe, 1975). African governments at the 1974 World Population Conference in Bucharest generally took the position that population should not be treated as an issue per se, that "The Best Pill is Development" (Pradervand, 1973b).[2] At present, only Ghana and Kenya have policies favoring less rapid growth of population; Nigeria, Tanzania, and others promote family planning on the grounds of health; some countries, such as Cameroon, Gabon, and the Ivory Coast, actively favor more rapid growth (Gwatkin, 1972).

A major constraint to active political commitment to population limitation programs is the continuing high mortality rates throughout Africa. Although mortality rates have fallen, they are still the highest of any continent, with crude death rates of about 21 per thousand and life expectancy of 45 years, compared to crude death rates of about 15 in Asia and only 9 in Latin America, and life expectancies of 52 and 61 respectively for those areas (Population Reference Bureau, 1973). Regarding infant and child mortality, the situation is even more grim. Twenty African countries have infant mortality rates above 150 per thousand live births, with some above 200 per thousand. Most Latin American countries now have rates below 100 per thousand. (The rate in the U.S. is about 20 per thousand.) For some African countries, combined infant and child mortality is above 250 per thousand, meaning one out of four children is likely to die before the age of five. The death of children may induce extra births; African parents possibly overcompensate for lost children (Snyder, 1973; Harrington, n.d.).[3]

Table 1 illustrates that in no part of the world has a fall in fertility preceded a fall in mortality, supporting at the aggregate level evidence from Africa that parents have many children to guarantee a large family in a high-mortality situation.[4] In this context, improved health and lower mortality are prerequisites to future reductions in population growth.

For Africa in the 1970s, those in the population field should adopt a strategy of strong support for health, and particularly for the restructuring of health systems. Only with better health services will demand for family planning services arise and supply of those services be justified by their costs.

I. PRESENT HEALTH EXPENDITURES

African governments devote as much as 10 percent of their total recurrent budgets to health (Table 2) and significant additional annual amounts to capital investment in health (Gwatkin, 1972:217). For a number of reasons, this effort in health is not likely to diminish. One is the growing conviction that a healthy

TABLE 1

Population Growth Rates in the World and Major Regions

Regions	High birth rate; high death rate[a]	High birth rate; low death rate	Low birth rate; high death rate	Low birth rate; low death rate	Total
Number of Countries					
World	76	29	–	49	154
Africa	45	3	–	1	47
Asia	24	10	–	7	41
Latin America	6	14	–	10	30
Europe, North America, USSR, and Oceania	1	2	–	31	34
Percent of Total Population					
World	40	30	–	30	100
Africa	98	2	–	–	100
Asia	49	45	–	6	100
Latin America	9	74	–	17	100
Europe, North America, USSR, and Oceania	–	–	–	100	100
Population Growth Rate (percent per year)					
World	2.6	2.1	–	0.9	2.0
Africa	2.5	3.3	–	1.7	2.5
Asia	2.7	1.9	–	1.4	2.3
Latin America	2.8	3.1	–	1.6	2.8
Europe, North America, USSR, and Oceania	2.4	2.6	–	0.8	0.8

[a]Birth rates 30 or higher are classified as high. Death rates 15 or higher are classified as high.

Source: Population Reference Bureau. 1973 World Population Data Sheet. Washington, D.C.: P.R.B. Arranged as above in *Population Policies and Economic Development*, a World Bank Staff Report, 1974, Annex Table I, p. 169.

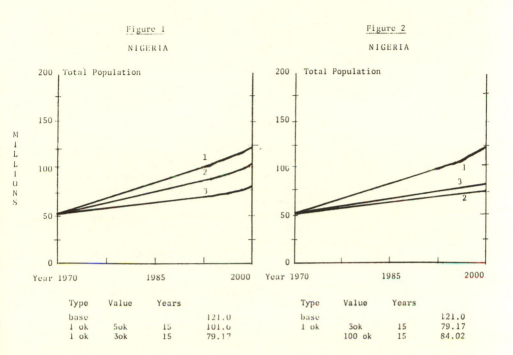

Figure 1

NIGERIA

200 Total Population

Figure 2

NIGERIA

200 Total Population

Type	Value	Years	
base			121.0
1 ok	5ok	15	101.6
1 ok	3ok	15	79.17

Type	Value	Years	
base			121.0
1 ok	3ok	15	79.17
	100 ok	15	84.02

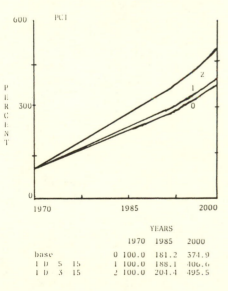

Figure 3

SIERRA LEONE

600 PCT

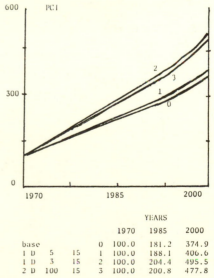

Figure 4

SIERRA LEONE

600 PCT

			YEARS			
				1970	1985	2000
base			0	100.0	181.2	374.9
1 D	5	15	1	100.0	188.1	406.6
1 D	3	15	2	100.0	204.4	495.5

			YEARS			
				1970	1985	2000
base			0	100.0	181.2	374.9
1 D	5	15	1	100.0	188.1	406.6
1 D	3	15	2	100.0	204.4	495.5
2 D	100	15	3	100.0	200.8	477.8

355

population is a prerequisite to economic development. The 1970–1974 Nigerian Plan states, "A healthy population is an economic asset since the assured supply of a strong and healthy labour force is an essential factor in development" (Federal Republic of Nigeria, 1974:247).[5]

Second is the subtle shift of attention on the part of development planners from growth per se, measured by annual increments to gross national product, to a more equitable distribution of increased wealth and the elimination of extreme poverty (McNamara, 1973). Brazil (where despite GNP growth of more than 9 percent annually over the past several years, a significant proportion of the population still is not adequately fed, housed, or educated) is compared to China, where a modest growth rate of perhaps 4 percent a year has permitted an apparent restructuring of the economy toward an equitable distribution of goods and services and the development of egalitarian health, educational, and employment programs. This comparison has provided legitimacy for health expenditures as a necessary and logical component of any development effort. The World Bank, which for years gave no loans for health or nutrition projections, is now active in these sectors.

Third is the low absolute amounts being spent on health, particularly if African countries are compared to other developing countries. Table 2 lists governmental health expenditures (both capital and recurring) for selected countries as a percent of total governmental expenditures and by annual absolute amounts per capita. The table indicates that though African governments spend relatively large proportions of national budgets on health, their per capita spending remains low. For example, Kenya, one of Africa's wealthier countries, in 1965 allocated about 4.4 percent of its total government spending to health. This amounted to $1.28 per capita. Chile, in contrast, allocating 7.9 percent of government spending to health, was able to spend $10.94 per capita in 1965. The United Kingdom, allocating 9.0 percent of government spending to health, spent $65.34 per capita in 1965.[6]

Finally, growing demand by citizens of African countries for improved health services is likely. Insofar as demand for health services is income-elastic (as suggested by Table 2, increases in per capita income will increase demand, as well better education and improved communications.

These factors point to spending by African governments at least at the present levels, with absolute increases as per capita income rises, if not increases in the amounts relative to other sectors. These amounts will be spent regardless of whether or not governments embark on family planning and other population programs. Persons concerned about rapid population growth would do well to regard these expenditures as inevitable, an investment made for reasons other than population concern.

However, this is not to say that this health investment should be written off, ignored, or underrated in terms of its potential impact on population growth. In Africa, this area of investment should be the chief concern at present of those interested in reducing long-term population growth: for though the size of this particular piece of pie is best viewed as fixed at a certain minimum level (not to be cut smaller in favor of other programs), the piece can be cut in a number of different ways, with significant differences in actual and potential results for population growth. The manner in which funds allocated for health are spent may be more important for the long term than the manner in which funds allocated specifically for family planning or other population-specific programs are spent. Amounts allocated specifically to family planning in even the most committed of governments are minuscule: India and Pakistan spend respectively only 1.6 percent and 1.9 percent of their national budgets on family planning, and even these amounts are made up in large party by foreign aid funds.[7] Developing countries would have to spend about 5 percent of their national budgets on family planning in order to carry out reasonably complete family planning programs on a national basis (IBRD, 1972), a figure which few governments anywhere are likely to reach in this century.

Let us, then, turn our attention to the strategy which will lay an adequate groundwork for future population programs, and which will also be consistent with the apparent desire of African countries to improve health services to their people.

II. STRATEGY FOR FUTURE HEALTH SPENDING: TOTAL AMOUNTS

To limit health spending on the grounds that it will radically increase population growth rates is ill-advised.[8] In addition to the clear necessity in the interests of social justice to improve the wellbeing of those already living, there is evidence that decreases in mortality (which can be expected in African countries in the next thirty years as a direct result of government health services) will have a relatively insignificant effect on future population size. This can be illustrated by the following figures.[9] Figure 1 represents a projection of the Nigerian population to the year 2000 under three different assumptions of fertility. The base line indicates that if the present total fertility rate (TFR)[10] of 6.63 continues to that year, the present population of about 55 million will grow to 121 million. The second line is a projection of population size should the fertility rate drop to 5.0 after fifteen years, and shows that under that assumption, the size of the population in the year 2000 would be under 100 million. The third line is a projection of population size should the fertility rate drop to 3.0 after fifteen years, and shows that under that assumption, the population in the year 2000 would be about 79 million.

Figure 2 shows the size of the population in the year 2000 at present fertility rates (line 1, upper), at a fertility rate reduced to 3.0 after fifteen years (line 2, lowest), and finally at the lowered fertility rate with a halving of infant and child mortality[11] (line 3, intermediate) from its present rate in fifteen years. The graph illustrates that the increase in the population in 2000 due to lowered infant and child mortality is of less

TABLE 2

Levels of Health Services in Selected Countries[a]

Country	U.S. $ per capita per year	Percent Total Government Expenditure	Approximate Percentage of Total Government Recurring Budget
Sweden	77.77	11.3	—
United Kingdom	65.34	9.0	—
United States	51.13	8.4	—
Japan	13.63	13.2	—
Netherlands	12.49	4.9	—
Chile	10.94	7.9	—
Malaysia	8.22	8.8	—
Iran	4.73	7.5	—
GABON	4.40	—	9
GHANA	3.66	5.3	—
SENEGAL	3.65	—	9
IVORY COAST	3.40	—	10
Ceylon (now Sri Lanka)	3.32	7.9	—
UNITED ARAB REPUBLIC	2.84	4.8	—
Colombia	2.66	8.7	—
Mexico	2.64	6.5	—
Peru	2.33	5.4	—
LIBERIA	2.50	—	7
Turkey	2.28	3.8	—
CAMEROON	1.75	—	11
DAHOMEY	1.75	—	12
Brazil	1.50	4.0	—
Philippines	1.39	5.0	—
KENYA	1.28	4.4	—
TOGO	1.15	—	9
SUDAN	.99	5.7	—
MALI	.98	—	11
Taiwan	.98	2.8	—
Thailand	.77	3.8	—
TANZANIA[b]	.75	6.4	—
UPPER VOLTA	.70	—	10
NIGER	.68	—	9
India	.53	2.2	—
Nepal	.40	4.6	—
ETHIOPIA	.38	6.7	—
Pakistan	.38	3.3	—
UGANDA	.10	6.4	—

[a]Figures are for 1965 or nearest available year.
[b]Figures are for Tanganyika.

Sources: Compiled by Corsa and Oakley (1971), pp. 381-82, from *United Nations Statistical Yearbook 1968* (New York, 1969) and *World Health Statistics Report* (vol. 21, no. 11, Geneva 1969), except Dahomey, Ivory Coast, Niger, Senegal, Upper Volta, Mali, Gabon, Cameroon, Togo, and Liberia, data on which were compiled by Gwatkin (1972), p. 218, from U.S. National Academy of Sciences, National Research Council, Division of Medical Sciences, *Public Health Problems in 14 French-speaking Countries in Africa and Madagascar*, vol. 11, *A Survey of Resources and Needs*, and United Nations, World Health Organization, *Third Report on the World Health Situation* 1961-1964 (Official Records of the World Health Organization, no. 155, Geneva, World Health Organization, April 1957).

TABLE 3

Urban-Rural Mortality Rates

Country	Urban Areas	Rural Areas
Central African Republic		
1959-1960	23.0	26.5
Dahomey 1961	11.9	27.5
Guinea 1955	31.2	43.1
Togo 1961	23.0	26.0[a]
Congo (Brazzaville) 1960-1961	13.0	24.0[a]
Ghana 1968-1969/infant mortality	98.0	148.0
Liberia 1970/infant mortality	82.0	158.0

[a]Figures are for capital city and rest of the country.

Sources: Conde (1971: 60) for CAR, Dahomey, Guinea, Togo, and Congo (Brazzaville); *Liberia Population Growth Survey* (1970: 53) for Liberia; Gaisie (1975: 29, Table 4) for Ghana.

TABLE 4

Zones	Infant mortality rates 1965-1967
1. A town with 5,000 with 8-bed health center and a maternity center	40
2. Villages with visiting medical and health services only	117
3. Other villages	141

Source: Child Mortality in the Khombol-Thienaba region 1964-1968, in *Study of Factors of Mortality*, J. Cantrelle, M. Diague, N. Raybaud, B. Vignac, ORSTOM, Series Sciences Humaines, vol. VI, no. 4, 1969. Cited by Conde (1971: 76-78).

magnitude than the decrease of the population due to a reduction of TFR. This halving of infant and child mortality results in a population of 84 million rather than 79 million, assuming a TFR of 3.0. At a TFR of 5.0, the population with the lower mortality would be 109.6 million rather than 101.6 million (now shown). Figure 2 represents a Nigeria in the year 2000 in which average family size has been reduced to three children and in which infant mortality has been reduced substantially.

A similar set of graphs can be used to illustrate the relatively minor effect of a lowered mortality rate on per capita income. According to Figure 3, per capita income in Sierra Leone, which would more than double over the next thirty years at the present TFR rate of 5.94, would almost quadruple if the rate were reduced to 3.0.[12] Figure 4 indicates that a significant reduction in the infant and child mortality rate, from the present 186.4 to 100, were it combined with the TFR of 3.0, would not significantly lower per capita income compared to the amount without any change in mortality.

These graphs are of simple, linear projections. They make no assumption regarding the highly complex relationship between infant mortality and fertility,[13] though it is likely that lowered infant mortality affects fertility, at least over the long term, as parents become more willing to limit the number of children when they know that more children will survive.

III. STRATEGY FOR FUTURE HEALTH SPENDING: STRUCTURAL CHANGE

The manner in which health resources are spent in African countries can have profound importance for a future population policy. Persons concerned for humane and developmental reasons with the pace of population growth would do well to focus increased attention on the structual aspects of health care spending of these countries.

Most spending on health care in African countries has been concentrated in the cities and on curative medicine. The training of highly-skilled doctors and the building of well-equipped hospitals have had the effect of providing good care for a small urban elite but almost no care for the 90 percent of Africa's population which resides in rural areas. Social and cultural factors responsible for rural-urban inequity have been adequately discussed elsewhere (King, 1966). During the colonial period, modern medical facilities were developed in the administrative centers where the Europeans resided. Today, doctors, nurses, and paramedicals educated in the city prefer to stay in the city.[14] Financial returns (especially to doctors) are higher in the cities (Sharpston, 1972: 214). A system which benefits the ruling elite (who are urban residents) is perpetuated for lack of political will to change it. (Few countries have restructured health systems to ensure that health care penetrates rural areas. The urban-rural dichotomy is merely more evident and more vexing in Africa because

TABLE 5

Capital Expenditures on Health Programs of Nigeria's State Governments
(£ million)

Project	1970-71	1971-72	1972-73	1973-74	Total
Benue-Plateau					
1. Curative Services	0.133	0.133	0.135	0.196	0.597
2. Public Health Services	0.047	0.060	0.060	0.010	0.177
East Central					
1. Curative Services	0.100	1.500	1.600	1.008	5.208
2. Public Health Services	0.400	0.500	0.500	0.161	1.561
Kano					
1. Curative Services	0.406	0.628	1.088	1.378	3.500
2. Public Health Services	0.474	0.348	0.222	0.155	1.199
Kwara					
1. Curative Services	0.204	0.749	0.785	0.962	2.700
2. Public Health Services	0.010	0.120	0.110	0.210	0.450
Lagos					
1. Curative Services	0.098	0.330	0.360	0.422	1.210
2. Public Health Services	0.035	0.065	0.095	0.105	0.300
Mid-Western					
1. Curative Services	0.986	0.986	0.987	0.988	3.947
2. Public Health Services	0.012	0.042	0.042	0.050	0.146
North-Central					
1. Curative Services	0.200	0.212	0.212	0.214	0.838
2. Public Health Services	0.100	0.100	0.186	0.200	0.586
North-Eastern					
1. Curative Services	0.488	0.327	0.341	0.347	1.503
2. Public Health Services and Training	0.135	0.490	0.415	0.590	1.630
North-Western					
1. Curative Services	0.525	0.500	0.750	0.750	2.525
2. Public Health Services	0.200	0.400	0.400	0.497	1.497
Rivers					
1. Curative Services	0.624	0.769	0.409	0.385	2.187
2. Public Health Services	0.050	0.100	0.200	0.200	0.550
South-Eastern					
1. Curative Services	0.295	0.248	0.200	0.257	1.000
2. Public Health Services	0.050	0.050	0.225	0.375	0.700
Western					
1. Curative Services	0.952	1.000	1.000	1.000	3.952
2. Public Health Services	0.110	0.110	0.220	0.220	0.660
TOTAL (all states)					
1. Curative Services	6.301	6.482	6.477	6.181	25.441
2. Public Health Services	1.543	1.870	1.860	1.598	6.871

Source: Second National Development Plan, 1970-74 of Nigeria (4), pp. 252-54.

of its low rates of urbanization.) A disproportionate share of resources is allocated to long and expensive training of doctors compared to paramedicals who can adequately deliver preventive medicine and deal with prevalent infectious diseases.

Other more subtle factors also help to explain the inappropriateness of African medical institutions to local needs. Public health and preventive medicine are a high priority in African countries, yet the system of health training inherited from the West places a low value on public health as a medical specialty. (Public health doctors worldwide are poorly paid compared to orthopedic surgeons and specialists in internal medicine.) Management and planning aspects of health service delivery are clearly important in Africa, where presently top heavy systems must be developed from the ground up, yet these skills are not emphasized in the training of health professionals.

In the absence of better data,[15] differentials between urban and rural mortality rates in African countries provide a crude illustration of the relative dearth of health services in rural areas. Though data are spotty, Table 3 illustrates the point. The results of a five-year study in Senegal are shown in Table 4. Though other factors besides health services contribute to lower urban mortality in African countries (e.g., better environmental sanitation, a more highly-educated population), the comparative standing of rural areas is symptomatic of the same general maldistribution of social services.

The urban-oriented health infrastructure, with its inadequate attention to preventive medicine and management, is inappropriate to the health needs of Africa's rural majority. Health statistics for Lagos (the capital city of Nigeria) indicate that between 1966 and 1967 about 44 percent of reported deaths were due to common diseases: pneumonia, dysentery and diarrhea, tetanus, malnutrition, tuberculosis, and measles, all of which are preventable through immunization, use of prophylactic drugs, public health education, personal hygiene, and environmental sanitation (Okediji, 1974: 315, cites P.O. Ahimie). Match this with data from Kenya on the relative costs of hospitals (which provide primarily curative facilities) and health centers. According to King and Jolly (1966: 2: 11-2: 12), the capital cost of a health center in Kenya serving one thousand people is about $2,200, a sum that would only purchase one-quarter of a hospital bed (or one bed for seventeen patients during a year). Annual recurrent costs of $1,100 for a health center serving the same one thousand people would be sufficient for 1.3 hospital beds (serving about one hundred in-patients a year).

The urban-oriented curative infrastructure is also inappropriate to any future public policy in support of family planning. With the exception of abortion, family planning services are intrinsically preventive. Many forms of contraceptives can be administered by persons with minimal medical training.[16] Such medical practitioners will have to work in rural areas if a large proportion of the population is to be serviced. They will have to be backed up by persons with training and experience in the more managerial aspects of medicine. Because of the sensitive nature of family planning and the need to relate use of contraception to the health and welfare of the family, a family planning program must include some provision for dissemination of information and education through an adequate program of extension.

There is scattered evidence that demand for family planning is lower where other health services are not also available. At the aggregrate level, there is in Africa the lowest rate of utilization of modern contraceptives anywhere in the world (Caldwell, 1974, estimates for all of West Africa an ever-used rate of 0.5 percent) combined with the lowest rates of health expenditure and the lowest doctor/patient ratios. Ghana and Kenya have had national family planning programs since the late 1960s; yet in Kenya, only about 2 percent of the women in reproductive ages were participating in the program in 1971 (Bondestam, 1972: 34); and in Ghana, perhaps 5 percent of women in urban coastal areas were participating -- the figure is much lower in rural areas (Caldwell, 1974). In recognition of this apparently low demand for family planning services per se, numerous donors have attempted to link family planning to the provision of more general health services, to health education and nutrition programs, and to training in literacy.[17] In the hope of specifying more precisely the degree to which demand for modern contraceptives is linked to provision of other health services, the United States Agency for International Development has funded a program in Danfa, Ghana, where family planning is delivered in different regions with varying degrees and amounts of accompanying health care, health education, nutrition education, etc. Acceptance of family planning appears to be greatest where comprehensive health care is available.[18]

Most health planners in African countries now recognize the importance of paramedical training, delivery of preventive services to persons in rural areas, and improved management; but few countries have actually launched programs based on this strategy. A look at the health plans of Nigeria and Tanzania illustrates the point.

During its First National Development Plan period 1962-1968, Nigeria incurred a total capital expenditure of Pound 7.46 million for health (including both the federal and regional governments). This figure was far short of the planned expenditure of Pound 17 million. Although the underspending can be in part attributed to the civil war which began in 1966, the health sector of all sectors showed one of the lowest levels of capital expenditure in relation to the planned estimate. ""Projects executed by the Federal Government included the Lagos University Teaching Hospital, reconstruction of the Lagos General Hospital and the establishment of health centers" (Okediji [1972: 314] maintains that the few health centers completed "in practice operated as curative centers" . "The proposed National Institute of Preventive Medicine and the planned expansion of Public Health Laboratories did not, however, materialize." Moreover, "the Regional programs placed greater emphasis on the curative services. In this connection all the former Regions undertook the construction of Hospitals in their various administrative areas" (Second National Development Plan, 1970: 247).

Although the current plan states that "in Nigeria, preventive measures should be the focus of health policy," actual allocation

of capital finances is still largely concentrated in curative
services. The Nigerian States, which will spend more than
four-fifths (Pound 43,681 million) of the total planned allocation
to health of Pound 53,811 million, are (to quote from the plan
itself), "still concentrating on the curative aspects of the health
service, although Kano State seems to be putting some emphasis on
Public Health services" (p. 250). Table 5 indicates the breakdown
by state of planned health expenditures between curative services
and public health services.

It can be argued that a minimum number of hospitals is needed
to serve as the backbone of a health delivery system, since
hospitals can be used as referral centers for those who cannot be
treated at smaller, less well-equipped health centers. However, a
survey of in-patients in Ghana's five major hospitals indicated
that 80 percent of in-patients came from the same urban area as the
one in which the hospital was located (Sharpston, 1972: 212).
Similar results obtained in Uganda, where King and Jolly (1967:
12:6) found that out-patient attendances per person per year halved
for every additional two miles distance from home to hospital.
In-patient care halved every three miles. Thus hospitals meant to
serve as referral centers do not necessarily do so; they are more
likely to serve primarily those in the urban centers where they are
situated. Moreover, since in Nigeria the present life expectancy
is about forty and the infant and child mortality rate over 200 per
thousand live births, we cannot assume that the present, largely
hospital-based infrastructure is adequate.

Tanzania places more emphasis on public control of all
resources and aspires toward a more egalitarian distribution of
goods and services. Tanzania's Second Five Year Plan (1969-1974)
also assigns priority to the improvement of rural services, calling
for the construction of 80 rural health centers in the five-year
period, with an ultimate goal of 240 centers (one for every 50,000
persons) by the mid-1980s (1969: 162-63).[19]

Like Nigeria, however, Tanzania has had difficulty with its
rural-oriented health plans. Because there is lag time in training
paramedicals for work in rural areas, and because it is more
difficult to plan and manage the expenditure of smaller amounts of
money on more novel infrastructure, the planned capital allocation
between programs in the 1969-1974 period was somewhat lopsided,
even taking into account that new hospitals were planned for
regional areas to serve rural persons.

However, the 1971/72 update of the Five-Year Plan (Annual Plan
for 1971/72) indicates that only seven new health centers had been
completed in the proceeding two years, well short of the target of
twenty new health centers for the period. "The health program
remains largely curative. It has not been possible to draw up a
sufficiently detailed plan to implement the preventive approach
outlined in the Five-Year-Plan" (1971: 48).

The Ministry of Health then raised the following issues for
discussion, asking for "planning guidelines . . . in order to
accomplish the goals of the Second Five-Year Plan" (p. 49):

1. the provision of rudimentary health service to all the
people before relatively sophisticated services are offered to a
few;

2. assigning priority to the improvement of rural health services, at necessary cost to further improvement to urban health facilities, and

3. a relatively balanced distribution of health manpower among regions and between major centers and rural areas.

These difficulties indicate the urgency of renewed attention to new approaches if the health services vacuum throughout much of rural Africa is to be filled. An adequate health delivery system, with ancillary services in nutrition and sanitation, is critical to a lowering of the death rate, particularly of the high infant mortality rate. Returning to Table 1 and to scattered survey data on the relationship between infant mortality and fertility (above), a lowering of the infant mortality rate appears to be a prerequisite to demand for modern contraceptives. Assuming such demand develops, contraceptives and other family planning services can be supplied effectively once a health infrastructure has been developed. In Africa, where political, moral, and social necessity dictate continued emphasis on health care and a limited public commitment to population limitation, health planners and population planners thus share a common priority: more health services more equitably delivered.

NOTES

[1]Caldwell reviews and summarizes the KAP survey results. See also Heisel (1973), Dow (1971), Morgan (1972).

[2]See also Pradervand's "The African Reaction to Foreign Initiatives in Population Programs" (1973a).

[3]For a comprehensive review of the social science literature on the fertility-mortality relationship, see Schultz (1975).

[4]An anonymous referee wonders why today's relatively lower mortality rates have not influenced fertility downward. Though existing data permit no certain conclusion, plausible explanations are: (1) reductions in mortality have affected different groups differentially -- fertility has dropped among the urban, best-educated, professional middle-class group (Caldwell, 1974), which group has probably benefited most from lower mortality1; (2) there may be some threshold level of mortality above which a fertility response will not be triggered -- this situation would obtain particularly if individual families make fertility decisions on the basis of their perception of community mortality levels.

[5]See also Okediji (1972: 313), who points out that "investments in public health, housing and social-welfare services have now been defined by most governments of the 'developing' nations as investments in human beings, which can contribute significantly to socio-economic development."

[6]Presumably health service expenditures refer primarily to doctors and other medical personnel working in hospitals and clinics. Yet potable water may be more important for health. The assumption here is that African government expenditures on environmental sanitation (and other health-related projects) are also low relative to such spending by richer governments.

[7]According to the World Bank, 38.3 percent of India's family planning budget and 77.9 percent of Pakistan's are made up of foreign aid funds (IBRD, 1972: 23).

[8]For an argument that "the evidence seems clear that the effects of health programs on population growth should rarely count on the positive side," see Preston (1975: 198). His argument is that the "replacement" of lost infants is not one hundred percent and has not been throughout the world. However, he does note (1975: 192) that "populations at the lowest level of development appear to display a stronger replacement effect than those at the next higher level," and that the absence of a volitional replacement mechanism in population at low levels of development may be explained because "[family size] goals . . . are so high that childbearing at a near maximum rate would be required to reach them even in the absence of child deaths" (p. 193). For the later argument directly applied to Africa, see Tabbarah (1971).

[9]These graphs are copies of computer projections programmed by the University of Illinois PLATO project (Paul Handler, Director), under contract to the United States Agency for International Development.

[10]Total fertility rate represents the total number of live births which a woman would bear at present age-specific birthrates for the population under study.

[11]Number of children between birth and the age of five who die per thousand.

[12]These are simple projections based on growth rates in the 1960-1970 period, holding investment ratio and rate of capital depreciations constant, and the rate of technological progress constant.

[13]For a recent review of this literature, see Schultz (1975).

[14]Veitch (1972:305) notes that in Zambia "the majority of the doctors [are] concentrated in the country's major towns, and an unknown number were in private practice, which probably catered

for a small section of the population."

[15]Health expenditures are seldom broken down between curative/ preventive and urban/rural. Hospitals do provide some "preventive" services, and urban services are available to rural people through referral systems. Rural health centers in turn provide "curative" services. The time of doctors and other medical personnel cannot easily be divided into categories, nor can resources spent on training and research. Governments in Africa seldom publish the wherabouts of medical personnel; where health services are not entirely state-run, such information may not be available. Data are sometimes available by district or state, but such aggregations do not correspond neatly to rural/urban breakdown.

[16]This will depend to some extent on policy decisions; however, in Pakistan, high school graduates with one year of training are performing IUD insertions (Corsa and Oakley, 1971).

[17]For example, the FAO's Better Family Living Program in Kenya, and World Education, Inc., New York's Literacy cum family planning programs in Ghana and Ethiopia.

[18]Visit of author to Danfa in October 1974. Progress reports on the project can be requested from the Unisted States Agency for International Development, Washington, D. C.

[19]Health planner Oscar Gish is largely responsible for Tanzania's plans. See his Doctor Migration and World Health (1971).

REFERENCES

Berelson, B. (1969) "Beyond Family Planning." Studies in Family Planning 38. New York: Population Council.

Bondestam, L. (1972) Population Growth in Kenya. Uppsala: Scandinavian Institute of African Studies Research Report no. 12.

Caldwell, J.C. (1968) "The Control of Family Size in Tropical Africa." Demography 5, 2 598-619.

_____. (1974) The Study of Fertility and Fertility Change in Tropical Africa. World Fertility Survey Occasional Paper no. 7. Voorburg (The Netherlands): International Statistical Institute.

Conde, J. (1971) The Demographic Transition as Applied to Tropical Africa with Particular Reference to Health, Education and Economic Factors. Paris: Organization for Economic Cooperation and Development.

Corsa, L. and D. Oakley. (1971) "Consequences of Population Growth for Health Services in Less Developed Countries -- An Initial Appraisal," pp. 368-402 in Rapid Population Growth: Consequences and Policy Implications. Johns Hopkins Press for the National Academy of Sciences.

Davis, K. (1967) "Population Policy: Will Current Programs Succeed?" Science 158: 730-39.

Evans, R.L. (1973) "The Role of Clinics in Family Planning." Paper delivered at International Labour Organization conference, Mwanza, Tanzania, March.

Federal Republic of Nigeria. (1970) Second National Development Plan, 1970-1974. Lagos.

Gaisie, S.K. (1975) "Levels and Patterns of Infant and Child Mortality in Ghana." Demography 12, 1 (February): 21-34.

Gish, O. (1971) Doctor Migration and World Health. London: G. Bell and Sons.

Gwatkin, D.R. (1972) "Policies Affecting Population in West Africa." Studies in Family Planning 3o (September): 214-21.

Harrington, J.A. (n.d.) "The Effect of High Infant and Childhood Mortality on Fertility: The West African Case." Mimeo.

Heisel, D.F. (1973) "Fertility Limitation among Men in Rural Kenya." Studies in Family Planning (December).

International Bank for Reconstruction and Development. (1972) "Population Planning: Sector Working Paper." Washington, D.C.

Jaffe, F.S. (1973) "Health Policy and Population Policy -- A Relationship Redefined." American Journal of Public Health (May): 401-41.

Jolly, R. and M. King. (1966) "The Organization of Health Services," pp. 2: 1-2:15 in M. King (ed.), Medical Care in Developing Countries. London: Oxford University Press.

_____., F. Komunvi, M. King, and P. Sebuliba. (1966) "The Economy of a District Hospital," pp. 12:1-12:9 in M. King (ed.), Medical Care in Developing Countries. London: Oxford University Press.

King, M. (ed.), (1966) Medical Care in Developing Countries. London: Oxford University Press.

McCabe, J. (1975) "Biological and Behavioral Determinants of Marital Fertility in Urban Zaire." Mimeo.

McNamara, R.S. (1973) "Address to the Board of Governors." Washington, D.C.: International Bank for Reconstruction and Development.

Morgan, R. (1972) "Family Planning Acceptors in Lagos, Nigeria."
Studies in Family Planning 3, 9 (September): 221-26.

Okediji, F. O. (1974) "Public Health and Nigeria's National
Development Plan," pp. 313-20 in S.H. Ominde and C.N. Ejiogu
(eds.), Population Growth and Economic Development in Africa.
London: Hienemann.

Population Reference Bureau. (1973) World Population Data Sheet.
Washington D.C.

Pradervand, P. (1973) "The African Reaction to Foreign Initiatives
in Population Programs." International Journal of Health Services
3,4 : 759-64.

Preston, S.H. (1975) "Health Programs and Population Growth."
Population and Development Review 1, 2 (December): 189-200.

Republic of Liberia, Ministry of Planning and Economic Affairs.
(1972) Demographic Annual of the Population Growth Survey 1970.
Monrovia.

Schultz, T.P. (1975) "Interrelationships between Mortality and
Fertility." Prepared for a conference on Policy Interventions to
Affect Fertility. Washington, D.C.: Resources for the Future. March
1975. Mimeo. 92 pp.

Sharpston, M.J. (1972) "Uneven Geographical Distribution of Medical
Care: A Ghanaian Case Study." The Journal of Development Studies
(January): 257-76.

United Republic of Tanzania. (1969) Second Five Year Plan for
Economic and Social Development. Dar es Salaam.

_____. (1971) The Annual Plan for 1971/72. Dar es Salaam.

Veitch, M.D. (1972) "Population Growth and the Health Services,"
pp. 304-12 in S.H. Ominde and C.N. Ejiogu (eds.), Population Growth
and Economic Development in Africa. London: Heinemann.

PART II
STATISTICAL
INFORMATION
AND SOURCES

Main purpose of this section is to provide a current bibliography of data sources related to health, food and nutrition, and Third world development. However, this bibliography should be supplemented with the complete directory of United Nations Information Sources provided in Part IV of this volume.

L BIBLIOGRAPHY OF INFORMATION SOURCES

AFRICAN STATISTICAL YEARBOOK, UN

Presents data arranged on a country basis for 44 African countries for the years 1965-1978. Available statistics for each country are presented in 48 tables: population; national accounts; agriculture, forestry, and fishing industry; transport and communications; foreign trade; prices; finance; and social statistics: education and medical facilities.

ASIAN INDUSTRIAL DEVELOPMENT NEWS, UN, Sales no. E.74.II.F.16

In four parts: (a) brief reports on the ninth session of the Asian Industrial Development Council and twenty-sixth session of the Committee on Industry and Natural Resources; (b) articles on multinationals and the transfer of know-how, acquisition of technology for manufacturing agro-equipment, fuller utilization of industrial capacity; (c) report of Asian Plan of Action on the Human Environment; and (d) statistical information on plywood, transformers, and transmission cables.

Banks, Arthur S., et al., eds.
ECONOMIC HANDBOOK OF THE WORLD: 1981. New York; London; Sydney and Tokyo: McGraw-Hill Books for State University of New York at Binghamton, Center for Social Analysis, 1981.

Descriptions, in alphabetical order, of all the world's independent states and a small number of non-independent but economically significant areas (such as Hong Kong). Data are current as of 1 July 1980 whenever possible. Summary statistics for each country include: area, population, monetary unit, Gross National Product per capita, international reserves (1979 year end), external public debt, exports, imports, government revenue, government expenditure, and consumer prices. Principal economic institutions, financial institutions, and international memberships are listed at the end of each description.

BULLETIN OF LABOUR STATISTICS. Quarterly, with supplement 8 times per year. Approx. 150 p.

Quarterly report, with supplements in intervening months, on employment, unemployment, hours of work, wages, and consumer prices, for 130-150 countries and territories. Covers total, nonagricultural, and manufacturing employment; total unemployment and rate; average nonagricultural and manufacturing hours of work per week, and earnings per hour, day, week, or month; and food and aggregate consumer price indexes.

COMPENDIUM OF SOCIAL STATISTICS, 1977. 1980, UN, Sales No. E-F. 80.XVII.6.

Contains a collection of statistical and other data aimed at describing social conditions and social change in the world. In four parts. Part 1 includes estimates and projections for the world, macroregions, and regions. Part 2 comprises data for countries or areas that represent key series describing social conditions and social change. Part 3 consists of general statistical series for countries or areas. Part 4 is devoted to information for cities or urban agglomerations. Includes a total of 151 tables, covering population, health, nutrition, education, conditions of work, housing and environmental conditions, etc. Provides an overall view of the world social situation and future trends.

DEMOGRAPHIC YEARBOOK, 1978. (ST-ESA-STAT-SER.R-7) 1979, UN, Sales No. E-F.79.XIII.I.

--Vol. 1. viii, 463 p. This volume contains the general tables giving a world summary of basic demographic statistics, followed by tables presenting statistics on the size distribution and trends in population, natality, fetal mortality, infant and maternal mortality, general mortality, nuptiality, and divorce. Data are also shown by urban/rural residence in many of the tables. --Vol. 2: Historical supplement.

DEVELOPMENT FORUM BUSINESS EDITION. DESI/DOP, UN, Palais des Nations, CH-1211 Geneva 10, Switzerland. 24 times a yr. 16 p.

A tabloid-size paper, published jointly by the United Nations Department of Information's Divison for Economic and Social Information and the World Bank. Presents articles on all aspects of the development work of the United Nations, with emphasis on specific development problems encountered by the business community. Contains notices referring to goods and works to be procured through international competitive bidding for projects assisted by the World Bank and the International Development Association (IDA). It also includes a Supplement of the World Bank, entitled "Monthly Operational Summary", and a similar supplement of the Inter-American Development Bank (IDB), once a month, which provide information about projects contemplated for financing by the World Bank and IDB, respectively.

DEVELOPMENT FORUM GENERAL EDITION

A tabloid-size paper, published jointly by the United Nations Department of Public Information's Division for Economic and Social Information and the World Bank, having as objective the effective mobilization of public opinion in support of a number of major causes to which the United Nations is committed. Presents articles reporting on the activities of various UN agencies concerned with development and social issues (health, education, nutrition, women in development). Includes a forum for nongovernmental organizations (NGO's) and book reviews.

DEVELOPMENT AND INTERNATIONAL ECONOMIC CO-OPERATION: LONG-TERM TRENDS IN ECONOMIC DEVELOPMENT. Report of the Secretary-General. Monograph. May 26, 1982.

Report analyzing world economic development trends, 1960's-81, with projections to 2000 based on the UN 1980 International Development Strategy, and on alternative low and medium economic growth assumptions. Presents data on GDP, foreign trade, investment, savings, income, population and labor force, housing, education, food and energy supply/demand, and other economic and social indicators.

DIRECTORY OF INTERNATIONAL STATISTICS: VOLUME 1. 1982 Series. Sales No. E.81.XVII.6

Vol. 1 of a 2-volume directory of international statistical time series compiled by 18 UN agencies and selected other IGO's. Lists statistical publications, and machine-readable data bases of economic and social statistics, by organization and detailed subject category. Also includes bibliography and descriptions of recurring publications, and technical descriptions of economic/social data bases.

VOLUME 2: INTERNATIONAL TABLES. Sales No. E.82.XVII.6, Vol. II

Presents analytical summary of major income and product accounts for approximately 160 countries, by country and world region.

ECONOMIC AND SOCIAL PROGRESS IN LATIN AMERICA: 1980-81 REPORT. 1981, IDB.

Provides a comprehensive survey of the Latin America economy since 1970, with particular emphasis on 1980 and 1981. Part One is a regional analysis of general economic trends, the external sector, the financing of development from internal and external sources, regional economic integration, and social development trends (women in the economic development of Latin America). Part Two contains country summaries of socioeconomic trends for 24 States members of IDB. Statistical appendix includes data on population, national accounts, public finance, balance of payments, primary commodity exports, external public debt, and hydrocarbons.

ECONOMIC AND SOCIAL SURVEY OF ASIA AND THE PACIFIC, 1977. The International Economic Crises and Developing Asia and the Pacific. 1978, UN, Sales No. E.78.II.F.1.

In two parts: (a) review of recent economic developments and emerging policy issues in the ESCAP region, 1976-1977; and (b) the impacts of the international economic crises of the first half of the 1970's upon selected developing economies in the ESCAP region and the market and policy response thereto. Topics discussed include: the food crisis; the breakdown of the international monetary system; fluctuations in the international market economy comprising the primary commodities export boom, the associated inflation and the subsequent recession, and, finally the sharp rise in the price of petroleum.

ECONOMIC AND SOCIAL SURVEY OF ASIA AND THE PACIFIC, 1979. Regional Development Strategy for the 1980's. 1981, UN, Sales No. E.80.II.F.1.

Analyzes recent economic and social development in the UN ESCAP region, as well as related international developments. Focuses on economic and social policy issues and broad development strategies. In two parts: (a) recent economic developments, 1978-1979, covering the second oil price shock economic performance of the developing countries of the ESCAP region, inflation, and external trade and payments; and (b) findings of a two-year study dealing with regional developmental strategies, covering economic growth, policies for full employment and equity, energy, technology, implementation systems, international trade, shipping, international resource transfers, and intraregional cooperation.

ECONOMIC SURVEY OF ASIA AND THE FAR EAST, 1973. 234 p. (also issued as Economic Bulletin for Asia and the Far East, vol. 24, no. 4), 1974, UN, Sales No. E.74.II.F.1.

Contains a general summary followed by Part One, which covers: education and employment--the nature of the problem; population, labor force and structure of employment and underemployment in the ECAFE [ESCAP] region; the role of location--assumptions underlying the education policies of developing countries in the ECAFE region; momentum and direction of expansion of education; structuring the flow of workers into the modern science of education for self employment--the traditional and informal sectors; and the search for new policies--a review of current thinking. Part Two covers: current economic developments--recent economic developments and emerging policy issues in the ECAFE region, 1972/73; and current economic developments and policies in 28 countries of the ECAFE region.

ECONOMIC SURVEY OF LATIN AMERICA. Series.

Series of preliminary annual reports analyzing recent economic trends in individual Latin American countries. Each report presents detailed economic indicators, including GDP by sector, agricultural and industrial production by commodity, foreign trade, public and private sector finances, and prices. Also includes selected data on employment and earnings.

THE ECONOMIST. THE WORLD IN FIGURES. Third edition. New York: Facts on File, Inc., 1980.

Compendium of figures on economic, demographic, and sociopolitical aspects of over 200 countries of the world. The first part is a world section with information on population, national income, production, energy, transportation, trade, tourism, and finance. The second part is organized by country (grouped by main region), containing statistics on location, land, climate, time, measurement systems, currency, people, resources, production, finance and external trade, and politics and the economy. The data, from many sources, cover through 1976. Country name and "special focus" indices.

FACTS OF THE WORLD BANK. Monthly (current issues).

A compilation of figures on World Bank lending, giving cumulative amounts and amounts for the current fiscal year of commitments by number of projects and by sector, as well as for each country by region. Also gives figures on sales of parts of Bank loans and IDA credits and on World Bank borrowings by currency of issue, original and outstanding amounts, and number of issues.

IMF SURVEY. Biweekly.

Biweekly report on international financial and economic conditions; IMF activities; selected topics relating to exchange rates, international reserves, and foreign trade; and economic performance of individual countries and world areas.

MAIN ECONOMIC INDICATORS: HISTORICAL STATISTICS, 1960-1979. 1980, OECD, Sales No. 2750 UU-31 80 20 3.

Bilingual: E-F. Replaces previous editions. Base year for all indicators is 1970. Arranged in chapters by country, the tables cover the period 1960 to 1979, and are followed by short notes describing some major characteristics of the series, and, where applicable, indicating breaks in continuity. Note: Supplements the monthly bulletin Main Economic Indicators.

MONTHLY BULLETIN OF STATISTICS. Monthly.

Monthly report presenting detailed economic data including production, prices, and trade; and summary population data; by country, with selected aggregates for world areas and economic groupings, or total world. Covers population size and vital statistics; employment; industrial production, including energy and major commodities; construction activity; internal and external trade; passenger and freight traffic; manufacturing wages; commodity and consumer prices; and money and banking. Each issue includes special tables, usually on topics covered on a regular basis but presenting data at different levels of aggregation and for different time periods. Special tables are described and indexed in IIS as they appear.

POPULATION AND VITAL STATISTICS REPORT. Quarterly.

Quarterly report on world population, births, total and infant deaths, and birth and death rates, by country and territorial possession, as of cover date. Also shows UN population estimates for total world and each world region.

QUARTERLY BULLETIN OF STATISTICS FOR ASIA AND THE PACIFIC. Quarterly.

Quarterly report presenting detailed monthly and quarterly data on social and economic indicators for 38 ESCAP member countries. Includes data on population; births and deaths; employment; agricultural and industrial production; construction; transportation; foreign trade quantity, value, and direction; prices; wages; and domestic and international financial activity.

1978 REPORT ON THE WORLD SOCIAL SITUATION. 1979, UN, Sales No. E.79.IV.1.

Deals with the global issues of population trends and employment; growth and distribution of income and private consumption; the production and distribution of social services; and changing social concerns. A supplement reviews the patterns of recent governmental expenditures for social services in developing countries, developed market economies, and centrally planned economies.

STATISTICAL INDICATORS FOR ASIA AND THE PACIFIC. Quarterly.

Quarterly report presenting selected economic and demographic indicators for 26 Asian and Pacific countries. Covers, for most countries, population size, birth and death rates, family planning methods, industrial and agricultural production, construction, transport, retail trade, foreign trade, prices, money supply, currency exchange rate, and GDP.

STATISTICAL YEARBOOK, 1979/80. 1981, UN, Sales No. E/F.81.XVII.1.

A comprehensive compendium of the most important internationally comparable data needed for the analysis of socioeconomic development at the world, regional and national levels. Includes tables (200) grouped in two sections: (a) world summary by regions (17 tables); and (b) remaining tables of country-by-country data, arranged in chapters: population; manpower; agriculture; forestry; fishing; industrial production; mining and quarrying; manufacturing; construction; development assistance; wholesale and retail trade; external trade; international tourism; transport; communications; national accounts; wages and prices; consumption; finance; energy; health; housing; science and technology; and culture. For this first time, this issue contains three new tables on industrial property: patents, industrial designs, and trademarks and service marks. Note: This issue is a special biennial edition, covering data through mid-1980, and in some cases for 1980 complete.

STATISTICAL YEARBOOK FOR ASIA AND THE PACIFIC, 1978. 1979, UN, Sales No. E-F.79.II.F.4.

Eleventh issue. Contains statistical indicators for the ESCAP region and statistics for period up to 1978 available at the end of 1978 for 34 countries and territories members of ESCAP, arranged by country, covering, where available: population; manpower; national accounts; agriculture, forestry, and fishing; industry; consumption; transport and communication; internal and external trade; wages, prices, and household expenditures; finance; and social statistics.

STATISTICAL YEARBOOK FOR LATIN AMERICA, 1979. 1981, UN, Sales No. E/S.80.II.G.4.

In two parts. Part 1 presents indicators of economic and social development in Latin America for 1960, 1965, 1970 and 1975-1978, including: population; demographic characteristics; employment and occupational structure; income distribution; living levels; consumption and nutrition; health; education; housing; global economic growth; agricultural activities; mining and energy resources; manufacturing; productivity; investment; saving; public financial resources; public expenditure; structure of exports and imports; intra-regional trade; transport services; tourist services; and external financing. Part 2 contains historical series in absolute figures for the years 1960, 1965 and 1970-1978

on population; national accounts; domestic prices; balance of
payments; external indebtedness; external trade; natural resources
and production of goods; infrastructure services; employment;
and social conditions.

SURVEY OF ECONOMIC AND SOCIAL CONDITIONS IN AFRICA, 1980-81 AND
OUTLOOK FOR 1981-82: SUMMARY

Examines growth in GDP, agricultural and industrial production,
trade and balance of payments, resource flows, energy
production/consumption, and selected other economic indicators,
1979-80, with outlook for 1981-82 and trends from 1960's.

TECHNICAL DATA SHEETS

Provides up-to-date information about projects as they are approved
for World Bank and IDA financing. In addition to a description
of the project, its total cost, and the amount of Bank financing,
each technical data sheet describes the goods and services that
must be provided for the project's implementation and gives the
address of the project's implementing organization.   On the
average, 250 such sheets will be issued annually. Requests for
sample copies are to be addressed to: Publications Distribution
Unit, World Bank, 1818 H St., N.W., Washington, D.C. 20433,
U.S.A.

UNESCO STATISTICAL YEARBOOK, 1978-79, 1266 p. 1980, UNESCO.

Composite: E/F/S (introductory texts).   Presents statistical
and other information for 206 countries on education; science
and technology; libraries; museums and related institutions;
theater and other dramatic arts; book production; newspapers
and other periodicals; film and cinema; radio broadcasting; and
television.   In this edition, the summary tables relating to
culture and communications, previously given in the introduction
to each of the corresponding chapters, have been grouped together
in a separate chapter.

World Bank. ANNUAL REPORT, 1982. 1982, WBG.

Presents summary and background of the activities of the World
Bank Group during the fiscal year ended 30 June 1982, covering:
the International Bank for Reconstruction and Development (IBRD);
the   International   Development   Association   (IDA);   and   the
International Finance Corporation (IFC). Chapters cover: brief
review of Bank operations in fiscal 1982; a global perspective
of the economic situation; Bank policies, activities and finances
for fiscal 1982; 1982 regional perspectives; and Executive
Directors. Lists projects approved for IBRD and IDA assistance
in fiscal 1982 by sector, region and purpose. Also reviews trends
in lending by sector for 1980-82 and includes statistical annex.

WORLD BANK COUNTRY STUDIES. Series.

Series of studies, prepared by World Bank staff, on development issues and policies, and economic conditions in individual developing countries. Studies may focus on specific economic sectors or issues, or on general economic performance of the country as a whole.

The World Bank.
WORLD DEVELOPMENT REPORT, 1978. August 1978.

First volume in a series of annual reports designed to provide a comprehensive, continuing assessment of global development issues. After an overview of development in the past 25 years, the report discusses current policy issues and projected developments in areas of the international economy that influence the prospects of developing countries. Analyzes the problems confronting policy makers in developing countries, which differ in degree and in kind, affecting the choice of appropriate policy instruments, and recognizes that development strategies need to give equal prominence to two goals: accelerating economic growth and reducing poverty. Reviews development priorities for low-income Asia, sub-Saharan Africa, and middle-income developing countries.

The World Bank.
WORLD DEVELOPMENT REPORT, 1979. Washington, D.C.

Second in a series of annual reports designed to assess global development issues. Focuses on development in the middle income countries, with particular emphasis on policy choices for industrialization and urbanization. Part one assesses recent trends and prospects to 1990 and discusses capital flows, and energy. Part two focuses upon structural change and development policy relevant to employment, the balance between agriculture and industry, and urban growth. Part three reviews development experiences and issues in three groups of middle income countries: semi-industrialized nations; mineral primary-producing countries; and predominantly agricultural primary-producing countries. Maintains that progress toward expanding employment and reducing poverty in developing countries lies not only in internal policy choices but also in a liberal environment for international trade and capital flows.

The World Bank.
WORLD DEVELOPMENT REPORT, 1980. New York: Oxford University Press for the World Bank, 1980.

Third in a series of annual reports. Parts one examines economic policy choices facing both developing and developed countries and their implications for national and regional growth. Projects, to the year 2000 but particularly to the mid to late 1980's, growth estimates for oil-importing and oil-exporting developing countries; and analyzes the fundamental issues of energy, trade, and capital flows. Part two focuses on the links between poverty, growth, and human development. It examines the impact of

education, health, nutrition, and fertility on poverty; reviews
some practical lessons in implementing human development programs;
and discusses the trade-offs between growth and poverty and the
allocation of resources between human development and other
activities. Stresses the views that growth does not obviate
the need for human development and that direct measures to reduce
poverty do not obviate the need for economic expansion. Concludes
that world growth prospects have deteriorated in the past year,
but higher oil prices have impoved the outlook [for the first
half of the 1980's] for the fifth of the developing world's
population that lives in oil-exporting countries; however, the
four-fifths that live in oil-importing countries will experience
slower growth for the first half of the decade. Includes a
statistical appendix to part one; a bibliographical note; and
a very lengthy annex of World Development Indicators.

The World Bank.
WORLD DEVELOPMENT REPORT, 1981. New York: Oxford University
Press for the World Bank, 1981.

With the major focus on the international context of development,
examines past trends and future prospects for international trade,
energy, and capital flows and the effects of these on developing
countries. Presents two scenarios for the 1980's, one predicting
higher growth rates than in the 1970's and one lower. Analyzes
national adjustments to the international economy, presenting
in-depth case studies. Concludes that countries pursuing
outward-oriented policies adjusted more easily to external shocks.
Contends that whichever scenario prevails, income differentials
will increase between the industrial and developing countries.
Low income countries have fewer options and less flexibility
of adjustment, therefore requiring continued aid from the more
affluent countries. Advocates policies to channel increased
resources to alleviate poverty.

The World Bank.
WORLD DEVELOPMENT REPORT, 1982.

The Report this year focuses on agriculture and food security.
As in previous years there is also a section on global prospects
and international issues, as well as the statistical annex of
World Development indicators.

The World Bank.
WORLD TABLES 1980: FROM THE DATA FILES OF THE WORLD BANK. Second
edition. Baltimore and London: Johns Hopkins University Press
for the World Bank, 1980.

A broad range of internationally comparable statistical information
drawn from the World Bank data files. Includes historical time
series for individual countries in absolute numbers for most
of the basic economic indicators for selected years (1950-77
when available); also presents derived economic indicators for
selected periods of years and demographic and social data for

selected years.   Although the number of social indicators is
fewer than those in the 1976 edition the quality of the data
has been improved through the use of more uniform definitions
and concepts, greater attention to population statistics, and
better statistics on balance of payments and central government
finance.   Includes an index of country coverage.

WORLD ECONOMIC OUTLOOK: A SURVEY BY THE STAFF OF THE INTERNATIONAL
MONETARY FUND.   1980, IMF.

An in-depth forecast of the world economy in 1980 and a preliminary
summary for 1981.   Chapters discuss: a profile of current
situation and short-term prospects; global perspectives for
adjustment   and   financing;   industrial   countries;   developing
countries--oil-exporting and non-oil groups; and key policy issues.
Appendixes include country and regional surveys; technical notes
on the world oil situation, estimated impact of fiscal balances
in   selected   industrial   countries,   and   monetary   policy   and
inflation; and statistical tables.

WORLD ECONOMIC OUTLOOK: A SURVEY BY THE STAFF OF THE INTERNATIONAL
MONETARY FUND.   [1982 ed.]   1982, IMF.

A comprehensive analysis of economic developments, policies,
and prospects through June 1981 for industrial, oil exporting
and   non-oil   developing   countries.   It   highlights   persistent
imbalances   in   the   world   economy,   high   inflation,   rising
unemployment, excessive rates of real interest, and unstable
exchange rates.   Appendix A includes supplementary notes providing
information on selected topics in greater depth or detail than
in the main body of the report: country and regional surveys;
medium-term scenarios; fiscal development; monetary and exchange
rate development; world oil situation; growth and inflation in
non-oil developing countries; developments in trade policy; and
commodity price developments and prospects.   Appendix B presents
statistical tables on: domestic economic activity and prices;
international   trade;   balance   of   payments;   external   debt;
medium-term projections; and country tables.

The World Bank.
WORLD BANK ATLAS.   Fourteenth edition.   1979.   Annual.

Presents estimates of gross national product (GNP) per capita
(1977), GNP per capita growth rates (1970-77), and population
(mid-1977), with population growth rates (1970-77) for countries
with populations of one million or more in three global maps;
a computer-generated map shows GNP per capita (1977) by major
regions.   Six regional maps give the same data for 184 countries
and territories, as well as preliminary data for 1978.   The base
years 1976-78 have been used for the conversion of GNP for both
1977 and 1978.   A Technical Note explains in detail the methodology
used.

The World Bank.
WORLD DEVELOPMENT INDICATORS. June 1979. 71 pages.

A volume of statistics prepared in conjunction with and
constituting the Annex to the World Development Report, 1979
to provide information of general relevance about the main features
of economic and social development, reporting data for a total
of 125 countries whose population exceeds one million. Countries
are grouped in five categories and ranked by their 1977 per capita
gross national product (GNP) levels. The volume contains 24
tables covering some 110 economic and social indicators. The
choice of indicators has been based on data being available for
a large number of countries, the availability of historical series
to allow the measurement of growth and change, and on the relevance
of data to the principal processes of development.

The World Bank.
WORLD ECONOMIC AND SOCIAL INDICATORS. Quarterly (current issues).

Presents most recent available data on trade, commodity prices,
consumer prices, debt and capital flows, industrial production,
as well as social indicators and select annual data (by countries
where applicable). Each issue contains an article on topics
of current importance. Strategies for improving the access to
education of the disadvantaged rural poor by serving areas out
of range of existing schools are discussed and programs in four
projects financed by the World Bank are described.

WORLD ECONOMIC OUTLOOK: A SURVEY BY THE STAFF OF THE INTERNATIONAL
MONETARY FUND. Annual. April 1982. (Occasional Paper No. 9)

Annual report on economic performance of major industrial and
oil exporting and non-oil developing countries, 1970's-81 and
forecast 1982-83, with some projections to 1986. Includes analysis
of economic indicators for selected industrial countries, world
economic groupings, and world areas, primarily for IMF member
countries. Covers domestic economic activity, including prices,
GNP, and employment; international trade; balance of payments;
and foreign debt. Also includes financial indicators for selected
industrial countries, including government budget surpluses and
deficits, savings, money supply, and interest rates.

WORLD ECONOMIC SURVEY. 1978, UN, Sales No. E.78.II.C.1.

Provides an overview of salient developments in the world economy
in 1977 and the outlook for 1978. Focuses on policy needs for
improving the tempo of world production and trade. Examines
in detail the course of production and trade and related variables
in the developing economies, the developed market economies,
and the centrally planned economies.

WORLD ECONOMIC SURVEY 1979-80. 1980, UN, Sales No. E.80.II.C.2.

A survey of current world economic conditions and trends, with chapters on salient features and policy implications; the growth of world output, 1979-1980; the accelerating pace of inflation; world trade and international payments; world economic outlook, 1980-1985; and adjustment policies in developing countries. Annexes cover external factors and growth in developing countries--the experience of the 1970's; supply and price of petroleum in 1979 and 1980; and prospective supply and demand for oil.

YEARBOOK OF NATIONAL ACCOUNTS STATISTICS, 1980. Annual. 1982.

Annual report presenting national income and product account balances for approximately 170 countries, and for world areas and economic groupings, selected years 1970-79, often with comparisons to 1960 and 1965. Data are compiled in accordance with the UN System of National Accounts (SNA) for market economies, and the System of Material Product Balances (MPS) for centrally planned economies. SNA data include GDP final consumption expenditures by type; production, income/outlay, and capital formation accounts, by institutional sector; and production by type of activity. MPS data include material and financial balances, manpower and resources, and national wealth and capital assets.

STATISTICAL NEWSLETTER. Quarterly. Approx. 15 p.

Quarterly newsletter on ESCAP statistical programs and activities, and major statistical developments in ESCAP countries. Includes brief descriptions of meetings, working groups, upcoming international statistical training programs, and regional advisory services; and an annotated bibliography of recent ESCAP and UN statistical publications.

BULLETIN OF THE PAN AMERICAN HEALTH ORGANIZATION. Quarterly.

Quarterly journal on health conditions and services, and disease prevention and control activities in Latin American countries. Articles with substantial statistics of broad research value are described and indexed in IIS. Data sources: Primarily national government agencies, original research, and international organizations.

BULLETIN OF THE WORLD HEALTH ORGANIZATION. Bimonthly.

Bimonthly journal presenting research articles on epidemiological and other biomedical and public health topics. Nontechnical articles with substantial statistical content of broad research interest are described and indexed in IIS as they appear. Data sources: Original research, and literature reviews.

FAO MONTHLY BULLETIN OF STATISTICS. Monthly.

Monthly report on world agricultural production and trade, by country, world area, and economic grouping; and prices on world markets. Includes data on crop areas and yields. Each issue includes production and trade data for 20-40 of approximately

70 commodities covered during the year; price series of international significance for 67 commodities; and a special feature presenting additional data on selected commodities or countries. Special features are described and indexed in IIS as they appear. Data sources: Primarily national government publications, responses to FAO questionnaires, and FAO estimates.

FOOD AND NUTRITION BULLETIN. Quarterly.

Quarterly research journal on topics related to worldwide nutrition, and dietary improvement methods and programs. Covers eating habits, perinatal nourishment, food processing and preservation, and various nutrition-related aspects of health care, agriculture, and social and economic development. Data sources: Primarily research papers presented at conferences, and national government and IGO publications.

FOOD OUTLOOK. Monthly.

Monthly report (combined Nov./Dec. issue) on actual and estimated world food supply and trade. Covers rice, wheat, and coarse grain production; foreign trade volume and prices; stocks, food aid; and freight rates; by commodity and/or country, with totals for selected world areas and economic groupings. Also includes notes on weather conditions; fertilizer and sugar price trends; selected data on other grain products, oils and oilseeds, and dried milk; and crop area estimates.

WORLD FOOD PROGRAMME NEWS. Quarterly.

Quarterly report on WFP activities and various food-related development issues. Includes data on new projects funded and emergency operations, by country; with cumulative project totals by world region, and total contributions and expenses by type. Articles and special features with substantial statistical content are described and indexed in IIS as they appear. Data sources: WFP records.

WORLD HEALTH STATISTICS ANNUAL, 1978. 3 volumes. WHO, 1978.

--Vol. 1: Vital Statistics and Causes of Death. Summary of most recent (mostly 1975-1976) vital statistics and causes of death, in 12 tables: (a) national area and population data; (b) population data by sex and age; (c) population, area, density, and selected health indicators; (d) natality, general mortality, and natural increase; (e) late fetal, infant, neonatal, post-neonatal, and perinatal mortality; (f,g) deaths according to cause, by sex, ICD "A" List; (h) deaths according to cause, by sex and age, ICD "B" List; (i) numbers and rates of infant mortality according to cause, by sex and age; (j) life expectancy at selected ages, by sex; (k) survival rates, at selected ages, by sex; and (1) chances of dying from specified causes, by sex. Four annexes contain: WHO membership; users' guide to standardized computer tape transcripts of WHO health statistics; tables of

numbers and rates of mortality due to accidents; and List B: List of 50 Causes for Tabulation of Mortality.
--Vol. 2: Infectious Diseases: Cases and Deaths.
--Vol. 3: Health Personnel and Hospital Establishments.

WORLD HEALTH STATISTICS ANNUAL, 1980: HEALTH PERSONNEL AND HOSPITAL ESTABLISHMENTS. WHO, 1980.

This volume contains statistics on health personnel and hospital establishments, showing the number of physicians, midwives and nurses working in the various countries, as well as the ratios to their population. It also provides information on the number of hospitals by category (general or specialized) and by type of administration (government or private), and on the bed complement, the number of admissions and of patient-days. Certain indices on hospital utilization, such as beds per 10,000 population, admissions per 10,000 population and per bed, bed occupancy rate, and average length of stay are also published.

WORLD HEALTH STATISTICS QUARTERLY. Quarterly.

Quarterly journal reporting on health research worldwide, including mortality and morbidity studies, methodology of statistics collection, and WHO statistical activities. Articles with substantial statistical content are described and indexed in IIS as they appear. Format and data presentation: Contents listing; 2-3 articles; and list of forthcoming WHO meetings related to statistics.

II. STATISTICAL TABLES AND FIGURES

In this section, an attempt is made to provide the reader with an overview of global trends related to health, food and nutrition, and Third world development, based on an analysis of the country data, as it is sometimes difficult to form any such general impression when faced with a general body of highly detailed data. Statistical information in the following pages have been reproduced from the following sources:

WORLD TABLES 1980: FROM THE DATA FILES OF THE WORLD BANK, Baltimore: Johns Hopkins University Press for the World Bank, 1980. (Reprinted by permission of the World Bank and Johns Hopkins University Press.)

WORLD ECONOMIC AND SOCIAL INDICATORS, October 1978. Report No. 700/78/04. Washington, D.C: WORLD BANK.

HEALTH: SECTOR POLICY PAPER, World Bank, 1975.

GLOBAL INDICATORS

TABLE 1. SOCIAL INDICATORS BY INCOME GROUP OF COUNTRIES

DEVELOPING COUNTRIES EXCLUDING CAPITAL SURPLUS OIL EXPORTERS
(ADJUSTED COUNTRY GROUP AVERAGES)

INDICATOR	LOW INCOME			LOWER MIDDLE INCOME			INTERMEDIATE MIDDLE INCOME		
	1960	1970	MOST RECENT ESTIMATE	1960	1970	MOST RECENT ESTIMATE	1960	1970	MOST RECENT ESTIMATE
GNP PER CAPITA (IN CURRENT US $)	67.4	107.4	162.0	136.1	239.6	398.6	225.6	410.9	817.9
POPULATION									
GROWTH RATE (%) - TOTAL	2.2	2.4	2.4	2.7	2.7	2.6	2.7	2.7	2.5
- URBAN	5.3	4.7	4.7	4.7	4.4	9.8	5.4	4.9	5.1
URBAN POPULATION (% OF TOTAL)	10.4	14.0	14.8	17.7	21.6	26.1	33.7	41.4	46.1
VITAL STATISTICS									
CRUDE BIRTH RATE (PER 1000)	47.5	46.9	45.2	47.1	45.5	42.6	44.6	41.2	38.2
CRUDE DEATH RATE (PER 1000)	26.1	21.7	18.2	21.4	16.1	12.7	18.6	13.5	11.1
GROSS REPRODUCTION RATE	2.9	3.1	3.1	3.4	3.2	3.3	3.0	2.8	2.6
EMPLOYMENT AND INCOME									
DEPENDENCY RATIO - AGE	0.8	0.9	0.9	0.9	0.9	0.9	0.9	0.9	0.9
- ECONOMIC	1.0	1.1	1.1	1.3	1.4	1.4	1.6	1.6	1.5
LABOR FORCE IN AGRICULTURE (% OF TOTAL)	65.4	62.0	59.3	70.4	65.9	62.5	62.8	54.5	47.0
UNEMPLOYED (% OF LABOR FORCE)	4.7	4.0	3.1	6.3	8.4	5.3	6.1	6.0	5.8
INCOME RECEIVED BY - HIGHEST 5%	24.5	23.3	20.3	25.1	23.1	25.5	31.5	27.0	19.3
- LOWEST 20%	4.6	5.1	6.5	4.8	4.9	4.8	4.4	3.9	5.7
HEALTH AND NUTRITION									
DEATH RATE (PER 1000) AGES 1-4 YEARS	43.6	33.0	33.0	9.3	6.8	7.5	8.5	3.6	2.7
INFANT MORTALITY RATE (PER 1000)	129.0	121.3	102.8	84.6	79.9	58.4	88.6	65.8	55.0
LIFE EXPECTANCY AT BIRTH (YRS)	39.2	43.8	46.0	45.0	50.8	53.2	51.1	57.0	59.1
POPULATION PER - PHYSICIAN	21790.7	15219.9	13235.9	16767.4	11977.3	10586.0	3299.7	2549.2	2412.7
- NURSING PERSON	8472.3	5215.0	4830.9	4078.2	1921.9	1683.8	3394.0	2205.1	1502.1
- HOSPITAL BED	1386.7	1267.8	1236.2	1037.6	815.3	793.1	721.8	629.2	507.1
PER CAPITA PER DAY SUPPLY OF:									
CALORIES (% OF REQUIREMENTS) - TOTAL	89.8	91.5	94.5	85.1	93.3	102.3	94.4	101.8	103.9
PROTEIN (GRMS) - TOTAL	50.5	51.6	53.9	47.4	53.0	56.9	54.4	58.7	60.6
- FROM ANIMALS & PULSES	14.9	14.4	16.4	17.7	18.1	18.8	21.8	22.1	23.0

TABLE 1. Social Indicators by Income Group of Countries (Continued)

(ADJUSTED COUNTRY GROUP AVERAGES)

DEVELOPING COUNTRIES EXCLUDING CAPITAL SURPLUS OIL EXPORTERS

INDICATOR	LOW INCOME			LOWER MIDDLE INCOME			INTERMEDIATE MIDDLE INCOME		
	1960	1970	MOST RECENT ESTIMATE	1960	1970	MOST RECENT ESTIMATE	1960	1970	MOST RECENT ESTIMATE
EDUCATION									
ADJ. ENROLLMENT RATIOS - PRIMARY	37.4	48.4	59.0	60.7	74.0	92.7	77.8	95.3	99.9
- SECONDARY	4.8	10.3	13.9	4.8	12.7	22.6	14.5	26.7	29.4
FEMALE ENROLLMENT RATIO (PRIMARY)	34.6	39.0	43.3	45.6	75.0	77.5	65.8	87.8	87.6
ADULT LITERACY RATE (%)	24.4	32.0	33.8	41.0	60.0	63.0	49.8	57.8	62.3
HOUSING									
PERSONS PER ROOM - URBAN	2.5	2.0	2.8	2.6	2.5	2.2	2.3	2.2	1.6
OCCUPIED DWELLINGS WITHOUT WATER	62.2	69.8	..	68.7	64.6	67.8	74.6	64.2	58.9
ACCESS TO ELECTRICITY (%) - ALL	..	..	..	17.3	23.3	40.4	28.4	49.6	71.9
- RURAL	..	..	..	..	..	..	5.6	26.7	34.1
CONSUMPTION									
RADIO RECEIVERS (PER 1000 POP.)	4.5	14.4	23.1	11.9	62.3	70.4	48.8	96.2	102.6
PASSENGER CARS (PER 1000 POP.)	1.3	2.5	3.0	3.0	6.5	8.6	4.2	7.5	11.1
ENERGY (KG COAL/YR PER CAPITA)	62.0	83.4	104.8	99.6	220.1	265.2	258.7	489.2	586.2
NEWSPRINT (KG/YR PER CAPITA)	0.2	0.4	0.3	0.6	0.8	0.8	1.1	1.8	2.4

(CONTINUED)

(ADJUSTED COUNTRY GROUP AVERAGES)

INDICATOR	DEV'G CTRIES. EXCL. CAP. SURP. OIL EXP. UPPER MIDDLE INCOME			CAP. SURP. OIL EXP. HIGH INCOME			CAP. SURP. OIL EXP.			INDUSTRIALIZED COUNTRIES		
	1960	1970	MOST RECENT EST.	1960	1970	MOST RECENT EST.	1960	1970	MOST RECENT EST.	1960	1970	MOST RECENT EST.
GNP PER CAPITA (IN CURRENT US $)	401.2	817.1	1648.7	689.4	1564.2	2911.1	1054.3	2858.9	5710.5	1417.4	3096.8	5297.7
POPULATION												
GROWTH RATE (%) - TOTAL	1.6	1.3	1.5	2.1	3.1	2.9	4.5	2.4	2.7	0.9	0.9	0.9
- URBAN	3.3	3.4	2.8	4.5	3.9	3.5	..	5.8	6.8	1.6	1.3	1.3
URBAN POPULATION (% OF TOTAL)	43.4	51.1	53.1	63.0	82.1	88.6	24.6	20.0	39.0	66.1	70.5	73.8
VITAL STATISTICS												
CRUDE BIRTH RATE (PER 1000)	26.2	28.5	20.8	41.7	37.4	33.6	48.3	49.4	45.0	21.3	20.0	18.7
CRUDE DEATH RATE (PER 1000)	10.4	9.1	8.9	9.6	8.3	8.0	21.2	22.8	14.7	9.7	9.0	8.8
GROSS REPRODUCTION RATE	1.7	1.8	1.8	2.3	2.5	1.8	..	3.5	3.3	1.3	1.3	1.2

TABLE 1. Social Indicators by Income Group of Countries (Continued)

(ADJUSTED COUNTRY GROUP AVERAGES)

INDICATOR	DEV'G CTRIES. EXCL. CAP. SURP. OIL EXP. UPPER MIDDLE INCOME			CAP. SURP. OIL EXP. HIGH INCOME			CAP. SURP. OIL EXP.			INDUSTRIALIZED COUNTRIES		
	1960	1970	MOST RECENT EST.	1960	1970	MOST RECENT EST.	1960	1970	MOST RECENT EST.	1960	1970	MOST RECENT EST.
EMPLOYMENT AND INCOME												
DEPENDENCY RATIO – AGE	0.7	0.7	0.6	0.8	0.6	0.6	0.9	0.9	0.9	0.5	0.6	0.4
– ECONOMIC	1.3	1.7	1.6	1.2	1.2	1.2	1.8	1.7	1.7	0.9	0.9	0.8
LABOR FORCE IN AGRICULTURE (% OF TOTAL)	48.5	42.5	36.3	26.1	17.8	21.0	54.7	44.5	29.0	19.8	13.2	10.0
UNEMPLOYED (% OF LABOR FORCE)	7.4	3.3	4.0	9.0	5.4	5.1	7.3	2.0	3.0	2.1	1.5	1.9
INCOME RECEIVED BY – HIGHEST 5%	32.5	28.2	21.3	18.9	16.1	..	13.3	..	..	19.3	14.0	15.5
– LOWEST 20%	4.2	3.8	4.7	5.8	6.6	..	10.1	..	..	4.2	7.0	5.7
HEALTH AND NUTRITION												
DEATH RATE (PER 1000) AGES 1-4 YEARS	4.8	2.9	1.9	..	1.3	1.3	..	3.6	3.6	1.2	0.9	0.8
INFANT MORTALITY RATE (PER 1000)	74.4	51.3	37.9	44.9	27.8	23.2	..	134.3	80.3	27.9	17.0	15.0
LIFE EXPECTANCY AT BIRTH (YRS)	64.6	67.3	68.4	66.2	64.0	68.2	45.4	44.9	52.9	69.5	71.4	72.5
POPULATION PER – PHYSICIAN	1625.8	967.5	718.2	1117.5	888.0	756.9	9853.7	6323.4	1260.0	895.2	825.6	656.0
– NURSING PERSON	1690.7	1279.6	1028.5	1165.0	605.9	683.5	5140.0	2856.8	460.0	279.6	199.6	167.1
– HOSPITAL BED	209.9	180.4	185.8	170.0	162.5	170.0	1093.2	727.5	230.0	96.1	86.0	81.9
PER CAPITA PER DAY SUPPLY OF:												
CALORIES (% OF REQUIREMENTS)	104.5	114.4	111.5	106.3	107.2	113.6	83.9	90.3	104.9	118.7	118.7	119.5
PROTEIN (GRMS) – TOTAL	75.5	84.9	77.8	78.5	79.2	89.9	53.6	57.0	65.1	90.3	94.1	94.8
– FROM ANIMALS & PULSES	27.0	29.0	27.5	33.0	40.1	48.0	11.0	14.8	18.2	49.7	55.0	54.9
EDUCATION												
ADJ. ENROLLMENT RATIOS – PRIMARY	94.6	97.9	95.7	104.4	120.1	107.6	18.2	47.1	145.0	106.7	104.3	103.3
– SECONDARY	22.7	36.6	46.7	18.1	40.1	46.2	3.1	12.4	47.0	59.5	79.1	79.8
FEMALE ENROLLMENT RATIO (PRIMARY)	89.7	87.9	86.1	100.2	100.0	102.0	3.5	31.6	40.4	111.4	104.6	104.0
ADULT LITERACY RATE (%)	51.4	67.8	66.1	81.8	86.2	87.2	25.2	17.1	..	98.0	99.0	99.0
HOUSING												
PERSONS PER ROOM – URBAN	1.4	1.2	..	1.1	..	..	..	1.9	..	0.8	0.7	0.9
OCCUPIED DWELLINGS WITHOUT WATER	59.1	75.3	67.1	57.1	20.0	..	..	69.0	..	7.2	3.1	4.3
ACCESS TO ELECTRICITY (%) – ALL	50.6	47.4	59.8	79.3	91.0	..	..	24.0	..	97.3	98.9	99.1
– RURAL	26.9	..	..	57.0	58.0	..	..	..	..	91.4	95.2	94.8
CONSUMPTION												
RADIO RECEIVERS (PER 1000 POP.)	76.3	137.2	200.4	170.7	174.3	185.6	13.8	17.5	18.4	277.1	359.7	379.3
PASSENGER CARS (PER 1000 POP.)	11.2	29.2	42.3	14.1	41.3	54.4	7.6	16.6	113.7	90.7	233.3	266.5
ENERGY (KG COAL/YR PER CAPITA)	676.2	1426.1	1618.7	798.4	1755.1	2467.6	302.5	1003.1	1419.4	2624.7	4575.2	4997.3
NEWSPRINT (KG/YR PER CAPITA)	1.4	1.9	2.3	3.5	8.7	6.6	0.2	0.2	0.1	16.4	22.3	22.2

TABLE 2. Social Indicators by Geographic Areas (Developing Countries)

(ADJUSTED COUNTRY GROUP AVERAGES)

INDICATOR	EUROPE			LATIN AMERICA & CARIBBEAN			N. AFRICA & MIDDLE EAST		
	1960	1970	MOST RECENT ESTIMATE	1960	1970	MOST RECENT ESTIMATE	1960	1970	MOST RECENT ESTIMATE
GNP PER CAPITA (IN CURRENT US $)	496.6	1018.0	2070.3	352.0	625.8	1015.6	307.7	579.0	1290.3
POPULATION									
GROWTH RATE (%) - TOTAL	1.0	0.8	0.9	2.5	2.7	2.6	2.7	2.9	3.0
- URBAN	3.8	2.8	2.1	4.2	4.1	4.2	6.4	4.5	5.1
URBAN POPULATION (% OF TOTAL)	32.1	40.7	38.7	48.3	54.3	58.5	33.8	39.6	44.3
VITAL STATISTICS									
CRUDE BIRTH RATE (PER 1000)	23.3	20.5	19.2	40.9	39.0	36.8	48.3	47.2	45.7
CRUDE DEATH RATE (PER 1000)	10.5	9.0	9.0	14.1	10.9	9.2	22.6	18.0	15.3
GROSS REPRODUCTION RATE	1.4	1.3	1.3	2.7	2.6	2.6	2.3	3.4	3.4
EMPLOYMENT AND INCOME									
DEPENDENCY RATIO - AGE	0.6	0.6	0.4	0.9	1.0	0.9	0.9	1.0	1.0
- ECONOMIC	1.1	1.1	1.0	1.6	1.5	1.7	1.6	2.0	1.9
LABOR FORCE IN AGRICULTURE (% OF TOTAL)	47.9	31.8	27.4	48.3	41.0	36.6	52.6	43.4	42.9
UNEMPLOYED (% OF LABOR FORCE)	3.0	4.0	6.0	7.6	6.2	8.8	6.3	3.4	4.1
INCOME RECEIVED BY - HIGHEST 5%	21.8	24.5	25.0	37.1	30.4	31.7	24.0	25.0	21.0
- LOWEST 20%	5.4	3.9	3.9	3.9	3.5	2.0	4.4	4.2	5.2
HEALTH AND NUTRITION									
DEATH RATE (PER 1000) AGES 1-4 YEARS	4.7	2.8	1.7	10.6	7.7	6.6	..	6.0	..
INFANT MORTALITY RATE (PER 1000)	60.4	39.7	34.5	77.4	67.3	56.2	127.8	111.6	97.8
LIFE EXPECTANCY AT BIRTH (YRS)	65.8	68.6	69.1	55.8	60.6	62.5	45.5	50.3	52.8
POPULATION PER - PHYSICIAN	1004.0	821.3	694.4	2058.1	1866.8	1796.9	5690.8	5760.2	4724.7
- NURSING PERSON	1343.2	653.9	339.2	4542.1	3389.5	2804.5	3286.6	2564.7	2383.1
- HOSPITAL BED	190.5	168.0	170.5	444.1	392.3	405.6	670.8	661.6	700.0
PER CAPITA PER DAY SUPPLY OF:									
CALORIES (% OF REQUIREMENTS)	109.3	118.0	118.0	97.6	103.2	105.5	80.9	91.0	96.0
PROTEIN (GRMS) - TOTAL	85.9	90.7	90.0	63.7	59.8	60.7	54.5	58.3	63.1
- FROM ANIMALS & PULSES	27.0	29.0	33.0	29.0	28.0	28.2	17.5	15.0	15.6
EDUCATION									
ADJ. ENROLLMENT RATIOS - PRIMARY	105.0	102.1	104.3	85.0	101.7	105.1	51.5	75.6	80.5
- SECONDARY	25.5	50.5	49.2	15.0	27.6	36.0	10.3	20.4	22.2
FEMALE ENROLLMENT RATIO (PRIMARY)	98.9	99.4	100.4	85.6	98.3	98.1	30.8	50.2	52.3
ADULT LITERACY RATE (%)	64.9	75.0	88.2	61.4	74.6	75.7	17.7	26.9	40.6
HOUSING									
PERSONS PER ROOM - URBAN	1.4	1.5	1.4	1.9	1.3	2.1	1.8	2.3	3.0
OCCUPIED DWELLINGS WITHOUT WATER	67.0	63.3	59.5	65.5	67.0	66.4	62.2	77.1	90.5
ACCESS TO ELECTRICITY (%) - ALL	51.4	46.3	57.9	44.4	54.2	53.1	40.1	31.0	39.1
- RURAL	18.1	20.9	33.8	9.3	12.5	12.6	..	..	..
CONSUMPTION									
RADIO RECEIVERS (PER 1000 POP.)	93.9	176.7	193.1	101.6	166.2	177.5	49.7	79.1	120.1
PASSENGER CARS (PER 1000 POP.)	6.8	49.9	90.0	11.7	22.1	29.9	7.5	11.5	15.4
ENERGY (KG COAL/YR PER CAPITA)	673.4	1334.0	1829.4	577.2	821.0	929.2	263.7	281.2	750.2
NEWSPRINT (KG/YR PER CAPITA)	2.3	3.2	3.3	2.2	3.1	3.0	0.3	0.3	0.3

TABLE 2. Social Indicators by Geographic Areas (Developing Countries), Continued

(ADJUSTED COUNTRY GROUP AVERAGES)

INDICATOR	AFRICA SOUTH OF SAHARA			SOUTH ASIA			EAST ASIA AND PACIFIC		
	1960	1970	MOST RECENT ESTIMATE	1960	1970	MOST RECENT ESTIMATE	1960	1970	MOST RECENT ESTIMATE
GNP PER CAPITA (IN CURRENT US $)	94.9	137.0	207.4	54.1	88.2	131.4	141.8	290.0	568.3
POPULATION									
GROWTH RATE (%) - TOTAL	2.2	2.4	2.6	2.2	2.6	2.1	3.0	2.8	2.3
- URBAN	5.6	6.0	6.0	5.2	4.1	4.3	5.4	5.0	5.2
URBAN POPULATION (% OF TOTAL)	9.1	12.5	13.5	7.8	9.8	12.4	28.1	27.1	38.1
VITAL STATISTICS									
CRUDE BIRTH RATE (PER 1000)	48.8	48.1	47.1	47.4	45.8	45.1	42.3	40.7	32.0
CRUDE DEATH RATE (PER 1000)	26.7	23.7	21.2	26.4	21.4	17.3	19.2	12.4	8.7
GROSS REPRODUCTION RATE	2.9	3.1	3.0	3.2	3.0	2.9	3.0	2.5	2.3
EMPLOYMENT AND INCOME									
DEPENDENCY RATIO - AGE	0.9	0.9	0.9	0.8	0.8	0.8	0.9	0.9	0.7
- ECONOMIC	1.1	1.1	1.1	1.5	1.4	1.2	1.4	1.4	1.3
LABOR FORCE IN AGRICULTURE (% OF TOTAL)	79.8	75.0	73.1	61.8	60.8	63.0	67.9	59.5	48.4
UNEMPLOYED (% OF LABOR FORCE)	5.1	4.6	5.1	..	..	11.0	5.1	5.1	4.1
INCOME RECEIVED BY - HIGHEST 5%	28.2	26.4	25.7	24.6	23.2	18.6	22.7	20.5	19.8
- LOWEST 20%	5.2	3.9	5.7	4.6	5.2	7.8	5.5	5.8	6.6
HEALTH AND NUTRITION									
DEATH RATE (PER 1000) AGES 1-4 YEARS	..	..	..	..	..	..	..	3.4	2.0
INFANT MORTALITY RATE (PER 1000)	153.9	129.6	127.5	136.2	124.3	104.0	61.2	31.1	27.4
LIFE EXPECTANCY AT BIRTH (YRS)	36.9	41.5	43.4	40.6	45.2	48.1	52.5	59.1	61.6
POPULATION PER - PHYSICIAN	31866.1	24906.5	21616.5	9920.9	8519.2	7412.6	3429.3	2268.9	2208.9
- NURSING PERSON	4558.4	3088.7	2496.5	14566.1	9168.6	8339.3	3096.6	1935.5	1465.5
- HOSPITAL BED	1234.7	819.9	799.9	2885.8	1998.5	1908.0	1270.8	921.7	662.1
PER CAPITA PER DAY SUPPLY OF:									
CALORIES (% OF REQUIREMENTS)	89.6	90.7	91.9	89.1	97.6	96.0	90.0	99.4	106.5
PROTEIN (GRMS) - TOTAL	56.6	59.0	60.6	47.8	53.2	50.8	48.1	53.4	55.6
- FROM ANIMALS & PULSES	19.2	19.8	23.1	15.0	16.0	15.5	19.0	22.1	22.1
EDUCATION									
ADJ. ENROLLMENT RATIOS - PRIMARY	27.7	42.4	50.0	36.9	47.9	55.2	95.0	105.7	110.0
- SECONDARY	1.9	5.6	6.9	9.1	15.5	20.0	17.3	26.9	51.1
FEMALE ENROLLMENT RATIO (PRIMARY)	21.7	37.4	43.2	22.2	53.8	44.5	88.5	102.0	104.7
ADULT LITERACY RATE (%)	9.8	17.4	18.4	16.0	20.0	21.0	47.7	66.4	72.6
HOUSING									
PERSONS PER ROOM - URBAN	2.7	2.4	1.7	..	..	..	2.5	2.3	..
OCCUPIED DWELLINGS WITHOUT WATER - URBAN	..	..	..	..	..	..	83.7	69.5	60.3
ACCESS TO ELECTRICITY (%) - ALL	..	..	..	..	..	..	22.6	40.7	50.5
- RURAL	..	..	..	..	..	..	12.0	20.1	23.4
CONSUMPTION									
RADIO RECEIVERS (PER 1000 POP.)	5.2	21.2	25.4	6.0	14.3	17.4	34.6	97.5	90.3
PASSENGER CARS (PER 1000 POP.)	2.1	3.4	3.9	0.9	2.2	2.1	2.7	7.0	9.3
ENERGY (KG COAL/YR PER CAPITA)	37.4	73.1	75.0	63.7	89.9	133.3	140.9	382.7	432.9
NEWSPRINT (KG/YR PER CAPITA)	0.2	0.2	0.3	0.5	0.6	0.3	1.1	2.1	2.3

TABLE 3. COMPARATIVE SOCIAL INDICATORS FOR DEVELOPING COUNTRIES (BY GEOGRAPHIC AREA AND COUNTRY)

GLOBAL INDICATORS (MOST RECENT ESTIMATE)

AREA AND COUNTRY	POPULATION & VITAL STATISTICS				EMPLOYMENT AND INCOME			HEALTH & NUTRITION			EDUCATION		
	POP. GROWTH RATE % (65-75)	URBAN POP. % OF TOTAL	CRUDE BIRTH RATE (/000)	CRUDE DEATH RATE (/000)	LABOR IN AGR. % OF TOTAL	INCOME RECD BY HIGHEST 5% HH	INCOME RECD BY LOWEST 20% HH	LIFE EXPECT. YRS AT BIRTH	CALORIE SUPPLY % CAP REQD.	PROTEIN SUPPLY GR/DAY /CAP	PRIMARY SCHOOL ENROLL RATIO %	FEMALE ENROLL. RATIO PRIMARY	ADULT LITERACY RATE % OF TOTAL
EUROPE													
CYPRUS	0.6	42.2	22.2	6.8	34.0	12.1	7.9	71.4	113.0	86.0	71.0	72.0	85.0
GREECE	0.6	64.8	15.4	9.4	34.0	18.7	6.3	71.8	132.0	102.0	106.0	104.0	82.0
MALTA	0.2	94.3	17.5	9.0	6.0	..	..	69.6	114.0	89.0	109.0	109.0	87.0
PORTUGAL	0.3	28.8	19.2	10.5	32.5	56.3	7.3	68.7	118.0	85.0	116.0	94.0	70.0
ROMANIA	1.2	43.0	19.7	9.3	36.0	..	..	69.1	118.0	90.0	109.0	109.0	98.0
SPAIN	1.0	59.1	19.5	8.3	23.0	18.5	6.0	72.1	135.0	94.1	115.0	115.0	94.0
TURKEY	2.6	42.6	39.4	12.5	52.5	28.0	3.5	56.9	113.0	75.7	104.0	94.0	55.0
YUGOSLAVIA	0.9	38.7	18.2	9.2	39.0	25.1	6.6	68.0	137.0	97.5	97.0	93.0	85.0
ALL COUNTRIES - MEDIAN	0.8	42.8	19.4	9.3	34.0	18.6	6.5	69.4	118.0	89.5	107.5	99.0	85.0
LATIN AMERICA & CARIBBEAN													
ARGENTINA	1.4	80.0	21.8	8.8	15.0	21.4	5.6	68.3	129.0	107.1	108.0	109.0	93.0
BAHAMAS	3.6	57.9	22.4	5.7	7.0	20.7	3.4	66.7	100.0	87.0	135.0	..	93.0
BARBADOS	0.4	3.7	21.6	8.9	18.0	19.8	6.8	69.1	133.0	82.5	117.0	116.0	97.0
BOLIVIA	2.7	34.0	44.0	19.1	65.0	36.0	4.0	46.8	77.0	48.5	74.0	65.0	40.0
BRAZIL	2.9	59.1	37.1	8.8	37.8	35.0	3.0	61.4	105.0	62.1	90.0	90.0	64.0
CHILE	1.9	83.0	27.9	9.2	19.0	31.0	4.8	62.6	116.0	78.3	119.0	118.0	90.0
COLOMBIA	2.8	70.0	40.6	8.8	39.0	27.2	5.2	60.9	94.0	47.0	105.0	108.0	81.0
COSTA RICA	2.8	40.6	31.0	5.8	36.4	22.8	5.4	69.1	113.0	60.8	109.0	109.0	89.0
DOMINICAN REPUBLIC	2.9	45.9	45.8	11.0	53.8	26.3	4.3	57.8	98.0	45.4	104.0	105.0	51.0
ECUADOR	3.4	41.6	41.8	9.5	43.5	..	..	59.6	93.0	47.4	102.0	100.0	69.0
EL SALVADOR	3.4	39.4	42.2	11.1	55.0	38.0	2.0	65.0	84.0	50.3	75.2	69.0	63.0
GRENADA	1.0	..	27.4	6.8	30.8	..	..	54.1	89.0	57.0	99.0	..	85.0
GUATEMALA	3.2	37.3	42.8	13.7	56.0	35.0	5.0	67.9	91.0	52.8	62.0	56.0	47.0
GUYANA	2.1	40.0	32.4	5.9	30.9	18.8	4.3	50.0	104.0	58.0	114.0	114.0	85.0
HAITI	1.6	23.1	35.8	16.3	77.0	..	..	50.0	90.0	39.0	70.0	37.0	20.0
HONDURAS	2.7	31.4	49.3	14.6	60.3	28.0	2.5	53.5	90.0	56.0	90.0	88.0	53.0
JAMAICA	1.7	37.1	32.2	7.1	26.9	30.2	2.2	69.5	118.0	68.9	111.0	112.0	86.0
MEXICO	3.5	63.3	42.0	8.6	41.0	27.9	3.4	64.7	117.0	66.9	112.0	109.0	76.0
NICARAGUA	3.6	48.0	48.3	13.9	48.0	42.4	3.1	52.9	105.0	68.4	85.0	87.0	57.0
PANAMA	3.2	49.6	36.2	7.1	30.0	22.2	4.6	66.5	105.0	61.0	124.0	120.0	82.2
PARAGUAY	2.6	37.4	39.8	8.9	49.0	30.0	4.0	61.9	118.0	74.5	106.0	102.0	81.0
PERU	2.9	55.3	41.0	11.9	40.0	28.8	3.1	55.7	100.0	61.7	111.0	106.0	72.0
TRINIDAD & TOBAGO	1.0	25.1	27.3	5.9	13.5	..	..	69.5	114.0	66.0	111.0	111.0	90.0
URUGUAY	0.4	80.6	20.4	9.3	13.2	19.0	4.4	69.8	116.0	98.1	95.0	94.0	94.0
VENEZUELA	3.3	75.7	36.1	7.0	21.0	21.8	3.6	66.4	98.0	63.1	96.0	96.0	82.0
ALL COUNTRIES - MEDIAN	2.7	43.7	36.2	8.9	37.8	27.9	4.0	63.0	104.0	61.7	105.0	105.0	81.0

(CONTINUED)

TABLE 3. Comparative Social Indicators for Developing Countries (By Geographic Area and Country)

Continued

AREA AND COUNTRY	POP. GROWTH RATE % (65-75)	URBAN POP. % OF TOTAL	CRUDE BIRTH RATE (/000)	CRUDE DEATH RATE (/000)	LABOR IN AGR. % OF TOTAL	INCOME REC'D BY HIGHEST 5% HH	INCOME REC'D BY LOWEST 20% HH	LIFE EXPECT. YRS AT BIRTH	CALORIE SUPPLY %/CAP REQD.	PROTEIN SUPPLY GR/DAY /CAP	PRIMARY SCHOOL ENROLL RATIO %	FEMALE ENROLL. RATIO PRIMARY	ADULT LITERACY RATE % OF TOTAL
NORTH AFRICA & MIDDLE EAST													
ALGERIA	3.3	39.9	48.7	15.4	42.8	..	..	53.3	88.0	57.2	77.0	72.0	35.0
BAHRAIN	3.3	78.1	49.6	18.7	..	..	..	44.5	113.0	70.7	72.0	55.0	40.0
EGYPT	2.4	44.6	37.8	14.0	43.9	21.0	5.2	52.4	98.0	56.0	90.0	67.0	50.0
IRAN	2.9	43.0	45.3	15.6	41.0	29.7	4.0	51.0	101.0	60.4	93.0	63.0	26.0
IRAQ	3.3	62.0	48.1	14.6	51.0	35.1	2.1	52.7	..	..	..	..	..
JORDAN	3.4	42.0	47.6	14.7	19.0	..	..	53.2	90.0	65.0	83.0	77.0	62.0
KUWAIT	7.7	88.0	45.4	..	2.0	..	..	64.0	..	..	90.0	86.0	55.0
LEBANON	2.8	60.1	39.8	9.9	17.8	26.0	4.0	63.3	101.0	67.9	132.0	125.0	68.0
LIBYA	4.2	30.5	45.0	14.7	19.5	13.3	10.1	52.9	117.0	62.0	145.0	135.0	27.0
MOROCCO	2.4	40.1	46.2	15.7	50.0	20.0	4.0	53.0	108.0	70.5	61.0	44.0	28.0
OMAN	3.1	5.0	49.6	18.7	48.0	..	..	47.0	..	..	44.0	..	20.0
QATAR	10.5	85.0	..	..	..	..	..	..	..	..	112.0	..	21.0
SAUDI ARABIA	1.9	17.9	50.2	24.4	61.0	..	..	42.0	86.0	56.0	34.0	27.0	15.0
SYRIAN ARAB REP.	3.1	46.2	45.4	15.4	49.9	17.0	5.0	56.0	104.0	66.7	102.0	81.0	40.0
TUNISIA	2.3	47.0	40.0	13.8	37.4	..	..	54.1	102.0	67.4	95.0	75.0	55.0
UNITED ARAB EMIRATES	13.1	80.0	..	..	..	..	..	..	..	..	75.0	..	21.0
YEMEN ARAB REP.	1.7	7.0	49.6	20.6	73.0	..	..	37.0	83.0	58.3	25.0	6.0	10.0
YEMEN PEOP. DEM. REP.	3.1	35.3	49.6	20.6	42.9	..	..	44.8	84.0	57.0	78.0	48.0	27.1
ALL COUNTRIES-MEDIAN	3.1	43.8	46.9	15.6	42.9	21.0	4.0	52.8	101.0	62.0	83.0	70.5	28.0
AFRICA SOUTH OF SAHARA													
BENIN PEOP. REP.	2.7	13.5	49.9	23.0	47.5	31.4	5.5	41.8	87.0	56.0	44.0	28.0	20.0
BOTSWANA	2.1	10.7	45.6	23.0	83.0	28.1	1.6	43.5	85.0	65.0	85.0	93.0	25.0
BURUNDI	2.0	3.7	48.0	24.7	86.0	..	..	39.0	99.0	62.0	23.0	17.0	10.0
CAMEROON	1.9	28.5	40.4	22.0	82.0	..	..	41.0	102.0	59.0	111.0	97.0	6.0
CENTRAL AFRICAN EMPIRE	2.2	35.9	43.4	22.5	91.0	..	..	41.0	102.0	49.0	79.0	53.0	15.0
CHAD	2.0	13.9	44.0	24.0	90.0	21.5	7.7	38.5	75.0	60.2	37.0	20.0	15.0
CONGO PEOP. REP.	2.3	38.0	45.1	20.8	56.0	..	..	43.5	98.0	44.0	153.0	140.0	50.0
EQUATORIAL GUINEA	1.3	11.2	..	..	..	..	..	..	..	..	..	..	..
ETHIOPIA	2.5	32.0	49.4	25.8	85.0	..	..	41.0	82.0	58.9	23.0	14.0	7.0
GABON	1.5	32.0	32.2	22.2	58.0	45.3	3.2	41.0	98.0	49.3	199.0	197.0	12.0
GAMBIA	2.3	14.0	43.3	24.1	79.6	..	..	40.0	98.0	64.0	32.0	21.0	10.0
GHANA	2.6	32.4	48.8	21.9	52.0	..	..	43.5	101.0	53.4	60.0	53.0	25.0
GUINEA	2.8	19.5	44.6	22.9	84.1	..	..	41.0	84.0	42.7	28.0	..	7.0
IVORY COAST	4.1	34.3	45.6	20.6	80.0	30.9	9.0	43.5	113.0	64.5	86.0	64.0	20.0
KENYA	3.4	13.0	48.7	16.0	84.0	20.2	3.9	50.0	91.0	59.6	109.0	101.0	40.0
LESOTHO	2.2	3.1	39.0	19.7	90.0	..	..	46.0	109.0	67.6	121.0	144.0	40.0
LIBERIA	3.3	27.6	43.6	20.7	72.0	61.7	5.3	43.5	87.0	39.0	62.0	44.0	15.0
MADAGASCAR	2.9	14.5	50.2	21.1	83.0	41.0	5.2	43.5	105.0	57.0	85.0	80.0	40.0
MALAWI	2.5	6.4	47.7	23.7	86.0	29.5	5.7	41.0	103.0	68.4	61.0	48.0	25.0
MALI	2.2	13.4	50.1	25.9	88.7	..	..	38.1	75.0	64.0	22.0	16.0	10.0

(CONTINUED)

(By Geographic Area and Country)   Continued

AREA AND COUNTRY	POPULATION & VITAL STATISTICS				EMPLOYMENT AND INCOME			HEALTH & NUTRITION			EDUCATION (MOST RECENT ESTIMATE)		
	POP. GROWTH RATE % (65-75)	URBAN POP. % OF TOTAL	CRUDE BIRTH RATE (/000)	CRUDE DEATH RATE (/000)	LABOR IN AGR. % OF TOTAL	INCOME RECD BY HIGHEST 5% HH	INCOME RECD BY LOWEST 20% HH	LIFE EXPECT. YRS AT BIRTH	CALORIE SUPPLY %/CAP REQD.	PROTEIN SUPPLY GR/DAY /CAP	PRIMARY SCHOOL ENROLL RATIO %	FEMALE ENROLL. RATIO PRIMARY	ADULT LITERACY RATE % OF TOTAL
MAURITANIA	2.6	23.1	44.8	24.9	85.0	..	4.5	38.5	81.0	63.2	17.0	9.0	10.0
MAURITIUS	1.4	48.3	25.1	7.8	30.3	31.0	..	65.5	108.0	55.8	80.0	78.0	80.0
MOZAMBIQUE	2.2	55.0	43.3	21.4	73.0	..	..	41.0	94.0	41.0	46.0	..	..
NIGER	2.7	9.4	52.2	25.5	91.0	23.0	6.0	38.5	78.0	62.1	17.0	12.0	5.0
NIGERIA	2.5	26.0	49.3	22.7	62.0	..	..	41.0	88.0	46.3	49.0	39.0	25.0
RWANDA	2.8	3.8	50.0	23.6	93.0	..	..	41.0	90.0	51.3	58.0	54.0	23.0
SENEGAL	2.7	38.8	47.6	23.9	73.0	36.8	3.2	40.0	97.0	67.1	43.0	33.0	10.0
SIERRA LEONE	2.3	15.0	44.7	20.7	73.0	36.2	1.1	43.5	97.0	50.9	35.0	28.0	15.0
SOMALIA	2.4	28.3	47.2	21.7	77.0	..	..	41.0	79.0	55.1	58.0	41.0	50.0
SUDAN	2.2	13.2	47.8	17.5	66.5	20.9	5.1	48.6	88.0	60.4	40.0	27.0	15.0
SWAZILAND	3.2	14.3	49.0	21.8	83.0	..	..	43.5	89.0	..	103.0	102.0	50.0
TANZANIA	2.8	7.3	47.0	20.1	83.1	33.5	2.3	44.5	86.0	47.1	57.0	46.0	49.0
TOGO	2.7	15.0	50.6	23.3	75.0	..	..	41.0	96.0	52.1	98.0	68.0	12.0
UGANDA	3.1	8.4	45.2	15.9	86.0	20.0	6.2	50.0	90.0	54.0	44.0	43.0	25.0
UPPER VOLTA	2.2	12.1	48.5	25.8	89.0	..	..	38.0	78.0	59.2	14.0	11.0	7.0
ZAIRE	2.7	26.4	45.2	20.5	77.0	..	..	43.5	85.0	32.0	88.0	87.0	15.0
ZAMBIA	2.9	36.3	51.5	20.3	52.0	23.0	3.8	44.5	89.0	58.8	88.0	86.0	43.0
ALL COUNTRIES-MEDIAN	2.5	14.8	47.4	22.1	82.5	30.9	4.5	41.0	90.0	57.0	58.0	47.0	15.0
SOUTH ASIA													
AFGHANISTAN	2.2	14.3	51.4	30.7	52.9	16.7	7.9	40.3	83.0	61.5	23.0	7.0	14.0
BANGLADESH	2.3	8.8	49.5	28.1	78.0	14.6	8.0	45.0	93.0	58.5	73.0	51.0	23.0
BURMA	2.2	22.3	39.5	15.8	67.8	25.0	4.7	50.1	103.0	58.0	85.0	81.0	67.0
INDIA	2.2	20.6	37.0	17.0	69.0	..	..	49.5	89.0	48.0	65.0	52.0	36.0
NEPAL	2.1	4.8	42.9	20.3	94.4	..	..	43.6	95.0	50.0	59.0	10.0	19.2
PAKISTAN	2.9	26.0	47.4	16.5	54.8	17.3	8.4	49.8	93.0	54.0	51.0	31.0	21.0
SRI LANKA	2.0	24.3	28.2	7.9	55.0	18.6	7.3	67.8	97.0	48.0	77.0	77.0	78.1
ALL COUNTRIES-MEDIAN	2.2	20.6	42.9	17.0	67.8	17.3	7.9	49.5	93.0	54.0	65.0	51.0	23.0
EAST ASIA & PACIFIC													
CHINA REP.	2.6	51.1	23.0	4.7	35.0	13.3	8.8	68.6	111.0	68.0	104.0	110.0	82.0
FIJI	2.2	38.5	25.0	4.3	43.3	19.0	5.1	70.0	..	..	111.0	75.0	75.0
INDONESIA	2.3	18.2	42.9	16.9	69.0	33.7	6.8	48.1	98.0	43.8	81.0	75.0	62.0
KOREA	2.1	48.5	28.8	8.9	44.6	18.1	7.2	68.0	115.0	75.7	109.0	109.0	92.0
LAO P.D.R.	2.7	15.0	44.6	22.8	85.0	..	..	40.4	94.0	58.0	57.0	47.0	20.0
MALAYSIA	2.7	30.2	31.7	6.7	45.2	28.3	3.5	59.4	115.0	56.5	93.0	91.0	60.0
PAPUA NEW GUINEA	2.5	12.9	40.6	17.1	83.0	..	..	47.7	98.0	48.2	59.0	44.0	31.0
PHILIPPINES	2.9	29.8	43.8	10.5	52.6	28.8	5.5	58.5	87.0	50.0	105.0	103.0	87.0
SINGAPORE	1.7	90.2	21.2	5.2	2.8	..	..	89.5	122.0	74.7	111.0	108.0	75.0
THAILAND	3.1	16.5	37.6	9.1	76.0	22.0	5.6	58.0	107.0	50.0	78.0	75.0	82.0
VIET NAM	2.6	21.5	36.9	6.7	67.0	..	..	58.0	100.0	52.7	91.0	..	97.8
WESTERN SAMOA	1.9	29.8	36.9	8.9	52.6	22.0	5.6	58.5	103.5	53.6	93.0	91.0	75.0
ALL COUNTRIES-MEDIAN	2.6												

COMPARATIVE ECONOMIC DATA

TABLE 4. Selected Economic Development Indicators: Population and Production
(average annual real growth rates)

Income group/ region/country	Population				Gross domestic product				GDP per capita			
	1950-60	1960-65	1965-70	1970-77	1950-60	1960-65	1965-70	1970-77	1950-60	1960-65	1965-70	1970-77
Developing countries	2.2	2.4	2.5	2.4	4.9	5.6	6.4	5.7	2.7	3.1	3.8	3.2
Capital-surplus oil-exporting countries	2.3	3.2	3.7	4.1	..	..	11.0	6.7	..	..	7.2	3.0
Industrialized countries	1.2	1.2	0.9	0.8	3.8++	5.3	4.9	3.2	2.5++	4.0	4.0	2.4
Centrally planned economies	1.7	1.8	1.6	1.4	..	6.2+	7.7+	6.4+	..	4.8+	6.7+	5.6+
A. Developing countries by income group												
Low income	2.0	2.4	2.4	2.2	3.8	3.8	5.3	4.0	1.8	1.4	2.8	1.7
Middle income	2.4	2.5	2.5	2.5	5.3	6.1	6.6	6.0	2.8	3.5	4.0	3.4
B. Developing countries by region												
Africa south of Sahara	2.3	2.5	2.5	2.7	3.6	5.0	4.9	3.7	1.3	2.4	2.3	0.9
Middle East and North Africa	2.4	2.6	2.7	2.7	5.1	6.4	9.4	7.1	2.6	3.7	6.5	4.3
East Asia and Pacific	2.4	2.6	2.5	2.2	5.2	5.5	8.0	8.0	2.8	2.8	5.4	5.7
South Asia	1.9	2.4	2.4	2.2	3.8	4.3	4.9	3.2	1.8	1.9	2.4	1.0
Latin America and the Caribbean	2.8	2.8	2.7	2.7	5.3	5.2	6.1	6.2	2.4	2.3	3.3	3.4
Southern Europe	1.5	1.4	1.4	1.5	6.1	7.5	6.5	5.3	4.5	6.0	5.0	3.8
C. Developing countries by region and country												
Africa south of Sahara												
Angola	1.6	1.5	1.6	2.3	..	5.9	3.2	-9.4	..	4.3	1.6	-11.5
Benin	2.2	2.5	2.7	2.9	..	3.1	2.7	2.7	..	0.6	0.0	-0.1
Botswana	1.7	1.9	1.9	1.9	2.9	4.2	9.8	15.7	1.2	2.2	7.8	13.5
Burundi	2.0	2.3	2.4	1.9	-1.3	2.8	5.8	2.3	-3.2	0.5	3.3	0.4
Cameroon	1.4	1.7	1.9	2.2	1.7	2.9	7.3	3.4	0.3	1.2	5.3	1.2
Cape Verde	3.1	3.1	2.7	2.1	..	..	..	..	..	..	..	..
Central African Republic	1.4	2.2	1.9	2.2	2.6	0.4	3.5	3.1	1.1	-1.7	1.3	0.9
Chad	1.4	1.8	1.9	2.2	..	0.5	1.6	1.2	..	-1.3	-0.3	-0.9
Comoros	3.0	3.2	3.3	3.8	..	9.5	3.2	-1.5		6.1	-0.1	-5.2
Congo, People's Republic of the	1.6	2.1	2.2	2.5	1.1	2.7	3.4	3.9	-0.5	0.8	1.2	1.4
Equatorial Guinea	1.5	1.7	1.9	2.2	..	13.8	2.0	-3.0	..	11.8	0.1	-5.0
Ethiopia	2.1	2.3	2.4	2.5	3.9	5.1	3.7	2.6	1.7	2.7	1.2	0.1
Gabon	0.2	0.5	0.7	0.9	11.5	3.9	5.3	9.1	11.3	3.3	4.6	8.1

TABLE 4. COMPARATIVE ECONOMIC DATA (Continued)

Income group/ region/country	Population				Gross domestic product				GDP per capita			
	1950-60	1960-65	1965-70	1970-77	1950-60	1960-65	1965-70	1970-77	1950-60	1960-65	1965-70	1970-77
Gambia, The	2.0	3.3	3.2	3.1	1.3	5.2	4.3	8.2	-0.7	1.9	1.1	4.9
Ghana	4.5	2.7	2.1	3.0	4.1	3.3	2.5	0.4	-0.4	0.6	0.4	-2.5
Guinea	2.2	2.7	3.0	3.0	:	3.9	3.0	5.4	:	1.2	0.0	2.4
Guinea-Bissau	0.2	-1.1	-0.2	1.6	:	:	:	:	:	:	:	:
Ivory Coast	2.1	3.7	3.8	6.0	3.6	10.1	7.4	6.5	1.5	6.1	3.5	0.5
Kenya	3.3	3.4	3.5	3.8	4.0	3.6	8.6	4.8	0.7	0.2	4.9	1.0
Lesotho	1.5	1.8	2.2	2.4	4.4	8.7	2.1	8.0	2.8	6.7	-0.1	5.5
Liberia	2.8	3.1	3.2	3.4	10.5	3.1	6.4	2.7	7.4	0.0	3.1	-0.6
Madagascar	1.8	2.1	2.3	2.5	2.3	1.4	4.9	-0.7	0.5	-0.7	2.5	-3.2
Malawi	2.4	2.7	2.9	3.1	:	3.3	4.5	6.3	:	0.6	1.5	3.1
Mali	2.1	2.5	2.4	2.5	3.2	3.2	2.9	4.7	1.0	0.7	0.5	2.1
Mauritania	2.2	2.5	2.6	2.7	:	9.9	4.6	2.2	:	7.2	2.0	-0.5
Mauritius	3.3	2.7	1.9	1.3	0.1	5.4	-0.3	8.2	-3.0	2.7	-2.2	6.8
Mozambique	1.4	2.1	2.3	2.5	3.1	2.3	8.3	-3.7	1.7	0.2	5.9	-6.1
Namibia	:	2.4	2.6	2.8	:	:	:	:	:	:	:	:
Niger	2.3	4.0	2.7	2.8	:	6.6	-0.3	1.2	:	2.5	-2.9	-1.5
Nigeria	2.4	2.5	2.5	2.6	4.1	5.3	4.5	6.0	1.6	2.7	1.9	3.3
Réunion	:	3.3	2.5	1.8	:	:	:	:	:	:	:	:
Rhodesia	4.1	4.2	3.7	3.3	:	3.2	6.1	3.2	:	-0.9	2.4	-0.1
Rwanda	2.3	2.5	2.7	2.9	1.0	-2.9	8.5	5.2	-1.2	-5.3	5.6	2.2
Senegal	2.2	2.4	2.5	2.6	:	3.6	1.3	2.8	:	1.1	-1.2	0.2
Sierra Leone	1.8	2.1	2.3	2.5	3.6	4.3	3.9	1.5	1.8	2.1	1.6	-1.0
Somalia	2.0	2.4	2.5	2.3	12.8	-0.5	3.4	1.2	10.6	-2.8	0.9	-1.1
South Africa	3.0	2.5	2.7	2.7	2.9	6.6	5.9	4.0	-0.1	4.0	3.1	1.2
Sudan	1.9	2.2	2.4	2.6	5.5	1.5	1.3	5.4	3.5	-0.7	-1.0	2.7
Swaziland	2.0	2.3	2.1	2.5	8.4	13.6	6.3	6.2	6.3	11.0	4.1	3.7
Tanzania, United Republic of	2.2	2.6	2.8	3.0	6.0	5.2	5.9	5.2	3.7	2.6	3.1	2.1
Togo	2.2	2.7	2.7	2.6	1.3	8.4	6.7	4.0	-0.9	5.6	3.9	1.4
Uganda	2.8	3.8	3.7	3.0	3.3	5.7	5.9	0.5	0.5	1.8	2.2	-2.4
Upper Volta	1.9	1.6	1.6	1.6	1.6	2.7	3.3	0.5	-0.3	1.0	1.6	-1.0
Zaire	2.3	1.9	2.1	2.7	3.4	3.7	4.3	1.0	1.1	1.7	2.2	-1.7
Zambia	2.4	2.8	2.9	3.0	5.6	5.4	2.8	2.8	3.1	2.6	-0.1	-0.2

See footnotes at end of table.

TABLE 4. COMPARATIVE ECONOMIC DATA (Continued)

Income group/ region/country	Population				Gross domestic product				GDP per capita			
	1950-60	1960-65	1965-70	1970-77	1950-60	1960-65	1965-70	1970-77	1950-60	1960-65	1965-70	1970-77
C. Developing countries by region and country (cont.)												
Middle East and North Africa												
Algeria	2.1	2.0	3.7	3.2	6.5	0.8	8.1	5.4	4.4	-1.2	4.2	2.2
Bahrain	3.5	4.2	2.9	7.1	..	..	..	10.7[d]	..	..	..	3.2[d]
Egypt, Arab Republic of	2.4	2.5	2.1	2.1	3.3	7.6	3.2	6.4	0.9	4.9	1.1	4.2
Iran	2.5	2.7	2.8	3.0	5.9	9.2	12.6	7.4	3.3	0.3	9.5	4.3
Iraq	2.8	3.1	3.2	3.4	9.9	7.7	4.1	8.1[e]	6.9	4.5	0.9	4.7[e]
Jordan	3.2	3.0	3.2	3.3	..	..	..	7.0[f]	..	..	..	3.6[f]
Lebanon	2.6	3.0	2.8	2.5	..	..	..	..	..	..	..	..
Morocco	2.7	2.5	2.9	2.7	2.0	4.2	5.7	6.4	-0.7	1.7	2.8	3.8
Syrian Arab Republic	2.7	3.1	3.3	3.3	..	8.8	5.6	9.6	..	5.4	2.3	6.2
Tunisia	1.8	1.9	2.1	2.0	..	5.2[c]	4.9	8.5	..	3.3[c]	2.8	6.4
Yemen, Arab Republic of	2.0	2.1	1.5	1.9	..	..	..	8.4	..	..	..	6.4
Yemen, People's Democratic Republic of	1.9	1.9	1.9	1.9	..	..	..	6.8[d]	..	..	..	4.8[d]
East Asia and Pacific												
Fiji	3.1	3.3	2.3	1.8	2.8	3.7	7.4	5.0	-0.3	0.3	5.0	3.1
Hong Kong	4.5	3.7	1.3	2.0	9.2	11.7	8.0	8.0	4.5	7.7	6.6	5.9
Indonesia	2.1	2.2	2.2	1.8	4.0	1.6	7.5	8.0	1.9	-0.6	5.2	6.1
Korea, Republic of	2.0	2.6	2.2	2.0	5.1	6.7	10.3	9.9	3.1	4.0	7.9	7.8
Malaysia	2.5	2.9	2.9	2.7	3.6	6.8	5.9	7.8	1.0	3.7	2.9	4.9
Papua New Guinea	1.8	2.3	2.4	2.4	4.8	6.4	5.7	5.0	2.9	4.0	3.3	2.5
Philippines	2.7	3.0	3.1	2.7	6.5	5.2	5.2	6.3	3.6	2.2	2.1	3.5
Singapore	4.8	2.8	2.0	1.6	..	5.5	13.0	8.6	..	2.6	10.7	6.9
Solomon Islands	2.6	2.6	2.6	3.5	10.7	3.7	2.5	5.4	7.9	1.1	-0.1	1.8
Taiwan	3.5	3.0	2.4	2.0	7.6	8.9	9.2	7.7	4.0	5.8	6.7	5.6
Thailand	2.8	3.0	3.1	2.9	5.7	7.4	8.4	7.1	2.8	4.2	5.1	4.0
South Asia												
Afghanistan	1.5	2.2	2.2	2.2	..	1.7	2.3	4.5	..	-0.4	0.2	2.2
Bangladesh	2.4	2.8	3.0	2.5	..	4.6	3.4	2.3	..	1.8	0.4	-0.1

TABLE 4. COMPARATIVE ECONOMIC DATA (Continued)

Income group/region/country	Population				Gross domestic product				GDP per capita			
	1950-60	1960-65	1965-70	1970-77	1950-60	1960-65	1965-70	1970-77	1950-60	1960-65	1965-70	1970-77
Bhutan	..	1.9	2.1	2.3	..	..	..	3.6	..	..	..	1.4
Burma	1.9	2.1	2.2	2.2	6.3	4.4	2.3	3.1	4.3	2.2	0.1	1.0
India	1.9	2.3	2.4	2.1	3.8	4.0	5.0	2.6	1.9	1.7	2.6	0.4
Nepal	1.2	1.9	2.2	2.2	2.4	2.7	2.2	2.6	1.2	0.8	0.0	0.7
Pakistan	2.3	2.7	2.9	3.1	2.4	7.2	6.9	3.8	0.1	4.4	3.8	1.1
Sri Lanka	2.6	2.5	2.3	1.7	3.9	4.0	5.8	2.9	1.3	1.5	3.4	1.2
Latin America and the Carribean												
Argentina	1.9	1.5	1.4	1.3	2.8	3.6	4.5	2.8	0.9	2.0	3.1	1.5
Bahamas	3.6	4.8	4.4	2.7	..	..	..	..	..	..	..	..
Barbados	0.9	0.3	0.3	0.5	5.9	4.5	7.9	2.0	4.9	4.1	7.6	1.4
Belize	3.1	2.8	2.8	0.9	..	..	..	6.0	..	..	..	5.0
Bolivia	2.1	2.5	2.6	2.7	..	5.0	4.8	5.9	..	2.5	2.1	3.1
Brazil	3.1	2.9	2.9	2.9	6.9	4.0	8.0	9.9	3.7	1.1	5.0	6.8
Chile	2.2	2.3	1.9	1.7	4.0	4.9	3.6	0.1	1.8	2.6	1.7	-1.6
Colombia	3.1	3.3	2.8	2.1	4.6	4.7	5.9	5.7	1.5	1.4	2.9	3.6
Costa Rica	3.7	3.7	3.2	2.5	..	5.3	6.9	6.0	..	1.5	3.6	3.3
Dominican Republic	2.9	2.9	2.9	3.0	5.8	4.6	6.6	8.0	2.8	1.6	3.6	4.9
Ecuador	2.9	3.0	3.0	3.0	..	..	5.8	9.2	..	..	2.7	6.0
El Salvador	2.8	3.4	3.5	3.1	4.4	6.7	4.2	5.3	1.5	3.2	0.7	2.1
Guatemala	2.8	2.8	2.9	2.9	3.8	5.5	5.9	6.0	1.0	2.7	2.9	3.0
Guyana	2.8	2.2	2.4	2.0	4.3	1.5	4.0	1.3	1.4	-0.8	1.5	-0.7
Haiti	1.9	1.5	1.6	1.7	..	0.6	0.1	3.8	..	-0.9	-1.5	2.1
Honduras	3.3	3.5	2.8	3.3	3.1	4.9	4.2	3.2	-0.2	1.4	1.4	-0.1
Jamaica	1.5	1.6	1.2	1.7	8.1	3.7	5.1	0.0	6.5	2.1	3.9	-1.7
Mexico	3.2	3.3	3.3	3.3	5.6	7.4	6.8	4.9	2.4	3.9	3.5	1.5
Netherlands Antilles	1.7	1.7	1.4	1.2	..	..	..	..	..	..	..	..
Nicaragua	2.9	3.0	3.0	3.3	5.2	10.4	4.1	5.8	2.2	7.2	1.1	2.4
Panama	2.9	3.1	3.1	3.1	4.9	7.9	7.8	3.5	1.9	4.7	4.8	0.4
Paraguay	2.6	2.6	2.7	2.9	2.7	4.5	4.3	7.0	0.1	1.9	1.6	4.0
Peru	2.6	2.9	2.9	2.8	4.9	7.1	4.3	4.5	2.2	4.1	1.4	1.7
Puerto Rico	0.6	1.6	1.3	2.8	5.3	8.1	7.0	3.6	4.7	6.5	5.6	0.7
Trinidad and Tobago	2.8	3.0	1.1	1.2	..	4.7	3.3	2.2	..	1.8	2.2	1.0
Uruguay	1.4	1.2	1.0	0.2	1.7	0.6	1.9	1.6	0.3	-0.6	1.0	1.3
Venezuela	4.0	3.6	3.3	3.4	8.0	7.4	4.9	5.6	3.8	3.7	1.6	2.2

TABLE 4. COMPARATIVE ECONOMIC DATA (Continued)

Income group/ region/country	Population				Gross domestic product				GDP per capita			
	1950-60	1960-65	1965-70	1970-77	1950-60	1960-65	1965-70	1970-77	1950-60	1960-65	1965-70	1970-77
C. Developing countries by region and country (cont.)												
Southern Europe												
Cyprus	1.5	0.6	0.8	0.7	4.0	3.7	8.1	1.0	2.5	3.0	7.2	0.3
Greece	1.0	0.5	0.6	0.7	6.0	7.7	7.2	4.6	5.0	7.2	6.6	3.9
Israel	5.3	3.9	3.0	2.8	11.3	9.8	8.7	5.0	5.6	5.6	5.5	2.2
Malta	0.5	-0.6	0.5	0.3	3.3	0.3	9.0	11.4	2.7	0.9	8.5	11.1
Portugal	0.7	0.2	-0.2	0.8	4.1	6.4	6.4	4.6	3.4	6.1	6.6	3.7
Spain	0.8	1.0	1.1	1.0	6.2	8.6	6.3	4.7	5.3	7.5	5.1	3.6
Turkey	2.8	2.5	2.5	2.5	6.3	5.3	6.3	7.3	3.4	2.8	3.7	4.6
Yugoslavia	1.2	1.1	0.9	0.9	5.6	6.6	6.2	6.2	4.4	5.4	5.2	5.2
D. Capital-surplus oil-exporting countries												
Kuwait	6.2	11.1	9.6	6.2	..	4.7[h]	5.7	-0.1	..	-5.8	-3.5	-6.0
Libyan Arab Republic	2.7	3.8	4.2	4.1	..	..	..	..	..	..	..	..
Oman	2.0	2.5	2.7	3.2	..	5.7	39.7	6.8	..	3.2	36.0	3.5
Qatar	2.4	7.1	6.9	10.3	..	..	..	..	..	..	..	..
Saudi Arabia	2.0	2.5	2.8	3.0	..	..	9.1	12.7	..	..	6.1	9.4
United Arab Emirates	2.4	9.3	13.7	16.7	..	..	..	12.5[f]	..	..	..	-2.1[f]
E. Industrialized countries												
Australia	2.3	2.0	1.9	1.7	4.7[i]	5.3	6.2	3.3	2.3[i]	3.2	4.2	1.6
Austria	0.2	0.6	0.5	0.2	5.6	4.3	5.1	4.0	5.4	3.7	4.6	3.8
Belgium	0.6	0.7	0.4	0.3	3.1[i]	5.2	4.8	3.7	2.5[i]	4.5	4.4	3.4
Canada	2.7	1.9	1.7	1.2	4.0[j]	5.8	4.8	4.7	1.3[j]	3.8	3.0	3.4
Denmark	0.7	0.8	0.7	0.4	3.6[j]	5.1	4.5	2.8	2.9[j]	4.3	3.7	2.4
Finland	1.0	0.6	0.2	0.4	4.9	5.0	5.1	3.4	3.9	4.4	4.9	3.0
France	0.9	1.3	0.8	0.7	4.8	5.9	5.3	3.8	3.8	4.5	4.5	3.1
Germany, Federal Republic of	1.0	1.3	0.6	0.2	7.3[j]	4.8	4.5	2.4	6.3[j]	3.5	3.9	2.2
Iceland	2.1	1.8	1.2	1.3	..	7.1	1.1	4.6	..	5.2	-0.2	3.2
Ireland	-0.5	0.3	0.5	1.2	..	4.0	5.3	3.4	..	3.7	4.7	2.3
Italy	0.7	0.7	0.7	0.7	5.5[k]	5.0	6.1	2.9	4.8[k]	4.3	5.4	2.2

TABLE 4. COMPARATIVE ECONOMIC DATA (Continued)

Income group/ region/country	Population				Gross domestic product				GDP per capita			
	1950-60	1960-65	1965-70	1970-77	1950-60	1960-65	1965-70	1970-77	1950-60	1960-65	1965-70	1970-77
Japan	1.3	1.0	1.1	1.2	8.0^i	10.1	12.4	5.0	6.6^i	9.0	11.2	3.7
Luxembourg	0.6	1.1	0.4	0.8	..	3.3	3.6	2.3	..	2.2	3.2	1.5
Netherlands, The	1.3	1.4	1.2	0.9	4.7	4.9	5.7	3.2	3.3	3.5	4.4	2.3
New Zealand	2.2	2.1	1.4	1.7	..	5.0	2.6	2.9	..	2.9	1.2	1.2
Norway	0.9	0.8	0.8	0.6	3.4^i	5.1	4.8	4.8	2.5^i	4.3	3.9	4.1
Sweden	0.6	0.7	0.8	0.4	3.4	5.3	3.9	1.7	2.7	4.6	3.1	1.3
Switzerland	1.3	2.1	1.1	0.2	4.6	5.2	4.2	0.2	3.2	3.0	3.1	0.0
United Kingdom	0.4	0.7	0.3	0.1	2.8	3.2	2.5	1.9	2.3	2.4	2.2	1.7
United States	1.7	1.5	1.1	0.8	3.3	4.7	3.2	2.8	1.5	3.2	2.1	1.9
F. Centrally planned economies^k												
Albania	2.8	3.0	2.8	2.5	..	..	..	..	..	..	..	..
Bulgaria	0.8	0.8	0.7	0.6	..	7.0	8.6	7.5	..	6.2	7.8	6.9
China	1.9	2.0	1.8	1.6	..	..	..	..	..	..	..	..
Cuba	2.6	2.1	1.9	1.6	..	..	..	..	..	..	..	..
Czechoslovakia	1.0	0.7	0.3	0.7	..	..	6.6^a	5.2	..	..	6.3^a	4.5
German Democratic Republic	-0.6	-0.3	0.0	-0.2	..	2.7^l	5.5^l	5.1^l	..	5.9	5.5	5.3
Hungary	0.7	0.3	0.4	0.4	..	4.5	6.8	6.2	..	4.2	6.4	5.8
Korea, Democratic People's Republic of	0.8	2.8	2.8	2.6								
Mongolia	2.2	2.8	3.1	3.0								
Poland	1.8	1.3	0.6	1.0	..	6.0	6.0	8.7	..	4.6	5.4	7.8
Romania	1.2	0.7	1.4	0.9	..	8.8	7.7	10.7	..	8.0	6.2	10.1^m
Union of Soviet Socialist Republics	1.8	1.5	1.0	0.9	..	6.6	8.2	6.1	..	5.0	7.1	5.5^m

+ Weighted average of the country growth rates; GDP in US dollars were used as weights; these are not strictly comparable to other group averages.   ++ 1955-60.   a. 1966-70.   b. 1967-70.
differences in national accounting system.   l. Based on NMP index (1960=100) constructed from 1975 constant price series.   m. 1970-76.

TABLE 4. COMPARATIVE ECONOMIC DATA (Continued)

| | Gross production | | | | | | | |
| | Agriculture | | | | Manufacturing | | | |
	1950-60	1960-65	1965-70	1970-77	1950-60	1960-65	1965-70	1970-77
Developing countries	3.9	2.8	3.4	2.7	4.9	7.6	7.5	7.4
Capital-surplus oil-exporting countries	..	..	2.2	4.4	..	..	..	..
Industrialized countries	2.3[+]	2.0	2.2	2.1	6.1[+]	5.9	5.8	2.8
Centrally planned economies	..	..	3.2[+]	2.4[+]	..	8.0[+]	8.3[+]	7.4[+]
A. Developing countries by income group								
Low income	..	1.6	4.1	2.2	..	8.4	3.3	5.2
Middle income	4.5	3.1	3.0	3.0	4.7	7.5	7.9	7.2
B. Developing countries by region								
Africa south of Sahara	4.8	2.6	2.4	1.3	..	8.3	6.6	5.6
Middle East and North Africa	..	1.3	3.6	2.8	..	10.0	6.9	12.1
East Asia and Pacific	4.8	4.6	3.4	4.1	..	4.8	11.9	11.6
South Asia	3.2	1.1	4.7	2.1	6.4	8.8	3.5	4.3
Latin America and the Caribbean	..	3.5	2.8	3.3	4.0	5.6	6.7	5.8
Southern Europe	4.4	3.2	3.2	3.1	8.4	11.4	9.3	6.1
C. Developing countries by region and country								
Africa south of Sahara								
Angola	..	3.2	2.0	-3.4	..	..	..	..
Benin	3.3	1.9	5.2	1.5	..	..	..	..
Botswana	..	2.4	0.4	4.5	..	..	..	..
Burundi	-1.5	1.7	1.7	2.0	..	..	..	..
Cameroon	3.7	7.2	4.4	1.8	..	..	10.7[a]	6.2
Cape Verde	..	..	..	..	..	..	..	..
Central African Republic	..	-1.2	3.3	2.1	..	4.1	8.1	6.0
Chad	..	0.9	-0.3	0.2	..	..	2.0[b]	5.7
Comoros	..	..	..	..	..	..	..	..
Congo, People's Republic of the	..	0.0	2.9	2.8	..	3.4	7.7	2.3
Equatorial Guinea	..	4.8[c]	-3.1	-4.9	..	..	..	..
Ethiopia	4.1	1.8	1.9	-0.1	..	..	..	..
Gabon	..	3.2[c]	1.9	1.3	..	..	..	..

TABLE 4. COMPARATIVE ECONOMIC DATA (Continued)

| | Gross production | | | | | | | |
| | Agriculture | | | | Manufacturing | | | |
	1950-60	1960-55	1965-70	1970-77	1950-60	1960-65	1965-70	1970-77
Gambia, The	0.4	7.1	-0.3	1.7	..	3.1	8.9	4.3
Ghana	7.0	3.5	3.8	-0.4	4.6	10.8	12.5	-1.9
Guinea	2.7	1.9	3.5	0.0	..	..	..	..
Guinea-Bissau	..	..	..	..	..	..	..	..
Ivory Coast	9.3	11.3	3.7	4.5	..	14.2	8.0	7.5
Kenya	4.7	2.9	1.1	3.0	..	..	..	..
Lesotho	..	0.1	1.5	2.0	..	..	..	..
Liberia	2.6	3.0	3.0	2.3	..	..	14.1	5.5
Madagascar	3.9	4.1	1.6	2.7	..	..	..	1.2
Malawi	..	3.8	3.4	3.8	..	..	..	10.6
Mali	1.8	2.3	3.2	2.7	..	..	4.0	9.2
Mauritania	..	3.4	2.2	-3.3	..	..	35.1	2.9
Mauritius	..	3.1	-1.4	2.6	..	..	..	..
Mozambique	..	0.8	4.4	-1.6	..	..	..	..
Namibia	..	..	..	..	..	..	..	..
Niger	5.5	5.2	0.6	0.4	..	14.6	8.8	8.6
Nigeria	5.1	2.1	1.7	1.7	..	11.1	10.4	8.1
Réunion	..	..	..	..	..	..	..	..
Rhodesia	..	2.9	0.0	3.9	5.0	6.2	7.5	3.8
Rwanda	..	-1.6	8.4	3.6	..	..	..	..
Senegal	4.8	4.1	-4.5	5.0	..	0.4	1.2	8.2
Sierra Leone	0.3	4.7	2.2	2.0	..	..	2.7	3.6
Somalia	..	2.7	1.9	0.0	..	..	..	..
South Africa	4.1	1.5	3.9	2.2	5.0	8.4	6.7	3.2
Sudan	-0.4	5.4	6.0	2.3	..	17.1c	..	..
Swaziland	..	4.6	7.0	3.6	..	..	21.9	7.3
Tanzania, United Republic of	6.9	2.9	3.0	1.2	..	..	..	..
Togo	9.3	31.3	1.4	-5.5	..	..	6.7	11.3
Uganda	6.9	1.4	4.2	0.8	..	..	..	..
Upper Volta	-0.2	7.2	2.2	1.6	..	..	3.8b	7.1
Zaire	1.0	-2.2	2.3	1.9	..	..	0.3	1.1
Zambia	..	1.2	1.9	4.7	..	12.1	8.6	1.7

TABLE 4. COMPARATIVE ECONOMIC DATA (Continued)

	Gross production							
	Agriculture				Manufacturing			
	1950-60	1960-65	1965-70	1970-77	1950-60	1960-65	1965-70	1970-77
C. Developing countries by region and country (cont.)								
Middle East and North Africa								
Algeria	-0.5	-2.2	4.1	0.4	..	..	..	..
Bahrain	..	..	1.6	4.0	..	..	..	..
Egypt, Arab Republic of	3.4	3.6	3.5	0.7	8.8	20.0	3.8	6.3
Iran	2.1	2.7	4.1	4.2	..	9.5	13.4	16.0
Iraq	1.5	4.0	4.0	-2.3	..	..	..	..
Jordan	..	20.7	-15.3	-1.6	..	..	..	..
Lebanon	5.0	9.1	0.7	-0.5	..	..	..	..
Morocco	3.0	5.1	4.1	-2.0	5.2	3.3	5.8	6.5
Syrian Arab Republic	2.1	10.8	-1.7	9.8	6.3	9.2	4.8	8.3
Tunisia	4.5	3.6	-0.5	5.6	..	2.9	4.8	5.6
Yemen, Arab Republic of	..	1.2	-4.3	3.1	..	..	..	..
Yemen, People's Democratic Republic of	..	2.6	1.2	3.8	..	..	..	..
East Asia and Pacific								
Fiji	..	11.2c	3.3	-0.4	..	..	5.4	3.0
Hong Kong	..	0.9	-0.3	-10.3	..	12.4	18.6	4.0
Indonesia	2.6	3.9	3.3	3.1	..	1.0	7.9	12.5
Korea, Republic of	5.5	6.3	3.1	4.9	16.4	13.9	25.6	23.5
Malaysia	0.9	5.2	6.4	4.3	..	..	11.5	12.6
Papua New Guinea	..	4.2	2.8	3.1	9.7g	..	..	..
Philippines	3.3	2.8	3.2	5.8	..	6.2	4.4	5.2
Singapore	..	1.4	15.8	1.0	..	7.7	15.8	11.2
Solomon Islands	..	1.4	0.9	1.9	..	..	..	..
Taiwan	4.8	4.8	2.9	3.1	15.4	13.6	21.0	13.3
Thailand	3.8	6.6	3.1	4.7	6.4	10.8	10.2	11.8
South Asia								
Afghanistan	..	1.6	1.0	4.0	..	..	8.0	9.3
Bangladesh	..	3.1	3.1	1.8	..	5.8	7.4	5.7

TABLE 4. COMPARATIVE ECONOMIC DATA (Continued)

	Gross production							
	Agriculture				Manufacturing			
	1950-60	1960-65	1965-70	1970-77	1950-60	1960-65	1965-70	1970-77
Bhutan	2.5	..	..	..	..	..	..	..
Burma	3.2	3.1	3.1	1.6	..	5.6	1.7	4.4
India	..	0.5	4.9	2.1	6.6	9.0	2.8	4.6
Nepal	..	0.9	1.7	1.2	..	..	..	..
Pakistan	..	4.6	5.9	2.6	..	12.1	9.4	2.6
Sri Lanka	2.3	3.6	2.1	2.4	-0.9	6.1	5.6	2.7
Latin America and the Carribean								
Argentina	..	3.0	3.0	3.3	0.4	3.9	6.1	3.0
Bahamas	..	..	..	..	..	..	..	..
Barbados	..	3.6	-2.5	-2.7	..	..	1.6*	6.5
Belize	..	13.7	5.4	2.6	..	..	..	..
Bolivia	4.5	4.1	4.2	4.4	1.3	7.0	3.4	7.1
Brazil	2.9	3.2	2.7	4.4	9.1	3.7	10.4	9.6
Chile	..	2.2	2.5	1.7	5.7	6.7	1.5	-4.4
Colombia	..	2.8	3.6	3.9	6.5	5.7	6.2	6.5
Costa Rica	..	3.4	5.6	3.5	..	9.2	8.0	8.1
Dominican Republic	..	-2.7	5.9	2.0	5.0	1.5	11.4	8.8
Ecuador	..	5.8	3.0	3.5	..	..	7.2	10.6
El Salvador	..	2.9	0.4	3.3	5.7	17.0	5.0	8.3
Guatemala	..	7.8	3.9	3.8	3.9	5.4	2.5	6.1
Guyana	..	-0.7	1.3	1.7	..	1.4	1.7	7.5
Haiti	..	3.5	0.8	0.6	0.3	0.9	0.8	7.0
Honduras	..	4.5	5.3	1.3	7.0	3.0	4.9	5.6
Jamaica	2.9	3.2	-1.3	1.1	..	7.8	3.0	0.6
Mexico	5.4	5.9	2.0	2.1	7.0	9.6	8.4	5.9
Netherlands Antilles	..	1.2	3.1	9.7	..	..	..	..
Nicaragua	1.1	13.0	1.2	5.0	10.7	..	..	..
Panama	..	4.3	6.5	3.5	..	12.6	9.6	1.2
Paraguay	..	4.9	2.4	4.8	..	3.5	5.9	3.1
Peru	3.6	2.4	2.3	0.7	7.3	9.7	6.7	5.8
Puerto Rico	..	..	..	..	..	..	..	..
Trinidad and Tobago	..	2.8	1.4	-0.5	..	..	6.1	-1.1
Uruguay	0.3	2.3	3.1	0.4	3.2	1.0	2.4	2.7
Venezuela	..	5.6	5.7	2.2	13.0	9.5	3.6	5.6

TABLE 4. COMPARATIVE ECONOMIC DATA (Continued)

| | Gross production | | | | | | | |
| | Agriculture | | | | Manufacturing | | | |
	1950-60	1960-65	1965-70	1970-77	1950-60	1960-65	1965-70	1970-77
C. Developing countries by region and country (cont.)								
Southern Europe								
Cyprus	3.8	7.7	5.4	0.8	..	2.5	10.1	1.4
Greece	4.7	6.5	2.4	3.8	7.9	7.9	8.7	7.7
Israel	12.0	8.1	5.8	4.9	11.8	13.6	11.8	6.1
Malta	..	2.7	6.7	0.4	..	..	..	1.2
Portugal	2.1	3.7	1.1	-1.1	6.7	8.7	8.9	7.9
Spain	2.9	2.6	3.3	3.4	8.8	12.6	10.1	7.9
Turkey	4.7	2.9	4.0	3.7	8.6	12.7	11.6	10.1
Yugoslavia	6.2	2.5	3.1	4.6	10.4	11.7	6.1	8.2
D. Capital-surplus oil-exporting countries								
Kuwait	..	..	3.0	1.5	..	..	..	..
Libyan Arab Republic	3.9	7.2	-2.0	11.4	..	..	..	..
Oman	..	..	2.8	2.1	..	..	..	..
Qatar	..	..	..	..	..	..	..	..
Saudi Arabia	..	2.8	2.9	2.8	..	..	11.9	4.0
United Arab Emirates	..	..	..	..	..	..	..	..
E. Industrialized countries								
Australia	3.8	0.5	3.6	1.9	6.3	6.1	4.9	1.3
Austria	4.7	0.7	3.6	1.9	7.5	4.5	6.4	3.3
Belgium	1.3	0.7	4.3	0.9	4.1	6.3	6.0	2.6
Canada	2.5	5.0	-1.2	2.8	3.5	6.3	4.9	3.7
Denmark	1.5	0.8	-1.1	1.2	3.5	6.9	4.6	1.8
Finland	3.4	2.4	1.4	1.4	6.4	6.2	7.5	3.3
France	3.2	2.7	1.6	1.3	6.8	5.5	9.8	2.8
Germany, Federal Republic of	3.3	0.8	3.7	0.4	9.8	5.7	6.5	1.6
Iceland	..	..	..	3.2	..	..	..	..
Ireland	2.2	0.3	3.2	3.9	3.0	6.6	7.1	4.1
Italy	2.2	3.0	2.4	1.0	9.3	6.3	7.3	3.0

TABLE 4. COMPARATIVE ECONOMIC DATA (Continued)

| | Gross production | | | | | | | |
| | Agriculture | | | | Manufacturing | | | |
	1950-60	1960-65	1965-70	1970-77	1950-60	1960-65	1965-70	1970-77
Japan	2.4	3.2	3.3	2.1	18.3	11.5	16.3	2.9
Luxembourg	1.3	0.7	4.5	0.9	4.4	1.8	4.5	0.0
Netherlands, The	2.9	0.1	6.6	3.0	5.9	6.2	7.4	2.1
New Zealand	3.0	3.0	2.2	1.0	..	..	..	..
Norway	0.6	-0.8	0.8	1.6	4.8	5.8	4.2	2.2
Sweden	-0.2	0.3	0.7	2.5	3.0	7.4	4.9	2.0
Switzerland	1.1	-0.9	2.5	1.9	6.0	5.1	5.8	-1.0
United Kingdom	2.7	3.1	1.1	0.8	3.5	3.4	3.0	0.5
United States	1.8	1.7	1.5	3.1	3.4	6.3	3.8	3.3
F. Centrally planned economies								
Albania	..	..	4.2	3.4	..	..	..	..
Bulgaria	..	..	1.5	1.6	..	11.0	11.0	8.4
China	..	..	2.5	3.0	..	..	..	..
Cuba	..	..	4.0	0.0	..	..	..	..
Czechoslovakia	..	..	3.8	2.9	..	4.5	6.8	6.7
German Democratic Republic	..	..	1.2	3.6	..	5.7	6.4	6.3
Hungary	..	..	2.7	3.7	..	7.7	5.9	6.2
Korea, Democratic People's Republic of	..	..	2.1	6.7	..	..	..	..
Mongolia	..	..	-2.0	2.3	..	..	..	..
Poland	..	..	1.6	1.3	..	8.7	8.9	10.7
Romania	..	..	-0.4	6.9	..	..	..	..
Union of Soviet Socialist Republics	..	..	4.1	1.8	..	8.4	8.6	7.2

c. 1961-65. d. 1973-77. e. 1970-75. f. 1972-77. g. 1951-60. h. 1962-65. i. 1952-60. j. 1953-60. k. GDP data are not strictly comparable to those of other countries because of

TABLE 5. GLOBAL PER CAPITA FOOD CONSUMPTION

Income group/ region/country	Total per capita consumption index (1970=100)				Food consumption per capita (calories per day)			
	1960	1965	1970	1977	1960	1966	1970	1977
Developing countries	75.3	84.6	100.0	125.7	2213.7	2144.4	2253.7	2290.2
Capital-surplus oil-exporting countries	..	..	..	..	2063.5	2171.8	2233.4	2718.7
Industrialized countries	70.5	83.7	100.0	121.6	3183.8	3201.1	3317.7	3376.5
Centrally planned economies	..	..	..	..	2265.3	3217.0	3323.2	3434.3
A. Developing countries by income group								
Low income	86.1	88.9	100.0	110.0	2059.3	1915.9	2062.0	2051.2
Middle income	72.8	83.5	100.0	128.6	2397.9	2430.6	2493.0	2583.8
B. Developing countries by region								
Africa south of Sahara	89.9	93.4	100.0	111.4	2276.6	2190.9	2286.1	2235.1
Middle East and North Africa	66.0	77.4	100.0	160.4	2161.5	2293.6	2338.6	2703.9
East Asia and Pacific	73.9	79.9	100.0	138.9	2037.4	2026.4	2169.8	2231.3
South Asia	87.7	90.3	100.0	102.9	2052.9	1896.2	2055.5	2036.1
Latin America and the Caribbean	77.0	85.9	100.0	125.0	2420.0	2487.0	2530.3	2565.3
Southern Europe	60.6	78.1	100.0	131.2	2927.5	2940.3	2978.1	3156.8
C. Developing countries by region and country								
Africa south of Sahara								
Angola	75.3	97.2	100.0	55.8	2008.0	1936.0	2008.0	2133.0
Benin	89.4	98.7	100.0	101.0	2164.8	2189.0	2214.0	2249.0
Botswana	60.6	70.7	100.0	161.1	1970.5	1998.0	2020.0	2186.0
Burundi	81.9	80.4	100.0	107.5	1879.7	2296.0	2293.0	2254.0
Cameroon	75.8	76.5	100.0	112.0	2411.0	2244.0	2411.0	2428.0
Cape Verde	..	..	100.0	..	..	1641.0	1920.0	2366.0
Central African Republic	96.4	87.0	100.0	102.8	2230.0	1969.0	2223.0	2242.0
Chad	108.1	108.6	100.0	93.6	2305.8	2288.0	2130.0	1762.0
Comoros	..	..	..	..	..	2285.0	2245.0	2166.0
Congo, People's Republic of the	108.2	96.7	100.0	120.4	2165.0	2035.0	2165.0	2284.0
Djibouti	..	..	..	72.8	..	..	..	..
Equatorial Guinea	78.6	84.4	100.0	110.0	2060.0	1905.0	1939.0	1754.0
Ethiopia	55.1	91.3	100.0	..	2177.0	2189.0	2207.0	2428.0
Gabon	84.3	77.1	100.0	128.8	2207.4	2227.0	2346.0	2318.0
Gambia, The	94.2	110.6	100.0	89.2	2086.3	2072.0	2239.0	1983.0
Ghana	..	94.8	100.0	98.2	2059.9	2072.0	2070.0	1943.0
Guinea	..	100.9	100.0	..	..	1970.0	2070.0	1943.0
Guinea-Bissau	..	..	100.0	..	..	1958.0	2099.0	2328.0
Ivory Coast	65.8	81.3	100.0	117.8	2077.6	2151.0	2384.0	2573.0

TABLE 5. (continued), Global Per Capita Food Consumption

Kenya	83.2	86.0	100.0	116.2	2316.2	2189.0	2287.0	2095.0
Lesotho	72.8	97.0	100.0	196.4		2102.0	2079.0	2245.0
Liberia	114.7	103.5	100.0	118.3	2179.2	2168.0	2234.0	2404.0
Madagascar			100.0	77.0	2460.0	2402.0	2460.0	2486.0
Malawi	93.3	97.5	100.0	122.2	2188.8	2033.0	2353.0	2237.0
Mali	95.4	96.4	100.0	128.0	2149.3	2079.0	2200.0	2117.0
Mauritania	63.2	109.8	100.0	121.4	1837.1	1934.0	1921.0	1976.0
Mauritius	95.1	108.6	100.0	163.1	2374.2	2311.0	2415.0	2588.0
Mozambique	78.3	80.4	100.0	68.6	1998.9	1963.0	2055.2	1906.0
Namibia							2256.0	2182.0
Niger	103.3	123.6	100.0	89.0	2090.0	2151.0	2090.0	2139.0
Nigeria	101.1	93.5	100.0	133.5	2479.4	2261.0	2327.0	2308.0
Réunion						2403.0	2440.0	2664.0
Rhodesia		93.0	100.0	96.9	2119.6	2420.0	2300.0	2576.0
Rwanda	84.0	70.3	100.0	94.0	2093.0	1967.0	2227.0	2284.0
São Tomé & Principe						2124.0	2195.0	2099.0
Senegal	96.5	111.9	100.0	97.7	2263.0	2282.0	2263.0	2261.0
Seychelles								
Sierra Leone		103.0	100.0	98.2	2207.2	2153.0	2204.0	2150.0
Somalia	112.2	99.7	100.0	93.0	2187.0	2179.0	2187.0	2221.0
South Africa	72.7	85.4	100.0		2994.6	2890.0	2899.0	2920.0
Sudan	116.7	116.9	100.0	136.5	1952.6	1824.0	2189.0	2282.0
Swaziland	37.8	52.3	100.0	142.5	1991.5	1941.0	2087.0	2357.0
Tanzania, United Republic of	78.8	86.6	100.0	123.5	2057.0	2134.0	2116.0	2063.0
Togo	68.9	78.8	100.0	101.5	2212.8	2209.0	2178.0	2069.0
Uganda	85.1	89.5	100.0	96.8	2063.9	2069.0	2274.0	2110.0
Upper Volta		94.5	100.0	90.2	2249.0	2041.0	1992.0	1875.0
Zaire	69.2	88.5	100.0	85.9	1896.1	2227.0	2249.0	2304.0
Zambia	80.6	91.1	100.0	87.3		1941.0	1934.0	2002.0
Middle East and North Africa								
Algeria	110.4	112.9	100.0	172.8	1910.9	1823.0	1878.0	2372.0
Bahrain								
Egypt, Arab Republic of	67.4	85.4	100.0	128.0	2444.8	2628.0	2599.0	2723.0
Iran	50.5	64.3	100.0	174.2	2224.4	2287.0	2325.0	3317.0
Iraq	80.0	108.1	100.0		1958.2	2054.0	2192.0	2134.0
Jordan					2184.2	2260.0	2283.0	2107.0
Lebanon	87.4	95.6	100.0		2200.2	2493.0	2470.0	2495.0
Morocco	87.3	89.6	100.0	125.3	1756.0	2269.0	2479.0	2534.0
Syrian Arab Republic		93.1	100.0	166.6	2407.0	2319.0	2407.0	2684.0
Tunisia		89.0	100.0	158.2	2092.8	1974.0	2103.0	2674.0
Yemen, Arab Republic of					1906.2	2104.0	1887.0	2192.0
Yemen, People's Democratic Republic of					2148.8	2234.0	2202.0	1945.0

TABLE 5. (continued), Global Per Capita Food Consumption

Income group/ region/ country	Total per capita consumption index (1970=100)				Food consumption per capita (calories per day)			
	1960	1965	1970	1977	1960	1966	1970	1977
C. Developing countries by region and country (cont.)								
East Asia and Pacific								
American Samoa	..	..	..	..	..	..	..	..
Brunei	..	..	..	..	..	2271.0	2493.0	2898.0
Fiji	79.2	85.5	100.0	145.8	..	2462.0	2410.0	2629.0
French Polynesia	..	..	..	..	..	2762.0	2820.0	2749.0
Gilbert Islands	..	..	..	..	..	..	..	..
Guam	..	..	..	..	..	..	..	..
Hong Kong	56.0	71.6	100.0	156.6	..	2639.0	2684.0	2883.0
Indonesia	83.4	81.1	100.0	147.2	1989.3	1812.0	1979.0	2117.0
Kampuchea (Cambodia)	105.6	107.3	100.0	..	2019.5	2077.0	2144.0	1914.0
Korea, Republic of	67.0	74.8	100.0	146.7	2124.9	2337.0	2584.0	2785.0
Lao People's Democratic Republic	..	..	..	..	1833.9	2055.0	2131.0	1929.0
Macao	..	..	..	..	..	2161.0	1895.0	2095.0
Malaysia	82.2	94.5	100.0	133.1	2393.9	2356.0	2531.0	2610.0
New Caledonia	..	..	..	..	..	2796.0	2872.0	2599.0
New Hebrides	..	..	..	..	..	2142.0	2272.0	2233.0
Papua New Guinea	..	83.5	100.0	87.5	2039.6	2100.0	2207.0	2288.0
Philippines	87.2	85.7	100.0	115.0	..	1975.0	2083.0	2189.0
Singapore	64.5	64.8	100.0	149.0	..	2496.0	2905.0	3074.0
Solomon Islands	..	..	..	..	..	2184.0	2117.0	2152.0
Taiwan	66.0	80.5	100.0	135.6	1915.9	2084.0	2259.0	2467.0
Thailand	68.8	78.7	100.0	129.4	2072.7	2281.0	2278.0	1929.0
Tonga	..	..	..	..	..	29380.0	29960.0	30900.0
Western Samoa	..	..	..	..	..	2372.0	2359.0	2192.0
South Asia								
Afghanistan	99.7	99.2	100.0	106.7	2115.4	2154.0	1955.0	1896.0
Bangladesh	90.2	98.2	100.0	92.5	..	2008.0	1967.0	1891.0
Bhutan	..	..	..	..	..	2043.0	2065.0	2028.0
Burma	90.9	98.0	100.0	110.8	1866.3	2004.0	2179.0	2199.0
India	89.8	91.4	100.0	103.1	2072.5	1849.0	2033.0	2021.0
Maldives	..	..	..	..	..	1733.0	1785.0	1771.0
Nepal	..	..	..	..	2070.3	2113.0	2101.0	2002.0
Pakistan	68.0	75.0	100.0	101.5	1908.5	1984.0	2243.0	2281.0

TABLE 5. (continued), Global Per Capita Food Consumption

Country								
Sri Lanka	96.0	92.6	100.0	109.4	2190.3	2258.0	2405.0	2055.0
Latin America and the Carribean								
Antigua						2189.0	2140.0	2064.0
Argentina	78.7	90.1	100.0	105.8	3349.5	3184.0	3448.0	3347.0
Bahamas						2418.0	2442.0	2317.0
Barbados[a]	62.0	66.7	100.0	102.9		2691.0	2902.0	3111.0
Belize						2353.0	2519.0	2503.0
Bermuda					1889.6	2976.0	3053.0	2761.0
Bolivia	82.8	94.2	100.0	128.1	2332.8	2001.0	2120.0	2137.0
Brazil[a]	76.0	81.5	100.0	152.6		2461.0	2496.0	2562.0
Chile	78.7	86.8	100.0	90.7[b]	2557.3	2751.0	2677.0	2656.0
Colombia	76.2	84.7	100.0	131.4	2082.1	2181.0	2149.0	2310.0
Costa Rica	79.3	88.4	100.0	118.2	2155.5	2360.0	2420.0	2550.0
Dominica						2085.0	2179.0	2094.0
Dominican Republic	71.7	82.4	100.0	125.7	2017.4	2012.0	1998.0	2104.0
Ecuador		91.2	100.0	150.4	1885.4	1953.0	2079.0	2051.0
El Salvador	86.0	98.2	100.0	116.7	1721.7	1838.0	1823.0	2545.0
French Guiana						2401.0	2617.0	2139.0
Grenada						2131.0	2308.0	2609.0
Guadeloupe						2455.0	2597.0	2156.0
Guatemala	82.0	90.0	100.0	118.5	1980.0	2108.0	2221.0	2502.0
Guyana	85.1	83.5	100.0	112.9	2290.0	2357.0	2313.0	2100.0
Haiti	108.2	113.5	100.0	123.8	1820.0	1951.0	1962.0	2015.0
Honduras	88.1	94.9	100.0	110.3	1993.3	2186.0	2287.0	2660.0
Jamaica	76.8	83.1	100.0	102.6	2097.7	2192.0	2487.0	2672.0
Martinique						2567.0	2589.0	2654.0
Mexico	73.1	84.2	100.0	112.2	2558.6	2638.0	2620.0	2726.0
Netherlands Antilles						2358.0	2471.0	2446.0
Nicaragua	74.5	98.2	100.0	114.5	2167.9	2477.0	2457.0	2341.0
Panama	69.0	86.3	100.0	107.0	2491.9	2346.0	2453.0	2824.0
Paraguay	79.5	92.1	100.0	127.1	2573.6	2608.0	2793.0	2274.0
Peru	66.7	87.1	100.0	116.1	2299.9	2294.0	2320.0	2192.0
Puerto Rico	56.1	75.2	100.0	117.8		2010.0	1951.0	
St. Kitts-Nevis						2012.0	2186.0	2233.0
St. Lucia						2218.0	2332.0	2335.0
St. Vincent						2416.0	2464.0	
Suriname					1994.2			2277.0
Trinidad and Tobago	69.0	82.5	100.0	110.8	2252.0	2517.0	2552.0	2694.0
Uruguay	95.3	88.2	100.0	94.8	3431.7	3141.0	3197.0	3036.0
Venezuela	87.2	92.3	100.0	125.4	2158.4	2280.0	2381.0	2543.0

TABLE 5. (continued), Global Per Capita Food Consumption

Income group/ region/country	Total per capita consumption index (1970=100)				Food consumption per capita (calories per day)			
	1960	1965	1970	1977	1960	1966	1970	1977
C. Developing countries by region and country (cont.)								
Southern Europe								
Cyprus	59.6	69.5	100.0	135.8	2934.0	2703.0	2934.0	3144.0
Gibraltar								
Greece	54.3	74.9	100.0	137.6	3212.1	3051.0	3105.0	3400.8
Israel	55.2	72.4	100.0	115.9	2877.4	2909.0	3063.0	3141.0
Malta	53.6	61.4	100.0	...	3108.0	2982.0	3108.0	3203.0
Portugal	55.8	71.5	100.0	144.9	2990.8	2813.0	3299.0	3397.0
Spain	56.7	79.2	100.0	127.1	2880.9	2886.0	2850.0	3149.0
Turkey	78.5	87.0	100.0	139.5	2792.0	2785.0	2792.0	2907.0
Yugoslavia	59.4	70.5	100.0	141.3	3082.1	3304.0	3303.0	3445.0
D. Capital-surplus oil-exporting countries								
Kuwait	...	111.8	100.0	...	...	...	...	...
Libyan Arab Republic	...	82.8	100.0	...	1731.6	2237.0	2471.0	2985.0
Oman	...	...	...	...	...	...	...	...
Qatar	...	...	...	...	...	...	...	...
Saudi Arabia	...	74.4	100.0	276.7	2157.0	2152.0	2157.0	2624.0
United Arab Emirates	...	...	...	...	...	...	...	...
E. Industrialized countries								
Australia	74.5	85.5	100.0	122.2	3420.0	3287.0	3322.0	3428.0
Austria	71.4	84.9	100.0	151.8	3249.0	3445.0	3445.0	3535.0
Belgium	70.7	82.9	100.0	133.9	3353.0	3420.0	3597.0	3583.0
Canada	73.8	84.7	100.0	133.5	3152.5	3269.0	3341.0	3374.0
Denmark	68.1	83.2	100.0	120.3	3538.2	3473.0	3441.0	3418.0
Finland	63.0	81.3	100.0	124.6	3255.4	3133.0	3141.0	3100.0
France	67.4	82.7	100.0	129.8	3342.5	3351.0	3417.0	3434.0
Germany, Federal Republic of	68.1	83.2	100.0	124.4	3239.8	3234.0	3354.0	3381.0
Iceland	71.2	86.2	100.0	128.3	...	2907.0	3017.0	2926.0
Ireland	71.5	82.0	100.0	118.4	3320.5	3404.0	3505.0	3541.0
Italy	61.8	77.6	100.0	114.1	3075.8	3178.0	3520.0	3428.0

TABLE 5. (continued) , Global Per Capita Food Consumption

Japan	47.5	68.3	100.0	134.0	2596.7	2630.0	2741.0	2949.0
Luxembourg	73.8	87.4	100.0	126.0	3160.0		3380.0	..
Netherlands, The	67.0	82.1	100.0	117.3	3233.2	3234.0	3273.0	3338.0
New Zealand^c	92.6	99.8	100.0	101.5	3600.6	3511.0	3416.0	3345.0
Norway	69.2	82.7	100.0	133.2	3062.5	3147.0	3073.0	3175.0
Sweden	71.4	86.0	100.0	133.0	3250.6	3022.0	3044.0	3221.0
Switzerland	72.9	86.6	100.0	113.4	3652.8	3488.0	3565.0	3485.0
United Kingdom	84.5	92.7	100.0	111.1	3477.7	3403.0	3434.0	3336.0
United States	76.9	87.2	100.0	117.5	3319.4	3349.0	3479.0	3576.0
F. Centrally planned economies								
Albania	55.6	..	..	..	2540.0	2461.0	2540.0	2857.0
Bulgaria	..	73.5	100.0	..	2822.1	3535.0	3475.0	3611.0
China	..	..	..	..	1870.0	..	..	..
Cuba	..	..	..	..	2594.0	2362.0	2594.0	2641.0
Czechoslovakia	63.1	..	100.0	130.1	3234.1	3473.0	3462.0	3459.0
German Democratic Republic	..	73.9	100.0	156.8	2754.1	3332.0	3430.0	3641.0
Hungary	63.5	75.5	100.0	132.9	3202.5	3232.0	3361.0	3521.0
Korea, Democratic People's Republic of	..	..	..	..	2388.5	2288.0	2443.0	2837.0
Mongolia	..	..	..	..	2074.6	2453.0	2293.0	2532.0
Poland	66.8	79.6	100.0	166.3	3558.0	3427.0	3473.0	3658.0
Romania	..	..	..	..	2705.2	3026.0	3036.0	3444.0
Union of Soviet Socialist Republics	..	..	..	..	3103.4	3258.0	3393.0	3460.0

a. Consumption includes changes in stocks.   b. 1976.   c. Consumption includes gross domestic investment.

TABLE 6. GLOBAL INDICATORS OF HEALTH AND NUTRITION

Income group/ region/country	Population per physician			Population per nursing person			Population per hospital bed		
	1960	1970	MRE	1960	1970	MRE	1960	1970	MRE
Developing countries	8043.5	6642.7	4638.3	3657.2	2751.3	1995.5	881.2	812.1	794.8
Capital-surplus oil-exporting countries	9566.0	5402.6	1598.6	1427.6	1875.2	348.6	1003.2	696.7	288.1
Industrialized countries	830.7	737.9	639.4	424.7	287.0	229.8	101.6	91.2	95.2
Centrally planned economies	742.5	586.8	514.1	349.2	239.0	210.7	126.5	115.7	111.6
A. Developing countries by income group									
Low income	28292.2	24702.1	12823.0	6143.6	5262.9	4358.1	1589.6	1489.1	1733.6
Middle income	4095.1	3445.8	2825.5	2671.3	1840.5	1228.8	753.2	655.5	570.5
B. Developing countries by region									
Africa south of Sahara	31435.6	23364.2	17493.5	4496.1	3253.3	2372.2	847.5	727.6	694.0
Middle East and North Africa	5658.5	5130.8	3973.3	..	..	2807.4	655.0	621.2	587.5
East Asia and Pacific	4890.7	4230.3	3508.8	2735.0	2419.3	987.4	1271.4	912.4	772.7
South Asia	12591.2	..	5288.6	1988.3	1426.2	1463.9	2450.1	2133.5	2738.4
Latin America and the Caribbean	2360.7	2229.0	1808.7	1321.8	792.5	677.1	443.2	565.3	571.2
Southern Europe	1000.8	839.4	634.8	..	..	..	201.5	189.6	180.1
C. Developing countries by region and country									
Africa south of Sahara									
Angola	14000.0	8460.0	..	..	1800.0	..	480.0	370.0	..
Benin	47000.0	28920.0	34380.0	..	2910.0	3100.0	710.0	870.0	780.0
Botswana	20870.0[a]	15460.0	9600.0	2380.0[a]	1250.0	1270.0	430.0[a]	370.0	340.0
Burundi	63000.0	59000.0	45430.0	5420.0	7500.0	6240.0	730.0	790.0	760.0
Cameroon	34000.0[a]	25960.0	13980.0	5210.0[a]	2470.0	1890.0	530.0[a]	310.0	380.0
Central African Republic	37000.0	38330.0	29410.0[c]	4300.0	2390.0	5880.0[c]	640.0	460.0	..
Chad	62000.0[a]	62880.0	41160.0[c]	..	5130.0	4820.0[c]	820.0	780.0	1140.0[c]
Comoros	18380.0[a]	12630.0	..	3500.0[a]	2050.0	2020.0[c]	500.0[a]	500.0	..
Congo, People's Republic of the	13000.0[a]	9160.0	7320.0[c]	1460.0[a]	670.0	800.0	220.0[a]	220.0[f]	190.0
Equatorial Guinea	5900.0	..	..	980.0	72250.0	..	200.0	..	..
Ethiopia	91000.0	74550.0	84850.0	..	24040.0	25670.0	3000.0	2980.0	..
Gabon	6120.0[a]	5210.0	4705.0	830.0	610.0	..	160.0	100.0	130.0
Gambia, The	..	18950.0	13120.0	..	1500.0[d]	3930.0[g]	650.0[a,h]	870.0[h,i]	1291.0

TABLE 6. GLOBAL INDICATORS OF HEALTH AND NUTRITION
(Continued)

Ghana	21000.0	12950.0[j]	10200.0	2740.0[a]	1070.0[j]	860.0	1370.0	760.0	600.0
Guinea	48000.0	31090.0	15500.0	3890.0	5000.0	2330.0	1110.0	980.0[h]	
Guinea-Bissau			6750.0		1610.0				760.0
Ivory Coast	25480.0[j]	15320.0	15220.0		2480.0[c]	1710.0[c]		850.0	840.0
Kenya	10000.0	7830.0[j]	8840.0[j]	2320.0[a,j]	1700.0[j]	1070.0[l,m]	830.0[a]	770.0	760.0[n]
Lesotho		26290.0	17800.0	7710.0	3800.0	3780.0	720.0[a]	570.0	560.0
Liberia	12000.0[o]	11590.0	10050.0	5710.0[o]	4590.0	3150.0	730.0	690.0	
Madagascar	8800.0	11390.0	10780.0		3760.0	3760.0	510.0	400.0	410.0
Malawi	35000.0[a]	38250.0	48500.0		16090.0	4570.0	940.0[j]	760.0	
Mali	39000.0[a]	41490.0	32459.0	4990.0[a,c]	3860.0	3040.0	1490.0[a,h]	1390.0[h]	1350.0
Mauritania	30000.0[a]	17210.0	14140.0	7130.0[a,c]	4320.0	3200.0	4140.0[a,h]	2780.0[h]	2580.0
Mauritius	5470.0[a]	4090.0	2550.0	1720.0[a]	800.0	620.0	230.0[a]	280.0	280.0
Mozambique	21000.0	14780.0		4660.0	4780.0			640.0	
Niger	71000.0[a]	58260.0	42970.0	8800.0[a]	7040.0	8220.0	2200.0	1850.0	1200.0
Nigeria	32000.0	20530.0	14810.0	6020.0[j]	4220.0	3210.0	2100.0	2220.0	1170.0
Rhodesia		6370.0						290.0	
Rwanda	144000.0[a]	57900.0	39350.0	11680.0[a]	20230.0	16000.0		790.0	580.0
Senegal	35000.0	16640.0	16450.0	4110.0[o]	2410.0	1880.0	940.0	810.0	730.0
Sierra Leone	26000.0	17110.0		4500.0[a]	3600.0		1880.0	1080.0	
Somalia	30000.0	21140.0	15560.0	5580.0	3690.0	2900.0	630.0	580.0	570.0[a]
South Africa	1900.0[e]	1970.0[e]	1970.0[e]	490.0[a]	560.0	440.0[e]	190.0[a]		150.0[e]
Sudan	31000.0	13660.0	9760.0	2940.0[a]	1940.0	1260.0	1000.0	930.0	960.0
Swaziland	10000.0[a]	8270.0	9200.0	3670.0[a]	1430.0	940.0	490.0[a]	300.0	290.0
Tanzania, United Republic of	21000.0[a]	20677.0	18490.0	8300.0[a,j]	4641.0	3300.0	575.0[a]	684.0	
Togo	35130.0[a]	27940.0	18360.0	4790.0[a]	4170.0	2040.0		660.0[h]	680.0
Uganda	13000.0[j]	9210.0[j]	28330.0	9450.0[j]	8030.0[j]	4410.0	760.0	640.0	640.0
Upper Volta	100000.0	92760.0	61798.0	4090.0[j]	4230.0	4893.0	1810.0[j]	1670.0	1518.0
Zaire	63000.0	30040.0			13230.0			320.0	330.0[e]
Zambia	12860.0	13520.0	10370.0	9950.0[j]	2430.0		350.0[j]	320.0	250.0

See footnotes at end of table.

TABLE 6. GLOBAL INDICATORS OF HEALTH AND NUTRITION (Continued)

Income group/ region/country	Population per physician			Population per nursing person			Population per hospital bed		
	1960	1970	MRE	1960	1970	MRE	1960	1970	MRE
C. Developing countries by region and country (cont.)									
Middle East and North Africa									
Algeria	7930.0^f	7860.0	5590.0	...	2730.0	1560.0	280.0^a	340.0	370.0
Egypt, Arab Republic of	2800.0	1910.0	1190.0^j	2730.0^j	1640.0^j	1150.0^j	480.0	460.0	460.0
Iran	3800.0	3300.0	2570.0	...	3230.0	1910.0	1100.0	790.0	650.0
Iraq	5600.0	3270.0	2530.0	6680.0	5490.0	3010.0	570.0	520.0	480.0
Jordan	5900.0	2680.0	2250.0	1650.0	1050.0	930.0	500.0	960.0	950.0
Lebanon	...	1430.0	...	...	1030.0^g	...	280.0	250.0	...
Morocco	9400.0^a	12650.0	11100.0	...	2820.0	1700.0	680.0^a	660.0	710.0^b,h,n
Syrian Arab Republic	4600.0	3860.0	2510.0	6660.0	4500.0	3810.0	900.0	1010.0	980.0
Tunisia	10000.0	5950.0	4800.0	...	730.0	1070.0	360.0	410.0	410.0
Yemen, Arab Republic of	...	31340.0	18770.0	...	...	7220.0	3300.0	...	2060.0
Yemen, People's Democratic Republic of	...	32380.0	9210.0	...	...	1650.0	...	1980.0	860.0
East Asia and Pacific									
Fiji	2100.0^a	2120.0	2300.0	800.0^a	640.0^g	630.0	270.0	340.0	...
Hong Kong	3100.0^a	1520.0	1350.0^c	3040.0^a	...	1060.0^c	390.0	240.0	240.0
Indonesia	41000.0^a	26830.0	16430.0	...	8010.0	4670.0	1370.0	1670.0	1560.0
Kampuchea (Cambodia)	...	...	...	...	...	...	...	...	...
Korea, Republic of	3000.0	2110.0	1677.0	3220.0^j	2170.0^j	517.0	2510.0	1900.0	1430.0
Lao People's Democratic Republic	38000.0^a	16550.0	21600.0	...	4530.0	2440.0	2400.0^a	1180.0	1020.0
Malaysia	7660.0	4540.0	4347.0^m	1810.0^a	1224.0	1210.0^m	300.0	280.0^v	270.0^v
Papua New Guinea	14390.0^o	11630.0	11990.0	2450.0^o	2370.0	2190.0	170.0^o	150.0^f	...
Phillippines	...	...	3150.0	...	3840.0	4990.0	1180.0	850.0	880.0
Singapore	2400.0	1520.0^j	1340.0	650.0^a	460.0	380.0	300.0	300.0	280.0
Taiwan	2330.0	2870.0	1590.0	3030.0^g	...	3740.0^g	2790.0	2510.0	450.0
Thailand	7800.0	8420.0	8370.0	4900.0	3340.0	1510.0	1340.0^a	890.0	800.0
Viet Nam	...	...	5340.0	...	...	880.0	...	...	290.0
Western Samoa	...	2880.0	2920.0	...	730.0	620.0	...	220.0	240.0
South Asia									
Afghanistan	40000.0^a	14900.0	28290.0^c	32030.0^a	21080.0	35680.0^c	5950.0^a	5240.0	5210.0
Bangladesh	...	7800.0^j	11350.0	...	72030.0^j	53700.0	11000.0^h	8120.0^h	4430.0

TABLE 6. GLOBAL INDICATORS OF HEALTH AND NUTRITION
(Continued)

Burma	9900.0^a	8970.0	5410.0		7540.0	6120.0	1400.0	1170.0	1220.0^n
India	5800.0^a	4890.0	3135.0	9630.0^a	5220.0	6320.0	2590.0^t	2020.0	1231.0
Nepal	72000.0	49770.0	38650.0		68320.0	52770.0^g	8130.0	6750.0	6630.0
Pakistan	11000.0	4310.0	3780.0		8440.0^l	10040.0^l	2070.0	1870.0	2020.0
Sri Lanka	4500.0		6230.0^l	4150.0	2730.0	2240.0	330.0	330.0	330.0
Latin America and the Caribbean									
Argentina	660.0	500.0	530.0		980.0	370.0	160.0	170.0	
Bahamas	1700.0	1230.0	1480.0	280.0	320.0^c			200.0	230.0
Barbados	2800.0^a	1890.0	1468.0	850.0	430.0	394.0	170.0	100.0	116.0
Bolivia	3900.0	2300.0	2120.0		2730.0	3520.0	580.0	510.0	
Brazil	3600.0	1910.0	1650.0		3220.0		275.0	260.0	260.0
Chile	1810.0	2210.0^c	2200.0	650.0		450.0	260.0	270.0	300.0
Colombia	2400.0	2170.0	1820.0	3740.0	2040.0		580.0	510.0	530.0
Costa Rica	2600.0	1630.0	1550.0	1700.0	1690.0	580.0		250.0	260.0
Dominican Republic		2100.0	1870.0^e		3930.0	1330.0^e	400.0	350.0	350.0^h
Ecuador	2600.0	2870.0	1570.0	2280.0	1605.0		520.0^a	430.0	
El Salvador	5400.0	4030.0	3459.0^m		1380.0	1308.0^m	460.0	500.0	
Grenada	4500.0^a	3550.0	3820.0	6400.0^a,g		4360.0	160.0		149.0
Guatemala	4200.0^a	3620.0	2500.0		1260.0			470.0	
Guyana	8100.0	4310.0	3270.0	1730.0^l	1070.0	1030.0	440.0^l	210.0	190.0
Haiti	10600.0	11730.0	11170.0	11880.0	7460.0	4170.0	1790.0	1370.0	1450.0^n
Honduras		3710.0^l	3300.0			1420.0	590.0	570.0	660.0
Jamaica	2800.0	2630.0	3510.0	1990.0^l	1710.0	540.0	250.0^l	240.0	280.0
Mexico	1700.0	1440.0			1570.0		1900.0	930.0	860.0
Nicaragua	2700.0	2060.0^l	1540.0		4880.0	760.0	440.0	410.0	400.0
Panama	2700.0	1550.0	1270.0	3460.0^l	1420.0	1440.0	250.0	288.0	266.0
Paraguay	2300.0	2340.0	1190.0		2310.0	2250.0	430.0	620.0	610.0^a
Peru	2200.0^o	1920.0	1580.0	3820.0^o	3200.0		490.0^a	470.0	500.0
Suriname	2400.0^l	2350.0	2030.0	1470.0^l	990.0^l	860.0	220.0^l	190.0	180.0
Trinidad and Tobago	2550.0^a	2330.0	1960.0		400.0	580.0	190.0^a	230.0	240.0^n
Uruguay	1100.0^a	940.0	700.0		3560.0		180.0	150.0	
Venezuela	1500.0	1080.0	870.0		520.0	420.0	270.0	310.0	340.0

See footnotes at end of table.

TABLE 6. GLOBAL INDICATORS OF HEALTH AND NUTRITION (Continued)

Income group/ region/country	Population per physician			Population per nursing person			Population per hospital bed		
	1960	1970	MRE	1960	1970	MRE	1960	1970	MRE
C. Developing countries by region and country (cont.)									
Southern Europe									
Cyprus	1390.0[a]	1290.0	1100.0	1080.0[a]	610.0	400.0	220.0[a]	190.0	200.0
Greece	790.0[a]	620.0	470.0	2081.0[a]	1530.0	1170.0	170.0	160.0	160.0
Israel	410.0[j]	400.0	350.0[j]	360.0	200.0[j]	:	150.0	170.0	170.0
Malta	:	950.0	790.0	630.0	230.0	140.0	150.0	100.0	:
Portugal	1200.0[a]	1100.0	800.0	1430.0[a]	1000.0	520.0	190.0	170.0	170.0
Spain	820.0[a]	750.0[j]	560.0[j]	1290.0[j]	950.0	900.0[j]	220.0[a]	220.0	190.0
Turkey	3000.0[a]	2250.0	1720.0	:	1880.0	1430.0	590.0[a]	490.0	460.0
Yugoslavia	1400.0[a]	1010.0	790.0	1350.0[a]	410.0	390.0	200.0	170.0	170.0
D. Capital-surplus oil-exporting countries									
Kuwait	760.0[a]	1070.0	850.0	190.0[a]	250.0	280.0	130.0[a,h]	210.0[h]	:
Libyan Arab Republic	5800.0	2650.0	1020.0	2390.0	720.0	290.0	320.0	280.0	240.0
Oman	:	8690.0	4938.0	:	5150.0	1850.0[g]	:	:	640.0
Qatar	1300.0[c]	1400.0[c]	930.0[c]	210.0[c]	390.0[c]	360.0[c]	120.0[h]	130.0[h]	130.0[e,h]
Saudi Arabia	13000.0[c]	8050.0[c]	2220.0[c]	:	:	:	1580.0[h]	1140.0[h]	:
United Arab Emirates	:	:	240.0	:	3010.0	150.0	:	:	:
E. Industrialized countries									
Australia	860.0	:	:	600.0[a]	360.0	270.0	90.0[a]	80.0	80.0[n]
Austria	550.0	540.0	440.0	:	410.0	250.0	90.0[a]	90.0	90.0
Belgium	780.0	650.0	500.0	:	160.0	130.0	130.0	120.0	110.0
Canada	910.0	680.0	580.0	300.0[a]	210.0	170.0	90.0	100.0	110.0
Denmark	810.0	690.0	510.0	270.0[a]	180.0	110.0	110.0[a]	100.0	:
Finland	1600.0	960.0	670.0	220.0[a]	370.0	200.0	100.0[a]	80.0	70.0
France	930.0	750.0	680.0	:	350.0	270.0	110.0	140.0	100.0
Germany, Federal Republic of	690.0	580.0	500.0	450.0[a]	240.0	180.0	100.0[a]	90.0	80.0
Iceland	810.0[a]	710.0	590.0	480.0	:	:	100.0	70.0	70.0
Ireland	950.0	980.0	830.0	180.0	170.0	200.0	70.0[a]	80.0	90.0
Italy	610.0	550.0	490.0	920.0	470.0	330.0	110.0	90.0	90.0

TABLE 6. GLOBAL INDICATORS OF HEALTH AND NUTRITION
(Continued)

Japan	920.0[a]	880.0	850.0	460.0[a]	240.0	290.0	100.0[a]	80.0	100.0
Luxembourg	1000.0[a]	940.0	880.0	:	410.0	280.0	90.0[a]	90.0	90.0
Netherlands, The	900.0	800.0	600.0	:	410.0	300.0	130.0	90.0	:
New Zealand	700.0	870.0	730.0	330.0[a]	180.0	200.0	90.0[c]	100.0	140.0
Norway	840.0	720.0	560.0	:	220.0	120.0	100.0[a]	90.0	70.0
Sweden	1100.0	730.0	580.0	:	200.0	140.0	70.0[a]	70.0	70.0
Switzerland	740.0	700.0	520.0	390.0[a]	300.0	230.0	80.0	90.0	:
United Kingdom	960.0	920.0	670.0	420.0[a]	350.0	180.0	270.0[h]	120.0[h]	110.0[h]
United States	780.0	630.0	600.0	340.0[a]	190.0	150.0	110.0[a]	130.0	150.0
F. Centrally planned economies									
Albania	2800.0[a]	1120.0	:	530.0[a]	520.0[n]	:	196.0	147.0	:
Bulgaria	710.0	540.0	450.0	550.0	340.0	240.0	161.0	129.0	116.0
China	1200.0	:	1110.0	910.0[a]	:	:	:	:	:
Cuba	570.0	480.0	400.0	280.0	200.0	160.0	224.0	213.0	231.0
Czechoslovakia	950.0	630.0	520.0	:	200.0	:	101.0	98.0	99.0
German Democratic Republic	640.0	510.0	440.0	440.0	230.0	200.0	84.0	90.0	92.0
Hungary	:	:	:	290.0[a]	:	:	144.0	123.0	117.0
Korea, Democratic People's Republic of	:	:	:	:	:	:	:	:	:
Mongolia	1010.0	590.0	480.0	660.0[j]	280.0	250.0	114.0	108.0	96.0
Poland	1110.0[j]	660.0	620.0	620.0[a]	320.0	270.0	143.0	131.0	129.0
Romania	780.0[a]	840.0	750.0	:	:	590.0	137.0	120.0	108.0
Union of Soviet Socialist Republics	520.0[a]	420.0	300.0	340.0[a]	230.0	210.0	123.0	91.0	85.0

a. 1962.   b. 1960–65.   c. Government personnel only.   d. 1963–64.   e. 1973.   f. 1967.   g. Includes midwives.   h. Government establishments only.   i. 1966.   j. Registered, not all Malaysia.   w. 1964–65.   x. 1965–70.   y. 1970–75.

TABLE 6. GLOBAL INDICATORS OF HEALTH AND NUTRITION (Continued)

	Access to water (percentage of total population)			Calorie supply per capita (percentage of requirements)			Infant mortality rate (per thousand live births)			Child (1-4 years) mortality rate (per thousand)		
	1960	1970	MRE	1960	1970	MRE	1960	1970	MRE	1960	1970	MRE
Developing countries	..	30.2	42.3	93.0	96.9	99.5	76.3	55.3	47.9	19.7	14.2	11.3
Capital-surplus oil-exporting countries	..	51.4	69.7				..			41.5	28.2	20.3
Industrialized countries	..	..	..	125.9	127.2	128.7	27.5	17.1	12.0	1.3	1.0	0.9
Centrally planned economies	..	..	..		126.7	135.8	47.1	30.6	23.2	2.5	1.1	1.1
A. Developing countries by income group												
Low income	..	13.7	25.8	89.1	91.7	92.5	..	..	..	31.8	24.1	20.6
Middle income	..	46.0	53.5	96.0	100.6	104.9	76.3	55.3	47.9	15.6	10.8	8.0
B. Developing countries by region												
Africa south of Sahara	..	13.2	20.3	89.5	92.4	89.5	..	..	..	35.2	28.3	22.3
Middle East and North Africa	..	39.4	55.4	84.6	91.5	98.7	60.2	50.3	41.2	28.1	20.2	15.5
East Asia and Pacific	..	7.2	21.9	90.9	108.1	103.6	..	..	..	13.1	7.2	4.5
South Asia	..	17.9	31.5	89.3	91.7	93.0	94.6	70.5	57.5	27.9	22.4	19.2
Latin America and the Caribbean	..	53.1	63.4	97.2	100.1	107.0	55.7	37.3	31.5	13.8	9.4	6.6
Southern Europe	..	..	73.3	114.0	120.3	134.2				2.9	1.6	1.3
C. Developing countries by region and country												
Africa south of Sahara												
Angola	..	..	..	81.0	81.0	86.0	..	20.8	..	49.0	41.0	34.0
Benin	..	..	20.0	96.0	97.0	87.0	206.0	..	..	41.0	32.0	27.0
Botswana	..	29.0	45.0	85.0	90.0	85.0	..	97.0	..	36.0	29.0	23.0
Burundi	..	..	..	82.0	99.0	99.0	..	140.0	..	41.0	36.0	28.0
Cameroon	..	..	26.0	96.0	96.0	102.0	167.0[b]	..	..	40.0	32.0	27.0
Central African Republic	..	..	16.0	96.0	96.0	102.0	190.0	..	..	40.0	32.0	27.0
Chad	..	27.0	26.0	94.0	89.0	75.0	190.0[d]	..	..	45.0	36.0	30.0
Comoros	..	..	50.0				..	..	..	32.0	29.0	27.0
Congo, People's Republic of the	..	27.0	38.0	97.0	97.0	98.0	180.0	..	..	40.0	32.0	27.0
Equatorial Guinea	..	..	..				35.7	..	..	..	..	..
Ethiopia	..	6.0	6.0	88.0	92.0	82.0	126.0[a]	119.0	..	43.0	39.0	37.0
Gabon	..	..	..	93.0	95.0	98.0	229.0	..	..	43.0	36.0	30.0
Gambia, The	..	12.0	11.5[e]	94.0	98.0	98.0	..	..	217.0	41.0	35.0	34.0

TABLE 6. GLOBAL INDICATORS OF HEALTH AND NUTRITION
(Continued)

Country												
Ghana	:	35.0	35.0	89.0	99.0	101.0	155.0	115.0	..	36.0	29.0	23.0
Guinea	:	..	10.0	83.0[k]	90.0	84.0	..	..	..	45.0	36.0	30.0
Guinea-Bissau	:	..	..	90.0	..	101.0	..	..	..	51.0	40.0	34.0
Ivory Coast	:	..	19.0	94.0	114.0	115.0	..	..	..	41.0	32.0	27.0
Kenya	:	15.0	17.0	103.0	98.0	91.0	126.0[a]	119.0	..	25.0	18.0	14.0
Lesotho	:	3.0	17.0	92.0	95.0	99.0	..	114.4	114.0	34.0	27.0	21.0
Liberia	:	..	20.0	86.0	84.0	87.0	..	159.0	..	36.0	29.0	23.0
Madagascar	:	11.0	26.0	104.0	108.0	105.0	..	177.0[p]	..	41.0	32.0	27.0
Malawi	:	..	33.0	86.0	103.0	103.0	..	149.0	..	41.0	32.0	27.0
Mali	:	..	9.0	85.0	75.0[n]	75.0	210.0	..	..	41.0	35.0	32.0
Mauritania	:	..	..	85.0	87.0	72.0	186.0[b]	..	..	41.0	35.0	32.0
Mauritius	:	81.0	60.0	103.0	106.0	108.0	69.5	59.0	40.4	11.0	5.7	4.1
Mozambique	:	..	..	83.0	94.0	84.0	..	93.0	..	..	..	..
Niger	:	20.0	27.0	93.0	83.0	78.0	212.0	..	..	41.0	35.0	32.0
Nigeria	:	..	..	91.0[m]	89.0	88.0	..	154.0[p]	..	38.0	33.0	24.0
Rhodesia	:	..	..	96.0	96.0	108.0	..	..	..	..	..	16.0
Rwanda	:	..	35.0	88.0	93.0	90.0	..	127.0	..	41.0	32.0	27.0
Senegal	:	..	37.0	97.0	91.0	97.0	..	..	..	41.0	35.0	32.0
Sierra Leone	:	12.0	..	89.0	100.0	97.0	..	..	..	41.0	32.0	27.0
Somalia	:	15.0	33.0	77.0	80.0	79.0	..	..	..	43.0	36.0	31.0
South Africa	:	..	..	114.0	117.0	118.0	..	92.0	..	17.0	13.0	10.0
Sudan	:	..	46.0	81.0	72.0	88.0	..	132.0[i]	..	46.0	38.0	31.0
Swaziland	:	..	37.0	..	90.0	89.0	..	168.0[i]	156.0	41.0	32.0	27.0
Tanzania, United Republic of	:	13.0	39.0	69.0	88.0	86.0	..	155.0[i]	125.0	32.0	25.0	20.0
Togo	:	17.0	16.0	89.0	94.0	96.0	177.0	..	..	41.0	32.0	27.0
Uganda	:	22.0	35.0	93.0	91.0	90.0	..	120.0	..	30.0	22.0	17.0
Upper Volta	:	..	10.0	85.0	78.0	78.0	263.0	..	..	41.0	35.0	32.0
Zaire	:	11.0	16.0	92.0	92.0	85.0	..	..	..	37.0	31.0	27.0
Zambia	:	37.0	42.0	80.0	84.0	90.0	..	144.0	..	36.0	29.0	23.0

TABLE 6. GLOBAL INDICATORS OF HEALTH AND NUTRITION
(Continued)

	Access to water (percentage of total population)			Calorie supply per capita (percentage of requirements)			Infant mortality rate (per thousand live births)			Child (1-4 years) mortality rate (per thousand)		
	1960	1970	MRE	1960	1970	MRE	1960	1970	MRE	1960	1970	MRE
C. Developing countries by region and country												
Middle East and North Africa												
Algeria	..	..	77.0	73.0	78.0	89.0	..	142.0	..	30.0	21.0	16.0
Egypt, Arab Republic of	..	..	66.0	95.0	106.0	113.0	..	..	108.0	31.0	23.0	18.0
Iran	..	35.0	51.0	82.0	90.0	98.0	..	155.0	..	24.0	18.0	14.0
Iraq	..	51.0	62.0	83.0	95.0	101.0	..	..	92.0	31.0	22.0	17.0
Jordan	..	..	56.0	90.0	92.0	90.0	..	..	..	30.0	22.0	16.0
Lebanon	..	92.0	..	85.0	100.0	101.0[x]	..	86.0	..	14.0	9.0	6.0
Morocco	..	51.0	55.0	90.0	102.0	108.0	..	65.0	..	30.0	22.0	17.0
Syrian Arab Republic	..	71.0	75.0	102.0	98.0	104.0	..	105.0	..	29.0	19.0	14.0
Tunisia	..	49.0	70.0	86.0	93.0	102.0	..	135.0	..	29.0	20.0	15.0
Yemen, Arab Republic of	..	4.0	4.0	82.0	71.0	83.0	..	..	..	55.0	38.0	31.0
Yemen, People's Democratic Republic of	..	..	24.0	84.0	84.0	84.0	..	..	..	54.0	38.0	31.0
East Asia and Pacific												
Fiji	..	37.0	69.0	109.0[q]	..	116.0[u]	..	..	41.0	5.0	2.0	1.0
Hong Kong	..	..	..	108.0	113.0	110.0	42.0	19.2	14.0	3.0	1.1	1.0
Indonesia	..	3.0	12.0	89.0	91.0	98.0	..	126.0	..	31.0	22.0	19.0
Kampuchea (Cambodia)	..	..	..	102.0	97.0	85.0	..	..	..	27.0	23.0	19.0
Korea, Republic of	..	58.0	62.0	85.0	114.0	112.0	120.0	43.0	37.0	13.0	8.0	5.0
Lao People's Democratic Republic	..	..	..	81.0	98.0	93.0	62.0	..	..	29.0	29.0	27.0
Malaysia	..	..	62.0	109.0[v]	112.0[v]	115.0[v]	75.0[t]	40.8	32.0	9.0	5.0	3.0
Papua New Guinea	..	..	20.0	88.0	86.0	98.0	..	106.0	..	32.0	24.0	19.0
Philippines	..	..	39.0	83.0	86.0	87.0	98.0	80.0	65.0	16.0	10.0	7.0
Singapore	..	83.0	100.0	105.0	119.0	122.0	35.0	21.0	12.0	4.0	2.0	1.0
Taiwan	..	..	..	102.0	113.0	119.0	53.0[t]	29.0	25.0	8.0	2.0	1.0
Thailand	..	17.0	22.0	96.0	103.0	107.0	..	86.0[w]	68.0	15.0	9.0	6.0
Viet Nam	..	..	..	..	..	106.0	..	..	62.0	..	..	6.0
Western Samoa	..	17.0	43.0	102.0	..	100.0	..	43.0	40.0	5.0	5.0	2.0
South Asia												
Afghanistan	..	3.0	6.0	86.0	78.0	83.0	..	226.0	..	42.0	33.0	27.0
Bangladesh	..	45.0	53.0	89.0[k]	89.0	93.0	..	153.0	140.0	29.0	25.0	23.0

TABLE 6. GLOBAL INDICATORS OF HEALTH AND NUTRITION
(Continued)

Burma	..	18.0	17.0	90.4	101.0	103.0	..	..	..	25.0	18.0	15.0
India	..	17.0	33.0	95.0	92.0	89.0	..	134.0	..	28.0	22.0	18.0
Nepal	..	2.0	9.0	92.0	94.0	95.0	..	152.0[f]	..	35.0	27.0	23.0
Pakistan	..	21.0	29.0	84.0	94.0	93.0	135.0	..	..	27.0	21.0	17.0
Sri Lanka	..	21.0	20.0	98.0	94.0	91.0	63.0	51.0	47.0[e]	7.0	3.0	2.0
Latin America and the Caribbean												
Argentina	..	56.0	66.0	115.0	129.0	129.0	..	59.0	..	6.0	4.0	3.0
Bahamas	..	65.0	65.0	93.0	95.0	100.0	52.0	35.2	25.0	7.0	6.0	4.0
Barbados	..	98.0	100.0	110.0	94.0	133.0	60.0	46.3	28.0	4.0	4.0	3.0
Bolivia	..	33.0	34.0	69.0	76.0	77.0	..	..	158.0	36.0	27.0	22.0
Brazil	..	56.3	77.1	102.0	104.0	105.0	..	..	..	13.0	10.0	9.0
Chile	..	56.0	83.0	96.0	113.0	117.0	108.0	82.0	61.0	14.0	7.0	5.0
Colombia	..	63.0	64.0	94.0	92.0	94.0	..	..	98.0[c]	17.0	13.0	9.0
Costa Rica	..	74.0	77.0	98.0	110.0	113.0	85.0[i]	70.0	37.6	10.0	4.6	3.0
Dominican Republic	..	37.0	55.0	92.0	88.0	98.0	..	96.0[g]	..	23.0	15.0	10.0
Ecuador	..	34.0	40.0	81.0	91.0	93.0	140.0	118.0	..	23.0	16.0	10.0
El Salvador	..	40.0	53.0	82.0	79.0	84.0	..	108.0	..	24.0	14.0	8.0
Grenada	..	..	38.0	79.0	..	89.0	77.9	34.0	23.5	6.0	5.0	4.0
Guatemala	..	38.0	40.0	86.0	92.0	91.0	..	87.1	77.0	31.0	21.0	15.0
Guyana	..	..	..	101.0	104.0	104.0	..	50.0[n]	..	10.0	5.0	4.0
Haiti	..	..	14.0	81.0	87.0	90.0	..	150.0[c]	..	39.0	29.0	23.0
Honduras	..	34.0	46.0	84.0	99.0	90.0	130.0	117.0	103.0	30.0	20.0	14.0
Jamaica	..	62.0	86.0	91.0	103.0	119.0	63.0	36.0	22.0	7.0	4.0	3.0
Mexico	..	54.0	62.0	107.0	105.0	117.0	78.0	74.0	..	14.0	9.8	6.0
Nicaragua	..	..	70.0	93.0	106.0	106.0	..	122.0[v]	..	30.0	..	17.0
Panama	6.0	70.0	79.0	102.0	116.0	105.0	90.0	53.0	47.0	9.6	6.0	3.0
Paraguay	..	11.0	13.0	112.0	121.0	118.0	..	64.0	..	16.0	10.0	8.0
Peru	..	35.0	47.0	97.0	99.0	100.0	..	122.0	..	28.0	20.0	16.0
Suriname	..	..	..	84.0	103.0	105.0	..	39.0	..	11.0	7.0	5.0
Trinidad and Tobago	..	96.0	..	100.0	97.0	105.0	45.0	34.4	26.9	8.0	5.0	3.0
Uruguay	..	92.0	98.0	115.0	114.0	116.0	..	..	49.0	4.0	3.0	3.0
Venezuela	..	75.0	..	90.0	100.0	98.0	72.0	51.0	..	12.0	5.4	5.0

TABLE 6. GLOBAL INDICATORS OF HEALTH AND NUTRITION (Continued)

	Access to water (percentage of total population)			Calorie supply per capita (percentage of requirements)			Infant mortality rate (per thousand live births)			Child (1-4 years) mortality rate (per thousand)		
	1960	1970	MRE	1960	1970	MRE	1960	1970	MRE	1960	1970	MRE
C. Developing countries by region and country (cont.)												
Southern Europe												
Cyprus	..	95.0	95.0	99.0	116.0	113.0	30.0	29.4	27.0	4.0	3.0	2.0
Greece	..	..	..	120.0	116.0	132.0	40.1	29.6	23.0	2.0	1.0	1.0
Israel	..	..	..	109.0	116.0	122.0	31.0	22.9	22.9	2.1	1.0	1.0
Malta	..	..	65.0	108.0	108.0	124.0	38.3	27.8	18.0	0.9	0.4	0.4
Portugal	..	..	..	107.0	118.0	141.0	77.5	58.0	39.0	7.0	4.0	2.2
Spain	..	..	..	116.0	124.0	135.0	43.7	27.9	11.0	2.0	1.0	1.0
Turkey	..	52.0	75.0	110.0	112.0	113.0	187.0	153.0[f]	118.0	24.0	16.0	10.0
Yugoslavia	..	..	..	115.0	124.0	136.0	88.0	55.5	35.0	4.0	3.0	2.0
D. Capital-surplus oil-exporting countries												
Kuwait	..	51.0	89.0	..	..	..	43.0	40.0	39.0	12.0	5.0	2.0
Libyan Arab Republic	..	58.0	100.0	75.0	108.0	117.0	..	..	..	30.0	22.0	17.0
Oman	..	..	32.0	..	..	..	..	..	..	48.0	37.0	29.0
Qatar	..	95.0	97.0	..	..	..	..	..	..	40.0	35.0	29.0
Saudi Arabia	..	49.0	64.0	86.0	86.0	102.0	..	..	..	48.0	36.0	28.0
United Arab Emirates	..	..	..	..	..	..	..	..	..	40.0	35.0	29.0
E. Industrialized countries												
Australia	..	..	..	122.4[q]	127.0[n]	124.4	20.2	17.9	14.3	1.1	0.9	1.0
Austria	..	..	..	128.0[q]	131.4[n]	131.0	37.5	25.9	17.0	1.3	1.0	0.7
Belgium	..	..	..	127.4[q]	133.4[n]	141.0	31.2	21.1	13.9	1.1	1.0	1.0
Canada	..	..	..	120.0[q]	128.0[n]	127.0	27.3	18.8	14.0	1.1	0.9	0.8
Denmark	..	..	..	127.0[q]	130.0[n]	127.0	21.5	14.2	9.0	1.0	1.0	1.0
Finland	..	..	..	118.0[q]	119.0[n]	118.0	21.0	13.2	12.0	1.0	0.6	0.6
France	..	..	..	133.0[q]	135.0[n]	135.4	27.4	18.2	11.0	1.2	1.0	1.0
Germany, Federal Republic of	..	..	..	122.0[q]	128.4[n]	129.0	33.8	23.6	17.4	1.3	1.0	1.0
Iceland	99.0	..	100.0	117.0[q]	109.0	113.0	16.8	13.0	7.7	1.1	0.6	0.7
Ireland	..	..	..	137.0[q]	136.0	141.0	29.3	19.5	14.6	1.3	1.0	1.0
Italy	..	..	..	120.0[q]	126.0	140.0	43.8	29.5	18.0	2.0	1.0	1.0

TABLE 6. GLOBAL INDICATORS OF HEALTH AND NUTRITION
(Continued)

Japan	:	:	109.0[q]	121.5	121.0	30.7	13.1	9.0	2.5	1.0	0.8
Luxembourg	:	:	127.4[q]	133.4[n]	141.0	31.5	24.6	18.0	1.9	1.1	1.0
Netherlands, The	:	:	120.4[q]	122.0	124.5	17.9	12.7	10.5	1.2	0.8	0.7
New Zealand	:	:	133.0[q]	130.0[n]	135.0	22.8	16.7	16.0	1.3	1.0	1.0
Norway	:	:	116.0[q]	119.9[n]	120.0	18.9	12.7	11.1	1.0	0.9	0.6
Sweden	:	:	118.0[q]	112.0[n]	114.0	16.6	11.0	8.0	1.0	1.0	0.4
Switzerland	:	:	131.0[q]	131.6[n]	128.0	21.1	15.1	10.7	1.3	0.9	0.7
United Kingdom	:	:	135.0[q]	133.0[n]	133.0	22.0	18.4	14.3	1.0	1.0	1.0
United States	:	:	127.0[q]	135.0[n]	133.0	26.0	20.1	15.1	1.1	0.8	0.7
F. Centrally planned economies											
Albania	:	:		98.0	105.0	83.0	:	:	6.0	3.0	2.0
Bulgaria	:	:		132.0	138.0	45.1	27.3	24.0	2.8	1.2	1.0
China	:	:		100.0	99.0	:	:	:	14.0	7.0	4.0
Cuba	:	:		115.0	117.0	35.4	35.9	23.0	8.0	4.0	5.0
Czechoslovakia	:	:		129.0	142.0	23.5	22.0	20.0	1.2	1.0	1.0
German Democratic Republic	:	:		130.0	133.0	38.8	18.5	13.0	1.7	1.0	1.0
Hungary	:	:		121.0	135.0	47.6	35.9	26.0	1.6	1.0	0.8
Korea, Democratic People's Republic of	:	:			113.0	:	:	:	13.0	8.0	5.0
Mongolia	:	:			102.0	:	:	:	14.0	8.0	5.0
Poland	:	:		125.0	134.0	56.8	33.2	23.8	1.7	1.0	0.8
Romania	:	:	105.0	118.0	123.0	75.7	49.4	31.0	3.0	2.4	1.0
Union of Soviet Socialist Republics	:	:		128.0	138.0	35.0	25.0	:	1.0	1.0	1.0

practicing in country.   k. 1961-65.   l. 1963.   m. 1978.   n. 1972.   o. 1984.   p. 1965-66.   q. 1961-63.   r. 1970-73.   s. 1969-74.   t. 1957.   u. 1972-74.   v. West

TABLE 7

**Measures of Health Status by Level of Per Capita
Gross National Product (GNP) in Selected Countries**

Country	Per[1] capita GNP	Crude[2] birth rate	Crude[2] death rate	Infant[3] mortality	Life[2] expectancy
Burundi	60	41.8	24.9	150[4]	39.0
Upper Volta	70	48.5	24.9	180	39.0
Ethiopia	80	49.5	23.8	162	40.0
Indonesia	80	44.8	18.9	125[4]	45.4
Yemen Arab Republic	90	49.5	20.0	160	45.5
Malawi	90	47.7	23.7	148[4]	41.0
Guinea	90	46.6	22.8	240[5]	41.0
Sri Lanka	100	28.6	6.3	50	67.8
Dahomey	100	49.9	23.0	110[4]	41.0
Tanzania	110	50.1	23.4	122[5]*	44.5
India	110	41.1	16.3	139	49.2
Sudan	120	47.8	18.5	130	47.2
Yemen, People's Democratic Republic of	120	50.0	22.7	160	45.3
Uganda	130	46.9	15.7	160[4]	50.0
Pakistan	130	47.6	16.8	130	49.4
Nigeria	140	49.3	22.7	150-175[6]	41.0
Central African Republic	150	43.2	22.5	190	41.0
Mauritania	170	48.8	23.4	187[5]	41.0
Bolivia	190	43.7	18.0	60	46.7
Liberia	210	50.7	22.3	159	43.5
Sierra Leone	210	41.9	20.2	197[5]	43.5
Thailand	210	43.7	10.4	23	58.6
Egypt, Arab Republic of	220	37.8	15.0	120	50.7
Viet-Nam, Republic of	230	41.8	23.6	100	40.5
Philippines	240	43.6	10.5	62	58.4
Senegal	250	47.3	22.2	93[4]	42.0
Ghana	250	48.8	21.9	156[4]	43.5
Congo	270	45.1	20.8	180	43.5
Paraguay	280	42.2	8.6	39	61.5
Syrian Arab Republic	290	46.9	14.4	24[4]	53.8
Honduras	300	49.3	14.6	37[4]	53.5
Ecuador	310	41.8	9.5	87[6]	59.6
Tunisia	320	41.0	13.9	76	54.1
El Salvador	320	42.2	11.1	58	57.8
Ivory Coast	330	45.6	20.6	138[4]	43.5
Turkey	340	39.4	12.7	153	56.4
Algeria	360	49.4	16.6	86[4]	51.5
Iraq	370	49.2	14.8	26	52.6
Colombia	370	40.6	8.8	81	60.9
Zambia	380	51.5	20.3	259[4]	44.5

Table 7 (continued)

Measures of Health Status by Level of Per Capita
Gross National Product (GNP) in Selected Countries (continued)

Country	Per[1] capita GNP	Crude[2] birth rate	Crude[2] death rate	Infant[3] mortality	Life[2] Expectancy
Guatemala	390	42.8	13.7	83	52.9
Malaysia	400	39.0	9.8	38	59.4
Dominican Republic	430	45.8	11.0	49	57.8
China, Republic of	430	26.7	10.2	18[7]	61.6
Iran	450	45.3	15.6	160[6]	51.0
Nicaragua	450	48.3	13.9	45[6]	52.9
Brazil	460	37.1	8.8	110[6]	61.4
Peru	480	41.0	11.9	67	55.7
Albania	480	33.4	6.5	87[4]†	68.6
Cuba	510	28.9	5.9	28	72.3
Costa Rica	590	33.4	5.9	56	68.2
Mexico	700	42.0	8.6	63	63.2
Jamaica	720	33.2	7.1	27	69.5
Portugal	730	18.4	10.1	50	68.0
Yugoslavia	730	18.2	9.2	44	67.5
Romania	740	19.3	10.3	40	67.2
Chile	760	25.9	8.1	71	64.3
Panama	820	36.2	7.1	34	66.5
Bulgaria	820	16.2	9.1	26	71.8
Hong Kong	900	19.4	5.5	17	70.0
Trinidad and Tobago	940	25.3	5.9	35[4]	69.5
Venezuela	1,060	36.1	7.0	52	64.7
Singapore	1,200	21.2	5.1	19	69.5
U.S.S.R.	1,400	17.8	7.9	23	70.4
Japan	2,130	19.2	6.6	12[4]	73.3
Israel	2,190	26.2	6.7	24	70.5
United States	5,160	16.2	9.4	19	71.3

Symbols: * for 1968
        † for 1965

Note:
Crude birth rates and death rates are births and deaths per 1,000 population per year. Infant mortality rate is number of deaths of children under one year of age per 1,000 live births per year. Life expectancy is expected length of life in years at birth.

Sources:
[1]World Bank. *World Bank Atlas,* 1973: "Population, Per Capita Product and Growth Rates," pp. 6-14. Washington: World Bank, 1973.
[2]United Nations projections, 1973. Unpublished data: averages for 1970-75.
[3]World Health Organization. *The Fifth Report on the World Health Situation, 1969-72—Part II: Review by Country and Territory,* "Population and Other Statistics," by country, except where other sources are indicated. Unless otherwise noted, figures are for 1970-72. Geneva: WHO, 1974.
[4]United Nations. *Statistical Yearbook 1972,* Table 21, latest available year. New York: United Nations, 1973.
[5]World Health Organization. *Malaria Control in Countries Where Time-limited Eradication is Impracticable at Present.* Report of a WHO Interregional Conference. WHO Technical Report Series No. 537, Annex 2, Table 2; figures are for 1971. Geneva: WHO, 1974.
[6]World Bank estimates, latest available year.
[7]United Nations. *Demographic Yearbook 1970,* Table 16; figure is for 1969. New York: United Nations, 1971.

TABLE 8

Health Resources in Developing Countries

Country	Population per hospital bed	Percentage of government hospitals in total number of hospitals	Population per physician	Percentage of government-employed physicians in total number of physicians	Population per non-physician primary health workers	Support personnel per physician
Rwanda	769	64	58,000	99	4,910	7.3
Burundi	787	—	59,066	—	11,770	7.5
Mali	1,389	—	41,471	100	43,630	15.9
Upper Volta	1,667	—	92,828	—	88,260	27.7
Bangladesh	8,333	—	8,932	—	87,250	0.1
Somalia	571	—	21,424	—	16,440	7.5
Afghanistan	6,667	94	17,698	100	19,670	1.0
Ethiopia	3,030	67	73,289	—	24,800	10.5
Indonesia	1,724	83	26,367	49	10,230	7.0
Burma	1,190	—	8,976	86	3,940	1.6
Chad	775	92	61,695	—	30,330	13.5
Nepal	6,667	—	50,045	—	11,830	0.8
Malawi	637	50	75,254	47	5,170	4.8
Zaire	318	50	26,184	—	10,460	13.1
Guinea	813	—	51,688	—	4,570	25.4
Niger	2,222	94	58,261	100	68,140	8.5
Sri Lanka	311	—	3,860	—	2,480	1.5
Dahomey	862	—	29,118	81	14,100	10.0
Tanzania	699	53	20,702	53	8,360	4.1
India	1,612	—	4,805	—	11,500	0.6
Haiti	1,369	71	13,481	—	20,200	4.1
Sudan	1,041	—	15,934	86	4,180	8.2
Laos	1,190	61	16,547	6	7,350	3.8
Khmer Republic	917	73	17,529	87	5,280	6.9
Uganda	641	69	9,215	33	5,410	0.9
Pakistan	1,667	—	4,329	—	10,200	0.3
Nigeria	1,851	81	20,525	32	3,830	4.9
Malagasy Republic	352	90	31,645	75	6,310	9.2
Togo	820	—	27,943	100	8,930	7.0
Central African Republic	465	—	36,952	—	3,910	27.8
Kenya	775	58	7,829	—	3,360	5.3
Mauritania	2,778	—	17,206	92	6,000	4.3
Bolivia	490	86	2,301	—	58,010	0.9
Cameroon	480	67	25,938	60	59,550	10.7
Liberia	526	51	13,818	—	5,020	4.8
Sierra Leone	1,041	69	17,148	67	1,630	6.7
Thailand	847	94	8,397	61	1,700	1.6
Egypt, Arab Republic of	463	87	1,913	—	2,130	1.2
Viet-Nam, Republic of	478	74	9,203	—	2,630	2.8
Philippines	855	45	9,097	—	7,880	1.9

TABLE 8   (Continued)

Health Resources in Developing Countries (continued)

Country	Population per hospital bed	Percentage of government hospitals in total number of hospitals	Population per physician	Percentage of government-employed physicians in total number of physicians	Population per non-physician primary health workers	Support personnel per physician
Senegal	730	–	14,715	–	12,990	9.0
Ghana	758	67	12,954	59	2,840	12.8
Jordan	962	68	3,805	34	3,870	2.9
Morocco	690	–	13,244	–	–	–
Congo	171	94	57,368	–	181,670	15.9
Paraguay	625	–	2,326	–	9,950	1.4
Mozambique	636	89	15,520	–	26,740	3.1
Korea, Republic of	1,923	–	2,207	8	3,370	1.4
Syrian Arab Republic	1,010	81	3,757	–	6,700	0.9
Honduras	568	76	3,621	–	21,720	3.6
Ecuador	434	–	2,929	–	58,030	1.9
Rhodesia	395	62	6,375	–	1,580	6.0
Tunisia	410	–	5,874	–	25,000	8.2
Papua New Guinea	152	47	11,635	–	5,280	6.6
El Salvador	526	94	4,039	–	–	4.5
Ivory Coast	676	–	13,918	81	26,140	4.9
Turkey	490	66	2,222	53	3,110	1.2
Algeria	341	–	8,439	–	21,290	3.1
Iraq	775	98	3,348	80	3,430	1.8
Colombia	446	77	2,285	–	2,500	2.1
Angola	362	42	8,463	–	26,070	4.9
Mongolia	108	–	–	–	510	2.3
Zambia	314	55	13,472	–	2,130	5.0
Guatemala	457	91	3,617	–	–	3.1
Malaysia	380	–	4,347	–	1,730	3.7
Dominican Republic	348	64	2,102	41	32,540	0.5
China, Republic of	2,941	–	3,224	–	7,430	0.3
Iran	775	56	3,297	90	7,820	1.5
Nicaragua	410	89	2,065	–	–	2.9
Brazil	262	–	1,963	–	46,570	0.6
Peru	474	84	1,978	–	13,670	2.6
Albania	167	–	1,875	–	1,330	3.5
Cuba	213	–	1,199	–	–	1.7
Saudi Arabia	1,136	–	9,558	–	10,950	2.2
Costa Rica	254	96	1,619	–	–	14.5
Lebanon	260	15	1,435	–	5,940	1.2
Mexico	935	–	1,491	–	–	0.9
Jamaica	244	92	2,659	–	21,950	1.7
Portugal	164	47	1,181	–	6,050	1.1
Yugoslavia	179	–	1,008	–	4,200	3.0

Sources: Derived from World Health Organization. *World Health Statistics Annual—Vol. III: Health Personnel and Hospital Establishments,* Table 1. Geneva: WHO, 1974. World Health Organization. *World Health Statistics Report,* 26(3), Table 2. Geneva: WHO, 1973.

TABLE 9

Health Expenditures in Developing Countries

Country	Source	Health budget as percentage of national budget	Health budget as percentage of GNP	Government health expenditures per capita (US$)
Rwanda	a	8.7	0.8	0.45
Upper Volta[1]	b	4.8	0.7	0.56
Somalia	c	6.7	2.0*	1.40
Ethiopia	a	6.9	0.8	0.67
Burma	a	6.2	1.1	0.85
Malawi	a	6.1	0.8*	0.50
Sri Lanka	b	8.1	3.6*	3.76
Tanzania	c	6.3	1.5*	1.68
India	c	4.9	0.9	0.91
Haiti	c	13.7	0.7*	0.78
Uganda	c	9.6	1.7*	2.24
Togo	c	6.5	1.0*	1.51
Central African Republic	b	8.4	1.9*	2.81
Kenya	a	6.4	1.7	0.14
Bolivia	b	3.6	2.0*	3.74
Cameroon	c	7.8	1.0*	2.02
Liberia	c	7.4	1.4*	2.90
Sierra Leone	c	6.2	0.9*	1.95
Thailand	b	6.0	1.2	2.45
Egypt, Arab Republic of	c	8.4	1.8*	3.91
Viet-Nam, Republic of	b	2.3	0.4*	1.00
Philippines	a	5.4	0.5	1.06
Senegal	b	9.1	1.4*	3.49
Ghana	a	7.3	1.3	3.76
Jordan	b	9.5	2.8	10.10
Congo	b	6.1	1.8*	4.82
Paraguay	b	26.4	2.4	6.77
Mozambique	c	4.9	0.9*	2.47
Korea, Republic of	a	1.4	0.5	1.33
Syrian Arab Republic	a-	2.6	0.7	2.03
Honduras	a	7.6	1.3	3.33
Ecuador	c	2.8	0.3	1.04
El Salvador	b	12.6	1.5	4.40
Turkey	b	21.4	2.6	8.21
Algeria	a	5.3	1.4	4.53
Colombia	a	10.4	0.6*	2.04
Angola	c	5.1	1.1*	3.95
Malaysia	b	6.7	2.5	7.18
Dominican Republic	b	8.6	1.4	7.71
Iran	c	2.5	0.6*	2.60
Brazil	c	1.4	0.2*	0.80
Lebanon	c	3.5	0.6*	3.80
Mexico	c	5.9	0.4*	2.64
Jamaica	c	10.0	2.7*	19.54

TABLE 9 (Continued)

Health Expenditures in Developing Countries (continued)

Country	Source	Health budget as percentage of national budget	Health budget as percentage of GNP	Government health expenditures per capita (US$)
Yugoslavia	a	38.2	10.1*	73.75
Romania	a	5.7	2.5	18.56
South Africa	c	1.8	0.3*	2.61
Panama	b	16.7	2.2	16.70
Trinidad and Tobago	a	7.8	1.8	14.27
Venezuela	b	18.4	4.1*	43.18
U.S.S.R.	c	5.8	3.4*	47.04
Libyan Arab Republic	c	5.8	2.4*	35.00
Japan	c	1.9	0.3*	5.45
United Kingdom	c	9.5	4.3*	105.16

*Calculated by dividing "per capita expenditure" figure in last column by estimates of per capita GNP for 1971, as published in *World Bank Atlas*, 1973.

(1)GNP extrapolated from 1968.

a = World Bank estimates.
b = World Health Organization. *The Fifth Report on the World Health Situation, 1969-72.* Geneva: WHO, 1974.
c = World Health Organization. *World Health Statistics Report*, Vol. 26, No. 11, Table 2. Geneva: WHO, 1973.

TABLE 10

Percentage Distribution of Health Expenditures in Selected Countries, 1961
(By focus of service)

Country	Personal medical services		Public health services (%)	Teaching and research (%)
	Inpatient (%)	Outpatient (%)		
Kenya	– – – – 89 – – – –		8	3
Sri Lanka	50	44	5	2
Tanzania	45	50	4	1
Yugoslavia	43	50	4	3
Czechoslovakia	48	44	2	6
United Kingdom	52	44	2	2
France	41	56	2	2
Sweden	53	42	1	4
United States	38	57	1	5

Source: Winkelstein, Jr., Warren. "Epidemiological Considerations Underlying the Allocation of Health and Disease Care Resources." *International Journal of Epidemiology,* 1(1), (1972): Table 1. London: Oxford University Press. (Data from the Epidemiology Program, School of Public Health, University of California, Berkeley.)

TABLE 11

Analysis of Government Health Expenditures in Selected Countries

Country	Year	Total public expenditures ($ millions)	Percentage for public health or prevention	Percentage for curative care	Percentage for training and research
Sri Lanka	1957–58	34.3	23.3	74.4	2.3
Tanzania	1970–71	19.5	4.9	80.3	4.4
India	1965–66	236.0	37.0	55.5	7.5
Laos[1]	1971–72	2.3	14.3[2]	19.9[3]	44.8
Kenya	1971	27.8	5.2	83.8	11.0
Thailand[1]	1971–72	83.6	28.1[4]	46.6[3]	19.1
Paraguay[1]	1972	10.0	10.5[5]	84.6[3]	–
Tunisia[1]	1971	15.8	–	86.3[3]	–
El Salvador[1]	1971	30.4	3.3[6]	52.9[3]	1.1
Turkey[1]	1972	303.7	16.3[7]	–	13.5
Colombia	1970	203.0	18.7	79.3	2.0
Mongolia[1]	1972	–	–	–	7.2
Chile	1959	63.8	18.3	77.0	4.0
Panama	1967	28.4	30.0	– – – – (70%) – – – –	
Venezuela	1962	–	18.0	76.5	5.5
Israel[1]	1959–60	82.7	4.9	80.3	4.4

[1]Classification of residual categories of expenditure is unknown.
[2]Expenditure for "environmental health services."
[3]Expenditure for government hospitals only.
[4]Expenditure for "control of communicable diseases, laboratory services, environmental health services and occupational health services."
[5]Expenditure for "campaigns against communicable diseases, maternal and child health and vaccinations and laboratory services."
[6]Expenditure for "immunization and vaccination activities, laboratory services and environmental health services."
[7]Expenditure for "mass campaigns against communicable diseases, immunization and vaccination activities, laboratory services and environmental health services."

Sources: Sri Lanka, Chile, Venezuela and Israel: Abel-Smith, Brian. *Paying for Health Services.* WHO Public Health Paper 17, Table 13. Geneva: WHO, 1963. Abel-Smith, Brian. *An International Study of Health Expenditures.* WHO Public Health Paper 32, Tables 12-14. Geneva: WHO, 1967.

India: Government of India. *Health Statistics of India.* Delhi: Publications Division, 1965.

Colombia: World Bank, Dragoslav Avramovic and associates. *Economic Growth of Colombia: Problems and Prospects.* Report of a Bank mission to Colombia in 1970. Baltimore and London: The Johns Hopkins University Press, 1972.

Kenya: Ministry of Health. *Recurrent and Development Budget, 1971-72.* Nairobi: Ministry of Health, 1972.

Panama: U.S. Office of International Health, Department of Health, Education and Welfare. *Syncrisis: The Dynamics of Health. Vol. I, Panama,* Table 45 and pp. 55-65. Washington: U.S. Government Printing Office, 1972.

Tanzania: Segall, Malcolm. "The Politics of Health in Tanzania." *Development and Change,* IV(1), (1972): Table 1.

Laos, Thailand, Paraguay, Tunisia, El Salvador, Turkey and Mongolia: World Health Organization. *The Fifth Report on the World Health Situation, 1969-72—Part II: Review by Country and Territory.* Geneva: WHO, 1974. "Government Health Expenditure," by country.

TABLE 12

**Distribution of Medical Doctors between the Capital
and the Remainder of the Country in Selected Countries, 1968**

	Population/medical doctors		
Country	Nationwide	Capital city	Remainder of country
Haiti	14,700	1,350	33,300
Kenya	10,999	672	25,600
Thailand	7,000	800	25,000
Senegal	19,100	4,270	44,300
Ghana[1]	18,000	4,340	41,360
Tunisia	6,486	2,912	10,056
Colombia[1]	2,220	1,000	6,400
Guatemala	4,860	875	22,600
Iran	3,750	906	6,220
Lebanon	1,470	650	3,000
Jamaica	2,280	840	5,510
Panama	1,850	760	4,400

[1]Major urban centers instead of capital city.

Sources: Panama, Colombia, Guatemala, Haiti: Pan American Health Organization. *Health Conditions in the Americas 1965-1968.* Scientific Publication No. 207, Table 58. Washington, D.C.: PAHO/WHO, 1970.

Jamaica, Senegal, Thailand, Iran: Bryant, John. *Health and the Developing World,* Table 14. Ithaca, New York: Cornell University Press, 1969.

Ghana: Sharpston, M. J. "Uneven Distribution of Medical Care: A Ghanaian Case Study." *Journal of Development Studies,* 8(2), (1972):206-213 and Tables IV-VI.

Tunisia: Le Ministère de la Santé Publique, unpublished data.

Kenya: Wheeler, Mark. "Medical Manpower in Kenya." *East African Medical Journal,* 46(2), (1969):93-101.

Lebanon: Zahlan, A. B. "Migration Patterns of the Graduates of the American University of Beirut." The Committee on the International Migration of Talent, *The International Migration of High-Level Manpower,* p. 293. New York: Praeger Publishers, Inc., 1970.

TABLE 13

**Population per Medical Doctor
in Urban and Rural Areas, in Selected Countries**

		Population /medical doctor		
Country	Year	Nationwide	Urban	Rural
Pakistan	1970	7,400	3,700	24,200
Kenya	1969	12,140	800	50,000
Philippines	1971	3,900	1,500	10,000
Honduras	1968	3,860	1,190	7,140
Colombia	1970	2,160	1,000	6,400
Iran	1967–70	3,752	2,275	10,000
Panama	1969	1,790	930	3,000

Sources: Panama, Honduras, Philippines: United States Office of International Health, Department of Health, Education and Welfare. *Syncrisis: The Dynamics of Health. Vol. I, Panama,* p. 59, Tables 6 and 37a; *Vol. II, Honduras,* p. 11, Tables 1 and 27; *Vol. IV, The Philippines,* pp. 37, 52-53, Tables 14 and 45. Washington: Government Printing Office, 1972.

Pakistan, Iran: Bowers, John Z., and Rosenheim, Lord. *Migration of Medical Manpower,* pp. 26, 91, 96. New York: Josiah Macy Foundation, 1971.

Colombia: World Bank, Dragoslav Avramovic and associates. *Economic Growth of Colombia: Problems and Prospects.* Report of a Bank mission to Colombia in 1970. Baltimore and London: The Johns Hopkins University Press, 1972.

Kenya: Wheeler, Mark. "Medical Manpower in Kenya." *East African Medical Journal,* 46(2), (1969):93-101.

TABLE 14

Indices of Hospital Utilization

Country	Year	Beds	Discharges	Patient days	Average days of stay	Occupancy rate (%)
General Hospitals						
Malawi	1965	1,025	24,528	293,817	12.0	78.5
Morocco*	1965	12,157	267,835	3,469,668	13.0	78.2
Senegal*	1967	2,424	33,944	813,237	24.0	91.9
Tunisia*	1967	6,655	222,813	2,059,619	9.2	84.8
Colombia	1967	34,399	871,911	7,226,563	8.3	57.6
Honduras	1967	3,408	78,488	980,737	12.5	78.8
Jamaica*	1967	3,034	82,565	914,679	12.5	78.8
Jordan	1967	1,980	43,087	293,618	6.8	40.6
Thailand	1967	20,161	790,338	4,606,036	5.8	62.6
Turkey	1967	32,686	895,912	7,235,542	8.1	60.6
Local and Rural Hospitals						
Dahomey*	1965	250	2,143	44,196	20.6	48.4
Malawi	1965	3,620	153,335	1,592,593	10.4	120.5
Morocco*	1965	1,639	30,826	288,255	9.4	48.2
Senegal	1967	591	14,327	132,575	9.3	61.5
Tunisia*	1967	2,317	86,364	602,640	7.0	71.3
Chile	1967	1,500	38,788	329,757	8.5	60.2
Costa Rica	1967	204	6,286	14,862	2.4	20.0
Surinam	1966	225	4,109	31,413	7.6	38.3
Cyprus*	1967	94	610	2,997	4.9	8.7
Laos*	1967	267	3,764	33,630	8.9	34.5

(*)Government hospitals only.
Source: World Health Organization. *World Health Statistics Annual, 1967—Vol. III: Health Personnel and Hospital Establishments,* Tables 4 and 5.2. Geneva: WHO, 1970.

TABLE 15

Utilization of Official Health Services in Selected Countries, 1962

Country	Population (millions)	Hospital admissions	Outpatient attendances at hospitals, health centers and dispensaries (millions)	Average visits per person per year
Jamaica	1.8	68,828	1.1	0.6
Guatemala	3.8	136,154	0.9	0.2
Senegal	3.1	65,673	7.8	2.5
Thailand	28.0	541,000	17.5	0.6
Kenya	9.3	146,740	5.2	0.5
Tanzania	10.0	231,598	26.0	2.6
Uganda	7.2	172,279	9.6	1.4

Source: Fendall, N.R.E. "Primary Medical Care in Developing Countries," *International Journal of Health Services,* Vol. 2(2), (1972): Table 4.

TABLE 16

Percentage of Deliveries Attended by a
Physician or by a Qualified Midwife in Selected Countries

Country	Year	In hospital	At home	In hospital or at home
Sri Lanka	1972	75.0[1]	20.0[1]	95.0[1]
Sudan	1971	–	–	10.0[2]
Malagasy Republic	1971	–	–	71.1[1]
Bolivia	1971	5.5[3]	12.8[3]	18.3[3]
Thailand	1971	19.2[3]	–	–
Viet-Nam, Republic of	1972	80.3[1]	0.7[1]	81.0[1]
Paraguay	1972	–	–	55.4[1]
El Salvador	1972	26.0[1]	–	–
Iraq	1971	6.5[3]	21.7[3]	28.2[3]
Guatemala	1970	–	–	25.0[2]
Dominican Republic	1972	40.2[3]	–	–
Peru	1971	15.2[3]	–	–
Panama	1972	–	–	69.2[1]
Venezuela	1972	61.5[2]	0.0[4]	61.5[2]
Singapore	1972	80.0[1]	8.2[1]	88.2[1]
Poland	1972	–	–	99.9[1]
Libyan Arab Republic	1972	48.8[2]	3.7[2]	52.5[1]
Israel	1972	–	–	98.3[1]
France	1971	97.0[1]	3.0[1]	100.0[1]

Note: Percentage figures which have been calculated from the total number of live births may overestimate the actual percentage by one or two points.

[1] Percentage figure given in the source.
[2] Percentage figure calculated by dividing number of deliveries by total number of live births.
[3] Percentage figure calculated by dividing number of deliveries given in the source by World Bank estimates of total number of live births.
[4] Only 141 deliveries out of 412,435 live births.

Source: World Health Organization. *The Fifth Report on the World Health Situation, 1969-1972—Part II: Review by Country and Territory,* "Population and Other Statistics" and "Specialized Units," by country. Geneva: WHO, 1974.

TABLE 17

Comparative Costs of Medical Education
in Selected Countries, 1965
(US$)

Country	Per medical doctor graduated[1]	Per medical assistant	Per nurse graduated	Per auxiliary nurse	Per health assistant	Per auxiliary sanitarian
Senegal	84,000	–	835	–	–	–
Jamaica	24,000	–	1,385	–	–	–
Guatemala	19,200	–	2,700	–	–	–
Thailand	6,600	–	1,200	–	700	350
Kenya	22–28,000	2,890	3,380	2,167	787	1,680
Pakistan	12,600	–	2,960	–	–	–
Colombia	29,000	–	3,000	1,000	–	–
United States	19,630	–	–	–	–	–

[1] Obtained by dividing total recurrent costs as assignable to medical education by number of students graduating.

Sources: Bryant, John. *Health and the Developing World,* Tables 27 and 43. Ithaca, New York: Cornell University Press, 1969. Fendall, N. R. E. "The Medical Assistant in Africa." *Journal of Tropical Medicine and Hygiene,* 71(4), (April 1968):90.

TABLE 18

Emigration of Medical Doctors to the Developed World

Country	Years	Medical doctors emigrating each year (as percentage of total graduates)	Permanent loss each year (as percentage of total medical doctors)
India	1961–64	18	7
Thailand	1968	67	4
Philippines	1962-67	20	13
Turkey	1964	22	17
Latin America,[1]	1965–68	5	—
comprising:			
Haiti		20	—
Colombia		14	—
Guatemala		8	—
Dominican Republic		16	—
Nicaragua		18	—
Brazil		1	—
Peru		2	—
Mexico		5	—
Jamaica		—	—
Chile		10	—
Argentina		3	—

[1]Some 80% of all Latin American medical doctors are produced by six countries—Argentina, Brazil, Colombia, Cuba, Mexico and Venezuela—and 67% are produced by Argentina, Brazil and Mexico alone.

Source: The Committee on the International Migration of Talent. *The International Migration of High-Level Manpower.* New York: Praeger Publishers, Inc., 1970.

India: Loc. cit. Domrese, Robert J. "The Migration of Talent from India," Table 9.1.

Thailand: Loc. cit. Ruth, Heather Low. "Thailand," p. 111.

Philippines: Loc. cit. Idem. "The Philippines," p. 63.

Turkey: Loc. cit. Franck, Peter Goswyn. "Brain Drain from Turkey," p. 305.

Latin America: Loc. cit. Kidd, Charles V. "Migration of Highly Trained Professionals from Latin America to the United States," Table 16.8.

PART III
RESOURCE
BIBLIOGRAPHY

This bibliography is entirely restricted to publications in English language and covers the literature since 1970. In a bibliography of this nature, it is essential that the material be as contemporary as possible, while at the same time it was thought desirable to provide a balanced weight of materials discussed over the last decade.

With respect to classification of the material, the form listed below seems to be appropriate. This classification is arbitrary, however much cross indexing is required.

A. **Problems, Issues and Trends;**
B. **Analytical Methods;**
C. **Strategies and Policies; and**
D. **Country Studies.**

Only the book section has been classified since the selected periodical articles and specialized publications dealt with specific categories from the above mentioned list of categories.

Many of the annotations in this section have been compiled from the Journal of Economic Literature, World Bank Publications, IMF-IBRD Joint Library Periodicals, Finance and Development, U.N. Documents and Publisher's Book Promotion Pamphlets.

I. BOOKS

DEVELOPMENT (GENERAL)

01   Abraham, M. Francis
A B   PERSPECTIVES ON MODERNIZATION: TOWARD A GENERAL THEORY
      OF THIRD WORLD DEVELOPMENT
      Washington, D.C.:   University Press of America, 1980.

02   Adelman, Irma and Morris, Cynthia Taft
B   ECONOMIC GROWTH AND SOCIAL EQUITY IN DEVELOPING COUNTRIES
      Stanford, Calif.: Stanford University Press, 1973.

      A quantitative investigation of the interactions among
      economic   growth,   political   participation,   and   the
      distribution of income in noncommunist developing nations.
      The study is based on data (presented in the earlier
      study, Society, politics, and economic development) from
      74 countries which is given in the form of 48 qualitative
      measures of the [countries] social, economic, and political
      characteristics, and it includes the use of discriminant
      analysis in an examination of the forces tending to
      increase political participation and the use of a stepwise
      analysis   of   variance   technique   in   analyzing   the
      distribution of income.

03   Albin, Peter S.
A B   PROGRESS WITHOUT POVERTY; SOCIALLY RESPONSIBLE ECONOMIC
      GROWTH
      New York: Basic Books, 1978.

      Examines   the   relationship   among   important   social
      tendencies, growth processes, and growth policies and
      argues for the return of the growth economy, with the
      caveat that social objectives and policy directions be

reformulated to avert ecological disaster and to improve economic welfare. Using a dualistic imbalance framework, explores the style and impact of unbalanced growth in modern industrial capitalism, focusing on educational policy, income distribution, and the control of technology, poverty, and urban decay. Concludes with policy recommendations for a program of social and technical advance that is geared to the intelligent management of a growth economy and the renovation of its distributive mechanisms. An appendix presents a dualistic-imbalance model of modern industrial growth.

04   Alexander, Robert J.
A B C   A NEW DEVELOPMENT STRATEGY
Maryknoll, N.Y.: Orbis Books, 1976.

Focusing on the demand side of the development equation, this monograph concerns itself with an economic development strategy of import substitution where industries are established to manufacture products for which a home market has already been created by imports. Analyzing the effect on development of this assured demand, and exploring the limit to which this strategy can be used, the author, looks in detail at the prerequisites for the use of this method (substantial imports and protection for newly created industries) and discusses the priorities for private and public investment in this phase. Contends that this process provides a basis for developing countries to decide which projects should be undertaken first and which can be postponed until later.

05   Alvarez, Francisco Casanova
A C   NEW HORIZONS FOR THE THIRD WORLD
Washington, D.C.: Public Affairs Press, 1976.

Presents the factors leading to approval of the Charter of Economic Rights and Duties of States by the United Nations General Assembly on 12 December 1974. Shows that the charter, with the main objective of overcoming the injustice prevailing in economic relations between nations and [elimination of] the dependence of Third World countries on industrial nations, owes its origin and adoption to President Luis Echeverria of Mexico. Argues that the developing nations remain essentially colonized and dependent entities of the industrialized world. Concludes that the future world will be less unjust and less ridden with anxiety, more secure and better able to care for its own if we respect the principles of the charter.

06   Anell, Lars and Nygren, Birgitta
A B C   THE DEVELOPING COUNTRIES AND THE WORLD ECONOMIC ORDER
New York: St. Marin's Press, 1980.

Explores the possible form, functioning, and enforcement
of a New International Economic Order (NIEO). Provides
an account of the demands of developing countries for
a better allocation of the world's resources and considers
the early cooperation between developing and developed
countries, particularly resolutions passed at various
U.N. General Assembly sessions. Also analyzes and comments
on the central NIEO demands. Among the possible actions
the authors suggest developing countries could take are:
(1) force industrialized countries to increase the flow
and quality of aid by threatening trade discrimination;
(2) establish a list of honest consultancy firms and
a file of information on technology procurement; and
(3) feel free to steal patents from big corporations
and make use of copyrights without compensation.

07   Angelopoulos, Angelos T.
A C   FOR A NEW POLICY OF INTERNATIONAL DEVELOPMENT
         New York: Praeger, 1977.

08   Angelopoulos, Angelos T.
A C   THE THIRD WORLD AND THE RICH COUNTRIES;
         PROSPECTS FOR THE YEAR 2000
         Translated by N. Constantinidis and C. R. Corner
New York: Praeger, 1972.

An examination and projection of the gap in incomes between
the developed and underdeveloped countries of the world.
The author brings data on and discusses the indicators
of poverty, the population explosion in the developing
world, the main causes of economic backwardness, the
"myth" of development aid, the need for a new international
development strategy, various strategies of development
financing, precipitating factors in the emergence of
the Third World, economic growth and forecasts of world
income in the year 2000, and the possibilities of China
becoming the spokesman for the Third World.

09   Arkhurst, Frederick S., ed.
B C D   AFRICA IN THE SEVENTIES AND EIGHTIES;
         ISSUES IN DEVELOPMENT
         New York and London: Praeger in cooperation with the
         Adlai Stevenson Institute of International Affairs, 1970.

Eleven experts in various fields express their views
in a symposium "Africa in the 1980's" which met in Chicago
in early 1969 under the auspices of the Adlai Stevenson
Institute of International Affairs. The purpose...was
to attempt to draw a portrait of Africa in the 1980's
on the basis of the experience of the past decade and,
also, on the basis of current trends in the area of
politics, economic development, population, agriculture,
trade, education and law - all viewed as composite and
interactive factors in the development process.

10   Arndt, H. W., et al.
A B C   THE WORLD ECONOMIC CRISIS: A COMMONWEALTH PERSPECTIVE
        London: Commonwealth Secretariat, 1980.

        Report of a group of experts from Commonwealth countries
        on obstacles to structural change and sustained economic
        growth, with recommendations for specific measures by
        which developed and developing countries might act to
        reduce or eliminate such constraints. Focuses on the
        implications of the world economic crises - inflation,
        slowdown of economic growth, and staggering disequilibria
        in balance of payments - for the developing countries
        of the Third World. Stresses the need for collective
        action in view of the interdependence of the world economy.

11   Bairoch, Paul
A C D   THE ECONOMIC DEVELOPMENT OF THE THIRD WORLD SINCE 1900
        Translated from the fourth French edition by Cynthia
        Postan
        Berkeley: University of California Press, 1975.

        The author covers a wide range of factors important to
        development, namely population, agriculture, extractive
        industry, manufacturing industry, foreign trade, education,
        urbanization, the labor force and employment, and
        macroeconomic data. Particular attention is devoted
        to the development of agriculture. Comparison is drawn
        between the economic progress of Third World countries
        and developed countries at a similar stage of
        industrialization. Twenty-four countries were selected
        for the analysis, representing 80 percent of the population
        of the Third World. These include seven countries from
        each of Africa, Latin-America, and Asia respectively,
        and three countries from the Middle East.

12   Bairoch, Paul and Levy-Leboyer, Maurice, eds.
A B   DISPARITIES IN ECONOMIC DEVELOPMENT SINCE THE INDUSTRIAL
        REVOLUTION
        New York: St. Martin's Press, 1981.

        Collection of thirty-five previously unpublished essays
        presented at the 7th International Economic History
        Congress in Edinburgh in August 1978. Main theme deals
        with disparities in economic development. Concerns
        differences in income at micro-regional and international
        levels. In four parts: (1) discussing economic
        disparities among nations (two papers on international
        disparities: ten on the Third World and five on the
        developed world); (2) covering regional economic
        disparities (eight essays on northern, western, and central
        Europe; three on France; two on Southern Europe and one
        on the Third World); (3) detailing relations between
        regional and national disparities (two papers); and (4)
        discussing the methodological aspects of measurement
        of economic disparities (two papers).

13   Baldwin, Robert E.
B C   ECONOMIC DEVELOPMENT AND GROWTH
        New York, London, Sydney and Toronto: John Wiley and
        Sons, Inc., 1972.

        This short text seeks to provide "an analysis of economic
        development that in terms of breadth and sophistication
        lies between the usual elementary and advanced approaches
        to the development topic."   It is organized around three
        themes, i.e., what the nature of growth problem is, what
        the main theories of growth and development are, and
        what the main policy issues facing less developed countries
        are.   Therefore, the chapters deal with the characteristics
        of   poverty,   various   classical   development   theories
        relatively more recent contributions to development theory,
        national and sectoral policies for growth, and issues
        in the financing of development.

14   Bauer, P.T.
B C   DISSENT ON DEVELOPMENT.   STUDIES AND DEBATES IN DEVELOPMENT
        ECONOMICS
        Cambridge, Mass.:   Harvard University Press, 1972.

        A collection of previously published articles, essays,
        and book reviews, some of which have been rewritten and
        expanded, dealing with various theoretical and empirical
        issues in economic development.   Part One ("Ideology
        and Experience") examines general problems of concept
        method, analysis, historical experience and policy in
        economic development, such as the vicious circle of
        poverty, the widening gap, central planning, foreign
        aid, Marxism, etc.   Part Two ("Case Studies") features
        five of the author's studies on developing countries,
        particularly Nigeria and India.   Part Three ("Review
        Articles") brings book reviews on such well known books
        as W. Arthur Lewis' The Theory of Economic Growth, Benjamin
        Higgins' Economic Development, Walt W. Rostow's The Stages
        of Economic Growth, Thomas Balogh's The Economics of
        Poverty, and other volumes by Gunnar Myrdal, John Pincus,
        Harry G. Johnson, E.A.G. Robinson, B.K. Madan and Jagdish
        Bhagwati.

15   Bauer, P.T.
A B   EQUALITY, THE THIRD WORLD AND ECONOMIC DELUSION
        Cambridge, Mass.: Harvard University Press, 1981.

        Critique of methods and finding of contemporary economics,
        particularly development economics, arguing that there
        is a hiatus between accepted opinion and evident reality.
        All but four chapters are extended and/or revised versions
        of previously published articles.   In the three parts:
        equality, the West and the Third World, and the state
        of economics.   Criticizes economics and especially
        development economics for disregard of personal qualities

and social and political arrangements as determinants
of economic achievement and for ignoring the role of
external contracts in extending markets. Notes that
the benefits of mathematical economics have been bought
at the cost of an uncritical attitude, which has led
to inappropriate use and in some cases to an emphasis
on form rather than substance.

16   Berry, Leonard and Kates, Robert W., eds.
A C   MAKING THE MOST OF THE LEAST
        New York: Holmes and Meier Publishers, 1979.

The poverty faced by Third World countries today seriously
challenges the stability of the world order. The
contributors look torward the restructuring of the present
economic order by establishing "harmonious linkages"
between the industrialized and nonindustrialized worlds.
A welcome addition to the literature on economic
development.

17   Bhatt, V. V.
A B C   DEVELOPMENT PERSPECTIVES: PROBLEM, STRATEGY AND POLICIES
        Oxford; New York: Sydney and Toronto: Pergamon Press,
        1980.

Discusses the dynamics of the socioeconomic system in
terms of the cumulative and cyclical changes in economic
institutions, ideologies, and technology. Stresses the
importance of: upgrading traditional technology and
adapting modern technology to given situations; the
financial system, since it affects savings and shapes
the pattern of resource allocation; and upgrading of
agricultural organization and technology. Sets forth
as necessary for the development process: the stability
of the international currencey and the international
monetary system, which the author proposes be linked
to prices of primary products; the shaping of the
international monetary-financial-trade system to be
consistent with LDC's development strategy; and viewing
the process of socioeconomic development as an integral
part of nation-building and of building the international
community.

18   Brown, Lester R.
A C   THE GLOBAL ECONOMIC PROSPECT: NEW SOURCES OF ECONOMIC
        STRESS
        Worldwatch Paper no. 20
        Washington, D.C.: Worldwatch Institute; New York, 1978.

Considers the relationship between the expanding global
economy and the earth's natural systems. Discusses the
increase in fuel costs, suggesting that the world is
running out of cheap energy; diminishing returns in grain
production and to fertilizer use; overfishing; global

inflation; capital shortages; unemployment; and the changing growth prospect. Concludes that future economic policies must shift from growth to sustainability; not advocating abandonment of growth as a goal, but with concern for carrying capacities of biological system. Fisheries, forests, grasslands, and croplands, require development of alternative energy sources and population policies consistent with resource availability.

19   Chenery, Hollis and Syrquin, Moises
A B C   PATTERNS OF DEVELOPMENT, 1950-1970
        Assisted by Hazel Elkington
        New York and London: Oxford University Press, 1975.

Examines principal changes in economic structure that normally accompany economic growth, focusing on resource mobilization and allocation, particularly those aspects needed to sustain further growth. These aspects are treated in a uniform econometric framework to provide a consistent description of a number of interrelated types of structural change and also to identify systematic differences in development patterns among countries that are following different development strategies. The major aim of the research is to separate the effects of universal factors affecting all countries from particular characteristics. The authors use data for 101 countries in the period 1950 to 1970. Countries are grouped into three categories: large country, balanced allocation; small country, industry specialization. Chapter 5 compares the results obtained from time-series data with those observed from cross-sectional data. Results are obtained from regression techniques, where income level and population are treated as exogenous variables. The demographic variables show how the movement of population from rural to urban areas and lowering of the birth rate and death rate have influenced demand and supply of labor. A technical appendix discusses the methods used, the problems encountered, and all the regression equations specified in this study.

20   Chenery, Hollis B., et al., eds.
A B C   STUDIES IN DEVELOPMENT PLANNING
        Cambridge, Mass.: Harvard University Press, 1971.

Attempts to bring together the contributors' varied backgrounds in both field work and the use of quantitative techniques and show how modern methods can be used in operational development planning.

21   Chodak, Szymon
A B   SOCIETAL DEVELOPMENT: FIVE APPROACHES WITH CONCLUSIONS
        FROM COMPARATIVE ANALYSIS
        New York: Oxford University Press, 1973.

A sociologist analyzes the development and change of societies using five different conceptual approaches, attempting to view the processes of development in society from a multidimensional synthesizing perspective. These five approaches are called: "Evolutionary Theories," "Development - The Growing Societal Systemness," "Development and Innovation in the Search for Security," "Economic and Political Development," and "Modernization." The author gives references to the societal development which has taken place in various parts of the world and under different political systems.

22   Colman, David and Nixson, Frederick
A B C   ECONOMICS OF CHANGE IN LESS DEVELOPED COUNTRIES
          New York: Wiley, Halsted Press, 1978.

Analyzes the changes that are occurring in the less-developed countries (LDC's); considers the problems generated by change; and examines the agents of change. Emphasizes the internal (rather than the international) aspects of development and focuses on economic inequality within LDC's and the impact on the development process in agriculture and industry of different income distributions. Although recognizing the impact of transnational corporations on the nature and characteristics of development within the LDC's, the authors argue that it is the LDC government that is responsible for the economic policies pursued. Also outlines the concepts and measurement of development, and reviews the literature on economic theorizing about development. A final chapter discusses inflation and migration in LDC's. Authors note that too often policy recommendations ignore political acceptability and recommend that the economist should cooperate with the political scientist in the study of inflation and with the sociologist in the study of rural urban migration.

23   Corbet, Hugh and Jackson, Robert, eds.
A B C   IN SEARCH OF A NEW WORLD ECONOMIC ORDER
          New York and Toronto: Wiley, Halsted Press, 1974.

Focuses on the reform of the international commercial systems for further liberalizations of world trade. Papers are grouped into four categories: (1) introduction, (2) general factors affecting negotiations, (3) outside issues of significance, (4) issues on the agenda.

24   Fields, Gary S.
A B C D   POVERTY, INEQUALITY, AND DEVELOPMENT
           New York and London: Cambridge University Press, 1980.

Focuses on the distributional aspects of economic
development and explores the impact of the rate and type
of growth on poverty and inequality in poor countries.
Findings show that in general growth reduces poverty,
but a high aggregate growth rate is neither necessary
nor sufficient for reducing absolute poverty or relative
inequality. Uses case studies of distribution and
development in Costa Rica, Sri Lanka, India, Brazil,
the Phillippines, and Taiwan to examine which combinations
of circumstances and policies led to differential
performance. Concludes that a commitment to developing
to help the poor does not guarantee progress, but it
helps a great deal. In its absence, the flow of resources
to the haves, with only some trickle down to the have-nots,
will be perpetuated.

25   Finger, J. M.
A B D   INDUSTRIAL COUNTRY POLICY AND ADJUSTMENT TO IMPORTS FROM
        DEVELOPING COUNTRIES
        World Bank Staff Working Paper no. 470, July 1981.

        A background study for World Development Report 1981.
        Reviews and interprets recent analyses of the policies
        established by industrial countries in response to
        increasing imports from developing countries.

26   Finger, Nachum
A C D   THE IMPACT OF GOVERNMENT SUBSIDIES ON INDUSTRIAL
        MANAGEMENT: THE ISRAELI EXPERIENCE
        New York: Praeger, 1971.

27   Fitzgerald, E. V.
A B   PUBLIC SECTOR INVESTMENT PLANNING FOR DEVELOPING COUNTRIES
        New York: Holmes and Meier, 1978.

28   Florence, P. Sargant
A B C   ECONOMICS AND SOCIOLOGY OF INDUSTRY: A REALISTIC ANALYSIS
        OF DEVELOPMENT
        Baltimore, Md.: Johns Hopkins University Press, 1969.

29   Frank, Andre Gunder
A B C   CRISIS IN THE THIRD WORLD
        New York: Holmes and Meier, 1981.

30   Frank, Andre Gunder
A B   DEPENDENT ACCUMULATION AND UNDERDEVELOPMENT
        New York and London: Monthly Review Press, 1979.

        Explains underdevelopment by an analysis of the production
        and exchange relations of dependence. Distinguishes
        the three main stages or periods in this world embracing
        process of capital accumulation and capitalist development:
        mercantilist (1500-1770), industrial capitalist (1770-
        1870), and imperialist (1870-1930). Analyzes each period

in terms of history, trade relations between the metropolis and the periphery, and transformation of the modes or relations of production, and the development of underdevelopment in the principal regions of Asia, Africa, and the Americas.

31   Frank, Charles R.,   r., and Webb, Richard C., eds.
A B D   INCOME DISTRIBUTION AND GROWTH IN THE LESS-DEVELOPED COUNTRIES
        Washington, D.C.: Brookings Institution, 1977.

Fourteen previously unpublished essays representing part of the results of a project undertaken jointly by the Brookings Institution and the Woodrow Wilson School of Public and International Affairs at Princeton University, dealing with the relation between income distribution and economic growth in the developing countries. The first two articles present an overview of income distribution policy and discuss the causes of growth and income distribution in LDC's, respectively. The next nine examine the relation between income distribution and different economic policies and factors, including: industrialization, education, population, wage, fiscal, agricultural, public works, health and urban land policies.

32   Gant, George F.
A B   DEVELOPMENT ADMINISTRATION - CONCEPTS, GOALS, METHODS
        Madison, Wisconsin: The University of Wisconsin Press, 1979.

Growth and modernization in the less developed countries (LDC's) during the past three decades has frequently depended upon the state's ability to plan and manage a range of developmental activities. Gant's study of development administration looks at some of the issues that could be of concern to managers in LDC's: in particular, coordination, budgeting, the selection of personnel, training, etc. He also delves into the administrative side of certain specific governmental concerns, such as family planning and education, drawing on examples from a number of Asian countries. This is not a book which goes into much technical detail. Nor does it tell one how to design an efficient administrative setup. Primarily for the general reader interested in an overview of these topics.

33   Garbacz, Christopher
A B D   INDUSTRIAL POLARIZATION UNDER ECONOMIC INTEGRATION IN LATIN AMERICA
        Austin, Texas: Bureau of Business Research, Graduate School of Business, The University of Texas, 1971.

The author discusses the problem of increased disparities in the levels of regional economic development that tend to come about as a result of economic integration. The political and economic implications of industrial polarization are studies within the context and experience of the Central American Common Market and the Latin American Free Trade Association. Finally, the author considers the problem in the light of the planned Latin American Common Market, discussing the various measures that could be taken as well as the implications for the future.

34   Garzouzi, Eva
A B C   ECONOMIC   GROWTH   AND   DEVELOPMENT: THE   LESS   DEVELOPED
        COUNTRIES
        New York: Vantage Press, 1972.

Essays to consolidate into one readable text the whole of the economics of growth and development. Part I discusses the meaning and theories of economic development, outlines historical patterns of development, and summarizes the impact of capital, agriculture, industry, monetary and fiscal policies, international trade, and foreign aid on economic growth. Part II presents comparative analyses of developing regions, including Latin America, the Middle East and North Africa, Africa south of the Sahara, and Southeast Asia.

35   Geithman, David T., ed.
A B C D   FISCAL   POLICY   FOR   INDUSTRIALIZATION   AND   DEVELOPMENT   IN
          LATIN AMERICA
          Gainesville: University Presses of Florida.

Collection of 10 previously unpublished papers (and related comments) presented at the Twenty-First Annual Latin American Conference held in February 1971. Central theme of the conference was the analysis and evaluation of the interaction among fiscal problems, fiscal tools, and fiscal systems in the industrializing economies of Latin America.

36   Ghai, D. P.
A B C   THE BASIC-NEEDS APPROACH TO DEVELOPMENT: SOME ISSUES
        REGARDING CONCEPTS AND METHODOLOGY
        ILO, Geneva, 1977.

Contains five papers which discuss issues which arise in the formulation of criteria and approaches for the promotion of employment and the satisfaction of the basic needs of a country's population. Presents the first results of the research and conceptual work initiated by the ILO to help countries implement the basic needs-oriented strategy recommended by the World Employment Conference in 1976.

37   Gianaris, Nicholas V.
A B C   ECONOMIC DEVELOPMENT: THOUGHT AND PROBLEMS
          North Quincy, Mass.: Christopher Publishing House, 1978.

          Part one examines the process of development, the
          historical perspective, mathematical models, and modern
          theories of development; part two considers domestic
          problems of development, specifically land and other
          natural resources, human resources (particularly the
          role of education), capital formation and technological
          change, the allocation of resources, and the role of
          government and planning; part three discusses the
          international aspects of development (foreign trade,
          aid, investment, and multinationals) and current issues
          such as environmental problems, the status of women,
          income inequalities, and discrimination.

38   Giersch, Herbert, ed.
A B C D INTERNATIONAL ECONOMIC DEVELOPMENT AND RESOURCE TRANSFER:
           WORKSHOP 1978
           Tubingen, Germany: J. C. B. Mohr, 1979.

          Twenty-four previously unpublished papers from a workshop
          held in June 1978 at the Institut fur Weltwirtschaft,
          Kiel University. Contributions organized under ten
          headings: Rural Industrialization, Employment and Economic
          Development; Choice of Techniques and Industries for
          Growth and Employment; Agricultural Patterns and Policies
          in Developing Countries; Hypotheses for the Commodity
          Composition of East-West Trade; The Relationship Between
          the Domestic and International Sectors in Economic
          Development; Patterns of Trade in Services and Knowledge;
          Changes in Industrial Interdependencies and Final Demand
          in Economic Development; Public Aid for Investment in
          Manufacturing Industries; Institutional and Economic
          Criteria for the Choice of Technology in Developing
          Countries; and Problems of Measuring the Production and
          Absorption of Technologies in Developing Countries.

39   Gierst, Friedrich and Matthews, Stuart R.
A B C   GUIDELINES FOR CONTRACTING FOR INDUSTRIAL PROJECTS IN
          DEVELOPING COUNTRIES
          New York: United Nations Publications, 1975.

          Designed to serve public and private organizations in
          developing countries as a guide in preparing contracts
          concerned with industrial investment projects. Examines
          various stages involved in the preparation of an industrial
          project and discusses the basic types of contacts involved
          (i.e. those with financial institutions, with consultants
          and with contractors).

40   Gill, Richard T.
A B C   ECONOMIC DEVELOPMENT: PAST AND PRESENT

Third Edition. Foundations of Modern Economics.
Englewood Cliffs, N.J.: Prentice-Hall, 1973.

Third edition of an introductory textbook with revisions
of the discussions. The Green Revolution, two-gap analysis
of foreign aid, Denison-Jorgenson-Griliches studies of
factors affecting United States economic growth and
Leibenstein's "X-efficiency" concept have been added.
Statistical tables have been updated to include figures
on Chinese economic growth. Six chapters cover: 1)
General factors in economic development, 2) Theories
of development, 3) Beginnings of development in advanced
countries, 4) Growth of the American economy, 5) Problems
of underdeveloped countries, and 6) Development in China
and India.

41   Goulet, Denis
A B C   THE CRUEL CHOICE: A NEW CONCEPT IN THE THEORY OF
        DEVELOPMENT
        Cambridge, Mass.: Center for the Study of Development
        and Social Change, Atheneum, 1971.

This work is intended to probe moral dilemmas faced by
economic and social development. Its central concern
is that philosophical conceptions about the "good life"
and the "good society" should be of more profound
importance in assessing alternative paths to development
than economic, political, or technological questions.
The theoretical analysis is based on two concepts:
"vulnerability" and "existence rationality." Vulnerability
is defined as exposure to forces that can not be
controlled, and is expressed in the failure of many
low-income countries to attain their development goals,
as well as in manifestations of mass alienation in certain
societies where prosperity has already been achieved.
Existence rationality denotes those strategies used by
all societies to possess information and to make practical
choices designed to assure survival and satisfy their
needs for esteem and freedom. These strategies vary
with a country's needs and are conditioned by numerous
constraints.

42   Griffin, Keith
A B C   INTERNATIONAL INEQUALITY AND NATIONAL POVERTY
        New York: Holms & Meier, 1978.

Nine essays, seven previously published between 1970
and 1978. Challenges the classical assumption that
unrestricted international intercourse will reduce
inequality and poverty. Argues that forces creating
inequality are automatic, and not due to malevolence
of developed nations or corporations, but that the motor
of change in the contemporary world economy is technical
innovation. Since the advances tend to be concentrated

in the developed countries where they are applicable to their technology, rich countries are able to extract supra-normal profits and rents from the poor countries through trade. The high level of factor earnings in rich countries attract the most valuable financial and human resources of the poor countries through induced international migration. Divided into two parts, part one deals with international inequality and discusses: the international transmission of inequality; multinational corporations; foreign capital, domestic savings, and economic development; emigration, and the New International Economic Order. The essays in part two focus on national poverty, discussing the facts of poverty in the Third World, analyzing models of development, and assessing the Chinese system of incentives.

43   Griffin, Keith B. and Enos, John L.
A B C   PLANNING DEVELOPMENT
        Reading, Mass.; Don Mills, Ontario; Sydney; London; and
        Manila: Addison-Wesley, 1971.

        Part of a series intended to serve as guidebooks on development economics, this book deals with practical problems of planning and economic policy in underdeveloped countries. Consists of four parts: 1) the role of planning, 2) quantitative planning techniques, 3) sector policies, and 4) planning in practice with reference to Chile, Columbia, Ghana, India, Pakistan and Turkey.

44   Hagen, Everett E.
A B C   THE ECONOMICS OF DEVELOPMENT
        Revised Edition. The Irwin Series in Economics.
        Homewood, Ill.: Irwin, 1975.

        Revised edition with two new chapters added, one dealing with the earth's stock of minerals and economic growth, and the other on the relationships between economic growth and the distribution of income. Chapters on population and economic planning have been extensively revised, with the former focusing on the relationship of food supply to continued world growth. Additional changes include: reorganization of the discussion of growth theories; a considerably augmented discussion of entrepreneurhsip; and a reorganization of the chapters on import substitution versus export expansion and external finance.

45   Helleiner, G. K., ed.
B C   A WORLD DIVIDED: THE LESS DEVELOPED COUNTRIES IN THE
        INTERNATIONAL ECONOMY
        Perspectives on Development, no. 5
        New York; London and Melbourne: Cambridge University
        Press, 1976.

Twelve papers discussing the new policies and instruments needed if the interests of poor nations are to be met. Within the realm of trade, consideration is given to the possibility of increased cooperation through: supply management schemes; bargaining capacity and power; closer ties with other less developed countries; and the development of alternative marketing channels and joint sales efforts. Relations between the less developed countries and transnational firms is then considered with special attention given to the factors affecting the bargaining position of the countries. Issues in international finance and monetary policy are: the borrowing of Eurodollars by less developed countries, internationally agreed upon principles for an honorable debt default, and interests of less developed countries in a new international monetary order. Another paper considers means by which a self-reliant but poor country can seek to conduct its economic affairs in the face of a most inhospitable and uncertain international environment. The concluding paper considers the implication of the new mood in the less developed countries for future international organisation.

46   Hermassi, Elbaki
A C D   THE THIRD WORLD REASSESSED
        Berkeley: University of California Press, 1980.

47   Horowitz, Irving Louis, ed.
A B C   EQUITY, INCOME, AND POLICY: COMPARATIVE STUDIES IN THREE
        WORLDS OF DEVELOPMENT
        New York and London: Praeger, 1977.

        Ten previously unpublished papers by sociologists and economists on the multiple ideologies of development and the drive toward equity congruent with different social systems. Six essays address the problems of the "First World," i.e. those types of societies dominated by a free market and an open society, where the main problem would seem to be how to maintain growth and development while providing distributive justice. Two papers look at the "Second World" of socialism; these assume the central role of state power as imposing its will to produce equity. The remaining papers consider the Third World, examining in particular income distribution in Tanzania and economic equality and social class in general.

48   Jalan, Bimal
A B C   ESSAYS IN DEVELOPMENT POLICY
        Delhi: S. G. Wasani for Macmillan of India, 1975.

        A common theme of the 11 essays (some previously published) is the explicit reference to political philosophies involved in the choices of means and objectives of development and social change. Essays include: discussion of self-reliance objectives; trade and industrialization policies; distribution of income; the project evaluation manual of Professors Little and Mirrlees; UNIDO guidelines for project evaluation; criteria for determination of appropriate terms of aid assistance; the definition and assessment of performance in developing countries; the history of the United Nations Capital Development Fund, the World Bank, and the International Development Association; and an analysis of the principal recommendations of the Pearson Commission Report (1969).

49   Jumper, Sidney R.; Bell, Thomas L. and Ralston, Bruce A.
B C   ECONOMIC GROWTH AND DISPARITIES: A WORLD VIEW
       Englewood Cliffs, N.J.: Prentice-Hall, 1980.

The authors emphasize understanding of real world differences in levels of human development, rather than sophisticated analytical procedures. In seven parts: geographical concepts; the factors influencing variations in levels of development; world food supplies; minerals; factors affecting intensity of manufacturing development; the service industries; and a summary of the role of geographers in facing these development problems.

50   Kahn, Herman
A B C WORLD ECONOMIC DEVELOPMENT: 1979 AND BEYOND
       With the Hudson Institute.
       Boulder: Westview Press, 1979.

Examines economic prospects focusing on the period 1978-2000, and particularly the earlier part of the period. In two parts, part one presents the general historical framework, concepts, and perspectives on economic growth and cultural change. Part two examines the major trends and problems of the real world, focusing on the elements of change and continuity in both the advanced and developing economies. Rejects attempts by some to stop the world and argues for and suggests strategies for rapid worldwide economic growth, for Third World industrialization, and for the use of advanced (or at least appropriate) technology.

51   Kasdan, Alan R.
A B C THE THIRD WORLD: A NEW FOCUS FOR DEVELOPMENT
       Cambridge, Mass.: Schenkman Publishing, 1973.

52   Kindleberger, Charles P. and Herrick, Bruce
B   ECONOMIC DEVELOPMENT
       Third Edition. Economics Handbook Series.
       New York; London; Paris and Tokyo: McGraw-Hill, 1977.

Textbook that survey[s] the present panorama of international poverty, the applications to it of economic analysis, and the policies for improvement that the analysis implies. This edition which has been completely rewritten and updated, includes new chapters on: population, urbanization, collective international action, employment, income distribution, and the theories of economic development.

53   Leipziger, Danny M., ed.
A B C   BASIC NEEDS AND DEVELOPMENT
        Foreword by Paul P. Streeten
        Cambridge, Mass.: Oelgeschlager, Gunn & Hain, 1981.

Five previously unpublished essays discuss the potential contribution of the basic needs approach to developmental theory and practice. Michael J. Crosswell gives his views in two essays on a development planning approach and on growth, poverty alleviation, and foreign assistance. Maureen A. Lewis discusses sectional aspects of the linkages among population, nutrition, and health. Danny M. Leipziger writes about policy issues and the basic human needs approach. Martha de Melo presents a case study of Sri Lanka focusing on the effects of alternative approaches to basic human needs. The authors are all economists.

54   Leontief, Wassily, et al.
A B C   THE FUTURE OF THE WORLD ECONOMY: A UNITED NATIONS STUDY
        New York: Oxford University Press, 1977.

Investigates the interrelationships between future world economic growth and availability of natural resources, pollution, and the impact of environmental policies. Includes a set of alternative projections of the demographic, economic, and environmental states of the world in the years 1980, 1990, and 2000 with a comparison with the world economy of 1970. Constructs a multiregional input-output economic model of the world economy. Investigates some of the main problems of economic growth and development in the world as a whole, with special accent on problems encountered by the developing countries. The findings include: (1) target rates of growth of gross product in the developing regions...are not sufficient to start closing the income gap between the developing and the developed countries; (2) the principal limits to sustained economic growth and accelerated development are political, social and institutional in character rather than physical; (3) the necessary increased food production is technically feasible, but dependent on drastically favorable public policy measure; (4) pollution is not an unmanageable problem.

55   Lin, Ching-Yuan
A C D   DEVELOPING COUNTRIES IN A TURBULENT WORLD: PATTERNS
          OF ADJUSTMENT SINCE THE OIL CRISIS
          New York: Praeger, 1981.

          Examines national authorities' policy reactions to changes
          in the world economy since 1973, to determine whether
          differences in national economic performances can be
          explained in terms of differences in their policy
          reactions. Investigates global patterns of absorption,
          production, and adjustment since the oil crisis; global
          expenditure flows before and after the crisis; and
          international bank transactions and world trade. Reviews
          the experiences of developing countries during the period,
          focusing on non-oil countries. Finds that collectively
          the non-oil developing countries experienced a much milder
          contraction of domestic demand and real ouput than the
          more developed countries after the disturbances in 1973-75,
          although individual experiences varied; however, inflation
          remains persistent. Argues that most developing countries
          did not pursue demand management policies early enough
          to counteract sharp changes in external demand.

56   Madhava, K. B., ed.
A B C D   INTERNATIONAL DEVELOPMENT, 1969:   CHALLENGES TO PREVALENT
          IDEAS ON DEVELOPMENT
          Dobbs Ferry: Oceana for Society for International
          Development, 1970.

          Contains the proceedings of the 11th World Conference
          of the Society for International Development held in
          1969 in New Delhi. The theme "Challenges to Prevalent
          Ideas on Development" was carried out through roundtable
          discussions centering on: the redefinition of goals;
          foreign aid; manpower, education, and development;
          population communication; social communication; political
          and social-cultural requisites; and challenges to theorists
          and strategists.

57   May, Brian
A C D   THE THIRD WORLD CALAMITY
          London and Boston: Routledge & Kegan Paul, 1981.

          Assessment of social conditions, politics, economics,
          and cultural barriers in the Third World, with particular
          reference to India, Iran, and Nigeria. Contends that
          the "chronic socio-economic stagnation" that characterizes
          these countries is not attributable to Western imperialism,
          maintaining that fundamental change in Third World
          countries was and is blocked by psychological and cultural
          facts. Compares relevant factors in Europe and in the
          three countries to show the constraints that block
          significant socioeconomic change.

58   McGreevey, William Paul, ed.
A B C   THIRD-WORLD POVERTY: NEW STRATEGIES FOR MEASURING
            DEVELOPMENT PROGRESS
            Lexington, Mass.:   Heath, Lexington Books, 1980.

            Five previously unpublished papers on the problems of
            measuring progress in alleviating poverty in the Third
            World, originally part of a series of seminars (1976-79)
            sponsored by the Agency for International Development.
            Editor McGreevey reviews the development progress from
            both a human capital and poverty alleviation standpoint;
            Gary S. Fields looks at absolute-poverty measures (i.e.,
            those not depending on income distribution considerations);
            Harry J. Bruton considers the use of available employment
            and unemployment data in assessing government poverty
            policy, and G. Edward Schuh and Robert L. Thompson discuss
            measures of agricultural progress and government commitment
            to agricultural development.   The fifth paper by Nancy
            Birdsall is a summary of discussion in two seminars on
            time-use surveys and networks of social support in LDC's.
            The authors find in part that: (1) existing data are
            inadequate to judge progress; (2) the best data gathering
            method is multipurpose household surveys; and (3) networks
            of social support are important (and unmeasured) means
            of income transfer between households.

59   McHale, John and McHale, Magda C.
A B C   BASIC HUMAN NEEDS: A FRAMEWORK FOR ACTION
            New Brunswick, N.J.:   Rutgers University, Transaction
            Books, 1978.

60   Meadows, Dennis L., ed.
A B C   ALTERNATIVES TO GROWTH--I: A SEARCH FOR SUBSTAINABLE
            FUTURES: PAPERS ADAPTED FROM ENTRIES TO THE 1975 GEORGE
            AND CYNTHIA MITCHELL PRIZE AND FROM PRESENTATIONS BEFORE
            THE 1975 ALTERNATIVES TO GROWTH CONFERENCE, HELD AT
            THE WOODLANDS, TEXAS
            Cambridge, Mass.:   Lippincott, Ballinger, 1977.

            Seventeen previously unpublished interdisciplinary papers
            on the transition from growth to a steady-state society
            i.e., a society with a constant stock of physical wealth
            and a constant stock of people.   In four parts: the
            relation between population and food or energy; economic
            alternatives; the rationales, mechanisms, and implications
            of various long-term planning proposals; and analysis
            of the determinants, nature, and implications of current
            paradigms, norms, laws, and religion.

61   Melady, Thomas Patrick and Suhartono, R. B.
A B   DEVELOPMENT -- LESSONS FOR THE FUTURE
            Maryknoll, New York: Orbis Books, 1973.

Investigation of what determines, economically, which countries are developing, based on examination of characteristics of nations agreed to be undergoing this experience. The study examines such facets of development as the nonhomogeneity of the developing countries; factors affecting economic growth, the sectoral aspect of growth (industry and agriculture), measurements of the phenomenon, and the applicability of economic theory in this work; and the effects of economic development on man and his role in society.

62   Morawetz, David
A B D   TWENTY-FIVE YEARS OF ECONOMIC DEVELOPMENT, 1950 TO 1975
        Johns Hopkins University Press for IBRD, 1977.

Assesses development programs of developing countries and global development targets adopted by international organizations over the past 25 years. Chapters cover: a) changing objectives of development; b) growth in GNP per capita, population and the gap between rich and poor countries; c) reduction of poverty, including employment, income distribution, basic needs, nutrition, health, housing and education; d) self-reliance and economic independence; and e) conclusions, hypotheses, and questions.

63   Morgan, Theodore
B C   ECONOMIC DEVELOPMENT: CONCEPT AND STRATEGY
        New York and London: Harper & Row, 1975.

Textbook in economic development with emphasis on policy, its appropriate definition, its targets, and its improvement of application. Diverts focus from GNP and average income growth rates and into issues such as income distribution, nutrition, disease, climate, and population increases and their effects on development. Surveys existing theoretical literature. Discusses development planning and the importance of the statistical foundation of decision-making, and planning techniques such as cost-benefit analysis. Provides sporadic data for less-developed countries, mostly for the post-World War II period, on various national variables.

64   Ramati, Yohanan, ed.
A B C   ECONOMIC GROWTH IN DEVELOPING COUNTRIES--MATERIAL AND
        HUMAN RESOURCES: PROCEEDINGS OF THE SEVENTH REHOVOT
        CONFERENCE
        Praeger Special Studies in International Economics and
        Development
        New York and London: Praeger in cooperation with the
        Continuation Committee of the Rehovot Conference, 1975.

Collection of 49 papers presented in September 1973. The papers are grouped into five sections following the structure of the conference. Part I includes papers setting the framework to analyze natural and human resources as factors in development and problems of planning and the quality of life. Part II includes papers on resources, technology, and income distribution. Part III deals with external constraints on development. Part IV examines planning and implementation. Part V contains the very brief closing addresses by Simon Kuznets and Abba Eban. Participants included 99 experts and policy makers for developing countries in Africa, Latin America, and Southeast Asia.

65   Rubinson, Richard, ed.
A B   DYNAMICS OF WORLD DEVELOPMENT
       Political Economy of the World-System Annuals, vol. 4
       Beverly Hills and London: Sage, 1981.

       Twelve previously unpublished papers, almost all by sociologists, presented at the Fourth Annual Political Economy of the World-System conference at Johns Hopkins University, June 1980. Papers are based on the assumption that the world's history is the history of capitalist accumulation; and that capitalist development is the development of a single...modern world-system. Papers cover: development in peripheral areas; development in semiperipheral states; development and state organization; cycles and trends of world system development; theooretical issues; and dynamics of development of the world economy.

66   Sachs, Ignacy
A C   THE DISCOVERY OF THE THIRD WORLD
       Cambridge, Mass., and London: M. I. T. Press, 1976.

       Focusing on a redefinition of development theory, discusses the role of ethnocentrism and domination by European and Western ideas in such areas as science, technology, and economics. Argues that discussions regarding economic development strategies attempt to apply Western theories and ignore the fact that Third World growth, unlike capital-intensive European growth, must be based on the use of labor. Proposes a general development theory to bridge the gap between European theory and Third World practice and discusses problems such as economic surplus and economic aid. Recommends that the U.N. assess Western nations and funnel the money to Third World nations on a "no-strings" basis.

67   Shafei, Mohamed Z.
A B   THREE LECTURES ON ECONOMIC DEVELOPMENT
       Beirut, Lebanon: Beirut Arab University, 1970.

       The first lecture focuses on the characteristics of developing countries. The second traces the process of economic development in the U.A.R. (Egypt) since 1952. The third is on the foreign assistance needs of developing countries.

68   Singer, H. W.
A C   THE STRATEGY OF INTERNATIONAL DEVELOPMENT: ESSAYS IN THE ECONOMICS OF BACKWARDNESS
       Edited by Sir Alec Cairncross and Mohinder Puri
       White Plains, N.Y.: International Arts and Sciences Press, 1975.

       A collection of 13 papers by the author, all published in past years, dealing with some of the central problems of economic development and development policy. Papers cover such issues as gains distribution among borrowing and investing countries, dualism, international aid, trade and development, employment problems, income distribution, science and technology transfers, etc. Introduction to the author's work and career by editor Sir Alec Cairncross.

69   Singer, Hans W. and Ansari, Javed A.
A   RICH AND POOR COUNTRIES
       Baltimore and London: Johns Hopkins University Press, 1977.

       Examines the changes that are required if the relationship between rich and poor countries is to make a more effective contribution to the development of the poor countries. Part one describes the structure of international economy and the nature of development process. Part two discusses the importance of the international trade sector to development in the poorer countries and reviews the trade policies of the rich and poor countries. Part three deals with the role of aid in the development process; and part four is concerned with international factor movement. Stresses the need for the formulation of an international development strategy...by the rich countries (both old and new), providing assistance in an increasing flow of resources through trade, aid capital and the transfer of skills and technology to the poor countries. Argues that such a strategy first must provide for some discrimination in international trade in favor of poor countries to provide more resources and secondly to enable the importation of more appropriate technologies.

70   Spiegelglas, Stephen and Welsh, Charles J., eds.
A B   ECONOMIC DEVELOPMENT; CHALLENGE AND PROMISE
       Englewood Cliffs, N.J.: Prentice-Hall, 1970.

       A collection of 33 reprinted readings, each representing an outstanding contribution, controversial issue, or synthesis of ideas in economic development. Major sections

include: an   introduction;   nature   and   techniques   of
planning; strategy and policy; and trade or aid.   The
selection of topics in these sections reflects recent
increased   emphasis   on   practical   development   problems,
particularly on human resources development and the need
to create exportable manufactured goods.   A matrix showing
how each selection fits into the scheme and sequence
of the seven widely used development textbooks is included.

71   T. N. Srinivasan
A B C D DEVELOPMENT, POVERTY, AND BASIC HUMAN NEEDS: SOME ISSUES
          World Bank Reprint Series, 76
          IBRD, 1977.

          Reprinted   from   Food   Research   Institute   Studies,   vol.
          XVI, no. 2 (1977), pp. 11-28.   Deals with the raising
          of standard of living of the poorest sections of the
          population   in   developing   countries.   Discusses   aid
          problems, distributional aspects of economic growth,
          employment goals, and the new perceptions of development.

72   Stein, Leslie
A C D   ECONOMIC REALITIES IN POOR COUNTRIES
          Sydney, London and Singapore: Angus and Robertson, 1972.

          This book surveys the problems of growth faced by the
          developing countries of the world.   The first part of
          the book describes the economic and social characteristics
          of Third World countries and presents some theories of
          development, including Baran's Marxian view, W. W. Rostow's
          non-Marxist   alternative,   balanced   growth   theory,   and
          Myrdal's view which considers non-economic as well as
          economic factors of growth.   Succeeding chapters discuss
          population growth, problems of education, the role of
          agriculture   and   industrial   development,   obstacles   to
          trade, and government plans which have been used in
          developing countries.   Designed for use as a text or
          for the layman.

73   Streeten, Paul
A B D   DEVELOPMENT PERSPECTIVES
          New York: St. Martin's Press, 1981.

          A combination of 17 previously published articles and
          7 new chapters, in five parts: concepts, values, and
          methods in development analysis; development strategies;
          transnational corporations; the change in emphasis from
          the growth approach to the basic needs approach; and
          two miscellaneous chapters on taxation and on Gunnar
          Myrdal.   Newly written chapters cover: the results of
          development strategies for the poor, alternatives in
          development, the New International Economic Order, the
          basic needs approach, human rights and basic needs, the

search for a basic-needs yardstick (with Norman Hicks), and transnational corporations and basic needs.

74   Thomson, W. Scott, ed.
A C   THE THIRD WORLD: PREMISES OF U.S. POLICY
        San Francisco: Institute for Contemporary Studies, 1978.

75   Tinbergen, Jan
A B   THE DESIGN OF DEVELOPMENT
        The Johns Hopkins University Press, 1958.

        Formulates a coherent government policy to further development objectives and outlines methods to stimulate private investments.

76   Todaro, Michael P.
A B C   ECONOMIC DEVELOPMENT IN THE THIRD WORLD: AN INTRODUCTION
        TO PROBLEMS AND POLICIES IN A GLOBAL PERSPECTIVE
        London and New York: Longman, 1977.

        In four parts: Part one discusses the nature of underdevelopment and its various manifestations in the Third World, and parts two and three focus on major development problems and policies, both domestic (growth, income distribution, population, unemployment, education, and migration) and international (trade, balance of payments, and foreign investment). The last part reviews the possibilities and prospects for Third World development.

77   Todaro, Michael P.
A B   DEVELOPMENT PLANNING: MODELS AND METHODS
        Series of undergraduate teaching works in economics, Volume V.
        London, Nairobi, and New York: Oxford University
Press, 1971.

        This is the last in a series of undergraduate teaching works in economics developed at Makere University, Uganda. This book is an introduction to development planning, with emphasis on plan formulation rather than implementation.

78   United Nations Department of Economic and Social Affairs
        THE INTERNATIONAL DEVELOPMENT STRATEGY: FIRST OVER-ALL
        REVIEW AND APPRAISAL OF ISSUES AND POLICIES. REPORT
        OF THE SECRETARY-GENERAL
        New York: United Nations, 1973.

        Deals with the issues and policies in the field of economic and social development...of prime concern in the first two years of the Second United Nations Development Decade. Emphasis is upon changes in the following areas: priorities of objectives, techniques of production, trade and aid relationships, and the external environment in which economic and social development takes place.

79   United Nations Department of Economic and Social Affairs
A C   SHAPING ACCELERATED DEVELOPMENT AND INTERNATIONAL CHANGES
      New York: United Nations Publications, 1980.

Contains views and recommendations of the UN Committee for Development Planning relating to the international development strategy for a third UN development decade. Chapters cover general premises and basic objectives; priority areas for action; means and implementation; and key goals and needed changes.

80   United Nations Department of Economic and Social Affairs
A C   DEVELOPMENT IN THE 1980'S: APPROACH TO A NEW STRATEGY;
      VIEWS AND RECOMMENDATIONS OF THE COMMITTEE FOR DEVELOPMENT
      PLANNING
      New York: United Nations Publications, 1978.

Reviews development issues for the 1980's with a discussion of the current situation and preliminary comments relating to a development strategy for the 1980's. Discusses economic cooperation among developing countries, covering trade, economic integration and other arrangements for economic cooperation.

81   United Nations Industrial Development Organization
A B C INDUSTRIALIZATION FOR NEW DEVELOPMENT NEEDS
      New York: United Nations Publication, 1974.

Emphasizes the reshaping of industrial development in the light of new development needs that the pervasive problems of unemployment, maldistribution of income, and poverty in general have brought to the fore in the developing countries.

82   UNRSID
A B C THE QUEST FOR A UNIFIED APPROACH TO DEVELOPMENT
      UNRSID: 1980.

Provides background information on UNRSID's efforts to formulate a unified approach to development analysis and planning, an approach which would bring together all the different aspects of development into a set of feasible objectives and policy approaches. Chapters cover: styles of development--definitions and criteria; strategies; the findings of the Expert Group; an assessment by Marshall Wolfe, former Chief of the Social Development Division of UN ECLA; and an annex containing the final report on the project by the UN Commission for Social Development, covering questions of diagnosis, monitoring, indicators, and planning and capicitation.

83   Uri, Pierre
A B C   DEVELOPMENT WITHOUT DEPENDENCE
          New York: Praeger for the Atlantic Institute for
          International Affairs, 1976.

          Monograph on foreign aid. Contends that the aid programs
          of the 1950's and 1960's were lopsided and failed to
          address the needs of the truly poor. According to Bundy,
          the author argues that although effective transfer of
          resources and skill remains a vital part of the need...such
          nation-to-nation aid...can only help to foster the very
          feelings of dependence...that are the deepest grievance
          of the developing world. Discusses control of population
          growth, the role and necessary scale of official foreign
          aid, stabilization of the raw materials market so as
          to assist consumers and producers alike, and the types
          of industries the developing countries should strive
          to build as a part of a rational world division of labor.
          Examines the control and regulation of multinational
          corporations and, focusing on Latin America, the extent
          to which regional cooperation can be developed. Recommends
          that development planning be based on future population
          growth and distribution.

84   Varma, Baidya Nath
A B C   THE SOCIOLOGY AND POLITICS OF DEVELOPMENT: A THEORETICAL
          STUDY
          International Library of Sociology Series
          London and Boston: Routledge & Kegan Paul, 1980.

          The author critically examines theories of development
          and presents his own theory. Considers general criteria
          used for evaluating the modernization process; describes
          a model for a general paradigm of modernization; surveys
          other models encompassing ideological, social scientific,
          anthropological and activistic theories; and discusses
          theoretical problems of planning and national
          reconstruction. Summarizes views of theorists in various
          social science disciplines and features of modernization
          in terms of guidance provided for economic, political,
          educational, and bureaucratic decision-making in a
          developing country. Concludes that both the socialist
          and capitalist systems of modernization are viable models
          for Third World countries.

85   Vogeler, Ingolf and De Souza, Anthony R., eds.
A C   DIALECTICS OF THIRD WORLD DEVELOPMENT
          Montclair: Allanheld, Osmun, 1980.

          Collection of previously published (some revised) papers
          designed for use by students of economics, political
          science, and development. Representing a variety of
          ideas and arguments relevant to Third World
          underdevelopment, the readings discuss climate and

resources, cultural traditions, European colonialism
(i.e., plantation agriculture), population, tourism,
and imperialism. An appendix provides "awareness"
exercises.

86   Wallman, Sandra, ed.
A B   PERCEPTIONS OF DEVELOPMENT
          New York: Cambridge University Press, 1977.

87   Ward, Richard J.
A C   DEVELOPMENT ISSUES FOR THE 1970'S
          New York and London: Dunellen, 1973.

An assessment of key issues and problems which emerged
from the Decade of Development and which will continue
to absorb the attention of students of development in
the present decade. The author, former Chief of Planning
of the U.S. Agency for International Development, presents
much data which has not been previously released and
which is unavailable elsewhere. The book is divided
into three parts: "Food and Human Welfare," "Development
Problems for This Decade," and "Planning Programs and
Strategies." The chapters specifically discuss such
issues as labor absorption in agriculture, means of
population control, the burden of debt service, the role
of foreign aid, big-push development, etc.

88   Waterston, Albert
A B   DEVELOPMENT PLANNING; LESSONS OF EXPERIENCE
          The Johns Hopkins University Press, 1979.

Analyzes the success of the development planning experience
in over 100 countries in Asia, Africa, Europe, and the
Americas. In two parts. Part 1 describes and analyzes
the problems associated with the implementation of planning
programs, the provision of basic data, the role of national
budget, and administrative obstacles. Part 2 contains
an extensive and comparative discussion of the experience
of the countries under review in setting up organizations
and administrative procedures for preparing and
implementing development projects; the distribution of
planning functions, types of central planning agencies,
and subnational regional and local planning bodies.

89   Watts, Nita, ed.
A B   ECONOMIES OF THE WORLD
          New York: Oxford University Press.

The purpose of this new series is to provide a brief
review of economic development during the post-war period
in each of a number of countries which are of obvious
importance in the world economy, or interesting because
of peculiarities of their economic structure or experience,
or illustrative of widespread economic development

problems. The series will be of interest to economists
in universities, and in business and government.

90   Wilber, Charles K., ed.
A B   THE POLITICAL ECONOMY OF DEVELOPMENT AND UNDERDEVELOPMENT
          New York: Random House, 1973.

          Emphasis in approach and content is on political economy
          in the sense of attempting to incorporate such noneconomic
          influences as social structures, political systems, and
          cultural values as well as such factors as technological
          change and the distribution of income and wealth. Readings
          are radical in that they are willing to question and
          evaluate the most basic institutions and values of society.
          Divided into eight groups concerned with methodological
          problems, historical perspective, trade and imperialism,
          agricultural and industrial institutions and strategies,
          comparative models of development, the human cost of
          development, and indications for the future.

91   Worsley, Peter
A C   THE THIRD WORLD
          Chicago: University of Chicago Press, 1972.

92   Wriggins, W. Howards and Adler-Karlsson, Gunnar
A C   REDUCING GLOBAL INEQUALITIES
          New York: McGraw-Hill, 1978.

          Two papers, plus an introduction on the role that
          developing countries themselves take to reduce the gap
          between rich nations and poor and to eliminate mass poverty
          within their own societies.   W. Howard Wriggins, U.S.
          ambassador to Sri Lanka and formerly professor of political
          science at Columbia University, analyzes the various
          bargaining strategies open to developing countries such
          as developing commodity or regional coalitions, or a
          variety of threats to developed countries.   The future
          is likely to see continued efforts at coalition building,
          but also periodic outbreaks of irregular violence against
          local opponents, neighbors, or Northern centers of power.

93   Zuvekas, Clarence, Jr.
A B C   ECONOMIC DEVELOPMENT: AN INTRODUCTION
          New York: St. Martin's Press, 1979.

          Text written from an interdisciplinary perspective
          stressing policy and empirical findings rather than an
          overall development theory.   Aims at balance between
          theory and policy, including historical development and
          empirical evidence.   After discussing the terminology
          of and the obstacles to development, the author examines
          population growth, trade and development, and the role
          of government. Also covers: the problems of agriculture

and industry, income distribution, employment, mobilization
of domestic and foreign savings, manipulation of trade
to the advantage of the developing country, and the limits
to growth controversy. Presumes acquaintance with basic
macro and micro theory.

HEALTH, FOOD AND NUTRITION IN THE DEVELOPMENT OF THIRD WORLD COUNTRIES

94   Alamgir, Mohiuddin
A C   THE DIMENSION OF UNDERNUTRITION AND MALNUTRITION IN
        DEVELOPING COUNTRIES: CONCEPTUAL, EMPIRICAL AND POLICY
        ISSUES
        Cambridge: Harvard   Institute   for   International
        Development, Harvard University, 1980.

95   Abel-Smith, Brian with Alcira Leiserson
A C   POVERTY, DEVELOPMENT, AND HEALTH POLICY
        WHO, 1978.

        Describes ways in which work in the health sector can
        support national planning of rural development aimed
        at the relief of poverty. In two parts: (a) health
        policy and national planning: the inequity of past
        development; health and development; economic growth
        and national planning; planning national health policy;
        and (b) economics of health services: analysis of
        expenditures; financing; cost-benefit/effectiveness
        analyses; and low-cost services.

96   Aldrich, Daniel G., Jr., ed.
A B   RESEARCH FOR THE WORLD FOOD CRISIS
        Washington, D.C.: American Association for the Advancement
        of Science, 1970.

97   Allaby, M.
A   WORLD FOOD RESOURCES: ACTUAL AND POTENTIAL
        Applied Science Publications, 1977.

98   American Public Health Association
A B C   THE STATE OF THE ART OF DELIVERING LOW-COST HEALTH SERVICES
        IN DEVELOPING COUNTRIES
        Washington, D.C.: APHA, 1977.

99   Austin, James E.
A B C   NUTRITION PROGRAMS IN THE THIRD WORLD: CASES AND READINGS
        Cambridge, Mass.: Oelgeschlager, Gunn & Hain, 1981.

        Five previously published but revised readings and fourteen
        case studies, prepared by the author and others, on
        nutrition policy and management in developing countries.

Covers: international agencies' programs dealing with malnutrition; supplementary feeding programs and formulated foods; food fortification and nutritional enhancement of corn; Mexico's efforts to improve nutrition by changing the food marketing system and by the use of subsidies; programs that combine nutrition, population, and health interventions; and design and implementation of a national nutritional plan.

100   Austin, James E. and Zeitlin, Marian F., eds.
A B C   NUTRITION INTERVENTION IN DEVELOPING COUNTRIES: AN OVERVIEW
        Camridge, Mass.: Oelgeschlager, Gunn & Hain, 1981.

This volume, part of a Harvard Institute for International Development study for the Office of Nutrition of U.S. Agency for International Development, summarizes seven separately published studies assessing the main types of nutrition programs employed in developing countries. The basic format followed by each author includes an overview, the intervention design, evaluation of the estimates of the costs and nutritional impact of the interventions, and a case study consisting of analyses of the field interventions to illustrate the methods used in each study. The individual studies cover supplementary feeding, nutrition education, fortification, formulated foods, consumer food price subsidies, agricultural production, technical change and nutritional goals, and integrated nutrition and primary health care programs. Aims at providing guidance to professionals in developing countries, international agencies, and research institutions involved in nutrition programs.

101   Aylward, Francis
A C   PROTEIN AND NUTRITION POLICY IN LOW-INCOME COUNTRIES
        New York: Wiley, 1975.

102   Aziz, Sartaj, ed.
A C   HUNGER, POLITICS AND MARKETS: THE REAL ISSUES IN THE FOOD CRISIS
        New York: NY University Press, 1975.

Contains papers and commentary arising from the Rome Forum, a two-day colloquy called together at the request of Sayed A. Marei, Secretary-General of the World Food Conference, and which immediately preceded the Conference in November 1974. Chapters cover: (a) text of the Declaration of the Rome Forum; (b) dimensions of the problem; (c) possible solution; (d) food and population; (e) science, technology and the small farmer; and (f) formulation of a world food policy.

103   Bachman, Kenneth L.
A C D   RAPID FOOD PRODUCTION, GROWTH IN SELECTED DEVELOPING

COUNTRIES: A COMPARATIVE ANALYSIS OF UNDERLYING TRENDS,
1960-1976
Washington, D.C.:   IFPRI, 1979.

104   Balderston, Judith B., et al.
A C   MALNOURISHED CHILDREN OF THE RURAL POOR: THE WEB OF
        FOOD,   HEALTH,   EDUCATION,   FERTILITY,   AND   AGRICULTURAL
        PRODUCTION
        Boston, Mass.:   Auburn House, 1981.

        Examines   the   connections   between   children's   individual
        growth and development, the economic and social conditions
        topics in health economics research and research progress
        during   the   period   1970-80;   the   role   of   government,
        measurement   of   health   status,   the   demand   for   medical
        services, and physician behavior.

105   Ball, Nicole
A C   WORLD HUNGER: A GUIDE TO THE ECONOMIC AND POLITICAL
        DIMENSIONS
        Santa Barbara, CA: Clio Press, 1981.

106   Bechtel, Rosanna M.
A B   SALUS: LOW-COST RURAL HEALTH CARE AND MANPOWER TRAINING
        IDRC, 1980.

        An annotated bibliography of many areas of health care,
        with special emphasis on developing countries.   Entries
        cover reference works; organization and planning; primary
        health-care implementation; the training and utilization
        of primary health manpower; and formal evaluative studies.

107   Beenstock, Michael
A D   HEALTH, MIGRATION AND DEVELOPMENT
        Farnborough, U.K.:   Gower Publishing Co., 1980.

        The essays published in this volume were prepared in
        the course of a two-year stint at the World Bank.   They
        cover a number of topics that are of continuing interest
        for developing countries, including the relation between
        the supply of basic needs and health, on the one hand,
        and the link between health and productivity, on the
        other.   Beenstock devotes the latter half of the book
        to analyzing the determination and effect of migration.
        The   Indonesian   transmigration   project   provides   the
        empirical leavening for this discussion.

108   Bekele, M.
A C   FAO STUDIES IN FOOD AND POPULATION
        Rome: FAO, 1976.

        This book gives an account of the development of the
        thinking on the issue of food and population over the
        last two decades as inspired by the work of FAO.   It

comprises speeches by world authorities, made at various major FAO meetings, seminars, etc. Topics covered: population in relation to the development of agriculture; population and food supply; demographic aspects of agricultural development and food supply; and the world's food supplies.

109   Bennett, M. K.
A B C   THE WORLD'S FOOD: A STUDY OF THE INTERRELATIONS OF WORLD
POPULATION, NATIONAL DIETS AND FOOD POTENTIALS
Arno Press, 1980.

110   Berg, Alan
A C   MALNOURISHED PEOPLE: A POLICY VIEW
Washington, D.C.: World Bank, 1981.

Discusses the importance of adequate nutrition as an objective, as well as a means of economic development. Outlines the many facets of the nutrition problem and shows how efforts to improve nutrition can help alleviate much of the human and economic waste in the developing world.

111   Berg, Alan with Muscat, Robert J.
A B C   THE NUTRITION FACTOR: ITS ROLE IN NATIONAL DEVELOPMENT
Washington, D.C.: Brookings Institution, 1973.

This study examines nutrition, its effects on economic development, and solutions to the problem of malnutrition as viewed from a national perspective. Begins with a discussion of the relationships between malnutrition and development, outlining the economic benefits of improved nutrition and its impact on population growth. The following chapters discuss various policies and programs--such as increased income and food supply, education, breast feeding of infants, use of nutritious foods, food distribution systems and government feeding programs--whose implementation would result in improved nutrition and a likely increase in national income. Stresses that no single policy is adequate to solve the malnutrition problem. The book's other features include a case study of India's experience in launching a national nutrition program and some conclusions regarding nutrition programs and their future needs.

112   Berg, Alan; Scrimshaw, Nevin S. and Call, David L.
A B C   NUTRITION, NATIONAL DEVELOPMENT, AND PLANNING
Cambridge, Mass.: MIT Press, 1973.

This book contains the proceedings of the International Conference [on Nutrition, National Development] held at MIT in October, 1971 in which world participants including economists, nutritionists, development planners and administrators, discussed nutritional problems and their effects on individuals and national development, means of alleviating those problems, and nutrition planning as part of national development programs in developing countries. The book is arranged in six parts: (1) the effects of nutrition on the individual (four papers); (2) the role of nutrition in national development (five papers); (3) diagnosis of food and nutrition problems (five papers); (4) determinants of malnutrition and nutrition intervention programs (seven papers); (5) conceptual approach to national nutrition program planning (six papers); (6) nutritional case studies (five papers).

113
B
Bloom, Gordon F.
PRODUCTIVITY IN THE FOOD INDUSTRY: PROBLEMS AND POTENTIAL
Cambridge, Mass.:   MIT Press, 1972.

114
B
Brewis, Francis
BIBLIOGRAPHY ON HEALTH PLANNING IN DEVELOPING COUNTRIES
Brighton, England: Institute of Development Studies, 1975.

115
B C
Burk, Marguerite C. and Pao, Eleanor M.
ANALYSIS OF FOOD CONSUMPTION SURVEY DATA FOR DEVELOPING COUNTRIES
Rome: FAO, 1980.

This manual deals with the uses and limitations of food survey data and analyses. Coverage includes: (a) analysis of important food and nutrition problems; (b) data reduction and other preparation for analysis; (c) variations in characteristics of survey participants and evaluation of samples; (d) variations in measures of food consumption; (e) comparing household food data with other types of data; (f) planning multivariate analyses of food consumption; (g) interpretations and use of relationships; (h) analyses of food intake of individuals; and (i) some technical problems.

116
A B C
Burki, Shahid Javed and Goering, T. James
A PERSPECTIVE ON THE FOODGRAIN SITUATION IN THE POOREST COUNTRIES
Working Paper No. 251; Washington, D.C.:   World Bank, 1977.

Examines secular trends in production, trade, and consumption and longer-term food prospects in a regional and global context. Lays out strategies that seem most appropriate for increasing availability of food in the poor countries, and estimates additional domestic and foreign resources required to meet output targets.

117
A C
Cadet, Melissa Lawson
FOOD AID AND POLICY FOR ECONOMIC DEVELOPMENT: AN ANNOTATED BIBLIOGRAPHY AND DIRECTORY
Sacramento, CA: Trans Tech Management Press, 1981.

118   Cahill, Kevin M., ed.
A C   HEALTH AND DEVELOPMENT
         Maryknoll, NY: Orbis, 1976.

119   Cairncross, J.
B C   AN APPROACH TO FOOD/POPULATION PLANNING
         Rome: FAO, 1978.

         Identifies and interprets the interactions between the
         relevant demographic, economic and social factors in
         the planning process. Chapters cover: food and population
         planning in developing regions; causes of a drop in
         fertility; and modelling economic-demographic interactions.
         Also includes evaluation of a summaries of papers delivered
         at the five seminars.

120   Caprihan, S. P.
A C   FIGHT AGAINST HUNGER IN DEVELOPING COUNTRIES
         Bhopal: J. K. Jain Brothers, 1975.

121   Chernichovsky, Dov
B C   THE ECONOMIC THEORY OF THE HOUSEHOLD AND IMPACT MEASUREMENT
         OF NUTRITION AND RELATED HEALTH PROGRAMS
         Working Paper No. 302; Washington, D.C.: World Bank,
         1978.

         Attempts to outline the conceptual framework and
         measurement of nutrition and related health programs
         in the context of the Narangwal nutrition experiment
         in India, and their relevance to evaluation research
         in nutrition. Narangwal is an interdisciplinary research
         project involving the School of International Health
         of The Johns Hopkins University and the World Bank's
         Development Economics Department.

122   Cheyne, James Inor
B C   DEVELOPMENT OF RURAL HEALTH SERVICES IN THE THIRD WORLD
         London: Center for Environmental Studies, 1975.

123   Chopra, R. N.
A D   EVOLUTION OF FOOD POLICY IN INDIA
         New Delhi: Macmillan of India, 1981.

124   Chou, Marylin, et al.
A B C   WORLD FOOD PROSPECTS AND AGRICULTURAL POTENTIAL
         New York and London: Praeger, in cooperation with the
         Hudson Institute, 1977.

         Second of a series under Hudson Institute's "Prospects
         for Mankind" program, this volume employs a 200-year
         outlook to examine various resource and institutional
         issues, to ascertain the problems that may hinder
         agricultural development, and to suggest ways to alleviate
         the problems. Deals with the dynamic side of agriculture

and associated resource and technology availabilities and issues, treats global and developing country institutional concerns, and examines the influence of technology on dietary changes. Concludes with two scenarios, (1) depicting the most likely course of agriculture as worldwide affluence and independence from nature increase and (2) a pessimistic case posited on the assumption the world is entering a long-term cooler period. Posits that the "world food problem" is regional rather than global, short-term rather than long-term, and institutional rather than a reflection of a lack of resources and technology.

125   Clay, Edward and others
A C   FOOD POLICY ISSUES IN LOW-INCOME COUNTRIES
Working Paper No. 473; Washington, D.C.:   World Bank, 1981.

A background study for World Development Report 1981. Discusses food distribution--especially its insecurity in the face of external economic pressures and potential conflicts with internal production concerns--in general and with reference to Bangladesh, Zambia, and India.

126   Conde, J.; Paraiso, M. J. and Ayassour, V. K.
A B C   THE INTEGRATED APPROACH TO RURAL DEVELOPMENT, HEALTH, AND POPULATION
Paris: OECD, 1979.

The need for rapid and effective rural development continues to preoccupy policymakers in the developed and developing world alike. This study, for the Development Center of the OECD, covers the problems associated with attempts to integrate population and health programs into rural development efforts. It attempts to formulate practical suggestions for economic and human development in the rural sector of developing countries.

127   Correa, Hector
B C   POPULATION, HEALTH, NUTRITION, AND DEVELOPMENT: THEORY AND PLANNING
Lexington, Mass.; Toronto and London: Heath; Lexington Books, 1975.

The author tries to show the usefulness of the application of systems analysis, operations research, and mathematical optimization to the macro problems of population, health, and nutrition planning. The first part of the book discusses the interrelationships between population growth, health, nutrition, and socioeconomic development. The second part of the book presents a collection of operations research models that would be useful for planning in these fields. The study is oriented toward planners

interested in the solutions to specific problems using
mathematical techniques. Where possible, there has been
at attempt to test conclusions with empirical evidence.

128   Cummings, Ralph Waldo
B C   FOOD CROPS IN THE LOW INCOME COUNTRIES: THE STATE OF
PRESENT AND EXPECTED AGRICULTURAL RESEARCH AND TECHNOLOGY
New York: Rockefeller Foundation, 1976.

129   Dalrymple, Dana G.
A B   DEVELOPMENT   AND   SPREAD   OF   HIGH-YIELDING   VARIETIES   OF
WHEAT AND RICE IN THE LESS DEVELOPED NATIONS
Washington, D.C.:   U.S. Department of Agriculture, Office
of ICD in cooperation with U.S. Agency for International
Development, 1978.

Sixth edition of a report that outlines the development
of high-yielding varieties (HYV's) of wheat and rice,
particularly   semi-dwarf   varieties,   and   documents   the
spread in their use for the 12-year period from 1965/66
to 1976/77.   Gives basic information on the origin and
interrelationships   of   the   current   HYV's   and   provides
estimates   of   areas   planted   or   harvested   in   individual
countries   by   crop   years,   including   some   preliminary
estimates for 1977/78.   Focuses on non-Communist nations,
but includes limited data on China, Laos, Vietnam, and
Cuba.

130   Development   Center   for   Economic   Co-operation   and
Development
B C   AN   APPRAISAL   OF   INCOME   ELASTICITIES   FOR   TOTAL   FOOD
CONSUMPTION IN DEVELOPING COUNTRIES
Paris: Quirino, 1970.

131   Duffy, John
A B   VENTURES IN WORLD HEALTH: THE MEMOIRS OF FRED LOWE SOPER
PAHO, 1977.

Traces   certain   phases   of   the   development   of   preventive
measures--locally,   nationally,   and   internationally.   The
basic approach is that of the public health administrator's
responsibility for disease prevention.   The study covers
a   sufficiently   long   period   of   time   to   reveal   some   of
the disastrous results of neglecting preventive measures.

132   Dumont, Rene
A B   THE GROWTH OF HUNGER: A NEW POLITICS OF AGRICULTURE
Australia: T. C. Lothian, 1980.

133   Elling, Ray H.
A B C   CROSS-NATIONAL STUDY OF HEALTH SYSTEMS: CONCEPTS, METHODS,
AND DATA SOURCES: A GUIDE TO INFORMATION SOURCES
Detroit: Gale Research, 1980.

Annotated bibliography of selected works in English written
between 1965 and 1977 on studies related to structural
arrangements of health and medical care systems; includes
studies referring to a single country. Sources include
collections of descriptions of health systems, monographs,
journal articles, official reports, unpublished
dissertations, and so forth. In ten parts according
to topic and type of entry: world political economy,
population, resources, development, and health; general
works; comparisons of two or more countries, framework
statements; regionalization of health service systems;
methods; data sources; bibliographies; journals; and
organizations.

134   El-Sherbini, A. A., ed.
C D   FOOD SECURITY ISSUES IN THE ARAB NEAR EAST
         New York: Pergamon Press, 1979.

This report of the United Economic Commission for Western
Asia provides data on production, consumption, stocks,
and trade of foodstuffs for Iraq, Lebanon, Jordan, the
Syrian Arab Republic, the Yemen Arab Republic, and the
People's Democratic Republic of Yemen. Policy options
for ensuring adequate food supplies are outlined briefly.

135   Ensminger, Douglas
A B C   CONQUEST OF WORLD HUNGER AND POVERTY
         Ames: Iowa State University Press, 1980.

136   Evenson, Robert E. and Kisley, Yoav
B C   AGRICULTURAL RESEARCH AND PRODUCTIVITY
         New Haven and London: Yale University Press, 1975.

A study of the discovery and diffusion of agricultural
technology and the economic effect emanating from it.
Concentrates on measurements and estimations of
agricultural research and technological change in an
international context with data on aggregate food
production, investment in research, and total factor
productivity by major Indian state, 1953-70. Empirical
studies of international agricultural productivity
determination are presented, and an analysis of
productivity change in Indian agriculture provides a
testing ground for the empirical models developed for
international comparisons.

137   Food and Agriculture Organization of the UN
A C   THE STATE OF FOOD AND AGRICULTURE, 1972
         Rome: FAO; New York: Unipub, 1972.

An assessment of food and agriculture throughout the
world, drawing on information available as of October
1, 1972. The report is divided into four parts; world
review of agriculture, including international trade

in agricultural products, food prices, production and trade of fishery and forest products, and development assistance for agriculture; review by geographical regions, with analysis of agricultural production, trade, prices, and agricultural policies and problems; a survey of education and training for development; and a report on advances in agricultural technology and research for the developing countries.

138   FAO
B C   NATURAL RESOURCES AND THE HUMAN ENVIRONMENT FOR FOOD AND AGRICULTURE; FAO Environment Paper, 1
        Rome: FAO, 1981.

Discusses the interrelationship--at a global level--of population pressure and natural resources use and management, with particular reference to increased food and agricultural demand and the ensuing environmental issues. Chapters cover: the state of natural resources; environmental impact of intensificaiton of agriculture; selected environmental problems of specific ecological zones; and legislative aspects of environmental problems.

139   FAO
B C   POPULATION AND AGRICULTURAL DEVELOPMENT: SELECTED RELATIONSHIPS AND POSSIBLE PLANNING USES NO. 7: PRODUCTIVITY, WAGES AND NUTRITION IN THE CONTEXT OF LESS DEVELOPED COUNTRIES
        New York: Unipub, 1978.

140   FAO
A B C   POPULATION, FOOD SUPPLY AND AGRICULTURAL DEVELOPMENT
        Rome: FAO; distributed by Unipub, New York, 1975.

Previously published world food survey that provided the basis for FAO's contribution to the World Population Conference. Discusses in particular: population and food supply, dimensions and causes of malnutrition, the demand for food, future food problems, possibilities for increasing production, and major policy implications. Concludes in part that enlargement in the scope of world trade in foodgrains required the evolution of a new system of exchange of data and information, more effective food reserve policies, flexible trading arrangements and harmonious adjustment policies. Demographic and food production information included in annex.

141   FAO
B C   STUDIES IN FOOD AND POPULATION
        New York: Unipub, 1978.

142   FAO
B C D   WOMEN IN FOOD PRODUCTION, FOOD HANDLING AND NUTRITION WITH SPECIAL EMPHASIS ON AFRICA.

Rome: FAO, 1979.

This report presents an appraisal of the information currently available concerning: (a) women's role in food production, food handling and nutrition in Africa; and (b) the extent to which the conditions under which women live and work have a bearing upon the availability of food and the nutritional levels of their families and communities.

143   FAO/ROAFE
B C D CONSULTATION ON IMPROVING NUTRITION OF THE RURAL POOR IN ASIA AND THE FAR EAST, BANGKOK, 1977
       Rome: FAO/ROAFE, 1977.

In four parts: (a) keynote papers; (b) case studies of nutrition programs in India, Korea, Malaysia, the Philippines and Thailand; (c) resource papers, covering public health nutrition in rural areas, nutrition surveillance and feeding programs at the village level, participation of women in development, and World Food Programme (WFP) assistance for supplementary feeding programs; and (d) four theoretical models for nutrition improvement programs.

144   FAO
A C   A RECORD OF EXPERIENCE: CATALOGUE OF FFHC/ACTION FOR DEVELOPMENT DOCUMENTS, 1971-1976
       Rome: FAO, 1977.

Presents a selection of reports on projects of FAO's Freedom From Hunger Campaign/Action for Development (FFHC/AD) program. Summaries of documents are classified by region and by country.

145   FAO
A C   FEEDING OF WORKERS IN DEVELOPING COUNTRIES
       Rome: FAO, 1976.

Presents information on food and work in relation to the feeding of workers in developing countries. Chapters cover: (a) food requirements of the worker; (b) problems of workers in meeting their energy needs; (c) food and working efficiency; (d) workers' feeding programs in practice; (e) planning workers' feeding programs; (f) consultancy and advisory services; and (g) training of managers and workers for feeding programs.

146   FAO
A B   FOOD, NUTRITION AND AGRICULTURE: GUIDELINES FOR AGRICULTURAL TRAINING CURRICULA IN AFRICA
       Rome: FAO, 1982.

Presents guidelines for the introduction of nutrition into pre-service agricultural education, deigned to help teachers develop a nutrition component for use in agricultural programs and to present the subject in a manner relevant to agricultural students.

147   FAO/WHO/UNICEF
A B C   LIVES IN PERIL: PROTEIN AND THE CHILD
          Rome: FAO, 1970.

148   Faruqee, Rashid
B C   ANALYZING   THE   IMPACT   OF   HEALTH   SERVICES: PROJECT
          EXPERIENCES FROM INDIA, GHANA, AND THAILAND
          Working Paper No. 546; Washington, D.C.:   World Bank,
          1982.

          Reviews four categories of health indicators (environment,
          services   offered,   services   received,   and   changes   in
          mortality, morbidity, and nutritional status) in order
          to evaluate the impact of health projects in India, Ghana,
          and Thailand.

149   Faruqee, Rashid
B C   INTEGRATING FAMILY PLANNING WITH HEALTH SERVICES: DOES
          IT HELP?
          Working Paper No. 515; Washington, D.C.:   World Bank,
          1982.

          Analyzes the findings of an experiment carried out in
          Narangwal, a village in Punjab, India, between 1968 and
          1974 related to health care and family planning.   The
          World Bank collaborated with The Johns Hopkins University
          in analyzing this data from one of the best known and
          well-documented field experiments in health care and
          family planning in the world.

150   Faruqee, Rashid and Johnson, Ethna
B C D   HEALTH, NUTRITION, AND FAMILY PLANNING IN INDIA: A SURVEY
          OF EXPERIMENTS AND SPECIAL PROJECTS
          Working Paper No. 507; Washington, D.C.:   World Bank,
          1982.

          Surveys   fourteen   experiments   and   special   projects   in
          health,   nutrition,   and   family   planning   in   India   and
          proposes guidelines for future Bank projects on the basis
          of the survey.

151   Feachem, Richard G.; Bradley, David J.; Garelick, Hemda
          and Mara, D. Duncan
B C   HEALTH   ASPECTS   OF   EXCRETA   AND   SULLAGE   MANAGEMENT--A
          STATE-OF-THE-ART REVIEW
          Washington, D.C.: World Bank, 1980.

          Provides information on the ways in which particular
          excreta disposal and reuse technologies affect the survival

and dissemination of pathogens. It is intended for planners, engineers, economists, and health workers.

152   Fuchs, Victor R.
A B   ECONOMIC ASPECTS OF HEALTH
        Chicago: University of Chicago Press, 1982.

The arguments for greater expenditure on health have tended to be more moral than economic in the past. This book, a conference report produced by the National Bureau of Economic Research, narrows the gap between health practitioners and economists by presenting economic studies of the determinants of health, the effects of sickness, and the issues facing policymakers. Although based on research on different income groups in the Untied States, it offers a number of theoretical tools for formulating health policy in less developed countries.

153   George, Susan
B C   THE HUNGER PROBLEMATIQUE AND A CRITIQUE OF RESEARCH
        UNU, 1980.

This report defines the "hunger problematique"; looks at its implications for research; and examines obstacles to relevant food/development scholarship. It suggests elements for a progressive research program and presents a programmatic diagram which could be a basis for education and training programs.

154   George, Susan
A C   FEEDING THE FEW: CORPORATE CONTROL OF FOOD
        Washington, D.C.: Institute for Policy Studies, 1978.

155   George, Susan
A C   HOW THE OTHER HALF DIES: THE REAL REASONS FOR WORLD
        HUNGER
        Montclair, NJ: Allanhold, Osmun, 1977.

156   Gish, Oscar
B C D   PLANNING THE HEALTH SECTOR: THE TANZANIAN EXPERIENCE
        New York: Holmes and Meier, Africana Publishing, 1976.

157   Golladay, Fredrick
A C   HEALTH
        Washington, D.C.: World Bank, 1980.

Draws on experience gained from health components of 70 World Bank projects in 44 countries between 1975 and 1978. Emphasizes the disproportionately high expenditures incurred on curative medicine, maintenance of expensive hospitals, and sophisticated training of medical personnel at the cost of preventive care for the majority of the people. Points out that low-cost health care systems are feasible and recommends that the Bank begin regular

and direct lending for health, in addition to having
health components as part of projects in other sectors.

158   Greve, J.
B C   CONSUMER PARTICIPATION AND RESPONSIBILITY IN THE PLANNING
AND DELIVERY OF HEALTH CARE
WHO/EURO, 1980.

Describes various forms of consumer participation and
responsibility in the field of health care; considers
their significance for the planning and delivery of health
care; and discusses some of the principal issues involved.

159   Gwatkin, Davidson, R.; Wilcox, Janet R. and Wray, Joe D.
A B C   CAN HEALTH AND NUTRITION INTERVENTION MAKE A DIFFERENCE?
Washington, D.C.:   Overseas Development Council, 1980.

Describes and evaluates the general characteristics and
reported results of ten direct intervention efforts that
sought both to reduce infant and child mortality in poor
rural areas and to keep adequate records about their
accomplishments (six of the projects were also concerned
with the physical growth of children, and four included
family planning and fertility reduction). The selected
projects served population ranging from 2000 to 65,000
and were located in different nations on several continents
(e.g., India, Nigeria, Jamaica, Peru, and the United
States). Declines in infant mortality occurred in all
areas served by the ten projects, and most of the declines
were large (one-third to one-half) and rapid (one to
five years). Evidence is persuasive that the mortality
declines in the majority of the people were notably more
rapid than they would have been without the project.
Concludes that health and nutrition interventions can
make a difference.

160   Hall, T. L. and Mejia, A., eds.
B C   HEALTH MANPOWER PLANNING: PRINCIPLES, METHODS, ISSUES
WHO, 1978.

Includes 12 papers which analyze various aspects of health
manpower planning as an integral part of overall health
planning in the context of socioeconomic development,
highlight common difficulties experienced, and describe
components of the planning process and techniques that
can be used, including their potential benefits and
limitations.

161   Harbert, Lloyd and Scandizzo, Pasquale L.
A B C   FOOD DISTRIBUTION AND NUTRITION INTERVENTION: THE CASE
OF CHILE
Working Paper No. 512; Washington, D.C.:   World Bank,
1982.

The impact of Chile's Complementary Feeding Program (CFP), both on the direct and indirect beneficiaries, is analyzed. Describes Chile's major nutrition intervention programs and establishes the relative importance of the CFP in terms of budgetary expenditures and number of beneficiaries reached. Reviews briefly the programs past limitation, recent reforms, and potential effectiveness.

162   Hardoy, Jorge E. and Satterthwaite, David
A B C   SHELTER: NEED AND RESPONSE: HOUSING, LAND AND SETTLEMENT POLICIES IN SEVENTEEEN THIRD WORLD NATIONS
Somerset, NJ: John Wiley, 1981.

163   Hetzel, Basil S.
BASIC HEALTH CARE IN DEVELOPING COUNTRIES: AN EPIDEMIOLOGICAL PERSPECTIVE
New York: Oxford University Press, 1979.

164   Hopkins, Raymond F. and Puchala, Donald J.
A B C   GLOBAL FOOD INTERDEPENDENCE: CHALLENGE TO AMERICAN FOREIGN POLICY
New York: Columbia University Press, 1980.

Enumerates the world's food problems, argues that the global food system has failed to perform satisfactorily in recent years, and analyzes the goals, formulation, execution, and impacts of American foreign agricultural policy. Reviews the U.S. participation in world food trade and international organizations dealing with world food problems; discusses issues concerning food aid; examines the processes and priorities of U.S. foreign agricultural policy; explores alternative development in global food supply and demand to the year 2000; and recommends courses of action that (1) guarantee greater stability in international food marketing, (2) promote rural modernization in poor countries, (3) coordinate domestic and international U.S. food policy and allow more effective decision-making, (4) support multilateral agencies, and (5) promote new programs of agronomic, economic, social, and political research.

165   Hopkins, Raymond F.; Puchala, Donald J. and Talbot, Ross B., eds.
A B C   FOOD, POLTIICS, AND AGRICULTURAL DEVELOPMENT: CASE STUDIES IN THE PUBLIC POLICY OF RURAL MODERNIZATION
Boulder, CO: Westview Press, 1979.

166   Hornby, P. and others
B C   GUIDELINES FOR HEALTH MANPOWER PLANNING: A COURSE BOOK
WHO, 1980.

A basic course for the training of health service administrators and educators, whether they occupy health manpower positions at the national, provincial, or local

level.   Coverage includes: health   manpower planning;
ten steps to health manpower planning; health manpower
report on existing manpower and services; future supply
of   manpower;   manpower   requirements--quantity,   quality
and   distribution;   mismatches   between   supply   and
requirements;   solving   mismatches;   organizational   and
management problems; manpower strategy and outline plan;
detailed   health   manpower   development   plan;   and
implementation and monitoring.

167   IDRC
B   LOW-COST RURAL HEALTH CARE AND HEALTH MANPOWER TRAINING:
        AN   ANNOTATED   BIBLIOGRAPHY   WITH   SPECIAL   EMPHASIS   ON
        DEVELOPING COUNTRIES
        IDRC, 1975.

        This series of bibliographies, issued at irregular
        intervals, is designed to coordinate information on
        nontraditional health care delivery systems in remote
        regions of the world, especially in developing countries.
        The literature abstracted focuses primarily on new models
        of   health   care   delivery,   and   on   the   training   and
        utilization of auxiliary health workers.   Each volume
        is divided into five sections: (a) reference works;
        (b) organization and planning; (c) primary health
        care--implementation; (d) primary health care--training
        and utilization; and (e) formal evaluative studies.

168   International Food Policy Research Institute
A B C   FOOD NEEDS OF DEVELOPING COUNTRIES: PROJECTIONS AND
        PRODUCTION AND CONSUMPTION TO 1990
        Washington, D.C.: IFPRI, 1977.

169   Institute for Food and Development Policy
A B C   FOOD FIRST RESOURCE GUIDE: DOCUMENTATION ON THE ROOTS
        OF WORLD HUNGER AND RURAL POVERTY
        San Francisco: The Institute, 1979.

170   International Food Policy Research Institute
A C D   FOOD POLICY ISSUES AND CONCERNS IN SUB-SAHARAN AFRICA
        Washington, D.C.: IFPRI, 1981.

171   International Food Policy Research Institute
A B C   MEETING FOOD NEEDS IN THE DEVELOPING WORLD: THE LOCATION
        AND MAGNITUDE OF THE TASK IN THE NEXT DECADE
        Washington, D.C.: IFPRI, 1976.

172   International Food Policy Research Institute
B C   RECENT AND PROSPECTIVE DEVELOPMENTS IN FOOD CONSUMPTION:
        SOME POLICY ISSUES
        Washington, D.C.: IFPRI, 1977.

173   Jazairi, N. T.
B C   APPROACHES TO THE DEVELOPMENT OF HEALTH INDICATORS
        Paris: OECD, 1976.

Contains a review of some approaches and measurements related to health in general, followed by a discussion of life expectancy at various ages as a social indicator of the length of life. Also discusses monitoring the healthfulness of life, the quality of health care, the delivery of health care, and the integration of the disabled in society.

174   Johnson, D. Gale, ed.
A B C   FOOD AND AGRICULTURAL POLICY FOR THE 1980'S
Washington, D.C. and London: American Enterprise Institute for Public Policy Research, 1981.

Seven previously unpublished papers and comments, read at the conference held 2 and 3 October 1980 in Washington, D.C., organized under three major topics: U.S. agricultural economic developments and consequences of farm policies during the 1970's; world food production, consumption, and international trade and their implications, and prospective changes in the agricultural structure; and U.S. agricultural policy in the 1980's.

175   Johnson, D. Gale
A B C   WORLD FOOD PROBLEMS
Enterprise, 1975.

176   Jones, David
A B C   FOOD AND INTERDEPENDENCE: THE EFFECT OF FOOD AND AGRICULTURAL POLICIES ON THE FOOD PROBLEMS OF DEVELOPING COUNTRIES
London: Overseas Development Institute, 1976.

177   Joy, Leonard and Payne, Philip
B C   FOOD AND NUTRITION PLANNING
Rome: FAO, 1975.

Presents a detailed account of the way in which nutritional concerns and objectives might become an integrated part of development planning. Chapters cover: (a) concept of food and nutrition planning; (b) approach to planning; (c) information required for nutrition planning; (d) social causes of malnutrition; (e) implications of introducing nutritional objectives into development planning; (f) nutrition planning; (g) food policy planning; (h) techniques for identification, design and choice of intervention measures; and (i) planning and administration. An appendix provides indices of nutritional status and their interpretation.

178   Junker, Louis ed.
B C   THE POLITICAL ECONOMY OF FOOD AND ENERGY: LECTURES GIVEN AT WESTERN MICHIGAN UNIVERSITY UNDER THE SPONSORSHIP OF THE DEPARTMENT OF ECONOMICS, ACADEMIC YEAR, 1975-76
Ann Arbor: University of Michigan, Graduate School of Business Administration, Division of Research, 1977.

Five previously unpublished papers with an introduction by the editor, dealing with food and energy problems. The authors analyze these problems from an "unorthodox" position and challenge some of the myths that prevail not only in our society in general but in the minds of professionals. The issues discussed include: world feeding, farming for profit in a hungry world, competition in the food manufacturing market, food and energy crises and the media, and a new look at the nature of economic activity.

179   Katz, F. M. and Snow, R.
B C   ASSESSING HEALTH WORKERS' PERFORMANCE: A MANUAL FOR TRAINING AND SUPERVISION
WHO, 1980.

This publication provides guidelines for teachers and supervisors in the health field in making an adequate assessment of their students' or workers' performance. In two parts. Part 1 outlines a general approach to performance assessment, establishes a set of principles essential to the effective assessment of individual performance, and discusses current instruments or techniques that can be applied in assessment. In addition, it describes a sequential set of steps in preparing a performance assessment and follows this up with illustrations of two performance assessment procedures, concerned with history-taking and blood-pressure measurement. Part 2 provides some examples of instruments currently in use in several countries for the assessment of students' and health workers' performance. These are classified into three categories of functions or tasks; clinical proficiency; multiple tasks (comprehensive assessment); and specific tasks.

180   Kaynak, Erdener
B C   FOOD RETAILING SYSTEMS IN A DEVELOPING ECONOMY
Cranfield, England: Cranfield Institute Press, 1975.

181   Ker, A. D. R.
A C   FOOD OR FAMINE: AN ACCOUNT OF THE CROP SCIENCE PROGRAM SUPPORTED BY THE INTERNATIONAL DEVELOPMENT RESEARCH CENTER
Ottawa: IDRC, 1979.

182   King, Maurice H.
A B C   NUTRITION FOR DEVELOPING COUNTRIES
Nairobi: Oxford University Press, 1972.

183   Knudsen, Odin K. and Scandizzo, Pasquale L.
A B C   NUTRITION AND FOOD NEEDS IN DEVELOPING COUNTRIES
Working Paper No. 328; Washington, D.C.: World Bank, 1979.

Assesses the problem of food supply and distribution in selected developing countries. On the basis of new evidence from household budget surveys and the availability of food supplies, shows that the pattern of calorie consumption is similar in the sample of countries considered (Bangladesh, India, Indonesia, Morocco, Pakistan, and Sri Lanka) and suggests that, if food prices increase or income distribution deteriorates, increases in general food supplies would be insufficient to eliminate malnutrition in the next two decades. Concludes that food programs and market intervention will be necessary to reduce the severity of malnutrition.

184   Kocher, James E.
B C   ACHIEVING HEALTH AND NUTRITIONAL OBJECTIVES WITHIN A
         BASIC NEEDS FRAMEWORK
         Cambridge, Mass.: Harvard University Press, 1979.

185   Konandreas, Panos
B C   FOOD SECURITY: AN INSURANCE APPROACH
         Washington, D.C.: IFPRI, 1978.

186   Kraul, S. N.
A D   JAMAICA: FOOD CROP DEVELOPMENT AND MARKETING FEASIBILITY
         SURVEY: AGRONOMIC CONSIDERATIONS
         FAO, 1971.

187   Lappe, Frances Moore
A   FOOD FIRST: BEYOND THE MYTH OF SCARCITY
         Boston: Houghton-Mifflin, 1977.

188   Latham, L.; Latham, M. and Basta, Samir S.
A C D   THE NUTRITIONAL AND ECONOMIC IMPLICATIONS OF ASCARIS
         INFECTION IN KENYA
         Working Paper No. 271; Washington, D.C.: World Bank,
         1977.

         The study, carried out by a research team from Cornell University, was undertaken to determine the impact of roundworm disease on the growth of children. Roundworm (ascaris) infection is believed to affect a quarter of the world's population, but few studies have been undertaken to determine its significance. Also discussed are the costs of medication, hopitalization, loss of income in the general population, and the cost-benefit ratio of a national control program.

189   Latham. M. C.
A B C D HUMAN NUTRITION IN TROPICAL AFRICA: A TEXTBOOK FOR HEALTH
         WORKERS WITH SPECIAL REFERENCE TO COMMUNITY HEALTH PROBLEMS
         IN EAST AFRICA
         FAO, 1979.

This revision first published in 1965. Although maintaining a bias toward the health worker, gives more attention to non-medical aspects of nutrition, including food and nutrition policies and the role of the agricultural sector in improving nutrition. Its main sections deal with the principles of nutrition, disorders of malnutrition, the nutritive value of specific foods, and various diets for family and institutional purposes. Policy aspects are also covered in terms of public health and social nutrition, and nutritional planning at the national level.

190   Lele, Uma
A B C THE DESIGN OF RURAL DEVELOPMENT: LESSONS FROM AFRICA
       Baltimore: Johns Hopkins University Press for IBRD, 1975.

191   Lele, Uma J.
A B C THE GREEN REVOLUTION: INCOME DISTRIBUTION AND NUTRITION
       Ithaca, NY: Cornell University Press, 1971.

192   Lindblad, Carl J.
B C   THE POTENTIAL FOR RENEWABLE ENERGY TECHNOLOGIES IN THE RURAL POSTHARVEST FOOD SYSTEM IN DEVELOPING COUNTRIES
       1981.

193   Linnemann, Hans, et al.
A B C MOIRA: MODEL OF INTERNATIONAL RELATIONS IN AGRICULTURE: REPORT OF THE PROJECT GROUP "FOOD FOR A DOUBLING WORLD POPULATION"
       Amsterdam; New York and Oxford: North-Holland, 1979.

Focuses on a description of MOIRA, an algorithmic simulation model constructed to analyze policy alternatives, which describes the food sector of individual countries and links these sectors through an equilibrium model of international trade. MOIRA was developed by a group, loosely associated with the Club of Rome, for studying future levels of food production and consumption under a variety of policy and state-of-the-world assumptions. Includes an assessment of potential world food production, a description of the model, the results of simulation runs, and a sensitivity analysis of simulated outcomes to changes in exogenous factors. Concludes that MOIRA has limited value as a prognostic tool, but represents a first step in understanding the international economic interrelations of food production and consumption.

194   Loftus, Tony
A B C FOOD AND ENVIRONMENT: RECONCILING THE DEMAND OF AGRICULTURE WITH GLOBAL CONSERVATION
       Rome: FAO, 1977.

Describes in general terms FAO's concern with the

environment, and presents some of the solutions developed by FAO to the dangers which threaten it. Topics covered: man, food and conservation; man as an environmental force; agricultural hazards; food supply; saving endangered nature; conservation; and natural resources for food and agriculture.

195   Manning, Diana H.
A C   SOCIETY AND FOOD: THE THIRD WORLD
       London: Butterworths, 1977.

196   Manocha, S. L.
A B C NUTRITION AND OUR OVERPOPULATED PLANET
       C. C. Thomas, 1975.

197   Martin, A. E., ed.
A B C HEALTH ASPECTS OF HUMAN SETTLEMENTS: A REVIEW BASED
       ON THE TECHNICAL DISCUSSIONS HELD DURING THE TWENTY-NINTH
       WORLD HEALTH ASSEMBLY, 1976
       WHO, 1977.

       Coverage includes: some basic concepts and a typology of human settlements; health in human settlements; priority needs in the provision of health services in human settlements; relative importance of individual influences on health; and the role of WHO. Annexes include summary of information contributed by Member States and review of previous work by WHO on health services in relation to human settlements.

198   Maxwell, Robert J.
B C   HEALTH AND WEALTH: AN INTERNATIONAL STUDY OF HEALTH-CARE
       SPENDING
       Lexington, Mass. and Toronto: Heath, Lexington Books
       for Sandoz Institute for Health and Socio-Economic Studies,
       1981.

       Draws from the latest data available (mostly through 1975 or 1977; some through 1979) to analyze health care expenditures for ten developed countries (Australia, Canada, France, West Germany, Italy, the Netherlands, Sweden, Switzerland, the United States, and the United Kingdom). Proposes a structure for national and international data collection and offers tentative conclusions.

199   May, Jacques M. and McLellan, Donna L.
B C D THE ECOLOGY OF MALNUTRITION IN MEXICO AND CENTRAL AMERICA
       New York: Hafner Publishing, 1972.

200   Mayer, Jean and Dwyer, Johanna T., eds.
A B C FOOD AND NUTRITION POLICY IN A CHANGING WORLD
       New York: Oxford University Press, 1979.

Condensed from the five-volume, 1975 UNICEF report, Priorities in Child Nutrition in Developing Countries, contains thirteen essays, on the need for national nutrition policy planning and the various aspects of formulating food and nutrition policy in developing countries, particularly with regard to the young child. Organized into five parts, part one, the introduction, focuses on demand, supply, and need and presents a systemized approach to dealing with malnutrition. Part two discusses long-term national planning, while part three considers specific interventions with immediate impact that are consistent with the long-term plan. Part four deals with problems and programs of nutritional deficiency, and part five discusses the role of the food industry. An appendix presents a "Nutrition Primer." Contributors come from many countries and are all experts in the field.

201   McIntire, John
B C D   FOOD SECURITY IN THE SAHEL: VARIABLE IMPORT LEVY, GRAIN RESERVES, AND FOREIGN EXCHANGE ASSISTANCE
Washington, D.C.: International Food Policy Research Institute, 1981.

Discusses findings of a five-year study (1979-83) in seven countries in the Sahel--Chad, Gambia, Mali, Mauritania, Niger, Senegal, and Upper Volta. Evaluates a food insurance scheme for the Sahel region. Identifies and compares the effects of different policy responses, and uses stochastic simulation to analyze two alternative cases of policy aimed at stabilizing food consumption in a situation with foreign exchange assistance and one without. Concludes that foreign exchange assistance schemes provide more security than grain reserves at lower costs; stresses specific responsibilities for the recipients and donors.

202   McLoughlin, Peter F. M., ed.
A C D   AFRICAN FOOD PRODUCTION SYSTEMS: CASES AND THEORY
Baltimore and London: Johns Hopkins Press, 1970.

Approximately a quarter of Africa's rural population is experiencing difficulty in feeding itself. Anthropologists and economists describe in detailed and descriptive case studies the food production of seven African societies. These studies attempt to provide the bases for the formulation of policy toward defining and solving the problems of rural African development.

203   Meyer, Evelyn E. and Sainsbury, Peter, eds.
A B C   PROMOTING HEALTH IN THE HUMAN ENVIRONMENT: A REVIEW BASED ON THE TECHNICAL DISCUSSION HELD DURING THE TWENTY-SEVENTH WORLD HEALTH ASSEMBLY, 1974
WHO, 1975.

In three parts: (a) describes the broad range of psycho-social aspects of the environment, including personal life stresses, cultural differences, socioeconomic factors, family patterns and the consequences of rapid social change; (b) outlines ways in which the health services can counter the negative effects of these environmental conditions and utilize knowledge about psycho-social factors in order to restore and promote health and well-being; and (c) conclusions and recommendations.

204   Miljan, Toivo, ed.
A B C   FOOD AND AGRICULTURE IN GLOBAL PERSPECTIVE: DISCUSSIONS IN THE COMMITTEE OF THE WHOLE OF THE UNITED NATIONS
New York; Oxford; Toronto and Syndey: Pergamon Press, for UNITAR and the Center for Economic and Social Studies of the Third World (CEESTEM), 1980.

Documents the activities and deliberations in March 1979 of the Second Session of the Committee of the Whole, which has been charged by the United Nations General Assembly with negotiating the adoption of guidelines toward achieving the objectives of the New International Economic Order. Focuses on the global problems of food and agriculture from the point of view of the specialized agencies of the UN and Member States. Consists of technical reference papers, statements by representatives of Specialized Agencies and Member States, and proposed negotiation texts; organized into two parts: (1) the problem and (2) specific issues, such as food production in LDC's, food aid, agricultural trade, rural development, and nutrition.

205   Mittendorf, H. J.
B C   PLANNING OF URBAN WHOLESALE MARKETS FOR PERISHABLE FOOD: WITH PARTICULAR REFERENCE TO DEVELOPING COUNTRIES
Rome: FAO, 1976.

Guide discusses the technical, economic, financial, and organizational problems involved in the planning, operation, and management of food wholesale markets in urban areas of developing countries. Detailed discussion of each aspect, drawing upon information from wholesale market authorities in Western Europe, North America, South America, Asia, Australia, and Africa.

206   Mondot-Bernard, Jacqueline
B C D   SATISFACTION OF FOOD REQUIREMENTS AND AGRICULTURAL DEVELOPMENT IN MALI
Paris: OECD, 1980.

Vol. 1: Results of Food Consumption Surveys. This study deals with the estimation of the "desirable intake" in the light of the real needs of the population in different ecological areas and the definition of an agricultural policy taking account of the food requirements and the other demands on agriculture. This volume describes the general methodology of the study and presents the analysis of food consumption surveys undertaken in Mali. Vol. 2: Results of Medical and Nutritional Surveys. This volume contains the results of the medical section of the nutritional surveys.

207   Morris, Morris D.
MEASURING THE CONDITION OF THE WORLD'S POOR: THE PHYSICAL QUALITY OF LIFE
Washington, D.C.:   Overseas Development Council, 1979.

208   Murdoch, William W.
A B C   THE POVERTY OF NATIONS: THE POLITICAL ECONOMY OF HUNGER AND POPULATION
Baltimore and London: Johns Hopkins University Press, 1980.

An analysis of the problem of the population expansion in LDC's in relation to the problem of food supply. Argues that rural poverty causes population explosion and limits food production. Low food production and inappropriate methods of production in turn lead to the persistence of rural poverty. Maintains that this poverty arises from the internal political and economic structure of LDC's and the LDC's unequal relationship to developed countries. Analyzes the relationship between population and poverty, discussing population growth, food production, agricultural development strategies, historical development of the dual economy and modern forms, and the structural causes of poverty in LDC's. The author contends that the world's nations can adequately meet the food requirements of their people if LDC economies are restructured along egalitarian lines.

209   Nelson, Jack A.
A B C   HUNGER FOR JUSTICE: THE POLTIICS OF FOOD AND FAITH
Maryknoll, NY: Orbis Books, 1980.

210   Newell, Kenneth W., ed.
A C D   HEALTH BY THE PEOPLE
WHO, 1975.

Consists of 10 chapters describing innovative methods of delivering primary health care to the population at large, particularly in rural areas, involving community action and participation. One chapter describes the approach taken in India to integrating a traditional system of medicine--the Ayurvedic system--into the health services as a whole. The remaining chapters fall into three groups dealing with countries where there were far-reaching changes at the national level (China, Cuba,

Tanzania), those where there was an extension of the existing system (Iran, Niger, Venezuela), and those where there was community development in a limited local area (Guatemala, India, Indonesia).

211   OECD
B C D   CRITICAL ISSUES ON FOOD MARKETING SYSTEMS IN DEVELOPING COUNTRIES; REPORT OF THE JOINT OECD/FAO SEMINAR, PARIS, 18-22 OCTOBER 1976.
        Paris: OECD, 1977.

Supported by quantitative information and experience, this report analyzes the role of a dynamic marketing system in accelerating development of semi-subsistence peasant farming areas and formulates strategies for marketing improvement. Emphasizes organizational, management and related economic and policy aspects. An annex includes case studies.

212   OECD
A C   FOOD POLICY
        Paris: OECD, 1981.

Discusses an integrated approach to policy making in the food-policy sector, with coverage on: the concept of food policy; the changing nature of the food economy; interdependence and policy; the case for food policy; the emerging policy context; guidelines; government measures; and future directions.

213   OECD/FAO
B C   FOOD MARKETING SYSTEMS IN DEVELOPING COUNTRIES, PARIS, FRANCE, 1976
        Washington, D.C.: OECD, 1977.

214   Oram, Peter
B C   INVESTMENT AND INPUT REQUIREMENTS FOR ACCELERATING FOOD PRODUCTION IN LOW INCOME COUNTRIES BY 1990
        Washington, D.C.: IFPRI, 1979.

215   PAHO
A B C   HEALTH FOR ALL BY THE YEAR 2000: STRATEGIES
        PAHO, 1980.

A compilation of the regional strategies representing the contribution of PAHO to the global strategies for attaining the worldwide goals of Health for All by the Year 2000. Coverage includes: developments in the health sector in the 1971-80 decade; a discussion of the goal and the necessary strategies and their implementation; national strategies; and the Declaration of Alma-Ata, USSR.

216   PAHO
B C D   THE NATIONAL FOOD AND NUTRITION SURVEY OF GUYANA
          Sponsored jointly by the Government of Guyana, PAHO,
          CFNI and FAO
          PAHO, 1976.

          Includes brief overview of the survey with an account
          of follow-up action, recommendations, and background
          information on Guyana and its people. Topics related
          to the survey are discussed by chapter as follows:
          sampling; characteristics of households; nutritional
          status of the population; young child feeding; food
          production; food consumption; ecological factors related
          to nutrition; three case studies; Amerindian villages
          in the hinterland; and the determination and significance
          of various associations.

217   Pearson, Paul B. and Greenwell, T. Richard, eds.
A B C   NUTRITION, FOOD AND MAN: AN INTERDISCIPLINARY PERSPECTIVE
          Tucson, AZ: University of Arizona Press, 1980.

          This collection of papers occupies an ill-defined middle
          space between highly technical studies of nutrition,
          on the one hand, and the informative survey written for
          the nonspecialist about various aspects of nutrition,
          on the other. The book covers a broad area and contains
          some fairly detailed and interesting articles on human
          adaptability to lack of nutrition, the relation between
          nutrition and immunity, and on restraints to accepting
          new foods.

218   Pearson, Scott R.; Stryker, J. Dirch and Humphreys,
          Charles P., et al.
B C D   RICE IN WEST AFRICA: POLICY AND ECONOMICS
          Stanford: Stanford University Press, 1981.

          Ten economists present twelve previously unpublished
          papers on rice policy in the Ivory Coast, Liberia, Sierra
          Leone, Senegal, and Mali. There are two chapters on
          each country, one using a microeconomic analysis of the
          efficiency of alternative techniques and location
          incentive, and the other analyzing the incentive effects
          of government trade, price, tax subsidy, and investment
          policies by measuring income transfer to or from farmers,
          millers, and traders. In addition, two papers compare
          the production efficiency of techniques and locational
          effectiveness of alternative policies.

219   Phillips, Richard for Agency for International Development
B C   BUILDING VIABLE FOOD CHAINS IN DEVELOPING COUNTRIES
          Manhattan: Kansas State University, 1973.

220   Porteous, Andrew, ed.
B C   DEVELOPMENTS IN ENVIRONMENTAL CONTROL AND PUBLIC HEALTH
          London: Applied Science, 1981.

Nine previously unpublished papers which deal with specific environmental problems of interest to engineers, public health officers, and scientists. Emphasizes the maintenance and control of the physical environment to safeguard public health. The topics discussed include: selection and operation of landfill sites; non-landfill methods of hazardous waste disposal; industrial noise and vibration control; measurement and control of sulphur dioxide emissions; diagnosis, prevention, and control of asbestosis and dust related diseases; water quality monitoring and control; water supply; biological monitoring of the environment.

221   Rechcigl, Miloslav, Jr., ed.
A B C   MAN, FOOD, AND NUTRITION: STRATEGIES AND TECHNOLOGICAL MEASURES FOR ALLEVIATING THE WORLD FOOD PROBLEM
        Cleveland, OH: CRC Press, 1973.

222   Reutlinger, Shlomo
A B C   FOOD INSECURITY: MAGNITUDE AND REMEDIES
        Washington, D.C.: World Bank Reprint Series, 1980.

        Argues that food security should not be made contingent upon arrangements for the stabilization of worldwide foodgrain supplies and suggests that food security could be attained through a food import bill insurance (FIBI) scheme; discusses alternative schemes and amounts. These tentative and intermediate findings of an ongoing World Bank research undertaking are presented because of the current public interest in this issue.

223   Reutlinger, Shlomo and Selowsky, Marcelo
A B C   MALNUTRITION AND POVERTY: MAGNITUDE AND POLICY OPTIONS
        World Bank Staff Occasional Papers, No. 23
        Baltimore: Johns Hopkins University Press, 1978.

        Presents the results of a first large research effort in the World Bank to determine the global dimension of malnutrition. The conclusion is that malnutrition is unlikely to disappear in the normal course of development. Only policies deliberately designed to reallocate food programs for target groups in urban areas and aimed at assisting low-income farm families to increase and stabilize food production for their own consumption can be more cost-effective than outright income distribution.

224   THE RISING TIDE: POPULATION, FOOD AND FAMINE
A B C   O'Brien Press, 1982.

225   Sai, Fred T.
A B C   FOOD, POPULATION AND POLITICS
        London: International Planned Parenthood, 1977.

226   Scandizzo, Pasquale L. and Swamy, Gurushri
B C D   BENEFITS AND COSTS OF FOOD DISTRIBUTION POLICIES: THE

INDIA CASE
Working Paper No. 509; Washington, D.C.: World Bank,
1982.

Analyzes some of the characteristics and the main
consequences of the food distribution policies followed
by the Indian government and provides a quantification
and a cost-benefit analysis of their effects on consumers,
producers, and the government budget.

227   Schaefer, Morris
B C   ADMINISTRATION OF ENVIRONMENTAL HEALTH PROGRAMMES: A
        SYSTEMS VIEW
        WHO, 1974.

In two parts: (a) explains what a system is, what basic
properties are common to all systems, and how environmental
health programs and agencies are best viewed as
administrative systems; describes and illustrates the
functions and processes of administrative systems, and
includes an application of systems theory to environmental
health; and (b) provides an overview of the administrative
process specifically oriented to environmental health
programs. Also examines phases of the administrative
process, including planning, decision making, and
evaluation.

228   Schmitt, Bernard A.
B C   PROTEIN, CALORIES AND DEVELOPMENT: NUTRITIONAL VARIABLES
        IN THE ECONOMICS OF DEVELOPING COUNTRIES
        Boulder, CO: Westview Press, 1979.

229   Schneider, Hartmut
A B C   FOOD AID FOR DEVELOPMENT: REPORT ON THE OECD DEVELOPMENT
        CENTRE EXPERT MEETING ON "SCOPE AND CONDITIONS FOR IMPROVED
        USE OF FOOD AID FOR DEVELOPMENT" HELD IN PARIS ON 30-31
        MARCH 1978
        Paris: OECD, 1978.

Discusses food aid versus other aid; the impact of food
aid; project versus program food aid; reorientation from
relief to development; the data base; food aid coordination
and donor constraints; and improved use of food aid for
development. Also economic incentives for noise abatement
in aircraft and traffic noise charges as well as damage
compensation.

230   Schofield, Sue
A B C   DEVELOPMENT AND THE PROBLEMS OF VILLAGE NUTRITION
        Montclair, NJ: Allanhold, Osmun, 1979.

231   Selowsky, Marcelo
A C   THE ECONOMIC DIMENSIONS OF MALNUTRITION IN YOUNG CHILDREN
        Working Paper No. 294; Washington, D.C.: World Bank,
        1978.

Some 400 million children below age ten are suffering from calorie deficient diets. The paper examines the effectiveness of alternative programs aimed at increasing calorie consumption in children. Specific programs, such as a subsidized food program for the household, a food stamp program, and a direct site-feeding program for children, are examined and changes to increase their effectiveness are suggested.

232   Sen, Sudhir
B C   REAPING THE GREEN REVOLUTION: FOOD AND JOBS FOR ALL
       Maryknoll, NY: Orbis Books; New Delhi: Tata McGraw-Hill,
       1975.

This is the author's second book in a planned trilogy on various aspects of international development. Discusses how to make the green revolution in agriculture successful; emphasizes the standpoint of the recipient countries. The focus is on India as a recipient of development assistance for new improved grains and fertilizers. Analyzes the foreign aid recipient's problems and studies ways of improving the efficiency of aid administration and allocation within the recipient country's economy in general and agricultural sector in particular. Takes a comprehensive look at food production shortages, with discussions of land reform, crop choice, population growth and employment problems, water control, access road construction, and agricultural credit development.

233   Shack, Kathryn W.
B C   TEACHING NUTRITION IN DEVELOPING COUNTRIES
       Santa Monica, CA: Meals for Millions Foundation, 1978.

234   Shah, Moin,; Shrestha, Mathura P. and Campbell, Marilyn,
       eds.
A B C RURAL HEALTH NEEDS: REPORT OF A SEMINAR: POKHARA, NEPAL,
       6-12 OCTOBER 1977
       IDRC, 1978.

Report on health services and needs in rural areas of Nepal, including information on the Nepal Health Manpower (medical personnel) Development Research Project. Examines survey methodology and data collecting procedures; application of research results; and the role of applied social research in health planning. Presents country papers from selected countries of South Asia and South East Asia, examining basic needs, personnel training, maternal child health, etc.

235   Sharpston, Michael J.
A B C A HEALTH POLICY FOR DEVELOPING COUNTRIES
       Washington, D.C.:   World Bank Reprint Series, No. 67.

Argues that factors other than conventional health services

such as better nutrition, better infrastructure, improved hygiene habits, and the elimination of poverty, are determinants for improved health. Proposes a health promotion system for developing countries that involves a whole community rather than individuals, grass-roots health training, and appropriate health management, and cautions that construction of new hospitals, which are very expensive to operate, should be avoided.

236   Sinclair, H. M. and Howat, G. R., eds.
A B C   WORLD NUTRITION AND NUTRITION EDUCATION
         Paris: UNESCO and Oxford University Press, 1980.

Covers a wide range of educational activities in the field of human activities. Topics covered include the nutrition of the individual, the family, and the community; nutritional problems and policies in the industrialized world and in developing countries, trends in curriculum development; the impact of new educational technology; education by international organizations, voluntary bodies, universities, colleges, and schools; adult education in nutrition; and reports of nutrition education programs from all over the world.

237   Sinha, Radha
A B C   FOOD AND POVERTY: THE POLITICAL ECONOMY OF CONFRONTATION
         New York: Holmes & Meier, 1976.

Examines the programs undertaken in developing countries (mainly Asian) from the viewpoint of internal and international inequalities and inequities. The book discusses: the world food problem and food production; employment creation; land reform; credit and marketing problems; development assistance. Finds all programs inadequate for alleviating hunger and poverty and stresses the "risk of confrontation."

238   Sinha, Radha
A B C   THE WORLD FOOD PROBLEM: CONSENSUS AND CONFLICT
         New York: Pergamon Press, 1978.

239   Smith, Richard A.
B C   MANPOWER AND PRIMARY HEALTH CARE: GUIDELINES FOR
         IMPROVING/EXPANDING HEALTH SERVICE COVERAGE IN DEVELOPING
         COUNTRIES
         Honolulu: University of Hawaii, 1978.

240   Smith, T. Lynn
B C D   THE RACE BETWEEN POPULATION AND FOOD SUPPLY IN LATIN
         AMERICA
         University of New Mexico Press, 1976.

241   Solimano, Giorgio and Taylor, Lance, eds.
A B C D FOOD PRICE POLICIES AND NUTRITION IN LATIN AMERICA:

PROCEEDINGS OF THE WORKSHOP ON IMPACT OF FOOD PRICE
POLICIES ON NUTRITION, MEXICO CITY, 22-25 MARCH 1978
UNU, 1980.

Contains the proceedings of the Workshop which dealt
with the impact of food price policies on nutrition and
the alleviation of world hunger. In three parts. Part
1 consists of two papers on the effects of price policy
and changes in real income on nutrition, together with
the discussions held at the Workshop. Part 2 presents
five case studies on food policies in Mexico, Jamaica,
Trinidad-Tobago, Chile, and the Dominican Republic. Part
3 discusses the basis for policy interventions and research
priorities.

242   Sorkin, Alan L.
A B C   HEALTH ECONOMICS IN DEVELOPING COUNTRIES
Lexington, Mass.; Toronto and London: Heath, Lexington
Books, 1976.

Analyzes the health sector in developing nations.
Considers topics such as the relationship between nutrition
and development, the impact of health services and
population on development, health planning, methods of
financing health services, hospitals and health centers,
and health manpower. Finds in part that health
expenditures are important determinants of the quality
and quantity of health services, and with the limitation
of funds in developing countries, emphasis must be on
the best allocation allowances. Observes also that capita
manpower is in critically short supply in developing
countries and that efforts should be made in training
health auxiliaries and in planning for greater efficiency
of resource allocation. Includes pertinent demographic
data and information on health expenditures and national
income for selected countries.

243   Spitzer, Robert R.
A B C   NO NEED FOR HUNGER: HOW THE U.S. CAN HELP THE WORLD'S
HUNGRY TO HELP THEMSELVES
Danville, IL: Interstate Printers and Pub., 1981.

244   Srivastava, Uma K. et al.
A B C   FOOD AID AND INTERNATIONAL ECONOMIC GROWTH
Ames: Iowa State University Press, 1975.

245   Stevens, Christopher
A B C D FOOD AID AND THE DEVELOPING WORLD: FOUR AFRICAN CASE
STUDIES
New York: St. Martin's Press, 1979.

Examines the impact of supplying and receiving food aid
on a continuing basis as a means of development assistance
to four widely differing African countries. In three

sections: section one introduces background data on donors (U.S., EEC, and Canada) and recipients--Botswana, Lesotho, Upper Volta, and Tunisia; section two outlines the uses of food aid for cash, nutrition, and wages in the cases studied; section three explores the direct and indirect effects of food aid on nutrition, consumer prices, and agricultural production in the recipient countries.   Argues that the view that food aid is not an inherently unsatisfactory form of development assistance but depends on the particular circumstances of the donor and recipient.   Concludes that food aid is unlikely to have a negative effect and may well have a positive impact if supplied in good time and in the form of locally acceptable commodities as part of a broader package of measures deisgned to assist a poverty-oriented development strategy; under the opposite circumstances, the impact is likely to be negative.

246   Tabah, Leon, ed.
A B C D POPULATION GROWTH AND ECONOMIC DEVELOPMENT IN THE THIRD WORLD
Dolhain, Belgium: Ordina Editions for the International Union for the Scientific Study of Population, Liege, 1976.

Twenty-one previously unpublished essays by economists and demographers presenting an approach to development that incorporates population planning.   Some specific topics include: the labor force in development and demographic transition; employment of women in developing countries; economic-demographic models; the impact of agricultural change on demographic development in the Third World; and impact of demographic change on the economic situation of families in developing countries. Other topics relate to education,   health,   environment, international economic relations, and demographic policies. Essays were prepared during 1972 and 1973.

247   Talbot, Ross B., ed.
A B C WORLD FOOD PROBLEM AND U.S. FOOD POLICIES, 1978
Ames: Iowa State University Press, 1979.

248   Thomas, Vinod
B C D DIFFERENCES IN INCOME, NUTRITION, AND POVERTY WITHIN BRAZIL
Working Paper No. 505; Washington, D.C.:   World Bank, 1982.

Regional disparities in living standards in Brazil are examined and estimates for real income and nutritional levels and poverty for major urban and rural areas are provided.   Although the growth rate of the country surpasses the average for most developing countries and the country performs as well as many middle-income countries in terms of a number of socioeconomic indicators, it is noted that there are large regional disparities between the northeast and the southeast with the northeast faring about the same as most low-income countries.

249   Tickner, Vincent
A B C   THE FOOD PROBLEM
London: Catholic Institute for International Relations, 1979.

250   Tolley, George S.
B C   AGRICULTURAL PRICE POLICIES AND THE DEVELOPING COUNTRIES
Baltimore: Johns Hopkins University Press, 1982.

251   Tuma, Elias H., ed.
B C D   FOOD AND POPULATION IN THE MIDDLE EAST
Washington, D.C.:   Institute of Middle Eastern and African Affairs, 1976.

Five revised papers, previously unpublished, and a related commentary; presented at the Eighth Annual Meeting of the Middle East Studies Association, held in Boston in November 1974. Hanna Rizk surveys population trends in selected Arab countries, 1955-73, and grain production, 1934-72; Michel Marto discusses trends in food production. Jared Hazleton looks at the role of agrarian reform policies in advancing Middle Eastern agriculture. Basheer K. Nijim considers internal migration and population movements in the Arab world. Kenneth Baldwin estimates the potentialities for expanded food production by the year 2000 (tables provided). The commentary, by Jerome Fried, notes the need to promote a more balanced development strategy between agriculture and industry and to reassess the relevance of various land tenure arrangements from a development standpoint.

252   Tune, George
A C   ENERGY, ENVIRONMENT, POPULATIONS AND FOOD: OUR FOUR INDEPENDENT CRISES
Krieger, 1976.

253   Ulin, Priscilla R. and Segall, Marshall H., eds.
B C D   TRADITIONAL HEALTH CARE DELIVERY IN CONTEMPORARY AFRICA
Syracuse, NY: Syracuse University, Maxwell School, 1980.

254   United Nations
B C   SIGNIFICANCE OF THE RELATIONSHIP BETWEEN NUTRITION AND HUMAN REPRODUCTION
New York: UN, 1981.

Assesses current analytical models defining the nutrition-fertility interaction and reviews recent field studies carried out in Asia, Latin America and Africa which examined such interrelationships. The Western experience is provided for contrast. Chapters cover: (a) a general analytical framework; (b) field studies with emphasis on sectoral linkages; (c) the dominant role of malnutrition in predisposing birth intervals; and (d) implications for policy makers.

255   UNU
B C   PROTEIN-ENERGY REQUIREMENTS UNDER CONDITIONS PREVAILING IN DEVELOPING COUNTRIES: CURRENT KNOWLEDGE AND RESEARCH NEEDS
UNU, 1980.

Discusses the issues regarding protein and energy requirements in developing countries and makes suggestions. In four major parts: (a) protein and energy requirements for body maintenance and healthy organ function; (b) the nutritional consequences of acute and chronic infections; (c) nutrient requirements for catch-up growth and tissue repletion; and (d) research considerations. Appendix on nitrogen-balance studies of protein requriements.

256   United Nations
B C   INTEGRATED APPROACH TO POPULATION, FOOD AND NUTRITION POLICIES AND PROGRAMMES FOR NATIONAL DEVELOPMENT: REPORT OF A REGIONAL SEMINAR
New York: UN/ESCAP, 1980.

Report on the Seminar, Bangkok, 24-31 July 1979. Describes the current population, food, and nutrition policies of the 11 countries represented in the Seminar. Also reports on rationale for integration; development of a food policy related to nutritional needs and to quality and size of population; review of experience in integrated action programs; potentials and problems in the development of integrated plans and programs; and guidelines for developing an integrated program.

257   UN Center on Transnational Corporations
B C   TRANSNATIONAL CORPORATIONS IN FOOD AND BEVERAGE PROCESSING
New York: UN, 1981.

258   United Nations
B C   ACTIVATING INTER-RELATED LINKS IN POPULATION, FOOD, AND NUTRITION PROGRAMMES: THEORY AND PRACTICE
New York: UN, 1980.

Based on the Seminar on an Integrated Approach to Population, Food and Nutrition Policies and Programmes for National Development, Bangkok, 24-31 July 1979. Reviews information on current population, food and nutrition policies and programs in countries of the region; formulates suitable strategies for effectively developing complementary policies in the field of action-oriented integrated programmes that will take into account available manpower and financial resources; and suggests measures to ensure the cooperation and coordination essential for the implementation of such programs.

259   U.S. General Accounting Office
B C   HUNGRY NATIONS NEED TO REDUCE FOOD LOSSES CAUSED BY STORAGE, SPILLAGE AND SPOILAGE
Washington, D.C.:   GAO, 1976.

260   Valdes, Alberta
A B C   FOOD SECURITY FOR DEVELOPING COUNTRIES
Boulder, CO: Westview Press, 1981.

Thirteen previously unpublished papers, prepared for the Conference on Food Security for Developing Countries (November 1978), discuss the nature and magnitude of the problem in LDC's (Africa, Asia, and Latin America) and assess the likely impact of national and international initiatives upon these countries' food security, i.e., the ability of food deficit countries to meet target consumption levels on a year-to-year basis. Conference was organized by the International Food Policy Research Institute and International Maize and Wheat Improvement Center. Concludes that the solution needs to be tackled at the national level and that each LDC should take initiatives to reduce this insecurity, which include large investments in food distribution systems, transport, and communications; early warning systems; and a mix of stock and trade policies. International initiatives include an international grain reserve system, consumption and production adjustments in developed countries, and food aid and financial approaches to alleviate the constraint in foreign exchange.

261   Von Ernahrung-Sproblemen, Losung
A B C   SOLUTION OF NUTRITIONAL PROBLEMS: THE CONTRIBTUION OF PRODUCERS, DISTRIBUTORS AND NUTRITIONALISTS
New York: Karger, 1979.

262   Weekley, James K.
A C D   WORLD HUNGER: FOCUS ON MEXICO
Toledo, OH: International Business Institute, Business Research Center, University of Toledo, 1979.

Examines the empirical data on the production, consumption, and prices of agricultural goods. Part one looks at this issue in a global perspective, with data for the period since the mid-1950's as well as projections to 1985. Part two focuses on Mexico and its agricultural, distributional, and demographic problems and their impact on nutrition and hunger. The last part provides a regional analysis of the food problems in Mexico, finding a correlation between regional development and incidence of hunger. The important implication is that Mexico's public policy, which supported growth in the stronger sectors, has been at the price of the stagnation and deprivation of people in the weaker sectors.

263   Weinbaum, Marvin G.
A B C D FOOD, DEVELOPMENT AND POLTIICS IN THE MIDDLE EAST
       Boulder, CO: Westview Press, 1982.

264   Weisbrod, Burton A., et al.
B C D   DISEASE AND ECONOMIC DEVELOPMENT: THE IMPACT OF PARASITIC
       DISEASES IN ST. LUCIA
       London and Madison: University of Wisconsin Press, 1973.

       This empirical study analyzes and quantitatively assesses the effects of parasitic diseases, particularly schistosomiasis, on the economic performance of certain of the inhabitants of St. Lucia, an island in the West Indies. Begins with a review of previous research conducted on the relationships between health and economic development, followed by a presentation of economic and social background information on St. Lucia. The study itself measures the impact of parasitic disease in three areas: 1) birth and death rates, 2) scholastic performance of children in school, and 3) labor productivity of workers living in two valleys, dominated by one plantation. Concludes that the diseases' effects are very modest, that they do not seriously retard economic development, and that development itself may cause the spread of disease. Statistical information is given on birth, deaths, prevalence of disease, and economic production.

265   Weiss, Thomas G. and Jordan, Robert S.
A B C   THE WORLD FOOD CONFERENCE AND GLOBAL PROBLEM SOLVING
       New York and London: Praeger in cooperation with the United Nations Institute for Training and Research, 1976.

       Examination of the World Food Conference held in Rome, November 5-16, 1974, from the standpoint of administrative decision-making to international organization; primary concern is with the impact of the growing concern with global welfare problems on the structure and the functioning of international organizations. The authors, both economists with the United Nations, see two functions of these global conferences: (1) to give publicity and redefinition to many issue-areas and (2) to initiate actions to strengthen the existing institutions.

266   Wells, Stuart and Klees, Steven
B C   HEALTH ECONOMICS AND DEVELOPMENT
       New York: Praeger, 1980.

Examines the relationship between major health problems, policy recommendations, and economic development. Reviews the nature of the health problem in developing countries and various health intervention strategies. Argues for a structural approach to public health programs; critically assesses the microeconomic analysis and the disaggregated approach to the delivery of health care or health education; analyzes measures and models of national economic growth and the impact of changes in health status and education on growth; discusses communications, technology, and research methodology in health education and health care; and examines a health education project in Tanzania. Concludes that public health programs that focus on economic structure are more likely to succeed than traditional, disaggregated programs directed at malnutrition and disease.

267   Whistler, Roy L. and Hymowitz, Theodore
B C   GUAR: AGRONOMY, PRODUCTION, INDUSTRIAL USE, AND NUTRITION
       West Lafayette, IN: Purdue University Press, 1979.

A detailed, technical study of a legume known to farmers in parts of South Asia for centuries and only now becoming a potential source of protein elsewhere. This book is based largely on research carried out in the United States that may be useful for agricultural researchers in other parts of the world.

268   Whyte, Robert Orr
B C D RURAL NUTRITION IN MONSOON ASIA
       New York: Oxford University Press, 1974.

269   Willet, Joseph W.
A B C THE WORLD FOOD SITUATION: PROBLEMS AND PROSPECTS TO 1985
       Dobbs Ferry, NY: Oceana Publications, 1976.

Includes reproductions of the following three UN documents: (a) "Assessment of the World Food Situation: Present and Future" (UN World Food Conference, Rome, 5-16 November 1974, Item 8 of the Provisional Agenda; E/CONF.65/3); (b) "The World Food Problem: Proposals for National and International Action" (UN World Food Conference, Rome, 5-16 November 1974, Item 9 of the Provisional Agenda; E/CONF.65/4); and (c) "Report of the World Food Conference" (Rome, 5-16 November 1974; E/CONF.65/20), which has been previosuly issued as a UN sales publication and listed in IBID, Vol. 3, no. 3, p. 165. Includes nine additonal reports and studies on the topics by various governmental, nongovernmental and university-affiliated bodies.

270   Williams, Douglas and Young, Roger
A B C TAKING STOCK: WORLD FOOD SECURITY IN THE EIGHTIES
       Ottawa: North-South Institute, 1981.

To aid in the discussion of Canada's role in promoting world food security, reviews the issues involved in attaing "food security," i.e., preventing global declines in food consumption in the intermediate term and increasing food availability in the Third World low-income food deficit countries over the longer term. Examines world food production and trade policies and current proposals for achieving food security. Recommends that Canada continue support for Third World agricultural and rural development, remove obstacles constraining Canadian food exports, continue efforts to increase the effectiveness of its Canadian International Development Agency food and program, assess present and potential contributions to world food security, and examine ways in which government policies contribute to world market instability.

271   Woods, Richard G.
A B C FUTURE DIMENSIONS OF WORLD FOOD AND POPULATIONS
Boulder, CO: Westview Press, 1981.

272   World Bank
A B C THE ASSAULT ON WORLD POVERTY: PROBLEMS OF RURAL
DEVELOPMENT, EDUCATION, AND HEALTH
Baltimore: Johns Hopkins University Press, 1975.

A compilation of sector policy papers on rural development, agricultural credit, land reform, education, and health, attempting to analyze the causes of poverty, to examine ways in which poverty can be alleviated, and to outline programs for World Bank assistance.

273   World Bank
A B C MALNUTRITION AND POVERTY: MAGNITUDE AND POLICY OPTIONS
World Bank Staff Occasional Papers, No. 23
Baltimore: Johns Hopkins University Press, 1976.

Assesses the character and magnitude of nutritional deficiency in the developing countries and analyzes the cost effectiveness of selected policy instruments in reducing the deficiency. Discusses some instruments for implementing a policy directed toward target groups. Appendixes include: basic country data; income distribution data; estimated calorie consumption functions based on cross-country data; projected calorie deficits; and cost of programs oriented to target groups.

274   World Food Program
B C   FOOD AID AND THE ROLE OF WOMEN IN DEVELOPMENT
WFP, 1976.

Gives some examples of practical ways in which food aid, combined with other forms of assistance, can be used to support efforts by governments to speed the integration of women into national economies.

275   World Health Organization
A C   PRIMARY   HEALTH   CARE: REPORT   OF   THE   INTERNATIONAL
        CONFERENCE ON PRIMARY HEALTH CARE, ALMA-ATA, USSR, 6-12
        SEPTEMBER 1978, JOINTLY SPONSORED BY WHO AND UNICEF
        WHO, 1978.

        Includes the Declaration of Alma-Ata, adopted at the
        Conference; the report of the Conference (background,
        organization of work, summary of discussions, and
        recommendations);   and   the   joint   report   of   the
        Director-General of the WHO and the Executive Director
        of UNICEF on primary care, covering its definition,
        operational aspects, relationship to development, and
        national strategies and international support.

276   World Health Organization
B C   APPLICATION OF SYSTEMS ANALYSIS OF HEALTH MANAGEMENT:
        REPORT OF A WHO EXPERT COMMITTEE, GENEVA, 16-22 DECEMBER
        1975
        WHO, 1976.

        Topics covered: (a) health management needs and systems
        analysis; (b) project systems analysis--an example of
        collaborative   development   of   methods;   (c)   further
        development of systems analysis in health management;
        (d) recommendations; and (e) summary statement. Annexes
        cover the work of WHO in project systems analysis;
        sturdiness and flexibility of procedures; and cost/benefit
        analysis.

277   World Health Orgnization
B C   HEALTH ECONOMICS: REPORT OF A WHO INTERREGIONAL SEMINAR,
        GENEVA, 2-16 JULY 1973
        WHO, 1975.

        Summarizes proceedings and some contributions to the
        seminar, with an introductory chapter which outlines
        the aims of health economics.   The two main sections
        of the report follow: (a) macro aspects of health
        economics, which covers the economic aspects of health
        services as a whole and includes such topics as cost
        trends, containing health service costs and monitoring
        costs; and (b) micro aspects of health economics, which
        deals with individual components of the health sector
        from the economic point of view.   Conclusions and
        recommendations.

278   World Health Organization
B C   NEW APPROACHES IN HEALTH STATISTICS: REPORT OF THE SECOND
        INTERNATIONAL CONFERENCE OF NATIONAL COMMITTEES ON VITAL
        AND HEALTH STATISTICS
        WHO, 1974.

        Covers recent developments in health statistics and
        achievements of national committees on vital and health

statistics. Provides information on users health and
vital statistics and their needs for information, as
well as methods for meeting these needs. The conference
was held at the WHO Regional Office for Europe, Copenhagen,
1-5 October 1973.

279   World Health Orgnization
B C   STATISTICAL INDICES OF FAMILY HEALTH: REPORT OF A WHO
        STUDY GROUP, GENEVA, 17-21 FEBRUARY 1975.
        WHO, 1976.

        Reviews (a) possible approaches to indices of family
        health (demographic, epidemiological [medical], social
        and economic approaches) and the methodological
        implications of these various approaches; (b) current
        state of family health statistics, particularly as regards
        problems of information collection and treatment; (c)
        types of demographic statistics that are available; and
        (d) development of some statistical indicators for family
        health.

280   World Health Orgnization
A B C   THE ROLE OF THE HEALTH SECTOR IN FOOD AND NUTRITION,
        REPORT OF A WHO EXPERT COMMITTEE, 23 SEPTEMBER-1 OCTOBER
        1980
        WHO, 1982.

        Topics discussed: the magnitude of the problem; past
        performance of the health sector; changing concepts of
        health and health services--new opportunities for nutrition
        promotion; role of the health sector in nutrition;
        diagnosis of nutrition problems; measures of primary
        and secondary prevention of malnutrition; administrative
        structure of nutrition services in the health sector;
        recent advances in nutrition knowledge and
        methodology--their applicability to the health sector;
        and nutrition research to support health measures.

281   World Health Organization
A B C   FOOD AND NUTRITION STRATEGIES IN NATIONAL DEVELOPMENT:
        NINTH REPORT OF THE JOINT FAO/WHO EXPERT COMMITTEE ON
        NUTRITION
        WHO, 1976.

        Briefly reviews the food and nutritional problems of
        the world and past approaches to their solution. Discusses
        the desirability of a new approach.

282   World Health Orgnization
A B C   HEALTH AND THE ENVIRONMENT
        WHO/EURO, 1977.

        Contains 14 articles which describe WHO:EURO activities
        related to environmental health problems. Topics covered

include, among others, development of rural water supplies and sanitation; housing hygiene; environmental pollution control project; environmental quality management; reductions in emission of pollutants from industrial sources; community noise study; food safety control; tourism and sanitation; permissable levels of toxic substances in the working environment; epidemiological studies of air pollution health effects; and manpower requirements in environmental health fields in Europe.

283   World Health Organization
B C   THE ROLE OF HEALTH ECONOMICS IN NATIONAL PLANNING AND
       POLICY-MAKING: REPORT ON A WORKING GROUP: COLOGNE,
       7-10 JUNE 1977
       WHO, 1978.

       Discusses the extent of impact of health economics advice on policy decisions, particularly on the cost and effectiveness of health care; and contains recommendations for improving the relevance of health economics to health planning and health policy formulation.

284   World Health Organization
A B C FORMULATING STRATEGIES FOR HEALTH FOR ALL BY THE YEAR
       2000
       Geneva: WHO, 1979.

285   World Health Organization
B C   INTEGRATED APPROACH TO HEALTH SERVICES AND MANPOWER
       DEVELOPMENT: REPORT OF A MINISTERIAL CONSULTATION,
       TEHERAN, 26 FEBRURARY2 MARCH 1978
       WHO/EMRO, 1978.

       Contains the report of the Consultation, covering the following aspects of health services and manpower development: the need for an integrated approach; obstacles to coordination; approaches to coordination; and ways and means of strengthening coordination. Also includes the background papers presented at the Consultation, discussing health services and manpower, development with particular reference to Eastern Mediterranean Region, and the experiences of the United Kingdom, Poland and Latin America regarding the integrated approach.

286   World Health Organization
B C   GUIDELINES FOR TRAINING COMMUNITY HEALTH WORKERS IN
       NUTRITION
       Geneva: WHO, 1981.

287   WORKING CONFERENCE ON APPROPRIATE TECHNOLOGY IN DEVELOPING
A B C COUNTRIES: APPROPRIATE TECHNOLOGY IN HEALTH IN DEVELOPING
       COUNTRIES
       Washington, D.C.:   1976.

288   World Health Organization
A B C   TOWARDS A BETTER FUTURE: MATERNAL AND CHILD HEALTH
        WHO, 1980.

        This book briefly examines the causes of maternal, infant,
        and childhood mortality and morbidity and discusses the
        different kinds of risk that might be expected to yield
        to more effective intervention. Recent developments
        and trends in technology, knowledge and health care are
        reviewed and preventive measures are suggested.

289   Wortman, Sterling
A B C   TO FEED THIS WORLD: THE CHALLENGE AND THE STRATEGY
        Baltimore: Johns Hopkins University Press, 1978.

II. SELECTED PERIODICAL ARTICLES

290   Abalu, G. O. I.
        Solving Africa's food problem. FOOD POLICY (GUILDFORD,
        ENG.) 7:247-56, August 1982.

291   Abdullah, M. and Saber, A.
        Prevalence of dietary inadequacy in energy and protein
        intake in rural Bangladesh. THE BANGLADESH DEVELOPMENT
        STUDIES (DACCA) 6, No. 3:322-30, 1968.

292   Acuna, Hector R.
        Health and development in Latin America. WORLD HEALTH
        FORUM (GENEVA) 2, No. 4:461-63, 1981.

293   Aftermath of the world food conference. CERES 8, No. 1,
        Jan/Feb 1975.

294   Alamgir, Mohiuddin
        The dimension of undernutrition and malnutrition in
        developing countries: conceptual, empirical and policy
        issues. HARVARD INSTITUTE FOR INTERNATIONAL DEVELOPMENT,
        DEVELOPMENT DISCUSSION PAPER No. 82:1-75, Feb. 1980.

295   Alamgir, Mohiuddin and Berlage, L.
        Foodgrain (rice and wheat) demand, import and price policy
        for Bangladesh. BANGLADESH ECONOMIC REVIEW 1:25-58,
        Jan. 1973.

296   Alderman, Harold C. and Timmer, C. Peter
        Food policy and food demand in Indonesia. BULLETIN OF
        INDONESIAN ECONOMIC STUDIES (CANBERRA) 16:83-93, Nov.
        1980.

297   Al-Isi, Ishmail L.,; Kanawati, A. A. and McLaren, D. S.
        Formal education of mothers and their nutritional behavior.
        JOURNAL OF NUTRITION EDUCATION 7:22-24, Jan-March 1975.

298   Anderson, Barbara A. and McCabe, James L.
        Nutrition and the fertility of younger women in Kinshasa,
        Zaire.   JOURNAL   OF   DEVELOPMENT   ECONOMICS   (AMSTERDAM)
        4:343-63, Dec. 1977.

        Examines the relationship between various measures of
        household nutrition and fertility in a less-developed
        country, Zaire, in which there is substantial malnutrition.

299   Andrews, Stanley
        Agriculture and the common market.   Ames, Iowa: Iowa
        State University Press, 1973.

300   Arena, Jay M.
        Nutritional status of China's children: An overview.
        NUTRITION REVIEWS 32:289-95, Oct. 1974.

301   Arthur, Henry B. and Cramer, Gail L.
        Brighter forecast for the world's food supply.   HARVARD
        BUSINESS REVIEW (May-June 1976).

302   Arua, E. O.
        Achieving food sufficiency in Nigeria through the operation
        "feed the nation" programme. AGRICULTURAL ADMINISTRATION
        (BARKING, ESSEX) 9:91-101, Feb. 1982.

303   Austin, James E.
        Agribusiness in Latin America. New York: Praeger, 1974.

304   Austin, James E.
        Institutional dimensions of the malnutrition problem.
        INTERNATIONAL ORGANIZATION (MADISON) 32:811-36, Summer
        1978.

        Critically examines the structure and capacity of existing
        international nutrition institutions. Concluding comments
        focus on prospects for improved institutional efforts.

305   Aziz, Sartaj
        Abolishing hunger: The complex reality of food.   THIRD
        WORLD QUARTERLY (LONDON) 1:17-27, Oct. 1979.

306   Aziz, Sartaj
        The Chinese approach to rural development. INTERNATIONAL
        DEVELOPMENT REVIEW 15, No. 4:2-7, 1973-74.

307   Aziz, Sartaj
        Hunger, politics and markets: The real issues in the
        food crisis. New York: NY University Press, 1975.

308   Balz, Daniel J.
        Politics of food aid presents U.S. with policy dilemma.
        NATIONAL JOURNAL REPORT. November 30, 1974, pp. 1787-92.

309   Banerji, D.
        Health and population control in the draft plan. ECONOMIC
        AND POLITICAL WEEKLY (BOMBAY) 13:1385-90, Aug. 1978.

        This paper examines the failure of health planning in
        India.

310   Banerji, D.
        Health as a lever for another development. DEVELOPMENT
        DIALOGUE (UPPSALA) No. 1:19-25, 1978.

        Argues that the present health services in India are
        unable to meet the real needs of the poor, and that a
        "people-oriented" health service would become an important
        factor in the creation of a just social order.

311   Bard, Robert L.
        Food aid and agricultural trade: A study in legal and
        administrative control. Lexington, Mass.: Heath, 1972.

312   Barnett, Andrew
        An introduction to the health planning and budgeting
        systems in India. INSTITUTE OF DEVELOPMENT STUDIES.
        DISCUSSION PAPER (BRIGHTON) No. DP121:1-13, Dec. 1977.

        Provides a guide to sources of material on health planning
        and budgeting in India and an initial analysis of
        government health expenditure on the basis of the data
        publicly available up to June 1976.

313   Barrow, D. J.
        Health and resettlement consequences and opportunities
        created as a result of river impoundment in developing
        countries. WATER SUPPLY & MANAGEMENT (OXFORD) 5, No.
        2:135-50, 1981.

314   Bates, Robert H.
        Food policy in Africa; political causes and social effects.
        FOOD POLICY (GUILDFORD, ENG.) 6:147-57, Aug. 1981.

315   Bates, Robert H.
        The rural factor: Rural responses to industrialization
        in Zambia. New Haven: Yale University Press, 1977.

316   Beckford, George L.
        Persistent poverty, underdevelopment in plantation
        economics in the Third World. London: Oxford University
        Press, 1972.

317   Benito, Carlos A.
        Policies for food production and consumption in
        underdevelopment: The case of Mexico. JOURNAL OF POLICY
        MODELING (NEW YORK) 1:383-98, Sept. 1979.

Presents a system analysis approach for the investigation of the most effective agricultural and nutrition intervening programs for improving the nutrition of the rural poor in a lesser developed economy. The empirical study is about the peasant economy of Puebla in Mexico.

318   Benyoussef, A.
Health service delivery in developing countries. INTERNATIONAL SOCIAL SCIENCE JOURNAL 29, No. 3:397-418, 1977.

319   Benyoussef, A. et al.
Health effects of rural-urban migration in developing countries. SOCIAL SCIENCE AND MEDICINE 8 (May 1974). About Senegal: 243-54; about Tunisia: 287-304.

320   Berg, Alan
A strategy to reduce malnutrition. FINANCE AND DEVELOPMENT (WASHINGTON) 17:23-26, March 1980.

Discusses the need for nutrition-oriented food policies. This article is based upon a longer paper, produced by the author for the World Bank.

321   Berg, Alan
Increased income and improved nutrition: A Shibboleth examined. INTERNATIONAL DEVELOPMENT REVIEW 12:3-7, Sept. 1970.

322   Berg, Alan
Nutrition, development, and population growth. POPULATION BULLETIN 29:1-37, 1974.

323   Berg, Alan
The new need: nutrition-oriented food policies. FOOD POLICY (GUILDFORD, ENG.) 6:116-22, May 1981.

324   Berg, Alan
Industry's struggle with world malnutrition. HARVARD BUSINESS REVIEW 50:130-41, Jan.-Feb. 1972.

325   Berg, A.; Scrimshaw, N. N. and Call, D. L.
Nutrition, national development and planning: Proceedings of an international conference. Cambridge, Mass.: MIT Press, 1971.

326   Berrebi, Z. M. and Silber, J.
Health and development: Socio-economic determinants of mortality structure. SOCIAL SCIENCE & MEDICINE (MED ECON) 15C:31-9, March 1981.

327   Berry, W. T.
Nutritional surveillance in affluenct nations. NUTRITION REVIEWS 30:127-31, June 1972.

328   Bigman, David and Reutlinger, Shlomo
       Food price and supply stabilization: National buffer
       stocks and trade policies. AMERICAN JOURNAL OF
       AGRICULTURAL ECONOMICS (LEXINGTON, KY.) 61:657-67, Nov.
       1979.

       The authors conclude that trade policies are likely to
       have a greater impact on the stability of a country's
       food grain supply than any reasonable size buffer stock.

329   Birdsall, Nancy
       Health planning and population policy in Africa. AFRICAN
       STUDIES REVIEW (WALTHAM, MASS.) 19:19-33, Sept. 1976.

       Recommends that for Africa in the 1970's, those in the
       population field should adopt a strategy of strong support
       for health, and particularly for the restructuring of
       health systems. Only with better health services will
       demand for family planning services arise and supply
       of those services be justified by their costs.

330   Blau, David M.
       Investments in child nutrition and women's allocation
       of time in developing countries. YALE UNIVERSITY.
       ECONOMIC GROWTH CENTER. CENTER DISCUSSION PAPER (NEW
       HAVEN) No. 371:1-41, March 1981.

       The purpose of this study is to investigate the
       determinants of fertility and home investments in the
       human capital of children in a context in which women
       have the option of working in the informal sector as
       well as the formal sector or no market work. The empirical
       analysis presented in Section III uses data from a 1977-78
       survey of households in Nicaragua.

331   Blau, G.
       International commodity arrangements and policies. Rome:
       FAO Commodity Policy Studies, no. 16, 1964.

332   Bocobo, D. Laurel
       The protein problem in the Asia and the Far East region.
       INDIAN JOURNAL OF NUTRITION AND DIETETICS 7 (Sept. 1970):
       307-16.

333   Bohrisch, Alexander
       Improving food procurement by developing countries.
       AGRIBUSINESS WORLDWIDE (WESTPORT, CONN) P. 24-29, Feb./
       March 1981.

334   Borgstrom, Georg
       The dual challenge of health and hunger: A global crisis.
       BULLETIN OF THE ATOMIC SCIENTISTS 26, No. 8:42-46, Oct.
       1970.

335   Bos, Andries Klaasse
       Food aid by the European Communities; policy and practice.
       ODI REVIEW (LONDON) No. 1:38-52, 1978.

       This article is based on a recent study undertaken by
       ISMOG, University of Amsterdam, of food aid procedures
       in Brussels and logistics in five African and Asian
       communities.

336   Boyce, James K. and Hartmann, Betsy
       Hunger in a fertile land. CERES, FAO REVIEW ON AGRICULTURE
       AND DEVELOPMENT (ROME) 14:32-35, March/April 1981.

       The authors suggest that inequitable patterns of land
       ownership result in underutilized resources.

337   Brandow, J. E.
       The place of U.S. food in eliminating world hunger. ANNALS
       OF THE AMERICAN ACADEMY No. 429 (Jan. 1977), p. 1-11.

338   Brinkerhoff, Derick W.
       Realities in implementing decentralization, coordination,
       and participation; the case of the Mali rural health
       project. HARVARD INSTITUTE FOR INTERNATIONAL DEVELOPMENT,
       DEVELOPMENT DISCUSSION PAPER (CAMBRIDGE, MASS) No.
       105:1-40, Nov. 1980.

339   Brookings Institute
       Toward the integration of world agriculture. Washington,
       D.C.: Brookings, 1973.

340   Brown, Lester R.
       Global food prospects; shadow of Malthus.   CHALLENGE
       (ARMONK, NY) 24:14-21, Jan/Feb 1982.

       Suggests that the period of global food security is over,
       and that soil erosion, cropland conversion, energy costs,
       and dropping yield response to chemical fertilizers are
       cutting the growth in world food output.

341   Brown, Lester
       Increasing world food output.   New York: Arno Press,
       1976.

342   Brown, Lester
       Seeds of change: The green revolution and development
       in the 1970's. New York: Praeger, 1970.

343   Brown, Lester
       The politics and responsibility of the North American
       breadbasket. Washington: Worldwatch Institute, Worldwatch
       paper #2, Oct. 1975.

344   Brown, Peter G. and Shue, Henry, eds.

Food policy: The responsibility of the United States in the life and death choices. New York: The Free Press, 1977.

345   Buvinic, Mayra and Leslie, Joanne
Health care for women in Latin America and the Caribbean. STUDIES IN FAMILY PLANNING (NEW YORK) 12:112-15, March 1981.

346   Calkins, Peter H.
Nutritional adaptations of linear programming for planning rural development. AMERICAN JOURNAL OF AGRICULTURAL ECONOMICS (LEXINGTON) 63:247-54, May 1981.

Through six model formulations for a representative Nepalese farm, linear programming identifies the most nutritious and profitable production patterns; trade-offs between nutrition and income; and the costs of constraints relating to levels of credit, market availability, and human capital development.

347   Campbell, Keith
Constraints on future world food supply: Real or imaginary? AUSTRALIAN QUARTERLY 48, No. 3:4-12, Sept. 1976.

348   Canby, Thomas Y. and Raymer, Steve
Can the world feed its people? NATIONAL GEOGRAPHIC MAGAZINE 148:2-31, July 1975.

349   Cardoso, Eliana A.
Food supply and inflation. JOURNAL OF DEVELOPMENT ECONOMICS (AMSTERDAM) 8:269-84, June 1981.

Presents an analytical version of the Latin American structuralist theory of inflation.

350   Caribbean Food and Nutrition Institute
Protein foods for the Caribbean. Kingston, Jamaica: Bolivar Press, 1969, 121 pp.

351   Chakravarti, A. K.
Foodgrain sufficiency patterns in India. GEOGRAPHICAL REVIEW 60:208-28, April 1970.

352   Chakrabarti, Santi K. and Panda, Manoj K.
Measurement of incidence of undernutrition. ECONOMIC AND POLITICAL WEEKLY (BOMBAY) 16:1275-78, Aug. 1, 1981.

353   Chambers, Robert
Health, agriculture, and rural poverty: Why seasons matter. JOURNAL OF DEVELOPMENT STUDIES (LONDON) 18:217-38, Jan. 1982.

354   Chen, Lincoln and Huda, Chaudhury R.
       Demographic change and food production in Bangladesh,
       1960-74. POPULATION AND DEVELOPMENT REVIEW 1:201-27,
       Dec. 1975.

355   Chenery, H. et al.
       Redistribution and growth. London: Oxford University
       Press, 1974.

356   Chowdhury, Zafrullah
       The paramedics of Savar: An experiment in community
       health in Bangladesh. DEVELOPMENT DIALOGUE (UPPSALA)
       No. 1:41-50, 1978.

       Describes the work of the People's Health Centre in primary
       health-care services, and some problems encountered there.

357   Christensen, Cheryl
       World hunger; a structural approach. INTERNATIONAL
       ORGANIZATION (MADISON) 32:745-74, Summer 1978.

       The argument of this essay is that radical inequality
       of income and wealth is reflected directly in the structure
       of food consumption and production, both nationally and
       internationally.

358   Clay, Edward J.
       Food aid and food policy in Bangladesh. FOOD POLICY
       (GUILDFORD, ENG.) 4:129-33, May 1979.

       Reviews the role of food aid in the Bangladesh economy
       during the first quinquennium of "planned" development,
       1972/3-1977/8.

359   Clay, Edward J.
       The Brandt report and international food problems. FOOD
       POLICY (GUILDFORD, ENG.) 5:310-13, Nov. 1980.

360   Cochrane, Willard W.
       Feast or famine: The uncertain world of food and
       agriculture and the policy implications to the United
       States. Washington: National Planning Assoc., 1974.

361   Cochrane, Willard W.
       Agricultural development planning: Economic concepts,
       administrative procedures and political process. New
       York: Praeger, 1974.

362   Cochrane, Willard W., and Ryan, Mary E.
       American farm policy, 1948-1973. University of Minnesota
       Press, 1976.

363   Committee for Economic Development
       A new U.S. farm policy for changing world food needs.
       New York, 1974.

364   Connelly, P. and Perlman, R.
       The politics of scarcity: Resource conflicts in
       international action. Rome: FAO, 1975.

365   Cooper, Michael
       The economics of health care. UNIVERSITY OF OTAGO.
       ECONOMICS DISCUSSION PAPERS (DUNEDIN) No. 7902:1-19,
       1979.

366   Cooper, Michael H.
       Resource allocation in the health services sector.
       UNIVERSITY OF OTAGO. ECONOMIC DISCUSSION PAPERS (DUNEDIN)
       No. 8104:1-21, Nov. 1980.

367   Correa, Hector and Hassouna, Wafik A.
       A model for the integration of health and nutrition
       planning DEVELOPMENT AND CHANGE (THE HAGUE) 6:51-61,
       Oct. 1975.

       Discusses the problem of choice between prevention and
       cure of several diseases. The fact that the incidence
       of disease and the final outcome depend upon the
       nutritional conditions of the population is taken into
       account. As an example, the approach is applied to the
       problem of minimizing infant and child mortality in Egypt.

368   Costa, E.
       The world food programme and employment: Ten years of
       multilateral food aid for development. INTERNATIONAL
       LABOUR REVIEW 107:209-21, March 1973.

369   Cottman, Grant
       The world food conference. FIELDSTAFF REPORT, West Europe
       Series, vol. 9, no. 5, Dec. 1974.

370   Cravioto, J. and De Licardie, E. R.
       The long-term consequences of protein-calorie malnutrition.
       NUTRITION REVIEWS 29:107-11, May 1971.

371   Crawford, Eric and Thorbecke, Erik
       The analysis of food poverty: An illustration from Kenya.
       PAKISTAN DEVELOPMENT REVIEW (ISLAMABAD) 19:311-35, Winter,
       1980.

       The study describes a methodology which is used to estimate
       the magnitude and regional distribution of food poverty
       among Kenyan smallholders.

372   Culyer, A. J. and Simpson, Heather
       Externality models and health: A Ruckblick over the
       last twenty years. UNIVERSITY OF OTAGO. ECONOMICS
       DISCUSSION PAPERS (DUNEDIN) No. 8006:1-25, 1980.

373   Dalton, Keith
       The undernourished Philippines. FAR EASTERN ECONOMIC
       REVIEW (HONGKONG) 101:35-36, Sept. 1, 1978.

       Shows how Manila's health drive is criticised as cosmetic
       while the scourge of malnutrition grows.

374   Dandekar, Kumudini and Bhate, Vaijayanti
       Maharashtra's rural health services scheme; an evaluation.
       ECONOMIC AND POLTIICAL WEEKLY (BOMBAY) 13:2047-52, Dec.
       16, 1978.

       The authors present an evaluation of the Community Health
       Workers (CHW) scheme launched by the Central government
       to extend health facilities to the country's remote
       villages.

375   Dandekar, V. M.
       On measurement of undernutrition. ECONOMIC AND POLTIICAL
       WEEKLY (BOMBAY) 17:203-12,, Feb. 6, 1982.

376   Dasgupta, Rajaram
       Undernutrition and poverty: Measurement problems. MARGIN;
       QUARTERLY JOURNAL OF THE NATIONAL COUNCIL OF APPLIED
       ECONOMIC RESEARCH (NEW DELHI) 14:83-88, Oct. 1981.

377   deLattre, Anne
       Food aid. OECD OBSERVER, No. 81:14-16, May-June 1976.

378   De Mel, Beatrice and Fernando, Marina W.
       Tradition, modernity and value movement: A study of
       dietary changes in a Sri Lanka village. MARGA QUARTERLY
       JOURNAL (COLOMBO) 6, No. 1:18-42, 1980.

379   De Mel, Beatrice V. and Jogaratnam, T.
       Population growth, nutrition and food supplies in Sri
       Lanka. MARGA QUARTERLY JOURNAL (COLOMBO) 4, No. 3:60-92,
       1977.

       The approach adopted here is first, to consider current
       levels of food consumption and relate them to requirements,
       and secondly to project requirements on the basis of
       population and income growth and consider the adjustments
       in supply necessary to meet demand.

380   Devadas, Rajammal P.; Prima, N. and Vijayalakshmi, R.
       Formulation, preparation and evaluation of diets based
       on the recommended allowance for foods and nutrients.
       INDIAN JOURNAL OF NUTRTION AND DIETETICS 10:1-7, Jan.
       1973.

381   Devadas, Rajammal P.; Anuradha, J. R. and Sharadambal, B.
       Evaluation of an applied nutrition feeding programme
       on the nutritional status of nursing women. INDIAN JOURNAL
       OF NUTRITION AND DIETETICS 8:143-48, May 1971.

382   Devadas, Rajammal P. and Chandrasekhar, Usha
       Nutrition education of illiterate people.   JOURNAL OF
       NUTRITION EDUCATION 1:13-16, Winter 1970.

383   Diesfeld, Hans-Jochen
       The significance of social security systems for health
       and population policies in developing countries. ECONOMICS
       (TUBINGEN) 19:58-67, 1979.

384   Dirks, Harlan J.
       Japan's strategy to stabilize food supplies. Washington,
       D.C.: U.S. Department of State Sixteenth Session Seminar
       in Foreign Policy, 1973-74.

385   Djukanovic, V. and Mach, E. P., eds.
       Alternative approaches to meeting basic health needs
       in developing countries. Geneva: WHO, 1975.   116 pp.

386   Donald, Brian L.
       India's experience--national, community, public or private
       health? PUBLIC ADMINISTRATION AND DEVELOPMENT (CHICHESTER)
       2:207-23, July/Sept. 1982.

       Outlines and comments upon recent developments in providing
       primary health care in rural communities in India.

387   Doxiadis, C. A.
       Systems of health care delivery.   EKISTICS 37 (March
       1974): 194-98.

388   Doxiadis, Spyros A.
       Individuality, nutrition and mental development.   EKISTICS
       35:223-26, April 1973.

389   Drummond, M. F.
       Welfare economics and cost-benefit analysis in health
       care. SCOTTISH JOURNAL OF POLITICAL ECONOMY (EDINBURGH)
       28:125-45, June 1981.

       The body of work upon which comments are based consists
       of over 100 cost-benefit and cost-effectiveness studies
       in the health care field published in the English language
       plus other papers, written by health economists, in which
       the conceptual issues surrounding the use of CBA are
       discussed.

390   Dugdale, A. E. and Doessel, D. P.
       A simulation model of infant feeding and family economics
       in developing countries. JOURNAL OF POLICY MODELING
       (NEW YORK) 2:345-69, Sept. 1980.

       The authors present a model which examines the problem
       of malnutrition in the Third World, and measures the
       extent to which it threatens economic growth and standards

of living.   The model is applied to the economy of Malaysia.

391   Dunn, James E.
Endangered species. Broadman, 1977.

392   Dustin, J.-P. and Lavoipierre, G. J.
Food aid as a capital investment.   WORLD HEATLH FORUM (GENEVA) 2, No. 1:106-13, 1981.

The authors show that food aid can become a substitute "currency" in financing part of the cost of such varied projects as rural water supplies and hospital surgical units, thereby saving scarce foreign exchange and giving project workers a greater sense of involvement in the completed project.

393   Eckholm, Erik and Record, Frank
Two two faces of malnutrition.   Worldwatch Paper 9. Washington, D.C.: Worldwatch Institute, 1976.   63 pp.

394   Ehrilich, Paul R. and Ehrilich, Anne H.
The world food problem: No room for complacency. SOCIAL SCIENCE QUARTERLY 57, No. 2:375-82, Sept. 1976.

395   Eliad Gebre-Egziabher
Health manpower problems of Ethiopia.   ETHIOPIAN JOURNAL OF DEVELOPMENT RESEARCH (ADDIS ABABA) 3, No. 2:33-53, Oct. 1979.

396   Elliott, Charles and Cole-King, Susan
Health and development: A policy for intersectoral action. WORLD HEALTH FORUM (GENEVA) 2, No. 4:567-75, 1981.

397   England, R.
More myths in international health planning.   AMERICAN JOURNAL OF PUBLIC HEALTH 68:153-59, Feb. 1978.

398   Esseks, John D.
The food outlook for the Sahel: Regaining self-sufficiency or continuing dependence on international aid?   AFRICA TODAY 22:45-56, April-June 1975.

399   Fasbender, Karl
Food for the world: Gloomy prospects.   INTERECONOMICS (Jan. 1975), pp. 26-28.

400   FAO
National grain policies. Rome: FAO, 1975.

401   FAO
The world food problem: Proposals for national and international action. Rome: FAO, 1974.

402   FAO
        Agricultural development: A review of FAO's field
        activities. Basic Study no. 23, Rome: FAO, 1970.

403   Feeding the poorest. ECONOMIST (LONDON) 268:87-88, Sept.
        16, 1978.

        Discusses the arguments that development effort ought,
        morally, to be concentrated on the poorest, and that
        wealth will not, as was once believed, "trickle down"
        to them from above.

404   Feldstein, Martin S.
        Health sector planning in developing countries. ECONOMICA
        (May 1970).

405   Fendall, N. R. E.
        Primary health care; issues and constraints. THIRD WORLD
        PLANNING REVIEW (LIVERPOOL) 3:387-401, Nov. 1981.

406   Feverstein, M. T.
        Rural health problems in developing countries: The need
        for a comprehensive community approach. COMMUNITY
        DEVELOPMENT JOURNAL 11:38-52, Jan. 1976.

407   Fleuret, P. and Fleuret, A.
        Nutrition, consumption and agricultural change. HUMAN
        ORGANIZATION 39:250-60, Fall 1980.

408   Food; amidst heavy odds. PAKISTAN ECONOMIST (KARACHI)
        21:24-29, Oct. 24, 1981.

        Discusses current food problems and possible solutions.

409   Food needs of developing countries; projections of
        production and consumption to 1990. BANGLADESH BANK
        BULLETIN (DACCA) 56:20-24, Feb. 1978.

        Summary of a Research Report (Report No. 3) published
        by International Policy Research Institute, Washington.

410   Food for Liberia. WEST AFRICA (LONDON) No. 3253:2129-30,
        Nov. 19, 1979.

        Reports on plans to develop agriculture to the point
        of self-sufficiency in food production.

411   Food policy and development strategy in Bangladesh. THE
        BANGLADESH DEVELOPMENT STUDIES (DACCA) 8:1-185,
        Winter/Summer 1980.

412   Franda, Marcus
        Food policy and politics in Bangladesh. INDIA QUARTERLY
        (NEW DELHI) 37:165-93, April/June 1981.

413   Frankel, Francine R.
       India's green revolution: Political costs of economic
       growth. Princeton University Press, 1971.

414   Frankenberg, Ronald
       Man, society and health: Towards the definition of the
       role of sociology in the development of Zambian medicine.
       AFRICAN SOCIAL RESEARCH (Dec. 1969), pp. 573-87.

415   Freeman, O. L.
       Food, jobs: A global solution. BUS & SOC REVIEW No.
       14:80, Summer 1975.

416   Freeman, W. H.
       Food and agriculture. Scientific American Books, 1976.

417   French, Carl B.
       Voluntary health programs, in NONALIGNED THIRD WORLD
       ANNUAL, 1970.

418   French, Charles E.
       Potential of research on world food and nutrition problems.
       AMERICAN JOURNAL OF AGRICULTURAL ECONOMICS (LEXINGTON,
       KY.) 59:838-54, Dec. 1977.

       The author gives some background about his experience
       with the World Food and Nutrition Study (WFNS) of the
       National Academy of Sciences, and suggests that
       agricultural economists have failed to produce an effective
       research agenda for tackling these problems.

419   Frisch, Rose E.
       Malnutrition and mental development: A critical review.
       INDIAN JOURNAL OF NUTRITION AND DIETETICS 8:149-62, May
       1971.

420   FUTURIST 9:293-306, Dec. 1975. Feeding the world poor
       in the year 2000 [symposium].

421   Gardner, Richard N., ed.
       The world food and energy crises: The role of
       international organization. Rensselaerville, NY: Institute
       on Science and Man, 1974.

422   Gelb, Leslie, and Lake, Anthony
       Washington dateline: Less food, more politics. FOREIGN
       POLICY, No. 17:176-89, Winter 1974.

423   Ghose, Ajit Kumar
       Food supply and starvation: A study of famines with
       reference to the Indian sub-continent. OXFORD ECONOMIC
       PAPERS (LONDON) 34:368-89, July 1982.

424   Girdner, Janet and Olorunsola, Victor
       Ghana's agricultural food policy; Operation feed yourself.
       FOOD POLICY (GUILDFORD, ENG.) 5:14-25, Feb. 1980.

       The authors discuss the successes and shortcomings of
       Operation feed yourself and suggest areas in which
       improvement might be made.

425   Gish, Oscar
       Health planning in developing countries.   JOURNAL OF
       DEVELOPMENT STUDIES 6:67-76, July 1970.

426   Goldberg, Ray A.
       International agribusiness coordination.   Cambridge,
       Mass.: Ballinger, 1975.

427   Goldman, H. Warrack and Ranade, C. G.
       Analysis of income effect on food consumption in rural
       and urban Philippines. JOURNAL OF AGRICULTURAL ECONOMICS
       AND DEVELOPMENT (LAGUNA) 7:150-65, July 1977.

       The authors' approach is to estimte well known demand
       functions for food items and to choose the most appropriate
       demand function on the basis of statistical and economic
       criteria.   Then they compute the expenditure elasticities
       for different income groups using the selected demand
       function.

428   Goldman, Richard H.
       Staple food self-sufficiency and the distributive impact
       of Malaysian rice policy. FOOD RESEARCH INSTITUTE STUDIES
       (STANFORD) 14, No. 3:251-93, 1975.

       Content: Prior to World War II; the post-war recovery
       and   the   origins   of   a   new   rice   policy, 1946-57;
       double-cropping and the drive toward self-sufficiency;
       per capita consumption, protection, and self-sufficiency;
       evaluation of policy instruments; and future policy
       developments and dilemmas.

429   Golladay, Frederick L.
       Community health care in developing countries. FINANCE
       AND DEVELOPMENT (WASHINGTON) 17:35-39, Sept. 1980.

       Concludes that health care systems in many developing
       countries need to be expanded and improved at the community
       level in order to reach the great majority of people
       who presently do not have access to adequate health care.

430   Gongora, Jose
       The UN/FAO World food programme--nutritional aspects.
       INDIAN JOURNAL OF NUTRITION AND DIETETICS 11:37-46, Jan.
       1974.

431   Goolsby, O. Galbert
       LDC's may need more aid to maintain food imports. FOREIGN
       AGRICULTURE (WASHINGTON) 18:18-19, Oct. 1980.

       Examines various sources of financing open to the less
       developed nations, including the IMF, the World Bank
       and OPEC.

432   Gopalan, G.
       Planning for better nutrition. YOJANA 17:561-64, Aug.
       1973.

433   Gordon, John E. and Scrimshaw, Nevin S.
       Evaluating nutrition intervention programs. NUTRITION
       REVIEWS 30:263-65, Dec. 1972.

434   Gosovic, B.
       UNCTAD, conflict and compromise: The Third World's quest
       for an equitable world order through the United Nations.
       Leiden: Sijthoff, 1975.

435   Gottinger, Hans W.
       Application of a multi-criteria evaluation procedure
       to health care delivery. ZEITSCHRIFT FUR NATIONALOKONOMIE
       (VIENNA) 41, No. 1/2:79-95, 1981.

436   Goulet, Denis
       World hunger: Putting development ethics to the test.
       SOCIOLOGY INQUIRY 45, No. 4:3-11, 1975.

437   Green, Christopher and Kirkpatrick, Colin
       A cross-section analysis of food insecurity in developing
       countries: Its magnitude and sources. JOURNAL OF
       DEVELOPMENT STUDIES (LONDON) 18:185-204, Jan. 1982.

438   Grewal, S. S. and Chatha, I. S.
       Prospects of foodgrain production in Punjab. ECONOMIC
       AFFAIRS (CALCUTTA) 26:17-24, Jan./March 1981.

439   Griffin, Keith
       Land concentration and rural poverty. New York: Holmes
       & Meier, 1976.

440   Griffin, Philip
       The impact of food aid; Peru, a case study. FOOD POLICY
       (GUILDFORD, ENG.) 4:46-52, Feb. 1979.

441   Groenwald, J. A.
       Nutritional and dietitic requirements of the individual
       and society; an agricultural economic perspective.
       AGREKON; QUARTERLY JOURNAL ON AGRICULTURAL ECONOMICS
       (PRETORIA) 19:1-7, Oct. 1980.

442   Gunjal, K. R. and Ram, G. S.
Nutritional management for farmers and landless
agricultural labourers in union territory of Delhi. INDIAN
JOURNAL OF AGRICULTURAL ECONOMICS (BOMBAY) 16-26,
July/Sept. 1977.

Seeks to examine the possibilities of minimizing diet
cost by optimal combinations of different foods in rural
Delhi in a manner that all the essential nutrients are
at or above the required levels and the physiological
needs of people are met.

443   Gwatkin, Davidson R.
Food policy, nutrition planning and survival; the cases
of Kerala and Sri Lanka. FOOD POLICY (GUILDFORD, ENG.)
4:245-58, Nov. 1979.

Concludes that in the two countries studied food and
nutrition efforts have served as central integrating
themes for a wide range of development activities directed
toward the alleviation of poverty.

444   Halse, Michael
Producing an adequate national diet in India: Issues
relating to conversion efficiency and dairying.
AGRICULTURAL SYSTEMS (BARKING, ENG.) 4:239-78, Oct. 1979.

Analyzes the relevance of the concept of conversion
efficiency to India's dairying, in particular.

445   Hamid, M. A.
Food demand-supply projections: Bangladesh 1978-2000.
THE BANGLADESH DEVELOPMENT STUDIES (DACCA) 8:169-85,
Winter/Summer 1980.

446   Hansen, R. Gaurth
An index of food quality. NUTRITION REVIEWS 31 (Jan
1973): 1-7.

447   Harris, Simon
The world commodity scene and the common agricultural
policy. Occasional Paper No. 1, Centre for European
Agricultural Studies, Wyde College, Ashford, Kent, England,
1975.

448   Hathaway, Dale E.
Food issues in North-South relations [based on conference
papers]. WORLD ECONOMY (LOONDON) 3:447-59, Jan. 1981.

449   Hayami, Yujiro
A century of agricultural growth in Japan: Its relevance
to Asian development. Minneapolis: University of
Minnesota Press, 1976.

450   Hayami, Yujiro
        Agricultural growth in Japan, Taiwan, Korea and the
        Philippines. Honolulu: University of Hawaii Press,
        1976.

451   Health. EUROPEAN COMMUNITIES. COMMISSION. COURIER
        (BRUSSELS) No. 34:24-55, Nov./Dec. 1975.

452   Heller, Peter S.
        An analysis of the structure, equity and effectiveness
        of public sector health systems in developing countries;
        the case of Tunisia, 1960-1972. UNIVERSITY OF MICHIGAN.
        CENTER FOR RESEARCH ON ECONOMIC DEVELOPMENT, DISCUSSION
        PAPER (ANN ARBOR) No. 43:1-105, Feb. 1975.

453   Heller, Peter S. and Drake, William D.
        Malnutrition, child morbidity and the family decision
        process. JOURNAL OF DEVELOPMENT ECONOMICS (AMSTERDAM)
        6:203-35, June 1979.

        This paper suggests a microeconomic model of the process
        by which infants and toddlers are subject to
        malnourishment, diarrhea and other illnesses in developing
        countries. It is econometrically estimated on a
        cross-section, time-series basis for 1200 children from
        Candelaria, Colombia.

454   Hemmer, Hans-Rimbert
        Possible consequences of nutritional improvements for
        the economic development. INTERECONOMICS, REVIEW OF
        INTERNATIONAL TRADE AND DEVELOPMENT (HAMBURG) No. 4:185-89,
        July/Aug. 1979.

        Attempts to answer the question: What possibilities
        exist for influencing the development process by measures
        of nutrition policy?

455   Henrichsmeyer, W.
        Trade negotiations and world food problems. London:
        Trade Policy Research Center, 1974.

456   Hepner, Ray and Maiden, Norma C.
        Growth rate, nutrient intake and "mothering" as
        determinants of malnutrition in disadvantaged children.
        NUTRITION REVIEWS 29:219-23, Oct. 1971.

457   Hillman, Jimmye; Johnson, D. Gale and Gray, Roger
        Food reserve policies for world food security: A
        consultant study on alternative approaches. Rome: FAO,
        ESC:CSP/75/2, Jan. 1975.

458   Hoke, Bob
        Healths and healthing: Beyond disease and dysfunctional
        environments. EKISTICS 37:169-72, March 1974.

459   Hopkins, Raymond F.
       How to make food work.   FOREIGN POLICY No. 27 (Summer
       1977), pp. 89-108.

460   Hopkins, Raymond F. and Puchala, Donald J.
       Perspectives on the international relations of food.
       INTERNATIONAL ORGANIZATION (MADISON) 32:581-616, Summer
       1978.

       The authors examine five current world food problems,
       and conclude that re-evaluation and reform of the major
       principles characterizing the food regime are needed.

461   Hopkins, R. F. and Puchala, D. J., eds.
       Global   political   economy   of   food   [symposium].
       INTERNATIONAL ORGANIZATIONS 32:579-880, Summer 1978.

462   Hospitals and health care; a special report on medical
       exports to the Arab countries and Iran.   TIME (LONDON)
       p. 13-15, Nov. 24, 1977.

463   Hu, S. M. and Seifman, Eli
       Revolution in Chinese medical and health work.   ASIAN
       AFFAIRS, JOURNAL OF THE ROYAL CENTRAL ASIAN SOCIETY
       (LONDON) 9:44-56, Feb. 1978.

       The authors examine the development of the "co-operative
       medical system" and the medical role of the "bare-foot
       doctor," and reforms in Chinese medical education.

464   Hunger: A growing specter.   COMRCIO EXTERIOR DE MEXICO
       ENGLISH EDITION (MEXICO) 25:379-83, Oct. 1979.

       Discusses world food availability with special reference
       to the situation in Latin America.

465   Hunter, Guy
       Administration of agricultural development: Lessons
       from India.   London: Oxford University Press, 1970.

466   Huq, Mahfuzul
       Food policy and national planning in Bangladesh.   THE
       BANGLADESH   DEVELOPMENT   STUDIES   (DACCA)   8:161-68,
       Winter/Summer 1980.

467   Hurtado, Maria Elena
       Feeding the billions of the Third World.   SOUTH; THE
       THIRD WORLD MAGAZINE (LONDON) No. 18:17-18, April 1982.

       Suggests that inequitable systems of land tenure must
       go, and political obstacles need to be cleared if food
       is to be distributed efficiently.

468   Hussain, M. Anwar
       A fresh look at the protein deficiency in Pakistan.

BRITISH JOURNAL OF NUTRITION 29:211-19, March 1973.

469   International Food Policy and Research Institute
        Recent prospective developments in food consumption:
        Some policy issues. New York: UN, 1977.

470   ILO
        Employment, growth and basic needs. NY: Praeger, 1977.

471   Iowa State University
        Proceedings: World Food Conference, 1976. Iowa State
        University Press, 1977.

472   Isenman, Paul J. and Singer, H. W.
        Food aid: Disincentive effects and their policy
        implications. ECONOMIC DEVELOPMENT AND CULTURAL CHANGE
        25:205-37, Jan. 1977.

473   Islam, Nasir
        Food aid: Conscience, morality, and politics.
        INTERNATIONAL JOURNAL (TORONTO) 36:353-70, Spring 1981.

474   Jacobsen, Michael and Lerza, Catherine
        Food for people, not for profit. New York: Ballantine
        Press, 1976.

475   Jagdish, V.
        Primary health care in rural India. WORLD HEALTH FORUM
        (GENEVA) 2, No. 2:218-21, 1981.

476   Jelliffee, D. B.
        Commerciogenic malnutrition? NUTRITION REVIEWS 30:199-205,
        Sept. 1972.

477   Jennings, Peter R.
        Rice breeding and world food production. SCIENCE
        186:1085-88, Dec. 20, 1974.

478   Johnson, D. Gale
        World food supply. New York: Arno Press, 1976.

479   Johnson, D. Gale
        Food for the future: A perspective. POPULATION AND
        DEVELOPMENT REVIEW 2:1-19, March 1976.

480   Johnson, D. Gale and Schnittker, John A.
        Agriculture in a world context: Policies and approaches
        for the next decade. New York: Praeger, 1974.

481   Johnston, Bruce F. and Meyer, Anthony J.
        Nutrition, health and population in strategies for rural
        development. UNIVERSITY OF NAIROBI. INSTITUTE FOR
        DEVELOPMENT STUDIES. DISCUSSION PAPER No. 238:1-43,
        Aug. 1976.

The authors suggest that a country's strategy for rural development should embrace a "composite package" approach for the delivery of nutrition, health and family planning services in rural areas.

482   Johnston, Bruce F. and Martorell, Reynaldo
Interrelationships among nutrition, health, population and development. FOOD RESEARCH INSTITUTE STUDIES (STANFORD) 16, No. 2:1-9, 1977.

The authors recommend giving a high priority to programs capable of improving nutritional status and health among the most vulnerable population groups and of slowing population growth.

483   Jones, David
Food and interdependence: The effect of food and agricultural of developed countries on the food problems of developing countries. London: Overseas Development Institute, 1976.

484   Josling, Timothy
An international grain reserve policy. Washington: National Planning Association, 1973.

485   Joy, Leonard
The segments of the world population at nutritional risk. AMERICAN JOURNAL OF AGRICULTURAL ECONOMICS (LEXINGTON) 61:977-81, Dec. 1979.

486   Kaldy, M. S.
Protein yield of various crops as related to protein value. ECONOMIC BOTANY 26:142-44, April-June 1972.

487   Karim, Rezaul and Levinson, F. James
A missing dimension of food and nutrition policy in Bangladesh. THE BANGLADESH DEVELOPMENT STUDIES (DACCA) 7:99-106, Winter 1979.

488   Kastens, Merritt L.
How government meddling threatens the world's food supply. FUTURIST (WASHINGTON) 15:5-10, Oct. 1981.

489   Kaul, J. L. and Grewal, S. S.
An economic analysis of nutrition problems in India. INDIAN JOURNAL OF AGRICULTURAL ECONOMICS (BOMBAY) 32:61-71, July/Sept. 1977.

The data analysed here are drawn from various reports published by the National Institute of Nutrition, Indian Council of Medical Research, Hyderabad and National Sample Survey of India and FAO.

490   Kaynak, Erdener

Government and food distribution in LDC's; the Turkish experience. FOOD POLICY (GUILDFORD, ENG.) 5:132-42, May 1980.

491   Keith, Robert G.
Conquest and agrarian change. Cambridge, Mass.: Harvard University Press, 1976.

492   Khan, M. Irshad
Role of IR-20 in solving the food problem of East Pakistan. PAKISTAN DEVELOPMENT REVIEW 11:63-70, Spring 1971.

493   Kidane, Asmerom
The demand and price structure for selected food products in Ethiopia; an econometric and spectral analysis. ETHIOPIAN JOURNAL OF DEVELOPMENT RESEARCH (ADDIS ABABA) 1:1-16, April 1974.

Investigates the demand and price structure for selected food products in Ethiopia. The food products selected for study are: teff, barley, wheat, maize and oilseeds.

494   King, K. W.
The place of vegetables in meeting the food needs in emerging nations. ECONOMIC BOTANY 25:6-11, Jan-March 1971.

495   King, Kendall W.
Nutrition education of the poor can be effective. INDIAN JOURNAL OF NUTRITION AND DIETETICS 9:351-56, Nov. 1972.

496   King, M. E.
Role of the skill-trained volunteer in international public health: Peace Corps' health programming and health policy in developing countries. AMERICAN JOURNAL OF PUBLIC HEALTH 71:408-09, April 1981.

497   Klatt, W.
China's food and fuel under new management. INTERNATIONAL AFFAIRS (LONDON) 54:60-74, Jan. 1978.

498   Kocher, James and Cash, Richard A.
Achieving health and nutrition objectives within a basic needs framework. HARVARD INSTITUTE FOR INTERNATIONAL DEVELOPMENT. DEVELOPMENT DISCUSSION PAPER (CAMBRIDGE, MASS.) No. 55:1-51, March 1979.

499   Konczaki, Zbigniew A.
Infant malnutrition in Sub-Saharan Africa: A problem in socio-economic development. CANADIAN JOURNAL OF AFRICAN STUDIES 6:433-50, 1972.

500   Konandreas, Panos and Huddleston, Barbara
Cost analysis of a food insurance scheme for developing

countries.   FOOD POLICY (GUILDFORD, ENG.) 4:3-14, Feb. 1979.

The authors describe a proposed tool to alleviate the food insecurity problems of developing countries.

501   Koppel, Bruce M.
Food policy options for secondary regions; a framework for applied research.   FOOD POLICY (GUILDFORD, ENG.) 6:33-46, Feb. 1981.

502   Krichta, J. M.; Rumsey, T. R. and Farkas, D. F.
Defining food R & D needs as a guide to the future. FOOD TECHNOLOGY 29:74-84, Oct. 1975.

503   Krishnamachari, K. A.; Rao, N. P. and Rao, K. V.
Food and nutritional situation in the drought affected areas of Maharshira.   A survey and recommendations. INDIAN JOURNAL OF NUTRITION AND DIETETICS 11:20-27, Jan. 1974.

504   Krone, Wolfgang
Fish as food; present contribution and potential.   FOOD SUUPLY (GUILDFORD, ENG.) 4:259-68, Nov. 1979.

Gives an account of the importance of fish as a source of animal protein and suggests that the relatively low cost of many fish-producing systems should encourage increased exploitation of fishery resources for food purposes.

505   Ladejinsky, W.
Wheat procurement in India in 1974 and related matters. WORLD DEVELOPMENT 3 (Feb.-March 1974), pp. 91-111.

506   Ladejinsky, Wolf
Food shortage in West Bengal; crisis or chronic?   WORLD DEVELOPMENT (OXFORD) 4:103-10, Feb. 1976.

507   Lampton, David M.
Development and health care; is China's medical programme exportable?   WORLD DEVELOPMENT (OXFORD) 6:621-30, May 1978.

Concludes that it is unlikely that Peking's policies will be easily adapted to quite different social and political circumstances, but in some cases, for example in Tanzania, the policies will not be entirely inappropriate.

508   Lane, Sylvia
The contribution of food aid to nutrition.   AMERICAN JOURNAL OF AGRICULTURAL ECONOMICS (LEXINGTON) 62:984-87, Dec. 1980.

509   Lappe, F. M. and Collins, j.
       More food means more hunger. FUTURIST 11:90-3, April
       1977.

510   Latham, Michael C.
       Health strategies for the control of chilhood malnutrtion.
       UNIVERSITY OF NAIROBI.   INSTITUTE FOR DEVELOPMENT STUDIES.
       DISCUSSION PAPER No. 228:1-18, Jan. 1976.

       Deals primarily with those interventions in which health
       personnel play a leading role.   The author presents a
       critical examination of three levels of treatment and
       prevention; the hospital, the nutrition rehabilitation
       centre and the health clinic.

511   Lawrie, R. A., ed.
       Proteins as human food. Westport, Conn.: Avi Publishing
       Co., 1970. 525 pp.

512   Lederer, Thomas H.
       Bangladesh food supply in uncertain balance.   FOREIGN
       AGRICULTURE (WASHINGTON) 15:12-14, June 20, 1977.

       Bangladesh's food situation in 1976 was the best in the
       country's short history.   But the balance between supply
       and demand may be precarious.

513   Leech, John
       Food   for   a   continent;   the   struggle   towards
       self-sufficiency.   AFRICA (LONDON) SUPPL., No. 1, Africa
       Agriculture, 6-9, 1981.

514   Lehmann, D.
       Agrarian reform and agrarian reformism. London: Faber
       & Faber, 1974.

515   Lele, Uma
       The design of rural development. Baltimore: Johns Hopkins
       University Press, 1975.

516   Leonard, David K.
       Reaching the peasant farmer, organization theory and
       practice in Kenya. Chicago: University of Chicago Press,
       1977.

517   Levin, Arthur, ed.
       Regulating health care; the struggle for control. ACADEMY
       OF POLITICAL SCIENCE, PROCEEDINGS (NEW YORK) 33, No.
       4:1-244, 1980.

       Content: Regulation: an overview; costs and constraints;
       assessing the effects; alternatives to regulation; the
       foreign experience.

518   Levinson, F. James
         Facilitating   effective   investment   in   nutrition.
         INTERNATIONAL DEVELOPMENT REVIEW 14:19-21, 1972.

519   Lewis, John P. and Kapun, Ishan
         The World Bank Group, multilateral aid, and the 1970's.
         Lexington, Mass.: Lexington Books, 1973.

520   Link, John E.
         Mexico aims self-sufficiency in basic foods, reduced
         imports. FOREIGN AGRICULTURE (WASHINGTON) 19:9-11, Jan.
         1981.

         Examines the prospects for a new program known as SAM
         (Sistema alimentario mexicano, or the Mexican food system).

521   Livingston, Sally K.
         What   influences   malnutrition?   JOURNAL   OF   NUTRITION
         EDUCATION 3:18-27, Summer 1971.

522   Lofchie, Michael F. and Commins, Stephen K.
         Food deficits and agricultural policies in tropical Africa.
         JOURNAL OF MODERN AFRICAN STUDIES (LONDON) 20:1-25, March
         1982.

523   Lofchie, Michael F.
         Political and economic origins of African hunger. JOURNAL
         OF MODERN AFRICAN STUDIES (LONDON) 13:511-67, Dec. 1975.

         Africa's problems of food are not reducible to a matter
         of rainfall levels. They have to do fundamentally with
         the dualistic structure of Africa's agricultural economies.
         Decades of over-concentration on export cultivation have
         left   the   continent's   food-producing   regions   badly
         under-supplied with infrastructure, deprived of government
         services, desperately short of capital for development,
         and technologically pre-feudal. As a result, any attempt
         to improve Africa's food-producing capability will need
         to   concern   itself   with   a   fundamental   structural
         transformation of the rural economy.

524   Longhurst, Richard and Payne, Philip
         Seasonal aspects of nutrition: Review of evidence and
         policy implications. INSTITUTE OF DEVELOPMENT STUDIES.
         DISCUSSION PAPER (BRIGHTON) No. 145:1-35, Nov. 1979.

         The authors examine evidence from developing countries
         which suggests a seasonal pattern in the balance between
         nutrient intake and requirements. They conclude by
         discussing the ways in which seasonal effects should
         be taken into account in programmes and policies relating
         to rural development.

525   Macaluso, Emmanuele
        The agricultural policy of the EEC. WORLD MARXIST REVIEW
        20, March 1977, pp. 110-118.

526   Maddock, R. T.
        The economic and political characteristics of food as
        a diplomatic weapon. JOURNAL OF AGRICULTURAL ECONOMICS
        (ASHFORD, KENT) 29:31-41, Jan. 1978.

        Considers the role of food as a diplomatic weapon and
        focuses attention on dominance of the U.S.A. in the
        production of the major grains and feedstuffs.

527   Mahler, Halfdan
        People. SCIENTIFIC AMERICAN (NEW YORK) 243:67-77, Sept.
        1980.

        Suggests that health for all is not just a by-product
        of development. In the author's opinion, it is a primary
        lever for initiating the development process itself.

528   Mahler, Halfdan
        The meaning of "health for all by the year 2000." WORLD
        HEALTH FORUM (GENEVA) 2, No. 1:5-22, 1981.

529   Makhijani, Arjun with Alan Poole
        Energy and agriculture in the Third World. Cambridge,
        Mass.: Ballinger, 1974.

530   Malhotra, Dina N.
        The book famine in developing countries. UNESCO BULLETIN
        FOR LIBRARIES 24:211-15, July-Aug. 1970.

531   Mair, Andrew J.
        Can the world's food production keep up with population
        growth? FOREIGN AGRICULTURE 11:8-9, 16, Aug. 23, 1973.

532   Majumder, Sanat K.
        Vegetarianism: Fad, faith, or fact? AMERICAN SCIENTIST
        60:175-79, March/April, 1972.

533   Manetsch, Thomas J.
        On food shortage forecasting with emphasis on the South
        Asia case. THE BANGLADESH DEVELOPMENT STUDIES (DACCA)
        5:349-58, July 1977.

        Suggests that there seem to be significant correlations
        between food shortages in this part of the world and
        solar activity and mean hemispheric temperature. The
        purpose of this discussion is to elaborate on these
        observed correlations and to indicate their implications
        for food shortage forecasting.

534   Marei, Sayed
        The world food crisis. New York: Longman, 1976.

535   Maru, Rushikesh M.
       Health manpower strategies for rural health services;
       India and China, 1949-1975. ECONOMIC AND POLTICAL WEEKLY
       (BOMBAY) 11:1253-68, Aug. 1976.

       Compares the health manpower strategies pursued in India
       and China and brings out the implications of these
       strategies for the birth control programmes. The three
       key areas discussed are: training medical manpower,
       redistribution of health manpower from urban to rural
       areas and utilization of practitioners of indigenous
       medicine.

536   Maxwell, S. J. and Singer, H. W.
       Food aid to developing countries; a survey. WORLD
       DEVELOPMENT (OXFORD) 7:225-47, March 1979.

       This paper reviews the evidence on the impact of food
       aid on growth and its associated factors and identifies
       a set of guiding principles for maximizing the
       effectiveness of food aid.

537   Mayer, Jean
       Coping with famine. FOREIGN AFFAIRS 53 (Oct. 1974):
       98-120.

538   Mazumdar, Subash
       Realistic food goals for Africa. CERES/FAO REVIEW ON
       AGRICULTURAL DEVELOPMENT (ROME) 76:36-40, July/Aug. 1980.

539   McCarthy, F. Desmond
       Nutrition planning; analysis of some policy options.
       PAKISTAN DEVELOPMENT REVIEW (ISLAMABAD) 16:165-80, Summer
       1977.

       The cost effectiveness of a general food subsidy is
       analyzed by a simple model and some alternative schemes
       treated briefly are fortification, income transfers,
       and food stamp programmes.

540   McCord, Colin
       Integration of health, nutrition, and family planning;
       the Companignaj project in Bangladesh. FOOD RESEARCH
       INSTITUTE STUDIES (STANFORD) 16, No. 2:91-105, 1977.

541   McCune, W.
       Who's behind our farm policy? Westport, Conn.: Greenwood
       Press, 1975.

542   McHenry, Donald F. and Bird, Kai
       Food bungle in Bangladesh. FOREIGN POLICY, no. 27 (Summer
       1977), pp. 72-88.

543   McLin, Jon

Surrogate international organization and the case of world food security, 1949-1969. INTERNATIONAL ORGANIZATION (MADISON) 33:35-55, Winter 1979.

Includes, as a case study: the international wheat economy in the 1950's and 1960's.

544   McPherson, A. T.
        Synthetic foods: Their present and potential contribution to the world food supply. INDIAN JOURNAL OF NUTRITION AND DIETETICS 9:285-308, Sept. 1972.

545   Mead, Margaret
        The changing significance of food. AMERICAN SCIENTIST 58:176-81, March-April 1970.

546   Mellor, John W.
        The economics of agricultural development. Itaca: Cornell University Press, 1966.

547   Mellor, John W.
        Food aid and nutrition. AMERICAN JOURNAL OF AGRICULTURAL ECONOMICS (LEXINGTON) 62:979-83, Dec. 1980.

548   Mencher, Joan P.
        Why grow more food? An analysis of some contradictions in the "grren revolution" in Kerala. ECONOMIC AND POLITICAL WEEKLY (BOMBAY) REVIEW OF AGRICULTURE, 13:A98-104, Dec. 23/30, 1978.

549   Mesarovic, Mihajilo and Pestel, Edward
        Mankind at the turning point. New York: Dutton, 1974.

550   Messing, Simon D.
        Social problems related to the development of health in Ethiopia. RURAL AFRICANA (Winter 1972), pp. 7-13.

551   Miller, D. C.
        Health care organizations in third and fourth world nations. PHYLON 38:236-48, Sept. 1977.

552   Montague, Joel
        School feeding in developing countries. WORLD AGRICULTURE 22:23-27, 1973.

553   Morgan, Dan
        The food aid business. THE WASHINGTON POST, March 9-14, 1975.

554   Morgan, Robert W.
        Basic health needs in Africa. BOSTON UNIVERSITY. AFRICAN STUDIES CENTER. WORKING PAPERS No. 29:1-34, 1980.

555   Morgan, Robert W.
        The Sopono cult and smallpox vaccinations in Lagos. BOSTON
        UNIVERSITY.   AFRICAN   STUDIES   CENTER.   WORKING   PAPERS
        No. 11:1-24, 1979.

556   Mott, Frank L.
        Some aspects of health care in rural Nigeria.   STUDIES
        IN FAMILY PLANNING 7:109-14, April 1976.

557   Munoz de Chavez, Miriam
        Improving nutrition in less developed areas.   JOURNAL
        OF NUTRITION EDUCATION 4:167-70, Fall 1972.

558   Muralidharan, M. A. and Kumar, P.
        An analysis of nutrition levels of farmers in Eastern
        Uttar Pradesh.   INDIAN JOURNAL OF AGRICULTURAL ECONOMICS
        (BOMBAY) 32:53-60, July/Sept. 1977.

        The data for this study are taken from the rural household
        schedules of the 25th Round of the National Sample Survey
        (1970-71).

559   Murdoch, William W.
        The poverty of nations: The political economy of hunger
        and population.   Baltimore: Johns Hopkins University
        Press, 1980.

560   Nagle, J. C.
        Agricultural trade policies. Lexington, Mass.:   Lexington
        Books, 1976.

561   Narayanaswamy, D. et al.
        Supplementary value of low cost protein food based on
        a blend of wheat and soyabean flours to poor Indian diets
        based on wheat and kaffir corn.   INDIAN JOURNAL OF
        NUTRITION AND DIETETICS 8:309-14, Nov. 1971.

562   Newland, Kathleen
        Infant mortality and the health of societies.   WORLDWATCH
        PAPER (WASHINGTON) No. 47:1-56, Dec. 1981.

563   Newman, James E. and Pickett, Robert C.
        World climates and food supply variations.   SCIENCE 186:
        877-81, Dec. 6, 1974.

564   Newman, James and Gulliver, Catherine
        Patterns   of   protein-energy   malnutrition   and   food
        deprivation among infants and toddlers in Africa south
        of the Sahara.   AFRICAN STUDIES REVIEW (WALTHAM, MASS.)
        22:65-76, Sept. 1979.

565   Nicholls, William H.
        The Brazilian food supply: Problems and prospects.
        ECONOMIC DEVELOPMENT AND CULTURAL CHANGE 19:378-90, April
        1971.

566   Nicholson, Norman K. and Esseks, John D.
        The politics of food scarcities in developing countries.
        INTERNATIONAL ORGANIZATION (MADISON) 32:679-719, Summer
        1978.

        The authors examine some of the domestic political factors
        which inhibit or influence solutions to the food crises
        in various Third World countries and the potential or
        real role of international forces upon them.

567   Oculi, Okello
        Dependent food policy in Nigeria, 1975-1979. REVIEW
        OF AFRICAN POLITICAL ECONOMY (LONDON) No. 15/16:63-74,
        May/Dec. 1979.

568   Odufalu, Johnson C.
        The performance of the Nigerian general hospitals.
        NIGERIAN JOURNAL OF ECONOMIC AND SOCIAL STUDIES (IBADAN)
        17:77-92, March 1975.

569   Olatunbosun, D. and Olayemi, J, K.
        A review of problem areas of Nigeria's food economy.
        EASTERN AFRICAN JOURNAL OF RURAL DEVELOPMENT 6:79-96,
        1973.

570   Olesen, Virginia
        Confluences in social change: Cuban women and health
        care. JOURNAL OF INTERAMERICAN STUDIES AND WORLD AFFAIRS
        17:398-418, Nov. 1975.

571   Oliveira, J. Santos and De Carvalho, M. Fidalgo
        Nutritional value of some edible leaves used in Mozambique.
        ECONOMIC BOTANY 29:255-63, July-Sept. 1975.

572   Omvet, Gail
        The political economy of starvation. RACE AND CLASS
        17, No. 2:111-30, Autumn, 1975.

573   Onokerhoraye, A. G.
        Spatial aspects of the health care problem in Nigeria;
        a case study of Kwara State. QUARTERLY JOURNAL OF
        ADMINISTRATION 12:241-55, April 1978.

574   Orfila, Alejandro
        The conquest of hunger. AMERICAS (WASHINGTON) 30:13-20,
        Nov/Dec 1978.

        Describes efforts to accelerate food production and to
        make available basic foodstuffs within the region.

575   Osmani, S. R.
        Poverty, inequality and the problem of nutrition in
        Bangladesh. THE BANGLADESH DEVELOPMENT STUDIES 8:121-42,
        Winter/Summer 1980.

576   Overseas Development Council
        The United States and world development, agenda 1977.
        New York: Praeger Publishers, 1977.

577   Paddock, William and Paddock, Paul
        Time of famines. Boston: Little, Brown, 1976.

578   Paige, Jeffrey M.
        Agrarian   revolution: Social   movements   and   export
        agriculture in the underdeveloped world. New York: The
        Free Press, 1975.

579   Pandey, V. K. and Shah, S. L.
        Nutritional status of farm households in Eastern Uttar
        Pradesh. INDIAN JOURNAL OF AGRICULTURAL ECONOMICS (BOMBAY)
        32:47-52, July/Sept. 1977.

        An attempt is made to study the nutritional level of
        farm households of the Eastern region of Uttar Pradesh
        and to analyze the factors affecting the same.

580   Panikar, P. G. K.
        Resources not the constraint on health improvement; a
        case study of Kerala.   ECONOMIC AND POLITICAL WEEKLY
        (BOMBAY) 14:1803-09, Nov. 3, 1979.

        Concludes the reason for the better health status of
        Kerala lies in the state having given equal importance
        to preventive and promotive measures like sanitation,
        hygiene,   immunization   programs,   infant   and   pre-natal
        care, health education, etc., as to curative medicine.

581   Pariser, E. R.
        Farming the sea: New horizons in food production.   FOOD
        PRODUCT DEVELOPMENT 8:43-44, 46, Nov. 1974.

582   Parr, John B.
        Health   care   facility   planning;   some   developmental
        considerations. SOCIO-ECONOMIC PLANNING SCIENCES (OXFORD,
        ENG.) 14, No. 3:121-27, 1980.

583   Pasricha, Swaran
        Possible calorie intake in young children fed cereal
        based diets.   INDIAN JOURNAL OF NUTRITION AND DIETETICS
        10:282-85, Nov. 1973.

584   Patel, Mahesh
        Environmental determinants of health and their influence
        on infant mortality: The case of Sri Lanka.   MARGA
        QUARTERLY JOURNAL (COLOMBO) 6, No. 1:67-80, 1980.

585   Pearce, I. O. and Odebiyi, I. A.
        The   impact   of   socio-economic   inequalities   on   health:
        The double burden of the Nigerian poor.   AFRICA DEVELOPMENT
        4:64-83, Oct./Dec. 1979.

586   Pereira, S. M. and Begum, Almas
       The manifestations and management of severe protein-calorie
       malnutrition (kwashiorkor). WORLD REVIEW OF NUTRITION
       AND DIETETICS 19:1-50, 1974.

587   Perrin, Richard K. and Scobie, Grant M.
       Market intervention policies for increasing the consumption
       of nutrients by low income households. AMERICAN JOURNAL
       OF AGRICULTURAL ECONOMICS (LEXINGTON) 63:73-82, Feb.
       1981.

588   Petersen, William
       The social roots of hunger and overpopulation [developing
       countries]. PUBLIC INTEREST (NEW YORK), p. 37-52, Summer
       1982.

589   A pilot study on the feasibility of using mass media
       for imparting nutrition education. Bombay: Protein
       Foods Association of India, July 1972.   22 pp.

590   Pinstrup-Anderson, Tweeten
       The value, cost, and efficiency of American food aid.
       AMERICAN JOURNAL OF AGRICULTURAL ECONOMICS 53, No.
       3:431-440, Aug. 1971.

591   Poleman, Thomas T.
       Quantifying the nutrition situation in developing
       countries.   FOOD RESEARCH INSTITUTE STUDIES (STANDFORD)
       18, No. 1:1-58, 1981.

592   Poleman, Thomas T.
       A reappraisal of the extent of world hunger. FOOD POLICY
       (GUILDFORD, ENG.) 6:236-52, Nov. 1981.

       Questions the basis of the major surveys of FAO, the
       World Bank and USDA, and suggests that they have grossly
       overestimated the extent of world hunger.

593   Popkin, Barry M.
       Nutrition planning; an application of benefit-cost analysis
       in Cebu. PHILIPPINE REVIEW OF BUSINESS AND ECONOMICS
       (DILIMAN) 12:223-49, Dec. 1975.

       This paper reports the results of a benefit-cost analysis
       of alternative nutrition programs in the Philippines
       based partially on the information of nutritionists and
       also on some research being conducted as part of this
       study.

594   Population and food supply in Asia.   ECONOMIC BULLETIN
       FOR ASIA AND THE FAR EAST, June 1973.

595   Preston, Samuel H.
       Health programs and population growth.   POPULATION AND
       DEVELOPMENT REVIEW 1:189-99, Dec. 1975.

596   Priebe, Hermann
        Tasks and objectives of agricultural development aid.
        ECONOMICS No. 14:107-22, 1976.

597   Priority of nutrition in national development. NUTRITION
        REVIEWS 28:199-204, Oct. 1970.

598   Prosterman, Ray L.
        Land reform as foreign aid. FOREIGN POLICY No. 6:128-42,
        Spring 1972.

599   Puchala, Donald J. and Hopkins, Raymond F.
        Toward innovation in the global food regime. INTERNATIONAL
        ORGANIZATION (MADISON) 32:855-68, Summer 1978.

        The authors examine various aspects of the present
        international forums and processes, and conclude that
        reform of the present global regime is urgently needed.

600   Pyke, Magnus
        Synthetic food. London: John Murray, 1970. 145 pp.

601   Qadeer, Imrana
        Reshaping health services; a note on draft plan on rural
        health services. ECONOMIC AND POLITICAL WEEKLY (BOMBAY)
        12:926-28, June 4, 1977.

602   Radetzki, Marian
        Stock-holding for the stabilization of the world food
        market. SKANDINAVISKA ENSKILDA BANKEN, QUARTERLY REVIEW
        (STOCKHOLM) No. 4:163-71, 1975.

        Content: 1) the importance and topicality of the problem;
        2) which goods are to be stocked?; 3) the aims of
        international stabilization; 4) how large stabilization
        stocks are required?; 5) what would stock-holding cost?;
        6) conclusions.

603   Ramalingaswami, V.
        Health aspects of development activities. WORLD HEALTH
        FORUM (GENEVA) 2, No. 4:563-66, 1981.

604   Ranatunga, Prienne
        The food chain. CERES 42:22-25, Nov/Dec. 1974.

605   Rao, B. Sarveswara and Krishna, K. S.
        Some economic aspects of nutritional deficiency (a case
        study of a small1 town in Andhra Pradesh). INDIAN JOURNAL
        OF AGRICULTURAL ECONOMICS (BOMBAY) 32:34-46, July/Sept.
        1977.

        The authors investigate from the economist's angle the
        nature and dimensions of undernutrition and malnutrition
        in a small town in Andhra Pradesh, namely, Anakapelle.

606   Rao, D. H. and Satyanarayana, K.
        Nutritional status of tribal preschool children of Andhra
        Pradesh. INDIAN JOURNAL OF NUTRITION AND DIETETICS 11:
        328-34, Nov. 1974.

607   Rasmussen, Wayne D. and Porter, Jane M.
        Strategies for dealing with world hunger; post-World
        War II policies. AMERICAN JOURNAL OF AGRICULTURAL
        ECONOMICS (LEXINGTON) 63:810-18, Dec. 1981.

608   Reflections on malnutrition in Mexico. COMERCIO EXTERIOR
        DE MEXICO, ENGLISH EDITION 24:93-97, March 1978.

        Discusses the deterioration in Mexico's food availability
        levels since 1965.

609   The relationship of nutrition to brain development and
        behavior: A position paper of the food and nutrition
        board. Washington: National Academy of Sciences, National
        Research Council, June 1973. 15 pp.

610   Reutlinger, Shlomo
        Food insecurity; magnitude and remedies. WORLD DEVELOPMENT
        (OXFORD) 6:797-811, June 1978.

        Examines various alternative schemes for food security,
        discusses the specific measures required to implement
        these proposals and shows that the resource capacity
        of the international community is sufficient to carry
        them out.

611   Reutlinger, Shlomo and Selowsky, Marcelo
        Malnutrition and poverty: Magnitude and policy options.
        Washington, D.C.: World Bank Staff Occasional Papers,
        No. 23, 1976.

612   Reutlinger, Shlomo
        Simulation of world-wide buffer stocks of wheat. AMERICAN
        JOURNAL OF AGRICULTURAL ECONOMICS. 58, No. 1:1-12, Feb.
        1976.

613   Reutlinger, Shlomo; Eaton, David; Bigman, David and Blum,
        David
        Stabilization, economic efficiency and income distribution
        implications of grain reserve investments by developing
        countries: A simulation approach. Washington, D.C.:
        World Bank working paper, 1976.

614   Revelle, Roger
        Ghost at the feast: World Food Conference. SCIENCE,
        March 21, 1975, 1026.

615   Richardson, Michael
        Asia's food drive lags. FAR EASTERN ECONOMIC REVIEW
        (HONGKONG) 97:68-77, Aug. 12, 1977.

Examines the conclusions of a study on food production in Asia carried out under the auspices of the Asian Development Bank.

616   Rifkin, Susan B.
Health services in China. BULLETIN [Institute of Development Studies] 4:32-38, June 1972.

617   Robbins, William
The American food scandal. New York: William Morrow and Company, 1974.

618   Roemer, Milton I.
The foreign experience in health service policy. ACADEMY OF POLITICAL SCIENCE, PROCEEDINGS (NEW YORK) 33, No. 4:206-23, 1979.

619   Romaniuk, A.
Increase in natural fertility during the early stages of modernization: Evidence from an African case study, Zaire. POPULATION STUDIES (LONDON) 34:293-310, July 1980.

620   Rosenfeld, Stephen S.
The politics of food. FOREIGN POLICY No. 14:17-29, Spring 1974.

621   Ross, Clark
A modeling of the demand and supply of food grains in Senegal. UNIVERSITY OF MICHIGAN. CENTER FOR RESEARCH ON ECONOMIC DEVELOPMENT. DISCUSSION PAPER (ANN ARBOR) No. 85:1-68, June 1980.

622   Rothschild, Emma
Food politics. FOREIGN AFFAIRS 54:285-307, Jan. 1976.

623   Russett, B. and others
Health and population patterns as indicators of income inequality. ECONOMIC DEVELOPMENT AND CULTURAL CHANGE 29:759-79, July 1981.

624   Ryan, James G.
Human nutritional needs and crop breeding objectives in the Indian semi-arid tropics. INDIAN JOURNAL OF AGRICULTURAL ECONOMICS (BOMBAY) 32:78-87, July/Sept. 1977.

Discusses the recent evidence on nutritional availabilities and needs within the semi-arid tropical (SAT) region in India and then proceeds to derive the implications of this for crop breeding and nutrition strategies.

625   Sambou Gassama, M. I.
Africa's food shortages. WEST AFRICA (LONDON) No. 3371: 709-10, March 15, 1982.

626   Saouma, Edouard
        Food security in the face of crises. CERES, FAO REVIEW
        ON AGRICULTURE AND DEVELOPMENT (ROME) 14:15-19, March/
        April, 1981.

        Proposes some steps that would help to protect the poor
        from calamities beyond their control.

627   Sarma, I. R. K.
        Balanced diet, its composition and cost. ECONOMIC RESEARCH
        JOURNAL (MANILA) 8:71-81, April 1976.

        The objective of this paper is to examine how much it
        would have cost per person per day to obtain a balanced
        diet in March 1975.

628   Sarris, Alexander H.; Abbott, Philip C. and Taylor, Lance
        International grain reserves and food aid (paper prepared
        for the Overseas Development Council, Oct. 1976).

629   Schertz, Lyle P.
        Nutrition realities in the lower income countries.
        NUTRITION REVIEWS 31:201-6, July 1973.

630   Schertz, Lyle P.
        World food: Prices and the poor. FOREIGN AFFAIRS (April
        1974): pp. 511-37.

631   Schneider, H.
        The effects of food aid on agricultural production in
        recipient countries. Paris: OECD Development Centre,
        1975.

632   Schneider, William
        Food, foreign policy, and raw materials cartels. New
        York: Crane Russak, 1976.

633   Schnittker, John A.
        Grain reserves--now. FOREIGN POLICY No. 20:225-231,
        Fall 1975.

634   Schofield, F.
        Health planning in developing countries. IMPACT OF SOCIAL
        SCIENCE 25:181-91, July 1975.

635   Schubert, James N.
        The impact of food aid on world malnutrition.
        INTERNATIONAL ORGANIZATION (MADISON) 35:329-54, Spring
        1981.

        Explores the long-term impact of U.S. Public Law 480
        food aid through a cross-national analysis of aggregate
        data on aid receipts and change in nutritional status
        from 1962 to 1974.

636   Schultz, T. W.
       Food for the world. New York: Arno Press, 1976.

637   Schultz, T. W.
       Transforming traditional agriculture. New York: Arno
       Press, 1976.

638   Scrimshaw, Nevin S. and Taylor, Lance
       Food. SCIENTIFIC AMERICAN (NEW YORK) 243:78-88, Sept.
       1980.

       The authors show that the task of feeding everyone
       adequately calls for an investment in the agriculture
       of developing countries of more than $100 billion, and
       that without a fairer distribution of income many will
       still go hungry.

639   Seagrave, J. R.
       World food needs and "new proteins": a comment. ECONOMIC
       DEVELOPMENT AND CULTURAL CHANGE 20:554-57, April 1972.

640   Selim, Robert
       The 1980's; a decade of hunger. FUTURIST (WASHINGTON)
       14:29-38, April 1980.

       Suggests that if wide-spread famine in the 1980's is
       to be avoided, corrective actions need to be taken soon
       to help the world's impoverished nations feed themselves.

641   Selowsky, Marcelo
       Target group-oriented food programs: cost effectiveness
       comparisons. AMERICAN JOURNAL OF AGRICULTURAL ECONOMICS
       (LEXINGTON) 61:988-94, Dec. 1979.

642   Selowsky, Marcelo and Taylor, Lance
       The economics of malnourished children: An example of
       disinvestment in human capital. ECONOMIC DEVELOPMENT
       AND CULTURAL CHANGE 22:17-30, Oct. 1973.

643   Sen, Amartya
       Famines. WORLD DEVELOPMENT (OXFORD) 8:613-21, Sept.
       1980.

       Text of the first annual lecture of the Development Studies
       Association, delivered in Reading, England, on 21 September
       1979. It investigates a variety of issues that arise
       in famine analysis, covering identification, causation
       and prevention.

644   Sen, Amartya
       Food problem: Theory and policy. THIRD WORLD QUARTERLY
       (LONDON) 4:447-59, July 1982.

645   Sen, Sudhir

Reaping the green revolution--food and jobs for all.
New York: Orbis Books, 1975.

646   Shah, C. H.
Food preferences and nutrition: A perspective on poverty
in less developed countries. INDIAN JOURNAL OF
AGRICULTURAL ECONOMICS (BOMBAY) 35:1-39, Jan/March 1980.

Examines the presumption that with rising levels of income,
food tastes or preferences substitute for calories. The
author presents examples from India.

647   Sharpston, M. J.
A health policy for developing countries. INTERNATIONAL
BANK FOR RECONSTRUCTION AND DEVELOPMENT. WORLD BANK
REPRINT SERIES No. 67:496-502, 1976.

648   Shaughnessy, Daniel E. and Shaffer, George E.
A systems approach to nutrition planning. WAR ON HUNGER
7:17-21, April 1973.

649   Shaw, John
The mechanism and distribution of food aid. JOURNAL
OF WORLD TRADE LAW 4:207-37, March-April 1970.

650   Shaw, R.
Strategies for employment-creating agriculture; Employment
creating in developing societies. New York: Praeger,
1973. pp. 156-183.

651   Shefrin, F.
Multilateral food aid development: A decade of WFP
operations. AGRICULTURE ABROAD 281:37-57, 1973.

652   Shenton, Bob and Watts, Mike
Capitalism and hunger in northern Nigeria. REVIEW OF
AFRICAN POLITICAL ECONOMY (LONDON) No. 15/16:53-62, May/
Dec. 1979.

653   Shepard, Jack
The politics of starvation. New York: Carnegie Endowment
for International Peace, 1975.

654   Shihata, I. M. I.
Food production in developing countries: Major constraints
and possible solutions. OPEC REVIEW (VIENNA) 3:27-38,
Autumn, 1979.

655   Siamwalla, Ammar and Valdes, Alberto
Food insecurity in developing countries. FOOD POLICY
(GUILDFORD, ENG.) 5:258-72, Nov. 1980.

The authors present a quantitative assessment of national
food insecurity for a sample of LDC's, and an examination

of the proposed international policies to enhance food security in food-deficit countries.

656   Simantov, A.
Food security: A shared responsibility. EUROPEAN REVIEW OF AGRICULTURAL ECONOMICS (THE HAGUE) 6, No. 1:5-16, 1979.

657   Simba, Iddi
We can't possibly grow too much food nowadays. CERES 8:47-49, Jan/Feb 1975.

658   Simmons, Emmy B.
The small-scale rural food-processing industry in northern Nigeria. FOOD RESEARCH INSTITUTE STUDIES (STANFORD) 14, No. 2:147-61, 1975.

This paper explores two aspects of this industry; the economic viability of the average firm and its characteristic self-employment pattern. The paper concludes with a brief essay on the probable future of the rural small-scale food processor in northern Nigeria.

659   Simon, Julian L. and Gardner, David M.
World food needs and "new proteins": A reply. ECONOMIC DEVELOPMENT AND CULTURAL CHANGE 20:558-59, April 1972.

660   Simon, Paul and Arthur
The politics of world hunger: Grass-roots politics and world poverty. New York: Harper's Magazine Press, 1973.

661   Singh, Amar J. and Cohen Jerome
The experiences of a management scientist in a health care system. COLUMBIA JOURNAL OF WORLD BUSINESS (NEW YORK) 12:58-65, Fall 1977.

Presents some experiences gained in developing and implementing management science studies in a health care facility and identifies some of the issues involved in changing such a system.

662   Singh, A. J. and Sidhu, D. S.
Economics of nutrition with special reference to the Punjab state. INDIAN JOURNAL OF AGRICULTURAL ECONOMICS (BOMBAY) 32:88-98, July/Sept. 1977.

663   Singh, B. N. and Pandey, R. K.
Study of nutrition status of rural families in Union Territory of Delhi. INDIAN JOURNAL OF AGRICULTURAL ECONOMICS (BOMBAY) 32:72-77, July/Sept. 1977.

A description of sampling design, review of literature and empirical results are presented.

664   Sinha, R. P.
        World food security. JOURNAL OF AGRICULTURAL ECONOMICS
        (ASHFORD, KENT) 27:121-35, Jan. 1976.

        Examines various proposals for a supranational grain
        authority which would operate in world markets so as
        to counteract excessive fluctuations in grain prices
        and relieve famine and other emergency situations.

665   Smith, Victor E.
        Agricultural planning and nutrient availability. NUTRITION
        REVIEWS 28:143-50, June 1970.

666   Snyder, Francis G.
        Health policy and the law in Senegal. SOCIAL SCIENCE
        AND MEDICINE 8:11-28, Jan. 1974.

667   Sobhan, Rehman
        Politics of food and famine in Bangladesh. ECONOMIC
        AND POLTIICAL WEEKLY (BOMBAY) 14:1973-80, Dec. 1, 1979.

        Examines the dependency of countries like Bangladesh
        on food aid and proposes the creation of a food reserve
        facility by Third World countries, in collaboration with
        OPEC, which could be used to stabilize the supply and
        price of foodgrains, and which could be availed of by
        these countries in time of crisis.

668   Sorenson, L. Orlo and Chung, Do Sup
        Bangladesh food grain storage and stock management study.
        KANSAS STATE UNIVERSITY OF AGRICULTURAL AND APPLIED
        SCIENCE. FOOD AND FEED GRAIN INSTITUTE. GRAIN STORAGE,
        PROCESSING AND MARKETING: REPORT No. 59:1-34, July 1976.

669   Srinivasan, T. N.
        Food security: Indian perspective. YALE UNIVERSITY.
        ECONOMIC GROWTH CENTER. CENTER DISCUSSION PAPER (NEW
        HAVEN) No. 373:1-27, April 1981.

670   Srinivasan, T. N.
        Malnutrition; some measurement and policy issues. JOURNAL
        OF DEVELOPMENT ECONOMICS (AMSTERDAM) 8:3-19, Feb. 1981.

671   Srivastava, J. B.
        Problems and prospects of health administration in India.
        JOURNAL OF PUBLIC ADMINISTRATION 19:138-47, April-June
        1973.

672   Srivastava, Uma K., et al.
        Food aid and international economic growth. Ames: Iowa
        State University Press, 1975.

673   Stanley, Robert G.
        Food for peace: Hope and reality of U.S. food aid. London:

Gordon and Breach, 1972.

674   Stevens, Christopher
        Food aid; good, bad, or indifferent? JOURNAL OF MODERN
        AFRICAN STUDIES (LONDON) 16:671-78, Dec. 1978.

675   Stevens, Robert D.
        Three rural development models for small farm agricultural
        areas in low income nations. JOURNAL OF DEVELOPING NATIONS
        8:409-20, April 1974.

676   Stewart, F
        Technology and employment in LDC's. WORLD DEVELOPMENT
        2, No. 3, March 1974.

677   Stirling, J.
        Third world health: Back to basics. FAR EASTERN ECONOMIC
        REVIEW 92:42-4, June 4, 1976.

678   Stockwell, Edward G. and Laidlaw, Karen A.
        A note on the association between population growth and
        economic development in low-income countries. RURAL
        SOCIOLOGY (COLLEGE STATION, TEXAS) 45:132-38, Spring
        1980.

        It is concluded that continuing efforts to slow down
        population growth through a reduction of the crude birth
        rate will have a positive impact on the rate of economic
        development in low-income countries.

679   Subramanian, C.
        A strategy for fighting protein hunger. INDIAN JOURNAL
        OF NUTRITION AND DIETETICS 8:268-80, Sept. 1971.

680   Svedburg, Peter
        World food sufficiency and meat consumption and, the
        price-disincentive effect of food aid revisited: a
        comment. UNIVERSITY OF STOCKHOLM. INSTITUTE FOR
        INTERNATIONAL ECONOMIC STUDIES. REPRINT SERIES No.
        108:661-66; 549-52, 1978-79.

681   Swaminathan, M.; Daniel, M. A. and Parpia, H. A. B.
        Protein-enriched cereal foods for overcoming malnutrition
        among pre-school children in India and other developing
        countries. INDIAN JOURNAL OF NUTRITION AND DIETETICS
        9:22-48, Jan. 1972.

682   Swanberg, Kenneth G. and Shipley, Elizabeth
        The nutritional status of the rural family in East
        Cundinamarca, Colombia. FOOD RESEARCH INSTITUTE STUDIES
        14:111-25, 1975.

683   Symposium: Food and agricultural policy. PUBLIC
        ADMINISTRATION REVIEW 36, No. 2 (March/April 1976).

684   Symposium on the chemical aspects of nutrition needs.
       JOURNAL OF AGRICULTURAL AND FOOD CHEMISTRY 20:455-537,
       May-June 1972.

685   Szczepanik, Edward F.
       Agricultural policies at different levels of development.
       Rome: FAO, 1976.

686   Talbot, R. B.
       The world food problem and U.S. food politics and policies:
       1972-76. Ames, Iowa: Iowa State University Press, 1977.

687   Talbot, Ross B.
       The European Community's food aid programme; an integration
       of ideology, strategy, technology and surpluses.   FOOD
       SUPPLY (GUILDFORD, ENG.) 4:269-84, Nov. 1979.

688   Tandon, Yash
       New food strategies and social transformation in East
       Africa.   AFRICA DEVELOPMENT (DAKAR) 6:86-107, April/
       June 1981.

689   Tarimo, Eleuther
       Health and self-reliance; the experience of Tanzania.
       DEVELOPMENT DIALOGUE (UPPSALA) No. 1:35-40, 1978.

       Describes the Tanzanian experience in the establishment
       of a network of rural health centres, the training of
       auxiliaries and involvement of the communities through
       mass mobilization campaigns.

690   Tarrant, J. R.
       Food policy conflicts in Bangladesh. WORLD DEVELOPMENT
       (OXFORD) 10:103-13, Feb. 1982.

691   Taylor, L.
       The misconstrued crisis: Lester Brown and world food.
       WORLD DEVELOPMENT 3, No. 11/12:827-38.

692   Thimmayamma, B. V., et al.
       The effect of socio-economic differences on the dietary
       intake of urban population in Hyderabad. INDIAN JOURNAL
       OF NUTRITION AND DIETETICS 10:8-13, Jan. 1973.

693   Thorp, Rosemary
       A note on food supplies, the distribution of income and
       national income accounting in Peru. BULLETIN OF THE
       OXFORD UNIVERSITY INSTITUTE OF ECONOMICS AND STATISTICS
       (Nov. 1969).

694   Tickner, Vincent
       New directions in food marketing policies in LDC's. FOOD
       POLICY (GUILDFORD, ENG.) 3:299-307, Nov. 1978.

695   Timmer, C. Peter and Alderman, Harold
       Estimating consumption parameters for food policy analysis.
       AMERICAN JOURNAL OF AGRICULTURAL ECONOMICS (LEXINGTON)
       61:982-87, Dec. 1979.

696   Timmer, C. Peter
       China and the world food system. HARVARD INSTITUTE FOR
       INTERNATIONAL DEVELOPMENT, DEVELOPMENT DISCUSSION PAPER
       No. 117:1-58, April 1981.

       Attempts to explain the mechanisms that would connect
       the Chinese food economy to international grain markets
       and the issues for both China and the world of that
       potential connection. After a brief review of Chinese
       food policy over the past 30 years the paper examines
       the current dilemma over future food policy directions.

697   Timmer, C. Peter
       Food prices and food policy analysis in LDC's.   FOOD
       POLICY 5:188-99, Aug. 1980.

       Report on the differential impacts of food prices in
       Indonesia and discusses the role of food prices in the
       policy process.

698   Timmer, C. Peter
       Food policy, food consumption, and nutrition. HARVARD
       INSTITUTE FOR INTERNATIONAL DEVELOPMENT, DEVELOPMENT
       DISCUSSION PAPER No. 124:1-23, Oct. 1981.

699   Tracey, Michael V.
       What we don't know about nutrition. ACROSS THE BOARD
       (NEW YORK) 15:62-66, May 1978.

       Concludes that in human nutrition there are many areas
       of ignorance, including energy needs, protein needs and
       vitamin needs.

700   Tracy, Michael
       Nutrition and food policy--an emerging issue for
       agricultural economists? JOURNAL OF AGRICULTURAL ECONOMICS
       (ASHFORD, KENT) 31:369-79, Sept. 1980.

701   The Transnational Institute
       World hunger: Causes and remedies.   Amsterdam:
       Transnational Institute Report, 1974.

702   Trezise, Philip H.
       Rebuilding grain reserves.   Washington, D.C.:   Brookings
       Institution, 1976.

703   Truran, James A.
       Brazil fine tuning farm policies to fight inflation,
       expand food production.   FOREIGN AGRICULTURE   p. 17-18,
       Nov. 1979.

704   Two papers on health aid. INSTITUTE OF DEVELOPMENT
        STUDIES. COMMUNICATIONS SERIES (BRIGHTON) No. 123:1-54,
        1979.
        Content: Cole-King, Susan, Primary health care and the
        role of foreign aid; White, Alastair and de Kadt, Emanuel,
        Health aid: A comparative study of three donor countries
        [Britain, the Netherlands and Sweden].

705   Udo, Reuben K.
        Food-deficit areas of Nigeria. GEOGRAPHICAL REVIEW
        61:415-30, July 1971.

706   U.N. World Food Conference
        Assessment of the world food situation: Present and
        future. Rome, 1974.

707   United States Congress, Office of Technology Assessment
        Food information systems. Washington: Office of
        Technology Assessment, 1976.

708   United States Congressional Budget Office
        U.S. food and agricultural policy in the world economy,
        April 26, 1976.

709   United States Congress, House of Representatives, Committee
        on Foreign Affairs, Subcommittee on International
        Organization and Movements
        International food reserves: Background and current
        proposals. Washington: U.S. Govt Printing Office, 1974.

710   United States Department of Agriculture
        International organizations and agricultural development.
        Prepared by Martin Kriesberg. Foreign Agriculture Economic
        Report No. 131, Washington: ERS, 1977.

711   United States Department of Agriculture
        PL 480 concessional sales: history, procedures,
        negotiating and implementing. By Amalia Vellianitis-Fidas
        and Eileen Manfredi, Washington: Foreign Agriculture
        Economic Report No. 142, Dec. 1977.

712   United States General Accounting Office
        Impact of U.S. development and food aid in selected
        developing countries. ID-76-53 April 22, 1976.

713   United States General Accounting Office
        Disincentives to agricultural production in developing
        countries. ID-76-2 November 26, 1975.

714   United States General Accounting Office
        U.S. participation in international food organizations:
        problems and issues. Aug. 6, 1976, ID-76-66.

715   United States General Accounting Office
       Grain marketing systems in Argentina, Australia, Canada,
       and the European community; soybean marketing system
       in Brazil. May 28, 1976, LD-76-61.

716   United States General Accounting Office
       Issues surrounding the management of agricultural exports.
       Report to the Congress, May 2, 1977.

717   United States General Accounting office
       Grain reserves: A potential U.S. food policy tool. March
       26, 1976, OSP-76-16.

718   United States House Committee on International Relations
       Implementation of recommendations of the World Food
       Conference. A report submitted by the Agency for
       International Development. Ninety-fourth Congress; second
       session, 1976.

719   United States House of Representatives
       The   right-to-food-resolution.   Subcommittee   on
       International Resources, Food, and Energy of the Committee
       on International Relations, June 22-24 and 29, 1976.
       Washington: GPO, 1976.

720   United States Senate
       Multinational corporations and United States foreign
       policy: International grain companies. Hearing before
       the Subcommittee on Multinational Corporations of the
       Committee on Foreign Relations, Ninety-fourth Congress;
       second session; June 18, 23 and 24, 1976 (Part 16);
       Washington: GPO, 1977.

721   United States Senate
       Who's making foreign agricultural policy? Hearings before
       the Subcommittee on Foreign Agricultural Policy of the
       Committee on Agriculture and Forestry; Ninety-fourth
       Congress; second session: January 22 and 23, 1976.
       Washington: GPO, 1976.

722   United States Senate
       Russian grain transactions. Report of the Permanent
       Subcommittee on Investigations, Committee on Government
       Operations, Washington: GPO, July 29, 1974.

723   United States Senate, Committee on Agriculture and Forestry
       U.S. agricultural outlook. Washington: GPO, 1977.

724   United States Senate
       The U.S., FAO and world food politics: U.S. relations
       with an International Food Organization. A staff report
       prepared for the Select Committee on Nutrition and Human
       Needs, Washington: GPO, 1976.

725   United States Senate Subcommittee on Foreign Agricultural
        Policy of the Committee on Agriculture and Forestry
        Hearings on foreign food assistance, April 4, 1974.

726   United States Senate
        World   food   situation,   trade   patterns   and   markets.
        Committee on Agriculture and Forestry. Washington: GPO,
        1976.

727   University of California
        A hungry world: The challenge to agriculture. University
        of California, 1974.

728   Utrecht, Ernst
        An alternative report on world hunger.   CULTURES   ET
        DEVELOPMENT 8, No. 1:145-50, 1976.

729   Valenzona, R. L.
        Poverty measurement and nutrition.   PHILIPPINE ECONOMIC
        JOURNAL (MANILA) 15, No. 3:543-60, 1976.

        This study is concerned with the development of a
        methodology that will consider income as the main factor
        that constrains the family's consumption and the actual
        estimation of incidence of poverty using the method
        proposed by the author.

730   Valliantos, E. G.
        Fear in the countryside: The control of agricultural
        resources in the poor countries by non-peasant elites.
        Cambridge, Mass.: Ballinger Pub., 1976.

731   Van Etten, Geert M. and Raikes Alanagh M.
        Training for rural health in Tanzania.   SOCIAL SCIENCE
        AND MEDICINE 9:89-92, Feb. 1975.

732   Van Thai, Vu
        Food from the basin: Senegal River.   CERES (July-Aug.
        1975): 25-28.

733   Veblen, Tom
        Redesigning the global food system. AGRIBUSINESS WORLDWIDE
        (WESTPORT, CONN.) p. 1-6, Oct./Nov. 1980.

        Attempts to determine whether the U.S. food system could
        provide the model for the global system of the year 2000.

734   Vengroff, Richard
        Food and dependency: P.L. 480 aid to black Africa. JOURNAL
        OF MODERN AFRICAN STUDIES (LONDON) 20:27-43, March 1982.

735   Vermeer, D. E.
        Food farming and the future: The role of traditional
        agriculture in the developing areas of the world.   SOCIAL
        SCIENCE QUARTERLY 57:383-96, S 1976.

736   Vicker, Ray
       This hungry world. New York: Scribner, 1975.

737   Vickery, James R.
       Possible developments in the supply and utilization of
       food in the next 50 years. FOOD TECHNOLOGY 25:55-60,
       June 1971.

738   Vijayalakshmi, R.; Jacob, Mary and Devadas, R. P.
       Relationship between diet during pregnancy and nutritional
       status of the new born. INDIAN JOURNAL OF NUTRITION
       AND DIETETICS 12:233-37, Aug. 1975.

739   Vis, Henri L., et al.
       The health of mother and child in rural central Africa.
       STUDIES IN FAMILY PLANNING 6:437-41, Dec. 1975.

740   Vogel, G. N.
       Economic development in food aid stressed by World Food
       Program. FOREIGN AGRICULTURE 17:25-27, June 1979.

741   von Blanckenburg, Peter
       Debit and credit factors of world nutrition; food supply
       balance in developing countries. ECONOMICS (TUBINGEN)
       18:77-96, 1980.

742   von Urff, Winfried
       Objective indicators of large-scale food shortages? Some
       remarks on their purpose and limitations. INTERECONOMICS,
       REVIEW OF INTERNATIONAL TRADE AND DEVELOPMENT (HAMBURG)
       No. 4:178-82, July/Aug. 1981.

743   Vyas, Rajendrat
       Blindness in the Third World. YOJANA 20:39-40, April
       1, 1976.

744   Wadekin, Karl-Eugen
       The place of agriculture in the European community
       economics. SOVIET STUDIES 29:238-54, April 1977.

745   Wade, Nicholas
       World food situation: Pessimism comes back into vogue.
       SCIENCE 181:634-38, Aug. 17, 1973.

746   Wagstaff, H. R.
       EEC food imports from the Third World and international
       responsibility in agricultural policy. EUROPEAN REVIEW
       OF AGRICULTURAL ECONOMICS 211:7-23, 1974/75.

747   Wallerstein, Mitchel B. and Austin, James E.
       The World Food Council at three years; global food system
       manager? FOOD POLICY (GUILDFORD, ENG.) 3:191-201, Aug.
       1978.

748   Wallensteen, Peter
        Scarce goods as political weapons: The case of food.
        JOURNAL OF PEACE RESEARCH 13, No. 4:277-298, 1976.

749   Walters, Harry
        Difficult issues underlying food problems. SCIENCE 188,
        No. 4188:524-30, May 9, 1975.

750   Warley, T. K.
        Agriculture in an interdependent world: U.S. and Canadian
        perspectives. Canadian-American Commission, May 1977.

751   Weisberg, Samuel M.
        Food acceptance and flavor requirements in the developing
        world. FOOD TECHNOLOGY 28:48-52, Nov. 1974.

752   Weiss, Jeffrey H. and Brodsky, Linda
        An essay on the national financing of health care. JOURNAL
        OF HUMAN RESOURCES 7:139-51, Spring 1972.

753   Weiss, Thomas G., and Jordan, Robert S.
        Bureaucratic politics and the World Food Conference.
        WORLD POLITICS 28, No. 3:422-39, April 1976.

754   Weiss, Thomas G. and Jordan, Robert S.
        The World Food Conference and global problem solving.
        New York: Praeger, 1976.

755   Wheeler, David
        Do the poor need nutrition education? Some methodological
        issues and suggestive evidence from Kinshasa, Zaire.
        BOSTON UNIVERSITY. AFRICAN STUDIES CENTER. WORKING
        PAPERS No. 2:1-34, 1977.

756   Wilford, W. T.
        Nutrition levels and economic growth: Some empirical
        measures. JOURNAL OF ECONOMIC ISSUES, Sept. 1973.

757   Williams, Glen and Satoto
        Socio-political constraints on primary health care; a
        case study from Java. DEVELOPMENT DIALOGUE (UPPSALA)
        No. 1:85-101, 1980.

758   Williams, Maurice
        Food in the context of the international development
        strategy: Measures for accelerated implementation. OPEC
        REVIEW (VIENNA) 5:3-56, Winter 1981.

759   Wilson, Christine S.
        Food habits: A selected annotated bibliography: A
        handbook of references, 1928-72, for all concerned with
        man's eating habits. JOURNAL OF NUTRITION EDUCATION
        5:39-72, Jan-March 1973.

760   Wilson, Christine and Knox, Sharron
        Methods and kinds of nutrition education (1961-72): A
        selected annotated bibliography. JOURNAL OF NUTRITION
        EDUCATION 5:71-107, Jan-March 1973.

761   Wisner, Ben
        Nutritional consequences of the articulation of capitalist
        and non-capitalist modes of production in Eastern Kenya.
        RURAL AFRICANA (EAST LANSING) No. 8/9:99-132, Fall 1981.

762   Wolf, Sidney K.
        Fortified loaf delivers superior nutriton--yet retains
        natural flavor appeal. FOOD PRODUCT DEVELOPMENT 8:18,
        24, 29, Nov. 1974.

763   The world food problem. EUROPEAN COMMUNITIES. COMMISSION.
        COURIER (BRUSSELS) No. 35:26-50, Jan/Feb 1976.

        Looks first at the progress made in 1975 to carry out
        the resolutions of the World Food Conference and then
        examines food aid and the action taken by the European
        Community in this vital field.

764   The world food situation and prospects to 1985. FOREIGN
        AGRICULTURAL ECONOMIC REPORT, No. 98. Washington: U.S.
        Department of Agriculture, December 1974. 90 pp.

765   World report: Food and nutrition. CERES (Nov.-Dec.
        1975), pp. 10-13.

766   Yamamoto, Mikio with Chikio Hayashi
        An ecological analysis of natioanl health in Japan.
        INTERNATIONAL SOCIAL SCIENCE JOURNAL (PARIS) 29, No.
        3:464-72, 1977.

        Lists the influence of living conditions on health. After
        three years of comparative study in 1960, 1965 and 1970
        several findings emerged.

767   Young, H. B.
        Effects of nutrition on growth and performance.
        AGRICULTURAL SCIENCE REVIEW 8:1-8, 1970.

768   Zukin,P.
        Health and economic development: How significant is
        the relationship? INTERNATIONAL DEVELOPMENT REVIEW 17,
        No. 2:17-21, 1975.

769   Zschock, Dieter K.
        Health care financing in Central America and the Andean
        region; a workshop report. LATIN AMERICAN RESEARCH REVIEW
        (CHAPEL HILL) 15, No. 3:149-68, 1980.

770   Zschock, Dieter K.
        Health planning in Latin America: Review and evaluation.
        LATIN AMERICAN RESEARCH REVIEW 5:35-56, Fall 1970.

III. SPECIALIZED PUBLICATIONS   DIRECTORIES)
(REPORTS, DOCUMENTS, AND DIRECTORIES)

771   The Institute for Food and Development Policy has issued
        several new publications. They are: Agrarian Reform
        and Counter-Reform in Chile, by Joseph Collins; Food
        First Resource Guide--Documentation on the Roots of World
        Hunger and Rural Poverty, Staff Report; and World
        Hunger--Ten Myths, by Frances More Lappe and Joseph
        Collins.   All publications may be ordered from the
        Institute for Food and Development Policy, 2588 Mission
        Street, San Francisco, California 94110, USA.

772   Application of Systems Analysis to Health Management,
        prepared by an expert committee of the World Health
        Organization, reports on the systems approach to health
        management and a particular WHO project using techniques
        of cost/benefit analysis.   New Trends and Approaches
        in the Delivery of Maternal and Child Care in Health
        Services is the sixth report of the WHO Expert Committee
        on Maternal and Child Health. Copies of both publications
        may be purchased from Distribution and Sales, World Health
        Organization, 1211 Geneva 27, Switzerland, or from
        booksellers throughout the world.

773   Approaches to Planning and Design of Health Care Facilities
        in Developing Areas, Volume 2, edited by B. M. Kleczkowski
        and R. Pibouleau; and Risk Approach for Maternal and
        Child Health Care.   Both publications may be ordered
        from Distribution and Sales Service, World Health
        Organization, 1211 Geneva 27, Switzerland.

774   Recent publications of the International Food Policy
        Research Institute include: Brazil's Minimum Price Policy
        and the Agricultural Sector of Northeast Brazil, by Roger
        Fox; Foodgrain Supply, Distribution, and Consumption
        Policies within a Dual Pricing Mechanism--A Case Study
        of Bangladesh, by Raisuddin Ahmed; Growth Potential of
        the Beef Sector in Latin America--Survey of Issues and
        Policies, by Alberto Valdes and Gustavo Nores; and Public
        Distribution of Foodgrains in Kerala--Income Distribution
        Implications and Effectiveness, by P. S. George.   Copies
        are available from the IFPRI, 1776 Massachusetts Avenue,
        Washington, D.C. 20036, USA.

775   The World Health Organization has issued its 1978 Catalogue
        of Health Film Titles. Copies may be obtained from Spears
        Associates, Box 1207, Arlington, Virginia 22210, USA.

776   The Central Treaty Organization Conference on the Methodology of National Health Planning was held in Istanbul, Turkey, January 8-12, 1973. The conference report contains papers presented on the current status of health planning in Iran, Pakistan, and Turkey. A CENTO Seminar on Hospital Administration, held in Karachi, Pakistan, March 19-24, 1973, contains fifteen papers on the training of hospital administrators in CENTO countries. Copies of both reports are available from the Office of U.S. Economic Coordinator for CENTO Affairs, Eski Buyuk Millet Meclisi Binasi, Ankara, Turkey.

777   Checkmate To Underdevelopment, by Fernando Monckeberg, uses Chile as a case study in the call for national nutrition policies to combat malnutrition and underdevelopment. To obtain this booklet, write to the author, c/o Department of Nutrition and Food Technology, University of Chile, Santiago, Chile.

778   Consultative Group on Food Production and Investment in Developing Countries--Report on the Second Meeting, held in Washington, D.C., February 10-12, 1976, is available from the CGFPI office, 1818 H Street, N.W., Washington, D.C. 20433, USA. Proceedings of a Conference on Capturing the Sun through Bioconversion, sponsored by some sixteen U.S. agencies, is available from the Washington Center, 1717 Massachusetts Avenue, N.W., Washington, D.C. 20036, USA.

779   The Delivery of Health Services in the People's Republic of China, by Peter Wilenski, gives an overview of China's health system. Copies are available from the International Development Research Centre, Box 8500, Ottawa, Canada 81G 3H9.

780   Development of Food Marketing Systems for Large Urban Areas reviews the situation and trends of food marketing systems in urban Latin America and discusses possible programs for food marketing development. Planning and Operation of Wholesale Markets discusses food wholesaling in Latin America and prospects of developing new wholesale markets. Both documents are available from the Agricultural Services Division, FAO, Via delle Terme di Caracalla, 00100 Rome, Italy.

781   Dimensions of World Food Problems, edited by E. R. Duncan, is a reference document covering a broad range of food-related issues current in the mid-1970's. Articles by noted authorities concentrate on agriculture and food provision for hungry people throughout the world. The book is available from the Iowa State University Press, Ames, Iowa 50010, USA.

782   Distant Hunger--Agriculture, Food, and Human Values, by Heather Johnston Nicholson and Ralph L. Nicholson, sets forth alternative conceptions of world food problems and the major variables and assumptions of each. The authors compare modern agriculture with traditional and subsistence forms of agriculture as biological systems. Copies are available from the Office of Publications, Purdue University, South Campus Courts-D, West Lafayette, Indiana 47907, USA.

783   Evaluation of Educational Programmes in Nursing, by Moyra Allen, presents a design for evaluating education programmes in nursing, developed in cooperation with the World Health Manpower Development. Copies are available from Distribution and Sales, World Health Organization, 1211 Geneva 27, Switzerland. Another WHO publication is Health Services: Concepts and Information for National Planning and Management, by K. L. White, et al. This is an excellent guide to strategies for planning change in health care systems, designed for planners and policy-makers in the health sector.

784   To Feed This World, by Sterling Wortman and Ralph Cummings, stresses the importance of agricultural assistance to the small farmer in developing countries. The book, also, looks at the current status of agricultural technology and describes successful aid projects in Colombia, Peru, Guatemala, and El Salvador. The publication is available from The Johns Hopkins University Press, Baltimore, Maryland 21218, USA.

785   Financing of Health Services is the report of a World Health Organization Study Group. The report looks at the problems in financing health services in developing countries, different approaches to improved financing, and presents some case studies of health sector financing. Two other WHO reports are Research in Human Reproduction: Strengthening of Resources in Developing Countries and Surveillance for the Prevention and Control of Health Hazards due to Antibiotic-resisitent Enterobacteria. Poverty, Development, and Health Policy, by B. Abel-Smith, with A. Leiserson, discusses health policy and national planning and the economics of health services. Copies are available from Distribution and Sales, World Health Organization, 1211 Geneva 27, Switzerland.

786   Finding the Causes of Child Malnutrition, by Judith and Richard Brown, is a handbook intended for workers in developing countries involved in community nutrition programs. The book also contains a listing of books and periodicals on nutrition education materials. Copies are available from the Task Force on World Hunger, 341 Ponce de Leon Avenue, N.E., Atlanta, Georgia 30308, USA.

787   Food Aid for Development, by Hartmut Schneider, reports on the OECD Development Centre Expert Meeting on the "Scope and Conditions for Improved Use of Food Aid for Development", held in Paris March 30-31, 1978. Copies are available from OECD Publication, 2 rue Andre-Pascal, 75775 Paris Cedex 16, France.

788   Food and Interdependence, by David Jones, deals with the effects of food and agricultural policies of developed countries on food problems in developing countries. Special attention is given to policies of the U.K. and the EEC. The study is available from Research Publications Services Ltd., Victoria Hall, East Greenwich, London SE10 ORF, United Kingdom.

789   Food Legume Improvement and Development, edited by Geoffrey C. Hawtin and George J. Chancellor, contains the proceedings of a workshop held at the University of Aleppo, Syria, May 2-7, 1978. Forty-one workshop papers on food legume production in the Middle East and North Africa are included in the document together with an extensive bibliography. Copies may be obtained from the Communications Division, International Development Research Centre, P.O. Box 8500, Ottawa, Canada K1G 3H9.

790   Food and Nutrition Strategies in National Development is the Ninth Report of the Joint FAO/WHO Expert Committee on Nutrition. Copies may be obtained from the Office of Publications, World Health Organization, 1211 Geneva 27, Switzerland.

791   Food Price Policy and Income Distribution in Low-Income Countries and Three Issues of Development Strategy--Food, Population, Trade are both by John W. Mellor. Impact of Subsidized Rice on Food Consumption and Nutrition in Kerala, by Shubh K. Kumar, and Intersectoral Factor Mobility and Agricultural Growth, by Yair Mundlak, are two papers in the IFPRI Research Report Series. India--A Drive Towards Self-Sufficiency in Food Grains, by J. S. Sarma, is a reprint from the American Journal of Agricultural Economics, December 1978. All publications may be obtained from the IFPRI, 1776 Massachusetts Avenue, N.W., Washington, D.C. 20036, USA.

792   Food, Population and Policies, by Fred T. Sai, highlights the interrelationship between nutrition, health, and fertility. Copies are available from the International Planned Parenthood Federation, 18-20 Lower Regent Street, London SW1Y 4PW, United Kingdom.

793   Food Production in India--A Perspective, by W. David Hopper, is an overview of agricultural development in India. Copies are available from the International Development Research Centre, Box 8500, Ottawa, Canada

K1G 3H9, or (USA orders only) UNIPUB, Box 433, Murray Hill Stn., NY, NY 10016, USA.

794   Food Security: An Insurance Approach, by Panos Konandreas, Barbara Huddleston, and Virabongsa Ramangkura, discusses some insurance principles designed to aid food deficit, in developing countries. The study is available from the International Food Policy Research Institute, 1776 Massachusetts Ave., N.W., Washington, D.C. 20036, USA.

795   Food for Thought: Three Recipes for Appraising Nutrition Programs, by John D. Montgomery, is based on a paper presented by the author at a seminar on "Nutrition Policy in Asia" in Malaysia, June 1976, sponsored by the Southeast Asia Development Advisory Group of the Asia Society. Copies may be obtained from SEADAG, 505 Park Avenue, New York, NY 10022, USA.

796   Health: The Family Planning Factor, by Erik Eckholm and Kathleen Newland, analyzes the relationship between health and family planning policies, particularly in developing countries. The study is available from the Worldwatch Institute, 1776 Massachusetts Avenue, N.W., Washington, D.C. 20036, USA.

797   Health Manpower Planning: Principles, Methods, Issues, edited by T. L. Hall and A. Mejia, is a comprehensive guide to health manpower planning in developing countries. The book contains some sixteen papers by experts in the field. Copies may be obtained from Distribution and Sales, World Health Organization, 1211 Geneva 27, Switzerland. Health Implications of Nuclear Power Production is another WHO publication containing the report of a Working Group that met in Brussels, December 1-5, 1975.

798   Health and Population: Research and Policy Issues, (Volume 3, Number 2) compiled by Anne S. McCook, is the sixth publication in a series of semi-annual annotated bibliographies issued by the Interdisciplinary Communications Program of the Smithsonian Institution. Most citations are based on research conducted in the Third World. Copies are available from the International Program for Population Analysis, Interdisciplinary Communications Program, Smithsonian Institution, 1717 Massachusetts Avenue, N.W., Washington, D.C. 20036, USA.

799   How the Other Half Dies--The Real Reason for World Hunger, by Susan George, presents a strong statement on the subject of hunger and related economic, social and political issues. Copies are available from Penguin Books, Ltd., Harmondsworth, Middlesex, United Kingdom.

800   Unipub has prepared an Information Kit on Food and

Nutrition. Over 200 publications on food and nutrition produced by the United Nations are described in the kit. In particular, reference is made to two new periodicals: Agrindex, a monthly bibliography of literature on food and agriculture prepared by the International Information System for the Agricultural Sciences and Technology (AGRIS); and Food and Nutrition, a quarterly concerned with world food and nutrition problems, published by the UN Food and Agriculture Organization. The information kit and subscriptions to the periodicals are availabe from Unipub, Box 433, Murray Hill Station, New York, New York 10016, USA.

801   The Interaction of Nutrition, Infection and Mortality during Recent Food Crises in Bangladesh, by A.K.M. Alauddin Chowdhury and Lincoln C. Chen, and Socio-economic Development and Fertility Change in Rural Africa, by James E. Kocher, are recent papers published by the Food Research Institute. Copies are available from the Institute, Stanford University, California, USA.

802   A Listing of U.S. Non-Profit Organizations in Food Production and Agricultural Assistance Abroad describes approximately 150 agencies administering agricultural and food production programs in developing countries. This broad spectrum of assistance includes community development, cooperatives, crop improvement, economic and development planning, education, equipment and material aid, food industry, land development, livestock, poultry and fish, and research. Copies of the guide are available from the Technical Assistance Information Clearing House of the American Council of Voluntary Agencies for Foreign Service, Inc., 200 Park Avenue South, New York, New York 10003, USA.

803   A Listing of U.S. Non-Profit Organizations in Medical and Public Health Assistance Abroad has been reprinted by the Technical Assistance Information Clearing House. Copies of the directory may be obtained from TAICH, 200 Park Avenue South, New York, New York 10003, USA.

804   Malnutrition and Poverty: Magnitude and Policy Options, by Shlomo Reutlinger and Marcelo Selowsky, assesses the nature and extent of malnutrition in developing countries, and analyzes the cost effectiveness of some policy options to reduce malnutrition in urban target groups. The study is available from The Johns Hopkins University Press, Baltimore, Maryland, USA and London, England.

805   Malnutrition and the Urban Poor is the theme of Assignment Children--No. 43, published by UNICEF. Four case studies are highlighted in this issue along with a general commentary on the plight of the urban poor. Copies are available from UNICEF, Palais Wilson, C.P. 11, 1211 Geneva 14, Switzerland.

806   Measurement of Levels of Health, edited by W. W. Holland, J. Ipsen and J. Kostrzewski, suggest the kinds of data necessary in determining the health status of populations and specifying health priorities. Some fifty-six authors contributed to the work. Copies are available from the Public Information Office, World Health Organization, 1211 Geneva 27, Switzerland.

807   Medicine and Public Health: Development Assistance Abroad is a listing of 300 U.S. non-profit organizations engaged in medical and public health programs abroad. The directory was prepared by the Technical Assistance Information Clearing House of the American Council of Voluntary Agencies for Foreign Service, Inc. Copies are available from TAICH, 200 Park Avenue South, New York, New York 10003, USA.

808   Nutrition, Development, and Social Behavior, edited by David J. Kallen, contains the proceedings of a conference on "The Assessment of Tests of Behavior from Studies of Nutrition in the Western Hemisphere" held in Puerto Rico in 1970. The meeting was cosponsored by the Pan American Health Organization and the U.S. Department of Health, Education and Welfare. The report discusses methodology in measuring aspects of mental growth affected by malnutrition and, also, the relation between malnutrition and social growth. It is available from the U.S. Government Printing Office, Superintendent of Documents, Washington, D.C. 20402, USA.

809   Nutrition--A Priority in African Development, edited by Bo Vahlquist, is based on a 1971 seminar sponsored by the Dag Hammarskjold Foundation in Uppsala, Sweden. The book is divided into three main sections: Problems of Human Nutrition, Factors Involved in Problem Solution, and The Necessity of Integration. Copies are available from Almqvist & Wiksell International Publishers and Booksellers, 26 Gamla Brogatan, P.O. Box 62, S-101 20 Stockholm 1, Sweden.

810   Nutrition and the World Food Problem, edited by Miloslav Rechcigl, Jr., contains three sections of papers contributed by authorities in the field. The first part discusses nutrition and health. The second examines the interrelationships between nutrition and disease, and the third section focuses on food habits and the nutritional aspects of food processing. The book is published by S. Karger with offices in Basel, Munich, Paris, London, New York and Sydney.

811   The Politics of Starvation, by Jack Shepherd, charges the international community with a cover-up of the Ethiopian drought during the last seven months of 1973 and calls for new international mechanisms to expedite

disaster relief quickly and effectively. The report is available from the Carnegie Endowment for International Peace, 345 East 46th Street, New York, New York 10017, USA.

812   Postharvest Food Losses in Developing Countries was prepared by an advisory panel of the Board on Science and Technology for International Development, Commission on International Relations of the U.S. National Research Council. The study summarizes existing work and information about losses of major food crops, and assesses both the potential of food loss reduction efforts and their limitations. A limited number of copies of the publication are available from the Commission on International Relations (JH 214), National Academy of Sciences--National Research Council, 2101 Constitution Avenue, Washington, D.C. 20418, USA.

813   Primary Health Care is the report of the International Conference on Primary Health Care, held in Alma Ata, USSR, September 6-12, 1978. The meeting, sponsored by the World Health Organization and UNICEF, covered primary health care and development, operational aspects of primary health care, and national strategies and international support. Copies are available from WHO, Geneva, Switzerland.

814   Protein-Energy Requirements under Conditions Prevailing in Developing Countries: Current Knowledge and Research Needs is based on the findings of a United Nations University expert group meeting in Costa Rica, February 1-3, 1977. The chief purpose of the report was to recommend new research needed in estimating protein and energy requirements for populations in developing countries. Copies are available from the United Nations University, Toho Seimei Building, 15-1 Shibuya 2-chome, Shibuya-ku, Tokyo 150, Japan.

815   Protein and Nutrition Policy in Low-Income Countries, by Francis Aylward and Mogens Jul, discusses the world food problem against the backdrop of United Nations programs in food and nutrition. The authors refer to the activities of the UN Protein Advisory Group from 1968-1974. A comprehensive bibliography is also included in the text. Copies are available from Halsted Press, John Wiley & Sons, 605 Third Avenue, New York, New York 10016, USA.

816   Public Health Education with Special Attention to Family Planning and Population Programmes is based on a Central Treaty Organization conference, held in Lahore, Pakistan, January 15-19, 1974. The report contains papers on health education policies in Iran, Pakistan, and Turkey, together with eleven reports on family planning, health education

and training programs in Cento countries. The publication
is available from the Public Relations Division, Central
Treaty Organization, Eski Buyuk Millet Meclisi Binasi,
Ankara, Turkey.

817   Recent and Prospective Developments in Food Consumption:
       Some Policy Issues--Research Report No. 2 discusses basic
       policy issues that need to be resolved at national and
       international levels if there is to be progress in
       alleviating hunger and malnutrition. The report provides
       estimates of the numbers of under-nourished people
       throughout the world and the amount of foodgrains required
       to give them the required energy standard. The report
       is available free of charge from the International Food
       Policy Research Institute, 1776 Massachusetts Avenue,
       N.W., Washington, D.C. 20036, USA.

818   Registers of Health Services Development Projects. The
       guides will provide information on research and development
       programs on the organization of community health services.
       For more information and copies of the Register write
       to the Division of Strengthening of Health Services,
       World Health Organization, 1211 Geneva 27, Switzerland.

819   A Report on the World Food Situation was published by
       the Agribusiness Accountability Project. The Report
       covers such issues as national food policy, grain reserves,
       free market export trade and the green revolution. Copies
       are available from the Agribusiness Accountability Project,
       1000 Wisconsin Avenue, N.W., Washington, D.C. 20007,
       USA.

820   Research Directions in Income Distribution, Nutrition,
       and the Economics of Food, by Lance Taylor, attempts
       to identify specific topics for research. Copies of
       the paper are available from the International Food Policy
       Research Institute, 1776 Massachusetts Avenue, N.W.,
       Washington, D.C. 20036, USA.

821   Selected European Markets for Tropical and Off-Season
       Fresh Fruits and Vegetables, prepared by the UNCTAD/GATT
       International Trade Centre, provides exporters in
       developing countries with information that will help
       them select the most suitable products for export to
       the most promising markets. The handbook is available
       from the International Trade Centre UNCTAD/GATT, Palais
       des Nations, 1211 Geneva 10, Switzerland.

822   The State of Food and Agriculture--1977 is the annual
       review of the United Nations Food and Agriculture
       Organization. The report gives an overall world review
       of food and agricultural production, discusses food and
       agriculture in developing countries, and includes a section
       on the state of natural resources and the human environment

for food and agriculture. Copies from any FAO sales agent or from Distribution and Sales, FAO, Via delle Terme di Caracalla, 00100 Rome, Italy.

823   The Public Health Service of the U.S. Department of Health, Education and Welfare has issued three studies on health conditions in developing countries and their impact on the country's socioeconomic development. They focus on Bangladesh, Pakistan and Senegal under the title of Syncrisis: The Dynamics of Health--An Analytical Series on the Interactions of Health and Socioeconomic Development. Copies may be obtained from the Office of International Health, Public Health Service, U.S. Department of Health, Education and Welfare, Rockville, Maryland 20852, USA.

824   The Office of International Health of the U.S. Department of Health, Education and Welfare is preparing a series of Syncrisis Studies which will analyze the health conditions of a country and their interrelationships with socioeconomic development. Studies on The Syrian Arab Republic (XXIII) and Afghanistan (XXIV) are now available. The publications may be ordered from Syncrisis Publications, DHEW/PHS/OASH/OIH, 5600 Fishers Lane, Room 18-87, Rockville, Maryland 20857, USA. Another companion publication is Health of Wealth: Reassessment of an Old Dilemma which contains articles on the relationships between health and economic development of developing countries. This document is available from the same address.

825   Systems for Monitoring and Evaluating Nutritional Interventions, prepared by Guido J. Deboeck for the World Bank, explains how Brazil's National Institute of Food and Nutrition developed systems to monitor the costs, nutrition effectiveness and achievement of objectives of a major nutrition programme. Available from the World Bank, 1818 H. Street, Washington, D.C. 20433.

826   Towards a Food Policy for Latin America's Urban Areas: Lima as a Case Study, by Marco A. Ferroni, and World Food: A Perspective, by Thomas T. Poleman, are monographs available from the Department of Agricultural Economics, New York State College of Agriculture and Life Sciences, Cornell University, Ithaca, New York 14850, USA.

827   Training and Utilization of Auxiliary Personnel for Rural Health Teams in Developing Countries is the Report of a WHO Expert Committee. The report also suggests a strategy for the development of rural health teams. Copies are available from Sales Service, World Health Organization, 1211 Geneva 27, Switzerland.

828   The Two Faces of Malnutrition, by Erik Eckholm and Frank
       Record, focuses on overnutrition as well as undernutrition,
       and calls on the affluent countries to develop national
       nutrition strategies to combat illnesses associated with
       high-calorie, high-fat diets in Western countries. Copies
       of the study are available from the Worldwatch Institute,
       1776 Massachusetts, Avenue, N.W., Washington, D.C. 20036,
       USA.

829   Vitamin A Deficiency and Blindness Prevention, edited
       by Vivian Beyda, is based on the proceedings of two
       seminars sponsored by the American Foundation for Overseas
       Blind and Nutrition Foundation. The papers consider
       examples of recent developments and needs in applied
       nutrition relative to blindness resulting from vitamin
       deficiency in order to plan for effective educational
       efforts. Bangladesh, Brazil, El Salvador, Indonesia,
       and Jordan are offered as case studies in blindness
       prevention programs. The publication is available from
       the American Foundation for the Blind, Inc., 15 West
       16th Street, New York, New York 10011, USA.

830   What Shall We Grow?--A Critical Survey of the Literature
       on Farmers' Decision Making, by Peggy F. Barlett,
       summarizes some of the effects of natural, cultural,
       economic, and political environments on the decision-making
       processes of small farmers. The report, also, includes
       recommendations for research in this area and an annotated
       bibliography. Copies are available from The Civic
       Participation Division, Bureau for Program and Policy
       Coordination, U.S. Agency for International Development,
       Washington, D.C., USA.

831   Who's Involved With Hunger: An Organization Guide lists
       over 200 agencies concerned with the world food problem.
       These include: International and multilateral
       organizations; U.S. Government agencies; food lobby
       organizations; policy research institutes; private
       nonprofit educational groups; and farm organizations.
       The directory is available from the American Freedom
       from Hunger Foundation, 1625 Eye Street, N.W., Washington,
       D.C. 20006, USA.

832   Working Against Hunger summarizes the Ford Foundation's
       international agricultural development program since
       1950. The report discusses the international agricultural
       research centers sponsored by Ford, as well as its projects
       in Asia, the Middle East, Africa, Latin America and the
       Caribbean. The publication is available from the Ford
       Foundation, 320 East 43 Street, New York, New York 10017,
       USA.

833   World Food and the Canadian "Breadbasket", prepared by
        The North-South Institute, discusses global food problems
        and improvements in Canadian assistance in this area.
        Copies are available from the North-South Institute,
        185 Rideau Street, Ottawa, Canada K1N 5X8.

834   World Food Crisis--An International Directory of
        Organizations and Infromation Resources, edited by Thaddeus
        C. Trzyna, with the assistance of J. D. Smith and Judith
        Ruggles, describes over 800 organizations and 275 major
        programs concerned with the food needs of poor countries.
        The directory is available from the Public Affairs
        Clearinghouse, P.O. Box 30, Claremont, California 91711,
        USA.

835   World Food and Nutrition Study: The Potential
        Contributions of Research is the final report of an ad
        hoc Steering Committee of the U.S. National Academy of
        Sciences. The study discusses the dimensions of the world
        food and nutrition problem, details priority areas for
        research, and offers recommendations for U.S. action
        in initiating this research. The study is available
        from the National Academy of Sciences, Printing and
        publishing Office, 2101 Constitution Avenue, N.W.,
        Washington, D.C. 20418, USA.

836   World Food: The Political Dimension, by Thomas W. Wilson,
        Jr., addresses the policy issues confronting governments
        in dealing with the world food crisis. The paper is
        based on several 1974 workshops sponsored by the Aspen
        Institute for Humanistic Studies Program in Environment
        and Quality of Life. Copies are available from the Aspen
        Institute for Humanistic Stuides, 1755 Massachusetts
        Avenue, N.W., Washington, D.C. 20036, USA.

837   The World Food Situation and Prospects to 1985 is Foreign
        Agricultural Economic Report No. 98, prepared by the
        Economic Research Service of the U.S. Department of
        Agriculture. The study analyzes factors which influenced
        food production, consumption, and trade in the two decades
        prior to 1972, as well as causes of the turbulent
        developments of 1972-74, and examines issues that will
        shape developments in the next decade. The report is
        available from the Economic Research Service, U.S.
        Department of Agriculture, Washington, D.C. 20250, USA.

838   World Food Supply--A Global Development Case Study,
        prepared by J. Carlisle Spivey of the Management Institute
        for National Development, is designed as a case study
        for global development studies at the secondary and college
        levels. The study covers past, present and future programs
        for handling world food shortages and also contains a
        basic bibliography and listing of organizations dealing
        with the food problem. The publication is available
        from the Management Institute for National Development,
        230 Park Avenue, New York, New York 10017, USA.

IV. BIBLIOGRAPHIC SUBJECT INDEX

PART IV
DIRECTORY OF INFORMATION SOURCES

I. UNITED NATIONS INFORMATION SOURCES

AUDIO MATERIALS LIBRARY
United Nations, Department of Public Information, Radio and Visual Services Division, United Nations Plaza, New York, NY 10017.

UNITED NATIONS DEMOGRAPHIC DATA BASE
United Nations, Department of International Economic and Social Affairs, Statistical office, New York, NY 10017.

DAG HAMMARSKJOLD LIBRARY
United Nations, Department of Conference Services, United Nations Plaza, New York, NY 10017.

UNITED NATIONS BIBLIOGRAPHIC INFORMATION SYSTEM
United Nations, Department of Conference Services, Dag Hammarskjold Library, United Nations Plaza, New York, NY 10017.

UNBIS DATA BASE
United Nations, Department of Conference Services, Dag Hammarskjold Library, United Nations Plaza, New York, NY 10017.

DEVELOPMENT INFORMATION SYSTEM
United Nations, Department of International Economic and Social Affairs, Information Systems Unit, Room DC 594, New York, NY 10017.

DEVELOPMENT INFORMATION SYSTEM DATA BASE
United Nations, Department of International Economic and Social Affairs, Information Systems Unit, Room DC 594, New York, NY 10017.

REFERENCE UNIT OF THE OFFICE FOR DEVELOPMENT RESEARCH AND POLICY ANALYSIS
United Nations, Department of International Economic and Social Affairs, Office for Development Research and Policy Analysis, New York, NY 10017.

MACRO-ECONOMIC DATA BANK AND TABLE PROCESSING SYSTEM
United Nations, Department of International Economic and Social Affairs, Office for Development Research and Policy Analysis, New York, NY 10017.

MACRO-ECONOMIC DATA BANK AND TABLE PROCESSING SYSTEM DATA BASE
United Nations, Department of International Economic and Social Affairs, Office for Development Research and Policy Analysis, New York, NY 10017.

REFERENCE UNIT OF THE OFFICE FOR SCIENCE AND TECHNOLOGY
United Nations, Department of International Economic and Social Affairs, Office for Science and Technology, New York, NY 10017.

UNITED NATIONS PHOTO LIBRARY
United Nations, Department of Public Information, Radio and Visual Services Division, United Nations Plaza, New York, NY 10017.

POPULATION INFORMATION NETWORK
United Nations, Department of International Economic and Social Affairs, Population Division, New York, NY 10017.

REFERENCE CENTRE OF THE POPULATION DIVISION
United Nations, Department of International Economic and Social Affairs, Population Division, New York, NY 10017.

INTEGRATED STATISTICAL INFORMATION SYSTEM
United Nations, Department of International Economic and Social Affairs, Statistical Office, New York, NY 10017.

UNITED NATIONS VISUAL MATERIALS LIBRARY
United Nations, Department of Public Information, Radio and Visual Services Division, United Nations Plaza, New York, NY 10017.

WORLD STATISTICS IN BRIEF
United Nations, Department of International Economic and Social Affairs, Statistical Office, New York, NY 10017.

UNCRD LIBRARY AND DOCUMENTATION SERVICES
United Nations Centre for Regional Development, Marunouchi 2-4-7, Naka-ku, Nagoya 460, Japan.

UNRISD LIBRARY AND DOCUMENTATION UNIT
United Nations Research Institute for Social Development, Palais des Nations, CH-1211 Geneva 10, 16 Avenue Jean Trembley, 1209 Geneva, Switzerland.

CAFRAD LIBRARY AND DOCUMENTATION CENTRE
United Nations, African Training and Research Centre in Administration for Development, BP 310, Tangier, Morocco.

CAIRO DEMOGRAPHIC CENTRE LIBRARY
United Nations, Cairo Demographic Centre, 109 Qasr Al Aini Street, Cairo, Egypt.

POPULATION INFORMATION AND DOCUMENTATION SYSTEM FOR AFRICA
United Nations, Regional Institute for Population Studies, University of Ghana, P.O. Box 96, Legon, Ghana.

INTERNATIONAL INSTITUTE FOR POPULATION STUDIES LIBRARY
United Nations, International Institute for Population Studies, Govandi Station Road, Deonar-Bombay 4000-88, India.

UNITED NATIONS-ROMANIA DEMOGRAPHIC CENTRE LIBRARY
United Nations, Demographic Centre, P.O. Box 1-550, 39 Boulevard Ana Ipatescu, 70100 Bucharest, Romania.

GROUP OF EXPERTS ON URBAN AND REGIONAL RESEARCH
Economic Commission for Europe, Environment and Human Settlements Division, Palais des Nations, 1211 Geneva 10, Switzerland.

ASIAN AND PACIFIC DEVELOPMENT INSTITUTE LIBRARY AND DOCUMENTATION CENTRE
Economic and Social Commission for Asia and the Pacific, Asian and Pacific Development Institute, P.O. Box 2.136, Sri Ayudhije Road, Bangkok, Thailand.

ESCAP LIBRARY
Economic and Social Commission for Asia and the Pacific, United Nations Building, Rajadamnern Avenue, Bangkok 2, Thailand.

ESCAP BIBLIOGRAPHIC INFORMATION MASTER FILE
Economic and Social Commission for Asia and the Pacific, Library, United Nations Building, Rajadamnern Avenue, Bangkok 2, Thailand.

POPULATION CLEARING-HOUSE AND INFORMATION SYSTEM
Economic and Social Commission for Asia and the Pacific, Clearing-house and Information Section, Population Division, United Nations Building, Rajadamnern Avenue, Bangkok 2, Thailand.

CURRENT RESEARCH IN FAMILY PLANNING
Economic and Social Commission for Asia and the Pacific, Clearing-house and Information Section, Population Division, United Nations Building, Rajadamnern Avenue, Bangkok 2, Thailand.

UNESCAP/STATISTICS INFORMATION SYSTEM
Economic and Social Commission for Asia and the Pacific, Statistics Division, United Nations Building, Rajadamnern Avenue, Bangkok 2, Thailand.

LATIN AMERICAN CENTRE FOR ECONOMIC AND SOCIAL DOCUMENTATION
Economic Commission for Latin America, Casilla 179-D, Edificio Naciones Unidas, Avenida Dag Hammarskjold, Santiago, Chile.

CLADBIB DATA BASE
Economic Commission for Latin America, Latin American Centre for Economic and Social Documentation, Casilla 179-D, Edificio Naciones Unidas, Avenida Dag Hammarskjold, Santiago, Chile.

CLADIR DATA BASE
Economic Commission for Latin America, Latin American Centre for Economic and Social Documentation, Casilla 179-D, Edificio Naciones Unidas, Avenida Dag Hammarskjold, Santiago, Chile.

CLAPLAN DATA BASE
Economic Commission for Latin America, Latin American Centre for Economic and Social Documentation, Casilla 179-D, Edificio Naciones Unidas, Avenida Dag Hammarskjold, Santiago, Chile.

CENTRAL AMERICAN CENTRE FOR ECONOMIC AND SOCIAL DOCUMENTATION
Economic Commission for Latin America/Central American Higher University Council, Apartado 37, Universidad de Costa Rica, San Jose, Costa Rica.

CEPAL/CSUCA-CEDESC DATA BASE
Central American Centre for Economic and Social Documentation, Apartado 37, Universidad de Costa Rica, San Jose, Costa Rica.

LATIN AMERICAN POPULATION DOCUMENTATION SYSTEM
Economic Commission for Latin America, Centro Latinoamericano de Demografia, Casilla 91, Edificio Naciones Unidas, Avenida Dag Hammarskjold, Santiago, Chile.

DOCPAL DATA BASE
Economic Commission for Latin America, Centro Latinoamericano de Demografia, Casilla 91, Edificio Naciones Unidas, Avenida Dag Hammarskjold, Santiago, Chile.

JOINT CEPAL/ILPES LIBRARY BIBLIOGRAPHICAL INFORMATION SYSTEM
Economic Commission for Latin America, Latin American Institute for Economic and Social Planning, Casilla 179-D, Edificio Naciones Unidas, Avenida Dag Hammarskjold, Santiago, Chile.

GLOBAL ENVIRONMENT MONITORING SYSTEM
United Nations Environment Programme, Programme Activity Centre, P.O. Box 30552, Nairobi, Kenya.

INTERNATIONAL REGISTER OF POTENTIALLY TOXIC CHEMICALS DATA BASE
United Nations Environment Programme, Pavillon du Petit Saconnex, 16, Avenue Jean Trembley, 1209 Geneva, Switzerland.

PROJECT INSTITUTIONAL MEMORY
United Nations Development Programme, Bureau for Programme Policy and Evaluation, One United Nations Plaza, New York, NY 10017.

PROJECT INSTITUTIONAL MEMORY DATA BASE
United Nations Development Programme, Bureau for Programme Policy and Evaluation, One United Nations Plaza, New York, NY 10017.

UNITED NATIONS FUND FOR POPULATION ACTIVITIES LIBRARY
United Nations Fund for Population Activities, 485 Lexington Avenue, Room 2018, New York, NY 10017.

UNITAR LIBRARY
United Nations Institute for Training and Research, 801 United Nations Plaza, New York, NY 10017.

UNITED NATIONS UNIVERSITY LIBRARY
United Nations University, Academic Services, 29th Floor, Toho Seimei Building, 15-1 Shibuya 2-chome, Shibuya-ku, Tokyo 150, Japan.

REFERRAL PROGRAMME OF ACADEMIC SERVICES DIVISION
United Nations University, Academic Services, 29th Floor, Toho Seimei Building, 15-1 Shibuya 2-chome, Shibuya-ku, Tokyo 150, Japan.

INTERNATIONAL OCCUPATIONAL SAFETY AND HEALTH INFORMATION CENTRE
International Labour Office, Working Conditions and Environment Department, Occupational Safety and Health Branch, 4 route des Morillons, 1211 Geneva 22, Switzerland.

AGLINET UNION LIST OF SERIALS
Food and Agriculture Organization of the United Nations, Department of General Affairs and Information, Library and Documentation Systems Division, Via delle Terme di Caracalla, 00100 Rome, Italy.

INTERNATIONAL INFORMATION SYSTEM FOR THE AGRICULTURAL SCIENCES AND TECHNOLOGY
Food and Agriculture Organization of the United Nations, Department of General Affairs and Information, Library and Documentation Systems Division, Via delle Terme di Caracalla, 00100 Rome, Italy.

AGRIS DATA BASE
Food and Agriculture Organization of the United Nations, Department of General Affairs and Information, Library and Documentation Systems Division, Via delle Terme di Caracalla, 00100 Rome, Italy.

AGRARIAN RESEARCH AND INTELLIGENCE SERVICE
Food and Agriculture Organization of the United Nations, Economic and Social Policy Department, Human Resources, Institutions and Agrarian Reform Division, Via delle Terme di Caracalla, 00100 Rome, Italy.

DEVELOPMENT EDUCATION EXCHANGE SERVICE
Food and Agriculture Organization of the United Nations, Development Department, Via delle Terme di Caracalla, 00100 Rome, Italy.

FOOD COMPOSITION DATA MANAGEMENT
Food and Agriculture Organization of the United Nations, Economic and Social Policy Department, Food Policy and Nutrition Division, Via delle Terme di Caracalla, 00100 Rome, Italy.

FILM LOAN LIBRARY
Food and Agriculture Organization of the United Nations, Department
of General Affairs and Information, Information Division, Via
delle Terme di Caracalla, 00100 Rome, Italy.

GLOBAL INFORMATION AND EARLY WARNING SYSTEM ON FOOD AND AGRICULTURE
Food and Agriculture Organization of the United Nations, Economic
and Social Policy Department, Commodities and Trade Division,
Via delle Terme di Caracalla, 00100 Rome, Italy.

INTERLINKED COMPUTERIZED SYSTEM FOR FOOD AND AGRICULTURAL STUDIES
Food and Agriculture Organization of the United Nations, Economic
and Social Policy Department, Statistics Division, Via delle
Terme di Caracalla, 00100 Rome, Italy.

DAVID LUBIN MEMORIAL LIBRARY
Food and Agriculture Organization of the United Nations, Department
of General Affairs and Information, Library and Documentation
Systems Division, Via delle Terme di Caracalla, 00100 Rome, Italy.

FOOD AND AGRICULTURAL INFORMATION STORAGE AND RETRIEVAL SYSTEM
Food and Agriculture Organization of the Untied Nations, Department
of General Affairs and Information, Library and Documentation
Systems Division, Via delle Terme di Caracalla, 00100 Rome, Italy.

FAIRS DATA BASE
Food and Agriculture Organization of the United Nations, Department
of General Affairs and Information, Library and Documentation
Systems Division, Via delle Terme di Caracalla, 00100 Rome, Italy.

FAO LIBRARY SERIALS INFORMATION SYSTEM
Food and Agriculture Organization of the Untied Nations, Department
of General Affairs and Information, Library and Documentation
Systems Division, Via delle Terme di Caracalla, 00100Rome, Italy.

LISIS DATA BASE
Food and Agriculture Organization of the United Nations, Department
of General Affairs and Information, Library and Documentation
Systems Division, Via delle Terme di Caracalla, 00100 Rome, Italy.

PHOTO LIBRARY
Food and Agriculture Organization of the United Nations, Department
of General Affairs and Information, Information Division, Via
delle Terme di Caracalla, 00100 Rome, Italy.

PULP AND PAPER CAPACITY SURVEY
Food and Agriculture Organization of the United Nations, Forestry
Department, Forest Industries Division, Via delle Terme di
Caracalla, 00100 Rome, Italy.

**JOINT FAO/WHO FOOD AND ANIMAL FEED CONTAMINATION MONITORING
PROGRAMME** Food and Agriculture Organization, Economic and Social
Policy Department, Food Policy and Nutrition Division, Via delle
Terme di Caracalla, 00100 Rome, Italy.

REGIONAL DATABANK ON TECHNOLOGIES IN AFRICA
United Nations Educational, Scientific and Cultural Organization/ National Science and Technology Development Agency, Publication and Information Division, PMB 12695, 8 Strachan Street, Lagos, Nigeria.

APPROPRIATE TECHNOLOGY FOR HEALTH INFORMATION SYSTEM
World Health Organization, Division of Strengthening of Health Services, ATH Unit, 20 avenue Appia, 1211 Geneva 27, Switzerland.

EPIDEMIOLOGICAL INFORMATION SERVICE
World Health Organization, Epidemiological Surveillance of Communicable Diseases Unit, 20 avenue Appia, 1211 Geneva 27, Switzerland.

HEALTH LEGISLATION INFORMATION
World Health Organization, Health and Biomedical Information Programme, Office of Publications, 20 avenue Appia, 1211 Geneva 27, Switzerland.

INFORMATION SERVICE OF THE PROGRAMME OF HEALTH MANPOWER DEVELOPMENT
World Health Organization, Division of Health Manpower Development, 20 avenue Appia, 1211 Geneva 27, Switzerland.

INTERNATIONAL DOCUMENTS SERVICE
World Health Organization, Health and Biomedical Information Programme/Office of Library and Health Literature Services, 20 avenue Appia, 1211 Geneva 27, Switzerland.

LIBRARY OF THE WORLD HEALTH ORGANIZATION
World Health Organization, Health and Biomedical Information Programme/Office of Library and Health Literature Services, 20 avenue Appia, 1211 Geneva 27, Switzerland.

PROGRAMME MANAGEMENT INFORMATION SYSTEM
World Health Organization, Reporting and Information Services, 20 avenue Appia, 1211 Geneva 27, Switzerland.

WHO TECHNICAL TERMINOLOGY SERVICE
World Health Organization, Health and Biomedical Information Programme, 20 avenue Appia, 1211 Geneva 27, Switzerland.

WORLD HEALTH STATISTICS DATA BASE
World Health Organization, Division of Health Statistics, 20 avenue Appia, 1211 Geneva 27, Switzerland.

HEALTH LITERATURE SERVICES OF THE WHO REGIONAL OFFICE FOR AFRICA
World Health Organization, Regional Office for Africa, P.O. Box 6, Brazzaville, Congo.

INFORMATION SERVICES OF THE WHO REGIONAL OFFICE FOR THE EASTERN MEDITERRANEAN
World Health Organization, Regional Office for the Eastern Mediterranean, P.O. Box 1517, Alexandria, Egypt.

INFORMATION SERVICES OF THE WHO REGIONAL OFFICE FOR EUROPE
World Health Organization, Regional Office for Europe, 8 Scherfigsvej, 2100 Copenhagen, Denmark.

WESTERN PACIFIC REGIONAL CENTRE FOR PROMOTION OF ENVIRONMENTAL PLANNING AND APPLIED STUDIES
World Health Organization, Regional Office for the Western Pacific, P.O. Box 2250, Kuala Lumpur, Malaysia.

WHO SOUTH-EAST ASIA REGION HEALTH LITERATURE, LIBRARY AND INFORMATION SERVICES NETWORK
World Health Organization, Regional Office for South East Asia, SEARO Library, World Health House, Indraprastha Estate, Mahatma Gandhi Road, New Delhi 110002, India.

HEALTH LITERATURE SERVICES OF THE WHO REGIONAL OFFICE FOR SOUTH EAST ASIA
World Health Organization, Regional Office for South East Asia, World Health House, Indraprastha Estate, Mahatma Gandhi Road, New Delhi 110002, India.

HEALTH INFORMATION OF THE WHO REGIONAL OFFICE FOR THE WESTERN PACIFIC
World Health Organization, Regional Office for the Western Pacific, P.O. Box 2932, United Nations Avenue, 12115 Manila, Philippines.

HEALTH LITERATURE SERVICES OF THE WHO REGIONAL OFFICE FOR THE WESTERN PACIFIC
World Health Organization, Regional Office for the Western Pacific, P.O. Box 2932, United Nations Avenue, 12115 Manila, Philippines.

REGIONAL LIBRARY OF MEDICINE AND THE HEALTH SCIENCES
World Health Organization/Pan American Health Organization, rua Botucatu 862, via Clementino, 0423 Sao Paulo, Brazil.

INFORMATION SERVICE OF THE PAN AMERICAN CENTRE FOR HUMAN ECOLOGY AND HEALTH
World Health Organization/Pan American Health Organization, Pan American Centre for Human Ecology and Health, Apartado Postal 37-473, Homero 418-6° pisoColonia Polaneo, Mexico 5, D.F., Mexico.

DOCUMENTATION AND HEALTH INFORMATION OFFICE
World Health Organization/Pan American Health Organization, 525 Twenty Third Street, N.W., Washignton, D.C. 20037.

HBR INFORMATION RETRIEVAL SYSTEM DATA BASE
World Health Organization/Pan American Health Organization, 525 Twenty Third Street, N.W., Washington, D.C. 20037.

PAN AMERICAN NETWORK OF INFORMATION AND DOCUMENTATION ON SANITARY ENGINEERING AND ENVIRONMENT
World Health Organization/Pan American Health Organization, Pan American Centre for Sanitary Engineering and Environmental Sciences, Los Pinos 259, Urbanizacion Camacho, Lima 100, Peru.

REPIDISCA CENTRAL BIBLIOGRAPHIC FILE
Pan American Centre for Sanitary Engineering and Environmental Sciences, Casilla Postal 4337, Los Pinos 250, Urbanizacion Camacho, Lima 100, Peru.

DOCUMENTATION REFERRAL SERVICE
World Bank, Records Management Division, Document Acquisition and Control, 1818 H Street, N.W., Washington, D.C. 20433.

INTERACTIVE BIBLIOGRAPHIC INDEXING SYSTEM
Records Management Division, Document Acquisition and Control, 1818 H Street, N.W., Washington, D.C. 20433.

SOCIAL INDICATORS
The World Bank, Economic Analysis and Projections Department, Economic and Social Data Division, 1818 H Street, N.W., Washington, D.C. 20433.

WORLD TABLES
The World Bank, Economic Analysis and Projections Department, Economic and Social Data Division, 1818 H Street, N.W., Washington, D.C. 20433.

JOINT BANK-FUND LIBRARY
International Monetary Fund, 700 19th Street, N.W., Washington, D.C. 20431.

II. BIBLIOGRAPHY OF BIBLIOGRAPHIES

ANNOTATED BIBLIOGRAPHY OF COUNTRY SERIALS is a listing of periodicals, annuals and other serials containing information of economic, business or trade interest. The listing is organized on a regional and country basis. Copies are available from the Documentation Service, International Trade Centre UNCTAD/GATT, 1211 Geneva 10, Switzerland.

BASIC-NEEDS APPROACH: A SURVEY OF ITS LITERATURE, edited by M. Rutjes, contains a brief analysis of the concept of basic needs, its targets, its strategy and implications, followed by a concise bibliography related to the topic. Copies may be obtained from the Centre for the Study of Education in Developing Countries, Badhuisweg 251, The Hague, The Netherlands.

DEVELOPMENT PLANS AND PLANNING - BIBLIOGRAPHIC AND COMPUTER AIDS TO RESEARCH, by August Schumacher, is arranged in three parts. The first contains more than 100 selected bibliographies on development plans and planning, the second is concerned with a new source of empirical materials for the development planner - the automated documentation centre, and the third analyzes recent work on computer aids for the research library. The publication is available from Seminar Press Ltd., 24-28 Oval Road, London NW1, England.

BIBLIOGRAPHY ON DEVELOPMENT EDUCATION lists books, manuals, resource materials, magazines, and articles in the field of development education. The listing was prepared by the Dutch Central Bureau of Catholic Education. Copies are available from the Central Bureau of Catholic Education, G. Verstijnen, Secretary Foreign Department, Bezuidenhoutseweg 275, The Hague, Netherlands.

BIBLIOGRAPHY OF GERMAN RESEARCH ON DEVELOPING COUNTRIES, prepared by the German Foundation for International Development, is divided into two sections: Part A contains an index of research institutes, author index, subject-matter index, and a geographical index. Part B contains specific information on each of the studies listed. The text is in German with explanatory notes in German, English, French and Spanish. Copies may be obtained from the Deutsche Stiftung fur Internationale Entwicklung (DSE), Endenicher Strasse 41, 53 Bonn, Federal Republic of Germany.

BIBLIOGRAPHY OF SELECTED LATIN AMERICAN PUBLICATIONS ON DEVELOPMENT is a listing of over 200 titles in Latin American development literature, including subject and author indexes. The document was prepared by the Institute of Development Studies Library. Copies are available from the Librarian, Institute of Development Studies, University of Sussex, Brighton BN1 9RE, England.

CANADIAN DEVELOPMENT ASSISTANCE: A SELECTED BIBLIOGRAPHY 1950-70, compiled by Shirley B. Seward and Helen Janssen, covers Canada's foreign aid programs and policies from 1950 to 1970. Copies are available from the Distribution Unit, International Development Research Centre, P.O. Box 8500, Ottawa, Canada KIG 3H9.

DEVINDEX CANADA is a bibliography of literature on social and economic development in Third World countries, which originated in Canada in 1975. Copies may be obtained from the International Development Research Centre, Box 8500, Ottawa, Canada KIG 3H9.

The UNESCO Division of Scientific Research and Higher Education has compiled **A DIRECTORY AND BIBLIOGRAPHY ON THE THEME "RESEARCH AND HUMAN NEEDS"**, listing organizations, journals, newsletters, reports and papers, information services and data banks. The bibliographical section includes headings such as food and nutrition, health, housing and sanitation, environment, energy, technology. For copies contact "Research and Human Needs", Division of Scientific Research and Higher Education, UNESCO, Place de Fontenoy, 75007 Paris, France.

GUIDE TO CURRENT DEVELOPMENT LITERATURE ON ASIA AND THE PACIFIC is published every two months by the Library and Documentation Centre of the Asia Pacific Development Information Service. For more information write to the Centre, United Nations Asian and Pacific Development Institute, P.O. Box 2-136, Sri Aydudhya Road, Bangkok, Thailand.

Hald, Marjorie W.
A SELECTED BIBLIOGRAPHY ON ECONOMIC DEVELOPMENT AND FOREIGN AID, rev. ed., Santa Monica, CA: The Rand Corporation, 1958.

Hazelwood, Arthur
THE ECONOMICS OF "UNDERDEVELOPED" AREAS: AN ANNOTATED READING LIST OF BOOKS, ARTICLES, AND OFFICIAL PUBLICATIONS. London: Oxford University Press for the Institute of Colonial Studies, 1954. 623 titles.

THE ECONOMICS OF DEVELOPMENT: AN ANNOTATED LIST OF BOOKS AND ARTICLES PUBLISHED 1958-1962. London: Oxford University Press, for the Institute of Commonwealth Studies, 1964.

INTERNATIONAL BIBLIOGRAPHY, INFORMATION DOCUMENTATION (IBID) provides bibliographic details and annotations necessary to identify the full range of publications prepared by the United Nations and its related agencies, plus those of ten organizations outside the UN system. IBID is published quarterly by Unipub. Available from Unipub, Box 433, Murray Hill Station, New York, New York 10016, USA.

THE 1978/79 PUBLICATIONS LIST OF THIRD WORLD PUBLICATIONS contains over 300 titles of pamphlets, books and teaching materials about the Third World. The listing is available from Third World Publications, Ltd., 151 Stratford Road, Birmingham B11 1RD, England.

A list of 200 books on **NORTH-SOUTH WORLD RELATIONS** has been compiled by the Developing Country Courier. The listing is organized by subject and region. For copies write to the Courier, P.O. Box 239, McLean, Virginia 22101, USA.

United States Agency for International Development
A PRACTICAL BIBLIOGRAPHY FOR DEVELOPING AREAS. Washington, D.C., 1966. 2 vols. (Vol. 1 - A selective, annotated and graded list of United States publications in the social sciences. 202 pp.) (Vol. 2 - A selective, annotated and graded list of United States publications in the physical and applied sciences. 332 pp.)

PUBLIC ADMINISTRATION--A SELECT BIBLIOGRAPHY, prepared by the British Ministry of Overseas Development Library is the second supplement to the 1973 revised edition. Copies may be obtained from Eland House, Stag Place, London SW1E 5DH, England.

PUBLIC ADMINISTRATION--A SELECT BIBLIOGRAPHY, prepared by the Library of the British Ministry of Overseas Development, is a supplement to the revised edition which appeared in 1973. It includes material published in the period 1972-1975 with 1,600 references. Copies may be obtained from the Library, British Ministry of Overseas Development, Eland House, Stag Place, London SW1E 5DH, England.

The OECD Development Centre has gathered together in the catalog **PUBLICATION AND DOCUMENT, 1962-1979** all the books and documents it has published since its establishment in 1962 up to August 1979. Copies available from OECD Development Centre, 94 rue Chardon Lagache, 75016 Paris, France.

REGISTER OF RESEARCH PROJECTS IN PROGRESS IN DEVELOPMENT STUDIES IN SELECTED EUROPEAN COUNTRIES was prepared by the Centre for Development Studies of the University of Antwerp at the request of the European Association of Development Research and Training Institutes. Copies are available from the Centre, St. Ignatius

Faculties, University of Antwerp, 13 Prinsstraat, 2000 Antwerp, Belgium.

Re Qua, Eloise and Statham, Jane
THE DEVELOPING NATIONS: A GUIDE TO INFORMATION SOURCES CONCERNING THEIR ECONOMIC, POLITICAL, TECHNICAL AND SOCIAL PROBLEMS. Detroit: Gale Research Company, 1965.

The East African Academy has published two new bibliographies. **SCIENCE AND TECHNOLOGY IN EAST AFRICA** contains more than 5,000 titles about research in the agriculture, medical technological, and related fields in East Africa, with short summaries on the problems and progress of research in these areas. **TANZANIA EDUCATION SINCE UHURU: A BIBLIOGRAPHY--1961-1971** was compiled by Dr. George A. Auger of the University of Dar es Salaam. Both publications are available from the East African Academy, RIPS, P.O. Box 47288, Nairobi, Kenya.

SELECTIVE ANNOTATED BIBLIOGRAPHY ON BRAZILIAN DEVELOPMENT has been prepared by the SID Sao Paulo Chapter. This first issue contains only references that have appeared in 1975. Copies are available from the Society for International Development, Sao Paulo Chapter, Caixa Postal 20.270-Vila Clementino, 04023-Sao Paulo-S.P. Brazil.

A SELECTED ANNOTATED BIBLIOGRAPHY: INDIGENOUS TECHNICAL KNOWLEDGE IN DEVELOPMENT, compiled by Liz O'Keefe and Michael Howes, is contained in the January 1979 IDS BULLETIN. This issue of the BULLETIN is devoted to the importance of indigenous technical knowledge in rural areas. Single copies of the BULLETIN are from the Communications Office, Institute of Development Studies, University of Sussex, Brighton Nl 9RE, United Kingdom.

SELECTED BIBLIOGRAPHY OF RECENT ECONOMIC DEVELOPMENT PUBLICATIONS covers a period of one year, from July 1977 to June 1978 and contains two main sections, one for general and theoretical works, the other for literature related to regions and countries. For copies write to the Graduate Program in Economic Development, Vanderbilt University, Nashville, Tennessee 37235, USA.

International Bank for Reconstruction and Development; Economic Development Institute
SELECTED READINGS AND SOURCE MATERIALS ON ECONOMIC DEVELOPMENT. A list of books, articles, and reports included in a small library assembled by the Economic Development Institute, Washington, D.C., 1961.

SOCIAL AND ECONOMIC DEVELOPMENT PLANS - MICROFICHE PROJECT is a cumulative catalogue listing the holdings of Inter Documentation Company AG on social and economic development plans around the world. About 1400 plans from over 180 countries are included. Copies of the catalogue and other catalogues of IDC's microfiche projects are free on request from Inter Documentation Company AG, Poststrasse 14, 6300 Zug-Switzerland.

Powelson, John
A SELECT BIBLIOGRAPHY ON ECONOMIC DEVELOPMENT. Boulder, Colorado:
Westview Press, 1979.

THIRD WORLD BIBLIOGRAPHY AND RESOURCE GUIDE features a wide range
of material on Third World issues. It is designed for students
and general readers. Copies may be obtained from the Development
Education Library Project, c/o OSFAM/Ontario, 175 Carlton Street,
Toronto, Canada.

The United Nations Asian and Pacific Development Institute has
prepared a **SPECIAL BIBLIOGRAPHY ON ALTERNATIVE STRATEGIES FOR
DEVELOPMENT WITH FOCUS ON LOCAL LEVEL PLANNING AND DEVELOPMENT**
in connection with a UNAPDI meeting, held in Bangkok, October
31 - November 4, 1978. Copies are available from the APDI Library
and Documentation Centre. UNAPDI, P.O. Box 2-136, Sri Ayudhya
Road, Bangkok, Thailand.

Vente, Role and Dieter Seul
MACRO-ECONOMIC   PLANNING: A   BIBLIOGRAPHY.   Nomos
Verlagsgesellshaft, Baden-Baden, 1970.

Volunteers in Technical Assistance (VITA) has published its 1979
CATALOGUE OF BOOKS, BULLETINS AND MANUALS. The listing contains
VITA documents related to appropriate technology, as well as
materials published by other development organizations around
the world. Copies are available from VITA, 2706 Rhode Island
Avenue, Mt. Ranier, Maryland 20822, USA.

AN ANNOTATED BIBLIOGRAPHY RELATING TO WORLD FOOD ISSUES, compiled
by Emmanuel H. D'Silva and Ruth M. Trace, contains 125 references
from the Cornell Library System using 1972-74 as the base period.
The selection covers a wide range of issues related to food supply.
Copies are free from the Center for the Analysis of World Food
Issues, Program in International Agriculture, Cornell University,
252 Roberts Hall, Ithaca, New York 14853, USA.

Ardell, Donald and James John
AUTHOR'S GUIDE TO JOURNALS IN THE HEALTH FIELD. Haworth Press,
1980.

Ash, Joan
HEALTH: A MULTI-MEDIA SOURCE GUIDE. Bowker, 1976.

Bailey, William J. and Gwynn, Stephen J.
BIBLIOGRAPHIC INDEX OF HEALTH EDUCATION PERIODICALS, 1981.
Cumulative edition. INU Department of Health, 1982.

Baker, Edward Alan
BIBLIOGRAPHY OF FOOD. Butterworth Scientific Publishers, 1958.

Bender, Arnold F.
THE FACTS OF FOOD. Oxford University Press, 1975.

Culyer, A. J.
AN ANNOTATED BIBLIOGRAPHY OF HEALTH ECONOMICS. Martin, 1977.

Employee Benefit Research Institute
BIBLIOGRAPHY OF RESEARCH: HEALTH CARE PROGRAMS. Employee Benefit, 1981.

FAO
BIBLIOGRAPHY OF FOOD CONSUMPTION SURVEYS. New York: Unipub, 1981.

FAO
LIBRARY SELECT CATALOGUE OF BOOKS, 1951-1958. New York: Unipub, 1961.

FOOD AND NUTRITION: ANNOTATED BIBLIOGRAPHY--AUTHOR AND SUBJECT INDEX, 1945-1972. New York: Unipub, 1974.

FOOD AND NUTRITION BIBLIOGRAPHY. Onyx Press, 1983.

Freedman, Robert L.
HUMAN FOOD USES: A CROSS-CULTURAL COMPREHENSIVE ANNOTATED BIBLIOGRAPHY. Westport, Conn.: Greenwood Press, 1981.

HEALTH CARE IN THE PEOPLE'S REPUBLIC OF CHINA--A BIBLIOGRAPHY WITH ABSTRACTS, by Shahid Akhtar, covers literature over the period 1949-1974. The material is useful to people concerned with providing health services and the training of auxiliary health workers in developing countries. Copies may be obtained from the International Development Research Centre, Publications, P.O. Box 8500, Ottawa, Canada KIG 3H9.

HEALTH SCIENCE BOOKS. Bowker, 1982.

Henderson, J. O.
BIBLIOGRAPHY OF INFANT FOODS AND NUTRITION. International Scholastic Book Service, 1979.

Ikhizama, Bose O.
A BIBLIOGRAPHY OF MAIZE PRODUCTION RESEARCH IN NIGERIA. National Cereals Research Institute, 1978.

Klemeyer, Charles D.
BIBLIOGRAPHY ON HUMANISTIC HEALTH CARE AND HEALTH CARE HUMANIZATION. Vance Bibliographies, 1979.

Langlands, B.
BIBLIOGRAPHY OF THE DISTRIBUTION OF DISEASE IN EAST AFRICA. Makere University College, 1965.

LOW-COST RURAL HEALTH CARE AND HEALTH MANPOWER TRAINING: AN ANNOTATED BIBLIOGRAPHY WITH SPECIAL EMPHASIS ON DEVELOPING COUNTRIES. VOLUMES 1 and 2, each contain some 700 entries with abstracts on all phases of rural health care in developing

countries.   Copies   may   be   obtained   from   the   International
Development Research Centre, Box 8500, Ottawa, Canada K1G 3H9.

NUTRITION   INFORMATION   RESOURCES   FOR   PROFESSIONALS.   Society   for
Nutrition Education, 1979.

Rees, Alan and Young, Blanche A.
CONSUMER HEALTH INFORMATION SOURCE BOOK.   Bowker, 1981.

Roper, Fred and Boorkman, Jo Anne
INTRODUCTION   TO   REFERENCE   SOURCES   IN   THE   HEALTH   SERVICES.   Med
Library Association, 1980.

Singer and Titus
**RESOURCES   FOR   THIRD   WORLD   HEALTH   PLANNERS: A   SELECTED   SUBJECT
BIBLIOGRAPHY.**   Trado-Medic Books, 1980.

Strauss, Marvin
BIBLIOGRAPHY OF PERIODICALS FOR THE HEALTH PLANNER.   Monticello,
Illinois: Council of Planning Librarians, 1969.

Taylor, Clara and Riddle, Katherine P.
ANNOTATED BIBLIOGRAPHY OF NUTRITION EDUCATION.   Teachers College,
1971.

Ullrich, Helen D.
**HEALTH   MAINTENANCE   THROUGH   FOOD   AND   NUTRITION: A   GUIDE   TO
INFORMATION SOURCES.**   Gale, 1981.

VILLAGE   NUTRITION   STUDIES: AN   ANNOTATED   BIBLIOGRAPHY,   compiled
by Sue Schofield, analyzes over 400 studies of village-level
dietary patterns and nutritional status.   The bibliography is
an excellent collection of micro-level nutrition data and is
a basic guide to the assessment of rural nutrition and specific
improvement   programs.   The   publication   may   be   purchased   from
Publications, The Institute of Development Studies, The University
of Sussex, Andrew Cohen Building, Falmer, Brighton BN1 9RE,
England.
Weise, Freda O.
HEALTH STATISTICS: A GUIDE TO INFORMATION SOURCES.   Gale, 1980.

WORLD   FOOD   PROBLEM: A   SELECTIVE   BIBLIOGRAPHY   OF   REVIEWS,   by
Miloslav Rechcigl, Jr., contains a listing of nearly 5,000 review
articles, books, chapters, and monographs on the food problem.
There are both subject and author indices for the user.   Copies
may be obtained from CRC Press, Inc., 18901 Cranwood Parkway,
Cleveland, Ohio 44128, USA.

DEVELOPMENT--A   BIBLIOGRAPHY,   was   compiled   by   Vaptistis-Titos
Patrikios   (Rome: FAO,   1974)   and   updates   the   first   edition,
published in 1970, to cover the 1970/73 period.   Contains eight
sections   relating   to   development: theories   and   problems;
perspectives of the Third World countries; population and food
production; aid, trade and international cooperation; agriculture;
manpower and employment; education; and environment.

III. DIRECTORY OF PERIODICALS

ACTUEL DEVELOPPEMENT, English Digest Edition, Paris.

AFRICA, London, Africa Journal, Ltd.

AFRICA INSTITUTE, Pretoria, Africa Institute.

AFRICA QUARTERLY, New Delhi, India Council for Africa.

AFRICA RESEARCH BULLETIN, Exeter, Eng. Africa Research, Ltd.

AFRICA, SOUTH OF THE SAHARA, London, Europa Publications.

AFRICA TODAY, New York, American Committee on Africa.

AFRICAN AFFAIRS, London, Journal of the Royal African Society.

AFRICAN DEVELOPMENT, London.

AFRICAN DEVELOPMENT BANK, Annual Report, Ibadan.

AFRICAN ENVIRONMENT, Dakar, United Nations Environmental Program.

AFRICAN STATISTICAL YEARBOOK, Addis Ababa, Economic Commission for Africa.

AFRICAN STUDIES REVIEW, Stanford, Boston, East Lansing, African Studies Association.

AFRICAN URBAN STUDIES, East Lansing, Mich., African Studies Center.

AGENDA, Washington, D.C, U.S. Agency for International Development.

APPROPRIATE   TECHNOLOGY,   London,   Intermediate   Technology Publications, Ltd.

APPROTECH, Ann Arbor, Mich., International Association for the Advancement of Appropriate Technology for Developing Countries.

ARTHA VIJNANA, Poona, Gokhale Institute of Politics and Economics.

ASIA AND THE WORLD MONOGRAPHS, Taipei, Asia and the World Forum.

ASIA YEARBOOK, Hong Kong, Far Eastern Economic Review.

ASIAN AFFAIRS, London, Royal Central Asian Society.

ASIAN DEVELOPMENT BANK, Annual Report, Manila.

ASIAN REGIONAL CONFERENCE OF THE INTERNATIONAL LABOR ORGANIZATION, Proceedings, Geneva, ILO.

ASIAN SURVEY, Berkeley, Institute of International Studies.

BANGLADESH DEVELOPMENT STUDIES, Dhaka, Bangladesh Institute of Development Studies.

BANGLADESH ECONOMIC REVIEW, Dhaka, Bangladesh Institute of Development Economics.

BULLETIN OF INDONESIAN ECONOMIC STUDIES, Canberra, Dept. of Economics, Australian National University.

CEPAL REVIEW, Santiago, Chile.

CANADIAN JOURNAL OF AFRICAN STUDIES, Montreal, Loyola College.

COMMUNITY DEVELOPMENT JOURNAL, Manchester, U.K., Oxford University Press.

DEVELOPING ECONOMIES, Tokyo, The Institute of Asian Economic Affairs.

DEVELOPMENT, Rome, Society for International Development.

DEVELOPMENT CENTER STUDIES, OECD, Paris.

DEVELOPMENT AND CHANGE, Beverly Hills, Calif.: Sage Publications.

DEVELOPMENT CO-OPERATION, Paris, OECD.

DEVELOPMENT DIGEST, Washington, D.C., U.S. Agency for International Development.

DEVELOPMENT DIALOGUE, Uppsala, Sweden, Dag Hammarskjold Foundation.

EASTERN AFRICA ECONOMIC REVIEW, Nairobi, Oxford University Press.

ECONOMIC DEVELOPMENT AND CULTURAL CHANGE, Chicago, University of Chicago Press.

ETHIOPIAN JOURNAL OF DEVELOPMENT RESEARCH, Addis Ababa, Institute of Development Research.

FAR EASTERN ECONOMIC REVIEW, Hong Kong.

FINANCE AND DEVELOPMENT, Washington, D.C.

IDS BULLETIN, Institute of Development Studies, University of Sussex, U.K.

IMPACT OF SCIENCE ON SOCIETY, Paris, UNESCO.

INDIAN JOURNAL OF INDUSTRIAL RELATIONS, New Delhi, India.

INDUSTRY AND DEVELOPMENT, Vienna, UNIDO.

INTERNATIONAL DEVELOPMENT REVIEW, Rome, Society for International Development.

INTERNATIONAL LABOR REVIEW, Geneva, ILO.

INTERNATIONAL STUDIES QUARTERLY, San Francisco.

JOURNAL OF AFRICAN STUDIES, Los Angeles, UCLA African Studies Center.

JOURNAL OF DEVELOPING AREAS, Macomb, IL, Western Illinois Univ.

JOURNAL OF DEVELOPMENT ECONOMICS, Amsterdam, North Holland Publishing Co.

JOURNAL OF DEVELOPMENT STUDIES, London, U.K.

JOURNAL OF ECONOMIC DEVELOPMENT, JOURNAL OF INTERNATIONAL AFFAIRS, New York, Columbia University.

JOURNAL OF MODERN AFRICAN STUDIES, New York, Cambridge University Press.

LATIN AMERICAN RESEARCH REVIEW, Chapel Hill, North Carolina.

MODERN ASIAN STUDIES, New York, Cambridge University Press.

MONOGRAPH, DEVELOPMENT STUDIES CENTER, AUSTRALIAN NATIONAL UNIVERSITY.

MONOGRAPH, OVERSEAS DEVELOPMENT COUNCIL, Washington, D.C.

ODI REVIEW, Overseas Development Institute, London, U.K.

OXFORD ECONOMIC PAPERS, Oxford, U.K.

PAKISTAN DEVELOPMENT REVIEW, Karachi, Pakistan.

PUBLIC   ADMINISTRATION   AND   DEVELOPMENT,   Sussex,   U.K.,   Royal
Institute of Public Administration.

THIRD WORLD QUARTERLY, London, Third World Foundation for Social
and Economic Studies.

WORLD BANK STAFF WORKING PAPER, IBRD, Washington, D.C.

WORLD DEVELOPMENT, Pergamon Press, N.Y.

NOTE:

For   more   information   on   relevant   periodicals   please   consult:

1.   **DIRECTORY OF UNITED NATIONS INFORMATION SYSTEMS**

2.   **REGISTER OF UNITED NATIONS SERIAL PUBLICATIONS**

Published   by   **Inter-Organization   Board   for   Information   Systems,**
IOB   Secretariat,   Palais   des   Nations,   CH-1211   Geneva   10,
Switzerland.

IV. RESEARCH INSTITUTIONS

INTERNATIONAL (GENERAL)

AFRICAN INSTITUTE FOR ECONOMIC DEVELOPMENT AND PLANNING
United Nations Economic Commission for Africa, Dakar, Senegal.

AFRO-ASIAN ORGANIZATION FOR ECONOMIC CO-OPERATION
Cairo Chamber of Commerce Building, Midan el-Falsky, Cairo, Egypt.

ASIAN ASSOCIATION OF DEVELOPMENT RESEARCH AND TRAINING INSTITUTES
P.O. Box 2-136, Sri Ayudhya Road, Bangkok, Thailand.

ASIAN DEVELOPMENT CENTER
11th Floor, Philippine Banking Corporation Building, Anda Circle,
Port Area, Manila, Philippines.

ASIAN INSTITUTE FOR ECONOMIC DEVELOPMENT AND PLANNING
P.O. Box 2-136, Sri Ayudhya Road, Bangkok, Thailand.

ATLANTIC INSTITUTE FOR INTERNATIONAL AFFAIRS
120, rue de Longchamp, 75016 Paris, France.

CARIBBEAN STUDIES ASSOCIATION
Inter-American University of Puerto Rico, P.O. Box 1293, Hato
Rey, Puerto Rico 00919.

CENTRE FOR STUDIES AND RESEARCH IN INTERNATIONAL LAW AND
INTERNATIONAL RELATIONS
The Hague Academy of International Law, The Hague, Netherlands.

CENTRE FOR THE CO-ORDINATION OF SOCIAL SCIENCE RESEARCH AND
DOCUMENTATION IN AFRICA SOUTH OF THE SAHARA
B.P. 836, Kinshasa XI, Zaire.

CLUB OF ROME
Via Giorgione 163, 00147 Roma, Italy.

COMMITTEE ON SOCIETY, DEVELOPMENT AND PEACE
Oecumenical Centre, 150, route de Ferney, 1211 Geneve 20, Suisse.

COUNCIL FOR ASIAN MANPOWER STUDIES
P.O. Box 127, Quezon City, Philippines.

COUNCIL FOR THE DEVELOPMENT OF ECONOMIC AND SOCIAL RESEARCH IN
AFRICA
B.P. 3186, Dakar, Senegal.

EAST AFRICAN ACADEMY RESEARCH INFORMATION CENTRE
Regional Building of East African Community, Ngong Road, (rooms
359-60), Nairobi, Kenya.

EASTERN REGIONAL ORGANIZATION FOR PLANNING AND HOUSING
Central Office: 4a, Ring Road, Indraprastha Estate, New Delhi,
India.

EASTERN REGIONAL ORGANIZATION FOR PUBLIC ADMINISTRATION
Rizal Hall, Padre Faura Street, Manila, Philippines.

ECONOMIC DEVELOPMENT INSTITUTE
1818 H Street, N.W., Washington, D.C.   20433, U.S.A.

EUROPEAN FOUNDATION FOR MANAGEMENT DEVELOPMENT
51, rue de la Concorde, Bruxelles, Belgique.

EUROPEAN   INSTITUTE   FOR   TRANSNATIONAL   STUDIES   IN   GROUP   AND
ORGANIZATIONAL DEVELOPMENT
Viktorgasse 9, 1040 Vienna, Austria.

EUROPEAN INSTITUTE OF BUSINESS ADMINISTRATION
Boulevard de Constance, 77 Fontainebleau, France.

EUROPEAN RESEARCH GROUP ON MANAGEMENT
Predikherenberg 55, 3200 Kessel-Lo, Belgique.

INSTITUTE OF INTERNATIONAL LAW
82, avenue de Castel, 1200 Bruxelles, Belgique.

INTERNATIONAL AFRICAN INSTITUTE
210, High Holborn, London WCIV 7BW, United Kingdom.

INTERNATIONAL ASSOCIATION FOR METROPOLITAN RESEARCH AND DEVELOPMENT
Suite 1200, 130 Bloor Street West, Toronto 5, Canada.

INTERNATIONAL CENTRE OF RESEARCH AND INFORMATION ON PUBLIC AND
CO-OPERATIVE ECONOMY
45, quai de Rome, Liege, Belgique.

INTERNATIONAL CO-OPERATION FOR SOCIO-ECONOMIC DEVELOPMENT
59-61, rue Adolphe-Lacombie, Bruxelles 4, Belgique.

INTERNATIONAL INSTITUTE FOR LABOUR STUDIES
154, rue de Lausanne, Case Postale 6, 1211 Geneve, Suisse.

INTERNATIONAL INSTITUTE FOR STRATEGIC STUDIES
18, Adam Street, London WC2N 6AL, United Kingdom.

INTERNATIONAL INSTITUTE OF ADMINISTRATIVE SCIENCES
25, rue de la Charite, Bruxelles 4, Belgique.

INTERNATIONAL MANAGEMENT DEVELOPMENT INSTITUTE
4, Chemin de Conches, 1200 Geneve, Suisse.

INTERNATIONAL SCIENCE FOUNDATION
2, rue de Furstenberg, 75006 Paris, France.

INTERNATIONAL SOCIAL SCIENCE COUNCIL
1, rue Miollis, 75015 Paris, France.

INTERNATIONAL STATISTICAL INSTITUTE
Prinses Beatrixlaan 428, Voorburg, Netherlands.

INTERNATIONAL TRAINING AND RESEARCH CENTER FOR DEVELOPMENT
47, rue de la Glaciere, 75013 Paris, France.

LATIN AMERICAN CENTRE FOR ECONOMIC AND SOCIAL DOCUMENTATION
Casilla 179-D, Santiago, Chile.

ORGANIZATION FOR ECONOMIC CO-OPERATION AND DEVELOPMENT
Chateau de la Muette, 2, rue Andre Pascal, 75775 Paris Cedex
16, France.

REGIONAL ECONOMIC RESEARCH AND DOCUMENTATION CENTER
B.P. 7138, Lome, Togo.

RESEARCH CENTRE ON SOCIAL AND ECONOMIC DEVELOPMENT IN
ASIA--INSTITUTE OF ECONOMIC GROWTH
University Enclave, Delhi 7, India.

SOCIETY FOR INTERNATIONAL DEVELOPMENT
1346 Connecticut Avenue, N.W., Washington, D.C. 20036, USA.

SOUTHEAST ASIAN SOCIAL SCIENCE ASSOCIATION
Chulalongkorn University, c/o Faculty of Political Science,
Bangkok, Thailand.

UNITED NATIONS INSTITUTE FOR TRAINING AND RESEARCH
801 United Nations Plaza, New York, NY, USA.

UNITED NATIONS RESEARCH INSTITUTE FOR SOCIAL DEVELOPMENT
Palais des Nations, 1211 Geneve, Suisse.

AUSTRALIA

AUSTRALIAN INSTITUTE OF INTERNATIONAL AFFAIRS
P.O. Box E181, Canberra, ACT 2600.

INSTITUTE OF ADVANCED STUDIES
The Australian National University, P.O. Box 4, Canberra ACT 2600.

STRATEGIC AND DEFENSE STUDIES CENTER
Research School of Pacific Studies, Australian National University,
P.O. Box 4, Canberra, ACT 2600.

AUSTRIA

AUSTRIAN FOUNDATION FOR DEVELOPMENT RESEARCH (OFSE)
Turkenstrasse 3, 1090 Vienna, Austria.

VIENNA INSTITUTE FOR DEVELOPMENT
Karntner Strasse 25, 1010 Vienna, Austria.

BANGLADESH

BANGLADESH INSTITUTE OF DEVELOPMENT STUDIES
Adamjee Court, Motijheel Commercial Area, Dacca 2.

BELGIUM

CATHOLIC UNIVERSITY OF LOUVAIN
Center for Economic Studies, Van Evenstraat 2b, 3000 Louvain,
Belgium.

FREE UNIVERSITY OF BRUSSELS
Department of Applied Economics, Avenue F-D Roosevelt 50, 1050
Brussels, Belgium.

UNIVERSITY OF ANTWERP
Centre for Development Studies, 13 Prinsstratt, 2000 Antwerp,
Belgium.

BRAZIL

BRAZILIAN INSTITUTE OF ECONOMICS
Fundacao Getulio Vargas, Caixa Postal 4081-ZC-05, Rio de Janeiro,
Brazil.

PROGRAMME OF JOINT STUDIES ON LATIN AMERICAN ECONOMIC INTEGRATION
Caixa Postal 740, Rio de Janeiro, Brazil.

BULGARIA

SCIENTIFIC RESEARCH CENTRE FOR AFRICA AND ASIA
Academy of Social Science, ul. Gagarin 2, Sofia 13, Bulgaria.

INSTITUTE FOR INTERNATIONAL RELATIONS AND SOCIALIST INTEGRATION
Bulgarian Academy of Sciences, Boul. Pencho Slaveicov, 15, Sofia,
Bulgaria.

CANADA

CANADIAN ASSOCIATION OF AFRICAN STUDIES
Geography Department, Carleton University, Ottawa, K1S 5B6.

CANADIAN COUNCIL FOR INTERNATIONAL CO-OPERATION
75 Sparks Street, Ottawa 4, Ontario.

CANADIAN INSTITUTE OF INTERNATIONAL AFFAIRS
Edgar Tarr House, 31 Wellesley Street East, Toronto 284, Ontario.

CENTRE FOR DEVELOPING-ASIA STUDIES
McGill University, Montreal.

INSTITUTE OF INTERNATIONAL RELATIONS
University of British Columbia, Vancouver 8.

INTERNATIONAL DEVELOPMENT RESEARCH CENTRE
60 Queen Street, P.O. Box 8500, Ottawa K1G 3H9.

REGIONAL DEVELOPMENT RESEARCH CENTER
University of Ottawa, Ottawa 2, Ontario.

CHILE

CATHOLIC UNIVERSITY OF CHILE
Institute of Economics, Avda. Libertador Bernardo O'Higgins,
No. 340, Santiago, Chile.

CATHOLIC UNIVERSITY OF CHILE
Centre for Planning Studies (CEPLAN), Avda. Libertador Bernardo
O'Higgins, No. 340, Santiago, Chile.

UNIVERSITY OF CHILE
Planning Centre (CEPLA), Avda, Libertado Bernardo O'Higgins,
No. 1058, Santiago, Chile.

COLOMBIA

UNIVERSITY OF ANTIOQUIA
Economic Research Centre, Apartado Aereo 1226, Medellin, Colombia.

CZECHOSLOVAKIA

INSTITUTE OF INTERNATIONAL RELATIONS
Praha 1 - Mala Strana, Nerudova 3, Czechoslovakia.

DENMARK

INSTITUTE FOR DEVELOPMENT RESEARCH
V. Volgade 104, DK-1552 Kobenhavn.

CENTRE FOR DEVELOPMENT RESEARCH
9, NY Kongensgade, 4K-1472 Copenhagen K, Denmark.

FRANCE

UNIVERSITY OF PARIS, INSTITUTE OF ECONOMIC AND SOCIAL DEVELOPMENT
STUDIES
58 Boulevard Arago, 75013 Paris, France.

INSTITUTE FOR RESEARCH INTO THE ECONOMICS OF PRODUCTION
2 rue de Rouen, 92000 Nanterre, France.

INTERNATIONAL CENTRE OF ADVANCED MEDITERRANEAN AGRONOMIC STUDIES
Route de Mende, 34000 Montpellier, France.

INSTITUTE FOR ECONOMIC RESEARCH AND DEVELOPMENT PLANNING
B.P. 47, 38040 Grenoble Cedex, France.

GERMANY, FEDERAL REPUBLIC OF

INSTITUTE FOR DEVELOPMENT RESEARCH AND DEVELOPMENT POLICY
Ruhr-Universitat Bochum, 463 Bochum-Querenburg, Postifach 2148,
Federal Republic of Germany.

INTERNATIONAL INSTITUTE OF MANAGEMENT
Wissenschaftszentrum Berlin, Criegstrasse 5-7, Berlin 33, D-1000.

GERMAN ASSOCIATION FOR EAST ASIAN STUDIES
Rothenbaumchaussee 32, 2 Hamburg 13.

GHANA

INSTITUTE OF AFRICAN STUDIES
University of Ghana, P.O. Box 73, Legon, Accra.

HUNGARY

INSTITUTE FOR WORLD ECONOMICS OF THE HUNGARIAN ACADEMY OF SCIENCES
P.O. Box 36, 1531 Budapest, Hungary.

INSTITUTE FOR ECONOMIC AND MARKET RESEARCH
P.O. Box 133, Budapest 62, Hungary.

INDIA

CENTRE FOR THE STUDY OF DEVELOPING SOCIETIES
29, Rajpur Road, Delhi 6, India.

INDIA INTERNATIONAL CENTRE
40 Lodi Estate, New Delhi 110003, India.

INDIAN COUNCIL FOR AFRICA
Nyaya Marg, Chankyapuri, New Delhi 21, India.

INDIAN COUNCIL OF WORLD AFFAIRS
Sapru House, Barakhamba Road, New Delhi 110001, India.

INDIAN INSTITUTE OF ASIAN STUDIES
23/354, Azad Nagar, Jaiprakash Road, Andheri, Bombay 38, India.

INDIAN SCHOOL OF INTERNATIONAL STUDIES
35, Ferozeshah Road, New Delhi 1, India.

INSTITUTE OF ECONOMIC GROWTH
University of Enclave, Delhi 7, India.

MADRAS INSTITUTE OF DEVELOPMENT STUDIES
74, Second Main Road, Gandhinagar Adyar, Madras 20, India.

INDONESIA

NATIONAL INSTITUTE OF ECONOMIC AND SOCIAL RESEARCH
Leknas, UC, P.O. Box 310, Djakarta, Indonesia.

ISRAEL

DAVID HOROWITZ INSTITUTE FOR THE RESEARCH OF DEVELOPING COUNTRIES
Tel-Aviv University, Ramat-Aviv, Tel-Aviv.

AFRO-ASIAN INSTITUTE FOR CO-OPERATIVE AND LABOUR STUDIES
P.O. Box 16201, Tel-Aviv.

ISRAELI INSTITUTE OF INTERNATIONAL AFFAIRS
P.O. Box 17027, Tel-Aviv 61170.

JAPAN

INSTITUTE OF DEVELOPING ECONOMIES
42 Ichigaya-Hommura-cho, Shinjuku-ku, Tokyo 162, Japan.

JAPAN CENTER FOR AREA DEVELOPMENT RESEARCH
Iino Building, 2-1-1 Uchisaiwai-cho, Chiyoda-ku, Tokyo, Japan.

KENYA

INSTITUTE FOR DEVELOPMENT STUDIES
University of Nairobi, P.O. Box 30197, Nairobi.

KOREA

INDUSTRIAL MANAGEMENT RESEARCH CENTRE
Yonsei University, Sodaemoon-ku, Seoul

INSTITUTE OF OVERSEAS AFFAIRS
Hankuk University of Foreign Studies, 270 Rimoon-dong, Seoul.

INSTITUTE OF THE MIDDLE EAST AND AFRICA
Rm. 52, Dong-A Building, No. 55, 2nd-ka, Sinmoonro, Chongro-ku, Seoul.

MEXICO

CENTRE FOR ECONOMIC RESEARCH AND TEACHING
Av. Country Club No. 208, Apdo. Postal 13628, Mexico 21, D.F.

NEPAL

CENTRE FOR ECONOMIC DEVELOPMENT AND ADMINISTRATION (CEDA)
Tribhuvan University, Kirtipur, P.O. Box 797, Kathmandu, Nepal.

NETHERLANDS

CENTRE FOR LATIN AMERICAN RESEARCH AND DOCUMENTATION
Nieuwe Doelenstraat 16, Amsterdam 1000, Netherlands.

INSTITUTE OF SOCIAL STUDIES
Badhuisweg 251, P.O. Box 90733, 2509 LS The Hague, Netherlands.

FREE UNIVERSITY, DEPARTMENT OF DEVELOPMENT ECONOMICS
De Boelelaan 1105, Amsterdam 1000, Netherlands.

CENTRE FOR DEVELOPMENT PLANNING
Erasmus University, Postbus 1738, Rotterdam, Netherlands.

DEVELOPMENT RESEARCH INSTITUTE
Hogeschoollaan 225, Tiburg 4400, Netherlands.

NEW ZEALAND

NEW ZEALAND INSTITUTE OF INTERNATIONAL AFFAIRS
P.O. Box 196, Wellington, New Zealand.

NEW ZEALAND INSTITUTE OF ECONOMIC RESEARCH
26, Kelburn Parade, P.O. Box 3749, Wellington, New Zealand.

NIGERIA

INSTITUTE OF AFRICAN STUDIES, UNIVERSITY OF NIGERIA
Univeristy of Nigeria, Nsukka, Nigeria.

NIGERIAN INSTITUTE OF INTERNATIONAL AFFAIRS
Kofo Abayomi Road, Victoria Island, G.P.O. Box 1727, Lagos,
Nigeria.

NIGERIAN INSTITUTE OF SOCIAL AND ECONOMIC RESEARCH
Private Mail Bag No. 5, U.I. University of Ibadan, Ibadan, Nigeria.

NORWAY

INTERNATIONAL PEACE RESEARCH INSTITUTE
Radhusgt 4, Oslo 1, Norway.

NORWEGIAN AGENCY FOR INTERNATIONAL DEVELOPMENT (NORAD)
Planning Department, Boks 18142 Oslo Dep., Oslo 1, Norway.

THE CHR. MICHELSEN INSTITUTE (DERAP)
Fantoftvegen 38, 5036 Fantoft, Bergen, Norway.

PAKISTAN

DEPARTMENT OF INTERNATIONAL RELATIONS
University of Karachi, Karachi-32, Pakistan.

PHILIPPINES

ASIAN CENTER
University of the Philippines, Palma Hall, Diliman D-505, Quezon
City, Philippines.

ASIAN INSTITUTE OF INTERNATIONAL STUDIES
Malcolm Hall, University of the Philippines, Diliman, Quezon
City, Philippines.

INSTITUTE OF ECONOMIC DEVELOPMENT AND RESEARCH
School of Economics, University of the Philippines, Diliman,
Quezon City, Philippines.

POLAND

RESEARCH INSTITUTE FOR DEVELOPING COUNTRIES
Rakowiecka 24, Warsaw, Poland.

CENTRE OF AFRICAN STUDIES
University of Warsaw, Al. Zwirki i Wigury 93, 02-089 Warsaw,
Poland.

SINGAPORE

INSTITUTE OF ASIAN STUDIES
Nanyang University, Jurong Road, Singapore 22.

INSTITUTE OF SOUTH-EAST ASIAN STUDIES
Campus of University of Singapore, House No. 8, Cluny Road,
Singapore 10.

SRI LANKA

MARGA INSTITUTE
P.O. Box 601, 61 Isipathana Mawatha, Colombo 5, Sri Lanka.

SUDAN

INSTITUTE OF AFRICAN AND ASIAN STUDIES
Faculty of Arts, University of Khartoum, P.O. Box 321, Khartoum,
Sudan.

SWEDEN

INSTITUTE FOR INTERNATIONAL ECONOMIC STUDIES
Fack S-104 05, Stockholm 50, Sweden.

STOCKHOLM SCHOOL OF ECONOMICS, ECONOMIC RESEARCH INSTITUTE
Box 6501, 11383 Stockholm, Sweden.

UNITED KINGDOM

CENTRE FOR SOUTH-EAST ASIAN STUDIES
University of Hull, Hull HU6 7RX

CENTRE OF AFRICAN STUDIES
University of Edinburgh, Adam Ferguson Building, George Square,
Edinburgh 8.

CENTRE OF LATIN AMERICAN STUDIES (CAMBRIDGE)
University of Cambridge, History Faculty Building, West Road,
Cambridge CB3 9ES, England.

CENTRE OF LATIN AMERICAN STUDIES (OXFORD)
Oxford University, St. Antony's College, Oxford OX2 6JF, England.

CENTRE OF WEST AFRICAN STUDIES
University of Birmingham, P.O. Box 363, Birmingham B15 2TT.

INSTITUTE FOR THE STUDY OF INTERNATIONAL ORGANISATION
University of Sussex, Stanmer House, Stanmer Park, Brighton BN1
9QA, England.

INSTITUTE OF DEVELOPMENT STUDIES
University of Sussex, Falmer, Brighton BN1 9QN, England.

INSTITUTE OF LATIN AMERICAN STUDIES
University of London, 31 Tavistock Square, London WC1, England.

INSTITUTE OF LATIN AMERICAN STUDIES (GLASGOW)
University of Glasgow, Glasgow.

ROYAL INSTITUTE OF INTERNATIONAL AFFAIRS
Chatham House, St. James' Square, London SW1Y 4LE, England.

UNITED STATES

AFRICAN STUDIES CENTER (BOSTON)
Boston University, 10 Lenos Street, Brookline, MA   02146.

BROOKINGS INSTITUTION
1775 Massachusetts Avenue, N.W., Washington, D.C.   20036.

CENTER FOR ASIAN STUDIES
Arizona State University, Tempe, AZ   85281.

CENTER FOR COMPARATIVE STUDIES IN TECHNOLOGICAL DEVELOPMENT AND
SOCIAL CHANGE
University of Minnesota, Minneapolis, Minnesota   55455.

CENTER FOR DEVELOPMENT ECONOMICS
Williams College, Williamston, MA   01267

CENTER FOR INTERNATIONAL AFFAIRS
Harvard University, 6 Divinity Avenue, Cambridge, MA   02138.

CENTER FOR INTERNATIONAL STUDIES
Massachusetts Institute of Technology, Cambridge, MA   02139.

CENTER FOR LATIN AMERICAN STUDIES, ARIZONA STATE UNIVERSITY
Arizona State University, Tempe, AZ   85281.

CENTER FOR LATIN AMERICAN STUDIES, UNIVERSITY OF FLORIDA
University of Florida, Room 319 LAGH, Gainesville, FL   39611.

CENTER FOR RESEARCH ON ECONOMIC DEVELOPMENT
506 East Liberty Street, Ann Arbor, MI   48108.

CENTER FOR STRATEGIC AND INTERNATIONAL STUDIES
Georgetown University, 1800 K Street, N.W., Washington, D.C.
20006.

CENTER OF INTERNATIONAL STUDIES, PRINCETON UNIVERSITY
Princeton University, 118 Corwin Hall, Princeton, NJ   08540.

HARVARD INSTITUTE FOR INTERNATIONAL DEVELOPMENT
Harvard University, 1737 Cambridge Street, Cambrdige, MA   02138.

INSTITUTE FOR WORLD ORDER
1140 Avenue of the Americas, New York, New York   10036.

INSTITUTE OF LATIN AMERICAN STUDIES
University of Texas at Austin, Sid. W. Richardson Hall, Austin,
TX   78705.

STANFORD INTERNATIONAL DEVELOPMENT EDUCATION CENTER
P.O. Box 2329, Stanford, CA   94305.

UNIVERSITY CENTER FOR INTERNATIONAL STUDIES
University of Pittsburgh, Social Sciences Building, Pittsburgh,
PA   15213.

WORLD FUTURE SOCIETY
4916 St. Elmo Avenue, Bethesda Branch, Washington, D.C.   20014.

UNIVERSITY OF HAWAII
Centre for Development Studies, Department of Economics, Porteus
Hall, 2424 Maile Way, Honolulu, Hawaii   96822

URUGUAY

LATIN AMERICAN CENTRE FOR HUMAN ECONOMY
Cerrito 475, P.O. Box 998, Montevideo, Uruguay.

VENEZUELA

UNIVERSITY OF ZULIA
Department of Economic Research, Faculty of Economic and Social
Sciences, Maracaibo, Venezuela.

YUGOSLAVIA

INSTITUTE FOR DEVELOPING COUNTRIES
41000 Zagreb, Ul. 8 Maja 82, Yugoslavia.

RESEARCH CENTRE FOR CO-OPERATION WITH DEVELOPING COUNTRIES
61 109 Ljubljana, Titova 104 P.O. Box 37, Yugoslavia.

INSTITUTE OF WORLD ECONOMICS AND INTERNATIONAL RELATIONS OF THE
ACADEMY OF SCIENCES OF THE U.S.S.R.
Yaroslavskaya Ul. 13, Moskva I-243.

Appendix

French Guiana
Guadeloupe
Hong Kong
Iran
Iraq
Isle of Man
Lebanon
Malta
Netherlands Antilles
Panama
Portugal
Puerto Rico
Reunion
Romania
Surinam
Trinidad & Tobago
Uruguay
Yugoslavia

Intermediate Middle Income ($551-1135)

Algeria
Antigua
Belize
Chile
China, Rep. of
Colombia
Costa Rica
Dominica
Dominican Republic
Ecuador
Ghana
Gilbert Islands
Guatemala
Ivory Coast
Jamaica
Jordan
Korea, Rep. of
Macao
Malaysia
Mauritius
Mexico
Namibia
Nicaragua
Paraguay
Peru
Seychelles
St. Kitts-Nevis
St. Lucia
Syrian Arab Rep.
Trust Territory of the Pacific
    Islands
Tunisia
Turkey

Lower Middle Income ($281-550)

Angola
Bolivia
Botswana
Cameroon
Cape Verde
Congo, P.R.
El Salvador
Equatorial Guinea
Grenada
Guyana
Honduras
Liberia
Mauritania
Morocco
New Hebrides
Nigeria
Papua New Guinea
Philippines
Rhodesia
Sao Tome & Principe
Senegal
St. Vincent
Sudan
Swaziland
Thailand
Tonga
Western Samoa
Zambia

Low Income ($280 or less)

Afghanistan
Bangladesh
Benin
Bhutan
Burma
Burundi
Cambodia
Central African Empire
Chad
Comoros
Egypt
Ethiopia
Gambia, The
Guinea
Guinea-Bissau
Haiti
India
Indonesia
Kenya
Lesotho
Madagascar
Malawi

Maldives
Mali
Mozambique
Nepal
Niger
Pakistan
Rwanda
Sierra Leone
Solomon Islands
Somalia
Sri Lanka
Tanzania
Togo
Uganda
Upper Volta
Viet Nam
Yemen Arab Rep.
Yemen P.D.R.
Zaire

**CAPITAL SURPLUS OIL EXPORTING
DEVELOPING COUNTRIES**

Kuwait
Libya
Qatar
Saudi Arabia
United Arab Emirates

CENTRALLY PLANNED COUNTRIES

Albania
Bulgaria
China, People's Rep. of
Cuba
Czechoslovakia
German Dem. Rep.
Hungary
Korea, Dem. Rep. of
Lao People's Dem. Rep.
Mongolia
Poland
U.S.S.R.

SOURCE : World Economic and Social Indicators
Document of the World Bank
Washington, D.C.

Index

About the Editor

Pradip K. Ghosh is President of the World Academy of Development and Cooperation, Washington, D.C. and Adjunct Associate Professor and Visiting Fellow at the Center for International Development at the University of Maryland, College Park. He is the author of *Thinking Sociology* and *Land Use Planning,* and editor of the International Development Resource Books series for Greenwood Press.